W9-CFU-452

Annual Review of

INFORMATION SCIENCE AND TECHNOLOGY

Annual Review of
INFORMATION SCIENCE AND TECHNOLOGY

Volume 45 • 2011
Blaise Cronin, Editor

Published on behalf of the
American Society for Information Science and Technology
by Information Today, Inc.

Information Today, Inc.
Medford, New Jersey

ISBN: 978-1-57387-402-1
ISSN: 0066-4200
CODEN: ARISBC
LC No. 66-25096

Published and distributed by
Information Today, Inc.
143 Old Marlton Pike
Medford, NJ 08055-8750

On behalf of

The American Society for Information Science and Technology
1320 Fenwick Lane, Suite 510
Silver Spring, MD 20910-3602, U.S.A.

Information Today, Inc. Staff
President and CEO: Thomas H. Hogan, Sr.
Editor-in-Chief and Publisher: John B. Bryans
Managing Editor: Amy M. Reeve
Proofreader: Penelope Mathiesen
VP Graphics and Production:
   M. Heide Dengler
Cover Designer: Victoria Stover
Book Designer: Kara Mia Jalkowski

ARIST Staff
Editor: Blaise Cronin
Associate Editor: Debora Shaw
Copy Editors: Dorothy Pike,
   Victoria Johnson
Indexer: Becky Hornyak

www.infotoday.com

Contents

SECTION I
Information Management

SECTION II
Information Retrieval

SECTION III
Scholarly Communication

SECTION IV
Technology Trends

SECTION V
Public Policy

Introduction

Blaise Cronin

In my introduction to Volume 40, I reflected on *ARIST*'s first four decades, describing briefly the sterling contributions of Carlos A. Cuadra, the founding editor, and those other good souls in the society's orbit whose efforts and farsightedness made the dream of a regular series of comprehensive reviews in information science a reality. The tone of my remarks was upbeat; after all, a ruby anniversary seemed an appropriate moment to look back with quiet satisfaction and take stock of developments and opportunities. For many of us, myself included, *ARIST* was a perennial in the field: authoritative, reliable, comprehensive. Much of the credit for that must go to Carlos Cuadra and his long-serving successor, Martha Williams, whose commitment to high standards, in terms of both content and production, served us well. Credit should go also to my diligent associate editor Debora Shaw for her punctiliousness over the course of the last decade.

The *ARIST* of today, though perhaps more international in character and broader in scope (this, I'll wager, is the first volume to have chapters from both IBM and Microsoft), is recognizably descended from the *ARIST* of the sixties and chapters from then continue to be highly cited. Donald King, who co-authored Chapter 7, "Some Economic Aspects of the Scholarly Journal System," in the present volume, published his first *ARIST* chapter in 1968; he is one of quite a few authors whose names have graced our pages on multiple occasions over the years. Some topics, too, appear with near regularity, even if the technological landscape has changed. Revenants from the sixties would surely recognize many of the conceptual issues that constitute the core of the chapters here in the sections on information management and scholarly communication; they would, I am quite confident, be impressed by progress in, for example, the world of pharmaceutical information management as described by David Bawden and Lyn Robinson.

It somehow seemed as if the serial could withstand the vicissitudes of the marketplace and disruptive advances in publishing technology. But it was not to be. The ineluctable decline in print sales, a consequence of cancellations in institutional subscriptions, coupled with high production costs and changes in readers' needs and expectations (e.g., swift, unfettered access), made matters impossible in spite of the best efforts of the publisher, Information Today, Inc. In addition, we have found it increasingly difficult to attract those authors who are committed to open access publication and thus uncomfortable with the *ARIST* model. This, then, is the final volume of *ARIST*, the 10th under my editorship, the 45th overall.

Ironically, the serial continues to receive glowing reviews worldwide and its impact factor is the envy of many a scholarly journal. *ARIST* is going out on top, but not by choice. I, personally, am saddened by the serial's demise, having used it routinely for more than 30 years. Like many others, I took reassurance from the fact that a treasure trove of first-rate reviews, a conspectus of our intellectual universe, was but a few feet away on the shelf behind me. Many of my colleagues in the United States and elsewhere felt similarly and, predictably, they now wonder whether and how the imminent gap can be filled. One way is the planned incorporation of review articles—"Advances in Information Science" as I have chosen to call them—which will be edited by Jonathan Furner from UCLA and appear in the pages of the *Journal of the American Society for Information Science and Technology*.

Because this is my valedictory piece, I can speak a little more openly than I might otherwise have about the trials and tribulations of an editor's life; the pleasures, of course, are easily imagined and, ultimately, there for all to see, bound and packaged annually in midnight blue. Jonathan Grudin's confident account of the evolution of the various strains of HCI (human–computer interaction) is the sort of chapter that makes it all worthwhile in the end. His chapter zips along, with documentation, library science, information science, and the iSchool movement weaving in and out of the narrative's major themes; this potted history of human factors, HCI, computer supported collaborative work (CSCW), and so on is as informative as it is pleasurable to read.

One of the things that distinguishes *ARIST* from its many competitors is the serial's meticulous attention to detail and an at times obsessive attention to style. Martha Williams was a stickler for bibliographic exactitude, as anyone who was commissioned to write a chapter under her tenure well knows. With experience one does indeed develop a sixth sense when it comes to references, of which a typical volume contains three to four thousand. There are times when something just doesn't seem right and a quick check (so much easier now than in my predecessors' days) confirms the initial suspicion. And Martha was not afraid to root out sloppy prose and demand that an author clarify what was meant by an infelicitous phrase or uncouth construction. We have tried to follow her example, but one never feels that the job has been done to one's complete satisfaction. Invariably, when we flick through the latest volume a blooper jumps off the page and one's heart sinks.

As editor, I read every word of every chapter, twice if not thrice, and mine are not the only eyes to engage with the text. Some chapters, a distinct minority, require little or no work; they are lucid and competently organized—Chapter 9, "The History of Information Technology," by Thomas Haigh in the present volume is a case in point, as is Tomas Lipinski's thorough tutorial on fair use in U.S. copyright law in Chapter 11. Regrettably, not all authors are always in full command of their own thoughts, or, if they are, something goes awry as their insights travel from the neocortex to the printed page. I sometimes wonder what they would say if they saw the blue-lined mess (think of a Cy Twombly painting) that once was their pristine submission; I wonder, too, if they even notice the improvements wrought by unseen editorial hands. Worse still are the no-shows; latterly we commissioned a third more chapters than we actually needed in any given year, such was the frequency with which one's peers failed to deliver the promised goods. As do airlines, we came to accept that overbooking was a necessary fact of publishing life, though not a fact much liked by commercial publishers I can assure you. It seems not to matter that authors sign a formal agreement and will be paid an honorarium for their service, or that they have 18 months lead-time and multiple opportunities to exit more or less gracefully from their contract; some still wait until the last minute before crying off. I have a file of excuses from otherwise sane and sensible people that would make an errant school kid blush.

But let us not carp; overall the 45 volumes of *ARIST* constitute an incomparable archive for scholars in our field, one that defines our spheres of intellectual activity and testifies with eloquence to the continuing vitality and maturation of information science. This may be the last *ARIST*, but it is certainly not the last we shall hear of *ARIST*.

Acknowledgments

Many individuals are involved in the production of *ARIST*. I gratefully acknowledge the contributions of our Advisory Board members and outside reviewers. Their names are listed in the pages that follow. Victoria Johnson and Dorothy Pike were enormously helpful with copy editing and bibliographic checking. Becky Hornyak produced the thorough index. As always, Debora Shaw did what a first rate associate editor is supposed to do.

ARIST Advisory Board

Chapter Reviewers

Mark Akerman
Karine Barzilai-Nahon
Micheline Beaulieu
Christine Borgman
Terrence Brooks
Cecilia Brown
Paul Ceruzzi
Kenneth Crews
Elisabeth Davenport
Tove Faber Frandsen
Jacek Gwizdka
Glynn Harmon
Brad Hemminger

Paul Jaeger
William Jones
Mike Koenig
Laura Marcial
Javed Mostafa
David Nichols
Charles Oppenheim
Carole Palmer
Neil Smalheiser
Bonnie Snow
Amanda Spink
Padmini Srinivasan
Wendy Warr

Contributors

David Bawden has a first degree in organic chemistry and master's and doctoral degrees in information science. He began his information career as a trainee in the information services of the Smith, Kline, and French pharmaceutical company and later worked as an information scientist for Pfizer Central Research. He is now Professor of Information Science at City University London and editor of the *Journal of Documentation*. He can be reached at db@soi.city.ac.uk.

Catherine Blake is an Associate Professor in the School of Library and Information Science at the University of Illinois at Urbana-Champaign where she teaches courses on text mining (first introduced in 2006), databases, data mining, evidence-based discovery, problem solving and programming, and information tools. Dr. Blake's research explores both human and automated methods to synthesize evidence from text, and her methods draw from human information behavior, scientific discovery, text mining, and natural language processing. She has held positions as a faculty member in the School of Information and Library Science at the University of North Carolina, a research scientist at BHP Research, and a programmer analyst at BHP Information Technology. She can be reached at clblake@illinois.edu.

Lutz Bornmann is a researcher at the Professorship for Social Psychology and Research on Higher Education of the ETH Zurich (Switzerland). Since the late 1990s, he has been working on issues in the promotion of young academics and scientists in the sciences and on quality assurance in higher education. Dr. Bornmann's current academic interests include research evaluation, peer review, and bibliometric indicators, especially the h-index. He is a member of the editorial board of the *Journal of Informetrics* (Elsevier) and of the advisory editorial board of *EMBO Reports* (Nature Publishing Group). He can be reached at lutz.bornmann@gess.ethz.ch.

Jonathan Grudin is a principal researcher in the Adaptive Systems and Interaction group at Microsoft Research and Affiliate Professor at the University of Washington Information School. Prior to joining Microsoft, he was Professor of Information and Computer Science at the University of California, Irvine. He has worked as a software engineer and in government research, and taught at Aarhus University, Keio University, and the University of Oslo. He has been involved in Association for Computing Machinery's (ACM) CHI and CSCW conferences since each began. He was Editor-in-Chief of *ACM Transactions on Computer-Human Interaction* from 1997–2003 and is *Computing Surveys'* Associate Editor for HCI. He writes and edits an *ACM Interactions* column on HCI history. He can be reached at jgrudin@microsoft.com.

Thomas Haigh is an Assistant Professor in the School of Information Studies at the University of Wisconsin, Milwaukee. He received his Ph.D. in History and Sociology of Science from the University of Pennsylvania and has published on many aspects of the history of computing including the evolution of database management systems, word processing, the software package concept, corporate computer departments, internet software, and the gendered division of work in data processing. He is chair of the Special Interest Group on Computers, Information and Society (SIGCIS) of the Society for the History of Technology and Biographies Editor of *IEEE Annals of the History of Computing*. He can be reached at thaigh@uwm.edu.

Noriko Hara is an Associate Professor of Information Science at Indiana University, Bloomington. Her research examines the means by which collective behaviors—including online activism, communities of practice, and knowledge sharing—are enabled and/or impeded by information technology, and is rooted in the social informatics perspective. She is the author of *Communities of Practice: Fostering Peer-to-Peer Learning and Informal Knowledge Sharing*. Her publications have appeared in the *Journal of the American Society for Information Science and Technology*; *Information, Communication & Society*; *The Information Society*; and *Instructional Science* among others. She can be reached at nhara@indiana.edu.

Bi-Yun Huang received her Ph.D. in Information Science from Indiana University, Bloomington in 2009. Her research spans several major areas of social informatics and is driven by an interest in incorporating social, economic, cultural, and political elements in order to understand information and communication technologies and the internet, in particular. She currently works in the area of digital activism. Current projects include a theoretical framework for web-based social movements and Falun Gong's use of the internet. She can be reached at bihuang@iupui.edu.

Donald W. King, a statistician, has described and evaluated information systems and services for nearly 50 years. His academic homes are the University of Tennessee and Bryant University. Recently, he has collaborated with José-Marie Griffiths, Carol Tenopir, and others in economic analysis of libraries and publishing. He gives invited speeches worldwide and is well published with two previous chapters in *ARIST*; 12 books (edited five others); more than 150 articles, chapters, reviews, and published presentations; and more than 150 other formal publications. His work has been recognized through, among other honors and awards, the Research Award and Award of Merit, American Society for Information Science and Technology (ASIST); Pioneer of Science Information, Chemical Heritage Foundation; and Fellow, American Statistical Association. He can be reached at donaldwking@gmail.com.

Stacy Kowalczyk is a Ph.D. candidate in information science at the School of Library and Information Science at Indiana University. Her research is focused on the preservation of digital objects and scientific data as well as barriers to, scalable models of, and the context of preservation. She is currently the Associate Director for Projects and Services for the Indiana University Digital Library Program, where she manages the development of new digital collection and management systems. She can be reached at skowalcz@indiana.edu.

Tomas A. Lipinski obtained his J.D. from Marquette University Law School, LL.M. from The John Marshall Law School, and Ph.D. from the University of Illinois at Urbana-Champaign. Professor Lipinski has worked in a variety of library and legal settings including the private, public, and nonprofit sectors. Professor Lipinski teaches, researches, and speaks frequently on various topics within the areas of information law and policy, especially copyright, free speech, and privacy issues in schools and libraries, and more broadly in society. He is a member of the American Library Association Office for Information Technology Policy Copyright Subcommittee. He can be reached at tlipinsk@uwm.edu.

Lyn Robinson has a first degree in pharmacology and master's and doctoral degrees in information science. She began her information career as an indexer for Derwent's pharmaceutical information databases; she later worked as an information officer and IT specialist in the toxicology laboratories and medical school of University College London. She is now director of the postgraduate Information Studies Scheme courses at City University London. Her book *Understanding Healthcare Information* was published by Facet in April 2010. She can be reached at lyn@soi.city.ac.uk.

Kalpana Shankar is an Assistant Professor in the School of Informatics and Computing at Indiana University, Bloomington. She completed her Ph.D. in Library and Information Science at the

University of California, Los Angeles (UCLA). Her research focuses on scientific work practices and documentation as well as uses of data in pervasive computing applications. She has worked as a postdoctoral researcher on data and metadata management for the Center for Embedded Networked Sensing at UCLA, as a Science Policy Fellow at the American Association for the Advancement of Science, and in the Office of Evaluation at the National Institutes of Health in Bethesda, Maryland. She can be reached at shankar@indiana.edu.

Carol Tenopir is a Chancellor's Professor in the School of Information Sciences, the Director of Research in the College of Communication and Information, and the Director of the Center for Information and Communication Studies, University of Tennessee. In 2009 she received the Award of Merit from ASIST, after previously receiving the ASIST Research Award and Outstanding Information Science Teacher Award. Tenopir is the author of five books (two with Donald W. King) and many journal articles on the topics of scholarly epublishing and reading patterns of scientists. Tenopir and King have done research on these topics together for many years. She can be reached at ctenopir@utk.edu.

Nina Wacholder is an Associate Professor at Rutgers University School of Communication and Information. Her background is in theoretical and computational linguistics and in information science. Her current research interests include the theory of query formulation, assessment of users' ability to recognize related words during interactive searching, and the expression of opposition in online text. She has also worked on assessment of query term quality, proper name identification, identification of significant topics in text, evaluation of question answering systems, and anatomical ontologies. Wacholder's research has been funded by the National Science Foundation, ARDA, and Google. She can be reached at ninwac@rutgers.edu.

Steve Whittaker is a research scientist at IBM Almaden. His research interests are in the design and evaluation of collaborative systems, personal information management, and digital systems that support memory. He has previously worked in industry for HP, Bell Labs, and AT&T, and was Chair of Information Retrieval at University of Sheffield, UK. He has published more than 100 refereed articles and holds 12 patents. He is a member of the ACM Computer Human Interaction Academy. He can be reached at sjwhitta@us.ibm.com.

About the Editor

Blaise Cronin is the Rudy Professor of Information Science at Indiana University, Bloomington, where he has been Dean of the School of Library and Information Science for 19 years. From 1985 to 1991 he held the Chair of Information Science and was Head of the Department of Information Science at the University of Strathclyde in Glasgow. He is concurrently an Honorary Visiting Professor at City University London, the University of Brighton, and Napier University, Edinburgh. For six years he was the Talis Information Visiting Professor of Information Science at the Manchester Metropolitan University. Dr. Cronin is the author of numerous research articles, monographs, technical reports, conference papers, and other publications. Much of his research focuses on collaboration in science, scholarly communication, citation analysis, and the academic reward system—the intersection of information science and social studies of science. His books include *The Citation Process* (1984), *The Scholar's Courtesy* (1995), and *The Hand of Science* (2005). He has also published on topics such as information warfare, information and knowledge management, strategic intelligence, and digital pornography. Dr. Cronin is Editor-in-Chief of the *Journal of the American Society for Information Science and Technology*.

He has extensive international experience, having taught, conducted research, or consulted in more than 30 countries. Clients have included the World Bank, NATO, Asian Development Bank, UNESCO, U.S. Department of Justice, Brazilian Ministry of Science and Technology, European Commission, British Council, Her Majesty's Treasury, Hewlett-Packard Ltd., British Library, Chemical Abstracts Service, and the Association for Information Management. He has been a keynote or invited speaker at scores of conferences, nationally and internationally. Dr. Cronin was a founding director of Crossaig, an electronic publishing start-up in Scotland, which was acquired in 1992 by Thomson Reuters. Dr. Cronin was educated at Trinity College Dublin (M.A.) and the Queen's University of Belfast (Ph.D., D.S.Sc.). In 1997, he was awarded the degree Doctor of Letters (D.Litt., *honoris causa*) by Queen Margaret University, Edinburgh for his scholarly contributions to information science. In 2006 he received the Award of Merit from the American Society for Information Science and Technology, the society's highest honor. He can be reached at bcronin@indiana.edu.

About the Associate Editor

Debora Shaw is a Professor at the Indiana University, Bloomington School of Library and Information Science. Her research focuses on information organization and information seeking and use. Her work has been published in the *Journal of the American Society for Information Science and Technology*, *Journal of Documentation*, *Library & Information Science Research*, and *First Monday*, among others. Dr. Shaw served as President of the American Society for Information Science (1997) and has also served on the society's Board of Directors. She has been affiliated with *ARIST* as both a chapter author and an indexer since 1986. Dr. Shaw received bachelor's and master's degrees from the University of Michigan and a Ph.D. from Indiana University. She was on the faculty at the University of Illinois before joining Indiana University. She can be reached at shawd@indiana.edu.

Information Management

CHAPTER 1

Personal Information Management: From Information Consumption to Curation

Steve Whittaker
IBM Research, Almaden, CA

Introduction

An implicit but pervasive view in the information science community is that people are perpetual seekers after new public information, incessantly identifying and consuming new information by browsing the web and accessing public collections. One aim of this review is to move beyond this *consumer* characterization, which regards information as a *public* resource containing *novel* data that we seek out, consume, and then discard. Instead, I want to focus on a very different view: where *familiar* information is used as a *personal* resource that we *keep, manage*, and (sometimes repeatedly) *exploit*. I call this *information curation*. I first summarize limitations of the consumer perspective. I then review research on three different information curation processes: keeping, management, and exploitation. I describe existing work detailing how each of these processes is applied to different types of personal data: documents, email messages, photos, and webpages. The research indicates people tend to keep too much information, with the exception of contacts and webpages. When managing information, strategies that rely on piles as opposed to files provide surprising benefits. And in spite of the emergence of desktop search, exploitation currently remains reliant on manual methods such as navigation. Several new technologies have the potential to address important curation problems, but implementing these in acceptable ways remains a challenge. I conclude with a summary of outstanding research and technical questions.

Information Seeking and Consumption

There is a long tradition within information and computer science of defining information in terms of its novelty and its ability to transform whoever consumes it (Shannon & Weaver, 1949). Consistent with this, a new set of computer science theories argues that our general information behavior is akin to the foraging behaviors of hunter-gatherer peoples (Pirolli, 2007; Pirolli & Card, 1995, 1999). According to this view, people actively *seek out* and *consume* new information from public resources. Although not as extreme in its focus on consumption, the information science literature also emphasizes *discovery* of new public information, rather than its exploitation. Many different models have been proposed to characterize how people find new information in public collections (Belkin, 1980; Ellis & Haugan, 1997; Kuhlthau, 1991; Marchionini, 1995; Wilson, 1981, 1994). As with information foraging, these models focus exclusively on the process of locating new information from public resources (e.g., archives or the web). Although such information seeking is acknowledged to be iterative, with people making repeated short-term efforts to satisfy information needs (Belkin, 1980; Marchionini, 1995), these models are silent about what happens once such valuable information is located. They do not discuss how this information is organized or curated for future use.

For example, in a very influential theory, Belkin (1980) proposes that people are motivated by ASK (anomalous states of knowledge) to discover new relevant information. He talks about the steps that people follow to address anomalous states. Kuhlthau (1991) describes various information seeking processes, including recognizing an information need and identifying a general topic, as well as stages for formulating and gathering information. Ellis and Haugan (1997) propose a similar *feature set model* and detail the activities involved in finding information, including browsing, chaining, monitoring, differentiating, extracting, and verifying it. Wilson (1999) provides a high-level macro-model, which characterizes how information needs arise and what aids or hinders these processes of information seeking, incorporating insights from Kuhlthau's and Ellis and Haugan's lower-level accounts. Marchionini's (1995) model is focused on more recent technologies, discussing how information seeking moves from high level framing of information needs to expressing those as some form of query, evaluation of the results of executing that query, and reiteration depending on the outcome of that evaluation.

However, all these models talk only about how public information is *found* and ignore what happens after finding has occurred. In a systematic meta-analysis of theoretical information science, Wilson (1999, p. 251) confirms that information science theories have not tackled what he calls "information use," that is, what happens after information seeking is completed. I will argue that this emphasis on information seeking is based on a partial and unrepresentative view of what people usually *do* with information. In contrast to the foraging and information-seeking viewpoints, this review is concerned with an increasingly important (but very different) set of behaviors which I call *personal information curation*. The collection management literature includes some studies of curation behaviors but these have tended to focus on the activities of information professionals who are trained to organize and manage *public* collections (Drew & Dewe, 1992; Osburn & Atkinson, 1991). Similar studies within computer-supported cooperative work look at how teams self-organize to create shared repositories (Ackerman, 1998; Ackerman & Halverson, 2004; Berlin, Jeffries, O'Day, Paepcke, & Wharton, 1993). In both of these cases, however, the focus of curation is on organization of *public* and not personal collections. Here I review evidence showing that people's everyday information habits are frequently focused around managing personal data and do not involve incessant access and immediate consumption of new public information. Instead, people keep and manage personal information for future exploitation. While reviewing the general literature, I will provide illustrative examples of each of these behaviors from my own research and that of my collaborators.

Curation Is the Rule and Not the Exception

One very strong argument for the incompleteness of the consumption model is that people *keep personal* information. Information seeking and foraging models argue that we are continually seeking out novel public resources. If these models are correct, then we should not expect people to conserve large amounts of information for future consumption. However, a minute's reflection will reveal that people persistently engage in active and extensive *preservation* and *curation* behaviors in their information environments. Much as we might want to, we do not immediately delete each email we receive, once we have read or replied to it. And after creating a document or presentation, we do not immediately transfer it to the trash. We take care to preserve personal photos over periods of years.

There are many, many examples of people preserving and managing personal materials for future exploitation. Here are some simple statistics about the huge amounts of information that people keep in their personal stores. Whittaker, Bellotti, and Gwizdka (2007) summarize eight studies of email use, showing that people archive a huge number of messages, with an average of around 2,846 messages being kept. Unsurprisingly, these personal email archives are growing larger, with more recent studies (Fisher, Brush, Gleave, & Smith, 2006) revealing that people have around 28,000 messages. People also keep a large number of personal files. Boardman and Sasse (2004) found an average of around 2,200 personal files stored on people's hard drives. And a recent study of digital photos found an average of over 4,000 personal pictures (Whittaker, Bergman, & Clough, 2010). Studies of web bookmarking show that people also preserve hundreds of bookmarks (Abrams, Baecker, & Chignell, 1998; Aula, Jhaveri, & Käki, 2005; Boardman & Sasse, 2004; Catledge & Pitkow, 1995; Cockburn & Greenberg, 2000). And of course these behaviors are not limited to the digital domain: Whittaker and Hirschberg (2001) looked at paper archives and found that people still amassed huge amounts of personal paper data. That study found that on average researchers had 62 kilograms of paper, equivalent to a pile of phone directories 30 meters high.

Furthermore, it is not just that people passively *keep* this information; they also make strenuous attempts to *organize it in ways that will promote future retrieval.* For email, Bellotti, Ducheneaut, Howard, Smith, and Grinter (2005) found that people spend 10 percent of their total time in email filing messages, leading to an average of 244 folders in their email collections. Personal computer files are organized in a similar way, with people averaging 57 folders with an average depth of 3.3 subfolders (Boardman & Sasse, 2004). Studies of web bookmarking also show active organizational efforts leading to an average of 17 folders with complex subfolder structure (Abrams et al., 1998; Aula et al., 2005). And Marshall (2008a, 2008b) describes the arcane organizations that result from attempts to preserve information over many years.

So, although it is obvious that consumption is important for some types of rapidly changing, transient public information (news, entertainment), it is not the norm. For most types of information, behavior seems to be much closer to *curation* than *consumption*. Furthermore, curation seems destined to become even more important. New technologies—such as ubiquitous sensors, digital video, and digital cameras—make it increasingly easy to capture new types of personal data. And this trend, along with continued increases in cheap digital storage, means that people's hard drives are now filling up with huge collections of personal photos, videos, and music (Bell & Gemmell, 2009; Kalnikaitė, Sellen, Whittaker, & Kirk, 2010; Marshall, 2008a, 2008b).

One obvious objection to the argument for curation is that we spend large amounts of time accessing public resources such as the web. However, new research shows that even here we are not seeking *novel* information. Accessing the web usually entails *re-accessing previously visited resources.* Various studies have shown that most of people's web behavior concerns *re-access*, that is, returning to information they have already viewed. Between 58 and 81 percent of all user accesses are of pages that the user has accessed previously (Cockburn & Greenberg, 2000; Obendorf, Weinreich, Herder, & Mayer, 2007; Tauscher & Greenberg, 1997). So, rather than people foraging for *new* information and resources, they instead revisit previously accessed information. Again this suggests a pattern of curation and re-use rather than one-time consumption.

If these arguments are correct, we need to rethink our theories of information. Prior systems and models of information describe consumption of public data. Indeed, until recently it was not possible to create and keep significant personal digital archives. The prevalence of keeping and re-use, however, suggests a need to develop theories of *curation*: the active preservation of personal information content for the future. We need to look beyond models of foraging and information seeking to think about practices of preserving and curating information. Agricultural practices allowed our ancestors to free themselves from the vagaries of an unpredictable environment. In the same way, we need new theories, tools, and practices for information curation to help support these pervasive activities. Although other work has neglected how we acquire and manage personal information, one exception is that of Jones and colleagues (Bruce, Jones, & Dumais, 2004; Jones, 2004, 2007a, 2007b; Jones & Teevan, 2007); we use a variant of Jones's Personal Information Management (PIM) lifecycle framework to organize this review.

The structure of the chapter is as follows. In the next section we present a framework for the *curation lifecycle,* which describes the processes by which we keep, manage, and access information, elaborating the relationships among these processes. We also discuss important distinctions between different properties of information that have implications for curation, such as whether information is unique and whether it requires action. The next three sections review the challenges of keeping, managing, and exploiting personal information. We present relevant research on how and why people keep information, the different ways they organize it, and finally how they access and exploit that stored information. In each case we review how different types of information (email messages, documents, photos, webpages) are treated differently. The final section looks ahead, exploring different technical developments that may influence the future of information curation, as well as outlining outstanding empirical and methodological issues.

The Curation Lifecycle

Curation involves *future oriented* activities, more specifically the set of practices that select, maintain, and manage information in ways that are intended to promote future consumption of that information. We begin by introducing a simple, three-stage model of the curation lifecycle that is a variant of one described by Jones (2007a, 2007b) and Jones and Teevan (2007). We talk about the relations between different phases of the lifecycle and clarify differences between our framework and Jones's work. We also introduce important distinctions between different *properties* of information that have implications for curation behaviors.

Keeping

We encounter new information all the time. Much of this encountered information may be irrelevant to us and other pieces of information, such as news or trivia, are of little future utility once we have registered them. But some of this new information we expect to need in the future; how do we decide what is worth keeping? What principles govern decisions about the sorts of information we keep (Jones, 2004, 2007a, 2007b)? There are *costs* to keeping, so how do we decide which information will have significant future value; and what makes it worth keeping (Marshall, 2008a, 2008b)? Keeping is clearly a complex decision that is influenced by many factors, including the *type* of information being evaluated, *when* we expect we will need it, as well as the *context* in which we imagine that it will be needed. There are also strategic trade-offs involved in keeping information *ourselves* rather than relying on regenerating that same information from public resources.

Information items (whether they are documents, email messages, photos, or webpages) have different utilities and will consequently be processed in very different ways. Transient information encountered on a webpage will be treated very differently from a personal document we have been working on for several days or an email sent by an important colleague. The technologies that we use to generate and encounter information will also have an effect on how likely we are to keep it. For example, digital photography has now made it much easier to take very many pictures. And preserving digital pictures is inexpensive because storage technology is now so cheap. One consequence is that people are keeping many more pictures, compared with the past when taking pictures was expensive, developing them was laborious, and careful physical organization and storage were needed. But the ease of generating pictures may have important downstream consequences for retrieval that need to be taken into account when deciding whether to keep them (Whittaker et al., 2010).

Management

Having decided *that* we want to keep certain information, how should we *manage* that information in ways that will guarantee it will produce future value? Again, this depends on the *type* of information, and once again there are strategic questions. A key decision people have to make is the trade-off between the *effort* to invest in managing information against the projected *payoff* during exploitation.

The different ways of managing information have different costs and payoffs. As information curators, we have to decide between *intensive* methods that are likely to engender higher information yields but at the cost of greater management efforts. These intensive methods must be compared with less intensive methods that may guarantee less predictable returns. For example, we might apply systematic structure to our paper files by filing incoming information into structured folders. This information should then be easier to access—providing that the structures match the context in which we wish to retrieve the information. However, this filing strategy imposes a heavy burden on the information curator because each new piece of information must be analyzed and structured in this way. Alternatively, we may adopt a more relaxed approach and allow physical information to accumulate in piles on our desk, or email messages to pile up in our inbox. This tactic reduces the costs of organizing the information, but may make it harder to locate critical information when we need it (Malone, 1983; Whittaker, 2005; Whittaker & Hirschberg, 2001; Whittaker & Sidner, 1996).

The management process is also organic and we modify our personal information systems in an adaptive way. We repeatedly revisit and restructure information related to ongoing tasks to meet our current needs. People may be able to remember more about the organization of recently or frequently visited information—making it straightforward to access. Other types of information may be infrequently accessed (e.g., photos that are stored for the long term). Infrequent access may mean that users do not discover that their photo collection needs to be systematically restructured for it to be effectively retrieved (Whittaker et al., 2010).

Management may also have repetitive properties. Some people habitually weed information that has turned out to be of little value and may be compromising the uptake of information with definite utility. People occasionally work through email inboxes, deleting old or irrelevant information (Whittaker & Sidner, 1996). However, it is abundantly clear that people find such cleanup activities difficult, not only because they require judgments about the projected value of information but also because there may be emotional connections with the information that they have invested time and effort in organizing (Bergman, Beyth-Marom, & Nachmias, 2003; Jones, 2007a, 2007b; Marshall, 2008a, 2008b; Whittaker & Hirschberg, 2001).

Exploitation

Exploitation is at the heart of curation practices. If we cannot successfully exploit the information we preserved, then keeping decisions and management activity will have been futile. But what are effective ways for accessing curated information? Successful exploitation clearly relates to keeping and management practices. Careful attempts to organize valuable information should make it easier to re-access the data. But technology potentially reduces the need to organize. Emerging technologies, such as desktop search (Cutrell, Dumais, & Teevan, 2006; Dumais, Cutrell, Cadiz, Jancke, Sarin, & Robbins, 2003; Russell & Lawrence, 2007), promise to reduce the overhead of organizing our files because we no longer have to navigate to them manually.

Two main methods can be used to exploit information:

- Navigation—which exploits structures the user has set up for retrieval and involves incremental manual traversal of these structures.

- Search—a more indirect way to find information—where the user generates textual labels that refer to the name of an information item, one of its attributes, or its contents.

There are advantages and disadvantages to both methods. Navigation, being incremental, offers the user feedback at each access stage (Barreau & Nardi, 1995; Bergman, Beyth-Marom, Nachmias,

Gradovitch, & Whittaker, 2008); but in the case of complex folder hierarchies can be laborious because of the multiple levels to traverse. Search is potentially more flexible, allowing users to specify multiple properties of the target file (Lansdale, 1988). However, it is reliant on being able to *remember* salient properties of the target item in order to generate appropriate search terms.

Relation to Jones's PIM Framework

The differences in terminology between our framework and that of Jones and Teevan (2007) and Jones (2007a) are shown in Table 1.1. The frameworks concur in their overall characterization of key personal information management processes, such as keeping and management. However, Jones and Teevan's (2007) main focus is on finding and refinding of public data, for example, if people want to repeatedly access a valued web resource. In contrast, in this review we are more concerned with information that people create themselves or that they receive in email. Where we focus on web data it is in the context of users' efforts to integrate such information into their personal information systems. Our stricter definition of personal information means we begin our model with keeping. Keeping is a prerequisite for later stages: People cannot manage or exploit information that they have not kept. In contrast, Jones and Teevan's (2007) concern is more with public data and they begin with (re)finding such information, because it already exists in the public domain without users making efforts to create or preserve it.

Table 1.1 Comparison of PIM activities proposed by Jones (2007a) and Jones and Teevan (2007) with those used in this chapter

PIM Activities (Jones, 2007a; Jones & Teevan, 2007)	Curation Lifecycle
(Re)finding	
Keeping	Keeping
Metalevel activities (managing, maintaining, …)	Management
	Exploitation

Interrelations Among Keeping, Management, and Exploitation

As will be obvious from the foregoing, there are close relations among the different processes in the curation lifecycle. For example, successful exploitation is highly dependent on the information people choose to preserve as well as the method they use to manage it. Keeping information does not necessarily guarantee that it will be successfully exploited: The more information we keep, the more effort has to go into organizing and maintaining it. Critically, having more information may increase the difficulty of exploitation because finding what one needs may be harder when there is more information to search.

Past outcomes may also influence future curation behaviors and exploitation success may influence future keeping and management practices. If certain information is difficult to re-access or maintain, people may conclude that there is little point in keeping it in future. In the same way, exploitation failure may cause people to change their management methods. If users realize that certain types of organization are less successful in promoting access, they may abandon those methods.

Information Properties

Not all information items are equivalent. We need to distinguish among various *information properties*, as these differences have implications for how each type of item will be curated.

Informative vs. Action-Oriented Items

Compare, for example, an average email message with a page found in a web search. One crucial property of many email messages is that they require the recipient *to do something*, whether it is to respond to a question, arrange a meeting, or provide some information. Such email messages are *action oriented*, because the message recipient is expected to *respond* in some way, often within a specific timeframe ("let me know about this within the next day"). In contrast, information items found during a web search are potentially *informative*—but do not usually require users to *act*: The page may be diverting but there is no *requirement* to process the information on the page to meet a given deadline. Of course this information vs. action distinction does not map neatly to computer applications. Not every message in email is action oriented (e.g., when people send us FYIs) and not every webpage is purely informative (e.g., when it contains a request to complete a form).

This distinction has critical implications for how we treat personal information. For reasons that will become clear, it is often impossible to discharge *action-oriented* items immediately. So, *reminding strategies* (e.g., creating task related email folders or leaving active documents on the desktop) have to be set up to prompt users about their commitments with respect to the undischarged item. Failure to set up such structures can have severe implications for job success and productivity; we must not forget to respond to that important request from our boss, even when we are inundated with other commitments. In contrast, how we deal with *informative* items is usually more discretionary: They usually do not need to be actively processed to meet deadlines, so it is less critical that we create dedicated reminding structures to ensure that they are dealt with appropriately.

Information Uniqueness

Another critical information property is *uniqueness*. Uniqueness has strong implications for how we deal with personal information. Certain types of information (such as personal files that we create ourselves) may be resident *only on our computer*. As a result we may be the only person in the world who has access to those items. Anyone who has lost data following a system crash is only too aware that if we do not take responsibility for storing and maintaining unique data, it will not be preserved for future access (Marshall, 2008a, 2008b). In contrast, public information such as web data may be resident on multiple servers and may be recoverable even if we personally take no action to store a local copy. Email data lie somewhere in between. We may be able to ask coworkers to regenerate a copy of an important message that we have temporarily mislaid, or lost in a system crash, but we cannot guarantee they will have kept that information.

It is important to note that uniqueness is defined *subjectively*: relative to our own goals and interests. Innumerable unique information items exist in the world, but as curators our only concern is to take decisive action to preserve those that are *relevant to us*. Other people's information may be equally important to them, but there is no reason we should be concerned to preserve it, unless of course we work with them. This personal uniqueness is often associated with information that we have invested *effort* in generating. If we have dedicated substantial time to generating an information item (e.g., an extended personal document, a carefully crafted presentation, or a collection of wedding photos), then that information will be something that we make enormous efforts to preserve, in part because of the effort involved in regenerating it.

Uniqueness has a huge impact on our management strategies. No one else will take care of our unique personal data. We personally need to create reliable structures for re-accessing highly personal data such as passwords, tax forms, passport details, or financial records, even when we rarely need to access this information. Personally produced documents also tend to be unique and need to be carefully organized. The same is largely true for email messages: We need to have reliable methods for re-accessing these because we cannot always rely on others to keep the important messages that we need. Webpages are rather different. They are generally more easily recoverable (via search or browsing) even if we have not bookmarked them. And in addition, because we have not usually been responsible for generating their content, we are not as concerned if we cannot recover the information they contain.

Table 1.2 shows the key properties of common classes of information, such as paper, electronic files, email, photos, and web documents. The table shows these are very different with respect to action orientation and also uniqueness. Current paper and electronic documents and email messages are often action oriented. Paper and electronic documents and personal photos tend to be unique. These differences have strong implications for curation. The uniqueness of paper or electronic personal documents

Table 1.2 Main properties of different information types

Information Type	Action or Information Oriented?	Uniqueness
Personal paper documents	Action oriented if self-created and current Long-term archives tend to be informational	Unique if self-created or annotated
Personal electronic documents	Action oriented if self-created and current Long-term archives tend to be informational	Unique if self-created
Email	Often action oriented Long-term archives tend to be informational	Range from unique to non-unique mass mailings
Personal photos	Affective	Predominantly unique
Web	Informational	Non-unique

and personal photos leads people to be very conservative and to keep most of these items. They also have to preserve action oriented items such as email messages and personal documents in ways that promote effective action.

We now turn to each of the main curation processes, describing how people keep, manage, and exploit their personal information. It will be clear from our prior discussion that there are huge dependencies among these processes. In what follows, we review each of these processes separately; but we should not lose sight of the relationships among them.

Keeping

Overview, Problems, and Strategies

We encounter too much information to keep it all because of various costs including:

- Management costs: We need to organize information if we are to obtain value from it. The more we keep, the more management effort is required. Some visions of new technology suggest that in the future our information will be organized automatically, but these technologies are not yet in place. Indeed, in future sections, we explore whether these technologies will *ever* effectively replace the need for manual organization.

- Exploitation costs: Keeping information of low value increases the difficulty of retrieval. Keeping too many items can be distracting if manual browsing is used for access. Nevertheless, there are those who contend that future retrieval will be entirely *search based*, reducing exploitation costs regardless of how much we keep.

Keeping decisions are a fact of life. Every day we receive new email messages, create new files and folders, and browse new websites. Some of this information is of little long-term value but some of it is task-critical and needs to be preserved for the long term. Boardman and Sasse's (2004) data suggest that users acquire an average of five new files per day, five email messages[1] per day, and one bookmark every five days. Other studies indicate people acquire one new contact per day (Whittaker, Jones, & Terveen, 2002a), and around five digital photos (Whittaker et al., 2010). But these statistics are an oversimplification of the complexity of keeping decisions. The statistics record *positive* decisions but fail to register the many decisions to reject information judged to be of little value. To be more specific, we know that users receive an average of 42 email messages per day; so focusing exclusively on the five they actively decide to keep overlooks the 37 decisions they make to delete irrelevant information. For email alone, making the highly conservative assumption that email volumes will not change over our lifetimes, this equates to around 1 million keeping decisions over a 60-year digital life.

We know from various interview and survey studies how difficult people find it to decide what information they want to keep (Bergman, Tucker, Beyth-Marom, Cutrell, & Whittaker, 2009; Boardman & Sasse, 2004; Jones, 2004, 2007a, 2007b; Whittaker & Hirschberg, 2001; Whittaker & Sidner, 1996). But why are keeping decisions so difficult? One reason is that they require us to predict the future. To decide what to keep, we have to determine the probable future value of an information item.

This may be a general psychological problem. A great deal of psychological research shows that people are poor at making many types of decisions that involve their future. Such prediction requires people to reason about hypothetical situations, at which they are notoriously poor. People's predictions are also subject to various types of bias. For example, they expect the future to be very much like the present; and their predictions are unduly influenced by recent, or easily recalled, events (Gilbert, 2006; Kahneman & Tversky, 1979).

In the PIM context, the keeping decision requires people to predict future informational contexts and assess future informational requirements. Jones (2004, online) argues that the decision whether "to keep or not to keep" information for future usage is prone to two types of costly mistakes. On one hand, information not kept is unavailable when it is needed later. On the other, keeping irrelevant information not only causes guilt about being disorganized (Boardman & Sasse, 2004; Whittaker & Sidner, 1996), it also increases retrieval time. Irrelevant information competes for the user's attention, obscuring important information relevant to the current task. Indeed, it is well known in psychology that in visual search the number of irrelevant distracters increases the time taken for people to identify a target object (Treisman & Gelade, 1980). Furthermore, there is a "deletion paradox": although unimportant information items distract attention and increase retrieval time for important items, it takes time and effort to review items to decide whether to delete them (Bergman et al., 2009, p. 269).

When people weigh the advantages of keeping versus deleting, some of the reasons for keeping are rational—after all, the user can always think of a situation when the information item may be needed (Whittaker & Hirschberg, 2001). However, there are also less rational reasons why people avoid deletion, which can be attributed to general psychological decision-making processes (Kahneman & Tversky, 1979). In making decisions, losses and gains are evaluated *asymmetrically*: Losses are more salient than gains and the possible loss of information emotionally influences the decision maker more than the gains of reduced retrieval time. Small objective probabilities are subjectively weighted more highly than their actual likelihood. Thus people perceive as significant the very small probability that a deleted information item will be needed.

We now review various studies looking at keeping decisions people make, when managing their paper archives, email messages, contacts, webpages, and personal photos.

Keeping Paper

Somewhat curiously, in spite of the prevalence of keeping decisions, relatively few studies have looked at this directly. One exception is a study of people's paper archiving behavior (Whittaker & Hirschberg, 2001). Although there is a common intuition that the world is shifting away from paper and becoming more digital, we will see that people treat paper in ways that are very similar to their treatment of digital information.

One methodological problem with investigating keeping behavior lies in finding contexts where people are explicitly focused on the keeping decision. Our study identified one such situation. Participants were about to move offices and had to decide which information to keep and what to throw away. When we interviewed them, they had all recently sorted through their paper archives in preparation for the move. Their new offices had reduced personal storage space compared with their existing offices, although extra storage was provided in public locations. This reduction in local storage motivated careful reflection as well as sorting and discarding existing data. In interviewing and surveying workers, we capitalized on the fact that they had very recently handled most of their paper data, forcing them to identify criteria for determining what to keep and what to discard.

Discarding Behavior

People experienced major problems in deciding what to keep and what to throw away. As the psychology literature would suggest, there was a bias toward preservation. Even after spending large amounts of time deciding what to discard, workers still retained huge archives after the move. In preparation for the move, people spent almost nine hours rationalizing their data and reported that this was a difficult process. In spite of these efforts, the amount of information that people actually threw away was small compared with what they kept: They discarded just 22 percent of their original archives, with the final preserved archive averaging more than 18 mover's boxes.

We looked at the characteristics not only of what people kept, but also of what was discarded. As expected, at least some of the discarded data constituted once-valuable information that had become *obsolete*. As jobs, personal interests, or company strategy changes, the value of particular information decreases. But not all discarded information underwent the transition from valuable to obsolete. For example, 23 percent of discarded data was *unread*. Two general problems led to this accumulation of superfluous information. First, people experience problems with *information overload*, leading them to only partially process incoming information. Second they engage in *deferred evaluation* of what to keep—causing them to acquire large amounts of data that later turn out to be extraneous.

Information overload occurs when people have insufficient time to process all the information to which they are exposed. One consequence of information overload is that non-urgent information is never processed. Non-urgent data are set aside (often in optimistically named "to read" piles), accumulating indefinitely, because the same time pressures that prevent complete processing of incoming data also prevent rationalizing ("clean-up") of archives. Consequently, people seldom discover that their unread non-urgent documents are superfluous until exceptional circumstances (such as an office move) force them to scrutinize their archives.

Yet even when people find the time to examine new information systematically, uncertainty of the future value of that information means they are often highly conservative—postponing final judgments about utility until some unspecified future date. Some people deliberately *defer evaluation* about incoming information, allowing time to pass so as to make better informed judgments about information utility. Often these post-hoc judgments are based on whether information was ever actually used.

Deferred evaluation means people retain information of unclear value—*just in case* it later turns out to be useful. Finally, judgments about potential utility are made more difficult because the value of data can change over time. Knowing that the value of information might change also leads some people to postpone the keeping decision while there is still archival space.

Accumulating unprocessed data and deferring evaluation are good from the (conservative) perspective that potentially valuable information is not lost. However, the problem with this approach is that people seldom revisit their archives to rationalize them, so they end up containing considerable amounts of information of dubious value. Thus, 74 percent of our users had not cleaned out their archives for over a year. Furthermore, very few clean-ups occur spontaneously: 84 percent arise from extrinsic events such as job changes or office moves. This infrequency of clean-ups means that documents are often not discovered to be superfluous until they have been stored for some time.

To sum up, our deletion data illustrate important aspects of keeping. When extraordinary events such an office move occur, people discard about 22 percent of their data, some of which is obsolete. However, other factors beside obsolescence, such as information overload and deferred evaluation, mean that archives are polluted by marginally relevant data. Rather than discarding once-valuable information that is now of little utility, much of what people later discard is unprocessed information they have never properly evaluated, or kept just in case.

What Do We Keep and Why Do We Keep It?

We also looked at the properties of the information people kept and their reasons for keeping it. One conjecture was that a large proportion of the information kept would be unique to that person. In contrast, we expected people to be much less likely to keep publicly available data. Why take responsibility for data that are available elsewhere?

Uniqueness was clearly important in determining whether users would preserve certain documents. Unique data are usually highly associated with their archiver. Three types of unique data accounted for 49 percent of people's archives: working notes, archives of completed projects, and legal documents.

But contrary to our expectations, uniqueness was not the sole criterion for deciding to keep data. Only 49 percent of people's original archive was unique: 15 percent was unread, but 36 percent consisted of *copies of publicly available documents*. We have already discussed why people preserve unread data, but why keep duplicates of public documents? Four main reasons were given: availability, reminding, lack of trust in external stores, and sentiment.

Availability allows relevant materials to be at hand when people need them. Several people mentioned not wanting to experience the delay associated with refinding information, or even accessing it on the web. In other words they wanted to reduce their exploitation costs by keeping valued information in a personal archive.

Reminding relates to availability. A personal copy prompts people about outstanding actions associated with a document, or simply reminds them they are in possession of that information. Documents in public or digital stores seemed less capable of supporting reminding. People also kept personal copies of public data because they did not trust other archival institutions to keep the documents they needed. Distrust of external stores also extended to digital resources such as the web.

In addition to these functional reasons, people described sentimental reasons for keeping information. People admit such information has little relevance for likely future activities but they still cannot part with it because it is part of their intellectual history and professional identity.

Another potential reason for keeping personal copies of publicly available documents is that they contain *personal annotations*. Other research has documented the utility of annotations for focusing attention and improving comprehension of what is read or heard (Kalnikaitė & Whittaker, 2007, 2008a; Sellen & Harper, 2002). Although most people made such annotations, they seemed of little long-term use. Many people stated that annotations had transient value, becoming uninterpretable after some time has elapsed. This is consistent with recent studies of long-term note taking, showing that the utility of handwritten notes decreases even after a month (Kalnikaitė & Whittaker, 2007, 2008a).

Keeping Email

Email is different from either self-created files or documents accessed on the web. One major difference is that a significant proportion of the information we receive in email is *actionable*: we have to respond to it or process it, often within a specific time frame. This contrasts with most web-based information which does not demand action. Another significant difference is that most email messages are generated by others (who in some cases are unfamiliar to the main user). This lack of familiarity sometimes makes it harder for people to decide on the utility of such email information. A final, rather different, characteristic of email is its sheer variability. In our inboxes we may see many different types of messages, including: tasks or to-do items, documents/attachments, fyis, schedules, social messages, and jokes. Again, this heterogeneity makes the keeping decision rather different from that for other information types.

Overall we keep about 70 percent of our email messages (Dabbish, Kraut, Fussell, & Kiesler, 2005). This seems a surprisingly high retention rate, given the apparent irrelevance of many of the email messages we receive, but there are reasons for this. We shall separately discuss people's keeping behaviors for informational versus actionable messages, because the keeping behavior is very different.

Informational Messages

Informational messages form about one third (34 percent) of what is delivered in email (Dabbish et al., 2005). Informational messages are treated in a similar manner to paper documents. As with paper, the keeping decision is often difficult. People find it hard to judge the value of incoming informational messages, so they use the *deferral strategy*.

Rather than investing valuable time in reading a new informational message, users register its arrival but defer dealing with it until they are more certain of its value. Deferred email messages are kept around, allowing more informed judgments to be made later.

Users are aware that deferred messages need to be re-evaluated at a later point. Some employ folders for this purpose: 28 percent of informational messages are filed for later reading (Dabbish et al., 2005). However, the problem with this strategy is that filing may lead these messages to be out of sight and out of mind because these folders are seldom revisited (Whittaker & Sidner, 1996). A more common strategy is to leave them in the inbox: Dabbish and colleagues (2005) found 42 percent of informational messages are left in the inbox, increasing the probability that deferred evaluation will actually take place. The inbox is an active workspace: Leaving information there increases the chance that information will be revisited as users re-access the inbox to process incoming messages. But there is an obvious downside to this strategy. Although the strategy increases the probability of revisiting yet-to-be-decided items, the presence of such unevaluated information makes it more difficult for people to locate important information, such as messages requiring action (Bellotti, Ducheneaut, Howard, & Smith, 2003; Whittaker, 2005; Whittaker & Sidner, 1996).

As with paper archives, people experience information overload in email. Overload may lead people to defer completely reading each message until they have more time. And of course because they are constantly bombarded with more incoming messages, they often never return to deferred messages (Whittaker & Sidner, 1996). One factor contributing to whether a message is read is its length; Whittaker and Sidner found that 21 percent of inbox messages contained enough text to fill more than five screens, consistent with the fact that people leave longer messages there for later reading.

Actionable Items

Actionable messages are those with which we have to do something specific. In an ideal world (such as that inhabited by management consultants), we might process these messages just once, carrying out the required action and then deleting them. This is often referred to as the one-touch model. The advantages of the model are obvious: Touching a message just once means that users do not forget to deal with it; and they do not have to repeatedly reconstruct the context of old messages when they eventually come to process these. And if messages are processed at once this keeps the inbox clear for important incoming messages.

Some users try to adhere to this model: Overall, users reply to 65 percent of actionable messages immediately (Dabbish et al., 2005). An immediate reply clearly reduces the chance that one will forget to act on a message. However, even when people do reply immediately *they still keep 85 percent of actionable messages*, suggesting that one touch does not describe actual practice.

Several reasons may account for such retention. In some cases, one touch and an immediate reply are not possible. Many important email tasks are too complex or lengthy to be executed immediately (Bellotti et al., 2005; Venolia, Gupta, Cadiz, & Dabbish, 2001; Whittaker, 2005; Whittaker & Sidner, 1996). This leads to deferral of 37 percent of actionable messages (Dabbish et al., 2005). Deferral is often a direct consequence of *interdependent* tasks: those involving tight collaboration with others (Bellotti et al., 2005; Whittaker, 2005). Interdependence results in both iteration and delays between messages relating to the task. Iteration arises because interdependent tasks often require multiple exchanges between participants (Bellotti et al., 2005; Venolia et al., 2001; Venolia & Neustaedter, 2003; Whittaker & Sidner, 1996). People may need to negotiate exactly what a collaborative email task involves or who will be responsible for each component. This consensus needs to be built and multiple responses often need to be collated. Delays occur because these negotiations take time and because collaborators often lack the necessary information to respond immediately to address their parts of the task. One way to estimate the prevalence of interdependent tasks is by determining how many email messages are part of a conversational thread, because threads indicate relations and common underlying activities among messages. Threading estimates range from 30 to 62 percent of messages (Bellotti et al., 2003; Whittaker et al., 2007).

The need to defer actionable messages has important consequences for keeping. Unless actions are discharged, messages are usually kept around as reminders that they are still incomplete. Actionable messages are therefore almost always kept (only 0.5 percent are deleted). This figure is much higher than for information messages, 30 percent of which are deleted. Furthermore, actionable messages have to be kept in a way that guarantees that they will be reencountered. It is no good deferring to-do email messages unless you have some method of guaranteeing that you actually return to them. We revisit this issue in the next section, when we talk about management strategies.

Keeping Contacts

Contact management is another area that demands careful keeping decisions. Whittaker, Jones, and Terveen (2002a) looked at people's address books, rolodexes, calendars, and contact management programs to explore the criteria they used for including someone in their contact lists. We are overloaded with respect to the contacts we encounter. We are copied on many messages and we read webpages or blogs from friends, colleagues, and strangers. Some of these are people with whom we want to interact again. Others may have been involved in one-off conversations that require no follow-up. Contact management requires decisions as to the people about whom you will keep contact information, as well as the types of information that you will keep about those people.

Deciding on important contacts from the many people that you are exposed to on a daily basis is complex. As with paper and email archives, it is hard to know whether you will need to communicate with that person in the future: whether someone is an *important contact* becomes clear only over time. Just as with the deferral strategy, our informants often *over-saved* information, leading to huge rolodexes, overflowing booklets of business cards, and faded post-it notes scattered around their work areas. But in spite of this strategy, participants were exposed to many more contacts than those about whom they recorded information.

We identified specific factors that were critical in determining important contacts. Just as with deferred evaluation in email and paper archives, the final decision to keep depends on past interaction with the contact, in particular *frequency* and *recency* of communication. People also noted how difficult it was to make decisions about the future based on short-term interactions and scanty evidence. Again we see the importance of *long-term* information in evaluating contacts: important contacts are those with whom we have repeated interactions over extended periods. In addition, the selection process is error-prone because of the difficulty of predicting long-term relationships on the basis of brief initial interactions.

In a follow-up study, we presented people with contacts mined from their email archives and asked them to distinguish between important and unimportant ones. The findings were striking. In spite of having huge archives of contacts (858 on average), participants rated only 14 percent (118) as important and worth keeping. Criteria for inclusion echoed those identified in our earlier interviews: Participants chose contacts with whom they interacted frequently and recently, as well as for a long time, and who were likely to respond to their email messages. They excluded spammers.

Overall, interesting parallels appear among contacts, paper, and email messages. People are exposed to many more contacts than they can record systematic information for, so they reserve judgment and overkeep data about contacts they do not need. Furthermore, the criteria people use to judge the value of contacts are based around usage and interaction: Valued contacts are those with whom they interact frequently and recently. However, one key difference between contacts, email, and paper is that users ignore or discard a much higher percentage of encountered contacts.

Keeping Webpages

Similar problematic keeping decisions also surface on the web (Jones, 2004), where we see errors of commission (overkeeping information that turns out to have little future value) and omission (failing to keep information that turns out to be needed later). There are clear errors of commission; for example, people expend energy creating bookmarks that they never subsequently use. Tauscher and Greenberg (1997) showed that 58 percent of bookmarks are never used, suggesting poor decision making.

At the same time, other studies of web behaviors reveal failures of omission—where people do not preserve information that turns out to be useful later. Wen (2003) coined the term *post retrieval value* to describe web resources that people have accessed but not preserved—only later realizing their utility. His study showed that people were able to later find only about 20 percent of information they have previously accessed and attended to in an earlier information retrieval session. Such failure originates in part from an unwillingness to make deliberate attempts to keep information; users were unwilling to create bookmarks as records of useful pages because these would clutter their current bookmark collection. These findings were replicated in similar studies (Aula et al., 2005). Instead, users preferred to try to retrace their original searches—a strategy that is often unsuccessful.

Keeping Photos

With the advent of digital photography, the number of pictures that people are now taking has increased massively (Bentley, Metcalf, & Harboe, 2006; Kirk, Sellen, Rother, & Wood, 2006; Whittaker et al., 2010; Wilhelm, Takhteyev, Sarvas, Van House, & Davis, 2004) and similar keeping issues are beginning to arise for digital photos. We looked at this in a study of parents with young families (Whittaker et al., 2010) who had an average of 4,475 digital pictures. All participants deleted some pictures, both when pictures were taken and when they were uploading from camera to computer. Participants estimated they deleted on average 17 percent of their pictures. The reasons they gave for deletion were that the pictures were of poor technical quality or did not capture an event of interest. In general, deletion was a difficult process, as evidenced by the fact that many of the pictures that were kept were near duplicates (i.e., multiple pictures of identical scenes), an observation that is confirmed in other studies (Kirk et al., 2006), suggesting that people are keeping their options open about the best view of a given scene. One of the reasons people gave for this overkeeping was that they perceived little cost in keeping many photos. They were not, therefore, focused on the exploitation/retrieval context when they made keeping decisions. As with paper and email, people had a strong expectation that they would return to their photo collection to rationalize it at a later date. And as in our paper and email studies, this rationalization seldom occurred.

Keeping Summary

Keeping decisions are difficult because they require people to: (1) predict their future retrieval needs, (2) take into account the possibility that those information needs may change, and (3) make utility decisions under conditions of information overload, often on incomplete readings of information.

Errors are made: the primary tendency is overkeeping—keeping things that are never accessed (observed with paper, email, contacts, and photo archives)—although there is evidence from some web studies of failing to keep information that later turns out to be relevant.

Consistent with overkeeping, deletion is relatively infrequent, varying from 17 percent for photos to 30 percent for email messages. Contacts are very different, however; it seems that because people are exposed to many more of these, they are happy to ignore 86 percent of the contacts they encounter.

The nature of the information item affects the keeping decision. This decision is relatively straightforward for certain items: We obviously need to keep actionable email messages that have not been handled or unique personally generated items that no one else will safeguard. However, it is very hard for people to determine the value of data such as public webpages or informational email messages.

Rather than viewing keeping as a one-time decision, people often used a deferral strategy—waiting to see whether information was useful. Two major weaknesses of deferral are: (1) people seldom return to their collections to carry out a re-evaluation of tentatively kept information; (2) deferral means that collections are full of items of dubious value, which makes it more difficult to find truly valuable information.

People do not generally seem to be aware of the implications of overkeeping. Although they complain about how full their inboxes are, they nevertheless delete only 30 percent of email messages; even after spending days working though paper archives they still preserve 78 percent of those. On the web, in contrast, there is a suggestion that people do not bookmark even though they are aware that this will make valued materials harder to find. This could be because they consider web information to be unimportant or because they think it is easily recoverable by other means.

Management

Overview, Problems, and Strategies

We first describe different methods for organizing information, as well as the trade-offs among them. We next discuss factors that influence users' choice of management strategies and studies evaluating the utility of these strategies. We then briefly talk about a radical alternative, which proposes that we forgo preparatory organization altogether and rely totally on search for information exploitation.

Management is a crucial curation process because it directly affects exploitation. We are constantly acquiring information and, over long periods, large amounts of personal information accumulate (Marshall, 2008a, 2008b). Using current estimates of how many documents, digital photos, and email messages we acquire on a daily basis (Boardman & Sasse, 2004; Whittaker et al., 2010), and making the conservative estimate that these will remain constant over our digital lifetimes, we will actively save around 125,000 documents, 115,000 email messages, and 120,000 digital photographs.

Certain types of management also take place more often than we might expect. For some items, such as files and email messages, people are perpetually and actively engaged in re-organization, as reflected by the frequent small modifications they make to their information. For example, a longitudinal study (Boardman & Sasse, 2004) found that people create a new file folder every three days and they make a new email folder every five days. In each case, the new structure demonstrates that people are constantly reflecting on how their information is currently organized and finding it to be inadequate. However, as mentioned in the keeping section, people seldom engage in major reorganizations or extensive deletion. Instead, they tend to modify existing structures incrementally. They are highly unlikely, however, to monitor and re-organize photos or contacts, for reasons that will become clear.

People also make management mistakes. They often engage in counterproductive behaviors in organizing their information. Studies of web bookmarking show that people construct complex hierarchical bookmarking systems (Abrams et al., 1998; Aula et al., 2005). Yet, we have already seen that users *never* access 42 percent of the bookmarks they organize for later retrieval (Tauscher & Greenberg, 1997). Efforts at organizing email messages may also not bear fruit. Email filing accounts for 10 percent of total time in email (Bellotti et al., 2005), yet information is usually accessed by browsing the inbox or search, rather than folder access (Tang, Wilcox, Cerruti, Badenes, Nusser, & Schoudt, 2008; Whittaker, 2005; Whittaker et al., 2007). With personal photos they may make the opposite type of mistake and fail to organize information when there is a clear need to do so. For example, a study of personal photo retrieval showed a failure to impose even rudimentary organization—in part because people believed that they would be able to retrieve their photos without needing to organize them (Whittaker et al., 2010).

Semantic Organization

Organizing information is a fundamental cognitive activity. One basic approach is to apply conceptual organization to information. Even newborn infants categorize objects, with natural psychological categories tending to be based around exemplars or prototypes. For example, an individual's concept of bird is based around exemplars such as robins, rather than unusual cases such as penguins. Our judgments and reasoning are influenced by the extent to which particular instances are similar to those exemplars (Rosch, 1978; Rosch, Mervis, Gray, Johnson, & Boyes-Braem, 1976).

When managing personal information, two different and separate aspects to organization are important for effective exploitation. We call these *mental* and *external* cueing. As many psychological studies have shown, the mental act of imposing organization on information makes it inherently more memorable. Organizing things within a consistent conceptual structure means that, at recall, one item may trigger memory of a related one; therefore, applying semantic organization is highly effective in promoting recall (Baddeley, 1997; Craik & Lockhart, 1972). Organization helps recall, even if people do not have direct access to their organizational scheme at retrieval. For example, in a recent study we showed that the simple act of organizing conversational information by taking notes increased recall even when people did not use their notes at retrieval time (Kalnikaitė & Whittaker, 2008b). Organization is also important because the products of organizational efforts can themselves be used as external retrieval cues. Appropriate notes can serve as cues to remind us about information items that we might otherwise have forgotten (Kalnikaitė & Whittaker, 2007, 2008b). Well chosen folder names cue people about their contents and organization (Bergman et al., 2003; Jones & Dumais, 1986; Jones, Phuwanartnurak, Gill, & Bruce, 2005; Lansdale, 1988).

Organization and labelling are mainstays of most computer operating systems. The primary way people organize their digital information is to sort it recursively into categories (in directories, folders, or subfolders) and then apply meaningful labels to these folders and subfolders. The act of applying organization may help retrieval by mental cueing, as well as generating a navigable conceptual structure with folder labels serving as external retrieval cues. Note also that folders usually contain a strong spatial component—with subfolders sitting inside; this, too, can help cue retrieval (Jones & Dumais, 1986).

Temporal Organization and Reminding

A second, less obvious, type of organization has been less extensively researched. We have already seen that some important information with which people deal is *actionable*. Further, it is usually the case that those actions are *required to happen by a certain time*, for example, to meet a certain deadline. People must therefore ensure that actionable information is organized in such a way that it is encountered at the right time, allowing the deadline to be met. This is the problem of *reminding*. It is no good having an extensive organizational structure allowing access to any item, if you forget the deadline relating to that information. Reminding is a critical problem, especially in the case of email, where actionable items are prevalent.

Most psychology research on organization has looked at natural categories (e.g., how we mentally organize places, events, names, and faces). It has not looked at the types of information we are addressing here, namely *synthetic,* human-generated information such as documents, email messages, photos or webpages. Nevertheless, human–computer interaction (HCI) and library science research have looked into people's preferences for organizing such personal data. For example, people prefer to relocate their documents *spatially* rather than using keyword search (Barreau & Nardi 1995; Bergman et al., 2008). This spatial organization works even better when the document space is three-dimensional, although this may not scale well to large numbers of files (Robertson, Czerwinski, Larson, Robbins, Thiel, & van Dantzich, 1998). However, there are limits to the utility of spatial organization: Semantic labels are stronger retrieval cues than spatial organization alone, although combinations of semantic and spatial organization can enhance performance (Jones & Dumais, 1986). And semantic and spatial cues are enhanced when these are *self-selected*, rather than being chosen by an external party (Bergman et al., 2003; Lansdale & Edmonds, 1992). There is also evidence for the utility of temporal organization as a retrieval cue. People can successfully retrieve documents by associating them with personal or public events that happened close to the time that the documents were encountered or created (Ringel, Cutrell, Dumais, & Horvitz, 2003). The importance of temporal factors is also shown by log files of search tools revealing a bias toward retrieval of *highly recent* information (Cutrell, Dumais, et al., 2006; Dumais et al., 2003).

In addition to these overall organizational preferences, other work has explored different types of management strategies and what motivates people to choose them. We now describe strategies for paper, digital files, email, web documents, and photos. We review the types of management strategies employed, what influences people's choice of strategy, and the trade-offs between strategies.

Several recent papers have argued that manual organization of our personal data will soon become obsolete. Improvements in desktop search will mean that documents, email messages, and webpages can be easily retrieved without the need for active organization (Cutrell, Dumais, et al., 2006; Russell & Lawrence, 2007). This is an appealing idea. We have seen that management activities are difficult for users, who may invest in organizational efforts that are not always directly successful. We consider these claims in more detail when we discuss exploitation techniques and evaluate the efficacy of different search tools.

Managing Paper

Malone (1983) conducted a pioneering study into people's organizational habits for paper, identifying two main strategies he called filing and piling. *Filing* involves constructing an exhaustive, hierarchical taxonomy, with semantically related items stored in each subcategory. In contrast, *piling* is more laissez-faire, usually resulting in shallower, less systematic hierarchies. Piles tend to be fewer in number with each pile containing more items, with looser associations between items stored in the same pile. Items may also be in a common pile because they were first generated or acquired at the same time.

There are clear trade-offs between these two organizational strategies. Piles are easier to create and maintain because they are less systematic. They have a less clear organizational structure with more items in each pile, which may make retrieval within each pile less efficient. But because there tend to be fewer piles in total, this leaves fewer potential locations to be searched, which may compensate for the lack of organization. Fewer piles may also mean that users visit each pile more frequently and end up being more familiar with the contents of each. Files, in contrast, require more effort at creation time and more maintenance. However, they offer benefits at retrieval, providing a more coherent retrieval structure along with more relevant labels as cues. These advantages may be offset by the fact that there may be more categories, so files may have more levels to navigate. Files may also fall into disrepair, with too many levels/distinctions being too infrequently visited, making distinctions between categories harder to remember.

In the move study described previously, we investigated when and why people choose filing or piling strategies. The distinction between filers and pilers was not absolute, being instead one of degree. All our respondents filed some information but kept other information in desktop piles. We classified users according to how likely they were to file information. Based on the predominant strategies that people described in our interviews, we identified a threshold of 40 percent for people to be categorized as filers.

Pilers often amass information without attempting to organize it systematically. This laissez-faire approach should lead to an accumulation of unscrutinized information before the office move. We found to our surprise that pilers had smaller original archives. They also had less preserved information than filers after cleaning out their archives. Why then did filers amass more information? Our interviews suggested one possible reason is *premature filing*: filers may file information that turns out to be of little utility and must be discarded later. If filers are more likely to incorporate documents of uncertain quality into their filing systems, we might expect them to throw away more reference materials than pilers in preparing for the move. This was not true for all documents, but was true for reference documents.

There were also differences between strategies in terms of data acquisition. We expected pilers to acquire information faster because they tend not to scrutinize incoming data as carefully. We looked at data acquisition rates, in separate analyses of original and preserved (i.e., post-move) information volumes. For both measures, pilers tended to be slower to acquire original as well as preserved information, when we allow for the number of years they had been in the company.

Given their more systematically organized systems, we expected filers to have an easier time of finding data and that they would access their data more often. Contrary to our expectations, pilers had accessed a greater percentage of documents than filers in the last year. Why were pilers more likely to access recent data? The interviews revealed both strategies had strengths and weaknesses. With a piling strategy, information is more accessible: It can be located in a relatively small number of piles through which people frequently sift. The result of this is that valuable, frequently accessed information moves to the top of the piles and less relevant material ends up located lower down. This pattern of repeated access allows people to identify important information, discarding unused or irrelevant information.

But the lack of a coherent system with piling has some disadvantages. Taken to excess, piles can dominate not just working surfaces but all areas of the office. However, even though filing is more systematic, it does not always guarantee easy access to information. With complex data, filing systems can become so arcane that people forget the categories they have already created, leading to duplicate categories. Accessing only one of these duplicates leads to incomplete retrieval because some part of the original information will be neglected. This illustrates a general disadvantage to filing strategies: They incur a large overhead for constructing, maintaining, and rationalizing complex organizations of documents. Similar findings are reported in a study comparing folders and tags as methods of organizing personal information (Civan, Jones, Klasnja, & Bruce, 2008).

A final possible reason that filers access proportionally less of their data is that they simply have more stuff. There are finite constraints on how much data one can access. Filers have more data and, as a consequence, they are able to access less of it. This is consistent with the observation that the absolute amounts of data accessed by both groups were very similar.

We also expected filers to be quicker to rationalize their data in preparing for the move, given the greater care they had initially taken to organize their data. But there were no differences in packing time for filers and pilers. This could be because filers' greater organization is offset by having more data through which to sift. And contrary to our predictions, pilers found it subjectively easier to rationalize archives in preparation for the move. Why was this? Even though filers discarded more reference information, they generally found it difficult to discard filed documents, partly because of the investment they had already made in managing that information. Filers therefore seemed less disposed to discard information they had invested effort in organizing. In contrast, unfiled information seemed easier to discard.

Finally, we looked at what determined strategy choice. Although job type influenced strategy somewhat (e.g., secretaries were more likely to be filers), in general strategy seemed to be more affected by dispositional factors.

Managing Digital Files and Folders

We access our files and folders on a daily basis and their organization has clear importance for our everyday digital lives, yet there have been relatively few studies of how people organize these files and what affects this organization. One exception is Boardman and Sasse's (2004) study, which looked at the structure of people's personal data; they found that on average people had 57 folders with a depth of 3.3 folders. That study also documented different filing strategies, finding that 58 percent of people systematically filed information items when they created them, a further 35 percent left many items unfiled (in a manner similar to paper piling), with a small proportion (6 percent) leaving most items unfiled. In some cases, people did not file actionable documents (i.e., those on which they were currently working), instead leaving them in obvious places such as the desktop where they would be reminded about them. Boardman and Sasse also looked at the types of folders that people created, identifying two main classes: project and role oriented. Finally, they looked longer term to see whether management strategies changed over time but found little evidence for this.

Two other studies looked at the structure of people's file systems. Gonçalves and Jorge (2003) studied the folder structure of 11 computer scientists using Windows (8), Linux (2), and Solaris OS (1). Their results show extremely deep, narrow hierarchies. The average directory depth was 8.45, with an average branching factor (an estimation of the mean number of subfolders per folder) of 1.84, indicating a deep and narrow hierarchy. In contrast, a larger scale study by Henderson and Srinivasan (2009) looked at the folder structure of 73 university employees using Windows OS. The structures they found were much shallower, being only 3.4 folders deep on average. Folders tended to be broader, with an average of 4.1 subfolders per folder for non-leaf folders. Both studies found relatively small numbers of files per folder: 13 for Gonçalves and Jorge (2003) and 11.1 for Henderson and Srinivasan (2009).

In another study probing why people generate specific folder structures, Jones and colleagues (2005) interviewed people about the nature of their folder systems. Consistent with external cueing, many folders were seen as *plans*—structures that people used to organize their future work. Folders represented main tasks and subtasks of ongoing projects, serving to remind people about aspects of their work activity that needed to be executed. People also used workarounds to make various types of information more salient, for example, labelling folders "aacurrent" instead of "current" to ensure that this information was more obvious when browsing an alphabetically ordered folder list.

Bergman and colleagues (2003, 2009) also document workarounds *within* folders, to make individual files and folders more salient while avoiding the need to delete information. They describe how people create subfolders for older, less relevant information and label these *archive* or *old* to reduce clutter and make relevant working items more visible in the main active folder.

Another important aspect of digital file organization is the *adaptive* nature of active folders. Bergman and colleagues (2008) showed that the most common strategy for accessing personal information is navigation through the folder system, with this type of access occurring many times per day. One implication of this continual re-access is that users are likely to discover suboptimal organization, leading them to modify their file and folder structures. Adaptive maintenance and modification will turn out to be important when we discuss archives that are much less frequently accessed, which often prove to be poorly structured. For example, people add an average of 5.9 new files to their work collection each day, creating a new file folder every three days. In contrast, with digital pictures, months may elapse between the creation of new folders, negatively affecting people's ability to retrieve those pictures (Whittaker et al., 2010).

More recently, new tools have been developed to support different types of organization. One example is *tagging*. The Phlat system (Cutrell, Robbins, Dumais, & Sarin, 2006) allows users to apply multiple labels to a given information item, rather than storing it in a single folder location. Tagging has the advantage of providing richer retrieval cues (because multiple labels are available as retrieval terms) as well as allowing users to filter sets of retrieved items in terms of their tagged properties (e.g., "pictures" + "personal" returns files with those tags). In contrast, current file and folder systems are more restricted in how data can be accessed and navigated. If a file is stored in the *work2008* folder, unless I can recall or navigate to that exact folder location, I will be unable to relocate the data. But in spite of these putative advantages, in a long-term field trial users made very little overall use of tagging, averaging only one query per week with the Phlat system. It seemed from user comments that the costs of creating tags may have been too high to generate sufficient tags to support flexible search and filtering. This led people to use the system more like a standard desktop search tool. Another study compared tagging and foldering, again failing to find clear benefits for tags (Civan, Jones, Klasnja, & Bruce, 2008). In the next section we discuss how social tagging may reduce some of the costs of creating personal tags.

Managing Email

Actionable Items

Managing email is complex and different from paper or standard digital files. A critical aspect of email is that it contains many actionable messages. To be effective, people need to organize actionable information in such a way that they are reminded of what they need to do and when. This means that users have to organize action-oriented information so that they will encounter it when they need to do so. We first describe *how* users process actionable messages. We then turn to what they do with informational messages, which are treated more like paper and standard digital files.

For actionable items, deferral is inevitable. Only a small proportion of actionable messages can be dealt with at once; most must wait to be processed. Dabbish and colleagues (2005) found that on average 37 percent of messages that require replies are deferred, which equates to about four deferred messages per day. Forgetting these deferred tasks can create major headaches both for the user and the organization.

Whittaker and Sidner (1996) found that the most prevalent strategy for reminding about actionable messages is to leave them in the inbox. Users know that they will return to the inbox to access incoming unprocessed messages and thus perhaps be reminded about their outstanding actionable messages. Dabbish and colleagues (2005) also report that actionable items are left in the inbox around 79 percent of the time. We called this strategy *no filing*.

Whittaker and Sidner also showed the importance of using the inbox to prompt visual reminding by observing the failure of other strategies: 25 percent of users had experimented with a strategy of filing actionable items in a to-do folder. In fully 95 percent of these cases, this folder was abandoned because people had to remember explicitly to go to it, open it, and review its contents. This extra effort contrasts with being reminded about outstanding actions merely by seeing them in the inbox when reading new email. Although other studies (Bellotti et al., 2003) suggest that some users change their work practices to exploit to-do folders, this demands extra cognitive steps. Paradoxically, these users have to remember actively to look for their reminders. In contrast, items in the inbox are encountered naturally as a side effect of accessing new messages.

Of course, there are also disadvantages to leaving actionable items in the inbox: These reminders may be difficult to spot if the user receives many new messages. Incoming messages visually displace older pending actionable items—requiring users continually to scroll through the inbox to ensure that these items are not out of sight and out of mind (Whittaker, 2005; Whittaker, Jones, & Terveen, 2002b; Whittaker & Sidner, 1996). Tang and colleagues (2008) looked at the proportion of the inbox that users had constantly visible, finding that on average only 25 percent of the messages were in view. The remaining 75 percent were not therefore serving as direct visual reminders for outstanding actions—compromising their ability to remind.

Other users try to keep the inbox clear by filing incoming actionable items in dedicated, task-related folders (Bellotti et al., 2005; Whittaker & Sidner, 1996). Whittaker and Sidner dubbed these people frequent filers and reported that 25 percent of users create such folders. There are obvious advantages to this strategy: Removing items from the inbox keeps it trim and also allows users to focus better on new and important information. However, these benefits may be outweighed by disadvantages: Users are required to create, maintain, and continually check these task folders. Failure to file appropriately can also have severe consequences, if one files important information and forgets about it.

A final strategy for actionable items is a hybrid of these. Whittaker and Sidner (1996) identified a final group accounting for 35 percent of their users who engaged in *spring cleaning*. These people would wait until huge amounts of information accumulated in their inboxes, making it hard to identify actionable items. They would then engage in extensive filing to rationalize the inbox. The process would be repeated with the inbox gradually growing in size until another crisis brought on extensive filing once more.

What determines which strategy people choose when processing actionable email messages? Whittaker and Sidner (1996) looked at the impact on strategy choice of organizational role and incoming volume of messages. Managers were more likely to receive greater volumes of email but there was no evidence of a direct relationship between strategy and role. As with our paper study, it may be that dispositional factors are an important determinant of strategy choice. This is supported by other research that demonstrated relations between cognitive style and strategy (Gwizdka, 2004a, 2004b).

Other studies of email have found some support for these management strategies (Bellotti et al., 2005; Dabbish et al., 2005; Fisher et al., 2006; Mackay, 1988; Whittaker, 2005; Whittaker et al., 2002a). However, later work indicates few instances of pure no filers: people with absolutely no folders who are totally reliant on their inboxes for task management. Bälter (2000) both extended the set of management strategies and also argued that people move sequentially from being an active filer to spring cleaner, and later no filer, as the volume of email they receive increases. He argues that those receiving the highest volumes of email are those with these least time to organize it.

Informational Messages

We now look at how users organize *informational* messages. A substantial percentage of email messages are informational as opposed to actionable (Dabbish et al., 2005; Whittaker & Sidner, 1996). Users also experience problems in processing informational email messages. Observations of email behavior show that users spend huge amounts of time organizing email messages: On average 10 percent of people's total time in email is spent filing messages (Bellotti et al., 2005).

Again Whittaker and Sidner (1996) examined why users have problems with filing such information. Creating folders for informational messages is hard for several reasons. Generating and maintaining folder collections requires considerable effort. Filing is a cognitively difficult task (Lansdale, 1988). Just as with the keeping decision, successful filing is highly dependent on being able to envisage future retrieval requirements. It is hard to decide which existing folder is appropriate or, if a new folder is needed, how to give it a memorable name that will be appropriate for the retrieval context in which it will be needed.

Again, as we saw in the keeping section, another reason for not filing is that users want to use the *deferral strategy* and postpone judgments about the value of information. Users do not want to create archives containing information that later turns out to be useless or irrelevant. They are aware that creating overly complex archives may make it harder to access truly valuable information.

Furthermore, folders may not be useful after they are constructed. One may not be able to remember folder labels, especially when one has large numbers of older folders. Research combining multiple studies shows that people have an average of around 39 email folders (Whittaker et al., 2007). When filing they therefore have to remember the definition of each and to be careful not to introduce duplication by creating new folders that are synonymous with pre-existing ones. Duplication of folders detracts from their utility at retrieval.

In addition, folders can be too small to be useful. A major aim of filing is to coerce the huge number of undifferentiated informational inbox items into a relatively small set of folders, each containing multiple related messages. Filing is clearly not successful if the number of messages in a given folder is small. If a folder contains only one or two items, then creating it has not significantly reduced the complexity of the inbox nor gathered together significant amounts of related material.

Our data show that filing often fails: On average 35 percent of users' folders contain only one or two items. Later studies duplicated these observations, but finding a lower percentage (16 percent) of such failed folders (Fisher et al., 2006). These tiny failed folders do not significantly reduce the complexity of the inbox; moreover, they introduce the dual overheads of: (1) creating folders in the first place and (2) remembering multiple folder definitions every time there is a decision about filing a new inbox item. This cognitive overhead is illustrated in that the larger the number of folders a user has, the more likely that person is to generate failed folders containing only one or two items (Whittaker & Sidner, 1996). Of course, a small number of these failed folders may represent new activities that the user is planning (Bergman et al., 2003; Boardman & Sasse, 2004; Jones et al., 2005) but such planning cannot account for all of these tiny folders.

Folders can also fail because they are too big. When there are too many messages in a folder, it becomes unwieldy. And as the relationships among messages within the folder become more tenuous, the benefit of keeping them together is much reduced. With large heterogeneous folders, it can be extremely difficult to collate related items or find a target item (Whittaker & Sidner, 1996).

Elsweiler, Baillie, and Ruthven (2008) looked at the impact of filing strategy on users' ability to remember their email messages. Frequent filers tended to remember less about their email messages. This is consistent with our earlier observations about premature filing. Filing information too quickly can lead to the creation of archives containing spurious information; quick filing also means that users are not exposed to the information frequently in the inbox, making it hard to remember its properties or even its existence.

Thus, email users experience cognitive difficulties in creating folders for informational messages. In addition, the payoffs for this effort may not be great: Folders can be too large, too small, or too numerous for people to remember individual folder definitions. In consequence, folders may be of restricted use either for retrieval or for collating related messages. As we have seen, some users finesse this problem: Instead of filing informational messages, they simply leave them all in their inbox. More recent work has tried to support this strategy by introducing new techniques such as thread-based viewers, which we describe in the technology trends section.

Managing Webpages

Unlike email, web information is largely not actionable: Users may want to ensure that they remember to read a webpage, but in general there are no negative consequences for failing to do this.

One prevalent form of managing web information is to bookmark encountered webpages. Numerous studies have looked into how people organize their bookmarks. Two early studies documented the number of bookmarks created as well as their underlying structure. For example, Abrams and colleagues (1998) found that 6 percent of respondents had no bookmarks, 10 percent had 1 to 10, 24 percent had 11 to 25, 44 percent had 26 to 100, 14 percent had 101 to 300, and 2 percent had more than 300 bookmarks. And Boardman and Sasse (2004) found that people organized their bookmarks into an average of 17 folders. Another study (Bruce et al., 2004) observed further strategies people use for organizing useful web information that they encounter. In addition to bookmarking, users might forward themselves a link in email, print the page, copy the link into a document, generate a sticky note, or rely on memory.

More recent work with more modern web browsers has revisited bookmarking. Aula and colleagues (2005) looked at people's bookmark collections and found that 92 percent have bookmarks, with an average of 220 links, although there is huge variance: 21 percent of people have fewer than 50 bookmarks and 6 percent have none. The largest collection contained 2,589 links with 425 folders. Most of Aula and colleagues' (2005) informants reported major problems in organizing and managing their collections. Consistent with other studies (Tauscher & Greenberg, 1997) users often bookmarked information that they never subsequently revisited. In contrast, other studies showed that users were unwilling to create new bookmarks, fearing that creating bookmarks for information of unclear utility would clutter their existing set of useful bookmarks—compromising the utility of useful items (Aula et al., 2005; Wen, 2003). Aula and colleagues also found that the key for success with complex bookmark collections is the extent to which users actively exploit and maintain their collection of links. A subgroup of heavy users of bookmarks had collections of over 500 links; these users tended (like email spring cleaners) to clean up their collections from time to time, deleting unused or no longer functioning links. They also carefully organized bookmarks into hierarchical levels (similar to a file system). For these users who invested organizational effort, bookmarks seemed to be an indispensable tool. Abrams and colleagues (1998) also looked at the types of strategies people used for organizing their bookmarks. They found four main types: About 50 percent of people were sporadic filers, a further 26 percent never organized bookmarks into files, around 23 percent created folders when they accessed a webpage, and around 7 percent created folders at the end of a session. Creating folders also seems to be a response to having too many bookmarks on a drop-down list, so that people with fewer than 35 bookmarks have no folders but, beyond this threshold, folders grow linearly with the number of bookmarks.

Some disadvantages of bookmarking relate to the costs of creating and maintaining collections, especially as information needs change. Recent social tagging systems, such as Delicious, Dogear, Onomi, and CiteULike, may finesse some of these problems. These social tagging systems allow users to create multiple labels for the same data, providing potentially richer retrieval cues (Cutrell, Robbins, et al., 2006; Lansdale, 1988). More importantly, they allow tags to be shared among users, reducing the cost of tag creation for each user. Of course, the approach raises important questions. Do different users agree on a common classification of information or do they generate inconsistent, orthogonal tag sets? Numerous studies have shown that, given sufficient numbers of users, tag sets tend to stabilize on common descriptions of web resources so that people can exploit others' tags (Golder & Huberman, 2006; Millen, Yeng, Whittaker, & Feinberg, 2007). Furthermore, with suitable user interface design (e.g., text completion) problems such as inconsistent spellings can be finessed and promote greater awareness of others' tags (Millen et al., 2007). If enough people are prepared to tag, social tagging seems a useful tool that removes some of the costs associated with standard, individual bookmarking methods.

Managing Photos

Photos are very different from email messages and webpages, tending to be *self-generated* (like many files), and are usually neither informational nor actionable. They are also perceived to be highly important and often irreplaceable (Petrelli, Whittaker, & Brockmeier, 2008; Whittaker et al., 2010). How, then, do people organize them? Recent studies show that people manage to organize photos using rather rudimentary structures (Kirk et al., 2006; Whittaker et al., 2010).

Whittaker and colleagues (2010) investigated how parents organized family photo archives. They found that these collections tended to have very little hierarchical structure and were organized more like piles than files. Participants typically relied on a single main picture storage location (such as the "My Pictures" folder). For participants with multiple computers or external hard drives there was usually a single main storage folder for each device. People usually stored their pictures in that location in a single-level, flat hierarchy with minimal subfolders.

Furthermore, when a target folder was opened and scanned, the folder often contained heterogeneous data, comprising pictures that related to multiple events (possibly because they were uploaded at the same time and never subsequently reorganized).

How can we explain this lack of organization? Previous work has highlighted how participants are able to exploit their familiarity with *recently taken* pictures to scan, sort and organize materials for sharing with others quickly (Kirk et al., 2006). Possibly because of these experiences with recent pictures, participants may have expected themselves to be very familiar with their *entire* picture collection, and as a result were not motivated to organize their collections carefully. In most cases, it seemed that people had not accessed the vast majority of their pictures since they were uploaded. We saw evidence of this during retrieval. Participants universally preferred to view pictures in the thumbnail view for easier scanning. Had the participants previously opened these folders, we would have expected to see thumbnails. Yet during retrieval, when participants first opened their folders, photos almost always appeared in the "list" view, suggesting folders had rarely been accessed. And because participants seldom accessed pictures, they did not discover how poorly organized these were. One reason for the lack of organization and unfamiliarity is that parents typically have very little spare time to organize their photos. One participant commented that his attitude to photos was "collect now—organize later—view in the future."

Another way to organize might be to *annotate* pictures. However, consistent with earlier studies (Frohlich, Kuchinsky, Pering, Don, & Ariss, 2002; Kirk et al., 2006; Rodden & Wood, 2003), we found very little evidence of annotation. One reason is that annotating is onerous. Another problem, also observed in earlier studies (Kirk et al., 2006; Rodden & Wood, 2003), is that users may not annotate because they are *unaware* that they are likely to forget key aspects of pictures. People can currently remember detailed information about recent pictures and this may mean they have little motivation to annotate pictures for the eventuality that they will forget.

Management Summary

Management is a difficult activity, because it requires people to predict when or how information will be accessed. To create effective organization, users have to anticipate the context in which they will be accessing information. And for action-oriented items, they have to anticipate exactly when they will need those items.

Information properties have a major impact on management strategy: *Actionable* items often require deferral, so people need to be *reminded* about them. Various tracking strategies facilitate reminding, including leaving actionable information in one's workspace, as well as using dedicated task folders. There are trade-offs between these strategies: Keeping information in a workspace affords constant reminding but it reduces efficiency because that workspace can become cluttered with many unrelated actionable items. A specific problem with using the email inbox for reminding is that as new items arrive they tend to displace older actionable items putting them out of sight and out of mind. The disadvantage of dedicated task folders is that these need to be constantly accessed and monitored.

For *informational* items, people use two main strategies, filing and piling. There are surprising advantages for a paper piling strategy. Pilers manage to build up smaller archives, with more frequent access to information in the archive. In addition, we found problems with filing, including premature filing of low value information, leading people to generate complex collections of information that are of little utility.

For *informational* items, users experience difficulty in categorizing information, failing to predict accurately the context in which they will want to retrieve that information. People create folders that are both too big—containing large collections of heterogeneous items—and too small—containing one or two items in a folder that is seldom used. People can also create duplicate folders for the same content. All this makes filing error prone.

Both users' dispositions and the volume of information they receive may influence the type of organizational strategy they employ. Users who receive large volumes of incoming information are under pressure to keep their workspaces clear (otherwise they may overlook important deferred actionable items) but they are the people who are least likely to have the time to file and organize their information.

Certain types of information, such as webpages and photos, are infrequently re-accessed. Infrequent access may mean that people fail to realize what information they have available and how poorly organized it is. Tags do not seem to be useful in the context of personal files but they do seem to have benefits in a web/intranet context, where people can reduce the cost of annotation by sharing others' labels.

Exploitation

Overview, Problems, and Strategies

In this section, we first contrast exploitation with classic information seeking and foraging behaviors, then go on to describe different strategies for exploitation as well as the costs and benefits of these strategies.

Exploitation Not Information Seeking

Exploitation is different from information foraging and classic information seeking. In both foraging (Pirolli, 2007; Pirolli & Card, 1999) and classic information seeking (Belkin, 1980; Marchionini, 1995; Wilson, 1999), the target information is seen as being *totally new*. Exploitation is different in several ways. First, retrieval structures are usually *self-* rather than *publicly* generated (Bergman et al., 2003; Lansdale, 1988).

In other words, people are searching their own organization and not a public database. Second, the exploiter may *remember* significant details about the target information item and how it has been organized.

For example, Gonçalves and Jorge (2004) asked participants to tell stories about three personal documents on which they had recently worked. People could remember a great deal about these documents with the most salient characteristics being age, location, and purpose of the document. Blanc-Brude and Scapin (2007) also found that location, format, age, keywords, and associated events were frequently remembered. Because people remember this information, access is not purely reliant on *external publicly provided* metadata ("scent" in the terminology of information foraging). Instead, it is mediated by *cueing*: where cues can be mental (the internal cognitive information users remember about the target before they begin to access it) or external (triggers provided by well-chosen folder or file names as users carry out their search). Indeed, as we saw earlier, management activities have the predominant purpose of constructing personal organizations that promote future exploitation.

Exploitation therefore involves reconstruction of partially familiar personally organized information, rather than evaluation of unfamiliar, publically organized data. A further difference concerns success criteria: While seeking information, it is often enough to access information that satisfies certain general properties ("cheap flights to Spain"), where multiple documents may satisfy this search. In contrast when accessing personal information, the user often has a specific document in mind—making the criterion for success much more stringent. Of course, such prior knowledge may make retrieval easier. During access, users may quickly recognize the target document, so they do not have to scrutinize it to determine its relevance as they would an unknown webpage. But in other ways, access to very specific information can be made harder when it is satisfied only if a specific item is found; and there may be strong feelings of frustration about failure to locate that item (Whittaker et al., 2010).

Exploitation Strategies

Exploitation success depends on the match between cues/structures generated for future retrieval and the extent to which they match that future retrieval context. Note that even if people rely on search, they still have to *generate* the relevant search terms to guarantee success; this requires them to reconstruct important aspects of the target document (e.g., title, keywords, date). If there is a good match between organizational cues and the retrieval context, retrieval will succeed. But to create effective retrieval cues, users need to anticipate successfully *when* and *how* they will consume information.

We access personal information in four main ways.

One very straightforward way to access information is to *navigate* for it. For information items such as files, we navigate within self-generated hierarchies of folders and subfolders. People usually traverse their organizational hierarchy manually. They visually and recursively scan within each folder (either actively by sorting the items by attribute or by using the system default) until they locate the folder that contains the target item.

Search is another way to access personal information. An important emerging technology for exploitation is desktop search, allowing users to locate information from within their own file systems, using keyword queries, in the same way they conduct web searches. First the user generates a query by specifying some property of the target item, including at least one word related to the name of the information item, and/or the text that it contains (full text search), and/or any metadata attribute relating to that item (e.g., the date it was created). The desktop search engine then returns a set of results from which the user selects the relevant item. Search has elsewhere been characterized as a form of teleporting whereby users move directly to the target information, without the intermediate steps that characterize navigation (Teevan, Alvarado, Ackerman, & Karger, 2004).

A third access method, *orienteering,* is a hybrid combining both navigation and search (Teevan et al., 2004). When orienteering, users may generate a search query to locate a particular resource page or folder and then manually navigate to the target; or they might begin by accessing a link and use information from that link to generate a new search query.

Finally, new technologies such as *tagging* allow users to apply multiple labels to an information item whether on the desktop (Cutrell, Dumais, et al., 2006) or on the web (Delicious, Flickr). This allows users more flexibility in how they categorize the item (more than one label can be applied). Multiple tags mean richer retrieval cues, because the same information can be accessed via several different tags.

These strategies apply to *personal* information. When people incorporate public information into their personal schemes (e.g., web bookmarking or history lists) more varied strategies are possible (Aula et al., 2005; Bruce et al., 2004; Jones, Bruce, & Dumais, 2003; Obendorf et al., 2007). For example, users can deliberately bookmark valued information or save it to disk and then navigate back to the data. Or they can apply less effortful strategies such as accessing information via the history list (a list of sites visited), or use the browser's back button to re-access recent information.

Costs and Benefits of Exploitation Strategies

If the fit between the organization that users construct and the retrieval context is inexact, even careful management strategies may not guarantee successful retrieval. The wrong classification of information can hide it from the user, reducing the chance of quick retrieval (Kidd, 1994; Malone, 1983; Whittaker & Sidner, 1996). Putting information in a folder may decrease its ability to remind, which may be vital for actionable information. In addition, because categorization is itself cognitively challenging, users may create spurious folders that are seldom accessed, which may make classification of new information harder (Fisher et al., 2006; Whittaker & Sidner, 1996).

What, then, are the trade-offs between navigation and search for accessing personal information items? There are clear benefits to navigation. Accessing information using a personally constructed organizational hierarchy is predictable and includes a spatial component that users find valuable (Barreau & Nardi, 1995; Bergman et al., 2008; Jones & Dumais, 1986; Robertson et al., 1998). Access takes place in incremental stages, so that users obtain rapid feedback about the progress of their access efforts, being able to backtrack if they find they have followed the wrong branch of their file hierarchy. At the same time, there are disadvantages to navigation, compared with search. In complex organizational structures, navigation can be inefficient; and taking a wrong step early in the access process may require extensive backtracking, depending on the precise nature of the organization scheme (Hearst, 1999). Furthermore, users have to remember at retrieval time how information was classified, which can be difficult when there are multiple categorization possibilities (Lansdale, 1988; Russell & Lawrence, 2007).

There are also potential advantages of *search* when accessing personal information. Search does not depend on users remembering the exact storage location or precisely how they classified their information; instead, they can specify in the query any attribute they happen to remember (date, name, filetype) (Lansdale, 1988). Search may also be more efficient: Users can potentially retrieve information in one step, via a single query, instead of using multiple operations to navigate to the relevant part of their folder hierarchy. More radically, search also has the potential to finesse the management problem, as users do not have to apply organizational strategies that exhaustively anticipate their future retrieval requirements.

The same dichotomy between navigation and search does not apply to actionable items. Here very different strategies must be used. *Reminding* is key; information must be organized in such a way that users encounter it opportunistically. Neither search nor navigation through complex file organizations is appropriate support for actionable items; both require *deliberate* acts to seek out data, whereas the primary characteristic of actionable items is that these should trigger *automatic reminding*. This is clearly a very hard problem: Effective reminding means users do not just want to *re-encounter* actionable information, they want to see it *exactly when or where they need it*. Actionable information presented at the wrong time may be highly distracting; it turns out that very different strategies are needed for actionable than informational items.

For public data (e.g., from the web) that people want to incorporate into their personal organizational schemes, it is apparent that users may have less incentive to manage public data because it is less highly valued, being less personally relevant or not unique (Boardman & Sasse, 2004; Whittaker & Hirschberg, 2001). There are also clear trade-offs between different exploitation strategies for public data (Bruce et al., 2004). Although browsers now offer support in the form of suggestions, regenerating prior searches still requires considerable effort in remembering search terms, especially because search is often iterative—involving multiple queries relating to a specific information need, some of which may result in dead ends (Morris, Ringel Morris, & Venolia, 2008). Retracing successful navigation is also hard. Users have to remember which links they traversed. Bookmarking requires people to remember which information they have bookmarked, as well as to maintain bookmark collections. And more passive strategies, (e.g., relying on the history list) means that users have to navigate through poorly structured traces of every piece of information they accessed rather than just information that they thought was valuable (Morris et al., 2008; Wen, 2003). In all cases, retrieval may be made more difficult by the changing nature of the web, which may alter the content of previously accessed pages.

We now discuss different strategies that people choose for exploitation of different types of information: namely, files, email messages, photos, and web information.

Accessing Files

Desktop search has seen significant recent developments. One limit of older search engines, such as those provided as part of the Windows and Macintosh operating systems, is that they allow users to search only one data format at a time. Following the Stuff I've Seen (SIS) initiative (Dumais et al., 2003), newer search engines support multiple formats—files, email messages, instant messages, and web history can be accessed within the same search query. They therefore have the potential to address the project fragmentation problem—where information items related to the same project are automatically stored in different locations, often because they depend on different applications (Bergman et al., 2003; Dragunov, Dietterich, Johnsrude, McLaughlin, Li, & Herlocker, 2005). Modern search engines are also substantially faster than older ones, with more sophisticated interfaces to specify their search choices (Farina, 2005; Lowe, 2006). Search is now also *incremental*, returning results as soon as the user begins typing the query. This incrementality allows users to refine their query in light of the results returned and truncate the query after typing just a few characters if the target item is already in view.

In a recent study (Bergman et al., 2008), we investigated whether advanced desktop search was replacing navigation as the main method for file access. We used multiple methods (longitudinal evaluation, large-scale cross-sectional surveys) and examined different search engines (Windows XP search, Google Desktop, Mac Spotlight, Mac Sherlock).

Users reported how often they searched versus navigated to their files. We verified the accuracy of the self-report data by collecting logfiles that allowed us to correlate self-report data with actual behavior. Self-reports were very accurate and highly correlated with actual behavior, with statistical correlations being around 0.94.

We know that organization requires effort—having to create and maintain appropriate structures that anticipate retrieval, as well as having to remember those structures during exploitation. Given these new search engine capabilities, we expected users to shift from relying on navigation for file access and become increasingly reliant on desktop search. We expected that people having access to desktop search engines with advanced features would be more likely to access their files using search than those who were using older search engines without those features.

Contrary to our expectations, we found that navigation was still users' preferred method for accessing their files. First, regardless of search engine properties, there was a strong overall navigation preference: Users estimated that they used navigation for 56 to 69 percent of file retrieval events and searched for only 4 to 16 percent of events. The remaining accesses were when users relied on shortcuts or used recent files to access items on which they had been working. Further, the effect of improving the quality of the search engine on search usage was limited and inconsistent. Although Google Desktop (which was fast, incremental, and supported cross-format search) led to more usage than Windows XP search, there was no evidence that other, more advanced features induced greater usage. For example, both Mac search engines were used equally often, even though the later version, Spotlight, was faster and supported cross-format, incremental search. Similar results using very different qualitative methods have also shown that pure search is uncommon. Instead, users often combine search with navigation (Teevan et al., 2004).

How can we explain why retrieval strategy seemed to be largely independent of search engine quality? One reason is that search often seemed to be used as a last resort when users could not remember a file's location. Bergman and colleagues (2008) asked users to characterize exactly when they used search as opposed to navigation and found that between 83 and 96 percent of the times when people searched, they did so because they were unable to remember the file's location. When they can remember, they rely on navigation.

It also seems that in the majority of cases users can remember where files are located. This is unsurprising if we think that for common tasks we are frequently accessing and modifying information related to specific, often recent, items (Dumais et al., 2003) and this reinforces our memory of those items and their locations. As we have seen, people are able to remember substantial amounts of information about recent files (Blanc-Brude & Scapin, 2007; Gonçalves & Jorge, 2004). The conclusion that search is used only when people cannot remember the location of a file is supported by other studies. Jones and colleagues (2005) found that only 7 percent of users were happy with the idea that they could dispense with folders even when desktop search was available.

Accessing Email

Accessing information in email is a critical problem, given the amount of time that people spend processing it and the fact that it is both a to-do list for actionable information as well as an archive for more informational data (Duchenaut & Bellotti, 2001; Whittaker, 2005; Whittaker & Sidner, 1996).

A critical aspect of email management is to ensure that actionable items are dealt with to meet specific commitments. The previous section noted that the most common reminding strategy is to leave such items in the email inbox, hoping that these will be re-encountered on returning to the inbox to process new incoming information (Bälter, 2000; Bellotti et al., 2005; Dabbish et al., 2005; Mackay, 1988; Whittaker, 2005; Whittaker & Sidner, 1996; Whittaker et al., 2007). Variants of the inbox as to-do list strategy include altering the status of actionable items that have been read and resetting the status of such messages so that they appear to be unread and hence bold in a standard browser (Whittaker, 2005).

In spite of the central role of email in everyday work, we know relatively little about how people actually retrieve information from email. One exception is a study by Elsweiler and colleagues (2008) that looked at people's ability to remember email messages. Participants were usually able to remember whether a message was in their collection. Also memory for specific information about each message was generally good, with users often remembering multiple attributes. People remembered content, purpose, or task-related information best, correctly recalling over 80 percent of this type of information—even when items were months old. They were less good at remembering sender information; memory for this type of information tended to decay rather quickly. Memory for temporal information was worst of all, dropping to around 50 percent correct over several months. In all cases, memory was affected by both the age and size of the email archive, with users remembering less when they had bigger archives or when they were required to remember older items.

Dumais and colleagues (2003) also examined email access in Stuff I've Seen. SIS is a cross-format search engine allowing users to access files, email messages, and webpages by issuing a query in a single interface. It also supports sorting of results via attributes such as date or author. The majority of searches (74 percent) was focused on email as opposed to files. This may be because, as we saw earlier (Bergman et al., 2008), if people want to access files, they do so using navigation rather than search. When searching for email messages, there was a very strong focus on recent items, with 21 percent of searched-for items being from the last week and almost 50 percent from the last month. Many of these searches (25 percent) included the name of the email sender in the query, suggesting (contrary to Elsweiler et al., 2008) that sender name is a useful retrieval cue for email messages. Elsewhere we exploit the salience of sender name in the ContactMap system, which provides a specific informational view of email data, centered around network models of sender data (Whittaker, Jones, Nardi, Creech, Terveen, Isaacs, et al., 2004). How can we explain the prevalence of name-based search observed by Dumais and colleagues, when compared with Elsweiler and colleagues' (2008) results? Part of the difference may be due to the Dumais group's observations of naturalistic behaviors, which tended to be focused around retrieving recent email messages. In contrast, the Elsweiler team looked at longer-term access, for more structured, lab-based tasks. In addition, Dumais and colleagues did not look at the success of searches; it may be that although sender information was used frequently in searches, these sender searches were often unsuccessful.

Accessing Photos

We have already described how people organize their digital pictures and the rudimentary management strategies that they employ. As with email research, there has been more focus on photo management and rather less examining exploitation. Digital photos are a highly valued resource (Petrelli et al., 2008; Whittaker et al., 2010), so we should expect people to create effective ways to access them. Indeed, work on accessing recently taken photos shows that people are good at retrieving these (Frohlich et al., 2002). When Kirk and colleagues (2006) asked people to sort recent pictures in preparation for sharing them with friends or family, they found that participants were effective in finding and organizing pictures taken within the last year.

These findings contrast with our own work on parents' ability to retrieve slightly older family pictures (taken more than a year ago). Although pictures were judged as being highly valued, participants were often unsuccessful in accessing such older pictures.

We asked participants to name significant family events from more than a year earlier that they had photographed digitally. In a subsequent retrieval task, participants were asked to show the interviewer digital pictures from 3 to 5 of these salient past events concerning their children. To prevent participants from choosing events that they could retrieve easily, they were not told about the retrieval task during the initial interview. The interviewer asked participants to sit at their computers and show him pictures relating to these key events.

In contrast to their expectations, our participants were successful in retrieving pictures in only slightly more than half of the retrieval tasks (61 percent). In the remainder (39 percent), participants simply could not find pictures of significant family events. Of the 28 unsuccessful retrieval tasks, 21 (75 percent) were pictures that the participants believed to be stored on their computer (or on CDs) but which they subsequently could not find. The remaining seven were pictures participants initially thought were stored digitally but during the retrieval process came to the conclusion that they were taken with an analog camera.

Based on participants' comments and behavior during and after search, we identified several potential reasons for their unexpectedly poor retrieval performance: too many pictures, distributed storage, unsystematic organization, false familiarity, and lack of maintenance. In our discussion of management we have already talked about the absence of systematic organization and the tendency to collect too many pictures; we now explore the implications of these for retrieval.

The most frequent explanation participants gave for their retrieval difficulties was that they had very large numbers of pictures to search. Consistent with previous work (Frohlich et al., 2002; Kirk et al., 2006; Rodden & Wood, 2003), participants felt that they were taking many more digital pictures than they had with analog equipment. All participants pointed to the low cost of capturing large numbers of digital pictures. However, during retrieval they realized that having too many pictures has its price when this mass of pictures competed for their attention, making it hard to locate specific ones. Average archive size was 4,475 pictures but with huge amounts of variation (SD 3,039). This is a striking finding because, consistent with other research (Kirk et al., 2006), participants all made definite efforts to reduce the overall number of pictures. For example, they deleted around 17 percent of poorly focused or unwanted pictures, both when pictures were first taken, as well as at upload.

Some participants attempted to account for their poor retrieval by arguing that they had not given folders meaningful names. However, 67 percent of participants made efforts to apply meaningful labels rather than relying on software defaults. But this did not seem to guarantee they could find their pictures, possibly because, as we saw in the management section, naming schemes were inconsistent. People who used meaningful labels were neither more successful nor faster at retrieving pictures. Participants' comments and behaviors also suggested that the meaning of such names was sometimes forgotten over time. Finally, participants commented on difficulties in remembering changes over the years in organizational schemes they had imposed or software they had used.

The lack of organization in people's collections meant that they were over-reliant on trial and error strategies for accessing their photos. Consistent with studies of autobiographical memory (Brewer, 1988; Wagenaar, 1986), some of our 18 participants tried to use knowledge of related events to remember the *approximate date* when the target event occurred and then navigate using date information to the folders they thought might contain these pictures. Specific folders were chosen because their names (if there was a meaningful name) were thought to relate to the target or because a folder date was close to the guessed date.

Others tried to remember the exact date when the event had occurred and to find folders from that date. This worked when folders had been labeled with correct dates, although in many cases folder labels were purely textual. We have already noted problems with this strategy. First, participants may be unable to remember the date of the target event accurately. Second, the date label itself may be inaccurate, either because of problems with camera settings or the folder date representing the upload date as opposed to when the picture was actually taken.

Overall, the retrieval strategy used most often seemed to resemble trial and error: Users would cycle through their entire photo collection, accessing folders to see whether they contained promising pictures and moving on to other folders if they did not.

Accessing Web Documents

The problems of accessing webpages have been much studied. Most people's intuitions about web accesses are that these follow the pattern of foraging: That people predominantly seek out *new* information from the web, which they then consume for the first time. These intuitions also lead people to think that we typically rely on *search* to access web information.

One possible reason for this belief in the dominance of search is that, historically, web tools moved from relying on navigation via human-generated categories to being search-based. Early web tools such as Yahoo! provided human-generated taxonomies of the then relatively small collection of web documents, supporting access by allowing users to navigate through these hierarchies. One limitation of these manual taxonomic techniques is that they are completely impractical for the billions of documents that are now estimated to be on the web. Self-report studies also suggest that usage of web navigation is now much less frequent, with people reporting a far greater reliance on search for foraging (Kobayashi & Takeda, 2000).

In reality, however, it turns out that search is less frequent than we might expect. Instead of foraging for new information, users tend to re-access previously visited data using a variety of simple browser techniques including following links, retyping the URL, or exploiting the back button (Aula et al., 2005; Bruce et al., 2004; Obendorf et al., 2007).

Many studies have attempted to document the extent to which web accesses involve information seeking versus refinding by analyzing logfiles and history lists. Early work looking at students' browsing behaviors showed that a characteristic web access pattern involved hub-and-spoke accesses, in which users would find a useful authoritative resource—a hub. They would then fan out to the various links from this page (spokes), usually traversing no more than two links before re-accessing the hub using the back button (Catledge & Pitkow, 1995).

Tauscher and Greenberg (1997) instrumented browsers and looked at the rate at which people returned to previously visited sites. They documented a recurrence rate of 58 percent, finding also that the majority of overall accesses targeted a small set of websites that the user frequently re-accessed. Revisits are prevalent, as indicated by the use of the back button, which accounts for around 30 percent of web actions. In addition, Tauscher and Greenberg found that people were much more likely to re-access sites that they had visited recently. Cockburn and Greenberg (2000) carried out a similar study, finding that a much higher frequency of accesses (81 percent) were revisits.

Another study conducted by Wen (2003) was unusual in looking at the *success* of refinding. He asked users to conduct typical web access sessions and then requested them to retrieve information that they had found useful in that search session. Users were able to re-access successfully only 20 percent of the sites they had visited. They often failed to bookmark useful information, believing that doing so would create clutter and compromise their existing bookmark collections. Finally, and consistent with other results (Teevan et al., 2004), Wen found that the general strategy for re-access was to try to retrace prior actions, rather than attempting to search or type in prior URLs.

Aula and colleagues (2005) looked at users' self-reported strategies for web search and re-access. They found that having multiple windows or tabs open was very common because re-access was prevalent. In addition, the most commonly reported ways to re-access information were to: re-access links, search for it again, directly type the URL, or save pages as local files. This confirms the results of an observational study by Bruce and colleagues (2004) that documented that the most prevalent strategy for refinding was to type in the URL. Other access strategies were much less prevalent, for example, emailing links to oneself, adding URLs to a website, or writing down queries. Finally, there is very little use of history lists for re-access. Aula and colleagues found various problems with history lists: Not only are page titles often misleading, the list shows important and unimportant results intermingled—making it hard for users to focus on valued information. Both Aula and colleagues (2005) and Wen (2003) also noted user problems with re-access: in particular, using search to exploit information is difficult because it is an iterative process often involving multiple queries. Users may try multiple routes to finding information, exploring sites that later turn out to be dead ends. In trying to recover from these dead ends, users often could not regenerate previous accesses that had been more successful. Users also could not recall the exact method that they had used for access; as a result they had problems in reconstructing search queries for information for which they had originally browsed.

In perhaps the best controlled study of revisiting, Obendorf and colleagues (2007) preprocessed sets of URLs for 25 users and found that revisiting rates in prior studies might have been artificially inflated by sites that automatically refreshed without user intervention. When they controlled for such automatic refreshes, revisitation levels were around 41 percent. They also documented a variety of general strategies used to access pages. The most common were: using a hyperlink (44 percent of accesses), using forms—including the use of search engines (15 percent), back button (14 percent), opening a new tab/window (11 percent), and typing in the URL directly (9 percent).

Turning specifically to revisits (as opposed to all searches), Obendorf and colleagues (2007) again found that the most common strategy for refinding information was to follow links (50 percent), with the back button being the next most common strategy (31 percent). The remaining direct access strategies (using bookmarks, homepage links, history, direct entry of URL) accounted for the final 13 percent of accesses. As in previous studies, re-accesses tended to be for recently visited sites: 73 percent of revisits occur within an hour of the first visit, which makes the reported use of the back button appear rather low. One possible reason for the relatively low numbers of back accesses may be that the tabbing facilities provided by new browsers mean that users are not as reliant on hub-and-spoke type re-accesses. They can, therefore, keep the context of their hub page while using tabs to manage follow-up spoke pages.

Finally, Obendorf and colleagues (2007) looked at how access strategies varied as a function of the length of time since the original page access. Again, there were huge recency effects; 50 percent of revisits occurred within three minutes and the dominant strategy here was to use the back button, presumably because the target information was readily available in the browser cache. For revisits occurring within the hour, the back button and links were the most common ways to refind data. Between an hour and a day, back button usage decreased hugely, with users becoming more reliant on links and direct access (typing in the URL). Between a day and a week, links and typing URLs were the most common strategies; and at intervals of greater than a week, use of links dominated. This greater reliance on links may reflect an orienteering strategy (Teevan et al., 2004), in which users generate plausible sets of links and then choose among these for the final stage of access. In any case, the results clearly show that access strategies are quite varied and are heavily dependent on the time interval between initial access and re-access. Part of the reason for this is technical: For very short-term re-accesses, information is directly available in the cache, whereas at longer intervals this is unlikely to be true. In addition, cognitive factors are at work here. At medium and longer re-access intervals, users may have generated several windows or tabs so they are unable to remember which of these they first used to access the data.

Finally, the majority of revisits (73 percent) occur within an hour, 12 percent between an hour and a day, 9 percent between a day and a week, and 8 percent at longer intervals. As we have seen, the time between accesses is a critical factor influencing retrieval and, because the majority of revisits is really short term, certain strategies (such as using the back button or link-based access) are prevalent overall.

To summarize, then, web retrieval often involves re-accessing previously visited pages. Use of links, tabs, and the back button is prevalent for more recently accessed pages. Search tends not to occur very often. Users also tend to access a small number of sites, and other research shows that familiarity also influences retrieval strategy (Capra & Pérez-Quiñones, 2005).

Exploitation Summary

During exploitation, people's preference is for manual methods (folder navigation/following links), whether this is for regular files or web data. Search is a less preferred option, even for web documents.

Search is not successful with personal photos (content-based techniques are weak and there is very little metadata); and people, therefore, have to rely on browsing, which turns out to be ineffective for older data in many cases.

Email messages are different from files: Search can be useful for *informational* items because people are able to remember certain information about messages (names/content), at least in the short term. However, reminding is needed for *actionable* items and search cannot be used because it is a deliberate act that implies the user has already remembered. Users therefore have to rely on scanning their inboxes, which is often inefficient because of the amount of heterogeneous information they currently contain.

In spite of people's intuitions, search is not the prevalent way to access web data. Re-accesses are very common, with people using the back button or hyperlinks as their main re-access methods. Re-accesses are usually for recently accessed information and the re-access strategy depends on how recently the target item was last accessed.

Mismatches sometimes occur between retrieval structures and their exploitation. For photos, there seems to be a failure to create retrieval-appropriate structures, which occurs in part because these are not frequently accessed; as a result, retrieval is often unsuccessful for older materials. For email messages, people spend large amounts of time creating folder structures that may not always be exploited. For web documents, people often create structures (such as bookmark collections) that are not used because there are less costly ways to access information. They also fail to create structures that are useful.

Retrieval has clear regularities—there is a strong bias toward access of recent items, as well as a bias toward accessing a small number of items very frequently.

Future Research

What, then, are pressing future issues for research into information curation? In particular, because technology is so important in this area, what impact will emerging technologies have on keeping, management, and exploitation?

Technology Trends

Keeping

Storage is now so cheap that we no longer need to delete items because they are consuming valuable space. One general shift will, therefore, be away from models where users delete information, either when it is first encountered or during later cleanups. Instead people will tend toward keeping everything (Jones, 2004; Marshall, 2008a, 2008b), but with interfaces that provide views onto what is important and valuable in the data.

There are clear advantages to this keep-everything approach. We know that users find deletion cognitively and emotionally difficult; and they are also concerned that they will end up deleting valuable information (Bergman et al., 2009). Keeping everything means that these difficult decisions can be at least partially avoided, although the consequence is that we need new approaches to management and exploitation if users are not to be overwhelmed by kept data. In this spirit, we have begun to build user interfaces that keep more (assuaging worries about deleting something valuable), but that privilege information that is valuable or important. For example, motivated by a study of users' current workarounds with files and folders, we built GrayArea (Bergman et al., 2009), which implements a two-tier view of each folder, with the main view showing critical documents. The secondary area (GrayArea) is for less important files, which are made less visually salient, but still potentially available. A user evaluation showed the utility of this interface compared with the standard Windows Explorer method of managing files. Of course, one problem with this approach is that it requires manual organization to generate two-tier views; we are exploring (semi-) automatic methods for learning distinctions between these two types of information in an attempt to reduce the burden of manual organization.

Other technical possibilities involve the direct application of machine learning to address the keeping decision. Indices and profiles could be built based on the structure and content of people's current email, files, and web documents. These could also include information about which items are accessed and changed most frequently. The data could be used to generate an interest profile for the user, which could then be applied to incoming email messages or recently accessed webpages. If, for example, an incoming email message or viewed webpage closely matches information that is already in the user's file system, this item would be a clear candidate for keeping. In contrast, an email message bearing no relation to the user's interests is a good candidate for deletion. One problem with this approach, however, is that it might be very effective at recognizing positive candidates for keeping but rather less good for deciding what should be rejected. Automatically deleting information that is unrelated to the user's current profile introduces various problems. Just because incoming information is unrelated to the user's current activity does not mean that it is irrelevant. Unrelated messages, files, or documents might just represent an exciting new opportunity, an emerging new area, or a potentially important new contact; they should not, therefore, be deleted.

Management

Programs built to support management have a long history (see Whittaker et al., 2007, for a review), in particular in email, where many systems try to file or filter incoming email messages automatically or semi-automatically. This approach has various problems, however.

One critical problem is that users fundamentally do not trust machine-learning programs (Pazzani, 2000). People are concerned that important incoming messages might be misfiled. It is clear that, in spite of large improvements in machine learning helped by the existence of new corpora, programs are still errorful (Whittaker, Hirschberg, Amento, Stark, Bacchiani, Isenhour, et al., 2002; Whittaker et al., 2007). And although programs promise to classify documents into folders correctly and with relatively low error rates, we still lack vital empirical data about what error rates are acceptable to users. Until we know clearly whether users will at best tolerate 5 percent of misfiling, we do not know what quality our machine-learning algorithms need to be.

One response to the errors problem is to use semi-automatic methods. Here the system suggests to the user where a document might be filed and the user confirms or corrects this. This approach is well liked by machine learning advocates because it provides a way for the user to generate structured feedback on the algorithm (Whittaker et al., 2004; Whittaker et al., 2007). But there is a downside: Unless the interface is well designed, so that suggestions and user feedback are handled in a lightweight manner, the effort of correcting system suggestions may be greater than manual filing. Feedback and suggestions need to be extremely subtle with good defaults, otherwise the purported solution (automatic filing) may require more effort than users' current manual filing practices.

Another, perhaps more promising approach might be to use public resources to organize personal data. For example, systems such as Phlat (Cutrell, Robbins, et al., 2006) and Dogear (Millen et al., 2007) use social tags to organize personal resources. For example, a document in my filing system may inherit tags that others have applied to that document in a public archive. This approach has the benefits that user-generated tags are often more appropriate than machine-generated ones; it also reduces the management costs to the individual user, who has access to rich tags without having to generate them. However, there are various unanswered questions here, such as how to weight the importance of personally generated versus social tags. In addition, as we have seen, many of the user's most important documents are unique, making it unlikely that public tags are available to describe them.

Yet another approach to automatic management is to analyze user activity to determine the importance of, and relatedness among, documents. A common intuition is that documents we access frequently are more likely to be important, as are recently accessed documents. The "my recent documents" shortcut in MS Windows capitalizes on the latter intuition, and more principled algorithms have also been built to capture more systematic aspects of recency (Tang, Lin, Pierce, Whittaker, & Drews, 2007). Other systems have used social information to profile documents, so that resources that are frequently accessed by others are visually privileged over those that are less frequently accessed (Kalnikaitė et al., 2010).

One specific area where machine learning might be extremely beneficial is for actionable items, which are often a user's greatest concern when processing email messages. Work on analyzing email content has been relatively successful in predicting whether a given message requires a response (Cohen, 1996). Annotating email messages with this information and presenting it in the interface might be very useful in helping people keep track of to-dos. Another approach to this problem is thread detection and visualization, which are now parts of newer email clients (e.g., Gmail) and research prototypes (Bellotti et al., 2003; Tang et al., 2008; Venolia and Neustaedter, 2003; Wattenberg, Rohall, Gruen, & Kerr, 2005). These thread-based viewers attempt to reduce inbox "clutter" by clustering related messages. This has the benefit of collating related information as well as reducing visual distraction in the inbox. Although there have been two small-scale evaluations of this technique (Bellotti et al., 2003; Tang et al., 2008), as yet we know little about how effective these techniques might be; one study (Tang et al., 2008), however, suggests that threading may interfere with established foldering practices.

Another specific area where we can expect developments in curation is with photos, where we have seen that users have major problems with management and exploitation (Whittaker et al., 2010). Standard metadata such as time and location might be supplemented with global positioning system (GPS) and compass data about where a camera is pointing (allowing inferences about what the shot might contain as well as content-based tagging). GPS data might also indicate where a photo was taken (Kalnikaitė et al., 2010). And specific content-based techniques such as face recognition might allow familiar people to be tagged in pictures, a tool already available in Picasa and on the Macintosh. However, the promise of face recognition needs to be evaluated in the light of practical concerns. Name tags may be most important for infrequently encountered people whose identity the user is likely to forget;

but will users be prepared to tag large numbers of people and will these programs work accurately for small numbers of relative strangers? And what about the success of these programs for people whose images change rapidly, such as infants and young children?

Machine learning has also been applied to task fragmentation. TaskTracer (Dragunov et al., 2005) is a system that analyzes user behaviors in an attempt to organize them according to activities. One major problem for users is fragmentation, whereby resources relating to a common project are placed in separate locations by applications. Thus the email messages, spreadsheet, presentation, and documents for a project may all be in different folders, making it hard for users to collate and organize task-related materials (Bergman et al., 2003; Boardman & Sasse, 2004). TaskTracer addresses this by analyzing temporal access patterns: If a webpage, document, email, and spreadsheet are repeatedly open at the same time, the system infers that they belong to the same task and constructs a virtual folder for that task. The user can choose to view resources in the virtual folder or in the regular file system, but the benefits of the virtual folder are that related materials are clustered together. Of course TaskTracer suffers from the same problems as many machine-learning programs in being imperfect but, because it is an alternative to manual files, users can employ it if and when it offers benefits.

Exploitation

Technology might also be beneficial for various aspects of exploitation. One obvious area is desktop search. Although we have seen that desktop search is currently an infrequent way to access personal data, it is nevertheless potentially useful as a last resort (Bergman et al., 2008). One current problem is that desktop search typically generates too many irrelevant results. Search might be improved by including either social information (e.g., Millen et al., 2007) or more specific data about frequency and recency of document access.

Automatically captured data could also provide different ways to view and hence access our personal information. One approach might be to project different views onto the user's data, employing readily available metadata (time-based, social, location). These views are not meant to replace existing folders but to provide alternative ways to access their contents. For example, we have seen that usage information might be automatically time aligned, so that all resources accessed around the same time can be accessed together (Dragunov et al., 2005). Radical alternatives such as Lifestreams (Fertig, Freeman, & Gelernter, 1996a, 1996b) promise to replace our current semantic file systems with operating systems that are purely time based. Other radical approaches suggest that we might want to view all our information around social relations or social networks (Nardi, Whittaker, Isaacs, Creech, Johnson, & Hainsworth, 2002; Whittaker et al., 2004); these systems have also proved useful as alternative email clients. Yet, other hybrid approaches combine search with key temporal events extracted from calendars or the public domain to allow people to access documents using these events as landmarks (Ringel et al., 2003). For example, a user might be able to look at the personal information that was accessed shortly before a business trip to Boston or just after Thanksgiving, where the events are extracted from a personal calendar (the Boston trip) or public resource (Thanksgiving).

Such views could potentially be extended to other types of metadata. With the development of cheap sensors, it is now possible to record all sorts of information about what the user is doing at any time. Thus, it might be possible to provide information about where the user was when he or she worked on a document; and photos or other recordings might be available about other activities that the user was engaged in when that document was produced (Kalnikaité & Whittaker, 2008b, Kalnikaité et al., 2010). For example, a user might recall working on a presentation for a business trip to London; and a locational view might allow access to relevant documents by using this cue. Of course, there are design challenges here: A huge amount of metadata available about users' activities already exists and interfaces will have to be carefully designed to ensure that the user is not overwhelmed by this richness.

Empirical and Methodological Issues

One striking observation about information curation is that we know very little about it, in spite of its prevalence in everyday computer use (Whittaker, Terveen, & Nardi, 2000). Further, most previous research has focused on one aspect of the problem, namely management. We know much less about keeping and exploitation processes. This is somewhat ironic given the vast amount of research effort dedicated to systems and tools for accessing public corpora. More critically we do not know much about the *relationships* among different aspects of information curation or, perhaps most importantly, how management strategies influence exploitation success. What, for example, is the relationship between a person's folder structure and his or her ability to retrieve and access files? Much more research is needed in this area. We also need to know more about when and why people keep or delete different types of information, exactly how they manage and reorganize, as well as the different methods that they use to access information.

Several practical reasons help explain why we know so little. First, it is extremely hard to gather data in this area. To understand information curation better, we need to collect data about people's personal information habits. This is potentially intrusive: It might require logging software to be installed on study participants' machines, or manual access to their personal data. And there are also problems with more system-oriented approaches: If we want to study the efficacy of new curation systems, these need to be both robust and fully featured. New curation software must be reliable because people use it on a regular basis for everyday work. If we want users to provide feedback about a new file system, email client, or web bookmarking system, that system had better be very effective or users will quickly switch back to their regular software. In the same way, the new system had better offer a comparable set of features to users' regular software, otherwise participants will quickly revert to that software to do their everyday work (Bellotti et al., 2005; Whittaker et al., 2004).

Further, methods for evaluating curation systems are complex and standard techniques cannot always be used (Kelly, 2006; Kelly & Teevan, 2007). For example, in evaluating information retrieval systems it is customary to use standard corpora and measures such as precision and recall, where documents have been manually tagged for relevance. With curation systems, however, we need to evaluate systems against participants' own information because the use of public data would be meaningless. Further, users will generate their own access tasks exploiting their own management structures, so that methods relying on relevance metrics generated against standard corpora cannot be applied. In part this may explain why promising results obtained by the machine learning community using standard public corpora have not yet transferred well to practical curation systems. For example, new algorithms are able to categorize email data in standard corpora with error rates around 10 percent. Yet we do not know: (a) what error rates users will tolerate for this type of task when carrying out everyday work; or (b) whether similar performance can be obtained with the user's own data. In our own work, we found that users were rather intolerant of automatic methods of clustering email contacts, instead preferring semi-automated methods (Whittaker et al., 2004). More studies need to be carried out and better evaluation methods developed for information curation. Elsewhere we have advocated that the community develop a set of reference tasks for personal information management, which would allow comparative analysis of different algorithms across a common set of user tasks (Whittaker, Terveen, & Nardi, 2000).

Summary

This review has argued that prevailing views of information behaviors are misleading. People's informational behavior has less to do with consumption of new public information than with curation, in which they keep and manage personal information for future access. We have outlined a three-stage model of the curation process, reviewing the central problems of keeping, management, and exploitation, and presented relevant data for each stage of the process, concluding with an overview of outstanding technical and empirical questions. In general, users tend to overkeep information, with the exception of contacts and webpages. With respect to organizing information, we found surprising benefits for piles as opposed to files, although organizing action-oriented information remains a major challenge. Exploitation remains reliant on manual methods such as navigation, in spite of the emergence of desktop search.

There are also mismatches between people's organizational structures and their actual retrieval requirements, for example, for email, web documents, and photos. Several new technologies have the potential to address important curation problems but implementing these in ways that users will find acceptable remains a challenge. Finally, research in this area remains in its infancy and new data and methods are still sorely needed.

Endnote

1. Although Dabbish et al. (2005) suggest higher keeping rates for email.

References

Abrams, D., Baecker, R., & Chignell, M. (1998). Information archiving with bookmarks: Personal web space construction and organization. *Proceedings of the ACM SIGCHI Conference on Human Factors in Computing Systems*, 41–48.

Ackerman, M. S. (1998). Augmenting organizational memory: A field study of Answer Garden. *ACM Transactions on Information Systems*, *16*(3), 203–224.

Ackerman, M. S., & Halverson, C. A. (2004). Organizational memory as objects, processes, and trajectories: An examination of organizational memory in use. *Journal of Computer Supported Cooperative Work*, *13*(2), 155–190.

Aula, A., Jhaveri, N., & Käki, M. (2005). Information search and re-access strategies of experienced web users. *Proceedings of the International World Wide Web Conference*, 583–592.

Baddeley, A. D. (1997). *Human memory: Theory and practice*. Hove, UK: Psychology Press.

Bälter, O. (2000). Keystroke level analysis of email message organization. In *Proceedings of the ACM SIGCHI Conference on Human Factors in Computing Systems*, 105–112.

Barreau, D. K., & Nardi, B. (1995). Finding and reminding: File organization from the desktop. *ACM SIGCHI Bulletin*, *27*(3), 39–43.

Belkin, N. J. (1980). Anomalous states of knowledge as a basis for information retrieval. *Canadian Journal of Information Science*, *5*, 133–143.

Bell, G., & Gemmell, J. (2009). *Total recall: How the e-memory revolution will change everything*. New York: Dutton.

Bellotti, V., Ducheneaut, N., Howard, M., & Smith, I. (2003). Taking email to task: The design and evaluation of a task management centered email tool. *Proceedings of the ACM SIGCHI Conference on Human Factors in Computing Systems*, 345–352.

Bellotti, V., Ducheneaut, N., Howard, M., Smith, I., & Grinter, R. (2005). Quality vs. quantity: Email-centric task-management and its relationship with overload. *Human-Computer Interaction*, *20*(1–2), 89–138.

Bentley, F., Metcalf, C., & Harboe, G. (2006). Personal vs. commercial content: The similarities between consumer use of photos and music. *Proceedings of the ACM SIGCHI Conference on Human Factors in Computing Systems*, 667–676.

Bergman, O., Beyth-Marom, R., & Nachmias, R. (2003). The user-subjective approach to personal information management systems. *Journal of the American Society for Information Science and Technology*, *54*(9), 872–878.

Bergman, O., Beyth-Marom, R., Nachmias, R., Gradovitch, N., & Whittaker, S. (2008). Advanced search engines and navigation preference in personal information management. *ACM Transactions on Information Systems, 26*(4), 1–24.

Bergman, O., Tucker, S., Beyth-Marom, R., Cutrell, E., & Whittaker, S. (2009). It's not that important: Demoting personal information of low subjective importance using GrayArea. *Proceedings of the ACM International Conference on Human Factors in Computing Systems,* 269–278.

Berlin, L. M., Jeffries, R., O'Day, V. L., Paepcke, A., & Wharton, C. (1993). Where did you put it? Issues in the design and use of a group memory. *Proceedings of the ACM SIGCHI Conference on Human Factors in Computing Systems,* 23–30.

Blanc-Brude, T., & Scapin, D. L. (2007). What do people recall about their documents? Implications for desktop search tools. *Proceedings of the International Conference on Intelligent User Interfaces,* 102–111.

Boardman, R., & Sasse, M. A. (2004). "Stuff Goes into the Computer and Doesn't Come Out": A cross-tool study of personal information management. *Proceedings of the ACM SIGCHI Conference on Human Factors in Computing Systems,* 583–590.

Brewer, W. (1988). Memory for randomly sampled autobiographical events. In U. Neisser & E. Winograd (Eds.), *Remembering reconsidered* (pp. 21–90). New York: Cambridge University Press.

Bruce, H., Jones, W., & Dumais, S. (2004). Information behavior that keeps found things found. *Information Research, 10*(1). Retrieved April 15, 2010, from informationr.net/ir/10-1/paper207.html

Capra, R., & Pérez-Quiñones, M. A. (2005). Using web search engines to find and refind information. *IEEE Computer, 38*(10), 36–42.

Catledge, L., & Pitkow, J. (1995). Characterizing browsing strategies in the World Wide Web. *Computer Networks and ISDN Systems, 27*(6), 1065–1073.

Civan, A., Jones, W., Klasnja, P., & Bruce, H. (2008). Better to organize personal information by folders or by tags? The devil is in the details. *Proceedings of the Annual Meeting of the American Society for Information Science and Technology* (CD-ROM).

Cockburn, A., & Greenberg, S. (2000). Issues of page representation and organisation in web browser-revisitation tools. *Australian Journal of Information Systems, 7*(2), 120–127.

Cohen, W. (1996). Learning rules that classify email. *AAAI Symposium on Machine Learning in Information Access,* 18–25.

Craik, F. I. M., & Lockhart, R. S. (1972). Levels of processing: A framework for memory research. *Journal of Verbal Learning and Verbal Behavior, 11,* 671–684.

Cutrell, E., Dumais, S., & Teevan, J. (2006). Searching to eliminate personal information management. *Communications of the ACM, 49*(1), 58–64.

Cutrell, E., Robbins, D., Dumais, S., & Sarin, R. (2006). Fast, flexible filtering with Phlat. *Proceedings of the ACM SIGCHI Conference on Human Factors in Computing Systems,* 261–270.

Dabbish, L. A., Kraut, R. E., Fussell, S., & Kiesler, S. (2005). Understanding email use: Predicting action on a message. *Proceedings of the ACM SIGCHI Conference on Human Factors in Computing Systems,* 691–700.

Dragunov, A. N., Dietterich, T. G., Johnsrude, K., McLaughlin, M., Li, L., & Herlocker, J. L. (2005). TaskTracer: A desktop environment to support multi-tasking knowledge workers. *International Conference on Intelligent User Interfaces,* 75–82.

Drew, P. R., & Dewe, M. D. (1992). Special collection management. *Library Management, 13*(6), 8–14.

Ducheneaut, N., & Bellotti, V. (2001). Email as habitat: An exploration of embedded personal information management. *Interactions, 8*(5), 30–38.

Dumais, S., Cutrell, E., Cadiz, J., Jancke, G., Sarin, R., & Robbins, D. (2003). Stuff I've Seen: A system for personal information retrieval and re-use. *Proceedings of the 26th Annual International ACM SIGIR Conference on Research and Development in Information Retrieval*, 72–79.

Ellis, D., & Haugan, M. (1997). Modelling the information seeking patterns of engineers and research scientists in an industrial environment. *Journal of Documentation, 53*(4), 384–403.

Elsweiler, D., Baillie, M., & Ruthven, I. (2008). Exploring memory in email refinding. *ACM Transactions on Information Systems, 26*(4), 1–36.

Farina, P. A. (2005). *A comparison of two desktop search engines: Google Desktop Search (beta) vs. Windows XP Search Companion*. Proceedings of the 21st Computer Science Seminar. Hartford, CT.

Fertig, S., Freeman, E., & Gelernter, D. (1996a). Finding and reminding reconsidered. *SIGCHI Bulletin, 28*(1), 66–69.

Fertig, S., Freeman, E., & Gelernter, D. (1996b). Lifestreams: An alternative to the desktop metaphor. In M. J. Tauber (Ed.), *Conference companion on human factors in computing systems: Common ground* (pp. 410–411). New York: ACM Press.

Fisher, D., Brush, A. J., Gleave E., & Smith, M. (2006). Revisiting Whittaker & Sidner's "Email Overload": Ten years later. *Proceedings of the 20th Anniversary ACM Conference on Computer Supported Cooperative Work*, 309–312.

Frohlich, D., Kuchinsky A., Pering C., Don, A., & Ariss, S. (2002). Requirements for photoware. *Proceedings of the ACM Conference on Computer Supported Cooperative Work*, 166–175.

Gilbert, D. (2006). *Stumbling on happiness*. New York: Knopf.

Golder, S., & Huberman, B. (2006). The structure of collaborative tagging systems. *Journal of Information Science, 32*(2), 198–208.

Gonçalves, D., & Jorge, J. A. (2003). An empirical study of personal document spaces. *Proceedings of the International Workshop on Design Specification, and Verification of Interactive Systems*, 46–60.

Gonçalves, D., & Jorge, J. A. (2004). Describing documents: What can users tell us? *Proceedings of the International Conference on Intelligent User Interfaces*, 247–249.

Gwizdka, J. (2004a). *Cognitive abilities and email interaction: Impacts of interface and task*. Unpublished doctoral dissertation, University of Toronto, Canada.

Gwizdka, J. (2004b). Email task management styles: The cleaners and the keepers. *Proceedings of the ACM SIGCHI Conference on Human Factors in Computing Systems*, 1235–1238.

Henderson, S., & Srinivasan, A. (2009). An empirical analysis of personal digital document structures. *HCI International*, 394–403.

Hearst, M. A. (1999). User interfaces and visualization. In R. Baeza-Yates & B. Ribeiro-Neto (Eds.), *Modern information retrieval* (pp. 257–322). Boston: Addison-Wesley.

Jones, W. (2004). Finders, keepers? The present and future perfect in support of personal information management. *First Monday*, 9(3). Retrieved April 3, 2010, from firstmonday. org/htbin/cgiwrap/bin/ojs/index.php/fm/article/view/1123/1043

Jones, W. (2007a). *Keeping found things found: The study and practice of personal information management*. San Francisco, CA: Morgan Kaufmann.

Jones, W. (2007b). Personal information management. *Annual Review of Information Science and Technology*, *41*, 453–504.

Jones, W., Bruce, H., & Dumais, S. (2003). How do people get back to information on the web? How can they do it better? *Proceedings of the International Conference on Human-Computer Interaction*, 793–796.

Jones, W., & Dumais, S. (1986). The spatial metaphor for user interfaces: Experimental tests of reference by location versus name. *ACM Transactions on Office Information Systems*, *4*(1), 42–63.

Jones, W., Phuwanartnurak, A. J., Gill, R., & Bruce, H. (2005). Don't take my folders away! Organizing personal information to get things done. *Proceedings of the ACM SIGCHI Conference on Human Factors in Computing Systems*, 1505–1508.

Jones, W., & Teevan, J. (2007). *Personal information management*. Seattle: University of Washington Press.

Kahneman, D., & Tversky, A. (1979). Prospect theory: An analysis of decision making under risk. *Econometrica*, *47*, 263–291.

Kalnikaitę, V., Sellen, A., Whittaker, S., & Kirk, D. (2010). Now let me see where I was: Understanding how lifelogs mediate memory. *Proceedings of the ACM SIGCHI Conference on Human Factors in Computing Systems*, 2045–2054.

Kalnikaitę, V., & Whittaker, S. (2007). Software or wetware? Discovering when and why people use digital prosthetic memory. *Proceedings of ACM SIGCHI Conference on Human Factors in Computing Systems*, 71–80.

Kalnikaite, V., & Whittaker, S. (2008a). Cueing digital memory: How and why do digital notes help us remember? *Proceedings of the British Computer Society Conference on Human Computer Interaction*, 153–161.

Kalnikaite, V., & Whittaker, S. (2008b). Social summarization: Does social feedback improve access to speech data? *Proceedings of ACM Conference on Computer Supported Co-operative Work*, 9–12.

Kelly, D. (2006). Evaluating personal information management behaviors and tools. *Communications of the ACM*, *49*(1), 84–86.

Kelly, D., & Teevan, J. (2007). Understanding what works: Evaluating personal information management tools. In W. Jones & J. Teevan (Eds.), *Personal information management* (pp. 190–205). Seattle: University of Washington Press.

Kidd, A. (1994). The marks are on the knowledge worker. *Proceedings of the ACM SIGCHI Conference on Human Factors in Computing Systems*, 186–191.

Kirk, D., Sellen, A., Rother, C., & Wood, K. (2006). Understanding "photowork." *Proceedings of the ACM SIGCHI Conference on Human Factors in Computing Systems*, 761–770.

Kobayashi, M., & Takeda, K. (2000). Information retrieval on the web. *ACM Computing Surveys*, *32*(2), 144–173.

Kuhlthau, C. C. (1991). Inside the search process: Information seeking from the user's perspective. *Journal of the American Society for Information Science, 42*(5), 361–371.

Lansdale, M. (1988). The psychology of personal information management. *Applied Ergonomics, 19*(1), 55–66.

Lansdale, M., & Edmonds, E. (1992). Using memory for events in the design of personal filing systems. *International Journal of Man-Machine Studies, 36*, 97–126.

Lowe, M. (2006). *Evaluation of desktop search applications* (Technical report). Kalio: Sydney, Australia.

Mackay, W. E. (1988). More than just a communication system: Diversity in the use of electronic mail. *Proceedings of the ACM Conference on Computer-Supported Cooperative Work*, 344–353.

Malone, T. W. (1983). How do people organize their desks: Implications for the design of office information systems. *ACM Transactions on Office Information Systems, 1*(1), 99–112.

Marchionini, G. (1995). *Information seeking in electronic environments*. Cambridge, UK: Cambridge University Press.

Marshall, C. (2008a). Rethinking personal digital archiving, Part 1: Four challenges from the field. *DLib Magazine, 14*(3/4). Retrieved April 29, 2010, from www.dlib.org/dlib/march08/marshall/03marshall-pt1.html

Marshall, C. (2008b). Rethinking personal digital archiving, Part 2: Implications for services, applications, and institutions. D-Lib Magazine, 14(3/4). Retrieved April 29, 2010, from www.dlib.org/dlib/march08/marshall/03marshall-pt2.html

Millen, D., Yeng., M., Whittaker, S., & Feinberg, J. (2007). Social bookmarking and exploratory search. *Proceedings of the European Conference on Computer Supported Cooperative Work*, 179–198.

Morris, D., Ringel Morris, M., & Venolia, G. (2008). SearchBar: A search-centric web history for task resumption and information re-finding. *Proceeding of the ACM SIGCHI Conference on Human Factors in Computing Systems*, 1207–1216.

Nardi, B., Whittaker, S., Isaacs, E., Creech, M., Johnson, J., et al. (2002, April). ContactMap: Integrating communication and information through visualizing personal social networks. *Communications of the ACM, 45*(4), 89–95.

Obendorf, H., Weinreich, H., Herder, E., & Mayer, M. (2007). Webpage revisitation revisited: Implications of a long-term click-stream study of browser usage. *Proceedings of the ACM SIGCHI Conference on Human Factors in Computing Systems*, 597–606.

Osburn, C. B., & Atkinson, R. (1991). *Collection management: A new treatise*. Greenwich, CT: JAI Press.

Pazzani, M. J. (2000). Representation of electronic mail filtering profiles: A user study. *Proceedings of the International Conference on Intelligent Use Interfaces*, 202–206.

Petrelli, D., Whittaker, S., & Brockmeier, J. (2008). Autotopography: What can physical mementos tell us about digital memories? *Proceedings of the ACM SIGCHI Conference on Human Factors in Computing Systems*, 53–62.

Pirolli, P. (2007). *Information foraging theory: Adaptive interaction with information*. Oxford, UK: Oxford University Press.

Pirolli, P., & Card, S. K. (1995). Information foraging in information access environments. *Proceedings of the ACM SIGCHI Conference on Human Factors in Computing Systems*, 51–58.

Pirolli, P., & Card, S. K. (1999). Information foraging. *Psychological Review*, *106*, 643–675.

Ringel, M., Cutrell, E., Dumais, S., & Horvitz, E. (2003). Milestones in time: The value of landmarks in retrieving information from personal stores. *Proceedings of Human-Computer Interaction (INTERACT '03)*, 184–191.

Robertson, G., Czerwinski, M., Larson, K., Robbins, D. C., Thiel, D., & van Dantzich, M. (1998). Data mountain: Using spatial memory for document management. *Proceedings of the ACM Symposium on User Interface Software and Technology*, 153–162.

Rodden, K., & Wood, K. (2003). How do people manage their digital photographs? *Proceedings of the ACM SIGCHI Conference on Human Factors in Computing Systems*, 409–416.

Rosch, E. (1978). Principles of categorization. In E. Rosch & B. B. Lloyd (Eds.), *Cognition and categorization* (pp. 27–48). Hillsdale, NJ: Erlbaum.

Rosch, E., Mervis, C. B., Gray, W., Johnson, D., & Boyes-Braem, P. (1976). Basic objects in natural categories. *Cognitive Psychology*, *8*, 382–439.

Russell, D., & Lawrence, S. (2007). Search everything. In W. Jones & J. Teevan (Eds.), *Personal information management* (pp. 153–166). Seattle: University of Washington Press.

Sellen, A., & Harper, R. (2002). *The myth of the paperless office*. Cambridge, MA: MIT Press.

Shannon, C., & Weaver, W. (1949). *A mathematical theory of communication*. Urbana: University of Illinois Press.

Tang, J. C., Lin, J., Pierce, J., Whittaker, S., & Drews, C. (2007). Recent shortcuts: Using recent interactions to support shared activities. *Proceedings of the ACM SIGCHI Conference on Human Factors in Computing Systems*, 1263–1272.

Tang, J. C., Wilcox, E., Cerruti, J. A., Badenes, H., Nusser, S., & Schoudt, J. (2008). Tag-it, snag-it, or bag-it: Combining tags, threads, and folders in email. *Proceedings of the ACM SIGCHI Conference on Human Factors in Computing Systems*, 2179–2194.

Tauscher, L., & Greenberg, S. (1997). How people revisit webpages: Empirical findings and implications for the design of history systems. *International Journal of Human-Computer Studies*, *47*(1), 97–137.

Teevan, J., Alvarado, C., Ackerman, M. S., & Karger, D. R. (2004). The perfect search engine is not enough: A study of orienteering behavior in directed search. *Proceedings of the ACM SIGCHI Conference on Human Factors in Computing Systems*, 415–422.

Treisman, A., & Gelade, G. (1980). A feature-integration theory of attention. *Cognitive Psychology*, *12*, 97–136.

Venolia, G., Gupta, A., Cadiz, J. J., & Dabbish, L. (2001). *Supporting email workflow* (MSR-TR-2001-88). Redmond, WA: Microsoft Research.

Venolia, G., & Neustaedter, C. (2003). Understanding sequence and reply relationships within email conversations: A mixed-model visualization. *Proceedings of the ACM SIGCHI Conference on Human Factors in Computing Systems*, 361–368.

Wagenaar, W. (1986). My memory: A study of autobiographical memory after six years. *Cognitive Psychology*, *18*, 225–252.

Wattenberg, M., Rohall, S., Gruen, D., & Kerr B. (2005). Email research: Targeting the enterprise. *Human Computer Interaction*, *20*(1–2), 139–162.

Wen, J. (2003). Post-valued recall webpages: User disorientation hits the big time. *IT & Society*, *1*(3), 184–194.

Whittaker, S. (2005). Supporting collaborative task management in email. *Human-Computer Interaction*, *20*(1–2), 49–88.

Whittaker, S., Bellotti, V., & Gwizdka, J. (2007). Everything through email. In W. Jones & J. Teevan (Eds.), *Personal information management* (pp. 167–189). Seattle: University of Washington Press.

Whittaker, S., Bergman, O., & Clough, P. (2010). Easy on that trigger dad: A study of long term family photo retrieval. *Personal and Ubiquitous Computing*, *14*(1), 31–43.

Whittaker, S., & Hirschberg, J. (2001). The character, value and management of personal paper archives. *ACM Transactions on Computer-Human Interaction*, *8*(2), 150–170.

Whittaker, S., Hirschberg, J., Amento, B., Stark, L., Bacchiani, M., Isenhour, P., et al. (2002). SCANMail: A voicemail interface that makes speech browsable, readable and searchable. *Proceedings of the ACM Conference on Human Computer Interaction*, 275–282.

Whittaker, S., Jones, Q., & Terveen, L. (2002a). Contact management: Identifying contacts to support long term communication. *Proceedings of the ACM Conference on Computer Supported Cooperative Work*, 216–225.

Whittaker, S., Jones, Q., & Terveen, L. (2002b). Managing long term conversations: Communication and contact management. *Proceedings of the 35th Annual Hawaii International Conference on System Sciences*. Retrieved May 7, 2010, from www.computer. org/portal/web/csdl/proceedings/h#4

Whittaker, S., Jones, Q., Nardi, B., Creech, M., Terveen, L., Isaacs, E., and Hainsworth, J. (2004). ContactMap: Organizing communication in a social desktop. *ACM Transactions on Computer-Human Interaction*, *11*(4), 445–471.

Whittaker, S., & Sidner, C. (1996). Email overload: Exploring personal information management of email. *Proceedings of the ACM SIGCHI Conference on Human Factors in Computing Systems*, 276–283.

Whittaker, S., Terveen, L., & Nardi, B. A. (2000). Let's stop pushing the envelope and start addressing it: A reference task agenda for HCI. *Human Computer Interaction*, *15*, 75–106.

Wilhelm, A., Takhteyev, Y., Sarvas, R., Van House, N., & Davis, M. (2004). Photo annotation on a camera phone. *Extended Abstracts on Human Factors in Computing Systems, CHI '04*, 1403–1406.

Wilson, T. D. (1981). On user studies and information needs. *Journal of Documentation*, *37*(1), 3–15.

Wilson, T. D. (1994). Information needs and uses: Fifty years of progress? In B. C. Vickery (Ed.), *Fifty years of information progress: A Journal of Documentation review* (pp. 15–51). London: Aslib.

Wilson, T. D. (1999). Models in information behaviour research. *Journal of Documentation*, *55*(3), 249–270.

CHAPTER 2

Pharmaceutical Information: A 30-Year Perspective on the Literature

David Bawden and Lyn Robinson
City University London, UK

Introduction

This chapter provides a selective review of the literature of pharmaceutical information from 1980 to the end of 2008, with a few significant earlier and later papers included. This relatively long time period is justifiable because there are no previous substantive reviews on the topic. It also allows an historical approach to be taken, showing developments over time and highlighting those aspects that have remained relatively constant. References are therefore cited from across the whole of this time period.

The chapter relies on published literature, mainly journal articles and mainly English language. With a very few exceptions, web resources have been omitted, because of their ephemeral nature. The material was identified from the authors' own resources, supplemented by searching of bibliographic databases—Library and Information Science Abstracts, MEDLINE, and Web of Science—and by following up citations.

The intention is not to provide anything like comprehensive coverage of a voluminous literature, but rather to illustrate the unique nature of pharmaceutical information and how its development has influenced the wider area of information science. Particular sources are mentioned as exemplars; this review is not intended to serve as a resource guide, although pointers are given to such listings.

The focus is on information sources, systems, and services and on information and knowledge management. Information technology, information systems, and informatics aspects—which form a large literature in their own right for pharmaceuticals—are mentioned only when directly relevant. We cite literature relating to information functions, resources, and so on in a variety of environments only if it refers directly to the pharmaceutical environment.

The structure and content of the review draws from the ideas of "domain analysis" (Hjørland, 2002, p. 422), whereby distinct approaches, of which Hjørland originally noted eleven, may be used to help to understand the information of a domain. The aspects used here, in respect of pharmaceutical information, are:

- Nature and structure of pharmaceutical information
- Existing literature guides and subject gateways
- Special classifications, taxonomies, and thesauri
- Specialist terminologies
- Resources, indexing, and retrieval
- User studies
- Structures and organizations in the communication of information
- Historical studies

The review, following this introduction, is divided into eight sections:

- The pharmaceutical information domain
- Previous reviews and monographs
- Pharmaceutical information producers and users
- Pharmaceutical information organization: classifications, thesauri, and terminologies
- Pharmaceutical information sources, services, and retrieval
- Pharmaceutical information and knowledge management
- Influence on information science

The Pharmaceutical Information Domain

Pharmaceutical information is usually taken to mean all the information required for, and produced during, the discovery, development, production, supply, regulation, and use of medicines. Usually, human medicines are meant, although the term may sometimes also cover information relevant to veterinary medicines. The term usually includes all remedial preparations and hence covers vaccines, antisera, diagnostics, and so on.

The terms *medicines information* and *drug information* have been used synonymously although the latter has, in recent years, mainly taken the meaning of information relating to the use of recreational drugs. Gagnon (1986), in a fairly typical view, considers the area to comprise five disciplines: medicinal chemistry, pharmaceutics, pharmacology and toxicology, pharmacy administration, and pharmacy practice.

Educational philosopher Paul Hirst argues that, because disciplines are closely associated with their knowledge base, we can understand a discipline by understanding its *form of knowledge* (Hirst, 1974; Hirst & Peters, 1970). Hirst identifies seven main domains or forms of knowledge, defined by the fundamental nature of the knowledge and concepts with which they deal: mathematics, physical sciences, human sciences, literature and the fine arts, morality, religion, and philosophy. Where a discipline equates to one of these forms, it is what would be regarded as a *pure* academic subject. Hirst also recognizes *practical disciplines*, based on one of the forms, but oriented toward solving practical problems. In his terms, pharmaceuticals would be, like all the other biomedical disciplines, a practical discipline based on the form of knowledge of the biological sciences. Like other healthcare topics, however, it also includes materials more related to the social sciences (Robinson, 2010).

We may expect, therefore, that pharmaceutical information will be of a diverse nature but will follow healthcare knowledge in having a generally clear and consistent structure, in the form of a complex hierarchy, with many levels (Blois, 1984, 1988; Patel & Kaufman, 2000; Robinson, 2010). This is confirmed by the nature of pharmaceutical information resources and information organization, as will be discussed.

Pharmaceutical information is created and used by a wide variety of groups, including:

- Scientists in academia and in the pharmaceutical industry

- Industry marketers, government regulators, health service purchasers and managers

- Doctors, pharmacists, and other healthcare professionals

- The general public, as consumers of prescription and over-the-counter medicines

Information about medicines is extensive and very varied in its nature and its intended use and users. Information is produced, and required, at all stages of the development and use of medicines, from the earliest stages of multidisciplinary pharmaceutical R&D, through clinical trials and regulatory approval, through the use of medicines on prescription and sold over the counter (see, for example, H. D. Brown, 1983; Haygarth-Jackson, 1987b; Robson, Bawden, & Judd, 2001). Kasarab (2006) notes one practical consequence of this—the need for very extensive document supply services for a pharmaceutical company. As early as 1963, a National Library of Medicine survey on drug literature commented that "drug literature is vast and complex. The very problem of defining what constitutes the literature is difficult. ... It is also increasingly complex, i.e., interdisciplinary and interprofessional in nature. Thus, drug information 'sprawls across' many professional journals of the most varied types" (Gora-Harper & Amerson, 2006, p. 1). The situation has not changed in the intervening half-century.

The scientist information producer/user group is very broad. Pharmaceutical information is of relevance not only to those sciences that focus on the topic—pharmacy, pharmacology, toxicology, and medicinal chemistry—but also to a range of associated sciences, including:

- Chemistry, particularly synthetic and analytical chemistry

- Biosciences, including biochemistry, molecular biology, genomics, bacteriology, and virology

- Medicinal sciences and medicinal practice, including public health and epidemiology

The economic and social importance of pharmaceuticals and the pharmaceutical industry has led to the need for extensive pharmaceutical business information on markets and competitors. The intensive regulation of the industry, and concerns about the safety of medicines, have led to extensive information systems in support of the regulatory function and also in support of pharmacovigilance—to identify side effects of drugs.

Recent moves toward *consumer health information* have led to a greatly increased need for the provision of pharmaceutical information directed to patients, carers, and other concerned members of the public, particularly through the internet.

This breadth of scope, plus its economic and social importance, lends pharmaceutical information a unique place within information science, with a particularly rich set of information resources and tools and systems for information handling. The pharmaceutical industry, in particular, is often referred to as the original "information intensive industry" (Haygarth-Jackson, 1987b, p. 75), and as an industry aware of the power of information (Nielsen, 1996), where "information is the lifeblood of the research based pharmaceutical industry" (Sherwell, 1997a, p. 35). In 1980, Hyams (1980, p. 2) identified it as one of three "information conscious industries" (the others being aerospace and food); H. D. Brown (1985, p. 218) considered the past and future of the "information facets" of a new drug in the 1980s; and Snow (2008) gave a picture of the extensive communication aspects of the drug development process thirty years later. As a consequence, particularly large investment has been made in information systems and services (Di Nallo & Schopfel, 2008), sometimes with the explicit aim of creating an "information rich environment" (Bawden, 1986, pp. 66–67; see also Lamb, King, & Kling, 2003). "The [pharmaceutical] industry," wrote Pickering (1990, p. 3), "spends very freely on information handling." This free spending, and that of health services and regulators, has provided the range of specialized and innovative services that distinguish this subject in information terms (Sillince & Sillince, 1993). Although the matter is controversial, there is some evidence that more information aware companies show greater research productivity (Koenig, 1990).

The pharmaceutical domain has often pioneered new forms of information systems and resources, influencing the development of information science and information management more generally. These developments have been promoted by specialists in pharmaceutical information, working within the pharmaceutical industry, health services, and professional institutions.

The nature of the pharmaceutical information domain, which is the focus of this review, is formed by the context in which this information is produced and used. This context has changed greatly over the time period of this review. Some of the causes of changes are directly information service related, for example, the almost total replacement of printed journals and reference works by electronic equivalents; these are dealt with in the appropriate places later. Changes in the environment are also of significance. Among the more important, six major and continuing clusters of changes can be identified.

The first is the continuing consolidation of pharmaceutical companies into multinational *big pharma* (e.g., Guay, 1988; Koenig & Mezick, 2004; Spilker, 1994). This has had direct consequences in a need for global information provision and for the merging of services (e.g., Culley, Hoffman, & Slavik, 2000; Di Nallo & Schopfel, 2008; Marsh, 2000; Riggins, Ferguson, Miller, & Gorham, 1999; Robson & Riggens, 2001; Schwartzer, 1995). Similar information-related issues arise from the creation of alliances of separate companies (Whitehead, Lomma, Tran, Miao, & Pikalov, 2009).

The second is the increasing focus of pharmaceutical research on continuous innovation, cost cutting, and shortening development times (e.g., Kennedy, 1997). Again, this has information consequences (e.g., Abbott, 1998; Gassman, Reepmeyer, & von Zedtwitz, 2004; Skaug, 1995; Steven, 2002).

The third is the changing nature of the science carried out in pharmaceutical research, with small molecule synthesis and testing complemented and replaced by methods from molecular biology and genomics, coupled with high throughput screening. Again, this has consequences for the type of information generated and needed (e.g., Cole & Bawden, 1996; Cunningham, 2000; Fischer & Heyse, 2005; Kshirsager, 2008; Ohlstein, Ruffolo, & Elliott, 2000; Ward & Warr, 1998).

The fourth is changes in health service requirements and expectations for the provision of medicines, particularly to address the problems of ageing populations, and chronic diseases (e.g., Andersen, Rice, & Kominski, 2007; Avgerou, Cornford, & Mossialos, 1996; Tovey, 2000).

The fifth is the increasing emphasis, as has been noted, on consumer health information and hence greater need for pharmaceutical information for the general public (Abbott, 1998; Cline & Haynes, 2001; Gann, 1987, 1991; Shulman, 1988).

The sixth involves information technology, in particular the advent of the internet, which has changed the information practices of consumers and professionals in a remarkable way (Dupuits, 2002; Johnson & Wordell, 1998). Commenting on this, in their monograph on drug information, Malone, Kier, and Stanovich (2006, p. xxiii) note that "the impact of the internet can be seen in this book. The first [1996] edition contained only two pages of information about the internet [but] in this new [2006] edition, it seems as if hardly a page can be found without some reference to internet material."

Even apart from the internet, the change in the technological environment has been profound and, as will be discussed later, driven in large measure by the pharmaceutical information sector. Just prior to the period covered by this review, a pharmaceutical company reported the replacement of its card catalog database by a punched card system (Bird, 1976). One of the authors of this review can recall as a trainee in a pharmaceutical information department having to carry out a search through in-house databases reflecting the industrial archaeology of information retrieval: card indexes, edge-notched cards, optical coincidence cards, punched cards, and finally computer files. The changes in the technologies of information have had perhaps the most dramatic effect on pharmaceutical information provision but must be considered in conjunction with the other changes.

These environmental changes over three decades form the backdrop to this review.

Previous Reviews and Monographs

The literature of pharmaceutical information is extensive. A search of the Library and Information Science Abstracts (LISA) database for the term "pharmaceutical" (a far-from-comprehensive search strategy in a far-from-complete data source) returns more than 1,600 journal articles and conference papers published between 1980 and 2008.

One journal is wholly devoted to the topic: *Drug Information Journal* has been published quarterly by the international Drug Information Association since 1967. Other articles are scattered across a wide variety of journals, largely in library and information science and information management, but also in journals of information systems and informatics, pharmacy, pharmacology, and medicine.

In spite of this plethora of primary materials, reviews and monographs are scarce. No previous *ARIST* review has focused on pharmaceutical information, although the topic is mentioned in reviews on medical, chemical, and toxicological information. Nor are there any substantive reviews of the whole area in other sources, although there are numerous summaries of sources and services, typically rather short and ephemeral; as an example of the more thorough of these, see Calam

(1992). However, a number of monographs produced over the period from 1980 to 2008 act in effect as extended reviews. Several of these will be described, so as to exemplify differences in approach and coverage, as well as changes over time.

Monographs published throughout the 1970s and 1980s took *pharmaceutical information* as largely synonymous with *the literature of pharmacy*. Sewell (1976), Andrews (1986), and Strickland-Hodge, Jepson, and Reid (1989) provide good examples of this approach. The first was aimed primarily at pharmacy students and practitioners, the second at librarians, the third at librarians and information workers; this change indicates the extent to which this area was becoming an important field within information science during the period. These books are essentially annotated lists of sources—largely printed, although some computerized sources are mentioned—and emphasizing the significance of specialist libraries and other information suppliers. All stick fairly close to the pharmacy remit, although both Sewell and Andrews include some materials on associated areas: chemistry, pharmacology, toxicology, and medicine.

An early example of a monograph taking a wider viewpoint is a volume in the Butterworth/Bowker-Saur series of "Information Sources ..." guides, which was aimed at a library/information audience and covered pharmaceutical information to the end of the 1980s (Pickering, 1990). Focusing, in accordance with the series aims, on information resources, this extensive (566 page) guide took, for the most part, an industry perspective. Its twenty chapters were divided into three sections. The first, dealing with information resources in detail, had chapters covering: chemical and physicochemical information, biological and biotechnology information, biological and biomedical information, toxicology and drug metabolism information, technical development and product information, intellectual property, marketing and business information, legal and regulatory issues, and post-marketing experiences. The second section, dealing with the institutions and organizations providing pharmaceutical information, had chapters on: publicly available drug information from a variety of sources, the industry as a source of information, and the World Health Organization. The third section, dealing with the variability of provision of pharmaceutical information in various regions of the world, covered the U.S., Western Europe, Japan, Australia, South America, Central Africa, and China.

Pickering's book sums up well what we might call the classical picture of pharmaceutical information, just before the changes brought about by restructuring in the industry and in healthcare provision and by the internet. It is a picture of a wide range of sources, printed and computerized, and a wide range of providers, even though use is largely restricted to professional groups; general public access is mentioned in only one chapter. The issues of a "pharma information divide" between rich and poor parts of the world looms large and has been a continuing theme; see, for example, Pakenham-Walsh, Eddleston, and Kaur (1999, p. 1265).

A more recent example is a book intended to accompany a U.K. master's course in pharmaceutical information management; it was aimed primarily at those working in pharmaceutical information functions in industry and the health service (Robson, Bawden, & Judd, 2001). Its substantive chapters covered: information sources, information technology, information and knowledge management, provision of information, analysis and evaluation of information, professional and managerial skills, medicines information in the U.K. health service, medical information services in the pharmaceutical industry, research information in the pharmaceutical industry, commercial information, pharmacovigilance, regulatory affairs, document and records management, end-user support and training, and codes of practice and ethics. These topics emphasize the wide scope of the topic, and illustrate the overlaps between pharmaceutical information per se and more general information science and information management.

Malone, Kier, and Stanovich's (2006) edition of their guide for pharmacists and pharmacy students provides a further example, typifying a number of "Pharmaceutical Information for ..." monographs aimed at particular professional groups and following in the mould of the earlier monographs mentioned, although with a considerably wider scope. Its eighteen chapters cover: concept of medication information, systematic approach to answering questions, effective responses and recommendations, drug information resources, electronic information management, clinical trial evaluation, literature evaluation, pharmacoeconomics, evidence-based practice, statistical analysis, professional writing, legal responsibilities, ethical issues, pharmacy and therapeutics committees, drug evaluation monographs, quality issues, adverse reactions and medication errors, and drug information through the licensing process. Again we see the overlap between the core of pharmaceutical information—information resources and the handling of information—and more general information-related activities, appropriate to a healthcare profession.

The last of the exemplar monographs, the third edition of a well-known guidebook, is a comprehensive and detailed resource guide aimed primarily at librarians and other specialized information providers (Snow, 2008). Chapters cover drug identification, government regulation and its information consequences, literature searching and evaluation, sources in pharmacology and therapeutics, sources for adverse reactions and drug interactions, sources for formulation and analysis, competitor intelligence resources, and business information sources. Emphasis is placed on choice of the best combination of sources, from an increased range and diversity, commonly now available in digital, and specifically web-based, formats.

These examples of monographs reviewing the pharmaceutical information area show two clear movements over time. The first is from a restricted, pharmacy-based viewpoint to a much broader subject domain. The second is a much wider range of resource types, largely brought about by the increased availability and diversity of digital information sources. They also illustrate the increasing recognition of pharmaceutical information as a specialism within information science.

Pharmaceutical Information Producers and Users

It is clear that the communication chain for pharmaceutical information is complex and involves an unusually large number of types of participants. They include academic and industrial research scientists and clinical researchers, healthcare professionals (particularly doctors and pharmacists), government regulators, pharmaceutical industry information units (typically categorized as research, medical, or commercial), consumers (mainly patients, carers, and support groups), and librarians, publishers, and database producers (Robson, Bawden, & Judd, 2001).

Typically, all these are both users and producers of pharmaceutical information; even patients, who have hitherto been assumed to be passive consumers of information on the medicines they use, are now generating information. This is accomplished both through formal channels, for example, communicating experiences of side effects (Craigle, 2007), and through informal channels, usually internet facilitated, such as blogs, forums, and newsgroups.

To help discussion of these issues, we adopt an extremely oversimplified model, regarding the lifetime of a medicine in three stages: discovery and development, regulatory approval, and use. We, necessarily, restrict the discussion to those aspects where clear information consequences have been discussed in the literature in the period reviewed.

Stage 1: Discovery and Development

In the first stage, medicines are discovered and developed to the point where an application can be made for their widespread use, either on prescription through a medical practitioner or sold over the counter, direct to the public.

Information users and producers here are primarily scientific and clinical researchers in academia and in industry; the wide variety of disciplines involved has already been noted. Other participants at this stage are involved in assessing viability of new medicines, whether in scientific areas such as epidemiology or in business areas such as marketing and competitor intelligence.

Studies of the information practices of research scientists have been widespread over several decades, to the extent that it could be said that information user studies until the mid-1980s were in fact studies of scientists' information behavior (T. D. Wilson, 1984): for overviews, see Case (2007) and Tenopir and King (2002). A proportion of such studies over the years has focused on scientists involved in pharmaceutical research, in both academic and industrial settings (e.g., Ash, Chubb, Ward, Welford, & Willett, 1985, pp. 15–41; Bawden, Devon, & Sinclair, 2000; Brown, 1984; Charton, 1992; Ljungberg & Tullgren, 1977; Rolinson, Al-Shanbari, & Meadows, 1996; Rolinson, Meadows, & Smith, 1995). These studies have shown, in broad terms, that pharmaceutical research scientists share the information behavior patterns of scientists in general, but with an added requirement for diversity of information from a wide variety of sources and a particular enthusiasm for using new technological aids. This reflects the diverse nature of the pharmaceutical information domain and the perceived requirement, and availability of funding, for the latest technical solutions.

In many respects, the information needs and practices of, and sources useful to, scientists in these early stages of pharmaceutical research are the same as those of chemical and biomedical scientists in other environments. This review cannot cover all of these issues, nor mention all of these sources; it focuses on specific pharmaceutical issues and applications.

Communication of information at this stage is facilitated by the usual infrastructure of scientific libraries and information services. For the pharmaceutical domain specifically, these include:

- Specialist pharmaceutical libraries (e.g., Bador, Locher, & Gallezot, 1991; Knoben, Phillips, & Szczur, 2004; Knoben, Phillips, Snyder, & Szczur, 2004; Lapidus, 2003; Ottlik, 1992; Strickland-Hodge, Jepson, & Reid, 1989, chapters 2.1 and 2.2), including those in industry (e.g., Dieckmann & Whittall, 1998; Haygarth-Jackson, 1977; Sandori, 1992; Schulte, 1986; Sherwell, 1997b). Such libraries are increasingly wholly digital in nature.

- Specialist library networks, which may include both academic and industrial libraries (e.g., Williams, Bliven, & Ladner, 1987).

- Pharmaceutical and other biomedical data services (e.g., Mendelsohn, 1999).

- Pharmaceutical database producers and publishers (e.g., Felter, 2005; Fowler, 2001; Lyon, Warr, & Brown, 1996).

At this early stage in the life of a medicine, information is usually communicated only to researchers and health professionals. However, the pressure for wider dissemination has led to initiatives to provide information to potential users of new medicines at an early stage; for example, publicly accessible databases of clinical trials of new drugs (Antonelli & Mercurio, 2009; Mi, 2005).

Within the pharmaceutical industry, provision of information at this stage is largely the remit of the *research* or *technical* information services

(Goodman, Whittall, & Morrison, 2001; Haygarth-Jackson, 1977; Nelson, 1989; Pay, 1991). These departments have an inward focus, their main task being to provide information services to R&D staff within the organization. This may, in turn, cover a wide scope of subject matter, from the purely scientific to information on markets and competitor activities. The traditional role has been that of an intermediary, carrying our searches and providing current awareness (Bawden, 1986), based largely on the scientific literature. With the advent of online systems aimed at the end-user (Leipzig, Kozak, & Schwartz, 1983; Mullan & Blick, 1987; Warr & Haygarth-Jackson, 1988), and particularly of web-based services, this has largely been supplanted by one of promoting user access, resource provision, database creation, and training and consultancy (Goodman & Boyce, 2001).

Another important function of research information departments has been the maintenance of databanks of internally generated information (Goodman, Whittall, & Morrison, 2001; McTaggart & Radcliffe, 1977). Here, there is increasing overlap with provision of bioinformatics and chemoinformatics systems and services (Cole & Bawden, 1996).

The pharmaceutical research information function has also shown most strongly the changing balance between the perceived merits of the information professional provider in an information department, and the information liaison function, embedded in scientific teams (e.g., Sze, 1985).

Most of the information provided by, or through, research information departments is strictly scientific in nature. However, two other important areas impinge on their work and may be handled by staff within the information unit or in conjunction with specialist departments.

The first is competitive intelligence, an essential issue for a particularly competitive industry (Bawden, 1998; Bexon, Stephens, & Pritchett, 2002; Desai & Bawden, 1993; Krol, Coleman, & Bryant, 1996). This function is located variously in different organizations, with the information department taking different roles. It is characterized by a need to access a very wide variety of sources, from science through business to news, and including numerous databases specifically created to serve this function (Blunck, Kalbfleisch, Mullen, & Rohbeck, 2003; Mullen, Blunck, Kalbfleisch, Möller, & Rohbeck, 1997).

The second is the handling of intellectual property, in particular patents; these latter having always been of great importance to the pharmaceutical industry both for their importance as scientific information resources, as well as indicators of competitor activity (Correa, 2004; Eisenschitz, 1990; Nolan, Oppenheim, & Withers, 1980; Yoo, Ramanathan, & Barcelon-Yang, 2005). Again, the information department may play various roles vis à vis intellectual property specialists, and again a variety of specialized resources is available (Goodman, Whittall, & Morrison, 2001; D. K. Wilson, 2007). Pharmaceutical patents may also be important information sources for information providers outside the pharmaceutical industry (Hogan & Scarborough, 1996).

Stage 2: Regulatory Approval

In this stage, when a new medicine has been shown in clinical trials to be safe and effective, approval is needed from national and international regulatory bodies before it is permitted to be used routinely (Griffin & O'Grady, 2003; Snow, 2008). Further approvals may be needed before it is recommended for use by national health services; and still further local approvals may be needed before it is included in a hospital formulary or local approved drugs lists. Legal frameworks, and the nature of regulatory agencies, differ across countries, although international harmonization is increasing, particularly within the European Union. Among the best known and most influential of the regulatory agencies are the U.S. Food and Drug Administration, the E.U. European Medicines Agency, and the U.K. Medicines and Healthcare Products Regulatory Agency and National Institute for Health and Clinical Excellence. Each country has its own equivalents.

This process of approvals, which may generate public controversy, is highly information intensive (see Snow [2008] for a detailed discussion of information products and services with respect to regulation; see also Beglin [2001], Goldwire and Rumore [1993], and Zimmer [2003]). The regulatory agencies are major consumers of information, analyzed and evaluated in order to reach decisions and make recommendations (e.g., Britt, 1996), and also major producers of data collections and guidelines, which are in themselves important sources of pharmaceutical information throughout the lifetime of the medicine. Consistent international terminology is of obvious importance. The Medical Dictionary for Regulatory Activities (MedDRA) vocabulary has been developed for this purpose, drawing terms and concepts from existing vocabularies such as the World Health Organization Adverse Reaction Terminology (WHO-ART), Coding Symbols for a Thesaurus of Adverse Reaction Terms (COSTART), and the International Classification of Diseases (ICD) (Brown, Wood, & Wood, 1999; Doan, 2002; Kubler, Vonk, Beimel, Gunselmann, Homering, Nehrdich, et al., 2005; Tucker, 2002; West, 2001).

The pharmaceutical companies' need to process and prepare very extensive sets of information for regulatory approvals has led to innovation in a number of areas such as records management (Pease, 1995), content management (Agoratus, 1999; Michalak, Matthews, Leslie, Kenkins, Mehta, & Asbjorn, 1996) (including a move to fully digital regulatory submission [Attridge, 2005]), and technical writing (Bonk, 1998).

Stage 3: Marketed Medicines

When a medicine enters general use, copious information is produced and used throughout its life; and indeed afterwards, because the information base on medicines no longer in use must be maintained in order to deal with the consequences of long-term adverse effects. Users and producers of information at this stage are again diverse; they include healthcare professionals, academic researchers, government regulators, the pharmaceutical industry, and the general public. Healthcare workers, doctors, and pharmacists, in particular, must make extensive use of such information in order to use medicines correctly. They also provide information, primarily through the medical and pharmaceutical literature and through systems for the reporting of adverse effects. As in the case of research scientists, numerous studies have investigated the information-related behavior of healthcare workers, doctors, and pharmacists (Bush, King, & Tenopir, 2004; Case, 2007; Stinson & Mueller, 1980). Several studies have examined this behavior as it relates to pharmaceutical information, most commonly for doctors and pharmacists in Western Europe and North America (e.g., Abate, Jacknowitz, & Shumway, 1989; Coumou & Meijman, 1994; Gaither, Bagozzi, Kirking, & Ascione, 1994; Gerrett & Clerk, 1997; "Internet influences doctors' clinical diagnosis," 2002; Joy, Arana, & Gallo, 1986; Ko & Sklar, 2009; Koo & Miller, 1992; Liddell, 1990; Lundborg, Hensjo, & Gustafsson, 1998; Schrimsher, Freeman, & Kendrach, 2006; Simon, Soares, & Aranda da Silva, 1987). They tend to show a general reliance on a small number of sources for pharmaceutical information: standard reference texts and formularies, colleagues, and pharmaceutical company representatives, joined now by internet sources. Formal sources, such as libraries, information centers, and bibliographic databases, have been relatively little used. The same is true for doctors and pharmacists in the developing world (Kreling & Dzvimbo, 1989) and for other healthcare workers having responsibility for medicines, including nurses (Haymond, Butler, Metts, & Brown, 1977; Hittel & Yost, 1981; Wolfgang, Perri, & Katzan, 1989), dentists (Murray, 1981; Parker & Reid, 1978), and clinical research coordinators (Wessel, Tannery, & Epstein, 2006).

Pharmacists, in particular, have been recognized as gatekeepers, having an important role as both recipients and providers of medicines information (e.g., Vainio, Airaksinen, Vaisanen, & Enlund, 2004; Watt, 1977); indeed, Byrd (2002, p. 68) has suggested that pharmacy could be a model for a "health informationist" profession. Pharmacists provide drug information to a variety of recipients, in community practice, in hospitals and clinics, and in specialized medicines information services. These are operated by national health services, with the aim of providing information on medicines to doctors, pharmacists, nurses, other healthcare workers, and also to patients (Hands, Judd, Golightly, & Grant, 1999; Hibberd, 1980; Judd, 2001; Smith, 1987). This may involve creation of centralized drug databases, input into creation of local formularies and prescribing policies, and assessment of new drugs, as well as advising on use of medicines for particular patients. Such services have been shown to have a direct and beneficial impact on patient care in providing information on adverse drug effects (Stubbington, Bowey, Hands, & Brown, 1998) but evidence of more general impact is limited (Hands, Stephens, & Brown, 2002; Rutter, Brown, & Rutter, 2004).

Academic researchers and industrial clinical investigators continue to carry out research on marketed medicines in order to study problems and to identify new opportunities for use. Government regulators monitor use of medicines and provide updated guidelines on appropriate use; there may be separate versions of guidance aimed at health professionals and at consumers.

Regulators have a particular responsibility to maintain pharmacovigilance systems for identifying unwanted effects of medicines, enabling the assessment and prevention of side effects. This process begins during the clinical development of drugs and extends through post-marketing surveillance to identify and assess adverse drug reactions through the time a drug is on the market, and indeed afterwards. It is a complex and information-intensive process, with numerous sources, regulations, legal issues, methods, and protocols (Mann & Andrews, 2007; Medicines and Healthcare Products Regulatory Agency, 2008; Talbot & Waller, 2003).

Numerous pharmacovigilance systems exist within government agencies, international organizations, and pharmaceutical companies for capturing, coding, storing and reporting data and information on adverse effects of drugs (Bess & Umrath, 2005; Fallowfield, 1995; Fucik & Edwards, 1996; Sakurai, Kugai, Kawana, Fukita, & Fukumoto, 1995; Soller, 2004; West, 2001). Sometimes these use standard vocabularies for indexing the data, although special coding schemes, such as WHO-ART, COSTART, and the newer MedDRA, may also be used, as for regulatory issues (Brown, Wood, & Wood, 1999; Fizames, 1997; Goldman, 2002). This information is increasingly made available to the general public through the internet (e.g., Mani, 2006).

The pharmaceutical industry also carries out many information-related activities at this stage. It must have systems for pharmacovigilance, as has been noted, and must identify information on the use of the company's products and competitors, in support of sales and marketing. It also has the responsibility to provide information on its own products to prescribers and users through medical information departments.

Pharmaceutical industry medical information departments have a two-fold role (Hopkins, Galligher, & Levine, 1999; Huntingford, O'Callaghan, Taylor, Turnbull, & Wells, 1990; Leighton & Davies, 2009; Pay, 1991; Roach, 1982; Robson, Blake, Chandler, Dellamy, Davies, Fleming, et al., 1996; Robson & Riggens, 2001; Robson & Robson, 2000; Royland, 1982; Yamamoto, Onaka, Hirai, Kuroko, Negi, Yamada, et al., 1995). Internally, they provide information services to a variety of customers within their organization, most particularly to the sales and marketing functions, but also to the medical and regulatory affairs departments. Externally—and the main reason for their existence—they provide information on their company's products to healthcare workers, particularly doctors and pharmacists. Although publicly available or externally produced sources may often be used by medical information departments, reliance is usually placed on in-house databases of publications and other material on the company's products, created and maintained by the department (Gretz & Thomas 1995; Hull, 1996; Robson & Riggens, 2001; van Putte & Peperkamp, 1983); as examples, see Ortelli and Ferrario (1990), Bauman and Bettenhausen (1994), and Gasperino and Lynn (1995). In some circumstances, such databases have been integrated with current awareness services (Hodge & Walker, 1984).

To a limited degree, and varying from country to country in the case of prescription medicines, information is provided to patients and the general public. This backs up the patient information leaflets required with all medicines; the best information content and presentation for this information has been extensively debated (Brown, 1989; Gustafsson, Kalvemark, Nilsson, & Nilsson, 2003; Newton, Newton, Clark, Kenny, Mossley, Purves, et al. 1998; Payne, 2002; Robson & Riggens, 2001; Smith & Ramseyer, 2002; Twomey, 2001). A perennial issue is the extent to which information provision from the industry overlaps with marketing and advertising, particularly where information provision to the public, and to patients and patients' organizations and support groups, is concerned (Herxheimer, 2003; Young, Paterniti, Bell, & Kravitz, 2005). This is of particular importance because sales representatives and marketing departments are among the most important users of medical information departments (Bauman & Bettenhausen, 1994; Robson & Riggens, 2001; Yamamoto, Iizuka, Negai, Shimizu, Funabashi, & Okada, 1998). The sensitive nature of this kind of information provision is evidenced by a unique concern for deceitful enquiries; for example, by members of the public claiming to be medical practitioners or by employees of competitor companies who do not identify themselves (e.g., Curran, 2002).

Provision of information within the pharmaceutical industry is sometimes carried out by specialist units, sometimes as an activity of research or medical information units. It involves provision of a variety of business, financial, and company information, with a particular focus on the competitor intelligence and environmental scanning, and is sometimes regarded as a specialism within pharmaceutical information (Berkien, 2006; Desai & Bawden, 1993; Snow, 2008).

The idea that the general public would have a need for information about medicines, or that it would be appropriate to provide such information to them, is of recent standing. Although information for the public about health and medical matters counts among the oldest writings—it was one of the first outputs of the printing press and has been a staple of publishers ever since (Robinson, 2010)—information about prescription medicines was felt to be a matter for the medical profession until relatively recently. None of the pre-1990 literature guides mentions it, but Barry (1991, p. 265) noted "the desire of an increasingly sophisticated public to know about commercial drugs ... patients know much more about drugs than they did even 10 years ago." Interest in providing information to the general public has increased dramatically, fuelled by the consumer health movement and the availability of the internet as a communications channel. We have noted the provision of public-friendly versions of regulatory guidelines, the opening to the public of databases of clinical trials information and of pharmacovigilance data, and the tensions implicit in the desire of the pharmaceutical industry to provide the public with information beyond that included in leaflets for patients. The web has proven useful in education on diseases and treatments, rather than promotion of particular products (e.g., Howe & Baker, 2007; Vigilante & Wogalter, 2005), and in supporting patients' organizations—itself controversial, as has been noted (Herxheimer, 2003).

Studies of the information-related behavior of members of the public seeking pharmaceutical information show a pattern that is typical of those seeking any form of health information (Case, 2007). A wide variety of sources is used, including books, magazines, newspapers, public libraries, radio and television, family and friends, support groups, and healthcare workers, but with the internet now usually taking a major role (e.g., Cantrill, Gray, Klein, Noyce, & Sesselberg, 2005; Dutta-Bergman, 2004; Farmer & Peffer, 1996; Keselman, Browne, & Kaufman, 2008; Trewin & Veitch, 2003; Nicholas, Huntington, Jamali, & Williams, 2007).

Pharmaceutical Information Organization: Classifications, Thesauri, and Terminologies

We have seen that pharmaceutical information is broad in scope and diverse in nature, with a wide range of resource types and users. Naturally it will require a variety of intellectual tools for its organization.

The first type to be considered is library classifications; these are important for the organization of printed sources and also useful with digital material. Sewell (1976) notes the Dewey Decimal Classification (DDC), the Library of Congress Classification (LCC), and the National Library of Medicine Classification (NLMC) as the three likely to be encountered in a pharmacy-related library in America. The same is likely to have been true anywhere in the world at that period, except for Continental Europe, where the Universal Decimal Classification (UDC) predominated. Strickland-Hodge and colleagues (1989) also mention these three leading schemes and note the use of a modified form of UDC in the library of the Royal Pharmaceutical Society (London). Lopez-Mertz (1997) reported a specific study on the adequacy of the NLMC for organizing pharmacy books. It is likely that these classifications will remain, for the foreseeable future, the default method for the organization of pharmaceutical collections.

These early guides mention the National Library of Medicine's Medical Subject Headings (MeSH) vocabulary as the main tool for detailed indexing of pharmaceutical literature; it retains that status today. The thesauri for the Biological Abstracts and the Excerpta Medica databases also cover pharmaceutical material in detail (Blair, 1980; Briggs & Crowlesmith, 1995; Excerpta Medica, 2008; Powell, 1980; Snow, 1991, 2008).

Examples of more subject-specific equivalents are the thesauri used in the indexing of the International Pharmaceutical Abstracts (Snow, 2008; Van Camp, 1984) and the Derwent Drug File (formerly RING-DOC) literature databases (Bawden & Devon, 1980; van Putte, 1990) and the thesaurus maintained by the U.K. Medicines Information Pharmacists Group, which is used to index that group's medicines information resources, particularly the Pharm-line bibliographic database on pharmacy practice and clinical use of drugs. Specialized thesauri are also used to index material in the Martindale pharmaceutical reference resource ("Martindale Online," 1984; Snow, 1988, 2008) and the drug pipeline databases, such as Adis R&D Insight and Pharmaprojects, as will be discussed (Snow, 2008).

Special purpose pharmaceutical vocabularies and taxonomies are numerous. Terminologies derived for regulatory purposes and for pharmacovigilance (WHO-ART, COSTART, and MedDRA) have been noted. Another example is the taxonomy used to organize material in the British National Formulary (produced jointly by the Royal Pharmaceutical Society and the British Medical Association) and also materials in the guidelines from the U.K. National Institute for Health and Clinical Excellence. Unique identification codes for all pharmaceuticals available in each country are widely used (Snow, 2008); studies have shown considerable inconsistency in the application of these codes in the U.S. Guo, Diehl, Felkey, Gibson, and Barker (1998) have created thesauri and classifications for the indexing of in-house databases (e.g., Leitmeyer & Gillum, 1993). The more recent tendency has been to adopt standard publicly available vocabularies for this purpose; see Harrison (1992) for an example of the adaption of the Excerpta Medica thesaurus for an in-house file.

The process of indexing pharmaceutical material, and the particular difficulties for the indexer, have been discussed with regard to books and journals (Gibson, 1983), abstracting and indexing services (Barber, Moffatt, Wood, & Bawden, 1988), and in-house bibliographic databases (Abbott, 1997).

Pharmaceutical Information Sources, Services, and Retrieval

Information resources may be categorized in various ways, so that an extensive set of diverse resources, as certainly exists for the pharmaceutical domain, may be better understood and organized (Bawden & Robinson, 2001; Robinson, 2000). Four general typologies are commonly used:

- By subject

- By format

- By location

- By type of material

To these we might add further categorizations by date, language, intended audience, and so on. Previous resource guides have used some or all of these, generally in combination.

Andrews (1986) has a separate, three-fold categorization: by subject (e.g., "pharmacology and toxicology"), by type of material ("pharmacopeias and standards"), and by format ("databases"). Strickland-Hodge and colleagues (1989) categorize resources by type of material (e.g., "bibliographies" and "textbooks and monographs") with some elements of format ("online databases and directories"). Pickering (1990) categorizes mainly by subject, such as "toxicology and drug metabolism information," with some elements of type of material (e.g., "intellectual property") and a separate categorization by location ("information needs and availability in the United States"). Shields and Lust (2006) in the drug information resources chapter of the monograph edited by Malone and colleagues (2006) make a partial distinction among primary, secondary, and tertiary but mainly use an essentially subject-based categorization (e.g., "general product information," "geriatric dosage recommendations," and "pharmacy law"). Snow (2008) also notes the categorization of scientific literature sources as primary, secondary, and tertiary but again primarily categorizes resources by their general subject (e.g., "adverse reactions and drug interaction") or purpose ("drug identification"). Bawden and Robinson (2001) have categorized pharmaceutical information resources by a three-fold framework for type of material, denoting resources as:

- Primary: the original information

- Secondary: value-added information, from some organization of primary material

- Tertiary: materials pointing to, and aiding the use of, primary and secondary materials

It is possible also to consider "zeroth" order information, raw information before it enters the communication chain—for example, the output from laboratory instrumentation. Although such information is certainly vital in the scientific and clinical investigation of pharmaceuticals, it is not discussed here because it does not constitute a generally available resource.

Similarly we may consider quaternary information resources, giving access to resource listings at a high level: bibliographies of bibliographies and lists of lists. A medical example of a list of lists, current at the time of writing, is Hardin MD (www.lib.uiowa.edu/hardin/md). Other examples of quaternary resources are lists of guides to literatures, such as that offered by Snow (2008, chapter 4), and the PINAKES (www.hw.ac.uk/libwww/irn/pinakes/pinakes.html) list of internet subject gateways.

The internet even offers quintenary resources: lists of lists of lists. These higher level resources are not usually specific to pharmaceutical information and so will not be considered here.

We can now consider, in outline, pharmaceutical resources in this three-way categorization. For more detail, see Bawden and Robinson's (2001) book, which lists pharmaceutical resources of importance at that date and includes resource listings for industrial research information services and for health services medicines information.

For virtually all these resources, the period 1980 to date has seen a general move from print-on-paper to online and CD-ROM formats, and then to web-based delivery. This information has scientific, medical, and economic importance particularly to the pharmaceutical industry; therefore sources, specifically those regarded as value added, have been relatively costly to use. This has led to a consistent demand for free or low-cost resources, especially for public-sector needs (e.g., Cooper, 2008).

Primary Resources

Because of its continuing importance, the journal literature is considered first in this section, followed by other forms of primary material.

Journals

Scientific and medical journals, now increasingly used in electronic form (Tenopir, King, Boyce, Grayson, Khang, & Ebuen, 2003), remain a major resource. They have been essential through the period from 1980 for all pharmaceutical information environments, whether as journal issues or separate articles (Barker & Jacknowitz, 1981; Brown, 1999; Cooper & McGregor, 1994; Ditchfield & Nielsen, 2008; Fong, 1985; Gagnon, 1986; Haygarth-Jackson 1987a; Okerson, 1992). The newer routes of access to journal material, through open access preprint and e-print servers, are also used (Ginestet & Miranda, 2002), although fully open access journals are still rare in this subject area (Clauson, Veronin, Khanfar, & Lou, 2008).

The range of journals of potential relevance to the topic is very wide and the precise number difficult to determine. Sewell (1976) points out that, as well as the core areas of pharmacy and pharmaceutical sciences, relevant material may appear in journals of medicine, the premedical sciences, chemistry, and even social science. Duckitt (1990, p. 82) states that "it is not possible to find a reliable figure for the number of journals in the fields which would encompass the full range of biological and medical biomedical interests within the pharmaceutical industry ... a reasonable estimate must be around 10,000 titles." Strickland-Hodge and colleagues (1989) list 220 journals of direct relevance to pharmacy, including 5 medical journals and 34 review journals; they encompass journals in 21 languages other than English. Other estimates for the number include: 318 "European pharmaceutical journals" (Bador, Picard, & Locher, 1994, p. 409); 289 "European pharmaceutical journals" (Bador, Romdhane, & Lafouge, 2003, p. 33); and 317 "pharmacy-focused journals" (Clauson, Veronin, Khanfar, & Lou, 2008, p. 1539).

Bringing matters up to date, Ulrich's periodicals directory for 2009 lists 2,717 journals under the *pharmacy and pharmacology* heading and 23,935 under *medical sciences*. The library of the Royal Pharmaceutical Society of Great Britain (www.rpsgb.org.uk) has a collection of more than 250 printed journal titles in pharmacy, pharmacology, pharmaceutics, and medicine and more than 2,000 ejournals in biomedical science. It can therefore be reasonably assumed that the journal literature of the subject consists of a core of about 300 titles, with a scatter through a very wide selection of others. Gorraiz and Schloegl (2008) reported a bibliometric analysis of the top-ranking journals of the area, focusing on the top 100.

Not all pharmaceutical journals are equivalent. Strickland-Hodge and colleagues (1989) distinguish three kinds: scientific journals; those concerned with a specific kind of pharmacy (e.g., retail), which might be termed trade journals; and those journals aimed at members of local professional associations or societies, which may have the character of newsletters. These local journals have evoked some controversy. As long ago as 1971, it was being argued that they should transform themselves into newsletters and give up the pretense of journal status (Provost, 1971); yet 20 years later some were more widely read and valued than higher status journals (Grussing & Wilkins, 1991).

This leads to other issues. These journals rely greatly on pharmaceutical industry advertising for viability. The ethics of allowing such advertisements, and the related question of whether to publish articles from industry sources, has been controversial; for a flavor of the arguments, see Williams (2007), Smith (2003, 2007), and Irving (2005).

The content of local journals may be partly or wholly in languages other than English, although it is increasingly regarded as the *lingua franca* of drug information; Strickland-Hodge and colleagues (1989) listed journals in 22 languages among their 220 pharmacy-related journals. A significant "language barrier" affecting the use of information from non-English sources has been identified among pharmaceutical research workers (Thorp, Schur, Bawden, & Joice, 1988, p. 17).

With increasing volumes of literature, abstracts of journal articles become more significant as a time-saving aid to literature searching. A study of one year's issues of seven pharmacy journals showed 60 percent of the abstracts to have omissions or inaccuracies (Ward, Kendrach, & Price, 2004).

The pharmaceutical journal literature has been used for bibliometric analysis to study the literatures of drugs and drug classes (Bordons, Bravo, & Barrigon, 2004; López-Muñoz, Alamo, Rubio, García-García, Martin-Agueda, & Cuenca, 2003; Windsor, 1975), to attempt to predict clinical success of drugs (Windsor, 1976), and to analyze the research performance of pharmaceutical companies (Gambardella, 1992; Koenig, 1983; McMillan & Hamilton, 2000; Narin & Rozek, 1988).

Other Primary Resources

Report series may offer an alternative form of primary publication, especially for government departments and agencies, as well as international organizations. Academic theses, dissertations, and project reports may also provide detailed information that does not appear in the published literature (Duckitt, 1990). Again, the influence of the web can be seen in improving access to these various forms of grey literature.

In addition to their importance for competitor intelligence and for legal and intellectual property issues, patents can provide scientific information not available elsewhere, although the reliability of their information may be questionable (Duckitt, 1990; Eisenschitz, 1990; Hogan & Scarborough, 1996; Norton, 1982). Windsor (1979) used bibliometric analysis of the patent literature to attempt to predict the clinical success of drugs in development.

Conference proceedings may provide information that never appears in the journal literature or is published only at a later stage (Duckitt, 1990). Conference reports databases are commonly provided by drug pipeline information suppliers, for example IDdb Meeting Reports (Snow, 2008). Even announcements of forthcoming conference papers can be valuable for current awareness and competitor intelligence. Providing advance notification of meetings and conferences, based on announcements in journals and specialist publications, used to be a common task for pharmaceutical information units (Forward & Selby, 1978); web-based communication has now largely taken over this function.

News media of all forms provide information particularly relevant to commercial, regulatory, and competitor aspects of the field; medical and scientific matters also appear here. Conventional news sources, with web feeds, are relevant; the use of consolidating services such as Reuters Health (Jenkinson & Kane, 2005) is replacing the scanning of printed newspapers, which was common in the past. Specific pharmaceutical news sources, in particular the Scrip/Pharmaceutical and Healthcare Industry News Database service, are also widely used (Brown, 1994; Chang, Caster, Morris, Nelson, & Larson, 1991; Snow, 2008).

For regulatory and legal purposes, access to legislation, regulations, standards, good practice guidelines, and so on, and to the frequent updates of these, is essential. Information about organizations, including company reports, and about individuals is now widely available through corporate and personal websites, replacing the files of paper brochures and contact lists kept in the past by many information services (Duckitt, 1990; Snow, 2008; Wisniewski, 1998).

Mailing lists, newsgroups, forums, blogs, and other internet communication media are used for scientific and medical purposes—and their archives may be searchable and valuable sources of specific information—but are of particular use in monitoring the views of the general public and of support groups for particular diseases (e.g., Boulos & Wheeler, 2007; Meier, Lyons, Frydman, Forlenza, & Rimer, 2007; Rimer, Lyons, Ribisl, Bowling, Golin, Forlenza, et al., 2005; Savino & Shick, 1998).

Publicly available information from the manufacturers of medicines, particularly the data sheets and patient information leaflets required by law to be produced in a standard format, are the fundamental source of information on each medicine. They are usually available as compendia or compilations for all the medicines available within a country; in the U.K., for example, such compendia have been provided by the Association of the British Pharmaceutical Industry ("ABPI opts for patient," 1987); in the U.S. they are made available through the National Library of Medicine's Daily Med service.

Not publicly available, but of importance within organizations and also required for regulation, is the internal information produced in the process of drug discovery, development, and clinical trials; both research and medical information services in the pharmaceutical industry need access. One specific example is the indexing, retrieval, and (more recently) digitization of laboratory notebooks and similar research documentation (Caporizzo, 2008; Cibbarelli, Tenopir, & Ott, 1978; Hentz, 2002; Le, 2003; Samuel, 1997). Increasing pressure toward openness and transparency in drug development and licensing has led some companies to make the results of clinical trials publicly available through the web, including negative results not published elsewhere.

Secondary Resources

In this section, we deal only with publicly available secondary sources; in-house databases have been discussed previously. Nor can we deal in detail with the many resources, particularly web resources, aimed primarily at the general public and consumers of medicines, often of dubious quality (for reviews, see Kelley & Chae, 2000; Perdue & Piotrowski, 2004; Perkins, 2001).

Secondary sources are considered under the three headings of database services, reference collections and databanks, and evaluated and summarized knowledge sources, with a final section on specialized searching facilities.

Database Services

Bibliographic abstracting and indexing services for the relevant scientific disciplines have been a mainstay of pharmaceutical information provision throughout the period. The sector has been such an important user of these services that it has considerably influenced their development. The seven most important such services were all noted by Sewell (1976) and remain dominant thirty years later (Snow, 2008):

- International Pharmaceutical Abstracts

- Chemical Abstracts

- Biological Abstracts/BIOSIS

- Index Medicus/MEDLINE/PubMed

- Excerpta Medica/EMBASE

- TOXLINE/Toxcenter/TOXNET

- Science Citation Index/Web of Science

These have been the subject of many comparisons and evaluations regarding their value in providing pharmaceutical information (e.g., Barillot, Sarrut, & Doreau, 1997; Bawden & Brock, 1985; Biarez, Sarrut, Doreau, & Etienne, 1991; Brown, 1998; Fishman, Stone, and DiPaula, 1996; Flory, 2002; Kruse, 1983; Robinson, McIlwaine, Copestake, & Anderson, 2000; Sayers, Joice, & Bawden, 1990; Simkins, 1977; Snow, 1982b, 1984; Sodha & Amelsvoort, 1994).

Comparative evaluation of these sources, together with the specific pharmaceutical information sources noted below, have generally concluded that, although one or the other may be preferred for particular searches, a combination is usually needed for effective retrieval. Variations in coverage and indexing have consistently subverted the desire of database producers to offer one-stop shopping for pharmaceutical information.

The Excerpta Medica/EMBASE database has tended to be particularly favored for good retrieval because of its responsiveness to the need for detailed pharmaceutical indexing (Brown, 1998; Hallam & Plaice, 1999; Powell, 1980; Snow, 1991). This kind of consideration has led to the creation of a number of databases specifically for pharmaceutical material, most notably Derwent's RINGDOC (latterly Derwent Drug File) database, with specific coverage and detailed intellectual indexing from several pharmaceutical perspectives (Bawden & Devon, 1980; Burcham, 1992; Hoover, 1981; van Putte, 1990). Other pharmaceutical-specific bibliographic databases include the Iowa Drug Information Service (Cornell, Gatewood, Davis, Fish, & Helmink, 1981; Hall & Foy, 1983; Milne, 1978; Rumschlag & Howes, 1993) and Pharm-line, produced by the U.K. National Health Service's medicines information service (Judd, 2001; Rodgers, 1985).

Chemical information sources and systems such as Beilstein and CAS/SciFinder are important in the pharmaceutical area, particularly for drug discovery and development, as with any chemical research environment (Arisumi & Turner, 1995; Bremner, Castle, Griffith, Keller, & Ridley, 2002).

The importance of competitor intelligence information reflects the need, of a kind unique to the pharmaceutical sector, for an awareness of drugs in the pipeline from discovery through development to clinical trials and marketing (Breton, 2003; Parkar & Toeg, 1999; Snow, 2008). Numerous database services have been developed to meet this need, originally provided via index card files (Bottle & Linton, 1971); examples are Pharmaprojects, Adis R&D Insight, IMS R&D Focus, Prous Ensemble, Derwent World Drug Index, MDL Drug Data Report, and the Investigational Drugs Database (Cheesman, 2002; Fenton & Hutton, 1993; Mullen et al., 1997; Mullen et al., 2003; Snow, 1993, 2008). These are typically structured by drug substance and provide value-added, evaluated, and summarized information. Studies have shown that there is little overlap in content (Snow, 2008); as with the bibliographic databases, a combination of sources is needed for comprehensive information collection. Sources of this kind, more than others, have undergone a constant process of rapid development, renaming, consolidation, and changes of ownership.

Patents information is, as noted previously, of considerable and continuing importance. It may be found in several disciplinary databases (Snow, 1989), in general patents services (Oppenheim, 1981), and also in sources specifically for pharmaceutical patent information (Borne, 1996; Cheesman, 1995; Gotkis, 1992; Johns, Andrus, de Voe, Myers, Smith, & Uhlir, 1979).

Other types of secondary data sources designed specifically for pharmaceutical information include databases for carcinogenicity studies (McAuslane & Lumley, 1993), for clinical trials details (Perkins, 2007), and for pharmaceutical news compilations (Chang et al., 1991).

Reference Collections and Databanks

The copious amount of structured data associated with the use of medicines has resulted in the availability of an array of reference tools. These range from small-scale reference books (for example, a local formulary for use in a hospital) to extensive databanks; they include sources for complementary and traditional medicines (Lapidus & Bond, 2008). Originally produced in print, virtually all have now migrated to digital form or to multiple print and digital format (Gretz, Stadler, & Thomas, 1996; Woodward, 1995); some are available on mobile devices (Barrons, 2004; De Groote & Doranski, 2004; Galt, Houghton, Remington, Rule, & Young, 2005; Gora-Harper & Amerson, 2006). Snow (2008) recommends acquisition of the print version of major resources to complement their digital equivalents. She also points out the value of retaining older copies of printed resources of this kind, because they may contain detailed information that has been omitted from more recent editions and cannot otherwise be found;

this point was demonstrated in a detailed comparison of secondary and tertiary sources (Bawden & Brock, 1982).

Most of these reference resources are pharmacopoeias, formularies, handbooks, drug information bulletins, drug dictionaries, and similar quick-reference tools, many of which are national or local in nature. Lists, descriptions, and comparisons of the more widely applicable resources of this type are given by Snow (2008), Shields and Lust (2006), Bawden and Robinson (2001), Andrews (1986), Strickland-Hodge and colleagues (1989), Smith (1996), Olsson and Pal (2006), and Hartel and Kupferberg (2004).

Important examples, which have retained their place throughout the period of this review, include *Martindale: The Extra Pharmacopoeia* (in print, now including digital versions, since 1883), the *Physicians' Desk Reference* (U.S.), the *Merck Manual Home Health Handbook*, the *Index Nominum* (drug name dictionary), and national drug lists (such as, for the U.K., the British National Formulary, the electronic Medicines Compendium, and the *Monthly Index of Medical Specialities [MIMS])* (Fijn, de Vries, Engles, Brouwers, de Blaey, & de Jong van den Berg, 1999; Fowler, 2001; Fryer, Baratz, & Helenius, 1991; Royal Pharmaceutical Society, 1996; Snow, 1988, 2008; Wills, 1986). Similar resources are available for veterinary medicines (Snow, 2008). These sources were invariably listed as commonly used tools in the studies of health professionals' information behavior, as has been noted.

Evaluated and Summarized Knowledge Sources

A third important category of secondary sources of pharmaceutical information is evaluative summaries of the knowledge base.

Throughout the period covered the review article, typically published in a specialist review journal, remained an important source, providing a critical evaluation of the literature. These are numerous for pharmaceutical information; Sewell (1976, p. 152) notes that "review publications occur in practically every area with which the pharmacist is concerned." One could say the same for the pharmacologist or medicinal chemist; these resources retain their traditional importance (Sayers et al., 1990).

A specific form of literature evaluation is the systematic review, geared to providing explicit advice on evidence-based best practice in an aspect of healthcare; these may be found in general bibliographic secondary sources or through specialist sources for evidence-based practice such as the Cochrane Database of Systematic Reviews (Fitzpatrick, 2000; Koonce, Giuse, & Todd, 2004). In turn, these feed into health service guidelines, which incorporate the reviewed literature (Linden, Vondeling, Packer, & Cook, 2007; Moores, 2006) and into public information guides (Dolovich, Burns, Cassel, Levine, Nair, McCormack, et al., 2006).

Encyclopaedias, monographs, and textbooks form another class of resource for presenting evaluated pharmaceutical knowledge. The latter, typically named after their originator and often running through many editions, generally now have both digital (online and/or CD-ROM) and printed versions; Snow (2008) gives a detailed listing. Well-known examples are: Goodman and Gilman's (2005) *Pharmacological Basis of Therapeutics*, in its 11th edition; Myler's (2006) *Side Effects of Drugs*, in its 15th edition; Stockley's (2007) *Drug Interactions*, in its 8th edition, Remington's (2005) *The Science and Practice of Pharmacy*, in its 21st edition; Rang and Dale's (2007) *Pharmacology*, in its 6th edition; and Burger's (2003) *Medicinal Chemistry and Drug Discovery*, a multivolume work with its 6th edition published between 2003 and 2008. A newer, arguably equivalent type of resource is a specialized, and usually proprietary, web portal, providing knowledge summaries in a particular area, with links to related resources: an example is Elsevier's xPharm service supporting drug discovery (Saimbert, 2006).

Specialized Searching Facilities

The sources noted previously have, among them, generated a number of unusual searching facilities. In some cases, these remain unique to the pharmaceutical sector; in others, they have been pioneered here, but have since become more widespread. They include:

- Chemical structure and substructure searching, similarity matching, and macromolecular sequence searching (Ash, Warr, & Willett, 1991)

- Searching features allowing for the multiple nomenclatures and terminologies used for medicinal substances (Kremin, 1979; Snow, 1992, 2008)

- Automated assistance for query formulation in databases with complex terminologies (Oakes & Taylor, 1998)

- Searching specifically for medicines dispensed in other countries, with unfamiliar names, uses, and standards (Snow, 1982a, 2008)

- Retrieval of the generic forms of chemical structure, so-called Markush structures, typically found in pharmaceutical patents (Barnard, 1991; Benichou, Klimczak, & Borne, 1997; Kaback, 1980; Lynch, Barnard, & Welford, 1981)

- Identification and distinction of medicines with names that either look similar or sound similar (Kondrak & Dorr, 2006; Lambert, Chang, & Lin, 2001)

- Identification of unknown medicines, in capsule or tablet form, by searching on shape, color, markings, etc., in systems such as TICTAC and IDENTIDEX, typically achieving 90 percent accurate identification (Popa & Robertson, 1994;

Raschke, Hatton, Weaver, & Belgado, 2003; Snow, 2008; Weaver, Hatton, & Doering, 2004)

Tertiary Resources

These resources, which point to and aid the use of lower order materials, have increased in number for the pharmaceutical domain over the period of this review, due in large part to the influence of the internet.

One type of such resource, which has retained its importance, is the subject guide, examples of which have been discussed in an earlier section. Another is the directory type of resource, providing structured and summarized information and data on pharmaceutical companies, research organizations, sales, markets, and so on. Most of these publications are now available on the web, with some integrated into pipeline database services; Snow (2008) gives numerous examples.

The new type of tertiary resource, which has proliferated with the internet, is the annotated list of sources, often packaged as a portal. These have been created in a number of formats:

- Public internet portals for pharmaceutical information, such as PharmWeb, the Virtual Library of Pharmacy, and Martindale's Virtual Pharmacy Center (De Manuele, 1998; Snow, 2008)

- Public internet portals for more general scientific information, including pharmaceuticals, such as the U.K. BIOME portal (Gray, 1999; MacKay, 2005)

- Portals created by information producers to integrate their pharmaceutically relevant sources and services, including both commercial providers, such as Thomson Pharma (Felter, 2005; Plosker, 2006), and public bodies, such as the U.S. National Library of Medicine (Knoben, Phillips, Snyder, & Szezur, 2004)

- In-house proprietary portals and intranets, integrating internal sources and services (e.g., Little & Millington, 2001; Srodin & Strupczewski, 2002)

Pharmaceutical Information and Knowledge Management

As has been discussed, the pharmaceutical industry, government regulatory agencies, and health services are all voracious producers and consumers of information. Naturally enough, the pharmaceutical domain has been the source of many innovations in information and knowledge management techniques and systems, including the management of documents and records, so as to make productive use of this plethora of information.

Some illustrative examples of these innovations, roughly categorized by topic, are discussed here. General strategic approaches to information management have been described, varying in their applicability from a single pharmaceutical company (Huotari, 1995) to the U.K. pharmaceutical profession ("Council approves information management," 1997).

Information Technology and Information Systems

The pharmaceutical area has been a major innovator and driver in this respect, the pharmaceutical industry in particular (e.g., Bruque-Cámara, Hernández-Ortiz, & Vargas-Sanchez, 2004; Lamb, King, & Kling, 2003; Schwartzer, 1995). Specific examples of technologies include database construction (Dugas, Weinzierl, Pecar, Endres, & Hasford, 2003), enterprise resource planning systems (Spremić & Vukšić, 2005), the provision of portals and intranets (Little & Millington, 2001; Srodin & Strupczewski, 2002), and data warehousing (Alshawi, Irani, & Saez-Pujol, 2003). Information technology has always played a major part in supporting the activities of pharmaceutical libraries and information units (e.g., Benfield, Haraki, & Venkataraghaven, 1981; Weaver & Porter, 1991). This environment has in turn contributed to the information systems field, for example, by the development of methods for "user sensitive" systems implementation (Goodman, 1998, p. 121).

Libraries and Document Delivery

The provision of documents through libraries has always been a major part of pharmaceutical information management. The industry has been a major user of, and innovator in, document supply services, particularly as the environment changed to mainly digital provision (Cooper & McGregor, 1994; Delaney, 2003; Haygarth-Jackson, 1987a; Kasarab, 2006; Sherwell, 1989; Stadler, Mernke, & Thomas, 1999).

Industry libraries have also been innovative in the provision of library services in general (He, Chaudhuri, & Juterbock, 2009). The optimal way of providing current awareness services, initially based on printed library materials and latterly on electronic sources, has been a perennial concern (Blick, Gaworska, & Magrill, 1982; Blick & Magrill, 1975; Hentz, 1996; Hodge & Walker, 1984; Law, 1989; McIntosh, 1993). Other innovations have concerned reference services (Delaney, 1999), maximizing use of the journal collection (Archer, 1997), and collection development (Law, 1989; Thorpe, 1979). Academic pharmaceutical libraries have also pioneered techniques for multifaceted collection evaluation (Bergen & Nemec, 1999).

Pharmaceutical libraries have been leaders in the move away from solely print resources, first to microforms (Blick & Ward, 1984) and then to digital resources (Brown, 1999; Gretz, Stadler, & Thomas, 1996), with development of a pharmaceutical model for the licensing of electronic journals (Ditchfield & Nielsen, 2008). Many pharmaceutical industry libraries were largely or wholly digital by the end of the period reviewed, with hard copy, if retained at all, moved to external stores.

Developments in library automation systems in pharmaceutical settings (Hentz, 1994; Zolezzi, 1991; Zom & Marshall, 1995) have led to the development of digital or hybrid libraries. This has come about in stages: from delivery of materials to users' desks (Hoskin, Lister, & Marsh, 1982), through provision of workstations in largely print-based libraries (Schulte, 1986), and then parallel physical and virtual libraries (Sherwell, 1997a, 1997b; Ward & Warr, 1998), to the fully digital library (Archer, 2004).

Facilitating Users

Proactive services led, particularly in industry, to the introduction of what was termed *end-user searching*, by which scientists and clinicians were encouraged to undertake their own searching in computerized sources: online bibliographic databases (Haygarth-Jackson, Holohan, & Shether, 1978; Leipzig, Kozak, & Schwartz, 1983; Marshall & Zorn, 1997), CD-ROM bibliographic databases (Mullan & Blick, 1987; Whittall, 1989), and specialized chemical information sources (Leipzig, Kozak, & Schwartz, 1983; Warr & Haygarth-Jackson, 1988). This emphasis on empowering users, pioneered in pharmaceutical settings and widely followed elsewhere, has led to pharmaceutical information services taking a largely consultant/advisor/facilitator stance, replacing the intermediary role (Goodman & Boyce, 2001; Goodman, Whittall, & Morrison, 2001).

Document Management

The information-intensive nature of drug development and use leads to extensive document production, particularly at the regulatory stage (Dobbs, 1993; Ehrhard, 2003; Hoefer, Geyer, Arnold-Gross, & von Jan, 2002; Zimmer, 2003), although also for R&D documentation (Samuel, 1997). Systems designed for the creation and management of paper documentation have been extended to deal with digital documentation.

Pharmaceutical companies were among the first users of large-scale electronic publishing (May, 1995; Warr, 1991; Wasserman, 1990) and electronic data capture (Grossman & Bates, 2008), and among the first to link such systems to documentation management processes (Lander, 1998). With increasing use of digital documents, specific measures for their preservation and archiving are an important issue ("ImageSolve II," 1992; Stamatoplos, 2005; Stephens, 2000). The practices of systematic document and records management, including file organization, were introduced at a relatively early stage and are of increasing importance (Chalmers, 2001; Curran & Sundar, 2002), with records management in particular identified as a significant component of information management in the pharmaceutical sector (Goodman, 1994; Samuel, 1998). Quality control and confidentiality of data sources has been a major focus (Chalmers, 2001; Ham, 1995; Pierredon, 1995), as have records management issues resulting from company mergers and restructuring (Marsh, 2000). The historical records of the pharmaceutical industry have also been noted as an archival resource worth preserving (Stevenson, 1997).

Knowledge Management

The pharmaceutical industry has been a leader in the transformation of library/information services from fulfilling a largely traditional role of provision of external published information to one placing equal importance on internally generated information. The practice of knowledge management as a means of maximizing the value of internal information and knowledge has been promoted widely within the pharmaceutical industry, although meeting some skepticism (Collins, Shaw, & Billington, 1999; Currie & Kerrin, 2004; Liebowitz, 2000; Pappa, Stergioulas, & Telonis, 2009; Wang, 2006). Practical solutions for knowledge sharing, involving both face-to-face facilitation and technical solutions, have been warmly received; see, for example, Robson, Bandle, and Ince (1999); Hynes, Getzi, McQuaid, Seward, and Field-Perez (1999); Hoffman, Pallansch, and Shafer (2000); Duffy (2000); Roth (2003); Evans and Brooks (2005); and Styhre, Ollila, Roth, Williamson, and Berg (2008). The idea of knowledge integration as a form of knowledge management has also been influential (Abbott, 1998, 2004; Millington & Walker, 2003). Other approaches to the sharing and management of pharmaceutical knowledge have included peer review of information (Bergquist, Ljungberg, & Lundh-Snis, 2001), structured writing (Bernhardt & McCulley, 2000), and integrated learning (Riedinger, 2008).

Quality Issues

The pharmaceutical environment is one of the most heavily regulated; it is controlled by codes of practice affecting many aspects, from the research laboratory to the community pharmacy. Guidelines for Good Clinical Practice, Good Laboratory Practice, Good Manufacturing Practice, and others have all had considerable information implications (Chalmers, 2001; Le, 2003; Lee & Lee, 2006; Olson, 2001; Rammell, 1997; Smith, 1997), as have the industry's own codes of practice for the promotion of medicines (Simmonds, 2001).

Not surprisingly therefore, pharmaceutical information providers in all environments, but particularly in the industry, have sought to apply quality principles to their activities. This has been particularly so in medical information departments, where a variety of quality mechanisms has been used, especially in response to ISO 9000 certification (Khan & Bawden, 2000). These include standardized and documented procedures and guidelines, such as objective quality measurements (Curran & Nowakowski, 1994; Curran, Sundar, & Westhe, 2003; Davies,

2001; Robson & Riggens, 2001), as well as more elaborate procedures such as benchmarking and organizational maps (Kinnell, 1997; Trzan-Herman & Kiauta, 1996). Wormleighton and Leighton (2009) describe an audit of medical information provision in the various national affiliates of a multinational pharmaceutical company. Outside the industry, standardized procedures have been recommended to pharmacists in providing drug information since the 1970s (Kirkwood & Kier, 2006), leading here also to a concern with more formal definitions of quality (Ninno & Ninno, 2006).

Assessing Value and Impact

A consistent theme in pharmaceutical information management has been the assessment of the value of information services, with a particular emphasis on cost/benefit; perhaps not surprisingly, in view of the resources invested in the area. Various methodologies have been explored, with growing emphasis on objective measurement, very different from the time when it could be said that "service evaluation is highly subjective," dependent purely on expressions of user satisfaction (Brown, 1983, p. 79).

A number of early studies examined the cost-effectiveness of particular services in industrial information units (Ashmole, Smith, & Stern, 1973; Blick, 1977a, 1977b); although the methods used may no longer be regarded as appropriate, their pioneering nature may still be recognized. User surveys, to obtain qualitative understanding of the value of aspects of services, have formed another standard approach (e.g., Albano & Santhouse, 2003; Baker, 1990; Bauman & Bettenhausen, 1994; Hoffman & Gumbhir, 1993). More holistic approaches to service evaluation have used a mixed-methods approach, linking cost analysis with user surveys and other means of assessing the value of information systems and services (Ljungberg & Tullgren, 1976, 1977; McElroy, 1982; Saltzman, 1995).

Some attempts have been made to measure the real value or direct impact of pharmaceutical information services. These have included the reporting of individual incidents of benefit (e.g., Fingerote & Blanchard, 1994) and the assessment of links between specific services and measurable impact—for example, between the overall stated satisfaction of doctors with information provided by a pharmaceutical company and the prescribing of that company's products (Albano & Santhouse, 2003) and between the provision of drug information services in a hospital and reduced mortality rates (Pitterle, Bond, Raehl, & Franke, 1994). Other approaches have been the identification of critical information needs (Huotari, 1995) and of the contribution of information to company priorities (He et al., 2009), information mapping and auditing (Ellis, Barker, Potter, & Pridgeon, 1993), and inter-company analysis of the relation between information environment and research productivity (Koenig, 1990).

Influence on Information Science

The pharmaceutical information domain, because of its numerous and diverse users and sources, its technical advances, and its economic and social significance, has played a major role in advancing the discipline of information science itself.

First, and most obvious, is the issue of information technology. Shepherd (2001) notes the applications of developing technology for delivering pharmaceutical information in health services, including microfiche, electronic publishing, CD-ROMs, online services, the internet (and latterly internet portals), and health service intranets. As has been shown, the pharmaceutical sector has always been in the forefront of applications in information technology to information communication: from pre-computer documentation technology (Bird, 1976), to the digital computer (Blakeman, 1985; Haygarth-Jackson, 1977; Lewi & Braet, 1970) and online searching (Bawden, 1986; Blick & Magrill, 1978, Goodemote, 1980; Haygarth-Jackson, Holohan, & Shether, 1978), to the personal computer (Bawden, 1988; Rudin, Hausele, & Stollak, 1985), to CD-ROMs (Whittall, 1989), the internet ("Stepping on to the Information Superhighway," 1996), and Web 2.0 (Warr, 2008).

The case of online database searching is particularly compelling. Bourne and Hahn (2003) give a number of examples of the pioneering role of the pharmaceutical industry in the development of online services. The first paying subscriber to the SDC service, itself the first to emphasize online biomedical databases, was the Pfizer pharmaceutical company library; the sector provided more than half the service's users for its first few years of operation.

Nor is it shaming to note pharmaceutical involvement in the development of information technologies that never really made their mark, from television as a medium for conveying medicines information (Springer, Yokel, Lorenzi, Sigell, & Nelson, 1978) to the short-lived videotex (Hull, 1994). It is also worth remembering that the idea, now taken for granted, of users doing their own searching in digital resources was pioneered in this sector.

Second, there is the influence of the pharmaceutical sector on the wider information industry. This is seen at the micro-level in the effect of the big users on the development of the online (and latterly CD-ROM) sector, in influencing the development of the disciplinary databases, and the creation of the pharmaceutically specific services. Associations of pharmaceutical information users—particularly the Pharma Documentation Ring (P-D-R) (Di Nallo & Schopfel, 2008), but also the Association of Information Officers in the Pharmaceutical Industry (AIOPI), recently absorbed into the Pharmaceutical Information and Pharmacovigilance Association (PIPA), in the U.K.—have been particularly important in this respect. On a larger scale, several significant information industry companies have developed largely to serve this sector: for example, the

Institute for Scientific Information (Garfield, 2001, 2008), Derwent Publications (Poynder, 2000), and Prous (Mason, 1999).

Third, there is the sector's influence on research and development within information science itself, the pharmaceutical sector being the locus for much practitioner research, sadly absent from most of the information world (Blick, 1983). The most obvious example is the development of chemoinformatics, which was to a great extent stimulated and promoted by the pharmaceutical industry (Chen, 2006; Willett, 2008). Another is the development of the user-oriented and contextualized style of comparative database evaluation (as has been noted) promoted by pharmaceutical sector collaboration (Bawden, 1980). Yet another is the pioneering work, again noted previously, on the assessment of the value and impact of information services, latterly taken up in other parts of the library/information world. Other examples where research techniques pioneered or developed in the pharmaceutical domain have been taken up more widely include data mining and text mining (Banville, 2009a, 2009b; Bremner et al., 2002; Olaleye & Tardiff, 2001) and the use of bibliometric analysis to make scientific and commercial predictions (Windsor, 1976, 1979). Finally, the development of the many and varied pharmaceutical classifications, thesauri, and other terminologies described earlier has influenced theory and practice in information organization generally.

In these various ways, the pharmaceutical sector has influenced the developing principles and practice of information science over the period of this review and has provided career opportunities for many information scientists (Alberts, 2008; Crawford & Weller, 1986). [Indeed, the authors of this review both began their information careers in this sector, as a trainee information officer in pharmaceutical research, and as an abstractor for Derwent's RINGDOC service, respectively.]

Windsor (1999) has argued that the roots of the information science discipline itself are to be found in industry, specifically in the pharmaceutical industry. The outline of the pharmaceutical information environment over three decades, presented in this review, suggests that this opinion is not without merit.

References

Abate, M. A., Jacknowitz, A. I., & Shumway, J. M. (1989). Information sources utilized by private practice and university physicians. *Drug Information Journal*, *23*(2), 309–319.

Abbott, R. (1997). "Aboutness" and other problems of text retrieval in the pharmaceutical industry. *Drug Information Journal*, *31*(1), 125–135.

Abbott, R. (1998). An overview of knowledge integration for innovation in healthcare and pharmaceuticals. *Drug Information Journal*, *32*(4), 905–915.

Abbott, R. (2004). Integration and structuring for enhanced knowledge management. *Drug Information Journal*, *38*(2), 187–196.

ABPI opts for patient information leaflets and compendium. (1987, October 31). *Pharmaceutical Journal*, *239*, 511.

Agoratus, S. (1999). Developing a knowledge interface for a document management system. *Drug Information Journal, 33*(1), 95–99.

Albano, D., & Santhouse, A. (2003). Evaluation of Wyeth medical communications written responses and the impact on prescribing. *Drug Information Journal, 37*(4), 445–450.

Alberts, D. (2008). The ever-changing role of the information professional in pharmaceutical R&D. *World Patent Information, 30*(3), 233–237.

Alshawi, S., Irani, Z., & Saez-Pujol, I. (2003). Data warehousing in decision support for pharmaceutical R&D supply chain. *International Journal of Information Management, 23*(3), 259–268.

Andersen, R., Rice, T. H., & Kominski, G. F. (2007). *Changing the U.S. health care system: Key issues in health services policy and management* (3rd ed.). New York: Jossey Bass.

Andrews, T. (1986). *Guide to the literature of pharmacy and the pharmaceutical sciences.* Littleton, CO: Libraries Unlimited.

Antonelli, M., & Mercurio, G. (2009). Reporting, access and transparency: Better infrastructure of clinical trials. *Critical Care Medicine, 37*(1S), 178–183.

Arisumi, P. P., & Turner, W. R. (1995). The introduction and role of SciFinder, a unique end-user search tool in a pharmaceutical company. *Abstracts of Papers of the American Chemical Society, 210*, 33.

Archer, M. (1997). The view from a special library. *Serials, 10*(3), 337–341.

Archer, M. (2004). Electronic only in the corporate environment. *Serials, 17*(1), 47–50.

Ash, J. E., Chubb, P. A., Ward, S. E., Welford, S. M., & Willett, P. (1985). The information needs of chemists. In J. E. Ash et al., *Communication, storage and retrieval of chemical information* (pp. 15–41). Chichester, UK: Ellis Horwood.

Ash, J. E., Warr, W. A., & Willett, P. (Eds.). (1991). *Chemical structure systems: Computational techniques for representation, searching, and processing of structural information.* Chichester, UK: Ellis Horwood.

Ashmole, R. F., Smith, D. E., & Stern, B. T. (1973). Cost effectiveness of current awareness sources in the pharmaceutical industry. *Journal of the American Society for Information Science, 24*(1), 29–39.

Attridge, P. (2005). Content management: The only cure for pharma's regulatory ills. *Information Management and Technology, 38*(3), 122–123.

Avgerou, C., Cornford, T., & Mossialos, E. (1996). Information infrastructures for the management of medical drug use: A European perspective. *Information Infrastructure and Policy, 5*(3), 205–215.

Bador, P., Locher, F., & Gallezot, J. (1991). Evaluation of the activity of the Pharmaceutical Documentation Centre of the Pharmacy Faculty of Lyon (France) from September 1990 to July 1991. *Health Information and Libraries, 2*(4), 169–180.

Bador, P., Picard, A., & Locher, F. (1994). Survey of European pharmaceutical journals in circulation in 1993. *Journal de Pharmacie de Belgique, 49*, 409–432.

Bador, P., Romdhame, M., & Lafouge, T. (2003). European pharmaceutical journals: Relationship between demand and indexation: The example of the main French document supplier. *Canadian Journal of Information and Library Science, 27*(2), 33–55.

Baker, R. P. (1990). User survey of an industry-based drug information service. *Drug Information Journal, 24*(1), 235–243.

Banville, D. L. (2009a). *Chemical information mining.* Boca Raton, FL: CRC Press.

Banville, D. L. (2009b). Mining chemical and biological information from the drug literature. *Current Opinion in Drug Discovery and Development, 12*(3), 376–387.

Barber, J., Moffat, S., Wood, F., & Bawden, D. (1988). Case studies of the indexing and retrieval of pharmacology papers. *Information Processing & Management, 24*(2), 141–150.

Barillot, M. J., Sarrut, B., & Doreau, C. G. (1997), Evaluation of drug interaction document citation in nine online bibliographic databases. *Annals of Pharmacotherapy, 31*(1), 45–49.

Barker, C. S., & Jacknowitz, A. T. (1981). Availability and use of pharmacy and medical journals by hospital pharmacists in West Virginia. *Drug Information Journal, 15*(1), 38–45.

Barnard, J. M. (1991). A comparison of different approaches to Markush structure handling. *Journal of Chemical Information and Computer Sciences, 31*(1), 64–68.

Barrons, R. (2004). Evaluation of personal digital assistant software for drug interactions. *American Journal of Health-System Pharmacy, 61*(4), 380–385.

Barry, C. (1991). Publicly-available information on marketed drugs. In W. R. Pickering (Ed.), *Information sources in pharmaceuticals* (pp. 265–277). London: Bowker-Saur.

Bauman, J. H., & Bettenhausen, D. K. (1994). Evaluation and effectiveness of a pharmaceutical-based drug information service. *Drug Information Journal, 28*(3), 657–665.

Bawden, D. (1980). The toxicology information working party: An exercise in user collaboration. *Aslib Proceedings, 32*(5), 226–227.

Bawden, D. (1986). Ten years of online information for pharmaceutical research. *Proceedings of the 10th International Online Information Meeting,* 63–67.

Bawden, D. (1988). Specific roles for microcomputer software in an information department. *Aslib Proceedings, 40*(1), 1–7.

Bawden, D. (1998). Competitor intelligence in the pharmaceutical industry. In A. Kent (Ed.), *Encyclopaedia of Library and Information Sciences* (vol. 63, supplement 26, pp. 33–52). Boca Raton, FL: CRC Press.

Bawden, D., & Brock, A. M. (1982). Chemical toxicology searching: A collaborative evaluation, comparing information resources and searching techniques. *Journal of Information Science, 5*(1), 3–18.

Bawden, D., & Brock, A. M. (1985). Chemical toxicology searching: A comparative study of online databases. *Journal of Chemical Information and Computer Sciences, 25*(1), 31–35.

Bawden, D., & Devon, T. K. (1980). RINGDOC: The database of pharmaceutical literature. *Database, 3*(3), 29–39.

Bawden, D., Devon, T. K., & Sinclair, I. (2000). Desktop information systems and services: A user survey in a pharmaceutical research organisation. *International Journal of Information Management, 20*(2), 151–160.

Bawden, D., & Robinson, L. (2001). Information sources. In A. S. Robson, D. Bawden, & A. Judd (Eds.), *Pharmaceutical and medicines information management: Principles and practice* (pp. 4–16). Edinburgh, UK: Churchill Livingstone.

Beglin, C. (2001). Regulatory affairs. In A. S. Robson, D. Bawden, & A. Judd (Eds.), *Pharmaceutical and medicines information management: Principles and practice* (pp. 186–198). Edinburgh, UK: Churchill Livingstone.

Benfield, L. K., Haraki, K. S., & Venkataraghaven, R. (1981). An online biomedical research information system. *Proceedings of the National Online Meeting,* 71–72.

Benichou, P., Klimczak, C., & Borne, P. (1997). Handling genericity in chemical structures using the Markush DARC software. *Journal of Chemical Information and Computer Sciences, 37*(1), 43–53.

Bergen, P. L., & Nemec, D. (1999). An assessment of collections at the University of Wisconsin-Madison Health Sciences Libraries: Drug resistance. *Bulletin of the Medical Library Association, 87*(1), 37–42.

Bergquist, M., Ljungberg, J., & Lundh-Snis, U. (2001). Practising peer review in organizations: A qualifier for knowledge dissemination and legitimization. *Journal of Information Technology, 16*(2), 99–112.

Berkien, T. (2006). Transforming information specialists into intelligence professionals. *Online, 30*(5), 27–31.

Bernhardt, S. A., & McCulley, G. A. (2000). Knowledge management and pharmaceutical development teams: Using writing to guide science. *Technical Communication, 47*(1), 22–34.

Bess, A. L., & Umrath, T. (2005). Establishing an adverse event collection team in a pharmaceutical safety department: Impact on report quality and customer satisfaction. *Drug Information Journal, 39*(1), 81–89.

Bexon, M., Stephens, D., & Pritchett, C. (2002). Competitive intelligence: A career opportunity for the information professional in industry. *Journal of Librarianship and Information Science, 34*(4), 187–196.

Biarez, O., Sarrut, B., Doreau, C. G., & Etienne, J. (1991). Comparison and evaluation of nine bibliographic databases concerning adverse drug reactions. *Annals of Pharmacotherapy, 25*(10), 1062–1065.

Bird, P. R. (1976). SCIDOC: A feature card system for retrieval of pharmacology literature. *Aslib Proceedings, 28*(4), 174–175.

Blair, J. C. (1980). Online drug literature searching: Excerpta Medica. *Online, 4*(4), 13–23.

Blakeman, K. (1985). The selection and implementation of a computerised information retrieval system in a small information unit. *Journal of Information Science, 11*(4), 187–193.

Blick, A. R. (1977a). Evaluating an in-house or bought-in service. *Aslib Proceedings, 29*(9), 310–319.

Blick, A. R. (1977b). The value of measurement in decision-making in an information unit: A cost-benefit analysis. *Aslib Proceedings, 29*(5), 189–196.

Blick, A. R. (1983). Information science research versus the practitioner. *Nachrichten für Dokumentation, 34*(6), 261–265.

Blick, A. R., Gaworska, S. J., & Magrill, D. S. (1982). A comparison of online databases with a large in-house information bulletin in the provision of current awareness. *Journal of Information Science, 4*(2/3), 79–86.

Blick, A. R., & Magrill, D. S. (1975). The value of a weekly in-house current awareness bulletin serving pharmaceutical research scientists. *Information Scientist, 9*(1), 19–28.

Blick, A. R., & Magrill, D. S. (1978). The effect of the introduction of on-line facilities on the choice of search tools. *Information Scientist, 12*(1), 25–31.

Blick, A. R., & Ward, S. M. (1984). A microform policy to reduce the physical growth of industrial libraries. *Aslib Proceedings, 36*(4), 165–176.

Blois, M. (1984). *Information and meaning: The nature of medical descriptions.* Berkeley: University of California Press.

Blois. M. (1988). Medicine and the nature of vertical reasoning. *New England Journal of Medicine*, *318*(13), 847–851.

Blunck, M., Kalbfleisch, E., Mullen, A., & Rohbeck, H. G. (2003). Using pharmaceutical development product databases for competitive intelligence. *Online*, *27*(3), 44–49.

Bonk, R. J. (1998). Writing technical documents for the global pharmaceutical industry. *Technical Communications Quarterly*, *7*(3), 319–327.

Bordons, M., Bravo, C., & Barrigon, S. (2004). Time-tracking of the research profile of a drug using bibliometric tools. *Journal of the American Society for Information Science and Technology*, *55*(5), 445–461.

Borne, P. (1996). PHARMSEARCH: The pharmaceutical patents database produced by INPI. *World Patent Information*, *18*(3), 125–132.

Bottle, R. T., & Linton, W. D. (1971). Quick reference sources. In R. T. Bottle & H. V. Wyatt (Eds.), *The use of biological literature* (2nd ed., pp. 118–140). London: Butterworth.

Boulos, M. N. K., & Wheeler, S. (2007). The emerging Web 2.0 social software: An enabling suite of sociable technologies in health and health care education. *Health Information and Libraries Journal*, *24*(1), 2–23.

Bourne, C. P., & Hahn, T. B. (2003). *A history of online information services: 1963–1976*. Cambridge, MA: MIT Press.

Bremner, J. B., Castle, K., Griffith, R., Keller, P. A., & Ridley, D. D. (2002). Mining the Chemical Abstracts database with pharmacophore-based queries. *Journal of Molecular Graphics and Modelling*, *21*(3), 185–194.

Breton, T. (2003). Working the pharmaceutical pipeline databases. *Searcher*, *11*(8), 32–42.

Briggs, K., & Crowlesmith, I. (1995). EMBASE: The Excerpta Medica database: Quick and comprehensive drug information. *Publishing Research Quarterly*, *11*(3), 51–60.

Britt, A. L. (1996). Safety information processing at the FDA. *Drug Information Journal*, *30*(1), 47–58.

Brown, C. M. (1998). The benefits of searching EMBASE versus MEDLINE for pharmaceutical information. *Online and CD-ROM Review*, *22*(1), 3–8.

Brown, E. G. (1989). Patient information leaflets from pharmaceutical companies: Survey of leaflets submitted to the Department of Health. *Pharmaceutical Medicine*, *4*(2), 123–129.

Brown, E. G., Wood, L., & Wood, S. (1999). The Medical Dictionary for Regulatory Activities (MedDRA). *Drug Safety*, *20*(2), 109–117.

Brown, H. D. (1983). A pharmaceutical information manager's viewpoint on R and D information resource management. *Journal of Chemical Information and Computer Sciences*, *23*(2), 78–80.

Brown, H. D. (1984). Information requirements for chemists in the pharmaceutical industry. *Journal of Chemical Information and Computer Sciences*, *24*(3), 155–158.

Brown, H. D. (1985). A drug is born: Its information facets in pharmaceutical research and development. *Journal of Chemical information and Computer Sciences*, *25*(3), 218–224.

Brown, P. J. (1994, March). Development of an international business information service for the pharmaceutical industry. *Pharmaceutical Historian*, *24*, 3–4.

Brown, R. (1999). What happens next? Ejournals in the corporate information service. *Serials*, *12*(2), 149–152.

Bruque-Cámara, S., Hernández-Ortiz, M. J., & Vargas-Sanchez, A. (2004). Organizational determinants of IT adoption in the pharmaceutical distribution sector. *European Journal of Information Systems*, *13*(2), 133–146.

Burcham, S. (1992). RINGDOC from Derwent and not patents! *Database*, *15*(3), 58–63.

Bush, A., King, D. W., & Tenopir, C. (2004). Medical faculty's use of print and electronic journals: Changes over time and in comparison with scientists. *Journal of the Medical Library Association*, *92*(2), 233–241.

Byrd, G. D. (2002). Can the profession of pharmacy serve as a model for health informationist professionals? *Journal of the Medical Library Association*, *90*(1), 68–75.

Calam, D. H. (1992). Pharmacology and therapeutics. In L. T. Morton & S. Godbolt (Eds.), *Information sources in the medical sciences* (4th ed., pp. 213–232). London: Bowker-Saur.

Cantrill, J. A., Gray, N. J., Klein, J. D., Noyce, P. R., & Sesselberg, T. S. (2005). Health information seeking behaviour in adolescence: The place of the internet. *Social Science and Medicine*, *60*(7), 1467–1478.

Caporizzo, M. (2008). Digitizing and securing archived laboratory notebooks. *Computers in Libraries*, *28*(9), 26–30.

Case, D. O. (2007). *Looking for information: A survey of research on information seeking, needs and behavior* (2nd ed.). New York: Academic Press.

Chalmers, S. (2001). Developments in records and document management. In A. S. Robson, D. Bawden, & A. Judd (Eds.), *Pharmaceutical and medicines information management: Principles and practice* (pp. 199–217). Edinburgh, UK: Churchill Livingstone.

Chang, C. W., Caster, J. G., Morris, J. C., Nelson, R. P., & Larson, D. L. (1991). Automated information delivery in a pharmaceutical company. *Drug Information Journal*, *25*(1), 55–61.

Charton, B. (1992). Chemists' use of libraries. *Journal of Chemical Information and Computer Sciences*, *32*(3), 199–203.

Cheesman, E. N. (1995). Patents Preview and Patents Fast-Alert. *Database*, *18*(4), 65–71.

Cheesman, E. N. (2002). IDdb3: Pharmaceutical intelligence for the next millennium. *Online*, *26*(1), 44–49.

Chen, W. L. (2006). Chemoinformatics: Past present and future. *Journal of Chemical Information and Modelling*, *46*(6), 2230–2255.

Cibbarelli, P., Tenopir, C., & Ott, R. Z. (1978). LIBNOTES a laboratory notebook retrieval system. *Proceedings of the Annual Meeting of the American Society for Information Science*, 67–69.

Clauson, K. A., Veronin, M. A., Khanfar, N. M., & Lou, J. Q. (2008). Open access publishing for pharmacy-focused journals. *American Journal of Health-System Pharmacy*, *65*(16), 1539–1544.

Cline, R. J. W., & Haynes, K. M. (2001). Consumer health information seeking on the internet: The state of the art. *Health Education Research*, *16*(6), 671–692.

Cole, N. J., & Bawden, D. (1996). Bioinformatics in the pharmaceutical industry. *Journal of Documentation*, *52*(1), 51–68.

Collins, M. A., Shaw, I., & Billington, D. C. (1999). Driving drug discovery and patient therapy via the encapsulation and fusion of knowledge. *Drug Design and Discovery*, *16*(3), 181–194.

Cooper, E. (2008). Online drug information resources: Free alternatives. *Medical Reference Services Quarterly, 27*(1), 97–103.

Cooper, M. D., & McGregor, G. F. (1994). Using article photocopy data in bibliographic models for journal collection management. *Library Quarterly, 64*(4), 386–413.

Cornell, J. A., Gatewood, L. C., Davis, T. D., Fish, S. S., & Helmink, R. (1981). Cost comparison of searching the Iowa Drug Information Service index manually and by computer. *American Journal of Hospital Pharmacy, 38*(5), 680–684.

Correa, C. M. (2004). Ownership of knowledge: The role of patents in pharmaceutical R and D. *Bulletin of the World Health Organization, 82*(10), 784–787.

Coumou, H. C. H., & Meijman, F. J. (1994). How do primary care physicians seek answers to clinical questions: A literature review. *Journal of the Medical Library Association, 94*(1), 55–60.

Council approves information management strategy for pharmacy. (1997, March 29). *Pharmaceutical Journal, 258*, 436–443.

Craigle, V. (2007). MedWatch: The FDA safety information and adverse event reporting program. *Journal of the Medical Library Association, 95*(2), 224–225.

Crawford, C. C., & Weller, A. C. (1986). Industrial drug information: Role of the library science professional. *Special Libraries, 77*(3), 157–161.

Culley, C. M., Hoffman, K. H., & Slavik, R. (2000). Merger mania: Impact on the medical information department. *Drug Information Journal, 34*(4), 1163–1168.

Cunningham, M. J. (2000). Genomics and proteomics: The new millennium of drug discovery and development. *Journal of Pharmacological and Toxicological Methods, 44*(1), 291–300.

Curran, C. F. (2002). Deceptive inquiries made to drug information departments. *Drug Information Journal, 36*(2), 435–438.

Curran, C. F., & Nowakowski, P. A. (1994). Optimizing inquiry activities in a corporate drug information department. *Drug Information Journal, 28*(2), 471–479.

Curran, C. F., & Sundar, M. N. (2002). Strategies for processing drug information documents and developing drug information files. *Drug Information Journal, 36*(3), 673–682.

Curran, C. F., Sundar, M. N., & Westhe, D. R. (2003). A same-day standard for responding to drug information requests by a pharmaceutical company. *Drug Information Journal, 37*(2), 241–249.

Currie, G., & Kerrin, M. (2004). The limits of a technological fix to knowledge management: Epistemological, political and cultural issues in the case of intranet implementation. *Management Learning, 35*(1), 9–29.

Davies, J. (2001). Providing information. In A. S. Robson, D. Bawden, & A. Judd (Eds.), *Pharmaceutical and medicines information management: Principles and practice* (pp. 60–74). Edinburgh, UK: Churchill Livingstone.

De Groote, S. L., & Doranski, M. (2004). The use of personal digital assistants in the health sciences: Results of a survey. *Journal of the Medical Library Association, 92*(3), 341–349.

De Manuele, A. (1998). PharmWeb: Pharmaceutical information on the internet. *Pharmaceutical Science and Technology Today, 1*(1), 2–4.

Delaney, E. L. (1999). Maximising reference services in a pharmaceutical R and D library. *Electronic Library, 17*(3), 167–170.

Delaney, E. L. (2003). GlaxoSmithKline Pharmaceuticals research and development: Document delivery in a global corporate environment. *Interlending and Document Supply, 31*(1), 15–20.

Desai, B. H., & Bawden, D. (1993). Competitor intelligence in the pharmaceutical industry: The role of the information professional. *Journal of Information Science, 19*(5), 327–338.

Di Nallo, L. A., & Schopfel, J. (2008). Insights into the issues facing pharmaceutical companies for information provision. *Interlending and Document Supply, 36*(3), 151–161.

Dieckmann, H., & Whittall, J. (1998). Managing information @ SmithKline Beecham. *Managing Information, 5*(7), 20–22.

Ditchfield, P. J., & Nielsen, H. P. (2008). The updated pharmaceutical model licence for ejournals: A continuing collaboration between publishers and the pharmaceutical industry. *Serials, 21*(1), 25–29.

Doan, T. V. T. (2002). Converting legacy data to MedDRA: Approach and implications. *Drug Information Journal, 36*(3), 659–666.

Dobbs, J. H. (1993). Overview of document management and document processing. *Drug Information Journal, 27*(2), 417–423.

Dolovich, L., Burns, S., Cassel, A., Levine, M., Nair, K., McCormack, J. P., et al. (2006). Using patient-oriented evidence-based information guides in practice: The family physician and community pharmacist perspective. *Drug Information Journal, 40*(1), 61–67.

Duckitt, P. (1990). Biologicals and biomedical information. In W. R. Pickering (Ed.), *Information sources in pharmaceuticals* (pp. 70–96). London: Bowker-Saur.

Duffy, J. (2000). Knowledge exchange at GlaxoWellcome. *Information Management Journal, 34*(3), 64–67.

Dugas, M., Weinzierl, S., Pecar, A., Endres, S., & Hasford, J. (2003). Design and implementation of a common drug information database for a university hospital. *Pharmacy World and Science, 25*(4), 156–161.

Dupuits, F. M. H. M. (2002). The effects of the internet on pharmaceutical consumers and providers. *Disease Management and Health Outcomes, 10*(11), 679–691.

Dutta-Bergman, M. J. (2004). Health attitudes, health cognitions, & health behaviours among internet health information seekers: Population-based survey. *Journal of Medical Internet Research, 6*(2), paper 15. Retrieved December 29, 2009, from www.jmir.org/2004/2/e15

Ehrhard, D. (2003). Erfolgskriterien für die Einführung eines elektronischen Dokumenten-Management-Systems zur Unterstützung der Erstellung von Zulassungsdossiers [Criteria for success in the implementation of electronic document management systems to support the compilation of registration dossiers]. *Pharmazeutische Industrie, 65*(5A), 498–502.

Eisenschitz, T. (1990). Intellectual property. In W. R. Pickering (Ed.), *Information sources in pharmaceuticals* (pp. 144–170). London: Bowker-Saur.

Ellis, D., Barker, R., Potter, S., & Pridgeon, C. (1993). Information audits, communication audits, & information mapping: A review and survey. *International Journal of Information Management, 13*(2), 134–151.

Excerpta Medica. (2008). *Emtree: The life science thesaurus*. Retrieved December 29, 2009, from www.info.embase.com/UserFiles/Files/emtree_white_paper.pdf

Evans, J., & Brooks, L. (2005). Collaborative working in a large pharmaceutical company: Developing better practices through a structuration schema. *International Journal of Information Management, 25*(6), 551–564.

Fallowfield, J. M. (1995). Adverse drug reactions from database to prescriber: The United Kingdom experience. *Drug Information Journal, 29*(1), 327–333.

Farmer, J., & Peffer, M. (1996). Comparing needs with available resources: A study of the use of drug information by rheumatology patients. *Journal of Librarianship and Information Science, 28*(4), 227–239.

Felter, L. M. (2005). Thomson Pharma: The cure for pharmaceutical research. *Searcher, 13*(9), 28–32.

Fenton, H., & Hutton, I. (1993). A unique drug activity search system. *Journal of Information Science, 19*(4), 303–308.

Fingerote, E., & Blanchard, L. (1994). Case report: The impact of information on prescribing patterns. *Bibliotheca Medica Canadiana, 15*(4), 202.

Fijn, R., de Vries, C. S., Engles, S. A. G., Brouwers, J. R. B. J., de Blaey, C. J., & de Jong van den Berg, L. T. W. (1999). The quality of Dutch hospital formularies: Evaluation of technical features and organisational information. *Pharmacy World and Science, 21*(3), 120–126.

Fischer, H. P., & Heyse, S. (2005). From targets to leads: The importance of advanced data analysis for decision support in drug discovery. *Current Opinion in Drug Discovery and Development, 8*(3), 334–346.

Fishman, D. L., Stone, V., & DiPaula, B. A. (1996). Where should the pharmacy researcher look first? Comparing International Pharmaceutical Abstracts and MEDLINE. *Bulletin of the Medical Library Association, 84*(3), 402–408.

Fitzpatrick, R. B. (2000). The Cochrane Library and Cochrane Collaboration. *Medical Reference Services Quarterly, 19*(4), 73–78.

Fizames, C. (1997). How to improve the medical quality of the coding reports based on WHO-ART and COSTART use. *Drug Information Journal, 31*(1), 85–92.

Flory, J. (2002). Pharmaceutical and drug resources. *Medicine on the Net, 8*(4), 11–27.

Fong, P. A. (1985). Using journals for drug information requests. *Drug Intelligence and Clinical Pharmacy, 19*, 765.

Forward, M. E., & Selby, M. A. (1978). Forthcoming event bulletin. *Aslib Proceedings, 30*(8), 298–301.

Fowler, J. (2001). The publications of the Royal Pharmaceutical Society. *Learned Publishing, 14*(3), 189–196.

Fryer, R. K., Baratz, N., & Helenius, M. (1991). Important full-text databases in the health sciences. *CD-ROM Professional, 4*(6), 92–96.

Fucik, H., & Edwards, I. R. (1996). Impact and credibility of the WHO adverse reaction signals. *Drug Information Journal, 30*(2), 461–464.

Gagnon, J. P. (1986). Ratings of scholarly journals in five pharmacy disciplines. *American Journal of Pharmacy Education, 50*(2), 127–134.

Gaither, C. A., Bagozzi, R. P., Kirking, D. M., & Ascione, F. J. (1994). Factors related to physicians' attitudes and beliefs towards drug information sources. *Drug Information Journal, 28*(3), 817–827.

Galt, K. A., Houghton, B., Remington, G., Rule, A. M., & Young, D. O. (2005). Personal digital assistant-based drug information sources: Potential to improve medication safety. *Journal of the Medical Library Association, 93*(2), 229–236.

Gambardella, A. (1992). Competitive advantages from in-house scientific research: The United States pharmaceutical industry in the 1980s. *Research Policy, 21*(5), 391–407.

Gann, R. (1987). The public their own physician: 2000 years of patient information. *Health Libraries Review*, *4*(3), 151–155.

Gann, R. (1991). Consumer health information: The growth of an information specialism. *Journal of Documentation*, *47*(3), 284–308.

Garfield, E. (2001). From laboratory to information explosions: The evolution of chemical information services at ISI. *Journal of Information Science*, *27*(2), 119–125.

Garfield, E. (2008). How I learned to love the Brits. *Journal of Information Science*, *34*(4), 623–626.

Gasperino, J., & Lynn, R. (1995). Responding to drug information requests using RAPID. *Drug Information Journal*, *29*(1), 99–106.

Gassman, O., Reepmeyer, G., & von Zedtwitz, M. (2004). *Leading pharmaceutical innovation: Trends and drivers for growth in the pharmaceutical industry*. Berlin: Springer.

Gerrett, J., & Clerk, J. C. (1997). General practitioners' approaches to accessing animate sources of drug information. *Drug Information Journal*, *31*(1), 221–227.

Gibson, J. (1983). The indexing of medical books and journals. *Indexer*, *13*(3), 173–175.

Ginestet, J., & Miranda, G. F. (2002). The attitude of pharmaceutical industry research scientists to browsing and publishing on internet preprint and e-print servers. *Drug Information Journal*, *36*(4), 831–837.

Goldman, S. A. (2002). Adverse event reporting and standardized medical terminologies: Strengths and limitations. *Drug Information Journal*, *36*(2), 439–444.

Goldwire, M. A., & Rumore, M. M. (1993). Sources of regulatory information for pharmacists. *American Journal of Hospital Pharmacy*, *50*(6), 1175–1181.

Goodemote, R. L. (1980). Planning online search service for a pharmaceutical company. *Science and Technology Libraries*, *1*(1), 69–73.

Goodman, E. C. (1994). Records management as an information management discipline: Case study from SmithKline Beecham Pharmaceuticals. *International Journal of Information Management*, *14*(2), 134–143.

Goodman, E. C. (1998). A methodology for user sensitive implementation of information systems in the pharmaceutical industry: A case study. *International Journal of Information Management*, *18*(2), 121–138.

Goodman, E. C., & Boyce, G. (2001). End-user support and training. In A. S. Robson, D. Bawden, & A. Judd (Eds.), *Pharmaceutical and medicines information management: Principles and practice* (pp. 218–233). Edinburgh, UK: Churchill Livingstone.

Goodman, E. C., Whittall, J., & Morrison, D. (2001). Research information in the pharmaceutical industry. In A. S. Robson, D. Bawden, & A. Judd (Eds.), *Pharmaceutical and medicines information management: Principles and practice* (pp. 144–155). Edinburgh, UK: Churchill Livingstone.

Gora-Harper, M. L., & Amerson, A. B. (2006). Introduction to the concept of medication information. In P. Malone, K. Kier, & J. Stanovich (Eds.), *Drug information: A guide for pharmacists* (3rd ed., pp. 1–28). New York: McGraw Hill.

Gorraiz, J., & Schloegl, C. (2008). A bibliometric analysis of pharmacology and pharmacy journals: Scopus versus Web of Science. *Journal of Information Science*, *34*(5), 715–725.

Gotkis, J. K. (1992). Current Patents Fast Alert. *Database*, *15*(6), 58–63.

Gray, L. (1999). BIOME: Incorporating the OMNI service. *Ariadne*, *22*. Retrieved December 29, 2009, from www.ariadne.ac.uk/issue22/biome

Gretz, M., Stadler, P., & Thomas, M. (1996). Silent revolution in the library: Electronic media replace printed products. Official pharmacopoeias: An example from the Boehringer Mannheim Central Library. *Electronic Library, 14*(5), 429–434.

Gretz, M., & Thomas, M. (1995). The in-house database: Nicety or necessity? *Drug Information Journal, 29*(1) 161–169.

Griffin, J., & O'Grady, J. (Eds.). (2003). *The regulation of medical products.* London: Blackwell.

Grossman, M., & Bates, S. (2008). Knowledge capture within the biopharmaceutical clinical trials environment. *VINE: The Journal of Information and Knowledge Management Systems, 38*(1), 118–132.

Grussing, P. G., & Wilkins, S. M. (1991). Member readership of state pharmaceutical association journals. *Journal of Pharmaceutical Marketing Management, 5*(3), 79–96.

Guay, Y. (1988). Internationalization of industrial research: The pharmaceutical industry, 1965–1979. *Scientometrics, 13*(5–6), 189–213.

Guo, J. J. F., Diehl, M. C., Felkey, B. G., Gibson, J. T., & Barker, K. N. (1998). Comparison and analysis of the national drug code systems among drug information databases. *Drug Information Journal, 32*(3), 769–775.

Gustafsson, J., Kalvemark, S., Nilsson, J. L. G, & Nilsson, G. (2003). A method to evaluate patient information leaflets. *Drug Information Journal, 37*(1), 115–125.

Hall, V., & Foy, E. (1983). The Iowa Drug Information Service (IDIS) and Medline: A comparison of their potential usefulness in answering selected drug information questions. *Bibliotheca Medica Canadiana, 5*(4), 125–129.

Hallam, E., & Plaice, C. (1999). An evaluation of EMBASE within the NHS: Findings of the Database Access Project working partnership to extend the knowledge base of healthcare. *Health Libraries Review, 16*(3), 192–203.

Ham, M. (1995). Confidentiality of medical databases and pharmaco-epidemiology. *Drug Information Journal, 29*(1), 343–349.

Hands, D. E., Judd, A., Golightly, P., & Grant, E. (1999). Drug information and advisory services: Past, present and future. *Pharmaceutical Journal, 262*(7039), 41–43.

Hands, D. E., Stephens, M., & Brown, D. (2002). A systematic review of the clinical and economic impact of drug information services on patient outcomes. *Pharmacy World and Science, 24*(4), 132–138.

Harrison, L. D. (1992). Implementing the MALIMET thesaurus on TRIP.TDBS. *Information Services and Use, 12*(4), 327–343.

Hartel, L. J., & Kupferberg, N. (2004). Evaluation of five full-text drug databases by pharmacy students, faculty, and librarians: Do the groups agree? *Journal of the Medical Library Association, 92*(1), 66–71.

Haygarth-Jackson, A. R. (1977). Library and technical information services: ICI Pharmaceuticals Division. *Aslib Proceedings, 29*(10), 337–347.

Haygarth-Jackson, A. R. (1987a). Journal holdings and interlibrary lending policies in the pharmaceuticals industry: A survey of ICI Pharmaceuticals Division. *Interlending and Document Supply, 15*(1), 3–6.

Haygarth-Jackson, A. R. (1987b). Pharmaceuticals: An information-based industry. *Aslib Proceedings, 39*(3), 75–86.

Haygarth-Jackson, A. R., Holohan, P. A., & Shether, M. J. (1978). Online retrieval of bibliographic information: Its introduction and evaluation based on the first year's experience. *Information Scientist*, *12*(1), 9–24.

Haymond, J. D., Butler, F. D., Metts, B. C., & Brown, W. D. (1977). Nurses' attitudes toward drugs and drug information. *Hospital Pharmacy*, *12*(2), 135–140.

He, L., Chaudhuri, B., & Juterbock, D. (2009). Creating and measuring value in a corporate library. *Information Outlook*, *13*(2), 12–26.

Hentz, M. B. (1994). Data conversion from Faxon's SC-10 serials control system into Techlib/Plus online card catalog. *Special Libraries*, *85*(3), 162–182.

Hentz, M. B. (1996). Comparison and utilization of electronic tables of contents delivery systems in a corporate library environment. *Journal of Interlibrary Loan, Document Delivery and Information Supply*, *7*(2), 29–41.

Hentz, M. B. (2002). How we set up enterprisewide access to our laboratory notebooks. *Computers in Libraries*, *22*(4), 22–27.

Herxheimer, A. (2003). Relationships between the pharmaceutical industry and patients' organisations. *British Medical Journal*, *326*(7400), 1208–1210.

Hibberd, P. L. (1980). The British drug information service. *Aslib Proceedings*, *32*(10), 408–415.

Hirst, P. (1974). *Knowledge and the curriculum*. London: Routledge and Kegan Paul.

Hirst, P., & Peters, R. S. (1970). *The logic of education*. London: Routledge and Kegan Paul.

Hittel, W. P., & Yost, R. L. (1981). Utilization of selected drug information resources by nurses. *Drug Information Journal*, *15*(2), 87–93.

Hjørland, B. (2002). Domain analysis in information science: Eleven approaches—traditional as well as innovative. *Journal of Documentation*, *58*(2), 422–462.

Hodge, G. M., & Walker, E. C. (1984). The use of the Macro/BIOSIS information transfer system at Ortho Pharmaceutical Corporation: A case study. *Information Services and Use*, *4*(6), 397–410.

Hoefer, J., Geyer, T., Arnold-Gross, K., & von Jan, K. (2002). Planung und Implementierung eines elektronischen Dokumenten-Managementsystems in einem pharmazeutischen Unternehmen [Planning and implementation of an electronic document management system within a pharmazeutical company]. *Pharmazeutische Industrie*, *64*(12), 1297–1302.

Hoffman, K. H., & Gumbhir, A. K. (1993). Evaluation of an industry-based drug information service. *Drug Information Journal*, *27*(2), 549–560.

Hoffman, K., Pallansch, P., & Shafer, S. (2000). Establishing a medical knowledge extranet to enhance medical communications. *Drug Information Journal*, *34*(4), 1063–1068.

Hogan, K., & Scarborough, R. (1996). Patents for medical librarians. *Medical Reference Services Quarterly*, *15*(2), 23–31.

Hoover, R. E. (1981). RINGDOC: The database for pharmaceutical manufacturers and researchers. *Online Review*, *5*(6), 435–468.

Hopkins, F., Galligher, C., & Levine, A. (1999). Medical affairs and drug information practices within the pharmaceutical industry: Results of a benchmarking survey. *Drug Information Journal*, *33*(1), 69–85.

Hoskin, A., Lister, W. C., & Marsh, M. M. (1982). The user-oriented library in an industrial setting. *Special Libraries*, *73*(4), 286–291.

Howe, S. M., & Baker, L. M. (2007). 1on1health. *Journal of Consumer Health on the Internet*, *11*(2), 81–90.

Hull, P. (1994). Videotex: A new tool for libraries. *Special Libraries*, *85*(2), 81–88.

Hull, P. (1996). Pharmaceutical published literature databases: A survey. *Medical Reference Services Quarterly*, *15*(1), 77–88.

Huntingford, A. L., O'Callaghan, R., Taylor, J., Turnbull, A. G., & Wells, F. O. (1990). A survey of industry medical information departments' activities. *Pharmaceutical Journal*, *245*, 238–239.

Huotari, M. L. (1995). Strategic information management: A pilot study in a Finnish pharmaceutical company. *International Journal of Information Management*, *15*(4), 295–302.

Hyams, M. (1980, May–June). Does industry make the most of information? *Inform*, *32*, supplement, 1–8.

Hynes, M. D., Getzi, S. A., McQuaid, L., Seward, C. M., & Field-Perez, R. R. (1999). Creation of a knowledge-based system to accelerate drug development. *Drug Information Journal*, *33*(2), 641–648.

ImageSolve II at ICI Pharmaceuticals: A case study of DIP used in a quality assurance department. (1992). *Information Management and Technology*, *25*(2), 71–72.

Internet influences doctors' clinical diagnosis, treatment, e-health survey indicates. (2002). *Medicine on the Net*, *8*(5), 9.

Irving, L. (2005). The pharmaceutical industry, researchers and publishers: The realities of competing interests within speciality journals. *Learned Publishing*, *18*(3), 228–230.

Jenkinson, V., & Kane, L. (2005). Reuters Health Information: A product review. *Journal of Electronic Resources in Medical Libraries*, *2*(3), 23–31.

Johns, T. M., Andrus, W. G., de Voe, S., Myers, J., Smith, R. G., & Uhlir, O. (1979). An evaluation of the leading patent equivalents services. *Journal of Chemical Information and Computer Sciences*, *19*(4), 241–246.

Johnson, S. T., & Wordell, C. J. (1998). Internet utilization among medical information specialists in the pharmaceutical industry and academia. *Drug Information Journal*, *32*(2), 547–554.

Joy, M. E., Arana, C. J., & Gallo, G. R. (1986). Use of information sources at a university hospital drug information service. *American Journal of Hospital Pharmacy*, *43*(5), 1226–1229.

Judd, A. (2001). Medicines information in the UK National Health Service. In A. S. Robson, D. Bawden, & A. Judd (Eds.), *Pharmaceutical and medicines information management: Principles and practice* (pp. 109–123). Edinburgh, UK: Churchill Livingstone.

Kaback, S. M. (1980). Chemical structure searching in Derwent's World Patents Index. *Journal of Chemical Information and Computer Sciences*, *20*(1), 1–6.

Kasarab, H. V. (2006). The impact of e-resources on document supply in a corporate pharmaceutical library: The experience of Novo Nordisk. *Interlending and Document Supply*, *34*(3), 105–108.

Kelley, L., & Chae, S. (2000). Evaluating sources of drug information on the World Wide Web. *Health Care on the Internet*, *4*(1), 27–42.

Kennedy, T. (1997). Managing the drug discovery/development interface. *Drug Discovery Today*, *2*(10), 436–444.

Keselman, A., Browne, A. C., & Kaufman, D. R. (2008). Consumer health information seeking as hypothesis testing. *Journal of the American Medical Informatics Association*, *15*(4), 484–495.

Khan, S., & Bawden, D. (2000). Quality standards in drug and medical information departments. *Aslib Proceedings*, *52*(4), 138–142.

Kinnell, M. (1997). Benchmarking for information service excellence: The pharmaceutical industry. *Total Quality Management*, *8*(1), 3–13.

Kirkwood, C. F., & Kier, K. L. (2006). Modified systematic approach to answering questions. In P. Malone, K. Kier, & J. Stanovich (Eds.), *Drug information: A guide for pharmacists* (3rd ed., pp. 29–38). New York: McGraw Hill.

Knoben, J. E., Phillips, S. J., Snyder, J. W., & Szczur, M. R. (2004). The National Library of Medicine and drug information. Part 2: An evolving future. *Drug Information Journal*, *38*(2), 171–180.

Knoben, J. E., Phillips, S. J., & Szczur, M. R. (2004). The National Library of Medicine and drug information. Part 1: Present resources. *Drug Information Journal*, *38*(1), 69–81.

Ko, P., & Sklar, G. E. (2009). Identification and evaluation of pharmacists' commonly used drug information sources. *Annals of Pharmacotherapy*, *43*(2), 347–352.

Koenig, M. E. D. (1983). A bibliometric analysis of pharmaceutical research. *Research Policy*, *12*(1), 15–36.

Koenig, M. E. D. (1990). The information and library environment and the productivity of research. *Inspel*, *24*(4), 157–167.

Koenig, M. E. D., & Mezick, E. M. (2004). Impact of mergers and acquisitions on research productivity within the pharmaceutical industry. *Scientometrics*, *59*(1), 157–169.

Kondrak, G., & Dorr, B. (2006). Automatic identification of confusable drug names. *Artificial Intelligence in Medicine*, *36*(1), 29–42.

Koo, J. M., & Miller, D. R. (1992). North Dakota pharmacists' need for drug information: 1990 vs 1980. *Drug Information Journal*, *26*(2), 237–242.

Koonce, T. Y., Giuse, N. B., & Todd, P. (2004). Evidence-based databases versus primary medical literature: An in-house investigation on their optimal use. *Journal of the Medical Library Association*, *92*(4), 407–411.

Kreling, D. H., & Dzvimbo, J. W. (1989). Drug information sources used by physicians and pharmacists: Study of public hospitals in Zimbabwe. *Journal of Social and Administrative Pharmacy*, *6*(4), 197–207.

Kremin, M. (1979). Chemical search reference tools. *Database*, *2*(1), 50–52.

Krol, T. F., Coleman, J. C., & Bryant, P. J. (1996). Scientific competitive intelligence in R&D decision making. *Drug Information Journal*, *30*(1), 242–256.

Kshirsager, T. (Ed.). (2008). *High-throughput lead optimization in drug discovery*. Boca Raton, FL: CRC Press.

Kruse, K. W. (1983). Online searching of the pharmaceutical literature. *American Journal of Hospital Pharmacy*, *40*, 240–253.

Kubler, J., Vonk, R., Beimel, S., Gunselmann, W., Homering, M., Nehrdich, D., et al. (2005). Adverse event analysis and MedDRA: Business as usual or challenge. *Drug Information Journal*, *39*(1), 63–72.

Lamb, R., King, J. L., & Kling, R. (2003). Information environments: Organizational contexts of online information use. *Journal of the American Society for Information Science and Technology*, *54*(2), 97–114.

Lambert, B. L., Chang, K. Y., & Lin, S. J. (2001). Effect of orthographic and phonological similarity on false recognition of drug names. *Social Science and Medicine, 52*(12), 1843–1857.

Lander, S. (1998). Structured document generation: Cornerstone of document management. *Drug Information Journal, 32*(3), 757–760.

Lapidus, M. (2003). Library services for pharmacy and health sciences students: Results of a survey. *Journal of Academic Librarianship, 29*(4), 237–244.

Lapidus, M., & Bond, I. (2008). Evaluation of the four most-used alternative medicine databases to answer common herbal information questions. *Journal of Electronic Resources in Medical Libraries, 5*(4), 338–345.

Law, D. T. (1989). Innovative use of in-house current awareness as a guide for collection development in a pharmaceutical library. *College & Research Library News, 50*(5), 372–374.

Le, K. S. (2003). Good laboratory notebook practices. *Drug Information Journal, 37*(2), 215–219.

Lee, C. S., & Lee, J. Y. (2006). Good laboratory practice (GLP) regulations: Interpretation techniques and review of selected compliance issues. *Drug Information Journal, 40*(1), 33–38.

Leighton, S., & Davies, J. E. (2009). Surveying medical information across Europe: The present and the future. *Drug Information Journal, 43*(6), 637–654.

Leipzig, N., Kozak, M. G., & Schwartz, R. A. (1983). Experiences with end-user searching at a pharmaceutical company. *Proceedings of the National Online Meeting*, 325–332.

Leitmeyer, J., & Gillum, T. (1993). Consistency in adverse event terminology: Merck's modified CLINTERM. *Drug Information Journal, 27*(2), 431–435.

Lewi, P. J., & Braet, W. W. (1970). Computer documentation system for small and medium-sized information collections. *Journal of Chemical Documentation, 10*(2), 95–97.

Liddell, H. (1990). General practitioners' awareness and use of drug information sources. *Pharmaceutical Journal, 244*(6590), 761–763.

Liebowitz, J. (2000). Knowledge management receptivity at a major pharmaceutical company. *Journal of Knowledge Management, 4*(3), 252–257.

Linden, L., Vondeling, H., Packer, C., & Cook, A. (2007). Does the National Institute for Health and Clinical Excellence only appraise new pharmaceuticals? *International Journal of Technology Assessment, 23*(3), 349–353.

Little, A., & Millington, K. (2001). Enabling end-user shopping on our corporate library's intranet. *Computers in Libraries, 21*(8), 46–49.

Ljungberg, S., & Tullgren, A. (1976). Investigation on the use of information in R and D at a research intensive company. Phase II: Possibilities of economic evaluation. *Tidskrift för Dokumentation, 32*(2), 17–23.

Ljungberg, S., & Tullgren, A. (1977). Investigation of the use of information in R and D in a research intensive company. *Proceedings of the 40th Annual Meeting of the American Society for Information Science*, [microfiche].

Lopez-Mertz, E. M. (1997). The adequacy of the National Library of Medicine Classification for organizing pharmacy literature, *Library Resources & Technical Services, 41*(2), 123–135.

López-Muñoz, F., Alamo, C., Rubio, G., García-García, P., Martin-Agueda, B., & Cuenca, E. (2003). Bibliometric analysis of biomedical publications on SSRIs during 1980–2000. *Depression and Anxiety, 18*(2), 95–103.

Lundborg, C. S., Hensjo, L. O., & Gustafsson, L. L. (1998). Drug information sources: Reported preferences by general practitioners. *Drug Information Journal, 32*(3), 777–785.

Lynch, M. F., Barnard, J. M., & Welford, S. M. (1981). Computer storage and retrieval of generic chemical structures found in patents, part 1: Introduction and general strategy. *Journal of Chemical Information and Computer Sciences, 21*(3), 117–146.

Lyon, J., Warr, W. A., & Brown, P. (1996, January). Focus on pharmaceutical information. *Information World Review, 110*, 15–18.

MacKay, D. M. (2005). Developing an internet resource discovery service for the U.K. health and life sciences community. *Journal of Electronic Resources in Medical Libraries, 2*(3), 13–22.

Malone, P., Kier, K., & Stanovich, J. (Eds.). (2006). *Drug information: A guide for pharmacists* (3rd ed.). New York: McGraw Hill.

Mani, N. S. (2006). Canadian Adverse Drug Reaction Monitoring Program (CADRMP): Adverse Reaction (AR) Database. *Journal of Consumer Health on the Internet, 10*(3), 93–101.

Mann, R. B., & Andrews, E. B. (Eds.). (2007). *Pharmacovigilance* (2nd ed.). New York: Wiley.

Marsh, M. (2000). Records in mergers and acquisitions: The records management perspective: Turning a threat into an opportunity. *Records Management Bulletin, 97*, 9–12.

Marshall, L., & Zorn, M. J. (1997). End-user reactions to a graphical MEDLINE interface in a scientific setting. *Medical Reference Services Quarterly, 16*(4), 19–28.

Martindale Online: Taking the work out of searching. (1984, July 7). *Pharmaceutical Journal, 233*, 12–13.

Mason, D. (1999). Complementary to medicine. *Information World Review, 153*, 52–53.

May, D. E. (1995). The impact of technology on everything else. *Drug Information Journal, 29*(2), 665–674.

McAuslane, J. A. N., & Lumley, C. E. (1993). Carcinogenicity studies for pharmaceuticals: Classification and misclassification. *Drug Information Journal, 27*(2), 509–514.

McElroy, A. R. (1982). Library-information service evaluation: A case-history from pharmaceutical R and D. *Aslib Proceedings, 34*(5), 249–265.

McIntosh, P. (1993). Scientific current awareness in an international pharmaceutical R and D environment. *Aslib Proceedings, 45*(3), 83–87.

McMillan, G. S., & Hamilton, R. D. (2000). Using bibliometrics to measure firm knowledge: An analysis of the US pharmaceutical industry. *Technology Analysis and Strategic Management, 12*(4), 465–475.

McTaggart, J. A., & Radcliffe, J. (1977). The construction and organization of computerized toxicology data banks. *Information Scientist, 11*(3), 101–111.

Medicines and Healthcare Products Regulatory Agency. (2008). *Good pharmacovigilance practice guide*. London: Pharmaceutical Press.

Meier, A., Lyons, E. J., Frydman, G., Forlenza, M., & Rimer, B. K. (2007). How cancer survivors provide support on cancer-related mailing lists. *Journal of Medical Internet Research, 9*(2), e12. Retrieved December 29, 2009, from www.jmir.org/2007/2/e12/HTML

Mendelsohn, S. (1999). Pharmaceutical information: Information sharing. *Information World Review, 143*, 21–22.

Mi, M. (2005). Clinical trials database: Linking patients to medical research http://clinical trials.gov. *Journal of Consumer Health on the Internet, 9*(3), 59–67.

Michalak, R. A., Matthews, R. A., Leslie, W. D., Kenkins, A. A., Mehta, M. S., & Asbjorn, D. T. (1996). The Query Response System: A database which captures regulatory questions/responses. *Drug Information Journal, 30*(1), 207–215.

Millington, K., & Walker, A. (2003). Business intelligence and knowledge management. *Information Outlook, 7*(8), 38–40.

Milne, A. (1978). Pilot study to examine comparative usefulness of Iowa Drug Information Service (IDIS) and Medline in meeting demands of a pharmacy-based information service. *Journal of Clinical Pharmacy, 2*(4), 227–237.

Moores, K. G. (2006). Evidence-based practice guidelines. In P. Malone, K. Kier, & J. Stanovich (Eds.), *Drug information: A guide for pharmacists* (3rd ed., pp. 289–338). New York: McGraw Hill.

Mullan, N. A., & Blick, A. R. (1987). Initial experiences of untrained end-users with a Life Sciences CD-ROM database: A salutary experience. *Journal of Information Science, 13*(3), 139–141.

Mullen, A., Blunck, M., Kalbfleish, E., Möller, E., & Rohbeck, H. G. (1997). Assessment, from an industrial user perspective, of some major competitor information files on pharmaceutical development products. *Journal of Information Science, 23*(1), 9–23.

Murray, B. P. (1981). Dentists' preferred sources of new drug information and their attitudes toward the use of drugs by patients. *Social Science and Medicine, 15A*, 781–788.

Narin, F., & Rozek, R. P. (1988). Bibliometric analysis of United States pharmaceutical industry research performance. *Research Policy, 17*(3), 139–154.

Nelson, R. P. (1989). Organization of information departments in the US pharmaceutical industry. *Drug Information Journal, 23*(1), 151–164.

Newton, L., Newton, D., Clark, J., Kenny, T., Mossley, D., Purves, I., et al. (1998). Patient information leaflets: Producing understandable PILs. *Journal of Information Science, 24*(3), 167–181.

Nicholas, D., Huntington, P., Jamali, H., & Williams, P. (2007). *Digital health information for the consumer: Evidence and policy implications*. Aldershot, UK: Ashgate.

Nielsen, H. P. (1996). Corporate intelligence in knowledge based industry: Information as a strategic resource in the company. *FID News Bulletin, 46*(4), 133–138.

Ninno, M. A., & Ninno, S. D. (2006). Quality improvement and the medication use process. In P. Malone, K. Kier, & J. Stanovich (Eds.), *Drug information: A guide for pharmacists* (3rd ed., pp. 557–598). New York: McGraw Hill.

Nolan, M. P., Oppenheim, C., & Withers, K. A. (1980). Patenting, profitability and marketing characteristics of the pharmaceutical industry. *World Patent Information, 2*(4), 169–176.

Norton, P. (1982). Central Patents Index as a source of information for the pharmaceutical chemist. *Drug Information Journal, 16*(4), 207–215.

Oakes, M. P., & Taylor, M. J. (1998). Automated assistance in the formulation of search statements for bibliographic databases. *Information Processing & Management, 34*(6), 645–668.

Ohlstein, E. H., Ruffolo, P. R., & Elliott, J. D. (2000). Drug discovery in the next millennium. *Annual Reviews of Pharmacology and Toxicology, 40*, 177–191.

Okerson, A. (1992). The changing journals environment. *American Journal of Pharmaceutical Education, 56*(4), 407–411.

Olaleye, D., & Tardiff, B. E. (2001). Practical issues in and applications of clinical data mining. *Drug Information Journal, 35*(3), 791–808.

Olson, L. (2001). Electronic record challenges for clinical systems. *Drug Information Journal, 35*(3), 721–730.

Olsson, S., & Pal, S. (2006). Drug bulletins: Independent information for global use. *Lancet, 368*(9539), 903–904.

Oppenheim, C. (1981). The past, present and future of the patents services of Derwent Publications Ltd. *Science and Technology Libraries, 2*(2), 23–31.

Ortelli, E., & Ferrario, A. (1990). Present and future of a private biomedical database. *Drug Information Journal, 24*(4), 775–783.

Ottlik, M. (1992). Library of the National Pharmaceutical Institute, Hungary. *Health Information and Libraries, 3*(2), 116–120.

Pakenham-Walsh, N., Eddleston, M., & Kaur, M. (1999). Developing world needs access to low cost pharmaceutical information. *British Medical Journal, 319*(7219), 1265.

Pappa, D. D., Stergioulas, L. K., & Telonis, P. (2009). The role of knowledge management in the pharmaceutical enterprise. *International Journal of Technology Management, 47*(1–3), 127–144.

Parkar, F., & Toeg, I. (1999). Analysis of drug pipeline databases for non-clinical scientists. *Database, 22*(3), 40–44.

Parker, W. A., & Reid, L. W. (1978). Dentist attitudes towards drug information resources. *Drug Information Journal, 12*(2), 81–84.

Patel, V. L., & Kaufman, D. R. (2000). Clinical reasoning and biomedical knowledge: Implications for teaching. In J. Higgs & M. Jones, *Clinical reasoning in the health professions* (2nd ed., pp. 33–44). Oxford, UK: Butterworth Heinemann.

Pay, S. (1991). Information provision in the pharmaceutical industry. *Aslib Information, 19*(3), 81–82.

Payne, S. A. (2002). Balancing information needs: Dilemmas in producing patient information leaflets. *Health Informatics Journal, 8*(4), 174–179.

Pease, J. (1995). Setting up a GCP archive. *Records Management Bulletin, 66*, 9–13.

Perdue, B., & Piotrowski, C. (2004). Bibliographic drug information: A guide for the public consumer. *Journal of Educational Media and Library Services, 42*(2), 157–166.

Perkins, E. (2001). Pharmaceutical decisions and the Net: More healthcare resources on the internet. *Searcher, 9*(2), 59–66.

Perkins, E. (2007). Clinical trial resources: Three of the best. *Searcher, 15*(5), 8–11.

Pickering, W. R. (Ed.). (1990). *Information sources in pharmaceuticals*. London: Bowker-Saur.

Pierredon, M. A. (1995). Confidentiality of databases: The view of one pharmaceutical company. *Drug Information Journal, 29*(1), 351–353.

Pitterle, M. E., Bond, C. A., Raehl, C. L., & Franke, T. (1994). Hospital and pharmacy characteristics associated with mortality rates in United States hospitals. *Pharmacotherapy, 14*(5), 620–630.

Plosker, G. R. (2006). Thomson Pharma and Infotrieve life science research center: New directions for online aggregators. *Online, 30*(2), 47–51.

Popa, D., & Robertson, W. O. (1994). Identifying unknown tablets and capsules: Use of a new tool. *Veterinary and Human Toxicology, 36*(2), 153–154.

Powell, J. R. (1980). Excerpt Medica (EMBASE) online: A reacquaintance. *Online, 4*(1), 36–41.

Poynder, R. (2000). Derwent keeps current: Managing director Peter McKay discusses the company's successful evolution. *Information Today, 17*(5), 74–75.

Provost, G. P. (1971). State pharmaceutical journals: Legitimate need or ego fulfilment? *American Journal of Hospital Pharmacy, 28*, 153.

Rammell, E. (1997). The trials of clinical records management: Making sense of GCP. *Records Management Bulletin, 81*, 3–5.

Raschke, C. G., Hatton, R. C., Weaver, S. J., & Belgado, B. S. (2003). Evaluation of electronic databases used to identify solid oral dosage forms. *American Journal of Health System Pharmacy, 60*(17), 1735–1740.

Riedinger, J. (2008). Using an applied learning centre as a vehicle for culture change. *VINE: The Journal of Information and Knowledge Management Systems, 38*(1), 95–103.

Riggins, J. L., Ferguson, K. J., Miller, S. I., & Gorham, E. (1999). Globalizing medical information services at Eli Lilly and Company. *Drug Information Journal, 33*(2), 515–524.

Rimer, B. K., Lyons, E. K, Ribisl, K. M., Bowling, J. M., Golin, C. E., Forlenza, M. J., et al. (2005). How new subscribers use cancer-related online mailing lists. *Journal of Medical Internet Research, 7*(3), e32. Retrieved December 29, 2009, from www.jmir.org/2005/3/e32/HTML

Roach, M. (1982). Six months in the life of an industry medical information unit. *Pharmaceutical Journal, 229*, 206–207.

Robinson, L. (2000). A strategic approach to research using internet tools and resources. *Aslib Proceedings, 52*(1), 11–19.

Robinson, L. (2010). *Understanding healthcare information.* London: Facet Publishing.

Robinson, L., McIlwaine, I., Copestake, P., & Anderson, C. (2000). Comparative evaluation of the performance of online databases in answering toxicological queries. *International Journal of Information Management, 20*(1), 79–87.

Robson, A. S., Bandle, E., & Ince, J. (1999). Medinfolink: A practical approach to knowledge management at SmithKline Beecham Pharmaceuticals. *Proceedings of the 23rd International Online Information Meeting*, 187–191.

Robson, A. S., Bawden, D., & Judd, A. (Eds.). (2001). *Pharmaceutical and medicines information management: Principles and practice*, Edinburgh, UK: Churchill Livingstone.

Robson, A., Blake, J., Chandler, R., Dellamy, L., Davies, J., Fleming, K., et al. (1996). Medical information services in the pharmaceutical industry: A survey of pharmacists' views with recommendations. *Pharmaceutical Journal, 256*, 864–866.

Robson, A. S., & Riggens, J. L. (2001). Medical information in the pharmaceutical industry. In A. S. Robson, D. Bawden, & A. Judd (Eds.), *Pharmaceutical and medicines information management: Principles and practice* (pp. 124–143). Edinburgh, UK: Churchill Livingstone.

Robson, A. S., & Robson, D. (2000). Industry based medical information in Europe: Practices and customer expectations. *Drug Information Journal, 34*(4), 1089–1095.

Rodgers, M. L. (1985). Development of a shared database for drug information in the United Kingdom. *American Journal of Hospital Pharmacy, 42*, 1702–1706.

Rolinson, J., Al-Shanbari, H., & Meadows, A. J. (1996). Information use by biological researchers. *Journal of Information Science, 22*(1), 47–53.

Rolinson, J., Meadows, A. J., & Smith, H. (1995). Use of information technology by biological researchers. *Journal of Information Science, 21*(2), 133–139.

Roth, J. (2003). Enabling knowledge creation: Learning from an R and D organization. *Journal of Knowledge Management, 7*(1), 32–48.

Royal Pharmaceutical Society. (1996). Martindale: The extra compendium. *Pharmaceutical Journal, 256*(6889), 579–585.

Royland, J. I. (1982). Providing drug information to health professionals and consumers: Role and responsibility of the pharmaceutical manufacturer. *Drexel Library Quarterly, 18*(2), 11–21.

Rudin, J., Hausele, N., & Stollak, J. (1985). Comparison of In-Search, Scimate and an intelligent terminal emulator in biomedical literature searching, *Proceedings of the National Online Meeting, New York*, 403–408.

Rumschlag, D., & Howes, B. (1993). IDIS: Iowa Drug Information Service. *CD-ROM World, 8*(5), 80–83.

Rutter, J., Brown, D., & Rutter, P. (2004). Primary care physicians' uptake of a secondary care-based medicines information service in the United Kingdom. *Drug Information Journal, 38*(4), 407–416.

Saimbert, M. K. (2006). xPharm a preclinical information portal for discovery researchers in institutions of higher learning. *Journal of Electronic Resources in Medical Libraries, 3*(1), 63–80.

Sakurai, Y., Kugai, N., Kawana, T., Fukita, T., & Fukomoto, S. (1995). A comprehensive adverse events management system for the pharmaceutical industry. *Drug Information Journal, 29*(2), 645–659.

Saltzman, A. (1995). Cost and value of information in American pharmaceutical companies. *Drug Information Journal, 29*(2), 531–544.

Samuel, J. (1997). Electronic laboratory notebooks consortium. *Records Management Bulletin, 81*, 11, 18.

Samuel, J. (1998). The intellectual infrastructure underpinning records management within Pfizer Central Research. *Records Management Journal, 8*(1), 11–23.

Sandori, Z. (1992). The technical library of chemical works of Gedeon Richter Ltd.: Facilities and services. *Health Information and Libraries, 3*(4), 258–265.

Savino, L. B., & Shick, J. A. (1998). Mailing lists for pharmacists and other interested health care professionals. *Health Care on the Internet, 2*(4), 45–51.

Sayers, M., Joice, J., & Bawden, D. (1990). Retrieval of biomedical reviews: A comparative evaluation of online databases for reviews of drug therapy. *Journal of Information Science, 16*(5), 321–325.

Schrimsher, R. H., Freeman, M. K., & Kendrach, M. (2006). A survey of drug information resources in Alabama pharmacy facilities. *Drug Information Journal, 40*(1), 51–60.

Schulte, L. (1986). A new pharmaceutical company library: The Upjohn Company corporate technical library. *Science and Technology Libraries, 7*(1), 18–30.

Schwartzer, B. (1995). Organising global IS management to meet competitive challenges: Experiences from the pharmaceutical industry. *Journal of Global Information Management, 3*(1), 5–16.

Sewell, W. (1976). *Guide to drug information.* Hamilton, IL: Drug Intelligence Publications.

Shepherd, I. (2001). The evolving technologies for delivering medicines information. *Hospital Pharmacist, 8*(6), 155–157.

Sherwell, J. R. (1997a). Building the virtual library: The case of SmithKline Beecham. *Managing Information, 4*(6), 35–46.

Sherwell, J. R. (1997b). Reaching for the virtual library. *Library Association Record, 99*(7), 376–377.

Sherwell, J. R. (1989). An electronic user request system for interlibrary loans. *Interlending and Document Supply, 17*(3), 89–93.

Shields, K. M., & Lust, E. (2006). Drug information resources. In P. Malone, K. Kier, & J. Stanovich (Eds.), *Drug information: A guide for pharmacists* (3rd ed., pp. 61–102). New York: McGraw Hill.

Shulman, J. (1988). Surviving the doctor's prescription: Do patients need more information? *Health Libraries Review, 5*(2), 66–75.

Sillince, J. A. A., & Sillince, M. (1993). Market pressure and government intervention in the administration and development of molecular databases. *Journal of the American Society for Information Science, 44*(1), 28–39.

Simkins, M. A. (1977). A comparison of databases for retrieving references to the literature on drugs. *Information Processing & Management, 13*(3), 141–153.

Simmonds, H. (2001). Codes of practice for the pharmaceutical industry. In A. S. Robson, D. Bawden, & A. Judd (Eds.), *Pharmaceutical and medicines information management: Principles and practice* (pp. 234–240). Edinburgh, UK: Churchill Livingstone.

Simon, A., Soares, T., Aranda da Silva, J. (1987). Comparative study of information needs of hospital and community pharmacists. *Journal de Pharmacie Clinique, 6*(4), 593–598.

Skaug, K. (1995). The changing focus in the pharmaceutical industry. *Drug Information Journal, 29*(2), 761–766.

Smith, C. (1997). Pharmaceutical regulatory guidelines: 1997 the year of change. *Records Management Bulletin, 81*, 7–10.

Smith, J. M. (1987). Drug information in Europe: State of the art and future prospects. *Journal de Pharmacie Clinique, 6*(1), 171–180.

Smith, N. V., & Ramseyer, K. E. (2002). Taking the package insert into the electronic age. *Drug Information Journal, 36*(2), 429–434.

Smith, R. (2003). Medical journals and pharmaceutical companies: Uneasy bedfellows. *British Medical Journal, 326*(7400), 1202–1205.

Smith, R. (2007). Should medical journals carry drug advertising? Yes. *British Medical Journal, 335*(7610), 74.

Smith, S. (1996). Drug information bulletins: An analysis of citations. *Journal of Information Science, 22*(5), 375–380.

Snow, B. (1982a). Foreign drug information retrieval. *Medical Reference Services Quarterly, 1*(3), 37–52.

Snow B. (1982b). Online retrieval of pharmaceutical information. *Drexel Library Quarterly, 18*(2), 64–83.

Snow, B. (1984). Online database coverage of pharmaceutical journals. *Database*, 7(1), 12–26.

Snow, B. (1988). Martindale Online: Drug info in a detective's toolkit. *Database*, 11(3), 90–98.

Snow, B. (1989). Patents in non-patent databases: Bioscience speciality files. *Database*, 12(5), 41–48.

Snow, B. (1991). EMBASE update for the pharmaceutical searcher. *Database*, 14(6), 93–96.

Snow, B. (1992). Trade names in medicine: Searching for brand name comparisons and new product news. *Database*, 15(3), 99–105.

Snow, B. (1993). Monitoring new drug development in IMSWorld R and D Focus and Pharmaprojects. *Database*, 16(4), 103–107.

Snow, B. (2008). *Drug Information: A guide to current resources* (3rd ed., Medical Library Association Guides). New York: Neal-Schumann.

Sodha, R. J., & Amelsvoort, T. V. (1994). Multi-database searches in biomedicine: Citation duplication and novelty assessment using carbamazepine as an example. *Journal of Information Science*, 20(2), 139–141.

Soller, R. W. (2004). Adverse experience reporting for OTC medicines: Scientific/regulatory framework and review of a hypothetical case study. *Drug Information Journal*, 38(2), 157–169.

Spilker, B. (1994). *Multinational pharmaceutical companies: Principles and practices*. New York: Raven Press.

Spremić, M., & Vukšić, V. B. (2005). ERP system implementation and business process change: Case study of a pharmaceutical company. *Journal of Computing and Information Technology*, 13(1), 11–24.

Springer, S. J., Yokel, R. A., Lorenzi, N. M., Sigell, L. T., & Nelson, E. D. (1978). Drug information to patient care areas via television: Preliminary evaluation of two years' experience. *Special Libraries*, 69(4), 155–163.

Srodin, S., & Strupczewski, J. (2002). Creating a global information portal: Our 9-month odyssey. *Computers in Libraries*, 22(2), 14–19.

Stadler, P., Mernke, E., & Thomas, M. (1999). Introduction of electronic book ordering with EDIFACT in a special library: A case study. *Electronic Library*, 17(1), 23–26.

Stamatoplos, A. (2005). Digital archiving in the pharmaceutical industry. *Records Management Journal*, 39(4), 54–59.

Stephens, D. O. (2000). Digital preservation: A global information management solution. *Information Management Journal*, 34(3), 68–71.

Stepping on to the information superhighway: The internet and the World Wide Web. (1996, August 24). *Pharmaceutical Journal*, 257, 251.

Steven, S. E. (2002). Focused portfolio measures to support decision making throughout the pipeline. *Drug Information Journal*, 36(3), 623–630.

Stevenson, J. (1997). The Business Archives Council survey of the historical records of the pharmaceutical industry. *Records Management Bulletin*, 81, 15, 23.

Stinson, E. R., & Mueller, D. A. (1980). Survey of health professionals' information habits and needs. *Journal of the American Medical Association*, 432(1), 140–143.

Strickland-Hodge, B., Jepson, M. H., & Reid, B. J. (1989). *Keyguide to information sources in pharmacy*. London: Mansell.

Stubbington, C., Bowey, J., Hands, D., & Brown, D. (1998, March). Drug information replies to queries involving adverse events: Impact on clinical practice. *Hospital Pharmacist, 5,* 81–84.

Styhre, A., Ollila, S., Roth, J., Williamson, D., & Berg, L. (2008). Heedful interrelating, knowledge sharing and new drug development. *Journal of Knowledge Management, 12*(3), 127–140.

Sze, M. C. (1985). The departmental information professional: A role of increasing importance. *Online Information Review, 9*(6), 467–470.

Talbot, J., & Waller, P. (Eds.). (2003). *Stephens' detection of new adverse drug reactions* (5th ed.). London: Wiley.

Tenopir, C., & King, D. W. (2002). Reading behaviour and electronic journals. *Learned Publishing, 15*(4), 259–265.

Tenopir, C., King, D. W., Boyce, P., Grayson, M., Khang, Y., & Ebuen, M. (2003). Patterns of journal use by scientists through three evolutionary phases. *D-Lib Magazine, 8*(5). Retrieved December 29, 2009, from www.dlib.org/dlib/may03/king/05king.html

Thorp, R. A., Schur, H., Bawden, D., & Joice, J. R. (1988). The foreign language barrier: A study among pharmaceutical research workers. *Journal of Information Science, 14*(1), 17–24.

Thorpe, P. (1979). Interlibrary loans analysis for journals acquisition. *Aslib Proceedings, 31*(7), 352–359.

Tovey, P. (Ed.). (2000). *Contemporary primary care: The challenge of change.* Buckingham, UK: Open University Press.

Trewin, V. F., & Veitch, G. B. (2003). Patient sources of drug information and attitudes to their provision: A corticosteroid model. *Pharmacy World and Science, 25*(5), 191–196.

Trzan-Herman, N., & Kiauta, D. (1996). The organizational map: An important aspect of achieving total quality management in a pharmaceutical and medical library: A Slovenian case. *Libri, 46*(2), 113–119.

Tucker, M. D. (2002). Data normalization techniques and autocoding algorithms for the medical dictionary for regulatory affairs (MedDRA). *Drug Information Journal, 36*(4), 927–933.

Twomey, C. (2001). An analysis of patient information leaflets supplied with medicines sold by pharmacists in the United Kingdom. *Library and Information Research News, 25*(80), 3–12.

Vainio, K., Airaksinen, M., Vaisanen, T., & Enlund, H. (2004). Assessing the importance of community pharmacists as providers of drug information. *Journal of Applied Therapeutic Research, 5*(1), 24–29.

Van Camp, A. (1984). IPA search aid kit. *Database, 7*(1), 79–80.

van Putte, N. W. (1990). The usefulness of RINGDOC in a medium-size pharmaceutical company. *Health Information and Libraries, 1*(3), 3–6.

van Putte, N. W., & Peperkamp, H. A. (1983). Online or inhouse? The advantages of an internal retrieval system for the literature on the products of a pharmaceutical company. *Proceedings of the Seventh International Online Information Meeting,* 207–211.

Vigilante, W. J., & Wogalter, M. S. (2005). Assessing risk and benefit communication in direct-to-consumer medication website advertising. *Drug Information Journal, 39*(1), 1–13.

Wang, M. (2006). The impact of information culture on managing knowledge: A double case study of pharmaceutical manufacturers in Taiwan. *Library Review, 55*(3), 209–221.

Ward, L. G., Kendrach, M. G., & Price, S. O. (2004). Accuracy of abstracts for original research articles in pharmacy journals. *Annals of Pharmacotherapy, 38*(7–8), 1173–1177.

Ward, S., & Warr, W. (1998). A virtual thinking space. *Information World Review, 132,* 19–20.

Warr, W. A. (1991). Some observations on piecemeal electronic publishing solutions in the pharmaceutical industry. *Journal of Chemical Information and Computer Sciences, 31*(2), 181–186.

Warr, W. A. (2008). Social software: Fun and games or business tools? *Journal of Information Science, 34*(4), 591–604.

Warr, W. A., & Haygarth-Jackson, A. R. (1988). End-user searching of CAS ONLINE: Results of a cooperative experiment between Imperial Chemical Industries and Chemical Abstracts Service. *Journal of Chemical Information and Computer Sciences, 28*(2), 68–72.

Wasserman, R. S. (1990). Use of an electronic publishing system for production of pharmaceutical product literature. *Drug Information Journal, 24*(4), 763–768.

Watt, J. W. (1977). Community pharmacist: Recipient and source of drug information. *Drug Information Journal, 11*(3), 209–212.

Weaver, R. H., & Porter, K. T. (1991). The role of information technology in ICI Pharmaceuticals group medical information department. *Drug Information Journal, 25*(2), 269–273.

Weaver, S. J., Hatton, R. C., & Doering, P. L. (2004). Evaluation of online drug references for identifying over-the-counter solid oral dose forms. *Journal of the American Pharmacists Association, 44*(6), 694–699.

Wessel, C. B., Tannery, N. H., & Epstein, B. A. (2006). Information-seeking behavior and use of information resources by clinical research coordinators. *Journal of the Medical Library Association, 94*(1), 48–54.

West, L. (2001). Pharmacovigilance. In A. S. Robson, D. Bawden, & A. Judd (Eds.), *Pharmaceutical and medicines information management: Principles and practice* (pp. 168–185). Edinburgh, UK: Churchill Livingstone.

Whitehead, R. E., Lomma, L. K., Tran, Q. V. N. D., Miao, Y. K., & Pikalov, A. (2009). A pharmaceutical alliance in medical information: Lessons learned in the life cycle. *Drug Information Journal, 43*(2), 123–129.

Whittall, J. (1989). CD-ROM in a specialist environment. *Proceedings of the Third Annual Conference on Small Computers in Libraries,* 119–121.

Willett, P. (2008). From chemical documentation to chemoinformatics: 50 years of chemical information science. *Journal of Information Science, 34*(4), 477–500.

Williams, G. (2007). Should medical journals carry drug advertising? No. *British Medical Journal, 335*(6710), 75.

Williams, T., Bliven, C. E., & Ladner, S. (1987). Mutual support for mutual benefit: The science and technology library and the academic health science library. *Science and Technology Libraries, 7*(3), 81–92.

Wills, B. A. (1986, May). Die Entwicklung des "Martindale" und der "British National Formulary" und ihre Rolle in der Bereitstellung von Informationen über Arzneimittel im Vereinigten Königreich [Evolution of Martindale and the British National Formulary and their role in providing information on medicines in the United Kingdom]. *Pharmazie, 41*, 354–456.

Wilson, D. K. (2007). Creating and managing a patent information group in a global environment. *World Patent Information, 29*(2), 136–139.

Wilson, T. D. (1984). The cognitive approach to information seeking behaviour and information use. *Social Science Information Studies, 4*(2–3), 197–204.

Windsor, D. A. (1975). Developing drug literatures. 1. Bibliometrics of baclofen and dantrolene sodium. *Journal of Chemical Information and Computer Sciences, 15*(4), 237–241.

Windsor, D. A. (1976). Could bibliometric data be used to predict clinical success of drugs? *Journal of Documentation, 32*(3), 174–181.

Windsor, D. A. (1979). Using bibliometric analyses of patent literature for predicting the clinical fates of developing drugs. *Journal of Chemical Information and Computer Sciences, 19*(4), 218–221.

Windsor, D. A. (1999). Industrial roots of information science. *Journal of the American Society for Information Science, 50*(12), 1064–1065.

Wisniewski, L. C. (1998). Sources for pharmaceutical industry research. *Business Information Alert, 10*(9), 1–3, 10–11.

Wolfgang, A. P., Perri, M., & Katzan, J. A. (1989). Hospital nurses' use of, and satisfaction with, sources of drug-related information. *American Journal of Hospital Pharmacy, 46*(10), 2052–2053.

Woodward, C. A. (1995). CPS [Compendium of Pharmaceuticals and Specialities] on CD-ROM: A review. *Bibliotheca Medica Canadiana, 17*(2), 70–75.

Wormleighton, C. V., & Leighton, S. (2009). Auditing medical information services across Western Europe: A cost-effectiveness approach, *Drug Information Journal, 43*(6), 655–662.

Yamamoto, M., Iizuka, T., Negai, H., Shimizu, M., Funabashi, S., & Okada, S. (1998). Utilization of drug information systems by medical representatives in the Japanese pharmaceutical industry. *Drug Information Journal, 32*(2), 761–767.

Yamamoto, M., Onaka, Y., Hirai, T., Kuroko, M., Negi, H., Yamada, A., et al. (1995). Drug information in the Japanese pharmaceutical industry: Analysis of an eight-year investigation. *Drug Information Journal, 29*(4), 1201–1209.

Yoo, H., Ramanathan, C., & Barcelon-Yang, C. (2005). Intellectual property management of biosequence information from a patent searching perspective. *World Patent Information, 27*(3), 203–211.

Young, H. N., Paterniti, D. A., Bell, R. A., & Kravitz, R. L. (2005). Do prescription drug advertisements educate the public? The consumer answers. *Drug Information Journal, 39*(1), 25–35.

Zimmer, G. (2003). Dokumenten-Management-Systeme als Basis für die Einreichung von Arzneimittel-Zulassungsdossiers [Document management systems as basis for the electronic submission of dossiers for the marketing authorisation process]. *Pharmazeutische Industrie, 65*(5A), 537–545.

Zolezzi, M. (1991). Management of the automation of the biomedical library services in a pharmaceutical group. *Health Information and Libraries, 2*(2), 96–102.

Zom, M. J., & Marshall, L. (1995). Graphical user interfaces and library systems: End user reactions. *Special Libraries, 86*(1), 28–35.

Information Retrieval

CHAPTER 3

Text Mining

Catherine Blake
University of Illinois, Urbana-Champaign, IL

Introduction

Changes in electronic publishing practices, the widespread adoption of the internet, and advances in the cyberinfrastructure provide students, scientists, and policy makers with access to more information than at any other time in history. Much of this information is text. For example, in the sciences, PubMed (the primary source of biomedical literature) comprises 18.8 million citations, CiteSeer (which has mainly computer science articles) has 1.4 million articles, the Association for Computing Machinery (ACM) digital library has 1.4 million pages, and in a single year the top chemistry journals published more than 110,000 articles. In addition to literature in the sciences, scholars in the humanities can now access more than 30,000 ebooks through Project Gutenburg (www. gutenberg.org) and the controversial Google Books project (books.google. com) will continue to add to the quantity of text available. Lastly, increasing adoption of collaborative technologies including blogs, wikis, email, chat, and Twitter bombard us with information throughout our daily lives. Although these information resources capture ideas from some of the greatest scientific minds in the world and offer new ways to engage with local and global communities, the quantity of information greatly exceeds our human cognitive processing capacity—a phenomenon called information overload.

Contrary to popular belief, information overload is not unique to the digital age. In 1613 Barnaby Rich stated that "One of the diseases of this age is the multiplicity of books; they doth so overcharge the world that it is not able to digest the abundance of idle matter that is every day hatched and brought forth into the world" (quoted in Price, 1986, p. 63).

One way to overcome information overload is to identify all (measured by recall) and only (measured by precision) the information resources that are relevant to a user's stated information need. Several premises underscore this information retrieval (IR) paradigm. First, there is an assumption that users can clearly articulate their information needs and that their expressions will match terms used in the given text collection. For example, a user could issue a search for "breast cancer" but the documents might use the phrase "mammary carcinoma."

The second premise is that a given collection contains a small number of books or articles that satisfy the information need completely. Consider a user who wants to know which of the many breast cancer treatments are best for her case. Although an IR system is considered perfect if it retrieves all and only articles that report breast cancer treatments, a user would probably first want to see recent, comprehensive articles that specifically refer to her case. An IR system has no way to prioritize based on date or credibility. Thus, the user faces the daunting task of finding collections of similar treatments, or side effects, without system support.

Text mining systems remove some of the underlying premises in the information retrieval paradigm and introduce others. Designers no longer assume that a user can clearly define his or her information need or that there will be only a small set of relevant information sources. Instead, a text mining system is data driven in that the starting point is the collection and not the user's specific searching need. Rather than provide the user with a ranked list of articles, a text mining system will allow a user to explore and interact with patterns of information from within a collection of potentially relevant documents. The goal of a text mining system is to help a user identify meaningful patterns and learn about the information space related to the information need.

Researchers from a variety of communities have developed new methods to mine text; three communities that have made the largest contributions are Knowledge Discovery from Databases (KDD), Information Science (IS), and Computational Linguistics (CL).

The KDD community, which borrows methods from machine learning and artificial intelligence, has made a significant contribution to text mining research. One approach common to many KDD techniques is that researchers treat text as simply another kind of structured data. Thus, systems first convert text into a collection of words in the preprocessing and transformation steps of the KDD process and then use standard data mining techniques such as clustering, classification, and association rules in the data-mining step. Researchers frequently publish in the ACM's Special Interest Group on Knowledge Discovery in Databases (SIGKDD).

Although it is tempting to align "text mining" with "data mining," data mining is just one of the steps within the knowledge discovery process. In contrast, text mining is more akin to the entire knowledge discovery process that comprises selection, preprocessing, transformation, data mining, interpretation, and evaluation steps (Fayyad, Piatetsky-Shapiro, & Smyth, 1996). Unlike the numeric, ordinal, and categorical data types that initially motivated the KDD community, text has inherent complexities—such as synonymy and polysemy—and cultural nuances, which means that the preprocessing and transformation steps have even more impact on the quality of the patterns produced using text than using non-text information resources.

Researchers in IS have also developed text mining methods that identify patterns from text. Rather than the inductive approach employed by many of the data mining methods in the KDD community, the IS community has explored deductive approaches such as literature-based discovery (LBD). LBD deduces a transitive association between A and C when given a known association between A and B and a second known association between B and C. Also under the IS umbrella are methods that synthesize evidence from literature and weighting methods developed within the information retrieval community.

The third key community from which text mining methods are drawn is computational linguistics (also called natural language processing [NLP]). Although the initial motivation for CL methods was to increase our understanding of language structure and form, the techniques developed by this community have recently reached a level of maturity where their value to non-linguistic areas of enquiry is starting to be realized. In contrast to the KDD and IS communities, models developed by the CL community typically consider both sentence- and document-level characteristics rather than simply the bag of words approach (see section on feature representations).

Although text mining has received attention from the popular press (Guernsey, 2003), no previous volume of the *Annual Review of Information Science and Technology* (*ARIST*) has focused on text mining. Chen and Chau's (2004, p. 291) review of web mining characterized the purpose of text mining as "finding new patterns or knowledge previously unknown," which is consistent with the definition used in this chapter. In contrast to the web mining chapter that explores a range of data types, this chapter considers text exclusively and includes techniques developed in the information science and computational linguistics communities. Similarly, this chapter relates closely to Kostoff and his colleagues' review of literature-based discovery (Kostoff et al., 2007) and their subsequent *ARIST* chapter titled "Literature-related Discovery" (Kostoff, Block, Solka, Briggs, Rushenberg, Stump, et al., 2009), but it is wider in scope than LBD alone.

Definitions and Scope

Feldman (1999, p. 182) defined text mining as "Determin[ing] the information of interest to any individual while minimizing the amount of search through irrelevant information." Feldman's definition aligns more closely to information retrieval (where the goal is to differentiate between relevant and irrelevant documents) than text mining (where the goal is to uncover patterns that are novel, interesting, and understandable). Other researchers suggest that text mining has two steps: the first provides structure to the initial corpora and the second enables knowledge discovery (Liddy, 2000; Nahm & Mooney, 2000).

Hearst (1999, p. 5) initially characterized "real" text data mining as finding novel nuggets from textual data. In subsequent work, she states that "text mining is the discovery by computer of new, previously unknown information, by automatically extracting information from different written resources" and that "a key element is the linking together of the extracted information together [sic] to form new facts or new hypotheses to be explored further by more conventional means of experimentation" (Hearst, 2003, online).

I characterize text mining as the process of identifying novel, interesting, and understandable patterns from a collection of texts. The subclass of information extraction (such as systems that identify people, places, and organizations from a given set of documents) is not text mining per se because the researcher knows in advance which facts the system should extract and thus the activity does not satisfy the novelty criterion. With that said, information extraction does help a user overcome information overload and is thus included in the feature representation section of this chapter. The true potential of text mining systems will be fully realized only when they habitually identify novel, plausible, useful patterns from collections of text that no single author has previously noted.

Review Organization

My goal in this review is to provide a unifying framework with which to compare and contrast automated techniques that identify patterns from textual resources. In contrast to structured data—such as ordinal, numeric, and categorical data types—there are varieties of ways to represent text that are described in the next section. If you were to create a matrix, where the cell (i,j) reflected the number of times that word i appeared in document j, then most of the cells would contain zero. Strategically reducing the dimensionality of the original sparse matrix can reduce noise and thus help subsequent algorithms avoid over-fitting the model to nuances in the original text collection. Dimensionality reduction techniques commonly used with text collections are described in the following section. With the representation and reductions in place, text mining systems then employ several analysis methods to address key application areas, which are described in the fourth major section of the chapter. Theoretically, you could combine any of the representations with any of the analysis methods; but in practice the representation limits the search space and constrains the type of patterns that the system can detect, thus research communities tend to cluster around both the representation and the analysis method. For example, researchers interested in recognizing textual entailment typically represent the syntax of a sentence, and researchers interested in extracting information from text employ surface level features, such as the number of uppercase characters in a word.

One area not well represented in the academic literature is the analysis of methods required to prepare documents for text mining, such as recognizing characters from scanned documents, table formats from HTML, or full sentences from PDF documents (although tools such as converting from Unicode to ASCII are available [Lu, Browne, & Divita,

2008]). Depending on the original format, document preparation can consume a significant proportion of the text mining effort; authors rarely describe the preprocessing effort, however, because many of the methods do not generalize well. For example, the formatting required to preprocess a collection of full-text breast cancer articles may not work for articles drawn from other journals or from other disciplines or text genres.

Candidate Text Representations

As with any well-posed machine learning problem (Mitchell, 1997), decisions about how to represent documents can have a significant impact on the quality of subsequently identified patterns. It comes as little surprise, therefore, that communities cluster around both the method used to represent text and the target text-mining pattern. This section describes common methods used to represent text.

Surface-Level Features

Surface-level features capture information about a word. For example, proper nouns typically start with an uppercase letter, regardless of where the word appears in a sentence; thus, identifying words that begin with an uppercase letter will help to discriminate people, places, and organizations from other words in a document. Gene names also contain surface-level features such as roman numerals, numbers, and a mix of upper and lower case letters. The length of a word, when combined with roman numerals and numbers, can be an effective way to identify gene names in a document.

In addition to identifying words, systems can use surface-level features to identify numeric values, such as four-digit numbers starting with 19 or 20 that usually indicate a year. Although this heuristic would not work well in certain text genres such as historical literature, a combination of surface-level features such as the name of a month followed by a number have good discriminatory power when identifying dates.

Vector-Based Representation

The most common text representation used in text mining is the bag of words (BOW) approach, where the system represents each document as a weighted vector of terms. The weight associated with each term is the number of times that a term appears in the document. The vector-based representation requires no domain knowledge and, because the representation ignores document and sentence structure, inconsistencies in formatting, page breaks, and tables have little impact on the accuracy of the document vector. The BOW representation also lends itself well to analysis methods that require a measure of similarity between documents (such as clustering) because systems measure the similarity among two documents as the cosine similarity between their corresponding vectors.

The biggest decision to make with respect to the vector-based representation is how to define a term. Systems that operate on Latin-based languages such as English typically define a term as the continuous set of alphanumeric characters that occurs between white spaces and punctuation. Floating-point numbers require an exception when a period follows a numeric character(s) and hyphens can be problematic. For example, a system that used a hyphen as a term delimiter would represent "eighty-four" as "eighty" and "four," which does not capture the original meaning. Moreover, a hyphen at the end of a line can indicate a word break (i.e., that the word starts on the first line and continues on the second) and thus the system should concatenate the last characters on the first line with the first characters on the second line. Choosing to partition terms on hyphens provides a potentially smaller vocabulary than if the hyphens are not removed, which can increase the speed of subsequent analysis steps in the text mining process. The domain can inform other punctuation choices, such as in chemistry articles where using parentheses to define a word boundary could result in an inconsistent representation of chemical names.

Concept Representation

A good text representation should resolve synonymy (when different words have the same meaning) and polysemy (when the same word has different meanings). One strategy to achieve this goal is to map multiple terms and phrases onto a higher order representation. Ironically, there has been much debate over how to refer to the higher order representations, with some researchers leaning toward *concept* (McCray, Srinivasan, & Browne, 1994) and others toward *ontology* (Smith, 2004).

The sciences have a long history of developing standard, widely adopted nomenclatures, such as the Gene Ontology (GO) project (www.geneontology.org). The National Library of Medicine has developed the Unified Medical Language System (UMLS), which provides several text mining resources (McCray, 2003). The current version of the UMLS (2009AA) can be downloaded or accessed online (umlsks.nlm.nih.gov). It includes a meta-thesaurus comprising more than 100 terminologies, classifications, and thesauri; a semantic network comprising 135 semantic types and 54 relationships; and a specialist lexicon comprising terms drawn from both general English and medical dictionaries (McCray et al., 1994). The meta-thesaurus maps terms from multiple ontologies onto a single concept unique identifier (CUI), thus accounting for synonymy. Similarly, a concept can be traced back to the source vocabulary and terms are mapped to one or more higher level concepts called semantic types (Aronson, 2001), which can be used to resolve the polysemy challenge.

A range of other general domain concept representations exist, including WordNet (Miller, 1995) which is so well used that the creators are currently planning the fifth global annual WordNet conference (wordnet.princeton.edu). The *CIA World Factbook* was developed as part of the TIPSTER challenge (www.cia.gov/cia/publications/factbook/index. html), and Cyc (Matuszek, Cabral, Witbrock, & DeOliveira, 2006) comprises general knowledge in a representation that is conducive to inference algorithms. As with the UMLS, these knowledge bases were not specifically developed for natural language processing applications or text mining, but can provide a higher level representation of text that has been shown to produce more plausible rules (Blake & Pratt, 2001).

Information Extraction

The desired product from an information extraction (IE) system is the accurate identification of a predefined set of entities from text such as names, organizations, places, proteins, genes, dates, times, currency amounts, and percentages. The question of information extraction is interesting from a text-mining perspective because the desired output for some systems is the entities, but for other systems information extraction provides the text representation and the subsequent processing step produces the desired patterns. This section describes key challenges that have prompted much of the information extraction research and the underlying methods used to identify entities from text automatically (see Appelt & Israel [1999] and Turmo, Ageno, & Català [2006] for more detailed descriptions).

Information Extraction Challenges

Organized challenges have driven many advances in methods to extract information automatically. The organizers of each challenge provide participants with annotated collections for system development (the training set) so that participants can focus on system design and implementation. After the system development period, the organizers provide a new collection of texts (the test set) that do not have annotations. Participants then run their systems over the new texts and submit the system-generated solutions to the organizers who calculate system accuracy. This strategy provides a level of independence between the system designers and the evaluators. Lastly, participants come together in a workshop where they can discuss different approaches and the final evaluations.

The goal of the Message Understanding Conferences (MUC) was to identify information from military messages automatically. The first MUC, MUC-1, took place in 1987, but unlike the subsequent challenges, each of the participants designed their own format for recording the required facts. Not until 1989, in MUC-2, did the challenge start to resemble the subsequent challenges MUC-3–6 (1991–1994). Each year organizers increased the number of entities required and improved the quality of the evaluation metrics (see Grishman & Sundheim, 1996). The last MUC challenge, MUC-7 (1995) included the following tasks: multi-lingual named entity, co-reference resolution, element, relationship, and scenario extraction.

Several other U.S. initiatives have guided work in information extraction, including the TIPSTER Program that started in 1989 following MUC-2 and ended in 1998 (Crystal, 1993). The related Text REtrieval Conferences (TREC) have a series of different tracks that address research questions in information retrieval. The Defense Advanced Research Projects Agency (DARPA)'s Translingual Information Detection Extraction and Summarization (TIDES) project started in 1999 and the Automatic Content Extraction (ACE) ran from 1999 to 2008. Both moved information extraction techniques forward, as did the Text Analysis Conference (TAC), which was initiated in 2008 and included tasks in question answering and document understanding. The 2009 TAC conference included a knowledge base population track, a recognizing textual entailment track, and the document understanding (summarization) track.

Information Extraction Strategies

Information extraction systems generally take either a machine learning or a knowledge-based approach. An example of a machine learning approach is the RIPPER system, which characterizes the text as pre-fillers, slot-fillers, and post-fillers (Califf & Mooney, 1999). An example rule from RIPPER that extracts the state from a job advertisement has (1) pre-filler consisting of the words *located* and *in*; (2) filler consisting of the word *Atlanta*; and (3) post-filler consisting of a *comma*, the word *Georgia*, and a *period*. Matching this complete pattern would extract *Atlanta* as the location from the job announcement. The authors evaluated the system on three types of textual resources: job announcements, seminar announcements, and the evaluation set from the Message Understanding Conference.

One difficulty with learning approaches is that they require training examples. To alleviate this, challenge researchers have developed interactive systems that semi-automate the training process where a user first annotates a subset of the resources; the system then proposes an extraction pattern and the information that will be extracted using the current pattern; and lastly the user validates the pattern (Caruana & Hodor, 2000; Day, Aberdeen, Hirschman, Kozierok, Robinson, & Vilain, 1997). The system developed by Caruana and colleagues enables a user to specify range checks between 0 and 1; Day and colleagues enable users to constrain the part of speech (such as noun and verb). The rules produced by Caruana and colleagues' system were regular expressions and evaluated by randomly selecting a record within the rule set and comparing it with the protein data bank. The system took an afternoon to extract information from a 5,200-record sample and revealed no errors: an estimated error rate of less than 0.05 percent. Day and colleagues' system (which generates LISP-like rules) took between 1.5 and 2.5 hours to extract information from a 25,000 MUC training sample.

Riloff (1996) also recognized the effort involved in manually labeling textual resources and reduced the effort needed by requiring that the user provide only a relevance judgment rather than annotate individual words. Results showed no significant difference between correct, correct and duplicate, and missing extractions between systems with different levels of annotation. Moreover, the less specific labels produced significantly fewer spurious extractions.

Knowledge-based approaches are also able to extract information from a textual resource, such as protein names in medical abstracts (Fukuda, Tsunoda, Tamura, & Takagi, 1998). After accounting for spelling variations and abbreviations, the system uses rules to determine character strings that are more likely to be protein names. Many of the knowledge-based approaches use existing knowledge resources (see section on concept representation).

Discourse Co-Reference Resolution

The goal of discourse co-reference resolution is to unify all text references to the same entity (also called a *referent*), where an entity is typically a proper noun, although entities can also be verbal relations (see Hirschman [1997] for a definition of co-reference annotations used in the MUC-7 co-reference task). Resolving pronominal anaphora such as *he* and *she* is particularly important in news texts if a text-mining system is to identify the source of a statement accurately. Co-reference resolution also applies to temporal and geographical entities, such as when a physician uses *yesterday* in a clinical note or when an author uses *southwest* in a tax report. Systems may require temporal or geographical context to resolve other referents. For example, the term *President*, when used in articles that were published in different decades from different countries, will probably refer to different persons. Although the scientific literature rarely refers to people, referents such as *it* or *the latter* become vitally important to identify entities.

Researchers have proposed several algorithms to resolve pronouns. Hobbs's (1978) algorithm uses a dependency-tree representation of sentences. The system starts with a predefined set of syntactic sentence structures and uses breadth-first search, starting with the pronoun to be resolved and working backward within the current and preceding sentences. The algorithm returns the first noun phrase that is consistent with the gender and number of the pronoun. The algorithm correctly resolved the four pronouns (he, she, it, and they) in 88.3 percent (265/300) of the cases. Interestingly, most of the pronouns in the test collections of technical writing, fiction, and news magazines were in the same sentence as the referent.

In contrast to Hobbs's algorithm that considers only the most recent noun phrase as the referent, Lappin and Leass (1994) propose an algorithm that assigns weights to previous candidate noun phrases. Only 46 percent of the pronouns in the corpus used to evaluate system performance, IBM computer training manuals, had more than one candidate referent. Subsequent work has explored methods such as decision trees (Ng & Cardie, 2002) and Markov models (Poon & Domingos, 2008) that learn to predict referent noun phrases accurately. A variety of empirical work has explored the degree to which syntactic and semantic features contribute to improved system performance (Bengtson & Roth, 2008; Ng, 2004).

Abbreviations

Abbreviations are a special case of co-reference resolution and are particularly important when working with scientific literature. One study found that 80 percent of abbreviations in the Unified Medical Language System were ambiguous (Liu, Aronson, & Friedman, 2002).

Initial work on abbreviations resulted in a series of dictionaries sourced from the web (Jablonski, 1993; Stahl & Kerchelich, 2001) and manually developed ontologies (National Library of Medicine, 2004). These dictionaries form the basis of several automated methods to identify abbreviations in literature. For example, Chang, Schutze, and Altman (2002) built an automatically generated and maintained lexicon of abbreviations; dictionaries informed Yu, Hripcsak, and Friedman's (2002) development of a software program called AbbRe, which identifies abbreviations automatically. Although the dictionary approach is effective in identifying existing abbreviations, authors introduce new abbreviations as fields unfold, so a universal dictionary is unsustainable.

The real difficultly with respect to abbreviations is not so much recognizing that the author has used an abbreviation, but rather identifying the correct expanded form, an activity called sense disambiguation. Several researchers have developed methods to extract abbreviations directly from scientific literature and thus are able to link the abbreviation and the expanded form on a document-by-document basis.

Automated methods to identify abbreviations and the correct sense cannot achieve 100 percent accuracy (Yoshida, Fukuda, & Takagi, 2000); however, Ao and Takagi's (2005) system ALICE achieved 97.5 percent precision and 98 percent recall; Schwartz and Hearst's system achieved 96 percent precision and 82 percent recall (Yoshida et al., 2000); and Yu and colleagues' system achieved 95 percent precision and 70 percent recall for abbreviations defined in scientific articles (Pakhomov, Pedersen, & Chute, 2005; Xu, Stetson, & Friedman, 2007).

Negation

Negation has received particular attention in medical notes where pseudo negation phrases such as *no change* and *not cause* (Chapman,

Bridewell, Hanbury, Cooper, & Buchanan, 2001) can have an enormous impact on the quality of the patterns produced. Negative test results (Friedman, Shagina, Lussier, & Hripcsak, 2004), abnormal test results (Sneiderman, Rindflesch, & Aronson, 1996), and contrasts with previous tests (Kim & Park, 2006) have also been explored. NegEx is a set of regular expressions that have been explored in the medical domain that is available for download (Chapman et al., 2001).

If negation is required in a text mining application, one should take care during the dimensionality reduction step (see next section) because negation terms, such as *not* and *no* typically appear on stop word lists.

Syntax

In contrast to the representations that focus on semantics, a syntactic representation captures information at a sentence level. Consider the following two sentences: (1) Slow down so you don't hit the cyclists on the side of the road; (2) Don't slow down so that you hit the cyclists on the side of the road. In spite of the very different meaning conveyed by sentences (1) and (2), the words in both sentences are identical. It is only through syntax that we can interpret the meaning correctly. Syntax tells us that negation applies to *hitting the cyclists* in the first sentence and *slowing down* in the second. In addition to identifying negation correctly, systems use syntax to reveal the subject, verb, and object of a sentence that in turn provide the raw materials for several application areas such as recognizing entailment and extracting relationships from text (see the section on applications). One last area where capturing syntax can be helpful is in document summarization and information synthesis. Here lexical pruning, such as removing noun appositives and gerundive clauses, can provide a powerful way to remove information from a sentence and still keep the original intent of the text (Blake, 2007; Conroy, Schlesinger, O'Leary, & Goldstein, 2006; Vanderwende, Suzuki, & Brockett, 2006; Zajic, Dorr, Schwartz, Monz, & Lin, 2005).

Several researchers have developed tools that generate the syntax of sentences automatically. Although a direct comparison of such tools is somewhat difficult because each parser uses a different set of branch labels, several studies have attempted to compare the quality of parsers. One (de Marneffe, MacCartney, Grenager, Cer, Rafferty, & Manning, 2006) reported that the Stanford Parser (see Figure 3.1) was more accurate than Minipar (Lin, 1998) and Link Grammar (Sleator & Temperley, 1993); another found that the dependency grammar was better suited to topic detection and tracking than the constituent structure (Lee, Lee, & Jang, 2007); and a third study (Clegg & Shepherd, 2007) found that the Charniak (1997) and Collins (1997) parsers were more accurate on biology abstracts.

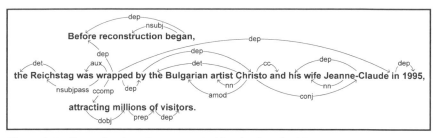

Figure 3.1 **Example of syntax generated by the Stanford Parser on a sentence from the recognizing textual entailment challenge (see Blake, 2007).**

Dimensionality Reduction Techniques

Reducing the dimensionality can reduce the noise in the original text collection and thus provide better patterns.

Stemming

Stemming attempts to identify the root form of a term; for example, the terms *differ, different, differing* and *differs* would all be represented as *differ* after stemming had been applied. One can characterize heuristic methods to identify the root form of a word as either light (terms are more likely to retain their original form) or heavy (terms are more likely to be stemmed). The Porter (1980) stemming algorithm, a light heuristic method, is frequently used for both text mining and information retrieval applications that employ English texts. Heuristic stemmers have also been developed for a variety of non-English languages including Indonesian (Adriani, Asian, Nazief, Tahaghoghi, & Williams, 2007); Finnish (Korenius, Laurikkala, Järvelin, & Juhola, 2004); Arabic (Al-Shammari & Lin, 2008); and the French, Portuguese, German, and Hungarian languages (Savoy, 2006).

Stop Words

Terms that occur frequently in text but have little discriminative power are called stop words. Several ways exist to identify stop words, such as removing the most frequent terms and removing words that have the following syntactic categories (parts of speech): determiners, prepositions, modals, auxiliaries, pronouns, and complementizers. In practice, text miners typically use one of the many stop word lists that are available online.

Although domain-specific terms may also carry little meaning within the scope of a particular collection, such as the term "baseball" in a collection of baseball texts, only a few text mining studies have considered domain-specific stop words (Blake & Pratt, 2001; Ha-Thuc & Srinivasan, 2008). Most stop word lists—even the list created by the National Library of Medicine for PubMed abstracts (www.netautopsy.org/umlsstop.htm)—do not include domain-specific terms.

Frequency Pruning

Including or excluding each of the features described in the previous section will reduce the time required to run the analysis methods described in the next section. Another method of feature reduction is to prune terms based on their frequency. The distribution of terms in a text collection conforms to a power law distribution (Blake, 2006); thus, removing words that appear in fewer than n documents (where n is usually around 5) or more than m times (where m is usually a percentage of the number of documents) can significantly reduce the time required to run the analysis methods described in the following section.

Latent Semantic Indexing

Latent semantic indexing (LSI), or latent semantic analysis (LSA), is a statistical technique that, given a matrix of documents and terms, generates a series of vectors that capture the variance within the original matrix (Deerwester, Dumais, Furnas, Harshman, Landauer, Lochbaum, et al., 1988; Furnas, Deerwester, Dumais, Landauer, Harshman, Streeter, et al., 1988). Also called principal component analysis (PCA) (Pearson, 1901), the output of this process is a series of orthogonal vectors called eigenvectors and a series of eigenvalues that reflect how much variance is captured in each of the eigenvectors. The benefit of using this approach is that eigenvectors capture words with a similar meaning, even though the words may not appear in a single document.

Once calculated, a user can reduce dimensionality by selecting only the n most informative eigenvectors. In addition to being statistically optimal, this also allows the user to calculate the proportion of variance captured by the first n eigenvalues. In Deerwester and colleagues' example (1990, appendix A), the sum of all nine eigenvalues was 14.45. If a user selected only the first four eigenvectors (which had corresponding eigenvalues of 3.34, 2.54, 2.35, and 1.64, respectively) the first four eigenvectors would account for 68.3 percent of the variance in the original matrix.

Analysis Methods

With the text representation in place and the dimensionality reduction applied, the researcher analyzes the collection of texts. This section describes domain-independent analysis methods that have been developed for non-text datasets.

Classification (a.k.a. Categorization)

A classification algorithm aims to create a model (the classifier) that accurately maps from a set of features used to represent each document to an existing class. Thus, the goal of a text-mining system is to create a classifier that, when provided with a set of features from a new document, accurately predicts the class of the new document. One well-used application of text classification is to assign controlled vocabulary terms to documents automatically. For example, several classifiers have been built that map journal abstracts to Medical Subject Headings.

Classification algorithms are typically supervised: Researchers provide the algorithm with training examples that include both the correct class (also called classification or category) and the features used to represent each document (such as the vector-based representation). The classification algorithm then constructs a model that best maps the given features to each class. When the training data have only two possible classes, a binary classifier is constructed; where there are more than two classes, a multi-class classifier is required. A white box classifier, such as decision trees, has the desirable property that a user can see which features the classifier uses when making a prediction. In contrast, a black box model, such as a neural network, has no explanation capability. A model built by a good classification algorithm will include features that together effectively discriminate among the possible categories.

The following classification algorithms developed by the KDD community have had much success when applied to text: Naïve Bayes, decision tree, decision rules, and neural network algorithms and support vector machines (see Sebastiani, 2002, for a longer description of these algorithms). The most straightforward approach is the Naïve Bayes algorithm that calculates the class probability of a new document using word-level prior probabilities from a training set.

Several researchers have compared the accuracy of classifiers built using different classification algorithms, including seminal work on automated classification of news stories (Yang & Liu, 1999; Yang & Pedersen, 1997). Current evidence suggests that support-vector machines consistently provide the highest classification and that system performance generally increases with the number of examples in the training set (Lewis, Yang, Rose, & Li, 2004).

Variations in how authors use natural language can introduce noise to the training data that makes it difficult for the algorithm to identify differentiating features. The large dimensionality of textual collections is also challenging for classification algorithms and can drastically increase running time. Researchers apply the dimensionality reduction techniques described in the previous section before running the classification algorithm to alleviate these challenges.

Clustering

The goal of a clustering algorithm is to group together documents such that each document group has a high degree of intra-class similarity and low degree of inter-class similarity. In contrast to classification, clustering is typically unsupervised in that researchers provide a training set comprising only the features that represent a document, and not the known class.

Several clustering algorithms have been used with text including hierarchical, portioning (such as the k-means algorithm [MacQueen, 1967]), mixture modeling (such as the Expectation Maximization [EM] algorithm [Dempster, Laird, & Rubin, 1977]), nearest neighbor algorithm, and self-organizing maps (see Jain, Murty, & Flynn [1999] for more details on each algorithm). Although hierarchical clustering is statistically optimal, researchers typically use the k-means algorithm to cluster text because k-means is less computationally expensive than hierarchical clustering. The k-means algorithm first selects k data points at random, which become the centroids of each cluster. The algorithm then assigns each data point to the closest centroid and recalculates the centroid as the average of all data points assigned to the cluster. The algorithm then repeats the process of assigning data points to the closest centroid and adjusting the centroid until there are no more data point reassignments or until the number of changes drops below a given threshold. The drawback of the k-means algorithm is that it is sensitive to the initial choice of centroids and that it is not statistically optimal.

Text clustering has been used to identify topics that are then used for browsing documents in a collection (Cutting, Karger, Pedersen, & Tukey, 1992). Mixture models such as a variation of the EM algorithm and latent Dirichlet allocation (Blei, Ng, & Jordan, 2003) have been used to identify cluster authors and topics (Steyvers, Smyth, Rosen-Zvi, & Griffiths, 2004), topics (Wang, Mohanty, & McCallum, 2005), and communities (Li, Nie, Lee, Giles, & Wen, 2008) and to disambiguate word senses (Boyd-Graber, Blei, & Zhu, 2007). The topics produced from clustering can be visualized, such as with self-organizing maps, or shown as topics over time (Havre, Hetzler, Whitney, & Nowell, 2002; Wang & McCallum, 2006).

Association Rules

Association rules capture co-occurrences between terms in a document collection. Such rules are often generated using the Apriori algorithm (Agrawal, Mannila, Srikant, Toivonen, & Verkamo, 1996) that presents patterns to the user in the form: $A \rightarrow B$, where A and B are sets of terms. The user must supply two parameters to the Aprori algorithm: support (the prior probability that A and B co-occur in the data set, which reflects the prevalence of a rule) and confidence (the conditional probability of B given A, which reflects the strength of the implication between A and B).

The KDT (Knowledge Discovery from Text) system was one of the first attempts to apply association rules that were originally developed for numeric and categorical data to text (Feldman & Dagan, 1995). The FACT system, also developed by Feldman, generates association rules based on the keywords assigned to a document (Feldman & Hirsh, 1996). In addition to the minimum support and confidence levels, users may specify semantic constraints on the keywords, where the constraints are sourced from the *CIA's World Factbook*. For example, a user could constrain the left-hand side of an association rule to be a *country* or a member of the *Arab League*.

Ahonen, Heinonen, Klemettinen, and Verkamo (1998) demonstrated that association rules generated over news stories could reveal useful phrases for subsequent analysis. The algorithm steps a window of size w over each sentence in the text, at each step recording the words that appear in the window. The system built by Lent, Agrawal, and Srikant (1997) first calculates the distribution of word terms for each time period, then allows a user to specify the shape of rules and the minimum and maximum window size, in addition to minimum levels of support and confidence. To improve the quality of association rules, the system imposes heuristics that separate words from different sentences and paragraphs before generating association rules. Nahm and Mooney (2000) also use the Apriori algorithm, but their system extracts information using a machine learning system called RIPPER.

Arimura (2000) used a suffix tree to identify patterns in text, which was subsequently shown to be capable of extracting RNA from full text documents. Kawahara and Kawano (2000) developed another system that works with document features to identify co-occurrences between authors and journals. Although it is feasible that the author-journal relationship depicts *publishes*, the system does not explicitly state the nature of the relationship (see next section).

Application Areas

In contrast to the methods discussed previously, this section describes text mining applications that have been formulated to resolve the following problems: relationship extraction, subjectivity detection, recognizing textual entailment, document summarization, information synthesis, and literature based discovery.

Relationship Extraction

Identifying relationships from text has been motivated in part by the bioinformatics community in response to the quantity of data produced by the human genome project (see the BioCreAtIvE challenge [Blaschke, Leon, Krallinger, & Valencia, 2005]). Early relationship extraction systems in biomedicine systems were provided with background knowledge such as the gene and protein names from the Saccharomyces Genome

Database (www.yeastgenome.org), the Swiss-Prot Databases (now merged with the unverified records in the TrEMBL Database to form the UniProt Database [www.uniprot.org]) or manually constructed collections of verbs that are indicative of a gene-protein relationship (Blaschke, Andrade, Ouzounis, & Valencia, 1999). Some would characterize this as an advanced form of text search.

RelEx is a system that identifies gene and protein relations based on the Stanford Parser (Klein & Manning, 2003) and tight constraints on terminal nodes; specifically the terminal node must be a gene or a protein (Rosario & Hearst, 2004). The latter authors use a multi-way classifier to classify the relationships when given the terminal noun phrases (Rosario & Hearst, 2005).

Rindflesch and Fiszman's (2003) hyponym detection uses verbs, prepositions, nominalizations, and the head-modifier relation in simple noun phrases to map text into a range of semantic relationships in the Unified Medical Language System. In later work, Fiszman, Rindflesch, and Kilicoglu (2006) expand the number of semantic types considered and experiment with 300 sentences drawn from MEDLINE abstracts.

Although researchers frequently use full-text biomedical articles in information retrieval experiments, relationship extraction experiments rarely consider the full text of an article. Two exceptions are Huang, Zhu, Hao, Payan, Qu, & Li (2004) who started with 50 full-text articles, but their experiments used only the 1,200 sentences that contain two proteins and the terms *inhibit* or *bind*. Saric, Jensen, Ouzounova, Rojas, and Bork (2006) examined 5,075 PubMed Central articles and found that only 133 of the 158 relations proposed by their approach satisfied their definition of a phosphorylation, dephosphorylation, or expression regulation.

In addition to biomedicine texts, relationships from news articles (Hearst, 1998) such as is-a (hypernyms) (Hearst, 1992; Ritter, Soderland, & Etzioni, 2009; Snow, Jurafsky, & Ng, 2004) and part-whole (meronymy) relationships (Girju, Badulescu, & Moldovan, 2006) have been explored. Many of these systems identify lexico-syntactic patterns that are indicative of the relationship. For example, the system built by Girju and her colleagues first identifies pairs of concepts where a known part-whole relationship exists. The system then uses both the semantics and syntax of the sentence to identify patterns between each concept pair. For example, the lexico-syntactic structures "consists of" and "made of" can be used to identify new part-of relationships. The latter system achieved 81 percent precision and 76 percent recall for the WordNet, TREC 9, and SemCor datasets. Lastly, the ACE challenge included relationships between people and their role in a company or society, such as a staff member, citizen, owner, or client, and personal relationships, such as spouse or sibling (Harabagiu, Bejan, & Morarescu, 2005).

Detecting Subjectivity

Wiebe, Wilson, Bruce, Bell, and Martin (2004, p. 277) define subjectivity in natural language as the "aspects of language used to express opinions, evaluations, and speculations." Detecting subjectivity can be useful for automated classification in a variety of genres, including political corpora (Mullen & Malouf, 2006), product reviews (Tang, Tan, & Cheng, 2009), government analysts, academics, public opinion, and crowdsourcing.

Several projects have tried to identify terms that are indicative of subjectivity, such as the Internet General Inquirer Project (www.webuse. umd.edu:9090) (Kelly & Stone, 1975; Stone, Dunphy, Smith, & Ogilvie, 1966). Terms from the Affect Control Theory (www.indiana.edu/~socpsy/ ACT/data.html) were generated by asking participants to rank terms with respect to subjectivity (Heise, 2001). In addition, researchers have identified lexico-syntactic patterns (Riloff & Wiebe, 2003) and adjectives (Hatzivassiloglou & McKeown, 1997; Hatzivassiloglou & Wiebe, 2000; Kamps & Marx, 2002) to detect subjectivity. One study (Wiebe, Wilson, & Cardie, 2005) has revealed interestingly that subjectivity clues can be adjectives, modals and adverbs, verbs, nouns, and various types of constituents. Turney and Littman (2003) provide a comprehensive set of experiments that measure the degree to which different linguistic clues can accurately capture subjectivity.

Recognizing Textual Entailment

A textual entailment system attempts to determine if a given hypothesis (H) is entailed by a given text expression (T). The hypothesis usually takes the form of a single sentence and the text can comprise one or more sentences. As with the research in summarization, entailment has been driven by a series of challenges that started with the PASCAL RTE-1 in 2005 (Dagan, Glickman, & Magnini, 2005; Giampiccolo, Dang, Magnini, Dagan, Cabrio, & Dolan, 2008). At about the same time Microsoft released a paraphrasing corpus (Dolan, Quirk, & Brockett, 2004). Participants in the RTE challenges develop systems based on a training set of sentences that organizers label as either entailed or not entailed. Participants then build a system that replicates the manually identified entailments. Organizers discard sentences where annotators do not agree on the entailment; thus, the sentences used in the challenge are unambiguous. In 2008, the challenge joined other National Institute of Standards and Technology (NIST) information activities including question answering and information retrieval; the organizers introduced a twist allowing participants to identify three classes—entailment, contradictions, and unknown (Giampiccolo et al., 2008)—rather than the two classes of entailment or not entailed. The current challenge (RTE-5) continues this trend but with longer texts.

Summarization

Researchers have tried since the late sixties to build systems that generate a summary of a single document automatically (Edmundson, 1969; see Mani & Maybury, 1999, for a collection of historical and recent summarization papers). The underlying methods can be characterized as extractive (when text within a document is selected) or abstractive (when the text from the original documents are transformed and new text is generated). In the latter case, the new summary may contain content that was not in the original texts. Early works were based on analyses of manually written document abstracts, such as Edmundson's (1969) insight that the lead sentence in a paragraph provides an overview of the issues discussed. Forty years later, researchers still use the lead sentences in many single document summarization systems. Moreover, the location of a sentence has been explored to generate extractive summaries from long documents (Yang & Wang, 2008). Unlike single document summarization, the sentence location heuristic is not as effective for multi-document summarization, but challenge organizers still use the first sentence as a baseline metric for both single and multi-document summaries.

A key challenge in both single and multiple document summarization is evaluating the quality of the subsequent summary because manually created summaries for the same document can vary greatly. In 2000, NIST started the Document Understanding Challenge (DUC) to help alleviate the effort required to develop evaluation collections, standardize evaluations, and motivate work in automated summarization. The specific tasks have evolved to include single and multi-document summary generation and a novelty track. For example, in 2007, the challenge was to develop a system that generates automatically a fluent 250-word summary from a set of 25 documents relevant to a given topic and query statements. In addition to the topics, queries, and initial documents for both a training and test collection, NIST provides challenge participants with four manually generated summaries and software to evaluate the quality of the summary produced automatically. Manual annotators rate the quality of each automatically generated summary using a score from 1 (excellent) to 5 (bad).

Early DUC challenges focused on developing metrics that correlated with the manual evaluations assigned to the automatic systems; the motivation being that such a metric would allow systems to use a generate-and-test model. In other words, the system could generate multiple potential summaries and then use the new metric to select the best summary. This work produced the Recall-Oriented Understudy for Gisting Evaluation (ROUGE) metric that uses n-grams to evaluate the quality of an automatically generated summary (Lin, 2004; Lin & Hovy, 2003). ROUGE has become the standard method to tune and evaluate systems (Radev, Lam, Elebi, Teufel, Blitzer, Liu, et al., 2003).

The underlying methods used to generate a summary vary widely; many systems use some form of query expansion, lexical simplification, clustering, and sentence selection. Blake, Kampov, Orphanides, West, & Lown (2007) suggest that query expansion using WordNet has had little effect, that lexical simplification and clustering have provided moderate performance improvement, and that sentence selection has had the most impact on performance. The method to select sentences appeared to have the greatest impact on performance, which was optimized when weights considered the similarity between a new sentence and the sentences already in the summary, and the similarity between the new sentence and the original topic and query—an approach similar to Maximal Marginal Relevance (MMR) (Carbonell & Goldstein, 1998). With respect to lexical simplification, Jing (2000) and Vanderwende, Suzuki, Brockett, and Nenkova (2007) each explored syntax to generate simplified sentences; Knight and Marcu (2002) explored compression algorithms.

Although the evaluations provided in DUC have played a large role in moving the summarization field forward, the text genre has only recently expanded from newspaper articles to include other texts, such as blogs. Beyond DUC, Paice and Jones (1993) explored single and multiple document summarization from scientific documents in agriculture (although some would argue that the approach resembles information extraction rather than summarization) and Kittredge (2003) studied paraphrasing as a way to identify short sentences, which are subsequently used to summarize biomedical literature.

Similar to Paice's work on full-text documents, Ou, Khoo, and Goh (2007) predefine the information expected in an abstract to include research variables, background, objectives, methods, results, and conclusions. Their approach uses sentence position, cue words, and a manually developed taxonomy of core concepts to identify sentences from the abstract that should be included in the final summary. A user study comparing an interface with and without the taxonomy suggests that students and researchers have different summary presentation preferences.

Paice and Ou's summarization methods each include a domain-specific component. In contrast, Rhetorical Structure Theory (RST) (Mann & Thompson, 1988) provides a more general framework that can be applied across domains. For example, Marcu and Echihabi (2002) focus on automated methods to identify contrast, cause-explanation-evidence, condition, and elaboration components and Blair-Goldensohn, McKeown, and Rambow (2007) focus on cause and contrast models of RST. In the latter work, the system first uses cue phrases to identify structures and frames the task as a classification problem.

Mani and Bloedorn (1999) created a system that identifies similarities and differences in a document collection; the first step is to identify entities. The system then connects terms based on proximity, pronoun resolution, and WordNet synonyms and antonyms. Lastly, the system uses spreading activation to identify clusters of sentences about the same topic.

Summarization research has matured to the point where two systems provide multi-document summarizations of daily news reports: NewsBlaster, which uses multi-gen, an approach that fuses information from multiple sentences (Barzilay & McKeown, 2009); and DEMS (Schiffman, Nenkova, & McKeown, 2002). NewsInEssence builds on the MEAD summarizer (Radev, Jing, Stys, & Tam, 2004), which clusters sentences from the original set of news stories and uses the centroid and MMR to identify sentences that will be used in the final summary (source code for MEAD is available [Radev, Allison, Blair-Goldensohn, Blitzer, Celebi, Dimitrov, et al., 2004]).

Information Synthesis

Although multi-document summarization is inherently a synthesis activity, research on the Collaborative Information Synthesis (CIS) model was informed by studies of human information behaviors surrounding the systematic review process (Davies & Crombie, 1998). The primary goal in a meta-analysis is to balance contradictory and redundant evidence in the scientific literature.

The Multi-User Extraction for Information Synthesis (METIS) system accelerates the systematic review process by automating the information extraction and analysis activities (Blake & Pratt, 2006a, 2006b). METIS extends traditional meta-analytic techniques by including secondary information—facts in an article that do not appear in the title, abstract, or as keywords. Consider an article that reports the relationship between residential magnetic fields and breast cancer risk (Davis, Mirick, & Stevens, 2002). Although the title, keywords, and abstract do not mention alcohol or a synonym, the study does state that 163 subjects with breast cancer never consume alcohol, 636 subjects consume more than one drink per day, and 14 subjects have unknown alcohol consumption behaviors. Thus, the reported information enables the researcher to calculate a case rate, but the absence of a control rate excludes the article from a traditional analysis. The system uses demographic, study, disease, and risk factor information reported in the article to generate a synthetic estimate for the missing control rate. For the alcohol example, METIS calculates the alcohol consumption rate from the Behavioral Risk Factors Surveillance system, a state-based telephone questionnaire that captures risk behaviors and preventive health practices in the U.S. (www.cdc.gov/BRFSS) based on the age and gender of the breast cancer subjects and the time-frame and location of the study. Such an estimate enables scientists to both identify and synthesize information from the scientific literature that would otherwise be hidden.

Literature-Based Discovery

Similar to information synthesis research, information overload in the biomedical literature prompted the development of literature-based discovery, which is a process of systematically searching existing literature to identify undiscovered public knowledge (Swanson, 1986). First, a user collects the A-literature, such as articles that report a medical condition. The system then identifies co-occurring terms, called B-terms, which might ideally indicate physiological mechanisms that underpin the medical condition. In the second search, the user collects articles that report any of the B-terms (the B-literature). Finally, the system scans the B-literature to identify C-terms, which might provide a candidate treatment.

The literature-based discovery model was used to identify fish oil as a treatment for Raynaud's disease (Swanson, 1986) and magnesium as a candidate migraine treatment (Swanson, 1988); both discoveries were subsequently verified in clinical trials (DiGiacomo, Kremer, & Shah, 1989; Ramadan, Halvorson, Vande-Linde, Levine, Helpern, & Welch, 1989). Literature-based discovery has since been used to identify connections between somatomedin C and arginine (Swanson, 1990), estrogen and Alzheimer's disease (Smalheiser & Swanson, 1996), myasthenia gravis and H.Pylori-induced gastritis and acute pancreatitis (Swanson, 1990), and thalidomide and hepatitis C (Weeber, Vos, Klein, Berg, Aronson, & Molema, 2003). Although most examples of this approach are in medicine, there have been attempts to apply the model to other domains, such as computing (Fox, Neves, Yu, Shen, Kim, & Fan, 2006).

The challenge with literature-based discovery is the branching factor. Each term in the A-literature co-occurs with hundreds or thousands of B-terms. Similarly, each term in the B-literature co-occurs with hundreds or thousands of C-terms. In the first experiment, the migraine-magnesium connection, manual pruning was used to control the branching factor; pruning 92 percent of the B-terms manually does not scale well, however. A variety of techniques has since been developed to control the branching factor, including variations of tf*idf weighting (Gordon & Lindsay, 1996; Lindsay & Gordon, 1999), thresholds and term co-occurrence (Swanson & Smalheiser, 1997), knowledge bases (Blake & Pratt, 2002), association rules (Pratt & Yetisgen-Yildiz, 2003), and concept profiles (Srinivasan, 2004).

Conclusions

We have never had more electronic text than we have today and, as the quantity of text continues to increase, so too does our need for text-mining systems that allow us to identify and explore patterns within these collections. This review identified key preprocessing and transformation methods used to work with text. General tools that enable automated preprocessing and transformations of text are still in their infancy and, because these approaches are specific to individual collections, it is unlikely that the academic community will address this gap.

Information science researchers are instead trying to intervene during the text generation stage through the development of standards; this will require ongoing collaboration between academe and industry partners who produce the software used to create text documents.

This review described several data analysis methods such as classification, clustering, and association rules that have been successful in identifying patterns from text collections. The review also demonstrated varying levels of success for specific text-mining applications such as relationship detection, sentiment analysis, recognizing textual entailment, document summarization, information synthesis, and literature-based discovery. Although some studies have explored the relationship between the underlying text representation and the subsequent analysis, experiments that systematically explore combinations of text representation, analysis method, and application are still rare.

Perhaps the greatest limitation of existing text-mining systems is that researchers have yet to study how these tools can be tightly woven into existing work environments. Such integration would enable text mining researchers to explore the types of patterns required by users on an ongoing basis, rather than the one-off experiments reported in the current literature. It is only in moving toward an integrative environment that we can improve understanding of the contributions of and interaction effects between individual components and, more importantly, start to realize the full potential of text-mining systems that identify novel, interesting, plausible patterns from collections of text.

References

Adriani, M., Asian, J., Nazief, B., Tahaghoghi, S. M. M., & Williams, H. E. (2007). Stemming Indonesian: A confix-stripping approach. *ACM Transactions on Asian Language Information Processing, 6*(4), 1–33.

Agrawal, R., Mannila, H., Srikant, R., Toivonen, H., & Verkamo, I. (1996). Fast discovery of association rules. In U. Fayyad, G. Piatetsky-Shapiro, P. Smyth, & R. Uthurusamy (Eds.), *Advances in knowledge discovery and data mining* (pp. 307–328). Menlo Park, CA: AAAI/MIT Press.

Ahonen, H., Heinonen, O., Klemettinen, M., & Verkamo, A. I. (1998). Applying data mining techniques for descriptive phrase extraction in digital document collections. *Proceedings of the IEEE Forum on Research and Technology Advances in Digital Libraries*, 2–11.

Al-Shammari, E. T., & Lin, J. (2008). Towards an error-free Arabic stemming. *Proceedings of the 2nd ACM Workshop on Improving non-English Web Searching, Conference on Information and Knowledge Management*, 9–16.

Ao, H., & Takagi, T. (2005). ALICE: An algorithm to extract abbreviations from MEDLINE. *Journal of the American Medical Informatics Association, 12*, 576–586.

Appelt, D. E., & Israel, D. J. (1999). *Introduction to information extraction technology.* Paper presented at the Tutorial for the International Joint Conference on Artificial Intelligence, Stockholm, Sweden. Retrieved January 12, 2010, from www.ai.sri.com/~appelt/ie-tutorial

Arimura, H. (2000, August). *Text mining: From the view of optimization data mining.* Paper presented at the International Workshop on Web Knowledge Discovery and Data Mining, Boston.

Aronson, A. R. (2001, February). *Effective mapping of biomedical text to the UMLS Metathesaurus: The MetaMap program.* Paper presented at the American Medical Informatics Association, LaJolla, CA. Retrieved January 12, 2010, from skr.nlm.nih.gov/papers/references/metamap_01AMIA.pdf

Barzilay, R., & McKeown, K. R. (2009). Sentence fusion for multidocument news summarization. *Computational Linguistics, 31*(3), 297–327.

Bengtson, E., & Roth, D. (2008). Understanding the value of features for coreference resolution. *Proceedings of the Conference on Empirical Methods in Natural Language Processing,* 294–303.

Blair-Goldensohn, S., McKeown, K., & Rambow, O. (2007). Building and refining rhetorical-semantic relation models. *Human Language Technology Conference of the North American Chapter of the Association of Computational Linguistics,* 428–435.

Blake, C. (2006). A comparison of document, sentence, and term event spaces. *International Committee on Computational Linguistics and the Association for Computational Linguistics,* 601–608.

Blake, C. (2007). The role of sentence structure in recognizing textual entailment. *Third Recognising Textual Entailment Challenge,* 101–106.

Blake, C., Kampov, J., Orphanides, A., West, D., & Lown, C. (2007, April). *UNC-CH at DUC 2007: Query expansion, lexical simplification, and sentence selection strategies for multidocument summarization.* Paper presented at the Document Understanding Conference, Rochester, NY.

Blake, C., & Pratt, W. (2001). Better rules, fewer features: A semantic approach to selecting features from text. *Proceedings of the IEEE Data Mining Conference,* 59–66.

Blake, C., & Pratt, W. (2002). Automatically identifying candidate treatments from existing medical literature. *AAAI Spring Symposium on Mining Answers from Texts and Knowledge Bases,* 9–13.

Blake, C., & Pratt, W. (2006a). Collaborative information synthesis I: A model of information behaviors of scientists in medicine and public health. *Journal of the American Society for Information Science and Technology, 57*(13), 1740–1749.

Blake, C., & Pratt, W. (2006b). Collaborative information synthesis II: Recommendations for information systems to support synthesis activities. *Journal of the American Society for Information Science and Technology, 57*(14), 1888–1895.

Blaschke, C., Andrade, M. A., Ouzounis, C., & Valencia, A. (1999, August). *Automatic extraction of biological information from scientific text: Protein-protein interactions.* Paper presented at the Seventh International Conference on Intelligent Systems for Molecular Biology, Heidelberg, Germany.

Blaschke, C., Leon, E. A., Krallinger, M., & Valencia, A. (2005). Evaluation of BioCreAtIvE assessment of task. *BMC Bioinformatics, 6*(S16).

Blei, D. M., Ng, A. Y., & Jordan, M. I. (2003). Latent Dirichlet allocation. *Journal of Machine Learning Research, 3,* 993–1022.

Boyd-Graber, J., Blei, D., & Zhu, X. (2007). A topic model for word sense disambiguation. *Proceedings of the Joint Conference on Empirical Methods in Natural Language Processing and Computational Natural Language Learning,* 1024–1033.

Califf, M. E., & Mooney, R. J. (1999). Relational learning of pattern match rules for information extraction. *Proceedings of the Sixteenth National Conference on Artificial Intelligence*, 328–334.

Carbonell, J., & Goldstein, J. (1998). The use of MMR, diversity-based reranking for reordering documents and producing summaries. *Proceedings of the Annual International ACM SIGIR Conference on Research and Development in Information Retrieval*, 335–336.

Caruana, R., & Hodor, P. G. (2000, August). *High precision information extraction*. Paper presented at the KDD-2000 Workshop on Text Mining, Boston.

Chang, J. T., Schutze, H., & Altman, R. B. (2002). Creating an online dictionary of abbreviations from MEDLINE. *Journal of the American Medical Informatics Association, 9*(6), 612–620.

Charniak, E. (1997). Statistical parsing with a context-free grammar and word statistics. *Proceedings of the Fourteenth National Conference on Artificial Intelligence*, 598–603.

Chapman, W. W., Bridewell, W., Hanbury, P., Cooper, G. F., & Buchanan, B. G. (2001). A simple algorithm for identifying negated findings and diseases in discharge summaries. *Journal of Biomedical Informatics, 34*, 301–310.

Chen, H., & Chau, M. (2004). Web mining: Machine learning for web applications. *Annual Review of Information Science and Technology, 38*, 289–329.

Clegg, A. B., & Shepherd, A. J. (2007). Benchmarking natural-language parsers for biological applications using dependency graphs. *BMC Bioinformatics, 8*(24). Retrieved January 12, 2010, from www.biomedcentral.com/1471-2105/8/24

Collins, M. (1997). Semantic tagging using a probabilistic context free grammar. *Proceedings of the 6th Workshop on Very Large Corpora*, 38–48.

Conroy, J. M., Schlesinger, J. D., O'Leary, D. P., & Goldstein, J. (2006, June). *Back to basics: CLASSY 2006*. Paper presented at the Document Understanding Workshop, Brooklyn, New York. Retrieved January 12, 2010, from duc.nist.gov/pubs/2006papers/ccs06.final.pdf

Crystal, T. H. (1993). TIPSTER program history. *Annual Meeting of the Association of Computational Linguistics*, 3–4.

Cutting, D. R., Karger, D. R., Pedersen, J. O., & Tukey, J. W. (1992). Scatter/gather: A cluster-based approach to browsing large document collections. *Proceedings of the 15th Annual International ACM SIGIR Conference on Research and Development in Information Retrieval*, 318–329.

Dagan, I., Glickman, O., & Magnini, B. (2005). The PASCAL recognising textual entailment challenge. *Proceedings of the PASCAL Challenges Workshop on Recognising Textual Entailment*, 175–180.

Davies, H. T. O., & Crombie, I. K. (1998). What is a systematic review? *Hayward Medical Communications, 1*(5), 1–5.

Davis, S., Mirick, D. K., & Stevens, R. G. (2002). Residential magnetic fields and the risk of breast cancer. *American Journal of Epidemiology, 155*(5), 446–454.

Day, D., Aberdeen, J., Hirschman, L., Kozierok, R., Robinson, P., & Vilain, M. (1997, March). *Mixed-initiative development of language processing systems*. Paper presented at the Fifth Conference on Applied Natural Language Processing, Washington, DC.

de Marneffe, M.-C., MacCartney, B., Grenager, T., Cer, D., Rafferty, A., & Manning, C. D. (2006, April). *Learning to distinguish valid textual entailments*. Paper presented at the

Second Pascal RTE Challenge Workshop, Venice, Italy. Retrieved January 12, 2010, from nlp.stanford.edu/pubs/rte2-report.pdf

Deerwester, S. C., Dumais, S. T., Furnas, G. W., Harshman, R. A., Landauer, T. K., Lochbaum, K. E., et al. (1988). *U.S. Patent No. 07/244,349*. Washington, DC: U.S. Patent and Trademark Office.

Deerwester, S. C., Dumais, S. T., Landauer, T. K., Furnas, G. W., & Harshman, R. A. (1990). Indexing by latent semantic analysis. *Journal of the American Society for Information Science, 41*(6), 391–407.

Dempster, A. P., Laird, N. M., & Rubin, D. B. (1977). Maximum likelihood from incomplete data via the EM algorithm. *Journal of the Royal Statistical Society, 39*(B), 1–38.

DiGiacomo, R. A., Kremer, J. M., & Shah, D. M. (1989). Fish-oil dietary supplementation in patients with Raynaud's phenomenon: A double-blind, controlled, prospective study. *American Journal of Medicine, 86*, 158–164.

Dolan, W. B., Quirk, C., & Brockett, C. (2004). Unsupervised construction of large paraphrase corpora: Exploiting massively parallel news sources. *Proceedings of the 20th International Conference on Computational Linguistics*, 350–356.

Edmundson, H. P. (1969). New methods in automatic extraction. *Journal of the ACM, 16*(2), 264–285.

Fayyad, U. M., Piatetsky-Shapiro, G., & Smyth, P. (1996). From data mining to knowledge discovery: An overview. In *Advances in knowledge discovery and data mining* (pp. 1–34). Menlo Park, CA: AAAI Press.

Feldman, R. (1999). Mining unstructured data. *Tutorial Notes of the fifth ACM SIGKDD International Conference on Knowledge Discovery and Data Mining*, 182–236.

Feldman, R., & Dagan, I. (1995). Knowledge discovery in textual databases (KDT). *Proceedings of the ECML-95 Workshop on Knowledge Discovery*, 175–180.

Feldman, R., & Hirsh, H. (1996). Mining associations in text in the presence of background knowledge. Proceedings of the 2nd International Conference on Knowledge Discovery, 343–346.

Fiszman, M., Rindflesch, T. C., & Kilicoglu, H. (2006). Summarizing drug information in Medline citations. *Proceedings of the American Medical Informatics Association Annual Symposium*, 254–258.

Fox, E. A., Neves, F. D., Yu, X., Shen, R., Kim, S., & Fan, W. (2006). Exploring the computing literature with visualization and stepping stones and pathways. *Communications of the ACM, 49*(6), 52–58.

Friedman, C., Shagina, L., Lussier, Y., & Hripcsak, G. (2004). Automated encoding of clinical documents based on natural language processing. *Journal of the American Medical Informatics Association, 11*, 392–402.

Fukuda, K., Tsunoda, T., Tamura, A., & Takagi, T. (1998). Toward information extraction: Identifying protein names from biological papers. *Pacific Symposium on Biocomputing, 3*, 707–718.

Furnas, G. W., Deerwester, S., Dumais, S. T., Landauer, T. K., Harshman, R. A., Streeter, L. A., et al. (1988). Information retrieval using a singular value decomposition model of latent semantic structure. *Proceedings of the Annual International ACM SIGIR Conference on Research and Development in Information Retrieval*, 465–480.

Giampiccolo, D., Dang, H. T., Magnini, B., Dagan, I., Cabrio, E., & Dolan, B. (2008). The Fourth PASCAL Recognizing Textual Entailment Challenge. *Proceedings of the First Text Analysis Conference*, 1–9.

Girju, R., Badulescu, A., & Moldovan, D. (2006). Automatic discovery of part-whole relations. *Computational Linguistics, 32*(1), 83–135.

Gordon, M. D., & Lindsay, R. K. (1996). Toward discovery support systems: A replication, reexamination and extension of Swanson's work on literature-based discovery of a connection between Raynaud's and fish oil. *Journal of the American Society for Information Science, 47,* 116–128.

Grishman, R., & Sundheim, B. (1996). Message Understanding Conference 6: A brief history. *International Conference on Computational Linguistics,* 466–471.

Guernsey, L. (2003, October 16). Digging for nuggets of wisdom. *The New York Times.* Retrieved February 1, 2010, from www.nytimes.com/2003/10/16/technology/circuits/16mine.html?pagewanted=all

Ha-Thuc, V., & Srinivasan, P. (2008). Topic models and a revisit of text-related applications. *Proceeding of the 2nd PhD Workshop on Information and Knowledge Management,* 25–32.

Harabagiu, S. M., Bejan, C. A., & Morarescu, P. (2005). Shallow semantics for relation extraction. *Nineteenth International Joint Conference on Artificial Intelligence,* 1061–1066.

Hatzivassiloglou, V., & McKeown, K. R. (1997). Predicting the semantic orientation of adjectives. *Proceedings of the 35th Annual Meeting of the ACL and the 8th Conference of the European Chapter of the ACL,* 174–181.

Hatzivassiloglou, V., & Wiebe, J. M. (2000). Effects of adjective orientation and gradability on sentence subjectivity. *Proceedings of the 18th Conference on Computational Linguistics,* 299–305.

Havre, S., Hetzler, E., Whitney, P., & Nowell, L. (2002). ThemeRiver: Visualizing thematic changes in large document collections. *IEEE Transactions on Visualization and Computer Graphics, 8*(1), 9–20.

Hearst, M. A. (1992). Automatic acquisition of hyponyms from large text corpora. *Proceedings of the 14th International Conference on Computational Linguistics,* 539–545.

Hearst, M. A. (1998). Automated discovery of WordNet relations. In C. Fellbaum (Ed.), *WordNet: An electronic lexical database and some of its applications* (pp. 1–26). Cambridge, MA: MIT Press.

Hearst, M. A. (1999). Untangling text data mining. *Proceedings of the 37th Annual Meeting of the Association for Computational Linguistics.* Retrieved January 12, 2010, from people.ischool.berkeley.edu/~hearst/papers/acl99/acl99-tdm.html

Hearst, M. A. (2003). *What is text mining?* Retrieved January 12, 2010, from people.ischool.berkeley.edu/~hearst/text-mining.html

Heise, D. R. (2001). Project Magellan: Collecting cross-cultural affective meanings via the internet. *Electronic Journal of Sociology, 5*(3).

Hirschman, L. (1997). *MUC-7 coreference task definition, version 3.0.* Retrieved June 30, 2009, from www-nlpir.nist.gov/related_projects/muc/proceedings/co_task.html

Hobbs, J. (1978). Resolving pronoun references. *Lingua, 44,* 311–338.

Huang, M., Zhu, X., Hao, Y., Payan, D. G., Qu, K., & Li, M. (2004). Discovering patterns to extract protein-protein interactions from full texts. *Bioinformatics, 20*(18), 3604–3612.

Jablonski, S. (1993). *Dictionary of medical acronyms and abbreviations* (2nd ed.). Philadelphia: Hanley & Belfus.

Jain, A. K., Murty, M. N., & Flynn, P. J. (1999). Data clustering: A review. *ACM Computing Surveys, 31*(3), 264–323.

Jing, H. (2000). Sentence reduction for automatic text summarization. *Proceedings of the Conference on Applied Natural Language Processing*, 310–315.

Kamps, J., & Marx, M. (2002). Words with attitude. *Proceedings of the First International Conference on Global WordNet*, 332–341.

Kawahara, M., & Kawano, H. (2000). An application of text mining: Bibliographic navigator powered by extended association rules. *Proceedings of the 33rd Hawai'i International Conference on System Sciences.* Retrieved February 1, 2010, from ieeexplore.ieee.org/stamp/stamp.jsp?tp=&arnumber=926651&isnumber=20043

Kelly, E., & Stone, P. (1975). *Computer recognition of English word senses.* Amsterdam: North-Holland.

Kim, J.-J., & Park, J. C. (2006). Extracting contrastive information from negation patterns in biomedical literature. *ACM Transactions on Asian Language Information Processing, 5*(1), 44–60.

Kittredge, R. (2003). Paraphrasing for condensation in journal abstracting. *Journal of Biomedical Informatics, 35*(4), 265–277.

Klein, D., & Manning, C. D. (2003). Accurate unlexicalized parsing. *Proceedings of the Annual Meeting of the Association for Computational Linguistics*, 423–430.

Knight, K., & Marcu, D. (2002). Summarization beyond sentence extraction: A probabilistic approach to sentence compression. *Artificial Intelligence, 139*(1), 91–107.

Korenius, T., Laurikkala, J., Järvelin, K., & Juhola, M. (2004). Stemming and lemmatization in the clustering of Finnish text documents. *Proceedings of the ACM International Conference on Information and Knowledge Management*, 625–633.

Kostoff, R. N., Block, J. A., Solka, J. L., Briggs, M. B., Rushenberg, R. L., Stump, J. A., et al. (2007). *Literature-related discovery: A review.* Arlington, VA: Office of Naval Research.

Kostoff, R. N., Block, J. A., Solka, J. L., Briggs, M. B., Rushenberg, R. L., Stump, J. A., et al. (2009). Literature-related discovery. *Annual Review of Information Science and Technology, 43*, 241–285.

Lappin, S., & Leass, H. (1994). An algorithm for pronominal anaphora resolution. *Computational Linguistics, 20*, 535–561.

Lee, C., Lee, G., & Jang, M. (2007). Dependency structure language model for topic detection and tracking. *Information Processing & Management, 43*(5), 1249–1259.

Lent, B., Agrawal, R., & Srikant, R. (1997). Discovering trends in text databases. *Proceedings of the Third International Conference on Knowledge Discovery and Data Mining*, 227–230.

Lewis, D. D., Yang, Y., Rose, T. G., & Li, F. (2004). RCV1: A new benchmark collection for text categorization research. *Journal of Machine Learning Research, 5*, 361–397.

Li, H., Nie, Z., Lee, W.-C., Giles, L., & Wen, J.-R. (2008). Scalable community discovery on textual data with relations. *Proceedings of the ACM Conference on Information and Knowledge Management*, 1203–1212.

Liddy, E. D. (2000). Text mining. *Bulletin of the American Society for Information Science, 27*(1). Retrieved January 12, 2010, from www.asis.org/Bulletin/Oct-00/liddy.html

Lin, C.-Y. (2004). ROUGE: A package for automatic evaluation of summaries. *Proceedings of the Workshop on Text Summarization Branches Out*, 74–81.

Lin, C.-Y., & Hovy, E. (2003). Automatic evaluation of summaries using n-gram co-occurrence statistics. *Proceedings of the 2003 Conference of the North American Chapter of the Association for Computational Linguistics on Human Language Technology*, vol. 1, 71–78.

Lin, D. (1998, May). *Dependency-based evaluation of MINIPAR*. Paper presented at the Workshop on the Evaluation of Parsing Systems, First International Conference on Language Resources and Evaluation, Granada, Spain.

Lindsay, R. K., & Gordon, M. D. (1999). Literature-based discovery by lexical statistics. *Journal of the American Society for Information Science, 50*(7), 574–587.

Liu, H., Aronson, A. R., & Friedman, C. (2002). A study of abbreviations in MEDLINE abstracts. *American Medical Informatics Symposium*, 464–468.

Lu, C. J., Browne, A. C., & Divita, G. (2008). Using lexical tools to convert Unicode characters to ASCII. *Proceedings of the Annual Symposium of the American Medical Informatics Association*, 1031.

MacQueen, J. B. (1967). Some methods for classification and analysis of multivariate observations. *Proceedings of the Berkeley Symposium on Mathematical Statistics and Probability*, 281–297.

Mani, I., & Bloedorn, E. (1999). Summarizing similarities and differences among related documents. In I. Mani & M. T. Maybury (Eds.), *Advances in automatic text summarization* (pp. 357–379). Cambridge, MA: MIT Press.

Mani, I., & Maybury, M. T. (1999). *Advances in automatic text summarization*. Cambridge, MA: MIT Press.

Mann, W. C., & Thompson, S. A. (1988). Rhetorical structure theory: Toward a functional theory of text organization. *Text, 8*(3), 243–281.

Marcu, D., & Echihabi, A. (2002). An unsupervised approach to recognizing discourse relations. *Proceedings of the Annual Meeting of the Association for Computational Linguistics*, 368–375.

Matuszek, C., Cabral, J., Witbrock, M., & DeOliveira, J. (2006). An introduction to the syntax and content of Cyc. *Proceedings of the 2006 AAAI Spring Symposium on Formalizing and Compiling Background Knowledge and Its Applications to Knowledge Representation and Question Answering*, 44–49.

McCray, A. T. (2003). An upper-level ontology for the biomedical domain. *Comparative and Functional Genomics, 4*, 80–84.

McCray, A. T., Srinivasan, S., & Browne, A. C. (1994). Lexical methods for managing variation in biomedical terminologies. *Proceedings of the Annual Symposium on Computer Applications in Medical Care*, 235–239.

Miller, G. (1995). WordNet: A lexical database for English. *Communications of the ACM, 38*(11), 39–41.

Mitchell, T. M. (1997). *Machine learning*. New York: McGraw-Hill.

Mullen, T., & Malouf, R. (2006). A preliminary investigation into sentiment analysis of informal political discourse. *Proceedings of the AAAI Symposium on Computational Approaches to Analyzing Weblogs*, 159–162.

Nahm, U. Y., & Mooney, R. J. (2000). Using information extraction to aid the discovery of prediction rules from text. *Proceedings of the KDD-2000 Workshop on Text Mining*, 51–58.

National Library of Medicine. (2004). *UMLS Metathesaurus fact sheet*. Retrieved October 20, 2004, from www.nlm.nih.gov/pubs/factsheets/umlsmeta.html

Ng, V. (2004). Learning noun phrase anaphoricity to improve coreference resolution: Issues in representation and optimization. *Proceedings of the 42nd Annual Meeting of the Association for Computational Linguistics*, 152–159.

Ng, V., & Cardie, C. (2002). Combining sample selection and error-driven pruning for machine learning of coreference rules. *Proceedings of the Association for Computational Linguistics Conference on Empirical Methods in Natural Language Processing*, 55–62.

Ou, S., Khoo, C. S. G., & Goh, D. H. (2007). Automatic multidocument summarization of research abstracts: Design and user evaluation. *Journal of the American Society for Information Science and Technology*, 58(10), 1419–1435.

Paice, C. D., & Jones, P. A. (1993). The identification of important concepts in highly structured technical papers. *Proceedings of the Annual International ACM SIGIR Conference on Research and Development in Information Retrieval*, 69–78.

Pakhomov, S., Pedersen, T., & Chute, C. G. (2005). Abbreviation and acronym disambiguation in clinical discourse. *Proceedings of the American Medical Informatics Association Annual Symposium*, 821–825.

Pearson, K. (1901). On lines and planes of closest fit to systems of points in space. *Philosophical Magazine*, 2(6), 559–572.

Poon, H., & Domingos, P. (2008). Joint unsupervised coreference resolution with Markov logic. *Proceedings of the Conference on Empirical Methods in Natural Language Processing*, 649–658.

Porter, M. F. (1980). An algorithm for suffix stripping. *Program*, 14(3), 130–137.

Pratt, W., & Yetisgen-Yildiz, M. (2003). LitLinker: Capturing connections across the biomedical literature. *Proceedings of the International Conference on Knowledge Capture*, 105–112.

Price, D. J. D. (1986). *Little science, big science ... and beyond*. New York: Columbia University Press.

Radev, D., Allison, T., Blair-Goldensohn, S., Blitzer, J., Celebi, A., Dimitrov, S., et al. (2004, May). *MEAD: A platform for multidocument multilingual text summarization*. Paper presented at the International Conference on Language Resources and Evaluation, Lisbon, Portugal.

Radev, D. R., Jing, H., Stys, M., & Tam, D. (2004). Centroid-based summarization of multiple documents. *Information Processing & Management*, 40(6), 919–938.

Radev, D. R., Lam, W., Elebi, A. C., Teufel, S., Blitzer, J., Liu, D., et al. (2003). Evaluation challenges in large-scale document summarization. *Proceedings of the Annual Meeting of the Association for Computational Linguistics*, 375–382.

Ramadan, N. M., Halvorson, H., Vande-Linde, A., Levine, S., Helpern, J. A., & Welch, K. M. (1989). Low brain magnesium in migraine. *Headache*, 29(9), 590–593.

Riloff, E. (1996). Automatically generating extraction patterns from untagged text. *Proceedings of the National Conference on Artificial Intelligence*, 1044–1049.

Riloff, E., & Wiebe, J. (2003). Learning extraction patterns for subjective expressions. *Proceedings of the Conference on Empirical Methods in Natural Language Processing*, 105–112.

Rindflesch, T. C., & Fiszman, M. (2003). The interaction of domain knowledge and linguistic structure in natural language processing: Interpreting hypernymic propositions in biomedical text. *Journal of Biomedical Informatics*, 36(6), 462–477.

Ritter, A., Soderland, S., & Etzioni, O. (2009). What is this, anyway: Automatic hypernym discovery. *Proceedings of the 2009 Association for the Advancement of Artificial*

Intelligence Spring Symposium on Learning by Reading and Learning to Read. Retrieved January 12, 2010, from turing.cs.washington.edu/papers/ritter_aaai_ss09.pdf

Rosario, B., & Hearst, M. A. (2004). Classifying semantic relations in bioscience texts. *Proceedings of the Annual Meeting of the Association for Computational Linguistics,* 430–438.

Rosario, B., & Hearst, M. (2005). Multi-way relation classification: Application to protein-protein interaction. *Proceedings of the Conference on Human Language Technology and Empirical Methods in Natural Language Processing,* 732–739.

Saric, J., Jensen, L. J., Ouzounova, R., Rojas, I., & Bork, P. (2006). Extraction of regulatory gene/protein networks from Medline. *Bioinformatics, 22*(6), 645–650.

Savoy, J. (2006). Light stemming approaches for the French, Portuguese, German and Hungarian languages. *Proceedings of the 2006 ACM Symposium on Applied Computing,* 1031–1035.

Schiffman, B., Nenkova, A., & McKeown, K. R. (2002). Experiments in multidocument summarization. *Proceedings of Human Language Technologies,* 52–58.

Schwartz, A. S., & Hearst, M. A. (2003). A simple algorithm for identifying abbreviation definitions in biomedical text. *Proceedings of the Pacific Symposium on Biocomputing,* 451–462.

Sebastiani, F. (2002). Machine learning in automated text categorization. *ACM Computing Surveys, 34*(1), 1–47.

Sleator, D., & Temperley, D. (1993, August). *Parsing English with a link grammar.* Paper presented at the Third International Workshop on Parsing Technologies, Tilburg, The Netherlands.

Smalheiser, N., & Swanson, D. (1996). Linking estrogen to Alzheimer's disease: An informatics approach. *Neurology, 47*(3), 809–810.

Smith, B. (2004, November). *Beyond concepts: Ontology as reality representation.* Paper presented at the International Conference on Formal Ontology and Information Systems, Turin, Italy.

Sneiderman, C. A., Rindflesch, T. C., & Aronson, A. R. (1996). Finding the findings: Identification of findings in medical literature using restricted natural language processing. *Proceedings of the American Medical Informatics Association Annual Fall Symposium,* 239–243.

Snow, R., Jurafsky, D., & Ng, A. Y. (2004, December). *Learning syntactic patterns for automatic hypernym discovery.* Paper presented at the Advances in Neural Information Processing Systems, Vancouver, Canada. Retrieved January 12, 2010, from books.nips.cc/papers/files/nips17/NIPS2004_0887.pdf

Srinivasan, P. (2004). Text mining: Generating hypotheses from MEDLINE. *Journal of the American Society for Information Science and Technology, 55*(5), 396–413.

Stahl, D., & Kerchelich, K. (Eds.). (2001). *Abbreviations dictionary* (10th ed.). Boca Raton, FL: CRC Press.

Steyvers, M., Smyth, P., Rosen-Zvi, M., & Griffiths, T. (2004). Probabilistic author-topic models for information discovery. *Proceedings of the Tenth ACM SIGKDD International Conference on Knowledge Discovery and Data Mining,* 306–315.

Stone, P. J., Dunphy, D. C., Smith, M. S., & Ogilvie, D. M. (1966). *The general inquirer: A computer approach to content analysis.* Cambridge, MA: MIT Press.

Swanson, D. (1986). Fish-oil, Raynaud's Syndrome, and undiscovered public knowledge. *Perspectives in Biology and Medicine, 30*(1), 7–18.

Swanson, D. (1988). Migraine and magnesium: Eleven neglected connections. *Perspectives in Biology and Medicine, 31*, 526–557.

Swanson, D. (1990). Somatomedin C and arginine: Implicit connections between mutually isolated literatures. *Perspectives in Biology and Medicine, 33*(2), 157–186.

Swanson, D., & Smalheiser, N. R. (1997). An interactive system for finding complementary literatures: A stimulus to scientific discovery. *Artificial Intelligence, 91*, 183–203.

Tang, H., Tan, S., & Cheng, X. (2009). A survey on sentiment detection of reviews. *Expert Systems with Applications, 36*(7), 10760–10773.

Turmo, J., Ageno, A., & Català, N. (2006). Adaptive information extraction. *ACM Computing Surveys, 38*(2), 1–47.

Turney, P., & Littman, M. (2003). Measuring praise and criticism: Inference of semantic orientation from association. *ACM Transactions on Information Systems, 21*(4), 315–346.

Vanderwende, L., Suzuki, H., & Brockett, C. (2006, June). *Microsoft Research at DUC 2006: Task-focused summarization with sentence simplification and lexical expansion.* Paper presented at the Document Understanding Workshop, Brooklyn, New York. Retrieved January 12, 2010, from duc.nist.gov/pubs/2006papers/duc2006_MSR_final.pdf

Vanderwende, L., Suzuki, H., Brockett, C., & Nenkova, A. (2007). Beyond SumBasic: Task-focused summarization with sentence simplification and lexical expansion. *Information Processing & Management, 43*(6), 1606–1618.

Wang, X., & McCallum, A. (2006). Topics over time: A non-Markov continuous-time model of topical trends. *Proceedings of the 12th ACM SIGKDD International Conference on Knowledge Discovery and Data Mining.* Retrieved January 12, 2010, from portal.acm.org.proxy2.library.uiuc.edu/toc.cfm?id=1150402&type=proceeding&coll=portal&dl=ACM&CFID=5764831&CFTOKEN=12441359

Wang, X., Mohanty, N., & McCallum, A. (2005). *Group and topic discovery from relations and text.* Paper presented at the Proceedings of the 3rd International Workshop on Link Discovery.

Weeber, M., Vos, R., Klein, H., Berg, L. T. W. d. J.-v. d., Aronson, A. R., & Molema, G. (2003). Generating hypotheses by discovering implicit associations in the literature: A case report of a search for new potential therapeutic uses for Thalidomide. *Journal of the American Medical Association, 10*(3), 252–259.

Wiebe, J., Wilson, T., Bruce, R., Bell, M., & Martin, M. (2004). Learning subjective language. *Computational Linguistics, 30*(3), 277–308.

Wiebe, J., Wilson, T., & Cardie, C. (2005). Annotating expressions of opinions and emotions in language. *Language Resources and Evaluation, 39*(2–3), 165–210.

Xu, H., Stetson, P. D., & Friedman, C. (2007). A study of abbreviations in clinical notes. *American Medical Informatics Association Annual Symposium*, 821–825.

Yang, C. C., & Wang, F. L. (2008). Hierarchical summarization of large documents. *Journal of the American Society for Information Science and Technology, 59*(6), 887–902.

Yang, Y., & Liu, X. (1999). A re-examination of text categorization methods. *Proceedings of the 22nd Annual International ACM SIGIR Conference on Research and Development in Information Retrieval*, 42–49.

Yang, Y., & Pedersen, J. O. (1997). A comparative study on feature selection in text categorization. *Proceedings of the Fourteenth International Conference on Machine Learning*, 412–420.

Yoshida, M., Fukuda, K., & Takagi, T. (2000). PNAD-CSS: A workbench for constructing a protein name abbreviation dictionary. *Bioinformatics, 16*(2), 169–175.

Yu, H., Hripcsak, G., & Friedman, C. (2002). Mapping abbreviations to full forms in biomedical articles. *Journal of the American Medical Informatics Association*, *9*(3), 262–272.

Zajic, D., Dorr, B., Schwartz, R., Monz, C., & Lin, J. (2005, October). *A sentence-trimming approach to multi-document summarization.* Paper presented at the HLT-EMNLP Workshop on Text Summarization, Vancouver, Canada.

CHAPTER 4

Interactive Query Formulation

Nina Wacholder
Rutgers University, New Brunswick, NJ

Introduction

Query formulation (QF) is the stage of the interactive information access process in which an information seeker translates an information need into a query and submits the query to an information access system such as a search engine (e.g., Google) or a library database (e.g., Factiva or PubMed). The system performs some computation to match the query with the documents most likely to be relevant to the query and returns a ranked list of relevant documents to the information seeker.

QF is a key component of the information access process (Bates, 1986; Belkin, Cool, Croft, & Callan, 1993; Blair & Maron, 1985; Hall, Negus, & Dancy, 1972; Kuhlthau, 1991; Marchionini, 1995; Oddy, 1977). It is also very hard (Beghtol, 1986; Belkin, Oddy, & Brooks, 1991, 1982; Swanson, 1960; Taylor, 1968; ter Hofstede, Proper, & van der Weide, 1996). The difficulty of QF is an impediment to development of optimally effective systems—if only users would formulate better queries, information retrieval systems could do a much better job of returning relevant documents.

In addition to being difficult to perform, QF is difficult to study. There are at least three reasons.

First, the QF process takes place inside the human mind. The user's mental representation of the information need and the process of translating that need into a query are not visible to outside observers. Self-reporting, although useful for studying some aspects of information seeking, is of limited use for studying mental representations and cognitive processes that take place below the level of consciousness (Wilson, 1994). Therefore the QF process must be studied indirectly, by analysis of queries or by other externally observable behaviors.

Second, the impact of user characteristics on QF is hard to isolate. It is very difficult to assess the effectiveness of the product of QF—the queries—outside of the context of particular users. For example, in her review of literature on the impact of domain expertise, Wildemuth (2004) concludes that it is possible to generalize about the impact of domain expertise on the vocabulary used in the queries but not about the impact of domain expertise on effectiveness of results. Designing human subject experiments that are carefully controlled, practical, and affordable is also hard; each experiment typically focuses on a very limited aspect of the problem.

Third, the goals of QF and system evaluation are the same. A query is the human-generated input to an automatic system. Therefore the goals of the user and the system are the same—to obtain relevant documents. Meadow, Boyce, and Kraft (2000, p. 313) discuss the challenge this creates for information system evaluation:

> [Is query composition] part of an information retrieval system? If we do not explicitly include it, then poor performance on the part of the user in understanding his or her information need or in explaining the need to an intermediary, or poor performance on the part of an intermediary in translating the need statement in query language may be attributed to poor performance on the part of the [information retrieval system]. On the other hand, to include these preliminary processes in an evaluation requires either that we be able to measure the translation process or that we apply an overall measure to the entire translation retrieval process. In the latter case, we may then be unable to identify the cause of any less than desirable overall system performance.

This observation emphasizes the need for query evaluation that is distinct from system evaluation.

There is also a surprising amount of variation in descriptions of the QF process, as the following examples show:

> Formulating a query—This step in a typical retrieval process entails composing a formulation of the information need in terms suitable for the retrieval system to use. (Meadow et al., 2000, p. 9)

> A query formulation process ... can be said to roughly consist of the following four phases:
>
> 1. The explorative phase. What information is there, how is it related, and what does it mean?
>
> 2. The constructive phase. Construction of the query.
>
> 3. The feedback phase. The result from the query formulated in phase 2 may not be completely satisfactory. In this case, phases 1 and 2 need to be re-done and the result refined.
>
> 4. The presentation phase. In most cases, the result of a query needs to be incorporated into a report or some other document. This means that the results must be grouped or aggregated in some form. (ter Hofstede et al., 1996, p. 256)

Formulation is thinking, developing an understanding, and extending and defining a topic for the information encountered in a search. The formulation of a focus or a guiding idea is a pivotal point in search when a general topic becomes clearer and a particular perspective is formed as the user moves from uncertainty to understanding. (Kuhlthau, 2004, p. 94)

Formulation (what happens before the search) ... is the most complex phase in that it involves decisions of several types, each of which may itself be complex. These decisions include the *sources* of the search, i.e., where to search; which *fields* of documents to search; what actual *text to search for;* and what *variants* of that text to accept. Some systems actually walk the user through each of these decisions in succession, but they cannot always be made in a predetermined order; nor are we convinced they exhaustively cover the query-formulation possibilities. (Shneiderman, Byrd, & Croft, 1997, online, emphasis in original)

These four definitions vary in scope and granularity. Meadow and colleague's definition is the narrowest; it includes only the actual process of translating an information need into a query. Ter Hofstede and colleagues' much broader definition includes the steps the user takes to develop and refine the information need, the initial formulation and reformulation of the query, and the presentation of results to the intended audience. Kuhlthau's definition focuses primarily on the process by which the user develops an understanding of the information need and moves from lack of clarity to a fuller understanding of the information need; but it does not explicitly mention the process of choosing and combining query terms. Shneiderman and colleagues describe some of the decisions that users make during development of the information need and selection of query terms and refer explicitly to the potential incompleteness of their description of the process.

We take it that the varying scope of the definitions reflects the complexity of QF and the difficulty of describing precisely what takes place during this process. The first part of this review therefore describes systematically the different phases of the process that have emerged to date in research on QF. To show the relationship of the different components of QF in an integrated model, we adopt a flow of information approach (Dretske, 1981; Israel & Perry, 1990), which depicts the entities involved in QF and the steps in which information moves between these entities. As represented in the generic model in Figure 4.1 (Wacholder & Liu, 2006), the QF process involves the cognitive processing required to develop and refine the information need and also includes the process of translating the information need into a query. After formulating the query, the user submits it to an automatic information access system

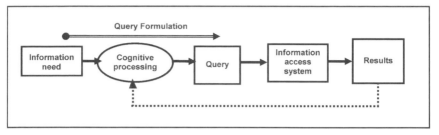

Figure 4.1 Generic model of the QF process.

either by typing a query into a search box or by selecting a query from a displayed list of index terms. With respect to the flow of information, the query mediates between the information seeker and the information access system; it is the observable component of the QF process.

The system processes the query and returns a set of results; depending on the results, the user may decide to quit or to formulate another query. The dotted arrow in Figure 4.1 represents the optional query reformulation process (Efthimiadis, 1996; Marchionini, 1995). This generic view is consistent with the definitions, except that it explicitly excludes the presentation of results; this stage of the information seeking process generally takes place after the cognitive processing involved in QF is complete.

The flow-of-information model allows us to distinguish the different types of research on QF and also to consider the process as whole. Five main approaches to studying interactive QF have emerged in the extensive research literature on this topic:

- Fully automatic QF. By definition, fully automatic information retrieval systems such as the vast majority of those created for the Text REtrieval Conference (TREC) typically are not evaluated with real users (Salton, Buckley, & Fox, 1983; Spärck Jones, 2005; Voorhees, 2003). Automatic QF nevertheless continues to be important for the study of interactive QF. First, the performance of automatically generated queries can be compared with the performance of human-created queries in the same systems. Second, automatic systems can model human processes. Third, fully automatic systems support large scale experiments with multiple controlled queries.

- Basic QF. Each single act of QF can in principle be studied in isolation, independent of previous or subsequent queries, and independent of the system used to process the queries. As has been noted (Meadow et al., 2000), it has been very difficult to figure out how to separate study of the QF process from system effectiveness. One reason is that basic QF, a component of all more complex QF processes, is purely cognitive—it takes place below the level of human consciousness. The importance of the cognitive approach has been widely acknowledged in the information science literature (e.g., Belew, 2000; Belkin, 1990; Ingwersen, 1999; Ingwersen & Järvelin, 2005) but most research has focused on (1) behavior that is observable or self-reportable and (2) techniques for increasing the effectiveness of IR systems.

- Contextualized QF. The literature on the information-seeking process has identified and attempted to measure a wide variety of factors that have an impact on the user's QF process. These factors include, but are not limited to, characteristics of the user, the setting, the system, the domain, and the collection. Other factors may have a major impact on QF: The strategies that users adopt to broaden their understanding of the kind of information that they seek; how they choose resources; and the ways they identify the vocabulary in which their results might best be described. Contextualized QF is one of the most active areas of QF research. However, the study of QF has often been limited by the difficulty of separating the impact of contextual factors from system effectiveness.

- Iterative query formulation. Iterative query reformulation involves creation of a new variant (reformulation) of a previous query (Efthimiadis, 1996; Marchionini, 1995). In the flow-of-information model, query reformulation is treated as a subprocess of the broader QF process. The same basic cognitive process is at the core of iterative QF as in basic QF, but it is more complicated by the iteration process.

- Assistance with query formulation. Recognition of the difficulty of QF has led to substantial effort to develop techniques to help users conduct better searches. Such assistance is something termed *query expansion* or *relevance feedback* (Fu, 2010; Salton & Buckley, 1990; Teevan & Kelly, 2003). This aspect of QF research has received substantial attention because researchers have recognition of the difficulty of QF and the ensuing need to help people use information retrieval systems successfully.

We use these models to distinguish the major streams of active QF research. Underlying the use of the flow-of-information models is the assumption that more specific models of the complex process of QF will make it easier to compare different approaches and lead to the identification of new and significant research questions. Such models will also lead to the development of information retrieval systems designed to respond to user behavior during QF.

This review is organized as follows. In the first section, we describe each type of QF, with a focus on the components of the process and on the extent to which it is possible to study QF in system- and user-independent ways. Next, we discuss cognitive frameworks in which QF can be studied. In the final section, we review emerging trends in three areas that have the potential to help advance our understanding of QF: search engine query logs, query quality (in the sense of "goodness"), and linguistic aspects of QF.

Before proceeding, a caveat is in order. The cited research represents only a subset of the available work. The impossibility of including all potentially relevant research has made the selection of sources for this review undesirably arbitrary.

Approaches to Studying Query Formulation

We start by looking at automatic QF. Although the focus of this review is on interactive QF, the study of automatic QF has much to contribute to our understanding of interactive QF. We begin the review of interactive QF in the next subsection, where we discuss a phase of QF that is basic in the sense that it is a component of every complex construal of QF. Because this process is cognitive, and not much research has focused on basic QF, we consider instead the potential of cognitive science to contribute to our understanding of what happens during QF. In the final subsection we extend the model to include other aspects of the process that cumulatively increase the complexity of interactive QF.

Automatic Query Formulation

In information access systems in which the query is generated by the system itself, there is no human interaction. The primary purpose of these systems and of related research and development is to improve the effectiveness of the system output, as discussed in the influential work of Salton and colleagues (1983). Nevertheless, such systems continue to be of substantial interest in the context of interactive QF. First, the effectiveness of automatically created queries can be compared with human-formulated queries. Second, automatic QF can be used to model interactive QF. Third, large-scale experiments in which characteristics of queries are carefully controlled can be conducted with automatic systems; experiments on such a scale are not feasible with human subjects.

Figure 4.2 depicts the information flow in a fully automatic system. The SMART Information Retrieval system (Salton, 1971) is one of the better known early information retrieval systems. Most systems used in TREC (except for the short-lived interactive track) are also examples (Voorhees, 2003).

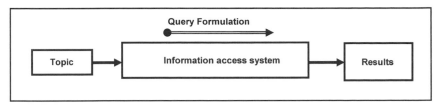

Figure 4.2 Fully automatic QF.

In the TREC experiments, the input is a set of topics composed by experts; the topics have been chosen to represent realistic information needs. The automatic QF process involves translating the topic into one or more queries that are then submitted to the system (Croft et al., 1991; Meadow et al., 2000).

TREC systems are usually evaluated using the Cranfield approach, in which evaluation is conducted in "a laboratory environment … freed as far as possible from the contamination of operational variables" (Cleverdon, 1991, p. 7). Findings from studies that take this approach do not always apply to real users; for example, Hersh, Turpin, Price, Chan, Kramer, and Sacherek (2000) suggest that improvements in system performance do not necessarily offer the same improvement in results to real users. One reason for the lack of such improvements is the difficulty of constructing effective queries.

In spite of criticisms about the inherent limitations associated with the absence of "real users" (Spärck Jones, 2000; Wacholder, Kelly, Kantor, Rittman, Sun, Bai, et al., 2007), TREC research has directly contributed to our understanding of QF by making possible studies that compare human and automatic QF. In a review of TREC achievements, Spärck Jones (2005, p. 428) concludes that fully automated systems "can do as well as minimal manual searching, though not as well as with heavy duty manual query development," where expert searchers engage in extensive effort to develop effective queries. The comparison of the capabilities of fully automatic retrieval systems is important, both for assessment of the quality of automatic systems and for professionals who need to decide what kind of systems to bring to their institutions.

As an alternative to the Cranfield approach, Jordan, Watters, and Gao (2006) use different language models and controlled query generation to construct queries that vary according to properties such as discrimination and length; the researchers systematically measure the impact of these characteristics on effectiveness in a single system. This approach can also be used to compare the impact of query characteristics on system effectiveness across systems.

If the relationship between users and query characteristics can also be studied independently of the relationships between query characteristics and query effectiveness, the results of these two types of research may be combined to produce a more nuanced understanding of the relationship between users and effectiveness.

Basic Query Formulation

We begin the review of interactive QF by looking at basic QF, which starts after the user has finished the process of development of the information need and ends when the query has been submitted. Figure 4.3 represents this stage of the QF process. The input is the information need; the output is the query. The span of QF represented by the double-lined arrow in Figure 4.3 explicitly excludes processing of the information need.

Basic QF is a component of every act of QF. The construal of basic QF conforms to Meadow's definition.

The stage of QF depicted in Figure 4.3 is purely mental and so lends itself to being studied with techniques developed in the increasingly important area of cognitive science (Thagard, 2005). Although there is much literature relating to the cognitive basis of information retrieval (e.g., Belew, 2000; Ingwersen, 1999), to date there has been relatively little in-depth research on basic QF. Lack of understanding of what happens at this stage is therefore a bottleneck in our understanding of interactive QF. Because the applicability of research on mental representations remains controversial in information science and because these techniques have not been applied to QF, we focus on the general applicability of studying mental representation and processes to the study of QF.

Cognitive Study of QF

The justification for the study of basic QF as a cognitive process derives from hypotheses that have emerged in the rapidly growing field of cognitive science.

> The central hypothesis of cognitive science is that thinking can best be understood in terms of representational structures in the mind and computational procedures that operate on those structures.

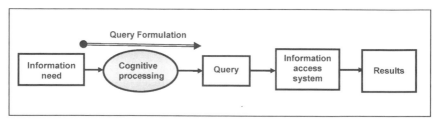

Figure 4.3 Basic query formulation.

Although there is much disagreement about the nature of the representations and computations that constitute thinking, the central hypothesis is general enough to encompass the current range of thinking in cognitive science. (Thagard, 2008, online)

Mental representations are "a theoretical construct of cognitive science" (Pitt, n.d., online), used to explain how people are able to think about entities and processes that exist in the real world (Johnson-Laird [1983], citing Craik [1967, a reissue of a 1943 publication]; see also Pinker [1999a]). Because QF is a cognitive process, it follows that the study of mental representations and mental computations (i.e., processing) are appropriate. A key challenge in the cognitive study of QF is the development of methods to characterize formally and compare the knowledge that users bring to the QF process and the ways in which they draw upon this knowledge to compose the query.

It is of no small interest that the cognitive process represented in Figure 4.3 is directly parallel to the process in which fully automatic systems engage when they are provided with an information need created by domain experts. The respective task of the user in the basic stage of interactive QF and of the system in fully automatic QF is to translate the information need (topic) into a query that will obtain the best results. The most obvious difference is in technology—humans use brains and computers use hardware (Searle, 1990).

Because it is a mental process, basic QF lends itself to study with the methods of cognitive science, including development of computational models and testing of models with computer programs.

A cognitive *theory* postulates a set of representational structures and a set of processes that operate on these structures. A computational *model* makes these structures and processes more precise by interpreting them by analogy with computer programs that consist of data structures and algorithms. Vague ideas about representations can be supplemented by precise computational ideas and data structures, and mental processes can be defined algorithmically. To test the model it must be implemented in a software *program*. (Thagard, 2005, p. 13, emphasis in original)

Our knowledge of the processes that take place during QF is as yet incomplete (Shneiderman et al., 1997). Two types of knowledge have received the most attention in the information science literature:

1. Mental models. Borgman (1985, p. 268) was among the first researchers to apply the notion of mental models to information science; she defined it as "the model of a system that the user has in his or her mind." Borgman's observations about the inaccuracy of users' mental models of information systems have been supported and extended by Aula, Jhaveri,

and Käki (2005), Ruthven (2003) and Muramatsu and Pratt (2001), among others. Although Borgman defines a mental model in terms of the user's understanding of the system, the notion of mental model can also be extended to other kinds of knowledge that have been extensively discussed in the literature. These mental models represent, at least, the user's understanding of the task, domain knowledge, general world knowledge (e.g., whether he or she knows that Kampala is the capital of Uganda), search experience, and any relevant resources that have recently been encountered.

2. Linguistic knowledge. Because queries are composed of words (or word stems), formulation of queries requires a user to call upon at least some linguistic knowledge. Blair (1990, 1992) emphasized the linguistic aspects of queries and document representation. Furthermore, processing of language is a mental process. As Lyons (1995, p. 21) says in his classic work on linguistic semantics, "It is, or ought to be, by now uncontroversial that what Chomsky calls competence in particular natural languages is stored neurophysiologically in the brains of individual members of particular language communities."

Because language competence is stored in the human brain, QF requires the user to draw upon linguistic competence. If a word is not part of one's vocabulary, it cannot be used in query. Basic QF also requires the user to draw upon other basic competencies, as well as general cognitive processes such as retrieval from memory (Anderson, 2007; Baddeley, 1998).

A key advantage of studying basic QF in this way is that it is system-independent—the output of the cognitive processing is the query itself, *before* it is submitted to the information retrieval system. Methodologically, this separates the study of the mental processing in basic QF from the processing of the query that is performed by the information retrieval system. If characteristics of queries (or of other observable behaviors, such as the speed at which queries are entered) can be identified, information retrieval systems can be trained to respond to these cues. A consequence of studying queries in a system-independent way is that techniques for comparing query characteristics are needed. We return to this problem in the section on queries.

Critiques of the Cognitive Approach in Information Science

Any discussion of the potential of cognitive science to contribute to the study of QF would be incomplete without reference to the strong anti-mentalist tradition in library and information science and to continued skepticism about the value of techniques that try to formally model processes that take place in the human mind. Critics of the cognitive approach, represented, for example, by Day (2007), Hjørland (2002), Jacob and Shaw (1998), and Frohmann (1990), argue that it is not useful, at least for information science. Jacob and Shaw criticize the assumption that "the brain is just a digital computer" (Jacob & Shaw [1998, p. 139], quoting Ingwersen [1992], who in turn attributes this quotation to an argument against a strong interpretation of artificial intelligence by Searle). More recently, Day (2007, p. 334) has argued that "The popular conception that performances reflect mental states and contents is ... wrong: such 'states' are cultural categories—not actual mental 'faculties' or other mental 'structures.'"

At a minimum, the claim that the study of cognition relies on the assumption that the brain is just a computer is controversial. Research dating at least from Johnson-Laird (1983) takes the position that studies of cognitive processing are best understood as attempts at simulation of how the mind works, not as attempts at duplication of mental processes. Anderson (2007, p. 10) identifies two key differences between the way information is processed in the brain and the way it is processed by computers: (1) "A brain consists of millions of units operating in parallel, but slowly, whereas the typical computer rapidly executes a sequence of actions"; and (2) "computers are discrete in their actions whereas neurons in the brain are continuous."

The reasonable argument that the cognitive viewpoint should not be seen as a "*total* theory" and as "the *only* theory" (Frohmann, 1992, p. 371, emphasis in original) need not be interpreted to mean that cognitive theory has no place in information science research (Westbrook, 2006). The focus in this review on the potential value of detailed simulations of mental processes can also be distinguished from the methodological approach adopted in the socio-cognitive literature on information retrieval (Ingwersen, 1996; Ingwersen & Järvelin, 2005; Larsen & Ingwersen, 2005; Larsen, Ingwersen, & Kekäläinen, 2006), a "holistic and explicitly cognitive framework for understanding the processes involved in Information Retrieval" (Larsen & Ingwersen, 2005, p. 43). In general, advocates of the socio-cognitive framework have stepped back from the use of methods that lead to studies of internal mental processing. For example, in her study of the theory of mental models within the socio-cognitive framework, Westbrook, citing Jacob and Shaw (1998), implies that techniques used in the sense-making approach to the study of information science are more informative.

> The primary difficulty in using mental model theory to support information system design lies in the mystery of the individual mind. The sense-making, grounded-theory approach of communication and information studies minimizes this difficulty through the use of interviews, observation, and think-aloud protocols. (Westbrook, 2006, p. 577)

Westbrook's objection is to the difficulty of studying mental representations, rather than to the importance of studying them.

The problem with the use of the methods preferred by Westbrook is that cognitive processing of information occurs very quickly, beneath the level of consciousness. For example, experiments show that one can retrieve words from one's mental lexicon in milliseconds (McNamara, 2005). People therefore have limited ability to report accurately on what happens during this processing (Johnson-Laird, 1983; Russo, Johnson, & Stephens, 1989; Wilson, 1994). Studies that rely on self-reporting by participants, such as that by Freund and Toms (2002), are important and interesting for the information they provide about users' perceptions of the QF process and their understanding of the system; but these studies provide only suggestive data for construction of a model of QF. Cognitive processing must be studied indirectly. Among the major contributions of cognitive science is the development of new techniques for collecting experimental data that can be used to develop and/or disprove models of human cognition. These techniques are already widely used in psychology, linguistics, and the study of human-computer interaction.

It is likely to take a substantial amount of work to identify promising models of QF; and it is also possible that the skepticism about the application of techniques that study mental processing to information science will ultimately be shown to be correct. At the same time, research on mental representations and processes has the potential to contribute to a more precise understanding of information-seeking behavior and ultimately to lead to the development of better systems.

Complex Query Formulation

In this section we look at research that is related to three increasingly complex construals of interactive QF: contextualized, iterative, and assisted.

Contextualized Query Formulation

We refer to the study of QF that includes development of the information need, especially as it affects QF, as contextualized QF. The term *contextualized* is used to indicate that characteristics of the user, setting, and domain directly affect the development of the information need and indirectly affect the query itself. The double arrow in Figure 4.4 indicates that in this construal, QF begins with the development of the information need. The dotted arrow represents the optional iterative processing of the information need that takes place, along with basic QF, during the contextualized QF.

Contextual QF takes into account the cognitive processing involved in development of the information need, as well as the cognitive process involved in basic QF. Like basic QF, contextualized QF can be studied in terms of the knowledge and processes involved in generation of a query, independent of the effectiveness of the query in any particular system.

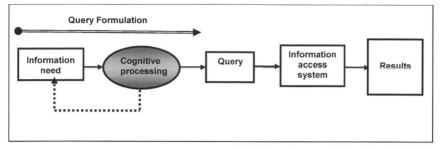

Figure 4.4   Contextual query formulation.

We can distinguish several components of the development of the information need that are likely to have a direct effect on the exact formulation of the query. This is in addition to the lower level processes, such as language processing and retrieval of information from memory, which are part of basic QF.

1. The process by which "knowledge in the world" becomes "knowledge in the head" (Norman, 1990, p. 54) is part of the cognitive processing that users engage in as they refine their understanding of an information need. As an example, Norman reports that students could not remember how digits and letters were arranged on a standard rotary telephone dial. Even for a familiar activity such as dialing a telephone (used to be), people need the cues provided by an external source—in this case, the symbols on the dial. In the same way, a user engaged in the process of mentally refining an information need may integrate information obtained from external sources such as lists of recommended terms or recently viewed pages.

2. More specifically, scanning or reading resources that extend the user's understanding of the information need and/or help identify language that may be useful in the query is a crucial part of good QF technique. Research on this part of the problem has been conducted, for example, by Spink and Saracevic (1997), who considered possibilities such as whether terms were derived from a thesaurus or from the user's domain knowledge and by Vakkari, Pennanen, and Serola (2003), who looked at the longitudinal evolution of search terms.

3. Choosing and carrying out what Bates (1990, p. 578) referred to as a "stratagem," a set of tactics or moves "designed to exploit the structure of a particular search domain thought to

contain desired information." For example, a user might browse a journal or search for citations. Developing a stratagem requires the user to decide what resources to use, to learn to use them, and to find useful results. Each stratagem is itself potentially complex.

4. User feelings such as uncertainty and anxiety (Kuhlthau, 1991, 2004) are known to affect the search outcome. As these feelings evolve, they may also play a role in the mental processing of the information need and the formulation of the query that the user develops. A fully integrated model of contextual QF will need to factor in the possible impact of psychological state on QF.

In contextualized QF, a key research goal is to focus on the relationship between processing the information need and its impact on QF. This includes study of characteristics of individuals that have an impact on QF. The most extensively studied characteristic of information seekers in the context of QF is domain expertise, (e.g., Allen, 1991; Hsieh-Yee, 1993; Shute & Smith, 1993; Sihvonen & Vakkari, 2004; Vakkari, 2002; Vakkari et al., 2003). In a review of this work, Wildemuth (2004, p. 257) distinguishes studies that assess the impact of domain knowledge on the choice of search terms from those that measure the effect of domain knowledge on the success of the retrieval process; she concludes that studies consistently "support the proposition that the searcher's level of knowledge in the domain of the search will affect the type and number of terms." In contrast, "the effects of a searcher's domain knowledge on search results are still in question" (p. 248). Wildemuth's conclusion suggests that the most promising approach to the study of contextualized QF is to look for relationships between characteristics of the user and characteristics of the queries rather than for relationships between characteristics of users and effectiveness of queries. In a study designed specifically to identify this relationship, Hembrooke, Granka, Gay, and Liddy (2005, p. 865) examined the characteristics of the queries used by domain novices and experts; they found a difference in the number of unique terms and in the overall complexity of the queries by "dividing the number of unique terms per search session by the total number of search terms in the session." As will be discussed, they relate the difference in performance to the conceptual knowledge that users bring to the search process.

Iterative Query Formulation

In the study of iterative QF, often referred to as query reformulation (Efthimiadis, 1996), the focus is on the change(s) that users make on new queries relative to earlier ones. It is only *after* the user has seen the results of a previous query that reformulation can begin. A reformulated query is therefore crucially distinguished from an initial query.

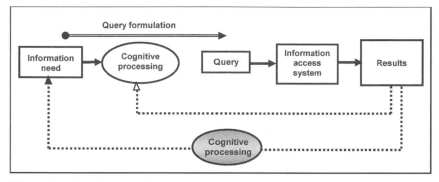

Figure 4.5   Iterative query formulation.

Figure 4.5 illustrates one of the key elements of query reformulation—the information seeker has input from the results of previous searches (from the same session). Basic QF is at the core of iterative QF but the process is modulated by the additional entities and increased complexity of the flow of information.

A user engaged in query reformulation therefore has at least some information about the effectiveness of the query and about how the system works.[1] The more one engages in reformulation, the greater the potential learning about how the system works.

Our ability to study query reformulation in particular has been vastly enhanced over the past ten or so years by the availability of search engine logs containing millions of queries (Brenes & Gayo-Avello, 2009; Downey, Dumais, & Horvitz, 2007; Jansen, Spink, & Saracevic, 2000; Rieh & Xie, 2006).[2] These queries are "real" or natural in the sense that they were created by information seekers engaged in their own pursuit of information, rather than in an experimental environment. Often each query is labeled with the time the query was submitted to the search engine and by a unique user ID; more recent search engine logs also contain a list of URLs presented in the most highly ranked results and the "clickthroughs," the webpages that the information seeker opened. These logs make it possible to track a sequence of queries submitted by a specific user and to study queries on a scale previously unimaginable. These search logs have opened up the study of query refinement. For example, before these logs became available we had no data about the extent to which users engaged in iterative QF; according to Rieh and Xie (2006), approximately half of all web users reformulate their initial queries.

The extraction of reformulated queries from these logs has led to the emergence over the last decade of a new stream of research focused on the type of changes in a reformulated query relative to earlier ones (e.g., Rieh & Xie, 2006; Sutcliffe & Ennis, 1998). The goal of much of this work is system improvement—predicting changes from one query to the next is a way to determine when to provide assistance to the user (Huang & Efthimiadis, 2009; Jansen, Booth, & Spink, 2009; Lau & Horvitz, 1998).

In any study where a user formulates queries that serve as input to a real system and also sees the results, iterative QF is system dependent. Turpin and Scholer (2006) and Allan, Carterette, and Lewis (2005) show that users adjust their search behavior in response to search results. However, it is possible to devise experimental approaches to query reformulation that are system independent. For example, Smith and Kantor (2008) report on an experiment in which results of Google-like searches were manipulated so that some subjects saw better results and others got worse results. Overall, searchers using the regular and the degraded systems achieved the same level of search success by adjusting the rate at which they submitted reformulated queries. Manipulating the results that experimental participants see is one way to conduct user studies of iterative QF independently of specific systems.

Assisted Query Formulation

Query assistance, sometimes referred to as term relevance feedback or query expansion, adds complexity to the flow of information by presenting to the user possible query terms while the user is engaged in the QF process. Query assistance is intended to help the user to formulate the query and obtain relevant results. Figure 4.6 shows the points where additional information may be inserted into the flow-of-information. If the suggestions are perceived as helpful by the user, they are likely to be welcomed; otherwise, the user may experience the suggestions as an unwelcome interruption of the QF process (Oard & Kim, 2001).

Point A occurs before the user has submitted a query. If an information access system provides the user with access to a list of descriptors, QF involves what Fidel (1991, p. 490) refers to as "selection of search keys": the information seeker must decide whether to consult the list of descriptors or to formulate the queries without assistance. Library databases traditionally have provided assistance at Point A in the form of displayed indexes. Earlier search engines did not do this but state-of-the-art search systems engines now provide assistance with QF at Point A (and at later points) in the form of recommended queries retrieved from search logs (Baeza-Yates, Hurtado, & Mendoza, 2005). At point B, the system provides query expansion such as synonyms or related terms; sources of query expansion might be, for example, a thesaurus or list of words in the document set being searched. Query assistance provided at point C may be more sophisticated, in that it may include queries identified based on terms used in other queries and also based on the results of those queries.

The study of assisted QF, like that of iterative QF, has received a great deal of attention because of its potential to help compensate for the indeterminacy of queries in real systems. Search engines now make extensive use of query suggestion techniques that are produced when the user begins to type a query into the search box; the system provides

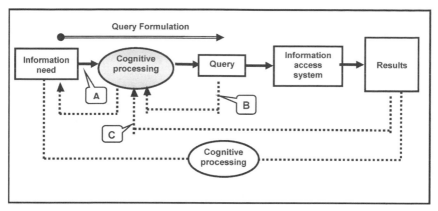

Figure 4.6   System-provided assistance to interactive QF.

suggestions for query completion. These suggestions may be based, for example, on popular queries, queries that have previously been success-ful, and/or characteristics of potentially relevant documents (Baeza-Yates et al., 2005; Billerbeck, Scholer, Williams, & Zobel, 2003; Fitzpatrick & Dent, 1997; Mei, Zhou, & Church, 2008; Smyth, Balfe, Freyne, Briggs, Coyle, & Boydell, 2004). At present, the primary source of terms for query recommender systems is search logs (Boldi, Bonchi, Castillo, Donato, & Vigna, 2009).

Research on users' responses (or lack thereof) to query suggestions is of particular interest to QF. Kelly and Fu (2006) provide a good sum-mary of the literature on the effectiveness of query suggestions. Factors that may affect user response to suggestions include, but are not limited to, the technique by which the suggested terms have been identified, the presentation of the suggestions such as time and method of display, the technique used to create the suggested terms, and the presentation of the suggested terms (Kelly, Gyllstrom, & Bailey, 2009; White & Marchionini, 2007). There is also evidence that users sometimes reject query recommendations, even when they are potentially useful (White & Morris, 2007).

In the real world, the effectiveness of query assistance that is pro-vided at points B and C depends both on the information retrieval sys-tem and on the system that generates the suggestions. But systematic control of the characteristics of the suggested terms and comparison of users' responses to these terms may also shed light on query quality.

QF: A Complex Process

We began this review with the acknowledgement that QF is hard for users to do well and hard for researchers to study. The varying descrip-tions of QF discussed in the first section reflect the complexity of QF and the variety of perspectives from which it can be studied. The definition by Meadow and colleagues (2000) corresponds to basic QF, the process that takes place after the user has finished the cognitive processing of the information need and encompasses only the formation of the query that the user then submits to the system. The definition from ter Hofstede and colleagues (1996) is the broadest; it includes the exploratory phase, which is an aspect of the processing that takes place as part of development and refinement of the information need; the constructive phase, which corresponds to what we refer to here as basic QF; and the feedback phase, which corresponds to iterative QF. The presentation phase that ter Hofstede and colleagues identify takes place after QF is complete; therefore it is not included in the flow-of-information models here. The process of interpreting and extending the information need that Kuhlthau (2004) describes also takes place at the point where the information need is being developed; the quoted definition does not incorporate basic QF. The definition by Shneiderman and colleagues (1997) is expressed in terms of the decisions the user needs to make during development of the information need and during basic QF; thinking about the decisions that must be made is one way to figure out what processes are involved in making these decisions. The varying definitions and the focus on different aspects of the process reflect the complexity of QF, as well as our incomplete understanding of the process.

To provide a holistic model of QF, we used the flow-of-information representation of QF that Wacholder and Liu (2006) proposed. In looking at research threads associated with the different QF models, it is clear that the basic QF process—a component of all types of interactive QF—has been less studied than contextualized, iterative, and assisted QF. The basic reasons are those listed in the introduction to this chapter: (1) QF takes place in the human mind, below the level of consciousness. Research methods that rely on user introspection are not sufficient. (2) Efforts to identify the impact of user characteristics on search effectiveness have enjoyed limited success. (3) In information access systems, the information system and the user of that system are two distinct, interacting entities. But there is only a single product of the interaction—a set of search results. It is therefore very hard to separate out the impact of the system from that of the user on the system output.

In the next section we talk about promising research approaches, results, and techniques that are likely to advance our knowledge of QF.

Emerging Approaches for Advancing Our Present State of Knowledge About QF

The review of the literature thus far has led to the identification (or re-iteration) of several challenges in QF research:

1. QF is very complex. Westbrook's (2006, p. 566) observation that "the more models are required for a task, the greater the

complexity of the work and, generally, the poorer the performance" certainly applies to QF.

2. Limitations in our ability to study the cognitive processes
   involved in basic QF constitutes a major research bottleneck.

3. We do not yet have (arguably) complete models of the types
   of mental representations and cognitive processing involved
   in QF.

This focus on what we do not yet know shows the breadth of opportunity for more research on all of these issues. In this section, we bring
together a potpourri of QF-related research that may serve as a foundation advancing our understanding of QF and become part of (perhaps
competing) integrated models of QF. First, we consider types of cognitive
models that are potentially useful for the study of QF.

Cognitive Models of the QF Process

In this section we consider the question of what kinds of theoretical models are appropriate for studying cognitive aspects of QF. One notion that
has received considerable attention in the information science literature
is that of mental models, a construct that emerged out of substantial
effort to understand how the mind works (Craik, 1967; Johnson-Laird,
1983). In the information science literature, this work generally emphasizes the discrepancy between a user's model of the information retrieval
system (including the documents in the system) and the reality of the
system, instead of developing a detailed representation of this model.

Some researchers have specifically suggested that aspects of the QF
process may call upon non-conscious processing that is generally studied
in cognitive science. For example, Willie and Bruza (1995) hypothesize
that query refinement and query assembly may call upon different levels of storage of knowledge in memory; they suggest that the behavior
they observed could be understood in terms of the difference between
Barsalou's feature lists and Minsky's frames. Cole (2000, p. 417) identifies three cognitive systems that come into play when a user receives a
message from an interactive system that shapes his or her model of the
information system: the perception subsystem, which involves visual
processing; the comprehension subsystem, in which the user processes
the content of the message, and the application system, in which the
user "interpret[s] the system message in terms of the user's task at
hand, and ... create[s] and send[s] a new message back to the system to
complete the interaction."[3]

Sutcliffe and Ennis (1998) propose some simple examples of non-
linguistic mental rules that information seekers might use for building
queries:

1. If the information need is simple, create a query using a
   single keyword.

2. If the information need is complex and the information seeker has a good understanding of how the information access system works, construct a Boolean query.

3. If the information need is complex and the information seeker has limited understanding of how the information access system works, create a query that consists of multiple terms; after seeing the results of this initial query, iterate.

As Sutcliffe and Ennis acknowledge, this is a very simple model and this work needs to be taken further.

Hembrooke and colleagues (2005, p. 868) adopted a methodology based on "inferences in cognitive psychology," which situates differences in the behavior of novices and experts in terms of the extent of their knowledge of the search topic. As with mental models of the information system, this knowledge may be incomplete or inaccurate. Hembrooke and colleagues draw an explicit connection between users' adaptive responses as displayed in iterative QF and the information foraging theory developed by Fu and Pirolli (2007); Chi, Pirolli, Chen, and Pitkow (2001); Pirolli & Card (1999); and Pirolli (1997). Information foraging theory is situated within the framework of the ACT-R (Adaptive Character of Thought) theory (Anderson, 2007; Anderson, Bothell, Byrne, Douglas, Lebiere, & Qin, 2004); the goal of ACT-R is to understand how all of the components of the mind work together to produce coherent results. More specifically, ACT-R is a cognitive architecture, defined as "a specification of the structure of the brain at a level of abstraction that explains how it achieves the function of the mind" (Anderson, 2007, p. 7).

The primary application of information foraging theory is to web browsing, where people look for information in electronic documents and then, based on the information need and the information they encounter, make a variety of decisions, such as which documents to view next. As such, it is not directly relevant to basic QF. The usefulness of information foraging theory to advancing our understanding of web navigation and the focus of ACT-R research on issues that are important to QF, such as the integration of different kinds of knowledge and the retrieval of vocabulary from memory, suggest that ACT-R theory may also provide a basis for advancing our understanding of the complex processes involved in basic QF.

Emerging Techniques in Cognitive Science

The inaccessibility of cognitive processing to introspection has led to the development of new techniques that are now well accepted as sources of information about mental processing. Eye tracking is a technique in which users wear headsets that allow a computer program to track the movements of their eyes as they focus on a particular part of a page or shift their gaze from one part of a page to another. Eye movements have been studied at least since the late 19th century; by now, the technology is able to track very fine movements and identify accurately the parts of a page that the user is looking at and for how long (Just & Carpenter, 1976; Rayner, 1998; Salvucci, 2001). There are two primary eye behaviors: saccades and fixations. During saccades, the eyes move very rapidly; saccades often reflect a shift of focus or attention. During fixations, the eyes hold relatively still; at this time, the user is perceiving information. Eye tracking has increasingly been adopted by the human-computer interface community in general (Jacob & Karn, 2004) and applied to information seeking and search engine use in particular. Several researchers (e.g., Clarke, Agichtein, Dumais, & White, 2007; Cutrell & Guan, 2007; Granka, Joachims, & Gay, 2004; Joachims, Granka, Pan, Hembrooke, & Gay, 2005; Joachims, Granka, Pan, Hembrooke, Radlinski, & Gay, 2007) use eye tracking to identify the parts of webpages that users look at when they are using search engines and to analyze how the webpages that people look at affect their subsequent actions. QF is mentioned in this literature, but not extensively discussed. However, it seems quite likely that eye tracking can be used to study, for example, the influence of what an individual has just seen on QF.

Semantic priming has been used, especially in psychology and psycholinguistics, to make inferences about people's perceptions of word relationships and on their ability to retrieve word knowledge in different contexts (McNamara, 2005). People respond significantly more quickly (measured in milliseconds) to semantically related words such as *egg* and *bird* than to unrelated words such as *egg* and *phone*. The semantic priming effect is quite robust, although there are competing theories for this phenomenon. Smith and Wacholder (2010) conducted an experiment in which semantic priming is used as an indicator of a searcher's perception of relationships among words.

Another technique that may be useful for studying QF involves monitoring cognitive load, a measure of the mental effort required to perform a task (Sweller, 1988). Dennis, McArthur, and Bruza (1998) measured the cognitive load imposed by two different query refinement mechanisms using a dual task methodology—for example, while users were engaged in information seeking, they were asked to perform another task as well. Physiological measures (such as pulse rate) that measure stress have also been used (Iani, Gopher, & Lavie, 2004).

Queries

In this section, we focus on the characteristics of queries, which are the visible product of the interactive QF process; here *visible* means that queries users submit to automatic systems can be logged, extracted, and studied by researchers. We consider three ways of studying queries: analysis of search logs, the linguistic characteristics of queries, and query quality.

Data Mining and Query Characteristics

Some of the most remarkable advances in information science over the last decade have arisen from the availability of search engine logs containing millions of queries. The application of data mining techniques to these logs makes them a rich source of information about queries and query characteristics (Baeza-Yates, 2005; Boldi et al., 2009; Srivastava, Cooley, Deshpande, & Tan, 2000). The development of sophisticated new techniques for finding patterns in search logs has enabled us to identify patterns across queries that were not evident in smaller-scale experimental studies conducted prior to the availability of search logs.

The early work in collecting information from search logs described query characteristics. It is now well known that most search engine queries are only two or three words long and do not make use of what search engines call "advanced search features"; in fact, more than half of all queries that use advanced features contain mistakes in them (Jansen, 2003; Spink, Wolfram, Jansen, & Saracevic, 2001). Because queries are short and usually do not include search operators, they are content-impoverished representations of the information need.

More recent research has attempted to go beyond description. User intention, for instance, has seen substantial work. Rose and Levinson (2004), refining the work of Broder (2002), identified three search goals: navigational, informational, and research. Jansen, Booth, and Spink (2008) developed a system for classifying search goals with 75 percent accuracy. White, Dumais, and Teevan (2009) linked queries that are ambiguous with regard to intent with patterns in query history and viewed documents. They also demonstrated that domain experts use move diverse vocabulary than do non-experts, as Hembrooke and colleagues (2005) also reported. Brenes, Gayo-Avello, and Pérez-González (2009) surveyed the techniques used for automatically identifying query intention; they suggested that in addition to systematic comparison of techniques, we need to develop an accurately annotated and labeled gold standard to compare different approaches to intent identification.

Query Quality

In this section we consider the issue of query quality, the characteristics of queries that make some better than others in the context of the information-seeking process (Wacholder & Liu, 2006, 2008). White and Marchionini (2007, p. 692) point out that "query quality is a complex construct that is dependent on many factors such as the searcher's knowledge about the need, search experience, system experience, and the mapping between the need and the information source." The standard metric for quality of information retrieval systems is effectiveness, a system-dependent measure of the quality of the results returned by the system (van Rijsbergen, 2004). The use of effectiveness as the primary measure of information retrieval success is one reason that it is difficult to separate the impact of these different factors. But, although it is easy to demonstrate the limitations of the effectiveness measure, it is harder to come up with meaningful and reliable measures of query quality outside of the context of particular systems.

Over the last decade or so, three approaches to system-independent assessment of query quality have emerged: (1) human assessment of query quality, (2) measurement of query characteristics that predict the effectiveness of the results of a query prior to the availability of ranked search results, and (3) controlled generation of queries with certain characteristics in order to compare query effectiveness within and across systems.

System-Independent Assessment of Query Quality

The obvious way to make system-independent judgments of query quality is to ask users to make them. The problem, of course, is how to determine what quality is. A couple of recent studies have attempted to develop system-independent measures of query quality and have also used techniques for assessment of quality that take into account the variability of human judgment. White and Marchionini's (2007) study of the effectiveness of real-time query expansion asked judges to assess the quality of queries in the context of a particular information need. Assessment was based on whether the queries included key concepts associated with the information need. The average score of two judges determined the quality rating.

Song, Luo, Wen, Yu, and Hon (2007) developed a taxonomy of query types (ambiguous, broad, and clear) and asked five human judges to make the assessment. The authors provide only limited details about how the judgments were collected. They found 90 percent agreement among subjects as to which queries were ambiguous but much less agreement about broadness and clarity of terms. The judgments of query quality techniques of White and Marchionini and of Song and colleagues were both developed to improve automatic information retrieval systems, rather than for the explicit study of query quality.

In an attempt to establish a cognitively valid, user-centered measure of query quality, Wacholder and Liu (2006, p. 1566) used a metric called "user preference" to measure the mental effort required of users in QF. Instead of formulating a query, participants selected from a displayed list of queries that had been developed by three different techniques. Having users select queries rather than compose them made it possible to present a limited set of possible queries and have the users determine which they preferred. Users showed a much stronger preference for queries composed by humans than for those generated by computer programs. Kelly and colleagues (2009), report similar results: Participants who received query suggestions created by humans used significantly more suggestions than those who received system-generated suggestions.

Query Performance Predictors

TREC-like systems that automatically generate queries have used a number of metrics that do not rely on human judgment to assess query quality. These metrics, such as length and ambiguity, can be used in a system-independent way but are usually employed to assess the performance of information retrieval systems. For example, queries of greater length have been associated with greater retrieval effectiveness in automatic systems (Buckley, Salton, & Allan, 1994). The lesser effectiveness of shorter queries is widely understood as applying to queries formulated by humans as well (Belkin, Kelly, Kim, Kim, Lee, Muresan, et al., 2003). However, long queries that contain too many descriptive words can also be problematic for information retrieval systems. Kumaran and Carvalho (2009) report that reducing the length of TREC queries improves precision by as much as 30 percent.

The clarity score predicts query effectiveness by measuring the relative entropy between the language of the query and the language of the documents in the collection (Carmel, Yom-Tov, Darlow, & Pelleg, 2006; Cronen-Townsend & Croft, 2002; Cronen-Townsend, Zhou, & Croft, 2002; Hauff, Hiemstra, & Jong, 2008; Hauff, Murdock, & Baeza-Yates, 2008; Liu, Yu, & Meng, 2005). This metric was designed to test a hypothesis about query effectiveness. Effective queries are not ambiguous in the sense that they are likely to retrieve relatively few documents. Ineffective queries are ambiguous in the sense that they are likely to retrieve many irrelevant documents. Whether the clarity score is system-independent depends on whether the collection is included in the definition of an information retrieval system. Still, clarity scores are typically used to *predict* query effectiveness using data about the language of the documents in the collection.

Humans cannot make this kind of prediction for large and diverse collections. Turpin and Hersh (2004) note that clarity of user queries submitted to the TREC Interactive Track did not correlate with greater search effectiveness. Furthermore, the overall clarity scores of the users, including those of advanced searchers, were very low. Liu (2009, p. 73) reports a similar result, that the TREC information retrieval systems generally performed much better than human searchers, including domain experts and search experts, at least on hard biomedical searches.

Controlled Generation of Queries

The impact of query characteristics on search results has been studied in a user-independent context, using controlled generation of automatic queries as a way both to study query effectiveness and also to understand user behavior. As mentioned, Jordan and colleagues (2006) use different language models and controlled query generation to construct systematically queries that vary according to properties such as discrimination and length. This makes possible direct study of the effect of query properties on effectiveness. Azzopardi (2009, p. 556) takes this research a step further by proposing that "query side evaluation," which focuses on characteristics of queries and their relationship to effectiveness, can lead to development of better systems and also advance our understanding of human QF. As an example of such an effort, he studies the relationship between query length and effectiveness using three strategies designed to simulate human behavior in QF: (1) discrimination; (2) frequency, which models user selection of terms likely to appear in documents; and (3) conditional querying, where the user's selection of query terms is conditioned by exposure to some information about a topic. The results show across these models of QF that queries with lengths of 3 to 5 terms are most effective. Based on these results, Azzopardi (p. 562) posits that queries of this length provide users with "the most bang for their buck" and argues that an economic model, whereby users seek to expend as little effort as possible, helps to account for user behavior; however, he does not draw an explicit connection between his research and the ecological aspects of the information foraging model.

To summarize the discussion of query quality, each of these approaches measures a dimension of query quality that can be studied in a system-independent way. But except with regard to relatively easily quantified features of queries such as length, demonstrably valid, broad generalizations about query quality across systems are limited.

Queries as Linguistic Entities

Blair (1992, p. 200) argues that "information retrieval systems are fundamentally linguistic in nature—in essence, the languages of document representation and searching are dialects of natural language." Blair's argument can be taken a step further by asking what are the linguistic properties of the query dialect. On one hand, queries are composed of words or word-bases, which are linguistic entities. On the other hand, queries typically do not consist of full sentences, or even of grammatical units such as noun phrases. The inability of current information retrieval systems to "understand" the syntax and semantics of a complete sentence, plus, perhaps, an economy of effort (Azzopardi, 2009), means that most users issue short queries.

Queries have been analyzed along three dimensions that are important for the study of natural language: query vocabulary—the words or word-bases used in a query; query syntax—the method for combining query terms using explicit or implicit operators; and query semantics— the meaning of the query and its terms.[4] In this section, we review linguistic aspects of QF.

Query Vocabulary

QF requires users to choose one or more words or word-bases that they believe are likely to retrieve relevant documents. Human language is characterized by extensive ambiguity (single words have multiple meanings) and synonomy (multiple ways to express the same idea). For example, WordNet 3.0 (wordnetweb.princeton.edu/perl/webwn) lists seven distinct senses for the noun *cell*; Thesaurus.com (thesaurus.reference.com/browse/anger) lists more than 35 synonyms for the noun *anger*. Because there are so many ways to express a concept, the process of formulating a query inevitably requires a choice of words on the part of users, even if they are not aware of making a choice.

The inconsistency people show in assigning labels to similar entities is well documented (e.g., Bates, 1998; Furnas, Landauer, Gomez, & Dumais, 1987; Gomez, Lochbaum, & Landauer, 1990; Saracevic & Kantor, 1988). Blair and Maron (1985) compare the challenge of formulating a query that will retrieve all and only relevant documents with that of figuring out how to open a combination lock without knowing the combination. The vocabulary problem is particularly challenging for people looking for information outside their domains of expertise (Hsieh-Yee, 1993; Vakkari et al., 2003).

A key concept from linguistics is the *mental lexicon*, a representation of the phonology, morphology, and semantics of the words in an individual's vocabulary (Aitchison, 2003). People can use or recognize only words that are part of their mental lexicons. Furthermore, there is robust evidence from psycholinguistics that when a word is *activated* in the brain (activation occurs when one is engaging in thought or speech acts that call upon the individual's knowledge of a particular word), semantically related words are also activated (McNamara, 2005). Mental lexicons can be studied both in terms of the words that are in the vocabulary of an individual and in terms of the kind of information that is available (Pinker, 1999b).

The study of vocabulary choice in QF involves assessing the extent to which users draw on the words in their mental lexicons and the users' judgments (whether or not the judgments are accurate) of the language used in relevant documents. Other factors such as exposure to possible search terms (e.g., in recently viewed documents), may also play a role. Spink and Saracevic (1997) identified sources of search terms such as a thesaurus or previously viewed pages. Kelly and Fu (2006) looked at use of words in queries that had appeared in the interface or come from suggestions formulated by human users; their results suggest that more terms came from the interface than from users. Ferber, Wettler, and Rapp (1995) used a lexical net to simulate the associative processes involved in word choice during QF. Smith and Wacholder (2010) have recently suggested that the very processing of the query may sometimes inhibit users from recognizing the potential usefulness of related words. The availability of search queries logs with large numbers of reformulated queries, discussed previously, has made it possible to study a user's modification of vocabulary (e.g., adding or removing words or word-bases) during the search process.

Query Syntax

In the linguistic sense, syntax refers "only to the ways in which words combine into phrases and phrases into sentences" (Sag & Wasow, 1999, p. 3). The linguistic use of the term *syntax* is different from its use in information science, where query syntax refers to the way that terms are combined in order to form a query. Each information access system "expects" one or more of three basic types of queries: unstructured, Boolean, and natural language. Unstructured (bag of word) queries (Croft, Turtle, & Lewis, 1991) consist of one or more words not connected by standard grammar or by search operators (e.g., *dog apple*). In Boolean syntax, query terms are combined using algebraic Boolean operators. Most non-professional searchers are not comfortable with strict Boolean syntax, which is based on set theory and Boolean algebra (Baeza-Yates & Ribeira-Neto, 1999). Search engines such as Google have adopted a simpler syntax, such as the "+" operator, which specifies that a search term should occur in the retrieved documents. Neither unstructured nor Boolean queries has syntax in the linguistic sense.

In natural language syntax, as understood in the information science literature, queries consist of a grammatical sequence of words that could be used in ordinary speech or writing. Natural language queries that consist of sentences or grammatical phrases thus have syntax in the linguistic sense. But, although a user can express a query using natural language syntax, the retrieval system may not treat the question as a syntactic unit. For example, automatic question-answering systems that accept queries structured as complex phrases or full sentences have sometimes been billed as systems that understand the user's intended meaning (Griffith, 1992). In practice, the systems decompose the questions into words or phrases and submit them to a standard information retrieval system (e.g., Radev, Qi, Zheng, Blair-Goldensohn, Zhang, & Fan, 2001; Soricut & Brill, 2006).

Searchers have responded to the behavior of information retrieval systems by using query terms that tend not to form coherent grammatical units. Recent work by Barr, Jones, and Regelson (2008, p. 1027), however, suggests that queries do "exhibit some degree of syntactical structure." Using automatic part-of-speech taggers developed for natural language processing, they studied part-of-speech (e.g., noun, verb) associated with query terms; the rationale for this research was the hypothesis "that queries exhibit their own partially predictable and unique linguistic structure different from that of the natural language of indexed documents" (p. 1022). Barr and colleagues observed that a purely non-linguistic model of QF is too simple.

From the perspective of Blair's observation that the language of searching is a dialect of language, teasing apart the extent to which query syntax draws on syntactic processes that have linguistic elements and on the extent to which it draws on non-linguistic processes of compositionality is an interesting question.

Query Semantics

Lyons (1995, p. xii) defines linguistic semantics as "the study of meaning as it is systematically encoded in the vocabulary and grammar of (so called) natural languages." Because natural language syntax is not a substantial component of QF, the main area of linguistic semantics of relevance to QF is lexical semantics—the relationship between the form of a word (its phonology and/or spelling) and its meaning (Fellbaum, 1998; Miller, Beckwith, Fellbaum, Gross, & Miller, 1990). The WordNet Project, which has been led primarily by Miller and Fellbaum, uses semantic relationships such as synonymy and antonymy to link related words.

The significance of semantic relations in information science was recently reviewed in *ARIST* (Khoo & Na, 2006). To the extent that QF was discussed, the focus was on the mixed results of using semantically related terms for automatic query expansion. Baeza-Yates and Tiberi (2007, p. 76) identified semantic relations among queries in a search log as an initial step toward identifying characteristics of "webslang." But in general, the study of semantic relations is likely to be less important for the study of interactive QF than will be the investigation of the semantics of vocabulary choice—what aspects of word meaning affect the user's decision to include a term in a query.

Summary of Linguistic Issues in QF

Although the linguistic dimension of QF and information retrieval has been recognized in the information science literature, progress on this front has been slow. However, in the past decade data-driven observations, enabled in part by the study of query logs, have started to emerge. Study of vocabulary use and vocabulary sources is likely to continue to make the most progress in the foreseeable future because of the availability of techniques to test people's knowledge of words, to compare the words they choose to use in search queries with the words that appear in resources that they have viewed relatively recently, and to analyze semantic relationships among the words users choose to include in queries.

Conclusion

Since the earliest research on information retrieval, there has been widespread recognition that interactive QF is hard to study. A review of the literature suggests three main reasons: (1) Basic QF takes place inside the human mind; (2) It is very hard to establish strong correlations between user characteristics and system effectiveness; and (3) When effectiveness is used as a measure of both the user's success and the system's success, it is difficult to separate the contribution of the user from the contribution of the system.

Although QF is a key part of the interactive information seeking process and has been studied extensively, much of this research has focused on particular aspects of QF that are potentially useful for the development of better information retrieval systems. The discrepancy between approaches is reflected in the definitions of QF cited previously. We have therefore felt it necessary to devote the first part of this review to development of a flow-of-information model that shows how the active streams of research are related in a holistic view of QF. Critics may object that this effort has exceeded the traditional scope of a review; however, without a close description of a process such as QF, it is hard to provide an overview of how it works. We hope that this overview adds clarity to discussion of QF and the many interesting questions that we can usefully ask about it.

Basic QF is the core of the QF process. During basic QF, users engage in mental processing to formulate queries that represent their information needs. The observable output of QF (extracted from search logs) is the query that is submitted to the information retrieval system after basic QF is complete. Basic QF is a component of all broader and more complex approaches to the study of QF that take into consideration the processing engaged in by the information system, the complexity added by iterative searching, and the different points at which systems may provide assistance in QF to the user. For example, when information systems provide recommendations the user chooses (or ignores), we have an example of basic QF (Wacholder & Liu, 2006).

We are fortunate to be conducting this research at a time when many exciting new sources of information and techniques for studying human-computer interaction and cognitive processing are available. Among the (surely incomplete set of) options that we have discussed here are:

1. System-independent study of QF, in which the relationship between users and the queries they formulate is assessed separately from the relationship between query characteristics and system effectiveness. Among the possibilities are: (a) study of basic QF, where the query formulated by the user is the product of cognitive processing and no system processing is involved; (b) controlled experiments in which system results are manipulated so that participants see mocked-up results that vary across factors such as result quality, as was done, for example, by Smith (2008) and Smith and Kantor (2008); and (c) development of system-independent metrics of query quality so that the product of QF can be studied separately from system effectiveness.

2. Assessment of the impact, across information retrieval systems, of queries whose characteristics are carefully controlled, as was done by Jordan and colleagues (2006) and Azzopardi, Rijke, & Balog (2007).

3. Adoption of the maturing techniques and approaches of cognitive science. The importance of such techniques has been recognized in the research literature. The diverse and scattered character of this research, however, suggests that we are at an early stage in developing models of QF that characterize the mental representation and cognitive processing involved in this process. Techniques from cognitive science are already being used extensively in the study of human-computer interaction, and so it makes sense to extend this effort to QF. These techniques include development of computational models that make falsifiable predictions about how people formulate queries under specific circumstances and the use of objective techniques such as eye tracking and assessment of cognitive load that provide information about mental processing without relying on user description of a process that takes place extremely quickly and below the level of consciousness.

4. Data mining of search logs with millions of queries may lead to the discovery of patterns of QF that could not be identified with a smaller corpus of queries.

5. Use of cognitive architecture such as ACT-R theory that provide scaffolding for identifying the types of mental representations and processing that are components of QF.

6. Exploration of the relationship between word knowledge and query formulation. Most queries are quite short, do not use search operators, and contain little (if any) explicit linguistic structure. This option includes studying users' choices of vocabulary in terms of the mental lexicon and the knowledge of words, including the relationships among the words, that people retrieve from the lexicon.

It is only fair to balance this optimistic anticipation of the potential of these emerging techniques for advancing our study of QF progress with explicit acknowledgment of some of the challenges we face.

1. QF is an extremely complex mental process; the complexity is a manifestation of human intelligence. Our ability to study our own mental processes may well be limited in that we have to use our own brains to study our own brains.

2. Among the impediments to doing research on cognitive processing are: (a) the intellectually challenging nature of this field, which is influenced by philosophy, psychology, and linguistics; (b) the large amount of study required to obtain more than a superficial understanding of parts of the process; and (c) the technical skills required to conduct experiments in

this area. Students in information science doctoral programs usually do not study this material in depth.

3. As noted, some researchers in information science question the usefulness of techniques that rely on measures other than user description and experimenter observation.

4. How far can research on system-independent QF go? For example, will we be able to develop metrics of query characteristics sufficiently specific to characterize different kinds of users? Will limitations of our ability to measure query characteristics, for example, make it hard to develop information systems that respond to cues provided by users during the QF process?

5. How much investment of effort in basic research is needed to reward adequately the investment of time and effort required to make substantial system improvements?

The rich combination of research opportunities and challenges is likely to make the study of QF a lively research area in the foreseeable future.

Endnotes

1. We set aside for the moment the issue of the user's previous experience with the system.

2. Concerns about privacy issues associated with the availability of these logs is not relevant to this review; however, Barbaro and Zeller (2006) recount an awkward incident.

3. The systems identified by Cole (2000) are key to iterative and assisted QF but play a much less important role in basic QF.

4. Fidel (1991, p. 490) focuses on the "semantics" of the request, which she defines as the "topic" and on the pragmatics of the request, which she defines as "the *purpose* of a request, or the use to which the information will be put" (emphasis in original). This is a different sense of semantics.

References

Aitchison, J. (2003). *Words in the mind: An introduction to the mental lexicon* (3rd ed.). New York: Basil Blackwell.

Allan, J., Carterette, B., & Lewis, J. (2005). When will information retrieval be "good enough"? *Proceedings of the Annual International ACM SIGIR Conference on Research and Development in Information Retrieval.* doi: 10.1145/1076034.1076109.

Allen, B. (1991). Topic knowledge and online catalog search formulation. *Library Quarterly, 61*, 188–213.

Anderson, J. R. (2007). *How can the human mind occur in the physical universe?* New York: Oxford University Press.

Anderson, J. R., Bothell, D., Byrne, M. D., Douglas, S., Lebiere, C., & Qin, Y. (2004). An integrated theory of the mind. *Psychological Review, 111*(4), 1036–1060.

Aula, A., Jhaveri, N., & Käki, M. (2005). Information search and re-access strategies of experienced web users. *Proceedings of the 14th International Conference on World Wide Web*, 583–592.

Azzopardi, L. (2009). Query side evaluation: An empirical analysis of effectiveness and effort. *Proceedings of the 32nd Annual International ACM SIGIR Conference on Research and Development in Information Retrieval*, 556–563.

Azzopardi, L., Rijke, M. D., & Balog, K. (2007). Building simulated queries for known-item topics: An analysis using six European languages. *Proceedings of the Annual International ACM SIGIR Conference on Research and Development in Information Retrieval*, 455–462.

Baddeley, A. (1998). Working memory. *Comptes Rendus de l'Académie des Sciences: Series III: Sciences de la Vie, 321*(2–3), 167–173.

Baeza-Yates, R. (2005). Applications of web query mining. *Proceedings of the 27th European Conference on Information Retrieval*, 7–22.

Baeza-Yates, R., Hurtado, C., & Mendoza, M. (2005). Query recommendation using query logs in search engines. *Current Trends in Database Technology—EDBT 2004 Workshops*, 588–596. Retrieved March 1, 2010, from www.springerlink.com/content/xrxlkhx07h376 dvd

Baeza-Yates, R., & Ribeira-Neto, B. (1999). *Modern information retrieval*. New York: Addison Wesley/ACM Press.

Baeza-Yates, R., & Tiberi, A. (2007). Extracting semantic relations from query logs. *Proceedings of the 13th ACM SIGKDD International Conference on Knowledge Discovery and Data Mining*, 76–85.

Barbaro, M., & Zeller Jr., T. (2006, August 9). A face is exposed for AOL searcher No. 4417749. *The New York Times*. Retrieved June 26, 2008, from www.nytimes.com/2006/08/09/technology/09aol.html?ex=1312776000&pagewanted=print

Barr, C., Jones, R., & Regelson, M. (2008). The linguistic structure of English web-search queries. *Proceedings of the Conference on Empirical Methods in Natural Language Processing*, 1021–1030.

Bates, M. J. (1986). Subject access to online catalogs: A design model. *Journal of the American Society for Information Science, 37*(6), 357–376.

Bates, M. J. (1990). Where should the person stop and the information search interface start? *Information Processing & Management, 26*(5), 575–591.

Bates, M. J. (1998). Indexing and access for digital libraries and the internet: Human, database and domain factors. *Journal of the American Society for Information Science, 49*(13), 1185–1205.

Beghtol, C. (1986). Bibliographic classification theory and text linguistics: Aboutness analysis, intertextuality and the cognitive act of classifying documents. *Journal of Documentation, 42*(4), 84–113.

Belew, R. K. (2000). *Finding out about: A cognitive perspective on search engine technology and the World Wide Web*. Cambridge, UK: Cambridge University Press.

Belkin, N. J. (1990). The cognitive viewpoint in information science. *Journal of Information Science, 16*(1), 11–15.

Belkin, N. J., Cool, C., Croft, W. B., & Callan, J. P. (1993). The effect of multiple query representations on information retrieval system performance. *Proceedings of the 16th Annual International ACM SIGIR Conference on Research and Development in Information Retrieval*, 339–346.

Belkin, N. J., Kelly, D., Kim, G., Kim, J.-Y., Lee, H.-J., & Muresan, G., et al. (2003). Query length in interactive information retrieval. *Proceedings of the 26th Annual International ACM SIGIR Conference on Research and Development in Information Retrieval*, 205–212.

Belkin, N. J., Oddy, R., & Brooks, H. M. (1982). ASK for information retrieval: Part I. Background and history. *Journal of Documentation, 38*(2), 61–71.

Belkin, N. J., Oddy, R., & Brooks, H. M. (1991). ASK for information retrieval: Part II. Results of a design study. *Journal of Documentation, 38*(3), 145–164.

Billerbeck, B., Scholer, F., Williams, H. E., & Zobel, J. (2003). Query expansion using associated queries. *Proceedings of the Twelfth International Conference on Information and Knowledge Management*, 2–9.

Blair, D. C. (1990). *Language and representation in information retrieval.* New York: Elsevier.

Blair, D. C. (1992). Information retrieval and the philosophy of language. *The Computer Journal, 35*(3), 200–207.

Blair, D. C., & Maron, M. E. (1985). An evaluation of retrieval effectiveness for a full-text document-retrieval system. *Communications of the ACM, 28*(3), 289–299.

Boldi, P., Bonchi, F., Castillo, C., Donato, D., & Vigna, S. (2009). Query suggestions using query-flow graphs. *Proceedings of the 2009 Workshop on Web Search Click Data*, 56–63.

Borgman, C. L. (1985). The user's mental model of an information retrieval system. *Proceedings of the 8th Annual International ACM SIGIR Conference on Research and Development in Information Retrieval*, 268–273.

Brenes, D. J., & Gayo-Avello, D. (2009). Stratified analysis of AOL query log. *Information Sciences, 179*(12), 1844–1858.

Brenes, D. J., Gayo-Avello, D., & Pérez-González, K. (2009). Survey and evaluation of query intent detection methods. *Proceedings of the 2009 Workshop on Web Search Click Data*, 1–7.

Broder, A. (2002). A taxonomy of web search. *SIGIR Forum, 36*(2), 3–10.

Buckley, C., Salton, G., & Allan, J. (1994). The effect of adding relevance information in a relevance feedback environment. *Proceedings of the 17th Annual International ACM SIGIR Conference on Research and Development in Information Retrieval*, 292–300.

Carmel, D., Yom-Tov, E., Darlow, A., & Pelleg, D. (2006). What makes a query difficult? *Proceedings of the 29th Annual International ACM SIGIR Conference on Research and Development in Information Retrieval*, 390–397.

Chi, E. H., Pirolli, P., Chen, K., & Pitkow, J. (2001). Using information scent to model user information needs and actions and the web. *Proceedings of the SIGCHI Conference on Human Factors in Computing Systems*, 490–497.

Clarke, C. L., Agichtein, E., Dumais, S., & White, R. W. (2007). The influence of caption features on clickthrough patterns in web search. *Proceedings of the Annual International ACM SIGIR Conference on Research and Development in Information Retrieval*, 135–142.

Cleverdon, C. W. (1991). The significance of the Cranfield tests on index languages. *Proceedings of the Annual ACM Conference on Information Retrieval*, 3–12.

Cole, C. (2000). Interaction with an enabling information retrieval system: Modeling the user's decoding and encoding operations. *Journal of the American Society for Information Science, 51*(5), 417–426.

Craik, K. (1967). *The nature of explanation*. Cambridge, UK: Cambridge University Press.

Croft, W. B., Turtle, H. R., & Lewis, D. D. (1991). The use of phrases and structured queries in information retrieval. *Proceedings of the 14th Annual International ACM SIGIR Conference on Research and Development in Information Retrieval*, 32–45.

Cronen-Townsend, S., & Croft, W. B. (2002). Quantifying query ambiguity. *Proceedings of the Second International Conference on Human Language Technology Research*, 104–109.

Cronen-Townsend, S., Zhou, Y., & Croft, W. B. (2002). Predicting query performance. *Proceedings of the 25th Annual International ACM SIGIR Conference on Research and Development in Information Retrieval*, 299–306.

Cutrell, E., & Guan, Z. (2007). What are you looking for? An eye-tracking study of information usage in web search. *Proceedings of ACM CHI Conference on Human Factors*, 407–416.

Day, R. (2007). Knowing and indexical psychology. In C. McInerny & R. Day, *Rethinking knowledge management* (pp. 331–348). Berlin: Springer. Retrieved August 13, 2009, from dx.doi.org/10.1007/3-540-71011-6_14

Dennis, S., McArthur, R., & Bruza, P. (1998). Searching the World Wide Web made easy? The cognitive load imposed by query refinement mechanisms. *Proceedings of the Third Australian Document Computing Symposium*, 65–71.

Downey, D., Dumais, S., & Horvitz, E. (2007). Heads and tails: Studies of web search with common and rare queries. *Proceedings of the 30th Annual International ACM SIGIR Conference on Research and Development in Information Retrieval*, 847–848.

Dretske, F. I. (1981). *Knowledge and the flow of information*. Cambridge, MA: MIT Press.

Efthimiadis, E. (1996). Query expansion. *Annual Review of Information Science and Technology*, *31*, 121–187.

Fellbaum, C. (Ed.). (1998). *WordNet: An electronic lexical database*. Cambridge, MA: MIT Press.

Ferber, R., Wettler, M., & Rapp, R. (1995). An associative model of word selection in the generation of search queries. *Journal of the American Society for Information Science*, *46*(9), 685–699.

Fidel, R. (1991). Searchers' selection of search keys: I. The selection routine. *Journal of the American Society for Information Science*, *42*(7), 490–500.

Fitzpatrick, L., & Dent, M. (1997). Automatic feedback using past queries: Social searching? *Proceedings of the 20th Annual International ACM SIGIR Conference on Research and Development in Information Retrieval*, 306–313.

Freund, L., & Toms, E. G. (2002). A preliminary contextual analysis of the web query process. *Proceedings of the 30th Annual Conference of the Canadian Association for Information Science*, 72–84.

Frohmann, B. (1990). Rules of indexing: A critique of mentalism in information retrieval theory. *Journal of Documentation*, *46*(2), 81–101.

Frohmann, B. (1992). The power of images: A discourse analysis of the cognitive viewpoint. *Journal of Documentation*, *48*(4), 365–386.

Fu, W., & Pirolli, P. (2007). SNIF-ACT: A cognitive model of user navigation on the World Wide Web. *Human-Computer Interaction*, *22*(4), 355–412.

Fu, X. (2010). Towards a model of implicit feedback for web search. *Journal of the American Society for Information Science and Technology*, *61*(1), 30–49.

Furnas, G., Landauer, T. K., Gomez, L. M., & Dumais, S. T. (1987). The vocabulary problem in human-system communication. *Communications of the ACM, 30*(11), 964–971.

Gomez, L. M., Lochbaum, C. C., & Landauer, T. K. (1990). All the right words: Finding what you want as a function of richness of indexing vocabulary. *Journal of the American Society for Information Science, 41*(8), 547–559.

Granka, L. A., Joachims, T., & Gay, G. (2004). Eye-tracking analysis of user behavior in WWW search. *Proceedings of the Annual International ACM SIGIR Conference on Research and Development in Information Retrieval*, 478–479.

Griffith, C. (1992, October 1). Westlaw's win: Not only natural, but new. *Information Today*, 9–10.

Hall, J., Negus, A., & Dancy, D. (1972). On-line information retrieval: A method of query formulation using a video terminal. *Program, 6*(3), 175–186.

Hauff, C., Hiemstra, D., & Jong, F. D. (2008). A survey of pre-retrieval query performance predictors. *Proceeding of the 17th ACM Conference on Information and Knowledge Management*, 1419–1420.

Hauff, C., Murdock, V., & Baeza-Yates, R. (2008). Improved query difficulty prediction for the web. *Proceeding of the 17th ACM Conference on Information and Knowledge Management*, 439–448.

Hembrooke, H. A., Granka, L. A., Gay, G. K., & Liddy, E. D. (2005). The effects of expertise and feedback on search term selection and subsequent learning. *Journal of the American Society for Information Science & Technology, 56*(8), 861–871.

Hersh, W., Turpin, A., Price, S., Chan, B., Kramer, D., & Sacherek, L. (2000). Do batch and user evaluations give the same results? *Proceedings of the 23rd Annual International ACM SIGIR Conference on Research and Development in Information Retrieval*, 17–24.

Hjørland, B. (2002). Epistemology and the socio-cognitive perspective in information science. *Journal of the American Society for Information Science and Technology, 53*(4), 257–270.

Hsieh-Yee, I. (1993). Effects of search experience and subject knowledge on the search tactics of novice and experienced searchers. *Journal of the American Society for Information Science, 44*(3), 161–174.

Huang, J., & Efthimiadis, E. N. (2009). Analyzing and evaluating query reformulation strategies in web search logs. *Proceedings of the 18th ACM Conference on Information and Knowledge Management*, 77–86.

Iani, C., Gopher, D., & Lavie, P. (2004). Effects of task difficulty and invested mental effort on peripheral vasoconstriction. *Psychophysiology, 41*(5), 789–798.

Ingwersen, P. (1992). *Information retrieval interaction*. London: Taylor Graham.

Ingwersen, P. (1996). Cognitive perspectives of information retrieval interaction: Elements of a cognitive IR theory. *Journal of Documentation, 52*(1), 3–50.

Ingwersen, P. (1999). Cognitive information retrieval. *Annual Review of Information Science and Technology, 34*, 3–51.

Ingwersen, P., & Järvelin, K. (2005). *The turn: Integration of information seeking and retrieval in context*. New York: Springer-Verlag.

Israel, D., & Perry, J. (1990). What is information? In J. Hanson (Ed.), *Information, language and cognition* (pp. 1–19). Vancouver: University of British Columbia Press.

Jacob, E. K., & Shaw, D. (1998). Sociocognitive perspectives on representation. *Annual Review of Information Science and Technology, 33*, 131–185.

Jacob, R. J. K., & Karn, K. S. (2004). Eye tracking in human-computer interaction and usability research: Ready to deliver the promises: Commentary on Section 4. In J. Hyona, R. Radach, & H. Deubel (Eds.), *The mind's eyes: Cognitive and applied aspects of eye movements*. Oxford, UK: Elsevier. Retrieved April 20, 2010, from citeseer.ist.psu.edu/ 538753.html

Jansen, B. J. (2003). Operators not needed? The impact of query structure on web searching results. *Proceedings of the Information Resources Management Association Conference*, 18–21.

Jansen, B. J., Booth, D. L., & Spink, A. (2008). Determining the informational, navigational, and transactional intent of web queries. *Information Processing & Management, 44*(3), 1251–1266.

Jansen, B. J., Booth, D. L., & Spink, A. (2009). Predicting query reformulation during web searching. *Proceedings of the 27th International Conference Extended Abstracts on Human Factors in Computing Systems*, 3907–3912.

Jansen, B. J., Spink, A., & Saracevic, T. (2000). Real life, real users, and real needs: A study and analysis of user queries on the web. *Information Processing & Management, 36*(2), 202–227.

Joachims, T., Granka, L., Pan, B., Hembrooke, H., & Gay, G. (2005). Accurately interpreting clickthrough data as implicit feedback. *Proceedings of the Annual International ACM SIGIR Conference on Research and Development in Information Retrieval*, 154–161.

Joachims, T., Granka, L., Pan, B., Hembrooke, H., Radlinski, F., & Gay, G. (2007). Evaluating the accuracy of implicit feedback from clicks and query reformulations in web search. *Transactions on Information Systems, 25*(2), 7.

Johnson-Laird, P. (1983). *Mental models: Towards a cognitive science of language, inference, and consciousness*. Cambridge, MA: Harvard University Press.

Jordan, C., Watters, C., & Gao, Q. (2006). Using controlled query generation to evaluate blind relevance feedback algorithms. *Proceedings of the 6th ACM/IEEE-CS Joint Conference on Digital Libraries*, 286–295.

Just, M. A., & Carpenter, P. A. (1976). Eye fixations and cognitive processes. *Cognitive Psychology, 8*(4), 441–480.

Kelly, D., & Fu, X. (2006). Elicitation of term relevance feedback: An investigation of term source and context. *Proceedings of the 29th Annual International ACM SIGIR Conference on Research and Development in Information Retrieval*, 453–460.

Kelly, D., Gyllstrom, K., & Bailey, E. W. (2009). A comparison of query and term suggestion features for interactive searching. *Proceedings of the 32nd Annual International ACM SIGIR Conference on Research and Development in Information Retrieval*, 371–378.

Khoo, C., & Na, J. (2006). Semantic relations in information science. *Annual Review of Information Science and Technology, 40*, 157–228.

Kuhlthau, C. C. (1991). Inside the search process: Information seeking from the user's perspective. *Journal of the American Society for Information Science and Technology, 42*(5), 361–371.

Kuhlthau, C. C. (2004). *Seeking meaning* (2nd ed.). Westport, CT: Libraries Unlimited.

Kumaran, G., & Carvalho, V. (2009). Reducing long queries using query quality predictors. *Proceedings of the 32nd Annual International ACM SIGIR Conference on Research and Development in Information Retrieval*, 564–571.

Larsen, B., & Ingwersen, P. (2005). Cognitive overlaps along the polyrepresentation continuum. In A. Spink & C. Cole (Eds.), *New directions in cognitive information retrieval* (pp. 43–60). Dordrecht, The Netherlands: Springer.

Larsen, B., Ingwersen, P., & Kekäläinen, J. (2006). The polyrepresentation continuum in IR. *Proceedings of the International Conference on Information Interaction in Context*, 88–96.

Lau, T., & Horvitz, E. (1998). Patterns of search: Analyzing and modeling web query refinement. *Proceedings of the 7th International Conference on User Modeling*, 119–128.

Liu, S., Yu, C., & Meng, W. (2005). Word sense disambiguation in queries. *Proceedings of the 14th ACM International Conference on Information and Knowledge Management*, 525–532.

Liu, Y. (2009). *The impact of MeSH terms on information seeking effectiveness*. Unpublished doctoral dissertation, Rutgers University. Retrieved March 20, 2010, from csusap.csu.edu.au/~yingliu/YHLiu_ThesisFinalVersion.pdf

Lyons, J. (1995). *Linguistic semantics: An introduction*. Cambridge, UK: Cambridge University Press.

Marchionini, G. (1995). *Information seeking in electronic environments*. Cambridge, UK: Cambridge University Press.

McNamara, T. P. (2005). *Semantic priming: Perspectives from memory and word recognition*. New York: Taylor & Francis.

Meadow, C. T., Boyce, B. R., & Kraft, D. H. (2000). *Text information retrieval systems* (2nd ed.). San Diego, CA: Academic Press.

Mei, Q., Zhou, D., & Church, K. (2008). Query suggestion using hitting time. *Proceedings of the 17th ACM Conference on Information and Knowledge Management*, 469–478.

Miller, G. A., Beckwith, R., Fellbaum, C., Gross, D., & Miller, K. J. (1990). Introduction to WordNet: An on-line lexical database. *International Journal of Lexicography*, *3*(4), 235–244.

Muramatsu, J., & Pratt, W. (2001). Transparent queries: Investigating users' mental models of search engines. *Proceedings of the 24th Annual International ACM SIGIR Conference on Research and Development in Information Retrieval*, 217–224.

Norman, D. A. (1990). *The design of everyday things*. New York: Doubleday.

Oard, D., & Kim, J. (2001). Modeling information content using observable behavior. *Proceedings of the Annual Meeting of the American Society for Information Science*, *38*, 481–488.

Oddy, R. (1977). Information retrieval through man-machine dialogue. *Journal of Documentation*, *33*(1), 1–14.

Pinker, S. (1999a). *How the mind works*. New York: W. W. Norton.

Pinker, S. (1999b). *Words and rules: The ingredients of language*. New York: Basic Books.

Pirolli, P. (1997). Computational models of information scent-following in a very large browsable text collection. *Proceedings of the SIGCHI Conference on Human Factors in Computing Systems*, 3–10.

Pirolli, P., & Card, S. (1999). Information foraging. *Psychological Review*, *106*(4), 643–675.

Pitt, D. (n.d.). *Mental representation*. Retrieved November 8, 2009, from plato.stanford.edu/entries/mental-representation

Radev, D. R., Qi, H., Zheng, Z., Blair-Goldensohn, S., Zhang, Z., & Fan, W. (2001). Mining the web for answers to natural language questions. *Proceedings of the Tenth International Conference on Information and Knowledge Management*, 143–150.

Rayner, P. (1998). Eye movements in reading and information processing: 20 years of research. *Psychological Bulletin*, *124*, 372–422.

Rieh, S. Y., & Xie, H. (2006). Analysis of multiple query reformulations on the web: The interactive information retrieval context. *Information Processing & Management*, *42*(3), 751–768.

Rose, D. E., & Levinson, D. (2004). Understanding user goals in web search. *Proceedings of the 13th International Conference on World Wide Web*, 13–19.

Russo, J. E., Johnson, E. J., & Stephens, D. L. (1989). The validity of verbal protocols. *Memory and Cognition*, *17*(6), 759–769.

Ruthven, I. (2003). Re-examining the potential effectiveness of interactive query expansion. *Proceedings of the 26th Annual International ACM SIGIR Conference on Research and Development in Information Retrieval*, 213–220.

Sag, I. A., & Wasow, T. (1999). *Syntactic theory: A formal introduction* (CSLI Lecture Notes, No. 92). Stanford, CA: Stanford University, Center for the Study of Language and Information.

Salton, G. (1971). *The SMART retrieval system experiments in automatic document processing.* Englewood Cliffs, NJ: Prentice-Hall.

Salton, G., & Buckley, C. (1990). Improving retrieval performance by relevance feedback. *Journal of the American Society for Information Science*, *41*(4), 288–297.

Salton, G., Buckley, C., & Fox, E. A. (1983). Automatic query formulations in information retrieval. *Journal of the American Society for Information Science*, *34*(4), 262–280.

Salvucci, D. D. (2001). An integrated model of eye movements and visual encoding. *Journal of Cognitive Systems Research*, *1*, 201–220.

Saracevic, T., & Kantor, P. (1988). A study of information seeking and retrieving: II. Users, questions and effectiveness. *Journal of the American Society for Information Science*, *39*(3), 177–196.

Searle, J. R. (1990). Is the brain a digital computer? *Proceedings and Addresses of the American Philosophical Association*, *64*(3), 21–37.

Shneiderman, B., Byrd, D., & Croft, W. B. (1997, January). Clarifying search: A user-interface framework for text searches. *D-Lib Magazine*. Retrieved August 12, 2009, from www.dlib.org/dlib/january97/retrieval/01shneiderman.html

Shute, S. J., & Smith, P. J. (1993). Knowledge-based search tactics. *Information Processing & Management*, *29*(1), 29–45.

Sihvonen, A., & Vakkari, P. (2004). Subject knowledge improves interactive query expansion assisted by a thesaurus. *Journal of Documentation*, *60*(6), 673–690.

Smith, C. L. (2008). *What might the system teach its user?* Unpublished doctoral dissertation, Rutgers University, New Brunswick, NJ.

Smith, C. L., & Kantor, P. B. (2008). User adaptation: Good results from poor systems. *Proceedings of the 31st Annual International ACM SIGIR Conference on Research and Development in Information Retrieval*, 147–154.

Smith, C. L., & Wacholder, N. (2010). Why do users neglect suggestions? Effects of semantic relatedness on word recognition. *Proceedings of the 2010 iConference*, 542–543. Retrieved December 15, 2009, from nora.lis.uiuc.edu/images/iConferences/2010posters.pdf

Smyth, B., Balfe, E., Freyne, J., Briggs, P., Coyle, M., & Boydell, O. (2004). Exploiting query repetition and regularity in an adaptive community-based web search engine. *User Modeling and User-Adapted Interaction, 14*(5), 383–423.

Song, R., Luo, Z., Wen, J., Yu, Y., & Hon, H. (2007). Identifying ambiguous queries in web search. *Proceedings of the 16th International Conference on World Wide Web*, 1169–1170.

Soricut, R., & Brill, E. (2006). Automatic question answering using the web: Beyond the factoid. *Information Retrieval, 9*(2), 191–206.

Spärck Jones, K. (2000). Further reflections on TREC. *Information Processing & Management, 36*, 37–85.

Spärck Jones, K. (2005). Metareflections on TREC. In E. M. Voorhees & D. K. Harman (Eds.), *TREC: Experiment and evaluation in information retrieval* (pp. 421–448). Cambridge, MA: MIT Press.

Spink, A., & Saracevic, T. (1997). Interaction in information retrieval: Selection and effectiveness of search terms. *Journal of the American Society for Information Science, 48*(8), 741–761.

Spink, A., Wolfram, D., Jansen, M. B. J., & Saracevic, T. (2001). Searching the web: The public and their queries. *Journal of the American Society for Information Science and Technology, 52*(3), 226–234.

Srivastava, J., Cooley, R., Deshpande, M., & Tan, P. (2000). Web usage mining: Discovery and applications of usage patterns from web data. *SIGKDD Explorations, 1*(2), 12–23.

Sutcliffe, A., & Ennis, M. (1998). Towards a cognitive theory of information retrieval. *Interacting with Computers, 10*(3), 321–351.

Swanson, D. R. (1960). Searching natural language text by computer. *Science, 132*(3434), 1099–1104.

Sweller, J. (1988). Cognitive load during problem solving: Effects on learning. *Cognitive Science, 12*, 257–285.

Taylor, R. S. (1968). Question-negotiation and information-seeking in libraries. *College & Research Libraries, 29*, 178–194.

Teevan, J., & Kelly, D. (2003). Implicit feedback for inferring user preference: A bibliography. *SIGIR Forum, 37*(2), 18–28.

ter Hofstede, A. H., Proper, H. A., & van der Weide, T. P. (1996). Query formulation as an information retrieval problem. *The Computer Journal, 39*(4), 255–274.

Thagard, P. (2005). *Mind: Introduction to cognitive science* (2nd ed.). Cambridge, MA: MIT Press.

Thagard, P. (2008). *Cognitive science*. Retrieved December 24, 2009, from plato.stanford.edu/entries/cognitive-science

Turpin, A. H., & Hersh, W. (2001). Why batch and user evaluations do not give the same results. *Proceedings of the 24th Annual International ACM SIGIR Conference on Research and Development in Information Retrieval*, 225–231.

Turpin, A., & Hersh, W. (2004). Do clarity scores for queries correlate with user performance? *Proceedings of the 15th Australasian Database Conference, 27*, 85–91.

Turpin, A., & Scholer, F. (2006). User performance versus precision measures for simple search tasks. *Proceedings of the 29th Annual International ACM SIGIR Conference on Research and Development in Information Retrieval*, 11–18.

Vakkari, P. (2002). Subject knowledge, source of terms, and term selection in query expansion: An analytical study. *Advances in Information Retrieval: Proceedings of the 24th BCS-IRSG European Colloquium on IR Research*, 101–106.

Vakkari, P., Pennanen, M., & Serola, S. (2003). Change of search terms and tactics while writing a research proposal: A longitudinal case study. *Information Processing & Management, 39*, 445–463.

van Rijsbergen, C. J. (2004). *Information retrieval* (2nd ed.). Retrieved March 20, 2010, from www.dcs.gla.ac.uk/Keith/Preface.html

Voorhees, E. (2003). Overview of TREC 2003. *Proceedings of the 12th Text Retrieval Conference*, 1–13.

Wacholder, N., Kelly, D., Kantor, P., Rittman, R., Sun, Y., Bai, B., et al. (2007). A model for quantitative evaluation of an end-to-end question-answering system. *Journal of the American Society for Information Science and Technology, 58*(8), 1082–1099.

Wacholder, N., & Liu, L. (2006). User preference: A measure of query-term quality. *Journal of the American Society for Information Science and Technology, 57*(12), 1566–1580.

Wacholder, N., & Liu, L. (2008). Assessing term effectiveness in the interactive information access process. *Information Processing & Management, 44*(3), 1022–1031.

Westbrook, L. (2006). Mental models: A theoretical overview and preliminary study. *Journal of Information Science, 32*(6), 563–579.

White, R. W., Dumais, S. T., & Teevan, J. (2009). Characterizing the influence of domain expertise on web search behavior. *Proceedings of the Second ACM International Conference on Web Search and Data Mining*, 132–141.

White, R. W., & Marchionini, G. (2007). Examining the effectiveness of real-time query expansion. *Information Processing & Management, 43*(3), 685–704.

White, R. W., & Morris, D. (2007). Investigating the querying and browsing behavior of advanced search engine users. *Proceedings of the 30th Annual International ACM SIGIR Conference on Research and Development in Information Retrieval*, 255–262.

Wildemuth, B. M. (2004). The effects of domain knowledge on search tactic formulation. *Journal of the American Society for Information Science and Technology, 55*(3), 246–258.

Willie, S., & Bruza, P. (1995). Users' models of the information space: The case for two search models. *Proceedings of the Annual International ACM SIGIR Conference on Research and Development in Information Retrieval*, 205–210.

Wilson, T. D. (1994). The proper protocol: Validity and completeness of verbal reports. *Psychological Science, 5*(5), 249–252.

Scholarly Communication

CHAPTER 5

Scientific Peer Review

Lutz Bornmann
Eidgenössische Technische Hochschule, Zurich, Switzerland

Introduction

Peer review is the principal mechanism for quality control in most scientific disciplines. By assessing the quality of research, peer review determines what scientific research receives funding and what research results are published. This review of the literature published on the topic of peer review describes the state of research on journal, fellowship, and grant peer review. The emphasis is on empirical research dealing with the reliability, fairness, and predictive validity of the process—the three quality criteria for professional evaluations.

Peer review, the instrument for ensuring trustworthiness (Cronin, 2005), grounds all scholarship (Ziman, 2000). Quality control undertaken by experts in the traditional peer review of manuscripts for scientific journals is essential in most scientific disciplines in order to create valid and reliable knowledge (Hemlin & Rasmussen, 2006). According to Lamont (2009), peers monitor the flow of ideas through the various gates of the academic community. But journal peer review influences not only scholarship: "The Intergovernmental Panel on Climate Change and other similar advisory groups base their judgments on peer-reviewed literature, and this is part of their success. Many legal decisions and regulations also depend on peer-reviewed science" (Alberts, Hanson, & Kelner, 2008, p. 15). The mid-18th century is cited as the beginning of reviewing. At that time the Royal Society in London took over fiscal responsibility for the journal *Philosophical Transactions* and established what they called a Committee on Papers (Kronick, 1990). Nowadays, innovative review possibilities have emerged on the World Wide Web, where peers can comment on internet-based materials in a review process sometimes called sky-writing (Harnad, 1990).

Almost all aspects of the contemporary scientific enterprise rely on quality evaluations by peers. Such evaluations determine, among other things, who gets which job, who gets tenure, and who gets which awards and honors (Feist, 2006). Research evaluation systems in various countries (e.g., the British research assessment exercise) are normally based on peer review. Whitley and Gläser's (2007) edited book shows how these systems are changing the organization of scientific knowledge production and universities in the countries involved (see also Moed, 2008). Aside from the selection of manuscripts for publication in journals, the most common contemporary application of peer review in scientific research is for the selection of fellowship and grant applications. Following World War II, and at first mostly just in the U.S., peer review became the process for allocating research funds (Biagioli, 2002). Today researchers rely less and less on regular research funds from their universities and more on external research grants that are allocated on the basis of peer review (Guston, 2003). For Wessely and Wood (1999) the peer review of grant proposals may be more relevant than publication practices to the health of science. Good papers will get published somewhere, as will bad ones, whereas applications for grants that do not succeed represent research that no one conducts.

Peers or colleagues asked to evaluate fellowship or grant applications or manuscripts in a peer review process take on the responsibility for ensuring high standards in their disciplines. Although peers active in the same field might be unaware of other perspectives, they "are said to be in the best position to know whether quality standards have been met and a contribution to knowledge made" (Eisenhart, 2002, p. 241). Peer evaluation in research thus entails a process by which a jury of equals active in a given scientific field convenes to evaluate the undertaking of scientific activity or its outcomes (i.e., applications for research fellowships and grants and manuscripts for publication). Such a jury of equals may be consulted as a group or individually, without the need for personal contacts among the evaluators. The peer review process lets the active producers of science, the experts, become the gatekeepers of science (McClellan, 2003). "By using the judgment and opinions of peers and members of the 'community of science,' the process of peer review is aimed at keeping the review 'in the family'" (Geisler, 2000, pp. 218–219). Nevertheless, keeping it "in the family" can result in intellectual closedmindedness.

The Formation of a Peer Review Process

Social psychology conceptualizes the peer review process as a social judgment process of individuals in a small group (for example, one or more reviewers and one or more editors of a disciplinary in-group in manuscript reviewing) (Krampen & Montada, 2002). In the review of manuscripts intended for publication and grant proposals for research funding, it is the reviewers' task to recommend for selection the "best" scientific research under the condition of scarce resources (such as limited space in journals, limited funds) (Hackett & Chubin, 2003). "With grants, an applicant submits a proposal, which is then reviewed by peers who make a judgement on its merits and eligibility for funding. With publications, an author submits a paper to a journal or a book proposal to a publisher, and peers are asked to offer a judgement as to whether it should be published" (British Academy, 2007, p. 2).

In journal peer review, reviewers sought by the editor normally provide a written review and an overall publication recommendation. "The editor, on the basis of the reviews and his or her own evaluation, decides to reject the submission, seek further review, ask the author to revise the manuscript in response to suggestions by the reviewers and the editor, or accept the manuscript" (Jayasinghe, Marsh, & Bond, 2001, p. 344). Most of the studies examining the relation of reviewers' (overall) ratings and editors' decisions on submissions at single journals have found that the reviewers' ratings are highly correlated with the editors' final decisions (Bakanic, McPhail, & Simon, 1987; Bornmann & Daniel, 2008a; Fogg & Fiske, 1993; Lock, 1985; Petty & Fleming, 1999; Sternberg, Hojjat, Brigockas, & Grigorenko, 1997; Zuckerman & Merton, 1971a). That means editors' decisions on manuscripts depend on the judgments of the reviewers. Peer review for fellowships shows similar associations between reviewers' ratings and the decisions of a selection committee (e.g., Bornmann, Mutz, & Daniel, 2007b).

Many aspects of the peer review process vary case by case and this variation largely depends on the type of application (see Hansson, 2002; Marsh & Ball, 1991; Shashok, 2005). Several publications describe the differing peer review processes at different research funding agencies, such as those by Geisler (2000), Kostoff (1997), and the U.S. General Accounting Office (1999). Weller (2002) specifically describes the journal peer review processes, which may proceed by highly formalized protocols or leave the choice of selection criteria to the peers in the committee (Hornbostel, 1997). Reviewers may work anonymously or openly. The persons reviewed may or may not be anonymous (double-blind versus single-blind). Reviewers may be assigned permanently or ad hoc (Geisler, 2000). A reviewer may represent one scientific discipline or a variety of disciplines (U.S. Office of Management and Budget, 2004). Funding agencies may select reviewers from academia, private industry, and/or government (U.S. General Accounting Office, 1999). A single reviewer or a committee may provide a peer review (Marsh & Ball, 1991). After a group of reviewers is assigned, the members may review either collectively or independently (Geisler, 2000). The peer review process can make its results public (Pöschl, 2004) or reveal them only to those directly involved. Accordingly, peer review practices can be characterized as heterogeneous processes across and among different disciplines, journal editors, funding agencies, rating schemas, and so on.

The Content of a Review

A review normally consists of a summarizing judgment regarding suitability for publication or funding, followed by comments, sometimes numbered by point or page, which may track criticisms in a sequential manner (Gosden, 2003). Negative comments predominate in review documents according to the findings of Bakanic, McPhail, and Simon (1989) in the analysis of manuscripts submitted to the *American Sociological*

Review; positive comments occur far less frequently. This result is in accordance with critical rationalism, the epistemological philosophy advanced by Popper (1961): critical rationalists hold that claims to knowledge can and should be rationally criticized so that scholarship moves forward. Bornmann, Nast, and Daniel (2008) examined the criteria employed in peer review. They conducted a quantitative content analysis of 46 research studies on editors' and reviewers' criteria for the assessment of manuscripts and their grounds for accepting or rejecting manuscripts. The 572 differing criteria and reasons from the 46 studies could be assigned to nine areas: (1) relevance of contribution, (2) writing/presentation, (3) design/conception, (4) method/statistics, (5) discussion of results, (6) reference to the literature and documentation, (7) theory, (8) author's reputation/institutional affiliation, and (9) ethics. The most significant criteria for editors and reviewers in manuscript assessment are those that relate to the quality of the research underlying a manuscript: theory, design/conception, and discussion of results.

Bornmann and Daniel (2005b) investigated the fellowship peer review process of the Boehringer Ingelheim Fonds (BIF, Heidesheim, Germany, an international foundation for the promotion of basic research in biomedicine). They found that fellowships were awarded to post-graduate researchers according to the following main criteria: (1) scientific quality as demonstrated by the applicant's achievements to date, (2) the originality of the proposed research project, and (3) the scientific standing of the laboratory where the research will be conducted. Even if the applicant's track record is a predictor of success in the grant peer review process of the National Science Foundation (NSF) (Abrams, 1991), classic studies by Jonathan R. Cole and Stephen Cole found that the characteristics of the proposal were more important than attributes of the applicant (see an overview in Cole, 1992).

Advantages of Peer Review

Proponents of the peer review system argue that it is more effective than any other known instrument for self-regulation in promoting the critical selection that is so crucial to the evolution of scientific knowledge. Putting it into a wider context: According to Popper's (1961) critical rationalism, intellectual life and institutions should be subjected to "maximum criticism, in order to counteract and eliminate as much intellectual error as possible" (Bartley, 1984, p. 113). If, for example, the editors of the journal *Social Text* had sent Alan D. Sokal's manuscript "Transgressing the boundaries: Toward a transformative hermeneutics of quantum gravity" to external peers, the manuscript would probably have been rejected and the well-known Sokal affair (Sokal, 2008) might not have happened. It can also be assumed that the fake paper Philip Davis submitted to the open-access journal *The Open Information Science Journal*, which the editor accepted for publication (Editor to quit over hoax open-access paper, 2009), would have been recommended for rejection if peers had been involved.

Evidence supports the view that peer review improves the quality of the reporting of research results (Goodman, Berlin, Fletcher, & Fletcher, 1994; Pierie, Walvoort, & Overbeke, 1996). Although alternatives to peer review have been suggested, they have not been implemented. For example, Roy (1985) developed the Peer-Reviewed Formula System, in which research money is allocated proportional to prior research productivity. This system certainly disadvantages younger scientists. Abelson (1980, p. 62), a proponent of peer review, writes: "The most important and effective mechanism for attaining good standards of quality in journals is the peer review system." According to Shatz (2004, p. 30) journal peer review "motivates scholars to produce their best, provides feedback that substantially improves work which is submitted, and enables scholars to identify products they will find worth reading."

The proponents of peer review are not the only people well disposed to the process. A series of surveys on grant and journal peer review have already reported on scientists' wide satisfaction with it. In a global survey on the attitudes and behavior of 3,040 academics, a large majority (85 percent) agreed that journal peer review greatly helps scientific communication, and 83 percent believed that without peer review researchers would have no control over scientific communication (Publishing Research Consortium, 2008). The majority of corresponding authors of papers published in *Academy of Management Journal* and *Academy of Management Review* agreed that the reviewers' recommended revisions improved their papers (Bedeian, 2003). Similar results obtained in surveys of authors for *Nature* (Overview: *Nature*'s peer review trial, 2006) and *Obstetrics & Gynecology* papers (Gibson, Spong, Simonsen, Martin, & Scott, 2008). Ninety-seven percent of more than a thousand *Astronomy & Astrophysics* authors reported that reviewers had dealt competently with their manuscripts (Bertout & Schneider, 2004). The Swiss National Science Foundation (SNSF) surveyed researchers at Swiss universities about its grant reviews and found that the evaluation process was regarded as good and its administration efficient (Hoffmann, Joye, Kuhn, & Métral, 2002). The German Research Foundation's (DFG) survey of subject reviewers yielded a similar positive result (Hornbostel & Olbrecht, 2007).

Critics of Peer Review

Critics of peer review argue that: (1) reviewers rarely agree on whether to recommend that a manuscript be published or a research grant be awarded, thus making for poor *reliability* of the peer review process; (2) reviewers' recommendations are frequently biased, that is, judgments are not based solely on scientific merit, but are also influenced by personal attributes of the authors, applicants, or the reviewers themselves (where the *fairness* of the process is not a given); (3) the process lacks *predictive validity* because there is little or no relationship between the reviewers' judgments and the subsequent usefulness of the work to the scientific community, as indicated by the frequency of citations of the work in later scientific papers; (4) reviewing is inefficient because it delays publications; inhibits the publication of new, innovative, and unconventional ideas; and is time consuming and costly; and (5) reviewing can be personally damaging, an experience that is particularly painful and distressing for new authors (for criticism on peer review see Eysenck & Eysenck, 1992; Ross, 1980).

Frey (2003, p. 206) holds that peer review constitutes a form of intellectual prostitution: The authors are forced to follow reviewers' demands "slavishly." Critics of peer review often cite the main results of the highly influential study on grant peer review at the NSF conducted by Cole, Cole, and Simon (1981, p. 885): "The fate of a particular application is roughly half determined by the characteristics of the proposal and the principal investigator, and about half by apparently random elements which might be characterized as 'the luck of the reviewer draw.'" The only reason for the further implementation of the peer review process—according to its skeptics—is the lack of any clear consensus on a better alternative (Young, 2003).

Nevertheless, if a workable synthesis could evolve between the diametrically opposed positions of proponents and opponents of peer review, perhaps an improved system could be developed.

Research on Peer Review

Because peer review is so central to what is published and funded, and because so much hinges on peer review in and outside of science, it is essential that it be carried out well and professionally (Hames, 2007). The research on peer review, which in recent years has addressed criticisms of the process, deals for the most part with journal peer review (see overviews in Armstrong, 1997; Campanario, 1998a, 1998b; Overbeke & Wager, 2003; Speck, 1993; Stieg Dalton, 1995) and somewhat less frequently with peer review for fellowship and grant proposals (see overviews in Demicheli & Pietrantonj, 2007; Kostoff, 2004; Wessely, 1998). Weller (2002), a former member of the editorial staff of the *Journal of the American Medical Association* (*JAMA*), has provided the most comprehensive review of research on journal peer review. Her book, *Editorial Peer Review: Its Strengths and Weaknesses*, covers 1,439 studies published in English between 1945 and 1997. Garfield's (2004) historiography shows that as of September 2006 some 3,720 publications in 1,228 journals by 6,708 different authors have focused on the peer review process. In addition to these publications, a multitude of monographs, compilations, and gray literature was not included in the historiography (which visualizes the results of literature searches in the *Web of Science*, provided by Thomson Reuters; this database covers only journal publications).

Over the past dozen years scientific research on journal peer review has been stimulated by *JAMA*'s conferences on the topic of journal peer review. The first *JAMA* conference on peer review and biomedical publication was held in 1989, and five more have been held in 1993, 1997, 2001, 2005, and 2009. *JAMA* published research articles from the first through fourth peer review congresses in peer review theme issues: March 6, 1990; July 13, 1994; July 15, 1998; June 5, 2002 (*Journal of the American Medical Association*, 1990, 1994, 1998, 2002). Weller (2002, p. 12) comments: "Overall, although isolated research endeavors were certainly taking place, the congress failed to uncover a large, coordinated research effort in the field of editorial peer review in biomedical publications."

Because comprehensive review articles of research on peer review have been published prior to August 2000, this review concentrates on research from the last decade. It particularly focuses on recent methodological developments, which have already been suggested or used in the investigation of peer review processes. According to Stieg Dalton (1995, p. 215) many peer review studies have methodological weaknesses, and "most of the publications on journal peer review are more opinion than research, often the ruminations of a former editor." This review focuses on studies concerning journal, fellowship, and grant peer review, where most of the research has focused. Peer review of completed research (e.g., research assessment exercises in various countries) and the review of conference papers or abstracts are dealt with only marginally.

The literature research for this review was conducted at the beginning of 2009. In a first step, studies were located using the reference lists provided by narrative reviews of research on journal and grant peer review and using tables of contents of certain journals (e.g., *JAMA*, *Nature*, *Research Policy*, *Scientometrics*). In a second step, in order to obtain keywords for searching databases, a bibliogram (White, 2005) was prepared for the studies located in the first step. The bibliogram ranks by frequency the words included in the abstracts of the studies located. Words at the top of the ranking list (e.g., peer review, quality, research, and evaluation) were used for searches in literature databases (e.g., Web of Science and Scopus) and internet search engines (e.g., Google). In the final step of the literature search, all of the citing publications for a series of articles (found in the first and second steps) which had a substantially large number of citations were examined.

In the following sections, empirical research is investigated with regard to the three assessment criteria for professional evaluations of peer review processes: reliability, fairness, and predictive validity. As an assessment tool, peer review is asked to be reliable (is the selection of scientific contributions reliable or is the result purely incidental?), fair (are certain groups of applicants or authors favored or at a disadvantage?), and predictively valid (do the selection decisions correlate with scientific performance measures subsequent to decision?). These three quantitative social science research tools used by psychologists are not only connected to the criticism on peer review, they are also uniquely appropriate for evaluating the peer review process (Marsh, Bonds, & Jayasinghe, 2007).

Reliability, Fairness, and Predictive Validity of Peer Review

Reliability of Peer Review

"In everyday life, intersubjectivity is equated with realism" (Ziman, 2000, p. 106). Therefore, scientific discourse is also distinguished by its striving for consensus. Scientific activity would clearly be impossible unless scientists could come to similar conclusions. According to Wiley (2008, p. 31) "just as results from lab experiments provide clues to an underlying biological process, reviewer comments are also clues to an underlying reality (they did not like your grant for some reason). For example, if all reviewers mention the same point, then it is a good bet that it is important and real." An established consensus among scientists must of course be voluntary and achieved under conditions of free and open criticism (Ziman, 2000). The norms of science make these conditions possible and regulate them (Merton, 1942): The norms of communalism (scientific knowledge should be made public knowledge) and universalism (knowledge claims should be judged impersonally, independently of their source) envisage eventual agreement. "But the norm of 'organized scepticism', which energizes critical debates, rules out any official procedure for closing them. Consensus and dissensus are thus promoted simultaneously" (Ziman, 2000, p. 255).

A group of peers normally reviews journal manuscripts, grant applications, and fellowship proposals and recommends acceptance or rejection. Cicchetti (1991, p. 120) defines inter-reviewer reliability "as the extent to which two or more independent reviews of the same scientific document agree." Manuscripts and applications are rated reliably when there is a high level of agreement between independent reviewers. In many studies of peer review the intraclass correlation coefficient measures the extent of agreement within peer review groups. "The intraclass correlation coefficient (ICC) ... is a variance decomposition method to assess the portion of overall variance attributable to between-subject variability. ... Raters are assumed to share common metric and homogeneous variance (i.e., *intra*class variance)" (von Eye & Mun, 2005, p. 116). The ICC can vary between -1.0 and +1.0. However, high agreement alone with low between-reviewer variability cannot result in high reliability because a certain level of agreement can be expected to occur on the basis of chance alone. Therefore the Kappa coefficient figures in many studies on peer review as a measure of between-reviewer variability. Kappa (κ) statistically indicates the level of agreement between two or more raters. If the raters are in complete agreement then $\kappa = 1$; if κ is near 0, the observed level of agreement is not much higher than by chance (von Eye & Mun, 2005).

If a submission (manuscript or application) meets scientific standards and contributes to the advancement of science, it can be expected that two or more reviewers will agree on its value. This is frequently not the case. Ernst, Saradeth, and Resch (1993) offer a dramatic demonstration of the unreliability of the journal peer review process. Copies of a paper submitted to a medical journal were sent simultaneously to 45 experts. They were asked to express their opinion of the paper with the journal's standard questionnaire containing eight quality criteria on a numerical scale from 5 (excellent) to 1 (unacceptable). The 31 completed forms demonstrate poor reproducibility with extreme judgments ranging from "unacceptable" to "excellent" for most criteria. Table 5.1 shows an overview of the results of some studies on reliability in the areas of journal (submission of manuscripts), meeting (submission of abstracts), and grant (submission of applications) peer review. The results indicate that the levels of inter-reviewer agreement, when corrected for chance, generally fall in the range from 0.2 to 0.4. A meta-analysis by Bornmann, Mutz, and Daniel (2009) of 48 studies on the reliability of agreement between reviewers' ratings in journal peer review reports overall agreement coefficients of $\sim$.23/ $\sim$.34 (ICC and Pearson product-moment correlation) and

Table 5.1   Reliability: agreement among reviewers

	Kappa coefficient/ intraclass correlation
Journal (submission of manuscripts)	
Social Problems (Smigel & Ross, 1970)	.40
Journal of Educational Psychology (Marsh & Ball, 1981)	.34
British Medical Journal (Lock, 1985)	.31
American Sociological Review (Hargens & Herting, 1990)	.28
Physiological Zoology (Hargens & Herting, 1990)	.28
Journal of Personality and Social Psychology (Scott, 1974)	.26
New England Journal of Medicine (Ingelfinger, 1974)	.26
Law & Society Review (Hargens & Herting, 1990)	.17
Angewandte Chemie International Edition (Bornmann & Daniel, 2008a)	.15
Angewandte Chemie (Daniel, 1993/2004)	.14
Physical Therapy (Bohannon, 1986)	.12
Meeting (submission of abstracts)	
National Meeting of the American Association for the Study of Liver Disease (Cicchetti & Conn, 1976)	.24
Annual Meeting of the Orthopaedic Trauma Association (Bhandari, Templeman, & Tornetta, 2004)	.23
Research funding organization (submission of applications)	
American Heart Association (Wiener, Urivetsky, Bregman, Cohen, Eich, Gootman, et al., 1977)	.37
National Science Foundation (solid states physics) (Cicchetti, 1991)	.32
Heart and Stroke Foundation, Medical Research Council of Canada (Hodgson, 1997)	.29

.17 (κ). According to Fleiss's (1981) guidelines, Kappa coefficients between 0 and 0.2 indicate a slight level of reviewer agreement.

Given these results, the norm of organized skepticism, which ensures that "much of the action in science is systematic controversy over the credibility of 'facts' and theories" (Ziman, 2000, p. 225), appears to be functioning effectively. The norm of organized skepticism is stronger than the norms of communalism and universalism, both of which envisage eventual agreement. Further examination of the data from various studies on the reliability of journal peer review by Cicchetti (1991, 1997) and Weller (2002, Chapter 6) shows that agreement is substantially higher in recommendations for rejection than for acceptance; reviewers are twice as likely to agree on rejection than on acceptance (Weller, 2002). "Although there seems to be satisfactory qualitative agreement as to what constitutes a manuscript of poor quality (a list of don'ts), there is little consistency among reviewers as to what constitutes good quality" (Kupfersmid, 1988, p. 639). With regard to grant reviewing, Opthof and Wilde (2009, p. 153) state that "the peer-review system is solid for recognising work that should not be granted, but is poor, if not unsuitable, for making a distinction between what is very good or excellent. This renders the whole process subject to personal bias." It can be surmised that the peer review process is better at encumbering the progress of bad research than at identifying the "best."

For Marsh and colleagues (2007), the lack of reliability constitutes the most important weakness of the peer review process. Bedeian (2004, p. 202) excludes the possibility of a "universal and articulable latent dimension of 'merit' or 'publishability,' against which manuscripts can be judged, as the definition of any such standard will inevitably vary from one reader to the next" (see also Campanario, 1998a; LaFollette, 1992). "The 'point faible' of the peer review system is not so much the referee and his human judgment (though that certainly is one of its weaknesses); it is the SELECTION of the referee, a function performed by the Editor" (Harnad, 1996, p. 111). Evidently the question becomes one of who constitutes a peer for a certain manuscript; journal editors answer that very differently. For one it constitutes a researcher in the same discipline, for another it could be someone who uses similar methods, and for a third, someone who conducts the same kind of research (Suls & Martin, 2009).

The fate of a manuscript depends on which small sample of reviewers underpins the editorial decision, as research such as that of Bornmann and Daniel (2009) for the AC-IE (Angewandte Chemie-International Edition) indicates. In AC-IE's peer review process, a manuscript is generally published only if two reviewers rate the results of the study as important and also recommend publication in the journal (what the editors have called the clear-cut rule). Even though the clear-cut rule is based on two reviewer reports, submitted manuscripts generally go out to three reviewers in total. An editor explains this process in a letter to an author as follows: "Many papers are sent initially to three referees (as in this case), but in today's increasingly busy climate there are many referees unable to review papers because of other commitments. On the other hand we have a responsibility to authors to make a rapid fair decision on the outcome of papers" (Bornmann & Daniel, in press). For 23 percent of those manuscripts, for which a third reviewer report arrived after the editorial decision was made (37 of 162), this rule would have led to a different decision if the third report had replaced either of the others. Thus, if the editor had been able to consider the recommendations from all three reviewers whom the editor judged to be suitable to review the manuscript, the editor would presumably have made a different decision.

According to J. R. Cole (2000, p. 115), a low level of agreement among reviewers reflects the lack of consensus that is prevalent in all scientific disciplines at the "research frontier." Cole says that usually no one reliably assesses scientific work occurring at the frontiers of research. Eckberg (1991) and Kostoff (1995) point out that differing judgments in peer review are not necessarily a sign of disagreement about the quality of a manuscript but may instead reveal differing positions, judgment criteria, and areas of competency among the reviewers. In addition, reviewers tend to be either more critical or more lenient in their judgments (Siegelman, 1991) if they direct their attention to "different points, and may draw different conclusions about 'worth'" (Eckberg, 1991, p. 146). The question of whether the comments of reviewers are in fact based on different perspectives, positions, and so forth has been examined by only a few empirical studies (Weller, 2002).

Fiske and Fogg (1990, p. 591), for example, found that reviewers of the same submission simply commented on different aspects of the manuscript: "In the typical case, two reviews of the same paper had no critical point in common. ... [T]hey wrote about different topics, each making points that were appropriate and accurate. As a consequence, their recommendations about editorial decisions showed hardly any agreement." Bedeian (2004) brings the perspective of social constructivism to bear on the issue. The argument runs as follows: "Knowledge-claims are socially constructed, being subject to the inevitable author-editor-referee tensions operating throughout the publication process. The impact of this social component, and the influence it has on referee judgments and, in turn, upon claims entering the list of science, offers an (as yet) overlooked explanation for the seeming randomness with which manuscripts are either accepted or rejected" (Bedeian, 2004, p. 204; see also Cole, 1992).

Although a high level of agreement among the reviewers is usually seen as an indicator of the high quality of the process, some scientists see high agreement as problematic: "Too much agreement is in fact a sign that the review process is *not* working well, that reviewers are not properly selected for diversity, and that some are redundant" (Bailar, 1991, p. 138). Many scientists see disagreement as a way of evaluating a contribution from a number of different perspectives. Although selecting reviewers according to the principle of complementarity (for example, choosing a generalist and a specialist) will lower inter-reviewer agreement, validity can be increased considerably because the decision makers (such as journal editors or grant program managers) can base their decisions about a manuscript or proposal on much broader information. "This may reflect a deliberate strategy by editors to have the paper reviewed by specialists with different strengths, although both are usually experts in the substantive topic of the paper" (Rossiter, 2003, p. 86).

Researchers who see low reliability as helpful for the decision-making process believe that reviewers should be selected precisely because of their different perspectives, judgment criteria, and so on (Stricker, 1991). Scientific merit is multifaceted; Hackett and Chubin (2003) therefore regard it as crucial that a valid review of a grant application attend to each of the many elements that make up a good proposal. "The combined assessments of several diverse experts may be needed to achieve a rounded evaluation of a proposal. With a multifaceted proposal evaluated from several divergent perspectives, it is not surprising that inter-rater agreement may be low. Different experts might properly reach different judgments about the quality of the proposal when their particular area of concern is given central importance and evaluated through their particular set of epistemic lenses" (Hackett & Chubin, 2003, p. 20).

Weller (2002) notes that experts have engaged in considerable debate on the subject of proper statistical tests for reviewer agreement studies. Although widely used, the Cohen's Kappa coefficient is prone to numerous methodological problems. Feinstein and Cicchetti (1990, p. 543) found that for Kappa the observed proportion of agreement can be "drastically lowered by a substantial imbalance in the table's marginal totals either vertically or horizontally." Furthermore, the true level of existing agreement may be systematically underestimated because diverging recommendations generally reflect not only the degree of discord, the factor of interest, but also inter-individual differences, called the dislocational component (Eckes, 2004; Lienert, 1987). For example, differences in strictness or leniency in reviewers' judgments (reviewer A may be inclined to rate all manuscripts one level lower than reviewer B) cannot be taken into account (Jayasinghe, Marsh, & Bond, 2003; Siegelman, 1991). In addition to the application of more appropriate coefficients (Cicchetti & Feinstein, 1990) such as Brennan and Prediger's (1981) Kappa, modeling approaches for the analysis of rater agreement have been discussed (Schuster, 2002). The modeling strategy aims not only to summarize the overall judgment concordance but also to model the assignment process of articles to the judgment categories.

Hargens and Herting (1990) took up the idea of latent class agreement models for journal peer review in the 1990s. They are critical of the fact that reviewers' assessments implicitly assume that judgments vary along one latent scientific quality dimension; the authors note that this assumption can hardly be tested by calculating κ or ICC. For this reason Hargens and Herting calculate row-column (RC) association models

(Goodman, 1984). Their investigation of five journals shows that in four cases one quality dimension accounts for the association in the reviewers' judgments. In contrast to the findings of the other studies on the reliability of peer review, Hargens and Herting report substantial statistical association among reviewers' judgments.

Bornmann, Mutz, and Daniel (2007b) stated the same hypothesis as Hargens and Herting (1990) in respect of fellowship peer review: For such reviews, does one quality dimension appear among reviewers? Using the data on applications for doctoral and postdoctoral fellowships that were assessed by means of a three-stage evaluation process, they tested the extent of the association between reviewers' recommendations (internal and external evaluation) and final decisions on fellowship applications by the BIF Board of Trustees. Using the RC association model, they showed that a single latent dimension was sufficient to account for the association between (internal and external) reviewers' recommendations and the fellowship award decision by the Board. Favorable ratings by the (internal and external) reviewers corresponded with favorable decisions by the Board (and vice versa). This indicates that the latent dimension underlying reviewers' recommendations and the Board's decisions reflects the merit of an application under evaluation. These results support Hargens and Herting's (1990) findings about the journal peer review system, although they contradict many other studies relating to the reliability of peer review.

Many general approaches are available to evaluate reliability, identify multiple sampling strategies, and choose which of many statistical tests to apply. The identification of appropriate testing assumptions and of appropriate tests appears to be critical to a sound reliability analysis.

Fairness of Peer Review

According to Merton (1942), the functional goal of science is the expansion of potentially true and secure knowledge. The norm of universalism prescribes that the evaluation of scientific contributions should be based upon objective scientific criteria. Journal submissions or grant applications are not supposed to be judged on the attributes of the author/applicant or on personal biases of the reviewer, editor, or program manager (Ziman, 2000). "First, universalism requires that when a scientist offers a contribution to scientific knowledge, the community's assessment of the validity of that claim should not be influenced by personal or social attributes of the scientist. ... Second, universalism requires that a scientist be fairly rewarded for contributions to the body of scientific knowledge. ... Particularism, in contrast, involves the use of functionally irrelevant characteristics, such as sex and race, as a basis for making claims and gaining rewards in science" (Long & Fox, 1995, p. 46). To the degree that particularism influences how claims are made and rewards are gained, the fairness of the peer review process is at risk (Godlee & Dickersin, 2003). Ever since Kuhn (1962) discussed the significance of different scientific or paradigmatic views for the evaluation of scientific contributions in his seminal work *The Structure of Scientific Revolutions* (see also Mallard, Lamont, & Guetzkow, 2009), researchers, in particular proponents of social constructivism, have expressed increasing doubts about the norm-governed, objective evaluation of scientific work (Hemlin, 1996). For Cole (1992), the constructivists' research supports a new view of science, which casts doubt on the existence of a set of rational criteria. According to Sismondo (1993, p. 548), social constructivist research has brought about the recognition that "social objects in science exist and act as causes of, and constraints on, scientists' actions." Because reviewers are human, factors influence their writing that cannot be predicted, controlled, or standardized (Shashok, 2005). Hames (2007), Hemlin (1996), and Ziman (2000) have indicated that reviewers' minds cannot be completely cleansed of individual interests and emotional factors and that their actions can lapse into bad behavior. Ziman (2000) finds the influence of non-cognitive factors on academic cycles of credibility and credit quite substantial in the more highly structured social world of post-academic science.

Proponents of Mertonian sociology of science have responded to the claim of social constructivists that Merton (1942) overestimates the effects of norms on research with the counterclaim that Merton's work "was later misinterpreted by members of the 'constructivist' school, who thought that Merton was arguing that this is how science actually is" (Cole, 2004, p. 839). Norms only affirm ideals; they do not describe realities. The moral order in any social system always involves a tense balance between its norms and the corresponding counter-norms. It would make no sense to insist on universalism if particularism were not a tempting alternative (Ziman, 2000).

Explicitly or implicitly, many researchers have studied biases in peer review against the backdrop of the norm of universalism (Mertonian sociology of science) or the existence of social objects in science as causes of, and constraints on, scientists' actions (social constructivism). Biases enter peer review when factors that are independent of the quality of a submission (manuscript or application) and are functionally irrelevant to the research correlate statistically with the judgment of reviewers or the decision of journals or funding organizations (Marsh, Jayasinghe, & Bond, 2008; Weller, 2002), For example, consideration of features such as:

- Authors' or applicants' academic status

- Research reported in a submission (e.g., the sub-field or the statistical significance of results)

- The reviewers' gender

- The peer review process, such as the practice of reviewing the applications in alphabetic order (Bornmann & Daniel, 2005a) or (as a recent study by Johnson [2008] on the system used by National Institutes of Health [NIH] has shown) the undue weight of the few reviewers who have read a proposal on the full committee's decision (see also Russo, 2008)

Grayson (2002, p. 8) holds the most fundamental charge of bias in peer review is that of "conservatism, or discrimination against innovatory, heretical, or dissenting opinions. This is in line with a Kuhnian [1962] view of scientific progress in which knowledge is shaped in line with conventional wisdom until the discrepancies between 'normal science' and observed reality become too glaring to ignore" (see also Stehbens, 1999).

Overviews of the peer review research literature (e.g., Hojat, Gonnella, & Caelleigh, 2003; Martin, 2000; Owen, 1982; Pruthi, Jain, Wahid, Mehra, & Nabi, 1997; Ross, 1980; Sharp, 1990; Wood & Wessely, 2003) have named up to 25 different sources of bias that can potentially compromise the fairness of the peer review process. These can be divided into sources closely related to the research (e.g., the reputation of the scientific institution to which an applicant belongs) and irrelevant to the research (e.g., author's gender or nationality). However, source of bias closely related to research may not in fact be functionally irrelevant in peer review. Such sources can contain important information for the reviewer. Biases can also be divided by valence into positive or negative: "that is, a bias may lead to a more negative evaluation of an article than the referee would give were it not for the biasing factor, or it may lead to a more positive evaluation, in which case we may speak of a 'halo effect,' whereby the quality of a work is exaggerated upward by the appraiser. Or the bias may make no difference: a biased evaluation might be identical with what an unbiased evaluation would yield" (Shatz, 2004, p. 36).

Godlee and Dickersin (2003, pp. 91–92) designate whichever biases lead to unfairness in peer review as bad biases, which they distinguish from good biases:

> By good biases we mean, for example, those in favour of important, original, well designed, and well reported science. Most editors and peer reviewers take these good biases for granted, as part of their responsibility to advance a particular field and to meet readers' needs. By bad biases we mean those that reflect a person's pre-existing views about the source of a manuscript (its authors, their institutions, or countries of origin) or about the ideas or findings it presents. Whether held by editors or peer reviewers, bad biases mean that decisions may be systematically influenced by factors other than a manuscript's methodological quality or relevance to the journal's readers.

Empirical research on peer review has dedicated itself to the investigation of potential sources of bias principally in two ways. On one hand, surveys ask scientists to estimate the fairness of particular peer review processes. As in the following examples, surveys often reveal that many grant applicants and authors have concerns about a lack of fairness in peer review. For the National Institute of Handicapped Research (now National Institute on Disability and Rehabilitation Research, NIDRR), a survey of applicants' opinions found that 41 percent of respondents did not agree with the following statement: "I think that as a whole, the peer reviewer comments were fair" (Fuhrer & Grabois, 1985, p. 319). In a survey of applicants for grants from the National Cancer Institute (NCI), 40 percent of applicants found that reviewers were biased against researchers in minor universities or institutions in certain regions of the U.S. (Gillespie, Chubin, & Kurzon, 1985).

Applicants to the Australian Research Council (ARC) claimed that "there is a strong element of luck or chance in being awarded a Large Grant, the outcome of applications depends too much on whom the ARC panel selects as assessors, panels favour applicants from some universities, there is an element of cronyism in the ARC evaluation processes, knowing panel members is a significant advantage in being funded under the Large Grants Scheme, and panel members are themselves advantaged when applying for a Large Grant" (Over, 1996, p. 25). A survey of the *Academy of Management Journal* and *Academy of Management Review* found that about one in ten respondents was dissatisfied with reviewers' objectivity (Bedeian, 2003). Further surveys showed similar results regarding the perceived fairness of peer review; these were published by Chubin and Hackett (1990), McCullough (1989, 1994), and Resnik, Gutierrez-Ford, and Peddada (2008). Predictably there is a close connection between satisfaction with the peer review process and both one's own success in a review and one's participation in a satisfaction survey: Successful applicants and authors are more satisfied and more often take part in surveys than unsuccessful applicants (Gillespie et al., 1985).

In addition to the surveys of grant applicants and authors, the research on the fairness of peer review has used process-generated data to examine the influence of bias variables on judgments. The total group of applicants, authors, or reviewers is divided into subgroups to see whether they consistently and systematically differ from each other in their judgments (e.g., differences in the mean ratings of male and female reviewers). This kind of research is as a rule very elaborate and costly because: (1) research has identified a large number of attributes (of applicants, authors, reviewers, etc.) that can represent potential sources of bias in the peer review process (as has been discussed); (2) the study design should meet the highest standards in order to establish unambiguously that the work from a particular group of applicants or authors has a higher rejection rate due to biases in the peer review process and not simply as a consequence of the lesser scientific merit of the group of applications or manuscripts; and (3) the peer review process is a secret activity (Tight, 2003) and reviews are secured with a guarantee of confidentiality.

Studies that have investigated systematic differences in the reviews of various subgroups primarily concern potential biases, which are attributed to specific features of applicants or authors. Features of reviewers, the peer review processes, or the research reported in a submission receive substantially less attention. Two studies are considered classics in the research on fairness: in a highly cited study of the reviewing process as practiced by scholarly journals, Zuckerman and Merton (1971a, 1971b) showed that the academic status of the author influences the probability that a manuscript will be accepted for publication. The results of the study by Wennerås and Wold (1997) on the fellowship peer review of the Swedish Medical Research Council, which appeared in the journal *Nature*, strongly suggest that reviewers cannot judge scientific merit independently of an applicant's gender. For Cole (1992) the results of such peer review studies suggest that the evaluation of scientific work is influenced by a complex interaction between universalistic factors, such as scientific merit, and scientific and non-scientific particularistic factors, such as gender. Given these findings, Cole (1992) assumes that there is no way to evaluate new scientific work objectively.

Even though numerous studies have reported a lack of fairness in the peer review process, a fundamental problem makes the findings difficult to generalize. Empirical studies have produced inconsistent findings. For example, some studies report that women scientists are at a disadvantage. However, a similar number of studies report only moderate gender effects, no effects, or mixed results (see Table 5.2). Inconsistent results also arise in the research on bias relating to an author's institutional affiliation, the second most frequently researched bias in the context of journal peer review. Some studies provide statistical evidence of discrimination against researchers coming from less prestigious institutions (e.g., Epstein, 1990). Other studies, however, have found little statistical evidence of systematic institutional bias (Lock, 1985; McIntosh & Ross, 1987) or describe contradictory results (Garfunkel, Ulshen, Hamrick, & Lawson, 1994; Pfeffer, Leong, & Strehl, 1977). Weller (2002) recommends more research on this particular topic in the future.

Meta-analysis could be a promising avenue for peer review research. The term meta-analysis (Glass, 1976) refers to a statistical approach that combines evidence from different studies to obtain an overall estimate of treatment effects (Shadish, Cook, & Campbell, 2002). Meta-analysis allows generalized statements on the strength of the effects, regardless of the specificity of individual studies (Matt & Navarro, 1997). It is necessary, of course, that each study be designed similarly with regard to certain properties (e.g., methods, sampling). Bornmann, Mutz, and Daniel (2007a) have presented the first meta-analysis in peer review research on one of the most frequently researched features, the gender of applicants. They were able to include in the meta-analysis data on proportions of women and men for 66 different sets of results

Table 5.2 Results of empirical studies on gender effects in journal peer review

Study results indicate a gender effect	Study results indicate no gender effect	Study results on gender effect are mixed
Author's gender		
Petty & Fleming (1999)	Caelleigh, Hojat, Steinecke, & Gonnella (2003)	Tregenza (2002)
Lloyd (1990)	Gilbert, Williams, & Lundberg (1994)	Levenson, Burford, Bonno, & Davis (1975)
Paludi & Bauer (1983)	Blank (1991)	
Paludi & Strayer (1985)	Patterson, Bailey, Martinez, & Angel (1987)	
Sahner (1982)	Bernard (1980)	
Ward (1981)	Lee, Boyd, Holroyd-Leduc, Bacchetti, & Bero (2006)	
Ferber & Teiman (1980)		
Goldberg (1968)		
Reviewer's gender		
Blank (1991)	Davo, Vives, & Alvarez-Dardet (2003)	
Lloyd (1990)	Gilbert, Williams, & Lundberg (1994)	
Paludi & Bauer (1983)	Nylenna, Riis, & Karlsson (1994)	
Paludi & Strayer (1985)		
Ward (1981)		
Levenson, Burford, Bonno, & Davis (1975)		

from 21 studies since the 1980s. The studies included findings relating to research funding organizations in Australia, North America, and Europe in the life sciences, exact sciences, social sciences, and humanities fields. The data were analyzed using a generalized linear mixed model (Skrondal & Rabe-Hesketh, 2004).

The results show a statistically significant gender effect on the distribution of fellowship and grant proposals: "Even though the estimates of the gender effect vary substantially from study to study, the model estimation shows that all in all, among grant applicants men have statistically significant greater odds of receiving grants than women by about 7 percent" (Bornmann et al., 2007a, p. 226). What importance can be attributed to this finding on the use of peer review for selection of applicants to receive fellowships or grants? Assume for a moment that worldwide in a certain time period decisions are made to approve or reject 100,000 applications (50,000 submitted by women scientists and 50,000 by men scientists). Half of these applications are approved, and half are rejected. Based on the results of the meta-analysis, an approval rate of 52 percent (26,000 approvals) for men and 48 percent (24,000 approvals) for women can be expected. This makes a difference of 2,000 approvals due to the gender of the applicants (Bornmann et al., 2007a).

Bornmann and colleagues (2007a) reported substantial heterogeneity in effect sizes for the different peer review processes considered in the meta-analysis that compromised the robustness of their results, but models incorporating variables to explain this heterogeneity failed to converge. In an extension and reanalysis of their data, Marsh, Bornmann, Mutz, Daniel, and O'Mara (in press) juxtapose traditional (fixed and random effects) and multilevel models, demonstrating important advantages to the multilevel approach and its appropriate application. (Marsh and Bornmann [2009] reported on the results of the reanalysis in *Nature*.) The results show that gender differences in peer review varied significantly in relation to the type of application (grant proposals or pre- and post-doctoral fellowships), but not in relation to the other covariates (e.g., publication year of the studies included in the meta-analysis). Gender differences in favor of men are larger for fellowship applications than for grant applications. Indeed, there are no gender differences for the 40 (of 66) sets of results based on grant proposals, but statistically significant gender differences in favor of men for the 26 sets of results that were for fellowship applications. These findings support Cole's (1979, p. 75) conclusion that "functionally irrelevant characteristics such as sex will be more quickly activated when there are no or few functionally relevant criteria on which to judge individual performance." The younger the applicants are, the shorter their track records. And the less information there exists on which to judge an application, the greater the risk of bias.

According to Marsh and colleagues (2008, p. 166) most peer review research is correlational; "it provides a weak basis for any causal inferences particularly in evaluating potential biases." These authors thus address a second principal problem, in addition to the heterogeneity of results, that affects bias research in general: the lack of experimental studies in which (1) an independent variable is varied or manipulated by an experimenter (e.g., applicant's gender), so that its effect on a dependent variable (e.g., selection decisions) may be measured and (2) the effect of the variable is monitored. Only very few researchers have attempted to study reviewer bias experimentally in the natural setting of actual reviewer evaluations (see Abramowitz, Gomes, & Abramowitz, 1975; Baxt, Waeckerle, Berlin, & Callaham, 1998; Mahoney, 1977; Nylenna, Riis, & Karlsson, 1994). Peters and Ceci (1982), for example, examined reviewers' evaluations of manuscripts submitted to American psychology journals in a natural setting (Duncan & Magnuson, 2003). They looked for reviewer bias that could be attributed to reviewers' knowledge of the authors' institutions or names. As test materials they selected already published research articles by investigators from prestigious and highly productive American psychology departments. With fictitious names and institutions substituted for the original ones, the altered manuscripts were formally resubmitted to the journals that had originally reviewed and published them. Eight of the nine altered articles that were peer reviewed a second time were rejected. Peters and

Ceci's bias study was criticized, however, for having violated ethical principles (Chubin, 1982; Fleiss, 1982; Honig, 1982; Weller, 2002).

Experimental research has been undertaken with regard to fellowship peer review as well as journal peer review. Noting that female applicants have had a consistently lower success rate when applying for the European Molecular Biology Organization's (EMBO) Long-Term Fellowship (LTF) and Young Investigator (YI) programmes, Ledin, Bornmann, Gannon, and Wallon (2007) conducted an experiment to test whether unconscious gender bias influenced the decisions made by the selection committee. First, they gender-blinded the committee for two rounds of applications in 2006. They eliminated all references to gender from the applications, letters of recommendation, and interview reports that were sent to the committee for scoring. Nevertheless, the committee reached the same conclusions when gender-blinded. Although the studies of Ledin and colleagues (2007) on fellowship peer review and Peters and Ceci (1982) on journal peer review used an experimental approach, they found different results regarding the effect of bias variables.

The lack of experimental studies makes it impossible to establish unambiguously whether work from a particular group of scientists (e.g., junior or senior researchers) receives better reviews (and thus has a higher approval or acceptance rate) due to biases in the review and decision-making process, or if favorable review and greater success in the selection process are simply consequences of the scientific merit of the corresponding group of proposals or manuscripts (Daniel, 1993/2004). As with non-experimental studies, it is almost impossible to demonstrate certain biases in the decision-making process of peer review. Marsh and colleagues (2008, p. 166) note that if "it may be possible to construct artificial laboratory studies with true random assignment in which potential biases are experimentally manipulated, researchers need to be careful that experimental manipulations reflect the actual bias being tested and that results generalize to actual peer-review practice."

Predictive Validity of Peer Review

The goal for peer review of grant/fellowship applications and manuscripts is usually to select the "best" from among the work submitted (Smith, 2006). The validity of judgments in peer review is often questioned. For example, the former editor of the journal *Lancet*, Sir Theodore Fox (1965, p. 8), wrote: "When I divide the week's contributions into two piles—one that we are going to publish and the other that we are going to return—I wonder whether it would make any real difference to the journal or its readers if I exchanged one pile for another." The selection function is a difficult research topic to investigate. According to Jayasinghe and colleagues (2001) and also Figueredo (2006) there exists no mathematical formula or uniform definition of what makes a manuscript worthy of publication, or of what makes a research proposal worthy of funding (see also Smith, 2006).

As a result of the increasing reliance on soft money in the financing of research and the use of publications as a measure of scientific performance (whether by individual researchers or groups of scientists) in nearly all scientific disciplines, the peer review system is faced with an ever-growing number of submissions (e.g., Gölitz, 2008). This trend creates new challenges. Previously, reviewers filtered out work that did not meet a certain minimum standard (negative selection), whereas today they need to select the "best" from a mass of high quality work (positive selection). Instead of minimum standards, today excellence is required (Koch, 2006). According to Yalow (1982, p. 401) the question for today's peer review is "how to identify the few, those who make the breakthroughs which permit new horizons to open, from the many who attempt to build on the breakthroughs—often without imagination and innovation."

One approach to testing the predictive validity of peer review is to investigate the fate of rejected scientific contributions. In journal peer review "a rejection usually does not kill a paper ... a rejected paper usually finds life at another journal" (Gans & Shepherd, 1994, p. 177). In the 1980s Abelson (1980) reported that almost all of the manuscripts rejected by the journal *Science* were published later in other journals. For manuscripts rejected by the journal AC-IE in 1984, Daniel (1993/2004) determined that 71 percent were subsequently published elsewhere; Bornmann and Daniel (2008a, 2008b) found 95 percent of manuscripts the journal rejected at the beginning of 2000 were published later elsewhere. (The follow-up study determined that no alterations or only minor alterations had been made to approximately three-quarters of the rejected manuscripts published elsewhere). Other studies on the fate of manuscripts rejected by a journal report subsequent publication figures ranging from 28 percent to 85 percent (Weller, 2002). Taken together, these studies demonstrate that in the peer review process of one manuscript submitted at various times, reviewers and editors arrive at different judgments: manuscripts that are rejected by a journal (after peer review) are then accepted by another journal (after peer review). This suggests that manuscript review is not based only on *generally* valid quality criteria; the review (or the outcome of the review) seems also to be dependent upon the local conditions under which the peer review process takes place.

Rejecta Mathematica (Wakin, Rozell, Davenport, & Laska, 2009)—a peer-reviewed open access journal—was launched in 2009 and is the first journal to publish only manuscripts that have been previously rejected from peer-reviewed journals in the mathematical sciences. As studies concerning the fate of rejected manuscripts show, this journal is not alone in publishing rejected manuscripts. The novelty is that rejections are made public and openly discussed. All research papers appearing in *Rejecta Mathematica* include an open letter from the authors discussing the manuscript's original review process, disclosing any known flaws in the manuscript and stating the case for the manuscript's value to the community.

Several studies have investigated the fate of rejected contributions in both grant and journal peer review. In a sample of projects rejected by the NIH at the beginning of the 1970s, 22 percent of proposals were subsequently carried out without substantial changes and 43 percent were not conducted after being rejected (Carter, Cooper, Lai, & March, 1978). Similarly, in a survey of applicants for grants from the NSF, 48 percent of researchers whose applications failed reported that they stopped that line of research (Chubin & Hackett, 1990). At the NCI two-thirds of unsuccessful applicants did pursue their research in spite of rejection and most were eventually published (Gillespie et al., 1985). In light of the paucity of studies on the fate of rejected applications,"further cohort studies of unfunded proposals are needed. Such studies will, however, always be difficult to interpret—do they show how peer review prevents resources from being wasted on bad science, or do they reveal the blinkered conservative preferences of senior reviewers who stifle innovation and destroy the morale of promising younger scientists? We cannot say" (Wessely, 1998, p. 303).

Following recommendations, such as those of Harnad (2008, p. 103), that "peer review ... [has] to be evaluated objectively (i.e., via metrics)," the second step in the research on the predictive validity of journal peer review consists of gauging the quality of journals that accepted previously rejected manuscripts. According to Jennings (2006, online) "there is a hierarchy of journals. At the apex of the (power law-shaped?) pyramid stand the most prestigious multidisciplinary journals; below them is a middle tier of good discipline-specific journals with varying degrees of selectivity and specialization; and propping up the base lies a large and heterogeneous collection of journals whose purviews are narrow, regional, or merely unselective." In her literature review covering research on journal peer review, Weller (2002) cites five studies (Chew, 1991; Cronin & McKenzie, 1992; Gordon, 1984; Weller, 1996; Whitman & Eyre, 1985) that have ranked the quality of the rejecting and the later accepting journals mostly by means of the Journal Impact Factors (JIF, provided by Thomson Reuters in the Journal Citation Reports, JCR). The JIF is the average number of times papers from the journal published in the past two years (e.g., 2005 and 2006) have been cited in the JCR year (e.g., 2007) (Bensman, 2007).

Seven further studies, which are not included in the literature review by Weller (2002), have been published by Armstrong, Idriss, Kimball, and Bernhard (2008); Bornmann and Daniel (2008a, 2008b); Daniel (1993/2004); Lock (1985); McDonald, Cloft, and Kallmes (2007); Opthof, Furstner, van Geer, and Coronel (2000); and Ray, Berkwits, and Davidoff (2000). In the total of twelve studies, between 0 percent (Daniel, 1993/2004) and 70 percent (Gordon, 1984) of the rejected manuscripts in a higher quality journal could be tracked. The results of these studies show "that authors do not necessarily move from 'leading' journals to less prestigious journals after a rejection" (Weller, 2002, p. 68). Authors seem to select a journal for a rejected manuscript based on the quality of the rejecting journal and the availability of additional high(er)-impact journals: the higher the quality ranking of the rejecting journal, the lower the chance that a rejected manuscript will appear in another journal ranked as higher quality.

Neither grant nor fellowship peer review has yet undergone similar analysis. At least no studies have compared the reputations of funding organizations, which rejected an application and/or funded a previously rejected application. This may have to do with the fact that the reputation of a grant-giving organization cannot be gauged as easily as the reputation of a journal (through its JIF or through circulation data).

A third, important step for the investigation of the predictive validity of peer review consists of comparing the impact of papers accepted or rejected (but published elsewhere) in journal peer review or the impact of papers that were published by applicants whose proposals were either accepted or rejected in grant or fellowship peer review. As the number of citations to a publication reflects its international impact (Borgman & Furner, 2002; Nicolaisen, 2007), and given the lack of other operationalizable indicators, it is common in peer review research to evaluate the success of the process on the basis of citation counts. Citation counts are attractive raw data for the evaluation of research output: They are "unobtrusive measures that do not require the cooperation of a respondent and do not themselves contaminate the response (i.e., they are nonreactive)" (Smith, 1981, p. 84). Although citations have been a controversial measure of both quality and scientific progress (e.g., scholars might cite because the cited source corroborated their own views or preferred methods, rather than because of the significance and relevance of the works cited), they are still accepted as a measure of scientific impact and thus as a partial aspect of scientific quality (Martin & Irvine, 1983).

Van Raan (1996, p. 404), holds that citations provide "a good to even very good quantitative impression of at least one important aspect of quality, namely international impact." For Lindsey (1989, p. 201), citations are "our most *reliable* convenient measure of quality in science—a measure that will continue to be widely used." For Pendlebury (2008, p. 1) "tracking citations and understanding their trends in context is a key to evaluating the impact and influence of research." Against the backdrop of these and similar statements (Borgman, 2007; British Academy, 2007; Evidence Ltd., 2007; Jennings, 2006), scientific judgments on submissions (manuscripts or applications) are said to show predictive validity in peer review research if the citation counts of manuscripts accepted for publication (or manuscripts published by accepted applicants) and manuscripts rejected by a journal but then published elsewhere (or manuscripts published by rejected applicants) differ statistically significantly.

Until now only a few studies have analyzed citation counts from individual papers as the basis for assessing predictive validity in peer review. A literature search found only five empirical studies into the level of predictive validity associated with the journal peer review process. Research in this area is extremely labor-intensive because a validity test requires information regarding the fate of rejected manuscripts and their citation counts (Bornstein, 1991). The editor of the *Journal of Clinical Investigation* (Wilson, 1978) undertook his own investigation into the matter of predictive validity. Daniel (1993/2004) and Bornmann and Daniel (2008a, 2008b) investigated the peer review process of AC-IE, and Opthof and colleagues (2000) did the same for *Cardiovascular Research*. McDonald, Cloft, and Kallmes (2009) examined the predictive validity of editorial decisions at the *American Journal of Neuroradiology*. All five studies confirmed that the editorial decisions (acceptance or rejection) for the various journals indicated a rather high degree of predictive validity, using citation counts as validity criteria.

Wilson (1978) was able to show that the 306 manuscripts accepted for publication in the *Journal of Clinical Investigation* during the 1970s were cited more frequently in the four years after their appearance than the 149 rejected manuscripts that subsequently appeared in other journals. Daniel (1993/2004) and Bornmann and Daniel (2008a, 2008b) reported similar results for manuscripts that were submitted to AC-IE, as did Opthof and colleagues (2000) and McDonald and colleagues (2009) for manuscripts that were submitted to *Cardiovascular Research* and the *American Journal of Neuroradiology*, respectively. Bornmann and Daniel (2008b) not only conducted a comparison of average citation counts of accepted and rejected (but published elsewhere) manuscripts, they also compared the average citation counts of both groups with international scientific reference standards using (1) mean citation rates for the journal set provided by Thomson Reuters corresponding to the field "chemistry" and (2) specific reference standards that refer to the subject areas of *Chemical Abstracts* (Bornmann, Mutz, Neuhaus, & Daniel, 2008; Neuhaus & Daniel, 2009). The comparisons reveal that mean citation rates below baseline values were significantly less frequent for accepted manuscripts than for rejected manuscripts.

Only six studies on the assessment of citation counts as a basis of predictive validity in selection decisions in fellowship or grant peer review have been published in recent years, according to a literature search. These studies tested whether papers by applicants whose proposals for funding were approved were cited more frequently than papers by applicants whose proposals were rejected. Armstrong, Caverson, Adams, Taylor, and Olley's (1997) study of the Heart and Stroke Foundation of Canada (HSFC); Bornmann and Daniel's (2005c, 2006) research on the BIF; and Bornmann, Wallon, and Ledin's (2008) work on the EMBO confirmed the predictive validity of the selection decisions. However, Hornbostel, Böhmer, Klingsporn, Neufeld, and von Ins (2009) investigated the Emmy Noether Programme of the DFG and Melin and Danell (2006) studied the Swedish Foundation for Strategic Research; neither group showed significant differences between the performance of accepted and rejected applicants. Van den Besselaar and Leydesdorff (2007) reported contradictory results regarding the Council for Social Scientific Research of the Netherlands Organisation for Scientific Research. Carter (1982) investigated the association between (1) assessments given by the reviewers for the NIH regarding applicants for research funding and (2) the number of citations obtained by journal articles produced with grant funding. This study showed that better votes in fact correlate with more frequent citations; however, the correlation coefficient was low. Unlike the clearer results for journal peer review, contradictory results emerge in research on fellowship or grant peer review: some studies confirm the predictive validity of peer review but others leave room for doubt.

Melin and Danell (2006) examined the publication histories of the top 8 percent of all applicants to the Swedish Foundation for Strategic Research and found only slight mean differences in scientific productivity between approved and rejected applicants. Similar results were reported by van den Besselaar and Leydesdorff (2007) when they compared in a second step of analysis the 275 successful applicants and the top performing 275 non-successful applicants (of all 911 non-successful applicants). Rejection decisions by the selection committees can be categorized as type I error (falsely drawn approval) or type II error (falsely drawn rejection). With type I error, the selection committee concluded that an applicant had the scientific potential for promotion (and was approved), when he or she actually did not (as reflected in an applicant's low scientific performance). With type II error, the selection committee concluded that an applicant did *not* have the scientific potential for promotion (and was rejected), when he or she actually did (as reflected in a high scientific performance).

Bornmann and Daniel (2007a) expanded on such approaches by determining the extent of type I and type II errors in the selection decisions of the BIF committee peer review. Approximately one third of the decisions to award a fellowship to an applicant showed a type I error, and about one third of the decisions not to award a fellowship to an applicant showed a type II error. In a similar manner, Bornmann, Mutz, and Daniel (2008) examined EMBO selection decisions (for two programs) to determine the extent of errors due to over-estimation (type I errors) and under-estimation (type II errors) of future scientific performance. The statistical analyses showed that between 26 and 48 percent of the decisions made to award or reject an application exhibited one or the other error type. It should be emphasized, of course, that even though the selection committees did not correctly estimate the applicants' performance, a statistically significant association emerged for both institutions between selection decisions and the applicants' subsequent scientific achievements.

Most studies on the predictive validity of journal, fellowship, and grant peer review rely on statistical methods, which strictly speaking should not be applied to bibliometric data. (Future peer review studies should adopt sound statistical methods.) For example, citation impact differences between accepted manuscripts and manuscripts that were rejected but published elsewhere were determined on the basis of arithmetic means. As a rule, the distribution of citation counts for a larger number of publications is skewed to the right according to a power law (Joint Committee on Quantitative Assessment of Research, 2008). In the face of non-normal distributed citation data, the arithmetic mean value is not appropriate because it can give a distorted picture of the kind of distribution and "it is a rather crude statistic" (p. 2). Arithmetic mean graphics show primarily where publications with high citation counts can be found. Evidence Ltd. (2007, p. 10), a British firm that has specialized in the evaluation of research, therefore recommends "where bibliometric data must stand alone, they should be treated as distributions and not as averages."

Comparisons drawn between groups of papers (e.g., of accepted or rejected applicants) in terms of reserach impact are, according to Bornmann, Mutz, Neuhaus, and colleagues (2008), valid only if (1) the scientific impact of the groups are looked at by using box plots, Lorenz curves, and Gini coefficients to represent the distribution characteristics of data (in other words, going beyond the usual arithmetic mean value); (2) different reference standards are used to assess groups' impact and the appropriateness of the reference standards undergoes critical examination; and (3) the comparative analysis of the citation counts for publications takes into consideration that, in statistical analysis, citations are a function of many factors in addition to scientific quality, including number of co-authors; location of the authors; the prestige, language, and availability of the publishing journal; and the size of the citation window. Including these factors in the statistical analysis makes it possible to establish the adjusted covariation between selection decisions and citation counts.

Hornbostel and colleagues (2009) incorporated not only bibliometric data into their study investigating predictive validity of the DFG peer review process, but also additional indicators of career success. Their results thus show that "a gratifyingly high number of the approved individuals were appointed to a professorship or had found a career position in research that they themselves described as satisfactory, either during the programme itself or after the funding had ended" (p. 188). Especially in fellowship peer review the evaluation of career data provides a good complement to the bibliometric analyses and should thus be applied in studies on predictive validity for determining the effectiveness of the peer review process (e.g., Wellcome Trust, 2001). Yet further performance measures in addition to citation counts can be employed not only for research on grant and fellowship peer review, but also for journal peer review. For example, publishers record the number of times that a paper in electronic form is accessed, which means the information on how many readers have downloaded it can be used. Many publishers are already members and vendors of COUNTER and provide the usage report "Number of Successful Full-Text Article Requests by Month and Journal" (see www.projectcounter.org). According to Perneger (2004) and Brody, Harnad, and Carr (2006), usage statistics can be used as early performance indicators for papers and authors.

Conclusions

For many years the peer review process has been a target for criticism. It has been criticized especially "in relation to traditional psychological research criteria of reliability, validity, generalizability, and potential biases" (Marsh et al., 2008, p. 160). On the other hand, defenders of the system argue that only qualified specialists can properly judge cutting-edge research and that peer review is necessary to maintain and improve the quality of submissions. This review has offered an overview of research on peer review processes and the arguments used by proponents and opponents in recent years. The most important research results are summarily described in the next section, thematic areas are pointed out, and recommendations for the conduct of future research are given.

Reliability of Peer Review

Most studies report a low level of agreement between reviewers' judgments on the basis of κ and/or ICC. Daniel (1993/2004) can certainly prove, at least for the AC-IE manuscript reviewing, that broad discrepancies between reviewers' judgments are rare, even if the chance-corrected agreement (measured on the basis of κ) between the judgments appears negligible. Agreement between reviewers appears less when measured with κ or ICC than it is in fact. Studies applying Hargens and Herting's (1990) RC association model to the analysis of reviewer agreement in journal and fellowship peer review report similar results. These studies show substantial association among reviewers' judgments. The dependence of results upon the statistical procedure raises an important issue for future research (Weller, 2002): What are the correct statistical procedures for reliability studies?

After reflecting on the abundance of studies reporting low inter-reviewer agreement, Weller (2002) considers a second issue significant: the meaning or importance of results of reliability studies. In Kostoff's (1995, p. 180) view, low agreement among reviewers is simply a response to the review of mediocre academic work:

> While a peer review can gain consensus on the projects and proposals that are either outstanding or poor, there will be differences of opinion on the projects and proposals that cover the much wider middle range. For projects or proposals in this middle range, their fate is somewhat more sensitive to

the reviewers selected. If a key purpose of a peer review is to insure that the outstanding projects and proposals are funded or continued, and the poor projects are either terminated or modified strongly, then the capabilities of the peer review instrument are well matched to its requirements.

As has been thoroughly discussed, a low reviewer agreement is seen as beneficial to the review process (Bailar, 1991). According to Marsh and Ball (1991), when varied perspectives are represented in the selection of reviewers, *reliability* declines, whereas the *validity* of the process is significantly increased.

However, very few studies have investigated reviewer agreement with the aim of identifying the actual reasons behind reviewer disagreement (e.g., by carrying out comparative content analyses of reviewers' comment sheets). LaFollette (1992), for example, noted the scarcity of research on such questions as how reviewers apply standards and the specific criteria established for making a decision on a manuscript. In-depth studies that address these issues might prove to be fruitful avenues for future investigation (Weller, 2002). Such research should dedicate itself primarily to the dislocational component in reviewers' judgments as well as differences in the strictness or leniency of the judgments (Eckes, 2004; Lienert, 1987).

Fairness of Peer Review

Although reviewers like to believe that they choose the "best" based on objective criteria, "decisions are influenced by factors—including biases about race, sex, geographic location of a university, and age—that have nothing to do with the quality of the person or work being evaluated" (National Academy of Sciences, 2006). Given that peers are not prophets, but ordinary human beings with their own opinions, strengths, and weaknesses (Ehses, 2004), a number of studies have examined potential sources of bias in peer review. Numerous studies have already shown an association between potential sources of bias and judgments in peer review and thus called into question the fairness of the process itself; however, research on bias faces two fundamental problems that make generalization of the findings difficult.

On one hand, the various studies have yielded heterogeneous results. Some have demonstrated the indisputable effects of potential sources of bias; others report moderate or slight effects. The heterogeneity of the results may possibly be explained by disparate definitions of the phenomena under investigation, or, alternatively, the application of different research designs and statistical procedures. With the application of meta-analyses in peer review research, however, Bornmann and colleagues (2007a) and Marsh and colleagues (in press) have introduced a promising possibility for arriving at *generalized* statements with a heterogeneous set of results on the effect of a potential source of bias, *regardless* of the specificity of individual studies. Therefore, future research should rely more heavily on meta-analyses in order to find a definitive answer to the question regarding the effect of specific sources of bias in peer review processes.

A second principal problem that affects bias research in general is the lack of experimental studies. This makes it impossible to establish unambiguously whether work from a particular group of scientists receives better reviews due to biases in the review and decision-making process, or if favorable reviews and greater success in the selection process are simply a consequence of the scientific merit of the corresponding group of proposals or manuscripts. Therefore, according to Wessely (1998, p. 304), "randomised controlled trials are needed to assess the role of ... sex and institutional bias. The absence of controlled trials in this area of scientific decision making is ironic." The conduct of experimental studies on peer review remains problematic and runs up against ethical limits.

In order to be able to arrive at results with greater accuracy and validity in the analysis of potential sources of bias in peer review, several suggestions for statistical analysis and/or research design are given. These suggestions should lead to significantly more robust results than heretofore (see also Weller, 2002).

- Cross-validation: The statistical analyses of fairness should be conducted not only for the group of first reviewers but also for the group of second (or further) reviewers of manuscripts or applications; the quality of the results can be tested using cross-validation (Efron & Gong, 1983): In statistics, cross-validation is the practice of partitioning a sample of data into subsamples, in this case the first and the second reviewers, such that analysis is initially performed on the first subsample and the second subsamples are retained "blind" for subsequent use in confirming and validating the initial analysis.

- Within-proposal analysis: To test the influence of potential sources of bias regarding the reviewer (e.g., his or her nationality) on judgments in peer review, a so-called within-proposal analysis can be undertaken. Jayasinghe and colleagues (2001, p. 353) analyzed reviewers' gender as a potential source of bias in the ARC peer review and conducted "a within-proposal analysis based on those proposals with at least one male external reviewer and at least one female external reviewer." The advantage of this statistical approach is that it controls for the many characteristics associated with a proposal (e.g., the applicant's gender). Differences in the mean ratings between both reviewer groups can be investigated with a statistical test for two related samples (e.g., the paired sample *t*-test).

- Multiple regression analysis: With multiple regression analysis, one can establish the association between a bias variable (which is included in the regression model as an independent variable) and the judgments in peer review (which constitute the dependent variable in the model), such that the scientific quality of the proposal or manuscript is controlled for (measured ex-post, for example, using bibliometric indicators). The indicator of scientific quality is also included in the model as an independent variable. This means the association between the bias variable and judgments is investigated, when manuscript quality is *statistically controlled*. In statistical bias analysis this procedure is called the control variable approach (Cole & Fiorentine, 1991).

- Interaction effects: Because attributes of the authors or applicants *and* attributes of the reviewers are potential sources of bias in peer review, both should always be included in the statistical analysis; the peer review process should be examined with regard to so-called interaction effects. An example of an interaction effect is when the regional origin of a submission influences the judgment of a U.S. reviewer but does not influence the judgment of a reviewer from another country (Bornmann & Daniel, 2007b; Jayasinghe et al., 2003).

- Multilevel regression analysis: Reviewers' ratings on proposals or manuscripts in a data set on peer review of a grant organization or a journal normally take the following form: (1) it has a multilevel structure, which means two or more reviewers for a journal are nested within manuscripts or two or more reviewers for a grant organization are nested within grant proposals. (2) the data structure is often cross-classified, which means the same reviewer reviews many submissions and one submission is reviewed by many reviewers. Calculating single-level regression models for these data is usually inappropriate (Jayasinghe et al., 2003). For Jayasinghe (2003, p. 341), an important finding from his investigation of the ARC peer review process is that "future peer review data need to be analysed using multilevel models with either categorical (e.g., accept, reject, fund, no fund for grant proposals) or continuous (e.g., assessor ratings for the quality of grant proposals) response variables."

- Case study: Biases in peer review might assume different configurations and exhibit different dynamics across different disciplines, professions, regions, time spans, funding organizations, journal editorial teams, and so forth. Accordingly, the case study method might be more heavily utilized to detect the possibly unique dynamics and configurations of bias in different settings, times, circumstances. Broad surveys and grand analyses appear to show too much inconsistency and to yield weak conclusions.

For research on journal peer review, Geisler (2001) has proposed that a journal's process should be studied continuously and that any evidence of bias in judgment should be brought to the attention of the editor for correction and modification. This naturally goes for research on both grant and fellowship peer review. According to Hojat, Gonnella, and Caelleigh (2003, p. 75), the controversy surrounding the peer review process demands "that the journal editors conduct periodic internal and external evaluations of their journals' peer review process and outcomes, with participation of reviewers, contributors, readers, and owners" to assure its integrity and fairness. In the most comprehensive review of research on editorial biases, Godlee and Dickersin (2003, p. 112) also conclude that "journals should continue to take steps to minimize the scope for unacceptable biases, and researchers should continue to look for them." In Weller's (2002, p. 100) view, the area of *editorial* bias is "ripe for more research." The investigations on potential sources of bias can help not only to minimize the scope of unacceptable biases, but also to prevent scientific misbehavior; Martinson, Anderson, Crain, and de Vries (2006, p. 51) report that "when scientists believe they are being treated unfairly they are more likely to behave in ways that compromise the integrity of science."

Investigations into the influence of bias variables on the peer review process are as a rule very elaborate and costly. Before a funding organization or a journal conducts an extensive evaluation study, it should therefore seek indications of the influence of potential sources of bias both in order to determine the necessity of an evaluation study and, if a necessity appears, then to identify the sources of bias that should be examined more closely. Bornmann, Mutz, and Daniel (2008) present a statistical method that program managers at a research funding organization or journal editors can use to obtain *initial indications* of potential sources of bias in their peer review process. To implement the method in grant peer review, the data required are the number of approved and the number of rejected applicants for grants among different groups (for example, women and men or natural scientists and social scientists). Editors of a journal require only data on specific manuscript groups for a number of years or a number of research fields. If these evaluations show an influence of bias variables in a peer review process, an in-depth evaluation study should be conducted.

Focusing on classical bias variables like an author's gender or an applicant's academic status in peer review studies can lead to the exclusion of other variables when such other variables are really more likely to produce unfair outcomes. The following merit further research:

- A high number of cited references in a submission appears to impress reviewers, perhaps more than a substantive or significant submission with a low number of cited references.

- Reviewers might tend to reward mathematical and statistical pyrotechnics irrespective of the significance of the contribution. Furthermore, do advanced statistical tests tend to be employed more than simple statistical tests when the simple test might be more appropriate?

- Is there a tendency for many reviewers to forget older contributions (particularly when their originators die—as in the case of Piaget's theories of child cognitive development) or to reward citations to current theories (or even academically fashionable theories) more than to old theories? Does knowledge (particularly inter-generational knowledge) tend to accumulate or to be cumulative (see Kuhn, 1962)?

- Is there a tendency for disciplines in traditional peer review processes to form intellectual silos (see Mallard et al., 2009) or editorial cliques?

- Does there exist a so called Oppenheim effect in scholarly publishing and if so, to what extent? Is external review just a formal exercise initiated by an editor because the publication decision is already clear to the editor? Gorman (2007) calls this phenomenon the Oppenheim effect.

Predictive Validity of Peer Review

The few studies that have examined the predictive validity of journal peer review on the basis of citation counts confirm that peer review represents a quality filter and works as an instrument for the self-regulation of science. Seven studies have investigated the predictive validity of selection decisions on the basis of citation counts for fellowship or grant peer review. Unlike with journal peer review, these studies have provided mixed results: Some confirm the predictive validity of peer review; others raise doubts.

The variable results on fellowship and grant peer review reflect the fact that "funding decisions are inherently speculative because the work has not yet been done" (Stamps, 1997, p. 4). Whereas in journal peer review the *results* of the research are assessed, grant and fellowship peer review is principally an evaluation of the *potential* of the proposed research (Bornmann & Daniel, 2005b). Evaluating the application involves deciding whether the proposed research is significant, determining whether the specific plans for investigation are feasible, and evaluating the competence of the applicant (Cole, 1992). Fellowship or grant peer review—when compared to journal peer review—is perceived as entailing a heightened risk for judgments and decisions with low predictive validity. Accordingly it is likely that studies on grant or fellowship peer review will have more difficulty confirming the predictive validity than studies on journal peer review.

The heterogeneous results can also be attributed to the widely differing designs and statistical procedures used. Some studies include all applicants in one cohort (or several cohorts) (e.g., Bornmann, Wallon, et al., 2008), whereas Melin and Danell (2006) examine only a highly select group of the "best" applicants among those accepted and rejected. The study by Carter (1982) includes only applicants with an approved proposal. In only two studies (Bornmann & Daniel, 2005c, 2006; van den Besselaar & Leydesdorff, 2007) did the researchers test for statistical significance. Only one study (Bornmann & Daniel, 2005c, 2006) applied discipline-specific reference standards (van Raan, 1999). This comparison with international scientific reference values revealed, for example, that (1) articles published by successful and non-successful applicants were cited considerably more often than the "average" publication in a certain (sub-)field, and (2) excellent research performance can be expected more from successful than non-successful applicants.

Such a comparison with international scientific reference values is an important step in the analysis of the predictive validity of peer review processes. If a study compares the impact of publications—not only by successful but also by non-successful applicants—with reference standards, the scientific performance of the total group of applicants for grants or fellowships can be determined. At an organization that claims to have a highly regarded grant program, even non-successful grant applicants should demonstrate research performance at a higher level—otherwise one cannot speak validly of this program's renown. (This certainly implies that applicants are familiar with a program's renown.) Highly regarded programs should have the ability to stimulate the "best" researchers in a certain discipline to submit their "best" applications.

On the other hand, as has been discussed, five studies on journal peer review have found a high degree of predictive validity through the comparison of mean citation rates for accepted manuscripts and rejected manuscripts published elsewhere. Cicchetti (1999) argued against this form of validity test, pointing out that papers accepted by journals may have been cited on average more frequently than those published elsewhere simply because they appeared in journals with a high impact factor. Higher citation rates are not necessarily the result of a paper's superior scientific quality; instead, they may just show the higher impact or higher visibility of a journal. Seglen (1994), however, reports that articles' citation counts do not seem to be detectably influenced by the status of the journals in which they are published. In spite of Cicchetti's (1999) criticism, this form of validity test for journal peer review decisions should produce useful results.

The limited comparability of accepted and rejected contributions in studies on the predictive validity of grant and fellowship peer review has been noted. Chapman and McCauley (1994, p. 428) write: "Criterion data for rejected applicants are difficult to obtain and difficult to interpret, even when available; those accepted are no longer comparable to those rejected because the two groups have had different experiences." According to Sonnert (quoted in Bornmann & Daniel, 2005c), fellowships clearly have a dual function. They reward prior excellence (i.e., they are given to the "best" applicants, who are selected according to merit criteria), but they also afford the successful applicants resources that might enable them to do excellent scientific work in their future careers. If a study establishes significant performance advantages for accepted applicants but not rejected ones, one can argue—with reference to Merton's (1948) concept of self-fulfilling prophecy—that the funding organization gives the fellows such an advantage in training, prestige, self-confidence, and so on that they later become superior scientists because of the fellowship, not because they were particularly promising at the point of application. Rather than picking the "best" scientists, the selection committee might, in this view, create them (see also Cole & Cole, 1967; Hagstrom, 1965; Merton, 1968).

There is accordingly a circularity in the study designs for the analysis of predictive validity that should be considered in future studies investigating grant or fellowship peer review. To control, for example, in statistical analysis of the influence of funding on subsequent publication and citation numbers, information is needed on the funding of rejected research by investigating in particular the fate of the rejected applicants and their research projects (Bornmann, Wallon, et al., 2008).

A general weakness of research on the predictive validity of peer review is the lack of studies; significantly more have been published on the reliability and fairness of peer review than on predictive validity. Weller (2002) has addressed this lack in journal peer review, and both Wessely (1998) and Jayasinghe and colleagues (2001) have done so for fellowship and grant peer review. Although the number of studies published in recent years has increased, particularly on fellowship peer review, comprehensive research is still lacking. Nonprofit and for-profit funding organizations and journals might be studied to provide an enhanced view of the peer review process.

Acknowledgments

This review of studies on journal, grant, and fellowship peer review is dedicated to my longstanding mentor Hans-Dieter Daniel, Professor at the ETH Zurich and Director of the Evaluation Office of the University of Zurich. The author wishes to express his gratitude to three anonymous reviewers for their helpful comments.

References

Abelson, P. H. (1980). Scientific communication. *Science, 209*(4452), 60–62.

Abramowitz, S. I., Gomes, B., & Abramowitz, C. V. (1975). Publish or politic: Referee bias in manuscript review. *Journal of Applied Social Psychology, 3*(5), 187–200.

Abrams, P. A. (1991). The predictive ability of peer review of grant proposals: The case of ecology and the United States National Science Foundation. *Social Studies of Science, 21*(1), 111–132.

Alberts, B., Hanson, B., & Kelner, K. L. (2008). Reviewing peer review. *Science, 321*(5885), 15.

Armstrong, A. W., Idriss, S. Z., Kimball, A. B., & Bernhard, J. D. (2008). Fate of manuscripts declined by the *Journal of the American Academy of Dermatology*. *Journal of the American Academy of Dermatology, 58*(4), 632–635.

Armstrong, J. S. (1997). Peer review for journals: Evidence on quality control, fairness, and innovation. *Science and Engineering Ethics, 3*(1), 63–84.

Armstrong, P. W., Caverson, M. M., Adams, L., Taylor, M., & Olley, P. M. (1997). Evaluation of the Heart and Stroke Foundation of Canada Research Scholarship Program: Research productivity and impact. *Canadian Journal of Cardiology, 13*(5), 507–516.

Bailar, J. C. (1991). Reliability, fairness, objectivity, and other inappropriate goals in peer review. *Behavioral and Brain Sciences, 14*(1), 137–138.

Bakanic, V., McPhail, C., & Simon, R. J. (1987). The manuscript review and decision-making process. *American Sociological Review, 52*(5), 631–642.

Bakanic, V., McPhail, C., & Simon, R. J. (1989). Mixed messages: Referees' comments on the manuscripts they review. *Sociological Quarterly, 30*(4), 639–654.

Bartley, W. W. (1984). *The retreat to commitment* (2nd ed.). La Salle, IL: Open Court.

Baxt, W. G., Waeckerle, J. F., Berlin, J. A., & Callaham, M. L. (1998). Who reviews the reviewers? Feasibility of using a fictitious manuscript to evaluate peer reviewer performance. *Annals of Emergency Medicine, 32*(3), 310–317.

Bedeian, A. G. (2003). The manuscript review process: The proper roles of authors, referees, and editors. *Journal of Management Inquiry, 12*(4), 331–338.

Bedeian, A. G. (2004). Peer review and the social construction of knowledge in the management discipline. *Academy of Management Learning and Education, 3*(2), 198–216.

Bensman, S. J. (2007). Garfield and the impact factor. *Annual Review of Information Science and Technology, 41*, 93–155.

Bernard, H. R. (1980). Report from the editor. *Human Organization, 39*(4), 366–369.

Bertout, C., & Schneider, P. (2004). Editorship and peer-review at A&A. *Astronomy & Astrophysics, 420*, E1–E14.

Bhandari, M., Templeman, D., & Tornetta, P. (2004). Interrater reliability in grading abstracts for the Orthopaedic Trauma Association. *Clinical Orthopaedics and Related Research, 423*, 217–221.

Biagioli, M. (2002). From book censorship to academic peer review. *Emergences, 12*(1), 11–45.

Blank, R. M. (1991). The effects of double-blind versus single-blind reviewing: Experimental evidence from the *American Economic Review*. *American Economic Review, 81*(5), 1041–1067.

Bohannon, R. W. (1986). Agreement among reviewers. *Physical Therapy, 66*(9), 1431–1432.

Borgman, C. L. (2007). *Scholarship in the digital age: Information, infrastructure, and the internet*. Cambridge, MA: MIT Press.

Borgman, C. L., & Furner, J. (2002). Scholarly communication and bibliometrics. *Annual Review of Information Science and Technology, 36*, 3–72.

Bornmann, L., & Daniel, H.-D. (2005a). Committee peer review at an international research foundation: Predictive validity and fairness of selection decisions on post-graduate fellowship applications. *Research Evaluation, 14*(1), 15–20.

Bornmann, L., & Daniel, H.-D. (2005b). Criteria used by a peer review committee for selection of research fellows: A Boolean probit analysis. *International Journal of Selection and Assessment, 13*(4), 296–303.

Bornmann, L., & Daniel, H.-D. (2005c). Selection of research fellowship recipients by committee peer review: Analysis of reliability, fairness and predictive validity of Board of Trustees' decisions. *Scientometrics, 63*(2), 297–320.

Bornmann, L., & Daniel, H.-D. (2006). Selecting scientific excellence through committee peer review: A citation analysis of publications previously published to approval or rejection of post-doctoral research fellowship applicants. *Scientometrics, 68*(3), 427–440.

Bornmann, L., & Daniel, H.-D. (2007a). Convergent validation of peer review decisions using the *h* index: Extent of and reasons for type I and type II errors. *Journal of Informetrics, 1*(3), 204–213.

Bornmann, L., & Daniel, H.-D. (2007b). Gatekeepers of science: Effects of external reviewers' attributes on the assessments of fellowship applications. *Journal of Informetrics, 1*(1), 83–91.

Bornmann, L., & Daniel, H.-D. (2008a). The effectiveness of the peer review process: Inter-referee agreement and predictive validity of manuscript refereeing at *Angewandte Chemie. Angewandte Chemie International Edition, 47*(38), 7173–7178.

Bornmann, L., & Daniel, H.-D. (2008b). Selecting manuscripts for a high impact journal through peer review: A citation analysis of communications that were accepted by *Angewandte Chemie International Edition*, or rejected but published elsewhere. *Journal of the American Society for Information Science and Technology, 59*(11), 1841–1852.

Bornmann, L., & Daniel, H.-D. (2009). The luck of the referee draw: The effect of exchanging reviews. *Learned Publishing, 22*(2), 117–125.

Bornmann, L., & Daniel, H. D. (in press). The manuscript reviewing process: Empirical research on review requests, review sequences and decision rules in peer review. *Library & Information Science Research.*

Bornmann, L., Mutz, R., & Daniel, H.-D. (2007a). Gender differences in grant peer review: A meta-analysis. *Journal of Informetrics, 1*(3), 226–238.

Bornmann, L., Mutz, R., & Daniel, H.-D. (2007b). Row-column (RC) association model applied to grant peer review. *Scientometrics, 73*(2), 139–147.

Bornmann, L., Mutz, R., & Daniel, H.-D. (2008). How to detect indications of potential sources of bias in peer review: A generalized latent variable modeling approach exemplified by a gender study. *Journal of Informetrics, 2*(4), 280–287.

Bornmann, L., Mutz, R., & Daniel, H.-D. (2009). *A reliability-generalization study of journal peer reviews: A multilevel meta-analysis of inter-rater reliability and its determinants.* (Submitted for publication)

Bornmann, L., Mutz, R., Neuhaus, C., & Daniel, H.-D. (2008). Use of citation counts for research evaluation: Standards of good practice for analyzing bibliometric data and presenting and interpreting results. *Ethics in Science and Environmental Politics, 8*, 93–102.

Bornmann, L., Nast, I., & Daniel, H.-D. (2008). Do editors and referees look for signs of scientific misconduct when reviewing manuscripts? A quantitative content analysis of studies that examined review criteria and reasons for accepting and rejecting manuscripts for publication. *Scientometrics, 77*(3), 415–432.

Bornmann, L., Wallon, G., & Ledin, A. (2008). Does the committee peer review select the best applicants for funding? An investigation of the selection process for two European Molecular Biology Organization programmes. *PLoS One, 3*(10), e3480.

Bornstein, R. F. (1991). The predictive validity of peer-review: A neglected issue. *Behavioral and Brain Sciences, 14*(1), 138–139.

Brennan, R. L., & Prediger, D. J. (1981). Coefficient kappa: Some uses, misuses, and alternatives. *Educational and Psychological Measurement, 41*(3), 687–699.

British Academy (2007). *Peer review: The challenges for the humanities and social sciences.* London: The Academy.

Brody, T., Harnad, S., & Carr, L. (2006). Earlier web usage statistics as predictors of later citation impact. *Journal of the American Society for Information Science and Technology, 57*(8), 1060–1072.

Caelleigh, A. S., Hojat, M., Steinecke, A., & Gonnella, J. S. (2003). Effects of reviewers' gender on assessments of a gender-related standardized manuscript. *Teaching and Learning in Medicine, 15*(3), 163–167.

Campanario, J. M. (1998a). Peer review for journals as it stands today: Part 1. *Science Communication, 19*(3), 181–211.

Campanario, J. M. (1998b). Peer review for journals as it stands today: Part 2. *Science Communication, 19*(4), 277–306.

Carter, G. (1982). *What we know and do not know about the peer review system* (Rand Report N-1878-RC/NIH). Santa Monica, CA: RAND Corporation.

Carter, G., Cooper, W., Lai, C., & March, D. (1978). *The consequences of unfunded NIH applications for the investigator and his research* (Rand Report R-2229-NIH). Santa Monica, CA: RAND Corporation.

Chapman, G. B., & McCauley, C. (1994). Predictive validity of quality ratings of National Science Foundation graduate fellows. *Educational and Psychological Measurement, 54*(2), 428–438.

Chew, F. S. (1991). Fate of manuscripts rejected for publication in the AJR. *American Journal of Roentgenology, 156*(3), 627–632.

Chubin, D., & Hackett, E. (1990). *Peerless science: Peer review and U.S. science policy.* Albany, NY: State University of New York Press.

Chubin, D. E. (1982). Reforming peer-review: From recycling to reflexivity. *Behavioral and Brain Sciences, 5*(2), 204.

Cicchetti, D. V. (1991). The reliability of peer review for manuscript and grant submissions: A cross-disciplinary investigation. *Behavioral and Brain Sciences, 14*(1), 119–135.

Cicchetti, D. V. (1997). Referees, editors, and publication practices: Improving the reliability and usefulness of the peer review system. *Science and Engineering Ethics, 3*(1), 51–62.

Cicchetti, D. V. (1999). Guardians of science: Fairness and reliability of peer review. *Journal of Clinical and Experimental Neuropsychology, 21*(3), 412–421.

Cicchetti, D. V., & Conn, H. O. (1976). A statistical analysis of reviewer agreement and bias in evaluating medical abstracts. *Yale Journal of Biology and Medicine, 49*(4), 373–383.

Cicchetti, D. V., & Feinstein, A. R. (1990). High agreement but low Kappa: II. Resolving the paradoxes. *Journal of Clinical Epidemiology, 43*(6), 551–558.

Cole, J. R. (1979). *Fair science: Women in the scientific community.* New York: The Free Press.

Cole, J. R. (2000). The role of journals in the growth of scientific knowledge. In B. Cronin & H. B. Atkins (Eds.), *The web of knowledge: A Festschrift in honor of Eugene Garfield* (pp. 109–142). Medford, NJ: Information Today, Inc.

Cole, S. (1992). *Making science. Between nature and society.* Cambridge, MA: Harvard University Press.

Cole, S. (2004). Merton's contribution to the sociology of science. *Social Studies of Science, 34*(6), 829–844.

Cole, S., & Cole, J. R. (1967). Scientific output and recognition: A study in operation of reward system in science. *American Sociological Review, 32*(3), 377–390.

Cole, S., Cole, J. R., & Simon, G. A. (1981). Chance and consensus in peer-review. *Science, 214*(4523), 881–886.

Cole, S., & Fiorentine, R. (1991). Discrimination against women in science: The confusion of outcome with process. In H. Zuckerman, J. R. Cole, & J. T. Bruer (Eds.), *The outer circle: Women in the scientific community* (pp. 205–226). London: W. W. Norton.

Cronin, B. (2005). *The hand of science: Academic writing and its rewards.* Lanham, MD: Scarecrow Press.

Cronin, B., & McKenzie, G. (1992). The trajectory of rejection. *Journal of Documentation, 48*(3), 310–317.

Daniel, H.-D. (1993/2004). *Guardians of science: Fairness and reliability of peer review.* Weinheim, Germany: Wiley-VCH. Retrieved July 16, 2004, from DOI: 10.1002/3527602208

Davo, M. D., Vives, C., & Alvarez-Dardet, C. (2003). Why are women underused in the JECH peer review process? *Journal of Epidemiology and Community Health, 57*(12), 936–937.

Demicheli, V., & Pietrantonj, C. (2007). Peer review for improving the quality of grant applications. *Cochrane Database of Systematic Reviews*, Issue 2. Art. No.: MR000003. DOI: 10.1002/14651858.MR000003.pub2

Duncan, G. J., & Magnuson, K. A. (2003). The promise of random-assignment social experiments for understanding well-being and behavior. *Current Sociology, 51*(5), 529–541.

Eckberg, D. L. (1991). When nonreliability of reviews indicates solid science. *Behavioral and Brain Sciences, 14*(1), 145–146.

Eckes, T. (2004). Rater agreement and rater severity: A many-faceted Rasch analysis of performance assessments in the "Test Deutsch als Fremdsprache" (TestDaF). *Diagnostica, 50*(2), 65–77.

Editor to quit over hoax open-access paper. (2009). *Nature, 459*, 901.

Efron, B., & Gong, G. (1983). A leisurely look at the bootstrap, the jackknife, and cross-validation. *American Statistician, 37*(1), 36–48.

Ehses, I. (2004). By scientists, for scientists. The Deutsche Forschungsgemeinschaft (DFG, German Research Foundation) and how it functions. *B.I.F. Futura, 19,* 170–177.

Eisenhart, M. (2002). The paradox of peer review: Admitting too much or allowing too little? *Research in Science Education, 32*(2), 241–255.

Epstein, W. M. (1990). Confirmational response bias among social-work journals. *Science, Technology, & Human Values, 15*(1), 9–38.

Ernst, E., Saradeth, T., & Resch, K. L. (1993). Drawbacks of peer review. *Nature, 363*(6427), 296.

Evidence Ltd. (2007). *The use of bibliometrics to measure research quality in UK higher education institutions.* London: Universities UK.

Eysenck, H. J., & Eysenck, S. B. G. (1992). Peer review: Advice to referees and contributors. *Personality and Individual Differences, 13*(4), 393–399.

Feinstein, A. R., & Cicchetti, D. V. (1990). High agreement but low Kappa: I. The problems of two paradoxes. *Journal of Clinical Epidemiology, 43*(6), 543–549.

Feist, G. J. (2006). *The psychology of science and the origins of the scientific mind.* New Haven, CT: Yale University Press.

Ferber, M. A., & Teiman, M. (1980). Are women economists at a disadvantage in publishing journal articles? *Eastern Economic Journal, 6*(3–4), 189–193.

Figueredo, E. (2006). The numerical equivalence between the impact factor of journals and the quality of the articles. *Journal of the American Society for Information Science and Technology, 57*(11), 1561.

Fiske, D. W., & Fogg, L. (1990). But the reviewers are making different criticisms of my paper: Diversity and uniqueness in reviewer comments. *American Psychologist, 45*(5), 591–598.

Fleiss, J. (1981). *Statistical methods for rates and proportions.* New York: Wiley VCH.

Fleiss, J. L. (1982). Deception in the study of the peer-review process. *Behavioral and Brain Sciences, 5*(2), 210–211.

Fogg, L., & Fiske, D. W. (1993). Foretelling the judgments of reviewers and editors. *American Psychologist, 48*(3), 293–294.

Fox, T. (1965). *Crisis in communication: The functions and future of medical publication.* London: Athlone Press.

Frey, B. S. (2003). Publishing as prostitution? Choosing between one's own ideas and academic success. *Public Choice, 116*(1–2), 205–223.

Fuhrer, M. J., & Grabois, M. (1985). Grant application and review procedures of the National Institute of Handicapped Research: Survey of applicant and peer reviewer opinions. *Archives of Physical Medicine and Rehabilitation, 66*(5), 318–321.

Gans, J. S., & Shepherd, G. B. (1994). How are the mighty fallen: Rejected classic articles by leading economists. *Journal of Economic Perspectives, 8*(1), 165–179.

Garfield, E. (2004). Historiographic mapping of knowledge domains literature. *Journal of Information Science, 30*(2), 119–145.

Garfunkel, J. M., Ulshen, M. H., Hamrick, H. J., & Lawson, E. E. (1994). Effect of institutional prestige on reviewers' recommendations and editorial decisions. *Journal of the American Medical Association, 272*(2), 137–138.

Geisler, E. (2000). *The metrics of science and technology.* Westport, CT: Quorum Books.

Geisler, E. (2001). The mires of research evaluation. *The Scientist, 15*(10), 39.

Gibson, M., Spong, C. Y., Simonsen, S. E., Martin, S., & Scott, J. R. (2008). Author perception of peer review. *Obstetrics and Gynecology, 112*(3), 646–651.

Gilbert, J. R., Williams, E. S., & Lundberg, G. D. (1994). Is there gender bias in *JAMA*'s peer review process? *Journal of the American Medical Association, 272*(2), 139–142.

Gillespie, G. W., Chubin, D. E., & Kurzon, G. M. (1985). Experience with NIH peer review: Researchers' cynicism and desire for change. *Science, Technology, & Human Values, 52*, 44–54.

Glass, G. V. (1976). Primary, secondary, and meta-analysis. *Educational Researcher, 5*, 3–8.

Godlee, F., & Dickersin, K. (2003). Bias, subjectivity, chance, and conflict of interest. In F. Godlee & J. Jefferson (Eds.), *Peer review in health sciences* (2nd ed., pp. 91–117). London: BMJ Publishing Group.

Goldberg, P. (1968). Are women prejudiced against women? *Transactions, 5*(5), 28–30.

Gölitz, P. (2008). Appeals. *Angewandte Chemie International Edition, 47*(38), 7144–7145.

Goodman, L. A. (1984). *The analysis of cross-classified data having ordered categories.* Cambridge, MA: Harvard University Press.

Goodman, S. N., Berlin, J., Fletcher, S. W., & Fletcher, R. H. (1994). Manuscript quality before and after peer review and editing at *Annals of Internal Medicine. Annals of Internal Medicine, 121*(1), 11–21.

Gordon, M. D. (1984). How authors select journals: A test of the reward maximization model of submission behavior. *Social Studies of Science, 14*(1), 27–43.

Gorman, G. E. (2007). The Oppenheim effect in scholarly journal publishing. *Online Information Review, 31*(4), 417–419.

Gosden, H. (2003). "Why not give us the full story?": Functions of referees' comments in peer reviews of scientific research papers. *Journal of English for Academic Purposes, 2*(2), 87–101.

Grayson, L. (2002). *Evidence based policy and the quality of evidence: Rethinking peer review.* London: Centre for Evidence Based Policy and Practice (ESRC).

Guston, D. H. (2003). The expanding role of peer review processes in the United States. In P. Shapira & S. Kuhlmann (Eds.), *Learning from science and technology policy evaluation: Experiences from the United States and Europe* (pp. 81–97). Cheltenham, UK: Edward Elgar.

Hackett, E. J., & Chubin, D. E. (2003, February). *Peer review for the 21st century: Applications to education research.* Paper presented at the conference Peer Review of Education Research Grant Applications: Implications, Considerations, and Future Directions, Washington, DC.

Hagstrom, W. O. (1965). *The scientific community.* New York: Basic Books.

Hames, I. (2007). *Peer review and manuscript management of scientific journals: Guidelines for good practice.* Oxford, UK: Blackwell.

Hansson, F. (2002). How to evaluate and select new scientific knowledge? Taking the social dimension seriously in the evaluation of research quality. *Vest, 15*(2–3), 27–52.

Hargens, L. L., & Herting, J. R. (1990). A new approach to referees assessments of manuscripts. *Social Science Research, 19*(1), 1–16.

Harnad, S. (1990). Scholarly skywriting and the prepublication continuum of scientific inquiry. *Psychological Science, 1*(6), 342–344.

Harnad, S. (1996). Implementing peer review on the net: Scientific quality control in scholarly electronic journals. In P. R. Peek & G. B. Newby (Eds.), *Scholarly publishing: The electronic frontier* (pp. 103–118). Cambridge, MA: MIT Press.

Harnad, S. (2008). Validating research performance metrics against peer rankings. *Ethics in Science and Environmental Politics, 8*, 103–107.

Hemlin, S. (1996). Research on research evaluations. *Social Epistemology, 10*(2), 209–250.

Hemlin, S., & Rasmussen, S. B. (2006). The shift in academic quality control. *Science, Technology, & Human Values, 31*(2), 173–198.

Hodgson, C. (1997). How reliable is peer review? An examination of operating grant proposals simultaneously submitted to two similar peer review systems. *Journal of Clinical Epidemiology, 50*(11), 1189–1195.

Hoffmann, H., Joye, D., Kuhn, F., & Métral, G. (2002). *Der SNF im Spiegel der Forschenden: Synthesebericht*. Neuchâtel, Switzerland: Schweizerischer Informations und Datenarchivdienst für die Sozialwissenschaften (SIDOS).

Hojat, M., Gonnella, J. S., & Caelleigh, A. S. (2003). Impartial judgment by the "gatekeepers" of science: Fallibility and accountability in the peer review process. *Advances in Health Sciences Education, 8*(1), 75–96.

Honig, W. M. (1982). Peer review in the physical sciences: An editor's view. *Behavioral and Brain Sciences, 5*(2), 216–217.

Hornbostel, S. (1997). *Wissenschaftsindikatoren: Bewertungen in der Wissenschaft*. Opladen, Germany: Westdeutscher Verlag.

Hornbostel, S., Böhmer, S., Klingsporn, B., Neufeld, J., & von Ins, M. (2009). Funding of young scientist and scientific excellence. *Scientometrics, 79*(1), 171–190.

Hornbostel, S., & Olbrecht, M. (2007). *Peer Review in der DFG: Die Fachkollegiaten* (iFQ-Working Paper No. 2). Bonn, Germany: Institut für Forschungsinformation und Qualitätssicherung.

Ingelfinger, F. J. (1974). Peer review in biomedical publication. *American Journal of Medicine, 56*(5), 686–692.

Jayasinghe, U. W. (2003). *Peer review in the assessment and funding of research by the Australian Research Council*. Greater Western Sydney, Australia: University of Western Sydney.

Jayasinghe, U. W., Marsh, H. W., & Bond, N. (2001). Peer review in the funding of research in higher education: The Australian experience. *Educational Evaluation and Policy Analysis, 23*(4), 343–364.

Jayasinghe, U. W., Marsh, H. W., & Bond, N. (2003). A multilevel cross-classified modelling approach to peer review of grant proposals: The effects of assessor and researcher attributes on assessor ratings. *Journal of the Royal Statistical Society Series a-Statistics in Society, 166*, 279–300.

Jennings, C. G. (2006). Quality and value: The true purpose of peer review. What you can't measure, you can't manage: The need for quantitative indicators in peer review. *Nature*. Retrieved July 6, 2006, from www.nature.com/nature/peerreview/debate/nature05032. html

Johnson, V. E. (2008). Statistical analysis of the National Institutes of Health peer review system. *Proceedings of the National Academy of Sciences, 105*(32), 11076–11080.

Joint Committee on Quantitative Assessment of Research (2008). *Citation statistics. A report from the International Mathematical Union (IMU) in cooperation with the International Council of Industrial and Applied Mathematics (ICIAM) and the Institute of Mathematical Statistics (IMS)*. Berlin, Germany: International Mathematical Union (IMU).

Journal of the American Medical Association. (1990). Guarding the guardians: Research on editorial peer review. Selected proceedings from the First International Congress on Peer Review in Biomedical Publication. *Journal of the American Medical Association, 263*(10), 1317–1441.

Journal of the American Medical Association. (1994). The 2nd International Congress on Peer Review in Biomedical Publication. Proceedings. *Journal of the American Medical Association, 272*(2), 79–174.

Journal of the American Medical Association. (1998). The International Congress on Biomedical Peer Review. *Journal of the American Medical Association, 280*(3), 203–306.

Journal of the American Medical Association. (2002). The International Congress on Biomedical Peer Review. *Journal of the American Medical Association, 287*(21), 2759–2871.

Koch, S. (2006). Die Begutachtungsverfahren der Deutschen Forschungsgemeinschaft nach Einführung der Fachkollegien. In S. Hornbostel & D. Simon (Eds.), *Wie viel (In-) Transparenz ist notwendig? Peer Review revisited* (Vol. 1, pp. 15–26). Bonn, Germany: Institut für Forschungsinformation und Qualitätssicherung.

Kostoff, R. N. (1995). Federal research impact assessment: Axioms, approaches, applications. *Scientometrics, 34*(2), 163–206.

Kostoff, R. N. (1997). The principles and practices of peer review. *Science and Engineering Ethics, 3*(1), 19–34.

Kostoff, R. N. (2004). *Research program peer review: Purposes, principles, practices, protocols* (DTIC Technical Report Number ADA424141). Arlington, VA: Office of Naval Research.

Krampen, G., & Montada, L. (2002). *Wissenschaftsforschung in der Psychologie*. Göttingen, Germany: Hogrefe.

Kronick, D. A. (1990). Peer review in 18th century scientific journalism. *Journal of the American Medical Association, 263*(10), 1321–1322.

Kuhn, T. S. (1962). *The structure of scientific revolutions*. Chicago: University of Chicago Press.

Kupfersmid, J. (1988). Improving what is published: A model in search of an editor. *American Psychologist, 43*(8), 635–642.

LaFollette, M. C. (1992). *Stealing into print: Fraud, plagiarism and misconduct in scientific publishing*. Berkeley: University of California Press.

Lamont, M. (2009). *How professors think: Inside the curious world of academic judgment*. Cambridge, MA: Harvard University Press.

Ledin, A., Bornmann, L., Gannon, F., & Wallon, G. (2007). A persistent problem: Traditional gender roles hold back female scientists. *EMBO Reports, 8*(11), 982–987.

Lee, K. P., Boyd, E. A., Holroyd-Leduc, J. M., Bacchetti, P., & Bero, L. A. (2006). Predictors of publication: Characteristics of submitted manuscripts associated with acceptance at major biomedical journals. *Medical Journal of Australia, 184*(12), 621–626.

Levenson, H., Burford, B., Bonno, B., & Davis, L. (1975). Are women still prejudiced against women? A replication and extension of Goldberg's Study. *Journal of Psychology, 89*(1), 67–71.

Lienert, G. A. (1987). *Schulnoten-Evaluation*. Frankfurt am Main, Germany: Athenäum.

Lindsey, D. (1989). Using citation counts as a measure of quality in science: Measuring what's measurable rather than what's valid. *Scientometrics, 15*(3–4), 189–203.

Lloyd, M. E. (1990). Gender factors in reviewer recommendations for manuscript publication. *Journal of Applied Behavioral Analysis, 23*(4), 539–543.

Lock, S. (1985). *A difficult balance: Editorial peer review in medicine*. Philadelphia, PA: ISI Press.

Long, J. S., & Fox, M. F. (1995). Scientific careers: Universalism and particularism. *Annual Review of Sociology*, *21*, 45–71.

Mahoney, M. J. (1977). Publication prejudices: An experimental study of confirmatory bias in the peer review system. *Cognitive Therapy and Research*, *2*, 161–175.

Mallard, G., Lamont, M., & Guetzkow, J. (2009). Fairness as appropriateness: Negotiating epistemological differences in peer review. *Science, Technology, & Human Values*, *34*(5), 573–606.

Marsh, H., & Bornmann, L. (2009). Do women have less success in peer review? *Nature*, *459*, 602.

Marsh, H. W., & Ball, S. (1981). Interjudgmental reliability of reviews for the *Journal of Educational Psychology*. *Journal of Educational Psychology*, *73*(6), 872–880.

Marsh, H. W., & Ball, S. (1991). Reflections on the peer review process. *Behavioral and Brain Sciences*, *14*(1), 157–158.

Marsh, H. W., Bonds, N. W., & Jayasinghe, U. W. (2007). Peer review process: Assessments by applicant-nominated referees are biased, inflated, unreliable and invalid. *Australian Psychologist*, *42*(1), 33–38.

Marsh, H. W., Bornmann, L., Mutz, R., Daniel, H.-D., & O'Mara, A. (in press). Gender effects in the peer reviews of grant proposals: A comprehensive meta-analysis comparing traditional and multilevel approaches. *Review of Educational Research*.

Marsh, H. W., Jayasinghe, U. W., & Bond, N. W. (2008). Improving the peer-review process for grant applications: Reliability, validity, bias, and generalizability. *American Psychologist*, *63*(3), 160–168.

Martin, B. (2000). Research grants: Problems and options. *Australian Universities' Review*, *43*(2), 17–22.

Martin, B. R., & Irvine, J. (1983). Assessing basic research: Some partial indicators of scientific progress in radio astronomy. *Research Policy*, *12*(2), 61–90.

Martinson, B. C., Anderson, M. S., Crain, A. L., & de Vries, R. (2006). Scientists' perceptions of organizational justice and self-reported misbehaviors. *Journal of Empirical Research on Human Research Ethics*, *1*(1), 51–66.

Matt, G. E., & Navarro, A. M. (1997). What meta-analyses have and have not taught us about psychotherapy effects: A review and future directions. *Clinical Psychology Review*, *17*(1), 1–32.

McClellan, J. E. (2003). *Specialist control: The publications committee of the Academie Royal des Sciences (Paris) 1700–1793* (Transactions of the American Philosophical Society, v. 93). Philadelphia, PA: American Philosophical Society.

McCullough, J. (1989). First comprehensive survey of NSF applicants focuses on their concerns about proposal review. *Science, Technology, & Human Values*, *14*(1), 78–88.

McCullough, J. (1994). The role and influence of the US National Science Foundation's program officers in reviewing and awarding grants. *Higher Education*, *28*(1), 85–94.

McDonald, R. J., Cloft, H. J., & Kallmes, D. F. (2007). Fate of submitted manuscripts rejected from the *American Journal of Neuroradiology*: Outcomes and commentary. *American Journal of Neuroradiology*, *28*(8), 1430–1434.

McDonald, R. J., Cloft, H. J., & Kallmes, D. F. (2009). Fate of manuscripts previously rejected by the *American Journal of Neuroradiology*: A follow-up analysis. *American Journal of Neuroradiology*, *30*(2), 253–256.

McIntosh, E. G., & Ross, S. (1987). Peer review in psychology: Institutional ranking as a factor. *Psychological Reports, 60*(3), 1049–1050.

Melin, G., & Danell, R. (2006). The top eight percent: Development of approved and rejected applicants for a prestigious grant in Sweden. *Science and Public Policy, 33*(10), 702–712.

Merton, R. K. (1942). Science and technology in a democratic order. *Journal of Legal and Political Sociology, 1*, 115–126.

Merton, R. K. (1948). The self-fulfilling prophecy. *Antioch Review, 8*, 193–210.

Merton, R. K. (1968). The Matthew effect in science. *Science, 159*(3810), 56–63.

Moed, H. (2008). UK Research Assessment Exercises: Informed judgments on research quality or quantity? *Scientometrics, 74*(1), 153–161.

National Academy of Sciences. (2006). *Beyond bias and barriers: Fulfilling the potential of women in academic science and engineering*. Washington, DC: The National Academies Press.

Neuhaus, C., & Daniel, H.-D. (2009). A new reference standard for citation analysis in chemistry and related fields based on the sections of Chemical Abstracts. *Scientometrics, 78*(2), 219–229.

Nicolaisen, J. (2007). Citation analysis. *Annual Review of Information Science and Technology, 41*, 609–641.

Nylenna, M., Riis, P., & Karlsson, Y. (1994). Multiple blinded reviews of the same two manuscripts: Effects of referee characteristics and publication language. *Journal of the American Medical Association, 272*(2), 149–151.

Opthof, T., Furstner, F., van Geer, M., & Coronel, R. (2000). Regrets or no regrets? No regrets! The fate of rejected manuscripts. *Cardiovascular Research, 45*(1), 255–258.

Opthof, T., & Wilde, A. A. M. (2009). The Hirsch-index: A simple, new tool for the assessment of scientific output of individual scientists: The case of Dutch professors in clinical cardiology. *Netherlands Heart Journal, 17*(4), 145–154.

Over, R. (1996). Perceptions of the Australian Research Council Large Grants Scheme: Differences between successful and unsuccessful applicants. *Australian Educational Researcher, 23*(2), 17–36.

Overbeke, J., & Wager, E. (2003). The state of the evidence: What we know and what we don't know about journal peer review. In F. Godlee & T. Jefferson (Eds.), *Peer review in health sciences* (2nd ed., pp. 45–61). London: BMJ Books.

Overview: *Nature*'s peer review trial. (2006). *Nature*. Retrieved May 18, from www.nature.com/nature/peerreview/debate/nature05535.html

Owen, R. (1982). Reader bias. *Journal of the American Medical Association, 247*(18), 2533–2534.

Paludi, M. A., & Bauer, W. D. (1983). Goldberg revisited: What's in an author's name. *Sex Roles, 9*(3), 387–390.

Paludi, M. A., & Strayer, L. A. (1985). What's in an author's name? Differential evaluations of performance as a function of author's name. *Sex Roles, 12*(3–4), 353–361.

Patterson, S. C., Bailey, M. S., Martinez, V. J., & Angel, S. C. (1987). Report of the managing editor of the *American Political Science Review*, 1986–1987. *PS, 20*, 1006–1016.

Pendlebury, D. A. (2008). *Using bibliometrics in evaluating research*. Philadelphia, PA: Research Department, Thomson Scientific.

Perneger, T. V. (2004). Relation between online "hit counts" and subsequent citations: Prospective study of research papers in the BMJ. *British Medical Journal, 329*, 546–547.

Peters, D. P., & Ceci, S. J. (1982). Peer-review practices of psychological journals: The fate of accepted, published articles, submitted again. *Behavioral and Brain Sciences, 5*(2), 187–195.

Petty, R. E., & Fleming, M. A. (1999). The review process at *PSPB*: Correlates of interreviewer agreement and manuscript acceptance. *Personality and Social Psychology Bulletin, 25*(2), 188–203.

Pfeffer, J., Leong, A., & Strehl, K. (1977). Paradigm development and particularism: Journal publication in three scientific disciplines. *Social Forces, 55*(4), 938–951.

Pierie, J. P. E. N., Walvoort, H. C., & Overbeke, A. J. P. M. (1996). Readers' evaluation of effect of peer review and editing on quality of articles in the *Nederlands Tijdschrift voor Geneeskunde*. *Lancet, 348*(9040), 1480–1483.

Popper, K. R. (1961). *The logic of scientific discovery* (2nd ed.). New York: Basic Books.

Pöschl, U. (2004). Interactive journal concept for improved scientific publishing and quality assurance. *Learned Publishing, 17*(2), 105–113.

Pruthi, S., Jain, A., Wahid, A., Mehra, K., & Nabi, S. A. (1997). Scientific community and peer review system: A case study of a central government funding scheme in India. *Journal of Scientific & Industrial Research, 56*(7), 398–407.

Publishing Research Consortium. (2008). *Peer review in scholarly journals: Perspective of the scholarly community: An international study*. Bristol, UK: The Consortium.

Ray, J., Berkwits, M., & Davidoff, F. (2000). The fate of manuscripts rejected by a general medical journal. *American Journal of Medicine, 109*(2), 131–135.

Resnik, D. B., Gutierrez-Ford, C., & Peddada, S. (2008). Perceptions of ethical problems with scientific journal peer review: An exploratory study. *Science and Engineering Ethics, 14*(3), 305–310.

Ross, P. F. (1980). *The sciences' self-management: Manuscript refereeing, peer review, and goals in science*. Lincoln, MA: The Ross Company.

Rossiter, J. R. (2003). Qualifying the importance of findings. *Journal of Business Research, 56*(1), 85–88.

Roy, R. (1985). Funding science: The real defects of peer-review and an alternative to it. *Science, Technology, & Human Values, 52*, 73–81.

Russo, G. (2008). Statistical analyses raise questions over NIH grant reviews. *Nature, 454*, 801.

Sahner, H. (1982). On the selectivity of editors: An input-output analysis of the *Zeitschrift für Soziologie*. *Zeitschrift für Soziologie, 11*(1), 82–98.

Schuster, C. (2002). A mixture model approach to indexing rater agreement. *British Journal of Mathematical & Statistical Psychology, 55*, 289–303.

Scott, W. A. (1974). Interreferee agreement on some characteristics of manuscripts submitted to the *Journal of Personality and Social Psychology*. *American Psychologist, 29*(9), 698–702.

Seglen, P. O. (1994). Causal relationship between article citedness and journal impact. *Journal of the American Society for Information Science, 45*(1), 1–11.

Shadish, W. R., Cook, T. D., & Campbell, D. T. (2002). *Experimental and quasi-experimental designs for generalized causal inference*. Boston: Houghton Mifflin Company.

Sharp, D. W. (1990). What can and should be done to reduce publication bias: The perspective of an editor. *Journal of the American Medical Association, 263*(10), 1390–1391.

Shashok, K. (2005). Standardization vs diversity: How can we push peer review research forward? *Medscape General Medicine, 7*(1), 11.

Shatz, D. (2004). *Peer review: A critical inquiry*. Lanham, MD: Rowman & Littlefield.

Siegelman, S. S. (1991). Assassins and zealots: Variations in peer review: Special report. *Radiology, 178*(3), 637–642.

Sismondo, S. (1993). Some social constructions. *Social Studies of Science, 23*(3), 515–553.

Skrondal, A., & Rabe-Hesketh, S. (2004). *Generalized latent variable modeling: Multilevel, longitudinal, and structural equation models*. London: Chapman & Hall/CRC.

Smigel, E. O., & Ross, H. L. (1970). Factors in editorial decision. *American Sociologist, 5*(1), 19–21.

Smith, L. C. (1981). Citation analysis. *Library Trends, 30*(1), 83–106.

Smith, R. (2006). Peer review: A flawed process at the heart of science and journals. *Journal of the Royal Society of Medicine, 99*(4), 178–182.

Sokal, A. D. (2008). *Beyond the hoax: Science, philosophy and culture*. Oxford, UK: Oxford University Press.

Speck, B. W. (1993). *Publication peer review: An annotated bibliography*. Westport, CT: Greenwood Press.

Stamps, A. E. (1997). Advances in peer review research: An introduction. *Science and Engineering Ethics, 3*(1), 3–10.

Stehbens, W. E. (1999). Basic philosophy and concepts underlying scientific peer review. *Medical Hypotheses, 52*(1), 31–36.

Sternberg, R. J., Hojjat, M., Brigockas, M. G., & Grigorenko, E. L. (1997). Getting in: Criteria for acceptance of manuscripts in *Psychological Bulletin*, 1993–1996. *Psychological Bulletin, 121*(2), 321–323.

Stieg Dalton, M. F. (1995). Refereeing of scholarly works for primary publishing. *Annual Review of Information Science and Technology, 30*, 213–250.

Stricker, L. J. (1991). Disagreement among journal reviewers: No cause for undue alarm. *Behavioral and Brain Sciences, 14*(1), 163–164.

Suls, J., & Martin, R. (2009). The air we breathe: A critical look at practices and alternatives in the peer review process. *Perspectives on Psychological Science, 4*(1), 40–50.

Tight, M. (2003). Reviewing the reviewers. *Quality in Higher Education, 9*(3), 295–303.

Tregenza, T. (2002). Gender bias in the refereeing process? *Trends in Ecology & Evolution, 17*(8), 349–350.

U.S. General Accounting Office (1999). *Peer review practices at federal science agencies vary*. Washington, DC: The Office.

U.S. Office of Management and Budget. (2004). *Revised information quality bulletin for peer review*. Washington, DC: The Office.

van den Besselaar, P., & Leydesdorff, L. (2007). *Past performance as predictor of successful grant applications. A case study*. Den Haag, The Netherlands: Rathenau Instituut.

van Raan, A. F. J. (1996). Advanced bibliometric methods as quantitative core of peer review based evaluation and foresight exercises. *Scientometrics, 36*(3), 397–420.

van Raan, A. F. J. (1999). Advanced bibliometric methods for the evaluation of universities. *Scientometrics, 45*(3), 417–423.

von Eye, A., & Mun, E. Y. (2005). *Analyzing rater agreement: Manifest variable methods.* Mahwah, NJ: Erlbaum.

Wakin, M., Rozell, C., Davenport, M., & Laska, J. (2009). Letter from the editors. *Rejecta Mathematica, 1*(1), 1–3.

Ward, C. (1981). Prejudice against women: Who, when, and why? *Sex Roles, 7*(2), 163–171.

Wellcome Trust. (2001). *Review of Wellcome Trust PhD research training: Career paths of a 1988 – 1990 prize student cohort.* London: The Trust.

Weller, A. C. (1996). Editorial peer review: A comparison of authors publishing in two groups of US medical journals. *Bulletin of the Medical Library Association, 84*(3), 359–366.

Weller, A. C. (2002). *Editorial peer review: Its strengths and weaknesses.* Medford, NJ: Information Today, Inc.

Wennerås, C., & Wold, A. (1997). Nepotism and sexism in peer-review. *Nature, 387*(6631), 341–343.

Wessely, S. (1998). Peer review of grant applications: What do we know? *Lancet, 352*(9124), 301–305.

Wessely, S., & Wood, F. (1999). Peer review of grant applications: A systematic review. In F. Godlee & T. Jefferson (Eds.), *Peer Review in Health Sciences* (pp. 14–31). London: BMJ Books.

White, H. D. (2005). On extending informetrics: An opinion paper. *Proceedings of the 10th International Conference of the International Society for Scientometrics and Informetrics, 2,* 442–449.

Whitley, R., & Gläser, J. (Eds.). (2007). *The changing governance of the sciences: The advent of research evaluation systems.* Dordrecht, the Netherlands: Springer.

Whitman, N., & Eyre, S. (1985). The pattern of publishing previously rejected articles in selected journals. *Family Medicine, 17*(1), 26–28.

Wiener, S., Urivetsky, M., Bregman, D., Cohen, J., Eich, R., Gootman, N., et al. (1977). Peer review: Inter-reviewer agreement during evaluation of research grant evaluations. *Clinical Research, 25,* 306–311.

Wiley, S. (2008). Peer review isn't perfect ... But it's not a conspiracy designed to maintain the status quo. *The Scientist, 22*(11), 31.

Wilson, J. D. (1978). Peer review and publication. *Journal of Clinical Investigation, 61*(4), 1697–1701.

Wood, F. Q., & Wessely, S. (2003). Peer review of grant applications: A systematic review. In F. Godlee & T. Jefferson (Eds.), *Peer review in health sciences* (2nd ed., pp. 14–44). London: BMJ Books.

Yalow, R. S. (1982). Is subterfuge consistent with good science? *Bulletin of Science Technology & Society, 2*(5), 401–404.

Young, S. N. (2003). Peer review of manuscripts: Theory and practice. *Journal of Psychiatry & Neuroscience, 28*(5), 327–330.

Ziman, J. (2000). *Real science. What it is, and what it means.* Cambridge, UK: Cambridge University Press.

Zuckerman, H., & Merton, R. K. (1971a). Patterns of evaluation in science: Institutionalisation, structure and functions of the referee system. *Minerva, 9*(1), 66–100.

Zuckerman, H., & Merton, R. K. (1971b). Sociology of refereeing. *Physics Today, 24*(7), 28–33.

CHAPTER 6

Data Sharing in the Sciences

Stacy Kowalczyk and Kalpana Shankar
Indiana University, Bloomington, IN

Introduction

Collaboration across disciplines, the increasing size of those collaborations, and the application of information technologies to scientific problems have contributed greatly to the data-intensive nature of scientific research. These trends have reduced the relevance of distance, allowed scientists to share resources remotely, and increased both the complexity and quantity of research data. They have also created numerous challenges for the sharing and reuse of data through data repositories. When institutions create repositories, they do so with several goals in mind: grant fulfillment, peer review, long-term archiving, disease management, daily scientific practice, the leveraging of scarce or endangered resources, and the exploiting of large infrastructures.

Tools for data mining and analysis foster the integration of existing datasets to answer and promote new lines of inquiry, enable multidisciplinary research, and facilitate educational efforts. Data may be archived within the research group, by an external organization, or in an institutional repository. Increasingly, it is not just researchers who reuse data, but also educators, policymakers, and the general public. Making data broadly available can promote public understanding of science, evidence-based advocacy, educational uses, and citizen-science initiatives. Promoting the effective sharing of data is increasingly part of national and international scientific discourse and held to be essential to the future of science (Interagency Working Group on Digital Data, 2009). Funding agencies argue that data sharing promotes the wisest use of public resources by reducing repetitive collection of expensive or sensitive data. Examples include datasets collected in fragile areas of the world, with national security implications, from unique circumstances such as natural or human-made disasters, or composed of rare or complex samples. In short, data sharing furthers the spirit of inquiry with a focus on interoperability and reuse by making experimental and observational data available (at least to the scientific community) and thus verifiable and replicable.

National initiatives to develop both an infrastructure to facilitate data sharing and a culture of sharing are gradually emerging (Research

Information Network, 2008) but the sharing of datasets is not simple nor is it practiced across all scientific disciplines. Data sharing is not universally practiced for numerous reasons. Organizations, as well as individual researchers, may consider themselves to be either friendly competitors or rivals for funding, leading them to view their data as a source of competitive advantage (Chaplin, 2004). Data and other by-products of research represent important and sometimes invaluable intellectual capital; dissemination strategies should be synchronized with the mission of the organization that collected the data (Association of Research Libraries, Association of American Universities, Coalition for Networked Information, & National Association of State Universities and Land-Grant Colleges, 2009). Individuals and organizations may fear being perceived as incompetent or inefficient if they have not extracted the full economic and institutional value from the data they share; further, organizations worry that trustees, donors, and other shareholders would not approve of unrestricted access that allows others to "free-ride" on institutional data resources (Hammond, Moritz, & Agosti, 2008, p. 3). Another concern is that data sharing may open up researchers to criticism of data collection methods and their research in general.

Minimally, for data sharing to be effective, the datasets must satisfy three criteria: persistence, longevity and sustainability, and quality (Interagency Working Group on Digital Data, 2009; Klump, Bertelmann, Brase, Diepenbroek, Grobe, Höck, et al., 2006). In other words, the data (and their location) must be findable over time via consistent pointers, preserved and accessible for the long term, and of sufficient quality to be usable. To meet these criteria, data repositories require the development of appropriate technical and organizational infrastructures for storage and retrieval, incentives for researchers to deposit and use the data, and enforceable policies. (Research groups and projects, academic and research institutions, funding agencies, and disciplinary bodies and societies may all have relevant data sharing policies.) Although the technologies exist to archive large datasets, making them readily accessible and easily described is not a trivial undertaking.

Many disciplines have successfully encouraged data sharing through its integration into the publication and peer review process (Piwowar & Chapman, 2008). For example, the Inter-university Consortium for Political and Social Research (ICPSR) has been active in archiving social science datasets, migrating them as necessary, and providing training for researchers from around the world in their use. In some disciplines, archiving data is a prerequisite for publication. A recent survey of the policies of journals in a subdiscipline of biology found that three quarters of the journals surveyed had at least some mention of a data sharing requirement for publication in the journal (Piwowar & Chapman, 2008). However, such policies do not always seem to work uniformly or effectively; one survey found that 28 percent of genetics researchers were unable to confirm published results because they could not access the relevant data (Campbell, Clarridge, Gokhale, Birenbaum,

Hilgartner, Holtzman, et al., 2002); many junior scientists reported in a 2006 survey that they had experienced data withholding (Vogeli, Yucel, Bendavid, Jones, Anderson, Louis, et al., 2006). In short, responsibility for making data available varies widely from discipline to discipline, and within disciplines, with differing formats, practices, and costs (and bearers of those costs).

For the information professions, several practical, significant questions arise around data sharing. These are intersections of storage, retrieval, preservation, management, access, and policy issues. The design and deployment of storage and retrieval mechanisms, metadata schema for data description, long-term preservation for data archives, the education of data curators and users, development of institutional and organizational policy, and access and use of repositories are some of the problems with which information professionals engage. More broadly, data sharing raises questions about the nature of research itself—the role of the public and the private sectors, citizen participation in the heavily taxpayer-supported scientific process, and the equitable distribution of the results of the research enterprise. Taken together, these disparate, complex challenges constitute the *data sharing problem*.

In this chapter we explore the many strands of data sharing and its myriad technical, social, ethical, and policy challenges. We focus specifically on the natural sciences, although many of the issues we discuss may be of equal relevance to the social sciences and humanities. We discuss the nature of data and the life cycle of creation and use, scale, formats, and provenance and the research problems these issues present. We then explore the policy, technical, ethical, and organizational dimensions of data sharing, present several case studies of data sharing in action, and conclude with an overview of current and future directions, including the use of Web 2.0 for data sharing and archiving.

Structure of the Chapter

Data sharing crosses many disciplines, professions, and literatures; at its core it is a sociotechnical enterprise. In framing this chapter, we found that this divergence presents a number of structural problems for both the writer and the reader in exploring the issues. Thus, we introduce a framework with which we explore the issues, noting that we could have presented the same information in many other ways.

We begin by discussing the nature of data—formats, the context in which they are created, measures of their quality, and their persistence (or lack thereof). We then explore aggregations of data into repositories, or data collections, and the nature of those aggregations.

Not surprisingly, the technical needs of data sharing command a considerable amount of resources, human and otherwise. We call this layer the technical infrastructure. The technical infrastructure for data sharing is a rich field of research. Most of the communities that have built data sharing infrastructures have developed unique solutions

(Rajasekar, Marciano, & Moore, 1999). Although this may seem wasteful, and some approaches undoubtedly are, there is no single infrastructure that will serve all of the varying needs of the scientific community. Infrastructure, which encompasses hardware, software, data formats, and protocols, needs to be built, implemented, and evaluated based on how the data are to be used (Geschwind, 2001). For technical infrastructure, we explore the three minimal criteria that Klump and colleagues (2006) articulate for data sharing: persistence, longevity, and quality. Data should be described, stored, accessible, and secure for these criteria to be applied.

The major interactions that need to be addressed in a technical infrastructure for data sharing include data discovery, data access, data context, data integrity, data security, and data management. We refer to this as the access and discovery layer. Descriptive standards, metadata, vocabularies, the context of creation and storage, and identifiers for data and their locations are critical to making data persistent, discoverable, and accessible.

The institutional, professional, and social conditions under which data are created and shared permeate these other layers, but can be most clearly explicated separately from the technical dimensions of data sharing. Many researchers are understandably concerned about the overhead entailed in making data publicly available, having their data used by other researchers before the data producers publish their findings (Toronto International Data Release Workshop, 2009), and the ways that outside (i.e., outside of the researcher's workgroup) entities manage data. They may also be concerned about the security of sensitive data in institutional repositories. Research ethics, disciplinary norms, complex institutional networks (including private and public partnerships), and resources (human and otherwise) for making data available can serve as either barriers or incentives for data sharing. Access policies and mechanisms also need to be developed that appropriately reflect the value of research data, particularly in the university setting. At this human infrastructure layer, explicit concerns about intellectual property, ethics and privacy, access and use policies, business models, sustainability, scientific practice, and professionalism arise. We conclude with a discussion of evaluation and suggest future research directions.

The Nature of Data

Defining Data

Data sharing begins with, of course, data. Although research data can be generated digitally, on paper, or in some hybrid form, most of the literature on data sharing focuses on data that is generated digitally. We generally adopt the definition of data as put forth by the U.S. National Science Board (NSB) (2005, p. 9): "any information that can be stored in digital form, including text, numbers, images, video or movies, audio, software, algorithms, equations, animations, models, simulations, etc. Such data may be generated by various means including observation, computation, or experiment." Hilgartner (1995) argues that data should be construed more broadly because conflicts over access have included tangible artifacts such as biological reagents and molecules, instrumentation, and other key resources. Including these artifacts is beyond the scope of this chapter. Data are inherently collective and come in sets— the collation of many individual data. In most scientific research, a researcher would need a number of datasets or databases. We refer to these sets of datasets as data collections.

Data collections "refer not only to stored data but also to the infrastructure, organizations, and individuals necessary to preserve access to the data" (U.S. National Science Board, 2005, p. 9). The NSB has developed a hierarchy by size of collection types: research data collections, community data collections, and reference data collections. We acknowledge that this hierarchy is not used by data creators themselves but, because this language is prevalent, we use the terms to structure discussion.

The process by which data are created, analyzed, and managed is complex; the experimental and observational data collection process is often referred to as the data life cycle. In general, although there may be significant differences in the individual stages, the life cycle is assumed to encompass the experimental design and capture, cleaning/integration, analysis, publication, and preservation processes, which occur in an iterative fashion.

The life cycle approach has been recognized as important to data preservation and sharing because active intervention early in that life cycle is essential for successful preservation (Beagrie, 2006). A high-level hypothesis or research question should be broken down into tasks that can be performed with appropriate workflow and data analysis. In e-science, such experiments are conducted *in silico* (performed computationally) but the same life cycle exists (Wroe, Goble, Greenwood, Lord, Miles, Papay, et al., 2004). However, different kinds of data (and disciplines) have different life cycles. Wallis, Borgman, Mayernik, and Pepe (2008) argue that the number of individuals and institutions involved at each stage of the life cycle increases as the complexity of the data increase. The cumulative weight of decisions made at each stage determines what is available at the next stage, how it is handled, and the purposes for which it is useful. Although the data themselves may be more or less easily depicted through various descriptive processes, documenting the decisions at each stage of the life cycle, and describing that cycle in detail, is more problematic and not easily automated (Borgman, 2007; Higgins, 2008; Wallis et al., 2008).

Format

Scientific data can be numeric, text-based, audio, video, or still images, depending on the nature of the studies that generated them. Data may be represented in a variety of formats that are domain- and community-dependent. Many communities have developed a set of standard formats to facilitate data sharing and system interoperability (Gardner, Toga, Ascoli, Beatty, Brinkley, Dale, et al., 2003; Westbrook, Ito, Nakamura, Henrick, & Berman, 2005). Researchers in astrophysics and genomics, for example, have a known set of widely accepted file formats that facilitate both data sharing and data archiving (Interagency Working Group on Digital Data, 2009).

Since the 1990s, the scientific community has been aware that effective data sharing depends on standard data formats and tool sets to build, read, and manage the data (Gardner et al., 2003; Rew & Davis, 1990). During the research life cycle, the original, raw data are often processed and transformed into a reduced or derived data product (Research Information Network, 2008). The wide variety of data formats used in different scientific disciplines is a barrier to data mining and sharing; conversion between different formats requires a substantial effort (Mann, Williams, Atkinson, Brodlie, Storkey, & Williams, 2002; Shiffrin & Börner, 2004). The ease or difficulty of data reuse, as well as the probability of long-term access and persistence, depends on the complexity and transparency of the file format itself (Abrams, 2004). Because formats depend on specific technologies and are bound to both a software environment and a hardware infrastructure for rendering and processing, changes to the format or to the environment can make the underlying data unrecognizable and unusable. One study, not surprisingly, discovered that it was easier to convert data in open formats such as Tagged Image File Format (TIFF). But the researchers also discovered that even open formats can have a proprietary, and thus secret, set of tags that may not be supported in future versions; they may also lack documentation for migration or conversion (Lawrence, Kehoe, Rieger, Walters, & Kenney, 2000). Because they manage and archive large collections of heterogeneous digital files, the Library of Congress; the National Archives of England, Wales and the United Kingdom; OCLC; and the National Archives of Australia have each developed separate sets of criteria for assessing the risks associated with formats. Although these four criteria differ in terms of complexity and thoroughness, a consensus exists that archival formats should be well documented and well understood; not wholly owned by a single commercial entity; widely adopted to increase the probability of commercial tools for migration and to ensure a long usage cycle to avoid repeated, short-term migration; self-contained; and not reliant on a specific technical environment (Kowalczyk, 2007).

Context

Context is defined as the information that documents the relationships of the data content to its environment (Consultative Committee for Space Data Systems [CCSDS], 2002). Context can include descriptions of the purpose of the data, its quality, formats, and many other variables. In short, context documents how datasets fit into their physical and technical environments (file formats and field descriptors) as well as into the scientific environment (experiment treatments and applications). Representing context—creating the relevant metadata—is as essential as representing datasets themselves. Moore, Baru, Rajasekar, Ludaescher, Marciano, Wan, and colleagues (2000a) contend that context, maintained in a representation that is not dependent upon the format of the data it describes, is a significant component of a persistent data infrastructure. As part of a project to develop a data sharing environment for a community of biologists, Chin and Lansing (2004) describe the context necessary for successful collaboration: biologists need to understand the relationships between the data and software applications, experiments, projects, and the scientific community. The specific properties of the data that should be included in the context are: general dataset properties (such as owner, creation date, size, and format); experimental properties (conditions and properties of the scientific experiment that generated or is to be applied to the data); data provenance (the relationship of data to previous versions and other data sources); integration (the relationship of data subsets within a full dataset); analysis and interpretation (such as notes, experiences, interpretations, and knowledge generated from analysis of data); physical organization (the mapping of datasets to physical storage structures such as a file system, database, or some other data repository); project organization (the mapping of datasets to project hierarchy or organization); scientific organization (the mapping of datasets to some scientific classification, hierarchy, or organization); task (the research task(s) that generated or applies to the dataset); experimental process (the relationship of data and tasks to the overall experimental processes); and user communities (different organizations' applications of the datasets) (Chin & Lansing, 2004).

These properties are represented in specific standardized formats, often unique to each scientific domain. Some are semi-structured representations for the digital objects and the data collection using an open schema definition (Moore, Baru, Rajasekar, Ludaescher, Marciano, Wan, et al., 2000a, 2000b). Some are multilevel representations with dataset level and variable/attribute level metadata (Jaiswal, Giles, Mitra, & Wang, 2006). Others are represented as graphs (Chen & Kotz, 2001), as topic maps (Goslar & Schill, 2004), as semantic networks (Henricksen, Indulska, & Rakotonirainy, 2002), or as trees (Gardner, Goldberg, Grafstein, Robert, & Gardner, 2008).

Creating and documenting this context is usually a manual effort. The researcher who creates the data can also create the metadata needed for preservation in a repository. Traditionally, this process has been a one-time event. However, new social networking paradigms of user-contributed metadata are emerging; collections are beginning to ask subsequent data users to add information via textual annotations

(Chin & Lansing, 2004; Ives, Halevy, Mork, & Tatarinov, 2003; Jaiswal et al., 2006; Michener, Beach, Bowers, Downey, Jones, Ludaescher, et al., 2005; Myers, Allison, Bittner, Didier, Frenklach, Green, et al., 2005) as well as visual annotations over images (Chin & Lansing, 2004). Research communities are developing algorithms and processes to generate dynamic community vocabularies and ontologies automatically, from both the human-generated metadata and the data themselves, for data integration and discovery in data collections (Jaiswal et al., 2006). The goals of automated context creation are to generate more accurate and consistent data, to create sufficient context for precise data discovery, and to ease the burden of creating metadata from the contributing scientist (Michener, 2005).

Data Integrity

Data integrity is the expectation of data quality—that is, the assurance that the data are whole or complete, consistent, and correct. Data integrity includes both intellectual and technical wholeness and can be compromised by human errors at any stage of creation and use. Because correcting data is always expensive, the best practice for all information systems is to ensure that the data are correct from the beginning (Galloway, 2004). Ensuring the integrity of the data is a significant factor in establishing trust within the designated community and the level of use of a data collection (Lyon, 2007).

Green and Gutmann (2007) advocate for collaboration among local, institution-based repositories, the data collection repositories, and the researcher that would both simplify and enhance the quality and the integrity of the data. Their model of the research data life cycle (discovery and planning, initial data collection, final data preparation and analysis, and publication and sharing) is designed to optimize persistent access to data. By involving the repository in all phases of the research project, from conceptualization and grant writing through publication, they argue that integrity issues such as data creation rules, processing requirements, data standards, and data confidentiality can be addressed early, creating a set of data and metadata with integrity and quality that is ready for long term archiving within repositories (Green & Gutmann, 2007).

Fixity is a significant data integrity issue because digital data can be changed easily, either maliciously or inadvertently (Hedstrom & Montgomery, 1998). Gladney (2004) argues that to ensure integrity the repository must be able to guarantee the fixity of each object. Technically, this is a simple process that includes creating a checksum or a digital signature for each object, be it a data file, a configuration file, rendering software, or documentation. The checksum should be created before the data are placed into the repository, stored in the repository with administrative data about the data object, and validated by a process that calculates the checksum for each digital file and compares it to the saved checksum on a regular schedule, reporting errors to the repository managers (Kowalczyk, 2007).

Versioning

Discussions of data sharing have generally focused on final data. The National Institutes of Health (NIH) defines "final data" as "recorded factual material commonly accepted in the scientific community as necessary to validate research findings" (National Institutes of Health, 2003, para. 4). The NIH accepts only data that support publications and explicitly excludes paper laboratory notebooks and other artifacts that document work in progress, even though these represent much of the data generated in the conduct of science. Much of the emphasis on data sharing thus focuses on finished or finalized datasets that can be used by groups and individuals beyond the original creators. However, it is not always clear which data should be considered final. Treloar, Groenewegen, and Harboe-Ree (2007) describe a fluid state for data, a continuum between informal pre-publication and more formal publication. Steinhart (2007) asserts that researchers need to share intermediate and supporting data and proposes that libraries provide both staging repositories, to allow researchers to add, delete, modify and share as they see fit prior to publication, and a process for moving completed datasets to an archival repository.

In some fields it is not sufficient to share the raw datasets; descriptors and the tools and methods by which data are generated, analyzed, and shared must be made available if the data are to be fully useful. The National Aeronautics and Space Administration (NASA) (1986), in its work developing earth observation data systems, developed a hierarchy of data levels to describe the nature of the data: Level 0, unprocessed instrument data at full resolutions; Level 1A, unprocessed instrument data at full resolution, time referenced, and annotated with ancillary information, including radiometric and geometric calibration coefficients and geo-referencing parameters; Level 1B, which are Level 1A data that have been processed within the range of the sensor filters; Level 2, derived environmental variables at the same resolution and location as the Level 1 source data; Level 3, variables mapped to uniform special and temporal grid scales, usually with some completeness and consistency properties; Level 4, model output or results from analyses of lower-level data (i.e., variables that were not measured by the instruments but instead are derived from these measurements). These levels are being reinterpreted in new domains as data provenance descriptors (Bose & Frew, 2005) and as text encoding levels (Renear, Dolan, Trainor, & Cragin, 2009).

Data Persistence

Various terms have been used to describe the process needed to maintain digital materials over time, including digital preservation, digital archiving, and digital curation. These terms are still evolving, are often used interchangeably, and are defined as "actions needed to maintain digital research data and other digital materials over their entire life cycle and over time for the current and future generations of users" (Beagrie, 2006, p. 4). Because persistence is a significant aspect of data sharing (Interagency Working Group on Digital Data, 2009; Klump et al., 2006), data archiving and curation are vital services of data collections (Green & Gutmann, 2007). Persistence through data curation requires organizational commitment and ongoing stewardship (Lynch, 2003). As an organizational issue, persistence requires long-term commitment for staffing, storage, and technology upgrades; thus persistence requires sustainable funding (Association of Research Libraries et al., 2009). Digital preservation policy development is a significant indicator of an organization's support for preservation activities (McGovern, 2007).

Moore (2008) characterizes digital preservation as a method of communication with both the future and the past. The conversation with the future conveys preservation properties such as authenticity, integrity, and maintenance of an object's chain of custody, so that future systems, as yet unimagined, will be able to interpret and display the information. The conversation with the past provides the characterizations of prior preservation processes and preservation management policies.

Assessing and managing risk are significant components of preservation management policy development. Kenney, McGovern, Botticelli, Entlich, Lagoze, Payette, and colleagues (2002) have identified four risk management stages: data gathering (risk identification) and characterization; simple risk declaration and detection; contextualized risk declaration and detection; and automated preservation policy enforcement. Digital preservation risk assessment methodologies include Digital Repository Audit Method Based on Risk Assessment (DRAMBORA) and INvestigation of FOrmats based on Risk Management (INFORM). The DRAMBORA methodology has three stages: identification of preservation objectives, identification of risks along with the probabilities and impact of the risks, and identification of risk mitigation strategies and measures (Whyte, Job, Giles, & Lawrie, 2008). The INFORM methodology defines six classes of risk: digital formats, software, hardware, associated organizations, the digital repository, and format migration preservation plans (Stanescu, 2005).

Data Collections

The U.S. National Science Board (2005) broadly defines data collections as the infrastructure, organizations, and individuals needed to provide persistent access to stored data. They developed a three-layer typology of data collections organized by size and scope: research data collections, community data collections, and reference data collections. Research data collections refer to the output of a single researcher or lab during the course of a specific research project. This collection may or may not use the data standards of its community or have use beyond its own original purpose. Community data collections generally serve a well defined arena of research. Often, standards are developed by the community to support the collection. At the highest level, reference data collections are broadly scoped, widely disseminated, well funded collections that support the research needs of many communities. In general, much of the focus of data research and development (and funding organizations' interest) has been on the trajectory of moving from local, somewhat informal research collections to more established, sustainable ones that can serve broader groups over time.

In the next section we use this framework—research collections, community collections, and reference collections—to describe the functions, structure, and organizational dimensions of such of datasets. We acknowledge that many contributors to and users of data collections generally do not use these terms to describe their own activities and repositories. Nevertheless, the framework provides a useful way of describing and categorizing many of the aspects of data collections and the changes that arise from scaling up and expanding the scope of use.

Research Collections

Research collections, the output from an individual researcher or project, are most often shared using technologies that are not specifically designed for sharing scientific data. These technologies include personal websites, email, electronic mailing lists, and online discussion groups (Gardner et al., 2003). Discovery of research collections is usually ad hoc, based on personal relationships or personal knowledge of reputation or published works (Chin & Lansing, 2004). The quality of the metadata for research collections varies widely from standardized schema to idiosyncratic labeling (Research Information Network, 2008). Data access is via simple technologies such as email attachments, File Transfer Protocol (FTP) (either secured or unsecured) or HyperText Transfer Protocol (HTTP) download. In this informal sharing environment, data security can be easily negotiated between the parties; however, determining and enforcing compliance with those security agreements can be difficult (Gardner et al., 2003). In research collections, the understanding of both data context and data integrity can benefit from the ad hoc, personal nature of the data exchange. The context of the data, as has been discussed, is a complicated interchange of implicit and explicit metadata. Direct communication between the data creator and the data user can facilitate efficient knowledge transfer. Personal relationships with the data creator and scholarly reputations typically increase confidence in the integrity of the data. Good data management practices vary widely for research collections due to a set of complex interactions among the technology environment of the academic institution and the nature of the data context, content, and format.

A new trend is emerging that might provide a more scalable model for data sharing for research collections. Academic institutions are beginning to develop programs to include data within their institutional repositories (Lyon, 2007; Parr & Cummings, 2005; Ruusalepp, 2008). Currently, adoption of institutional repositories as an infrastructure for storing and disseminating scientific data is not widespread (Lyon, 2007) but, as the barriers to self-archiving are reduced by streamlining workflows and simplifying metadata capture, researchers may find a more formal model useful to share their collections of data (Crow, 2002; Lyon, 2007).

Community Collections

Community collections integrate local, research level collections into more structured forms with the resources needed to undertake the task. They often face multiple challenges of standardization of data formats, metadata, and harmonizing diverse data management practices. To take one example of such a transitional community collection, coastal resource assessment and management relies heavily on numerous computer applications and data sources that are created and used by local, state, and federal government agencies; academic units; and nonprofit organizations. To manage coastal resource information and integrate data from multiple organizations, a partnership was formed among entities in the state government, Oregon State University, and a regional nonprofit to produce a data portal entitled the Oregon Coastal Atlas. This portal was designed to provide access to datasets, mapping tools, and other resources for decision making and research by interested parties. However, even experienced creators and users of the Atlas's data have had serious problems finding and using relevant data. They are confounded by multiple versions of the same data over time (not surprising for an ever-changing coastline), the inability to find the appropriate dataset, incomplete or unclear restrictions on use, software and hardware incompatibility, and integration problems with other data resources (Wright, 2009).

This case illustrates some of the many technical, policy, organizational, and other considerations in the creation, use, and reuse of scientific data, but yet others also exist. For example, a great deal of anxiety persists in the larger scientific community that researchers will not be adequately recognized, that data will be reused improperly, and that data quality in general may suffer (Borgman, 2007; Gardner et al., 2003). Other concerns include worries about privacy protection for research subjects that may be identifiable in specific datasets, licensing agreements, and the legal and policy frameworks within which scientific data sharing occurs (Eckersley, Egan, De Schutter, Yiyuan, Novak, Sebesta, et al., 2003). These concerns supplement many of the purely technical challenges, such as the development of controlled vocabularies and usable interfaces for simple access and ingest.

Neuroscience is a discipline in which community-level data sharing has been successful due to standardization. Palmer, Cragin, and Hogan (2004) note that neuroscience is highly reliant on the integration of data—including models, clinical data, and basic science data—across scales and research products. One initiative, entitled Collaborative Research in Computational Neuroscience (CRCNS), has been jointly funded by the National Science Foundation (NSF) and the National Institutes of Health since 2002 to facilitate the sharing of high-quality datasets in neuroscience. Researchers polled at the onset of its development overwhelmingly expressed the need for shareable datasets to advance their work. Previous data collections in the field focused narrowly on specific data types, analytical tools, and neuroimaging data (Whyte et al., 2008). CRCNS attempts to mitigate problems through a simple and sustainable administrative structure, a stripped-down metadata scheme to tag the datasets, peer validation of datasets, and levels of access control. Subsequent funding is being made available for further projects that will contribute data to CRCNS. Another community-level collection through which neuroscience data can be shared is a visual one—an atlas of the brain that is connected to other kinds of information (Boline, Lee, & Toga, 2008). Semantic linking and spatial registration link key information to areas of the brain mapped in the atlas.

The Visible Human Project is another such collection with similar goals—the construction of a suite of minutely detailed representations of the human form. The datasets serve as anatomical references to test medical imaging algorithms; the data have also been used for a much wider range of scientific and other applications (including virtual reality and digital art). The long-term goal is to permit visual knowledge of the human body to be connected with what the National Library of Medicine (2009, online) calls "symbolic knowledge" (such as the names of body parts). Other open access medical image repositories are similarly useful for purposes ranging from regulatory review to the development of new methods for data analysis (Vannier, Staab, & Clarke, 2003).

Community-level collections represent an intermediate scale and scope between the often ad hoc self-archiving initiatives of individual research groups and large-scale reference collections. These collections face challenges in obtaining sustainable funding and other resources; implementation of standards; and the integration of multiple, often informally managed, datasets from many researchers.

Reference Collections

Reference collections, the broadly scoped, widely disseminated, well funded collections that support the research needs of many disciplines, enable data sharing in a highly formalized technical infrastructure. The underlying technologies are generally opaque with a sophisticated set of tools with structured processes designed for ingestion, normalization, and validation of both the data and metadata. These reference collection infrastructures provide additional tools for data access, such as searching, browsing, and downloading. Several of these collections also provide analysis tools and data readers either to download material for use on the researcher's own computer or for use within the collection's infrastructure.

The oldest of these reference collections is the Worldwide Protein Data Bank (wwPDB), the international archive for biomacromolecular structural data (Berman, Bhat, Bourne, Feng, Gilliland, Weissig, et al., 2000; Berman, Henrick, & Nakamura, 2003). The wwPDB has a number of supporting organizations including the Research Collaboratory for Structural Bioinformatics (RCSB) PDB (U.S.), PDBe (Europe), and PDBj (Japan) (Berman, Henrick, & Nakamura, 2003). The wwPDB is typical of large reference collections and serves as an exemplar. Originally developed in 1971 at the Brookhaven National Laboratories as an archive for biological macromolecular crystal structures, it grew from seven to 59,000 structures (as of June 9, 2009) through improved data gathering technologies, such as nuclear magnetic resonance (NMR), and through changing research norms. Specifically, changes in the community's views about data sharing, many journals' requirement to provide a wwPDB accession code for publication, and funding agencies' requirement of data deposition for all structures led to the rapid growth of the data in the wwPDB (Berman, Westbrook, Feng, Gilliland, Bhat, Weissig, et al., 2002; Westbrook, Feng, Chen, Yang, & Berman, 2003).

With the primary goal of open access to data, a reference collection such as the wwPDB needs to have a nuanced approach to data security that balances open access and data integrity. Search, discovery, and data access are completely open. Anyone with an internet connection and a web browser can find protein structures; read the research papers; and download the data, metadata, documentation, and data analysis tools. The wwPDB has a login function but, rather than restricting or securing data or functions, it allows users to execute personalized queries either on command or on a schedule. The personalized data are stored in a secure server and not shared with third parties. No authorization or authentication is required to deposit data into the wwPDB. In addition to the automated tools that verify technical accuracy and compatibility, the wwPDB embargos new deposits until a peer-reviewed paper is published, thus ensuring intellectual verification. The wwPDB regularly reviews the embargoed data and notifies the depositors of the status of their data (Research Collaboratory for Structural Bioinformatics Protein Data Bank, 2009).

Reference collections such as the wwPDB have become an integrated component of the scientific workflow for entire domains by providing significant incentives for both the deposit of original data and the reuse of existing data. These reference collections have acquired commitments for long-term funding; they have invested in organizational and management infrastructure to ensure the persistence of the service and the data.

Technical Infrastructure

Repositories

For many data collections, a data repository is a significant component of the technical infrastructure. Through much of the literature on the technology infrastructure of scientific data sharing, the term *repository* refers to a simple data store for datasets (Venugopal, Buyya, & Ramamohanarao, 2006). We take a broader view and define a repository as a system and set of services designed as an archive for digital data with context, fixity, and persistence. Moore and colleagues (2000a; 2000b, online) describe such a digital repository as a "persistent archive" that is modular, allowing any component to be replaced without affecting the rest of the system. The low-level functional components can be updated as technology evolves so the archive remains stable in the context of rapid change. Persistent archives provide repository services to ensure the long-term archiving of and continuous access to data including backups, contingency planning, process resumption planning, hardware and network redundancy, automatic failover, and site mirroring (Kowalczyk, 2007). Repository services are mindful of the entire data life cycle (Hank & Davidson, 2009) and increase in importance as the amount of data grows (Choudhary, Kandemir, No, Memik, Shen, Liao, et al., 2000).

Ensuring that a repository is trustworthy has been a significant concern of the digital preservation community from its inception. In a seminal work, Waters and Garrett (1996) proposed an audit and certification process to evaluate repository services. Multiple initiatives have launched criteria and metrics for repository audits as methods of control and assessment (Day, 2008). In the U.S., the Trustworthy Repositories Audit and Certification: Criteria and Checklist (TRAC) is a set of digital preservation best practice criteria used to review the organizational infrastructure, digital object management, technologies, technical infrastructure, and security of a repository service (Center for Research Libraries & Online Computer Library Center, Inc., 2007). The TRAC criteria are based on four principles: documentation as evidence for audits; transparency in practice, design, and policy; adequacy of implementation decisions to ensure that the preservation objectives can be met; and measurability to provide objective goals for evaluation. Several European initiatives have been undertaken in this arena and some have international import. For example, Germany has several certification initiatives including the Network of Expertise in Long-term Storage of Digital Resources (NESTOR) that evaluates the technical, organizational, and financial characteristics of a digital repository (Dobratz & Neuroth, 2004) and the German Initiative for Network Information criteria that uses visibility of the services, policy, security, authenticity, data integrity, and metadata as evaluation criteria (Deutsche Initiative für Netzwerkinformation, 2007). Ross and McHugh (2006) argue that much of the effort in repository audit and certification has been to define the characteristics of a trusted repository; insufficient effort has been spent on developing metrics for evaluating a repository within its context and environment. They propose an evidence-based evaluation process using documentary evidence, observation of practice evidence, or testimonial evidence.

In general, specific technology infrastructures for data collections are difficult to discern from the data sharing literature. The repository services provided by data collections are not specifically addressed. The repository system software underlying data collections is generally opaque. But a number of digital repository systems exist that are used or could be used for data collections. The three major repository systems, DSpace, Fedora, and iRODS, are all open source projects governed by nonprofit foundations. Both DSpace and Fedora were developed within the library community and are jointly governed by DuraSpace. iRODS was developed in the cyberinfrastructure, grid computing, and supercomputing communities and is governed by the Data Intensive Cyberinfrastructure Foundation (Rajasekar, Wan, Moore, & Schroeder, 2006).

DSpace

Originally a joint project of the Massachusetts Institute of Technology (MIT) and Hewlett-Packard, DSpace is an open source repository system for the dissemination of digital research and educational materials (Smith, Barton, Bass, Branschofsky, McClellan, Stuve, et al., 2003). DSpace is a three-tiered system with an application layer, a business logic layer, and a storage layer (Massachusetts Institute of Technology, 2004). The layers have a strict hierarchy. Each layer has its own Application Programming Interface (API). Authentication and authorization are controlled at the application layer. DSpace is specifically designed to allow different communities within an organization to define their "space" with a set of depositors and an intellectual organization of the contents. Access to the content is through a customizable web portal.

DSpace is often implemented as an institutional repository. As a data repository, it provides a simple interface for both context data entry by the data producer and for researchers looking for data but, because it supports only Dublin Core as a metadata format, DSpace has limited ability to support robust data sharing. However, several projects use DSpace as their repository platform, including the DataShare project at the University of Edinburgh and the U.S. National Evolutionary Synthesis Center's Dryad project (DSpace, 2010).

Fedora

Fedora—the Flexible and Extensible Digital Object Repository Architecture—was originally developed as a research project at Cornell University's Computer Science Department with funding by the U.S. Department of Defense Advanced Research Projects Agency (DARPA) and NSF, and was further developed by the University of Virginia Library and Cornell University through a grant from the Andrew W. Mellon Foundation (Lagoze, Payette, Shin, & Wilper, 2005). The major functions of Fedora are Extensible Markup Language (XML) submission and storage where digital objects are stored as XML-encoded files that conform to an extension of the Metadata Encoding and Transmission Standard (METS) schema. Fedora is the underlying repository system for a number of major digital libraries as well as several data-centric applications, such as the eSciDoc project for the research results and materials of the Max-Planck Society and the Islandora project to create a collaboration and digital data stewardship environment (Fedora Commons, n.d.).

iRods

The Integrated Rule-Oriented Data System (iRODS) is a data grid repository system developed at the University of California San Diego to support data grids, digital libraries, and persistent archives (Data Intensive Cyber Environments, 2009). As its name suggests, iRODS is a rules-based system, enforcing management policies that are sets of assertions about the digital collections. The iRODS Rule Engine interprets the management policies that have been expressed as rules determining the appropriate responses to requests, events, and conditions (Rajasekar et al., 2006). iRODS can function as a stand-alone system or can be integrated with other repository systems such as DSpace and Fedora to provide additional preservation functions; because of the rules-based processing, preservation functions such as format migration and fixity validation can be automated (Moore & Smith, 2007). iRODS is the underlying repository system for the production environments for the Teragrid and the Southern California Earthquake Center and for the National Archives and Records Administration's (NARA) transcontinental persistent archive prototype (TPAP) project.

Data Storage

For data repositories, storage infrastructure is an important component of data archiving and preservation. Although storage has become an increasingly cheaper commodity (Association of Research Libraries, 2006; Atkins, 2003; Hacker & Wheeler, 2007), carefully designing an infrastructure is important (Brown, 2003; Rajasekar et al., 1999). Moore and colleagues (2000a, 2000b) contend that a persistent archive needs a scalable storage infrastructure. Creating an expandable and extendable storage architecture based on new but proven technologies is the most efficient and likely the least expensive approach (Moore et al., 2000a, 2000b; Morris & Truskowski, 2003).

Criteria to assess scalability, expandability, and extensibility of storage technologies should include longevity, capacity, viability, obsolescence, cost, and susceptibility. The criteria can be used to develop a matrix to measure media usability both in life span and in technical relevance, the amount of data that can be stored, data safety in terms of environmental trauma and data errors, and the total costs of implementing and maintaining the technologies (Brown, 2003).

Infrastructure Models

Data collections have to deal with four types of heterogeneity as defined by Koutrika (2005): system heterogeneity—different hardware platforms and operating systems; syntactic heterogeneity—different protocols and encodings within the system; structural heterogeneity—multiple data models and schemas; and semantic heterogeneity—multiple and conflicting name spaces giving different meanings to the same data and metadata. These multiple heterogeneities result in a recurrent struggle to find a balance between open access and security, standards and flexibility, rich metadata, and ease of submission. This heterogeneity necessitates complex tools to simplify the process of data sharing by facilitating interactions between data repositories (Ruusalepp, 2008). The federal government initiated development of large-scale infrastructures to deal with the heterogeneity of scientific data during the 1990s (Zimmerman, 2003). Much of the early infrastructure provided universal access to the raw data generated by "big science" instruments; the models that were developed have evolved and now support data generated by a wide variety of methods. Throughout the literature, these infrastructures are discussed in the abstract.

Centralized Infrastructure

In the centralized infrastructure model, technology and support are managed in a single organization. All services—data discovery, access, context, integrity, security, and data management—are delivered through this centralized infrastructure. The centralized model has a number of significant benefits including standardization, economies of scale, and reliability. It provides a standard platform for discovery, access, and context that is knowable by the designated community; simply put, there is a commonly understood and reliably consistent way of finding and accessing the data. A centralized infrastructure can also provide economies of scale. Hardware, particularly storage, has a lower cost of initial purchase in large quantities. Data loading processes can be automated, customized, and optimized for large-scale ingestion, which can reduce costs overall. A centralized infrastructure has the potential for exceptional reliability. With control from end to end, the infrastructure can be developed with redundancy at every level, with a high degree of normalization, and with smooth transitions between software components, which all contribute to a consistent and reliable service.

The centralized infrastructure, however, also has significant drawbacks. Unless there is a robust disaster recovery and business resumption plan, the centralized infrastructure is a single point of failure; that is, if a critical piece of the infrastructure fails, the service would be unavailable to researchers. A centralized infrastructure can also be seen as a monopoly that controls all aspects of the data. Reduced diversity of input is also possible: A few individuals could have disproportionate influence over the service interface and functions. Although all shared data collections require community buy-in, with a centralized infrastructure it is even more vital to serve the needs of the research community. The alternative is massive failure. Ongoing funding can be a major issue for centralized infrastructure. Although economies of scale often exist, a centralized infrastructure is generally very expensive to build and maintain. With a large budget to maintain, it can be difficult to find funding agencies willing to provide ongoing support in the absence of significant new and groundbreaking research.

Decentralized Infrastructure

In the decentralized, or distributed, infrastructure model, the technology and support are independently managed by multiple organizations. In this model, each organization stores a set of datasets and provides services. These datasets and services may be overlapping or unique. The decentralized model implies a diversity of technologies and implementation strategies providing flexibility and creativity in both software development and end-user functionality. This model allows for multiple interfaces with different functionalities, permitting researchers to choose the best system for their work; such freedom of choice, however, can be more confusing than liberating. In this model, users can become confused by the different interactions as well as the different data available in each interface. A decentralized infrastructure introduces the potential for lack of interoperability. Effort must be expended to develop standards to allow data to be exchanged and merged.

Geographic dispersion can result in multiple redundancies; that is, if one site and its data are offline, other sites with their data can still be available. A decentralized infrastructure also implies duplication of effort in hardware implementation, software development, and management, which can increase operational costs. Ongoing support in a decentralized infrastructure is a complex puzzle. Unlike the large, integrated, centralized approach, a decentralized infrastructure generally has many smaller components. With these smaller components, it may be easier to find funding in a piecemeal manner to replace or enhance a specific component. Securing large-scale funding can often mean sharing among a large number of partners, with each receiving a small amount.

Federated Infrastructure

Federated infrastructure was first conceived in 1985 as "an approach to the coordinated sharing and interchange of computerized information" implemented with a set of distributed components, minimizing central authority (Heimbigner & McLeod, 1985, p. 253). The federated infrastructure model is a multi-tiered environment with a central authority and independent yet interconnected partners. This implies an established distribution of power in which the central authority has a clearly defined set of responsibilities and control, documented in a binding agreement. The central authority sets standards, resolves conflicts, and provides resources (Semantic Counteroperability Community of Practice, 2008; Weill & Ross, 2004). A federated infrastructure provides a seamless interface to multiple, heterogeneous, and noncontiguous data sources. This implies a technology infrastructure that can query disparate databases, integrate results sets, and manage authentication and authorization across multiple independent organizations. Federations are complex, both organizationally and technologically.

A federated infrastructure can be implemented in a wide variety of configurations. Rajasekar, Wan, Moore, and Schroeder (2004) have developed a set of ten possible federation infrastructure models. The *occasional interchange* is the model with the greatest degree of autonomy for each partner, using the federation as an infrequent resource. In the *replicated catalog* model, each partner in the federation has an identical copy of the metadata catalog and the data; this allows for a high degree of fault tolerance. The *resource interaction* model allows a set of resources such as data or metadata to be replicated between partners. In the *replicated data zones* model, a subset of the partners (two or more) replicate data between themselves to form subnets of redundancy. The *master-slave zones* model has a central site, the master, at which new data are created and then replicated to the partner (slave) sites. This model provides a high degree of data security but limits the autonomy of the partners. The *snow-flake zones* model is a slight variation on the master-slave model, using a tiered replication: The master site replicates data to a set of slave sites, which in turn replicate to another set of slaves. The *user and data replica zone* model is a slight variation on the replicated data zones model, adding user data to the data that are replicated across subsets of the federation. The *nomadic zones* and the *free-floating zones* are very similar models involving individual, independent partners with asynchronous copies of the data and metadata for use by researchers in the field who cannot be online. The Nomadic zone implies no interconnectivity at all; the Free-floating zone implies occasional connectivity and data exchange. The *archival zone* model implies an offline site for backup purposes only (Rajasekar et al., 2004). The differences among these models include the degree of autonomy of each site, constraints on cross-registration of users, degree of replication of data, and degree of synchronization (Venugopal et al., 2006).

The federated infrastructure model facilitates powerful collaborations that can provide simple access to a wide array of data for researchers. But these collaborations take effort to build and nurture. Care is needed to maintain the balance of power among partners to keep the collaboration and partnership going. Implied in the federated model is cooperative software development. Coordinating this type of development effort across partners is challenging but can bring a sense of ownership to the partners. The federated infrastructure model is highly configurable and thus is often complex and difficult to understand and support. Finding problems, primarily with access or data synchronicity issues, can be costly both in resources and time.

Cyber/Cloud Infrastructure

Cyberinfrastructure (or e-science in the U.K.) describes a suite of internet-based services around scientific information (Atkins, 2003) but not a specific technology or implementation. Both the grid and the cloud are strongly associated with cyberinfrastructure (Arms, Calimlim, & Walle, 2009; Berman, Fox, & Hey, 2003; Venugopal et al., 2006). Buyya, Yeo, and Venugopal (2008) describe the grid as a set of resources—such as supercomputers, storage systems, data sources, and specialized devices—that may be geographically dispersed and owned by multiple organizations used to solve large-scale, computing-intensive problems. By integrating resources, a grid creates a "virtual platform for information" (F. Berman et al., 2003, p. 9). This platform is used by a number of cyberinfrastrucure projects that have data sharing as a core mission, including Linked Environments for Atmospheric Discovery (LEAD), the Network Workbench, and the Social Informatics Data-Grid (SID-Grid). Data grids are designed specifically for distributed data-intensive applications that create massive datasets by providing shared and distributed data collections and specialized services for data integrity and security (Venugopal et al., 2006). The Resource Storage Broker (Baru, Moore, Rajasekar, & Wan, 1998), iRODS (developed at the University of California San Diego [Moore & Smith, 2007]), and the NERC DataGrid (Hey & Trefethen, 2002) are some of the major initiatives in the area of data grids for e-science research. The term is meant to include the human resources needed to make the technical infrastructure function, but the discourse suggests a technologically deterministic vision for web services in science (Jankowski, 2007).

The cloud is defined as a distributed system of networked computers using virtualization that allows for real-time provisioning to create the appearance of a single computing resource when used. The amount of computing power and/or storage provided is defined by service level agreements between the service provider and each customer (Buyya et al., 2008). Although this may seem to be just another cluster of grids, the model is very different. In cloud technology, virtual nodes are created on demand with a specific quality of service agreement that is negotiated via Web 2.0 interfaces. Buyya and colleagues contend that cloud services are a transformative technology. Cloud technology provides a "shared storage system than can provide powerful abstractions for convenient, efficient, and large-scale inter-service data sharing" (Geambasu, Gribble, & Levy, 2009, p. 1). Yet, it is not without challenges. Geambasu and colleagues identify three major challenges for large-scale data sharing using the cloud: creating a generalized and flexible data sharing abstraction, resolving file/element naming and data protection issues, and resource allocation. The cloud provides technology as a service; the two major services are Software-as-a-Service (SaaS) and Infrastructure-as-a-Service (IaaS) both of which can simplify data sharing. Software-as-a-Service provides access to a suite of software tools, either as a monthly or per-use cost for commercial software, or at no cost for non-commercial software. This enables a computing environment with no capital investment, few set-up costs, and no maintenance. Infrastructure-as-a-Service provides on-demand computing cycles and data storage via a virtual machine that can be configured to execute requests. The impact of the cloud is not fully understood and the future is unclear. Although Geambasu and colleagues argue that the cloud infrastructure will eliminate the need for traditional data centers within organizations, Arms and colleagues (2009) argue that local systems operations help to diffuse expertise across an organization and thus will continue to be valuable.

Access and Discovery

Metadata, Ontologies, and Vocabularies

Access to and discovery of data resources require sufficient, targeted description of the resources themselves. This description is generally accomplished with metadata, ontologies, and vocabularies. The words metadata and ontologies have been used in multiple ways, but it is worth defining them briefly for our purposes. Ontologies are hierarchical, formal representations of the objects that constitute a specific area of interest (Gruber, 1995). In general, metadata has been used in information science to mean information about a particular representation of data (a document or set of documents, a dataset, images, or similar digital objects) (Duval, Hodgins, Sutton, & Weibel, 2002). A vocabulary consists of the properties that characterize the particular metadataset. For example, Dublin Core, which may be the most common metadata vocabulary, is applied to data to describe them for resource discovery and content management. It includes thirteen properties—such as title, author, and publication data—that characterize a particular digital resource.

Metadata can be informal or maintained and created in a more structured way as part of the dataset itself. Metadata can be as straightforward as the date a particular dataset was generated, the creators/custodians of the data, and the experimental or observational procedures that generated the data, to much more complex information about potential uses, geographic location of the data, its quality, or its state of completeness. Some metadata are also used to describe the kinds of web services that generated and maintain the dataset, associated tasks, and previous uses by others. Metadata can be human-generated or automatically generated and can be intended either for human use or for use by automated processes. Scientific communities, national scientific bodies, and international scientific organizations have all created metadata standards for datasets; their complexity and use depend extensively upon the expense and resource-intensiveness of the data collection procedures. The integration of standards is necessary to make workflows and resources reliable and discoverable. Lack of metadata is cited as one of the major barriers to data sharing because it affects both machine-readable processes and human searching (Wright, 2009).

Ontologies are more complex because they purport to offer a closer match to the real world than do metadata. Ontologies offer a structured view by representing more information in the form of types, properties, and relationships. The terms that actually constitute the ontology may vary widely, but the purpose of ontologies is to model concepts for a specific domain.

A key issue with metadata and ontologies, with respect to data sharing, is the sheer diversity of both and the lack of common vocabulary among the different systems, which hinders compatibility. How should we differentiate among types of metadata? One typology of metadata from the digital library field comprises administrative, structural, and descriptive metadata. Administrative metadata describe the data necessary to manage the digital object and include such data as terms and conditions of use, provenance, and technical data (file format, data schema, etc.). Structural metadata make the object usable, such as file sequencing and time-based data and file interrelationships. Descriptive metadata include data about the intellectual content, such as creator name, title, and description (Schwartz, 2000). Rajasekar and Moore (2008) developed a layered architecture to characterize metadata: 1) kernel metadata is the most basic metadata that includes information about how the metadata is organized, information about catalogs, information about how two sets of metadata can be interoperated, and so on; 2) system-centric metadata contain systemic information including data replicas, location, size, ownership, access control information, the use of resources (computation platforms used for deriving the data, methods used, etc.), and information about users and storage resources; 3) standardized metadata include metadata that implement agreed-upon generalized standards (such as Dublin Core, MARC [MAchine-Readable Cataloging, a standard data format for bibliographic information exchange], and METS [a standard for encoding metadata in digital libraries]); 4) domain-centric metadata include metadata that implement agreed upon standards inside (and possibly across) scientific disciplines such as FITS (Flexible Image Transport System, a data standard for the transfer of astronomical data), FGDC (Federal Geographic Data Committee, pertains to the transfer of geospatial metadata), and AIML (Artificial Intelligence Markup Language); 5) application-level metadata include information that is particular to an application, experiment, group, or individual researcher and may include creation or derivation notes by individual researchers.

Provenance is an important category of metadata that tracks the steps used to derive the data from their origins to their current state

(Buneman, Khanna, & Tan, 2000). Also known as lineage, provenance is an audit trail from data creation to final state, a record of each migration, transformation, and/or process applied to a set of data (Pearson, 2002). Provenance data have no metadata standard and have been represented as graphs, semantic networks, and entity relationships (Bose, 2002). In data sharing, whether generalized or domain specific, data provenance is difficult to collect, convey, and preserve. Defining the data required to prove provenance is specific to each data type and/or domain. Although much of the research is focused on describing data for sharing, it is also an important component to preserving data. Understanding the full history of a dataset and describing its transformations is a primary function of a digital archive. Without provenance data, objects cannot be considered preserved (Chen, 2004).

Developing appropriate and effective ontologies is an essential but often thankless task (Saltz, 2002). Domain specific provenance schemas are being developed—SNOMED and LOINC for medical research (Saltz, 2002) and Karma for atmospheric research (Plale, Ramachandran, & Tanner, 2006; Simmhan, Plale, & Gannon, 2005, 2006) are cases in point. But a more generalized solution is needed. Self-describing data and the software to process those data are not yet realities (Bose & Frew, 2005). Chimera, a prototype generalized data provenance system, has attempted to abstract data representation by using types, descriptors, and transforms. Types provide an abstraction layer for semantic content, the format of the physical representation and the format's encoding; descriptors define an interpretable schema that defines the data—number of files, types of files, and so forth; and forms are a generic, typed abstraction for computational procedures (Foster, Vockler, Wilde, & Zhao, 2002). Although many research efforts have focused on acquiring and presenting provenance data seamlessly, how such metadata are applied and used in practice and how the presence of structured and searchable metadata influences and facilitates data sharing is still under investigation (Niu & Hedstrom, 2008).

One highly successful case of scientific metadata and their uses is the Flexible Image Transport System. First developed in the 1970s as a format for file exchange of astronomical data, it became widely used as a machine-readable format for online data that can be read and analyzed by data analysis software. FITS also contains a human-readable ASCII component that allows users to investigate a file of particular interest fairly readily. FITS is endorsed by NASA and the International Astronomical Union. A working group at NASA is responsible for regular updates to the content and structure of FITS.

Data Access

Within the context of data sharing, data access is defined as the process by which a researcher can obtain data in order to act upon them. The most challenging technical issue is actually how to deliver large, often petabyte, datasets to researchers over networks with insufficient bandwidth (Gray, Liu, Nieto-Santisteban, Szalay, DeWitt, & Heber, 2005). Lubell, Rachuri, and Mani (2008) define a taxonomy of access scenarios for data collections—reference, reuse, and rationale. Reference is the ability to read the digital object; reuse is the ability to modify the digital object in an appropriate system environment; and rationale, the highest level of access, is the ability to explain any decisions that are made about the content of the digital object. In order for researchers to be able to reference and reuse data, they must have access.

Three models of data access have emerged: moving the data to the tools; moving the tools to the data; and building virtual views and dynamic access. Moving the data to the tools was the first model. Before organized data collections developed, data were shared by moving the data from the data owner's computer to another researcher's computer via email, FTP, Network File System (NFS), and other simple technologies (Birnholtz & Bietz, 2003; Gardner et al., 2003). As early data collections developed, this first model was prevalent. It was simple to implement and allowed the researchers to use their preferred tools within their own computing environments. Over time, both the size of datasets and the use of the collections grew, resulting in longer download times and increased demands on the collections' network infrastructure (Arms et al., 2009).

With the expansion of data collections, a second model has developed. Rather than moving the data to the researcher, the software tools are moved to the data (Arms et al., 2009; Gray et al., 2005; Michener et al., 2005; Myers et al., 2005). The tools can be specific to a data format, such as mesoscale weather analysis (Droegemeier, Gannon, Reed, Plale, Alameda, Baltzer, et al., 2005), or specific to a function, such as spatial mapping (Michener et al., 2005). The number of tools is proliferating, raising yet another discovery issue: How do researchers find the right tool for their needs? Many data collections provide a discovery portal for the tools that they offer (Myers et al., 2005). Providing a generalized infrastructure for tool delivery is a new research stream with emphasis on data conversion and integration (Myers et al., 2005; Schuchardt, Pancerella, Rahn, Didier, Kodeboyina, Leahy, et al., 2007).

A third model is evolving: data integration. This consists of providing the infrastructure to build new, dynamic data resources on demand by creating virtual views of slices of different data collections. Two methods are emerging; one uses schema mapping and the other semantic annotations and ontologies. The schema mapping method focuses on replication, synchronicity, and constraint issues of dynamic data exchange between collaborating researchers. Arenas, Kantere, Kementsietsidis, Kiringa, Miller, Mylopoulos, and colleagues (2003, p. 54) refer to mappings between seemingly unconnected databases as "mediation across multiple worlds" that can apply rules to check automatically for data consistencies and infer new constraints. Ives, Khandelwal, Kapur, and Cakir (2005) suggest that trust policies could specify the conditions under which a database is shareable and could score the incoming data based on perceived quality or relevance. These scores would then be used to reconcile conflicts. Like other rules-based processing, schema mapping requires a significant investment to build the necessary rules. The second method for an infrastructure for data integration uses semantics mediation to link datasets to ontologies explicitly. The semantic annotations are used to drive a knowledge-based data integration service that performs a series of integration transformations, such as scale resolution and geographic projection reconciliation, as well as data mining services, such as sampling data to create vectors with layers associated with an occurrence point. Ontologies built for data integration can have multiple purposes, such as thematic searching and metadata creation (Michener, 2005). Developing automated tools to build the ontologies and generate variable-names metadata in datasets that lack attribute-level metadata is ongoing (Jaiswal et al., 2006).

Metadata and ontologies function as identification for data; but sustainable access to data requires a method for providing persistent identification (Helly, Elvins, Sutton, & Martinez, 1999; Helly, Elvins, Sutton, Martinez, Miller, Pickett, et al., 2002; Lubell et al., 2008; Rajasekar et al., 2004). That is, sustainable access requires a unique, permanent, location-independent identifier for a network-accessible resource, which, using the language of the World Wide Web, is commonly known as a Universal Resource Identifer (URI) (World Wide Web Consortium, 2001). The URI is a generalized concept that is implemented in a number of different schemes: Persistent URLs, Digital Object Identifiers, and many others. In general, a Universal Resource Locator (URL) cannot be a persistent identifier because it conflates two important but separate functions—item location and item identification. By separating location from identification, URIs help avoid the problem of broken links. URIs are generally implemented as URLs that require a multiphased resolution process. Figure 6.1 shows the generalized model of this process (Harvard University Library, 2003). The first level resolution is to find the right resolution server. Once the resolution server is located, the second level resolution finds the resource. The second phase of the resolution is relatively simple. The resolution service uses a database that stores both the persistent ID and a location of the object (usually in the form of a URL) to redirect the http transaction using the location URL. As the problem of persistent identification of digital resources has become more prominent, a number of competing URI schemes have been developed.

The Online Computer Library Center (OCLC) uses a PURL—a persistent URL. This technology is similar to the Harvard persistent identification system but with a different syntax (Shafer, Weibel, & Jul, 2001). With funding from DARPA, the Corporation for National Research Initiatives (CNRI) created another unique persistent identifier syntax, the Handle System. The Handle System is an open source, downloadable technology specification with a set of open protocols and a

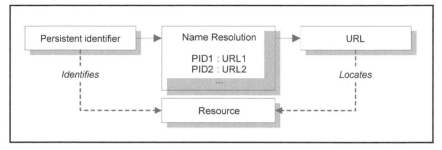

Figure 6.1   Harvard University's Name Resolution Service.

namespace (www.handle.net). The DSpace digital repository system uses Handle to identify its contents uniquely and persistently. The International DOI Foundation developed the semantics for the Digital Object Identifier (DOI), which has been implemented using the Handle syntax and resolution system (www.doi.org). Although the DOI specification was originally developed by publishers of electronic information to provide persistent and controlled access to journal articles, DOIs are often used to cite data in experiments and in provenance schemas (Simmhan, Plale, & Gannon, 2005). The California Digital Library has developed the Archival Resource Key (ARK), which provides access to a digital information resource. The ARK is architected to deliver three parameterized services: the digital object metadata, digital object content files, and a commitment statement made by the owning organization concerning the digital object (Kunze, 2003).

Data Discovery

Data discovery needs for data collections are both general and specific. The problem is "finding both needles in the haystack and finding very small haystacks" (Gray et al., 2005, p. 34). Researchers need a query interface that allows for a general overview of the complete collection to understand the breadth and depth of the data available. Beyond the general view, the data discovery system within a data collection commonly allows queries by subject terms, by data creator, and by data format, as well as by a more general set of terms (Treloar & Wilkinson, 2008). Domain specific ontologies are beginning to be used for concept-based searching (Jaiswal et al., 2006; Michener, 2005). Other types of discovery are emerging, such as geographic and spatially oriented searches and navigating provenance trees (Myers et al., 2005). Although researchers have indicated an interest in discovering data across domains, data sharing that crosses such boundaries is inhibited by the innate differences in the information-seeking behaviors of researchers within those different domains as well as the disparate vocabularies used (Kingsley, 2008; Treloar & Wilkinson, 2008). Parsons and Duerr

(2005) contend that data discovery interfaces require multiple views based on the designated user community in order to minimize unanticipated, inappropriate use of data.

Many of these data collections provide discovery services through a portal (Ruusalepp, 2008). A metadata portal is an internet site that provides an integrated access interface to distributed information resources (Myers et al., 2005; Schindler & Diepenbroek, 2008; Wright, 2009). Portals are also used for cross-domain searching (Treloar & Wilkinson, 2008). Portals can reduce the complexity of the underlying infrastructure for researchers. In distributed search infrastructures, every data provider has a separate metadata catalog and search interface; a domain portal can create a unified interface by federating searches and integrating result sets (Schindler & Diepenbroek, 2008). Although some projects use the library-oriented, client-server protocol Z39.50 to support federated searching (Altman, Andreev, Diggory, King, Sone, Verba, et al., 2001; Schindler & Diepenbroek, 2008), the U.K.'s Joint Information Systems Committee (JISC) recommended the A9 OpenSearch specification, a Web 2.0 technology for sharing search results as syndications and aggregations, in its most recent report on portal development in e-science (Allan, Crouchley, & Ingram, 2009).

Portals used to harvest data from a wide variety of sources, and then integrate those beyond the original scope of the data collection, are emerging (Ruusalepp, 2008). The primary technology for this harvesting is the Open Archives Initiative Protocol for Metadata Harvesting (OAI-PMH), a simple, six-step protocol for metadata exchange (Duke, Day, Heery, Carr, & Coles, 2005; Jaiswal et al., 2006; Schindler & Diepenbroek, 2008). As a simple protocol, OAI-PMH is difficult to implement in a multifaceted data environment because Dublin Core is the only natively supported metadata format, creating difficult choices when mapping complex data streams. Consider the following OAI-PMH data mapping example from a crystallography data collection project:

> [The] duality of the role of data contained within the data files, which at times was part of the data, but at other times fulfilled the role of exchanged metadata, or simply additional information displayed to a user, made discussion and reconciliation of views difficult, particularly at the initial stages when a common ground of understanding between the different partners was still being established. (Duke et al., 2005, p. 52)

To resolve the issues of mapping complex data into a simple data structure, the Open Archive Initiative has developed a new data representation protocol specifically for complex data objects, the Object Exchange and Reuse, commonly referred to as OAI-ORE (Lagoze & Van de Sompel, 2007). The OAI-ORE was designed to make the information within a complex object discoverable, reusable, machine readable, and actionable (Cheung, Lashtabeg, Drennan, & Hunter, 2008). Complex data objects are composite objects; that is, they consist of multiple independent data objects such as a binary dataset, a set of TIFF images, and a text document. The OAI-ORE protocol uses named graphs to describe the relationships among the many parts of a complex object. Each individual data object (a node) has one or more relationships (arcs) to other objects. Nodes and arcs are web resources and have URIs. Each element can be reused and recombined to make new named graphs, meaning that a dataset can be linked to multiple published and working papers with minimal duplication of data (Cheung et al., 2008). The Center for Embedded Networked Sensing (CENS) used the OAI-ORE protocol to provide interoperability for its content (Borgman, Wallis, Mayernik, & Pepe, 2007; Pepe, Borgman, Wallis, & Mayernik, 2007).

Data Security

Data security refers to the "protection of data from accidental or intentional but unauthorized modification, destruction or disclosure through the use of physical security, administrative controls, logical controls, and other safeguards to limit accessibility" (U.S. Social Security Administration, 2009, para. 10). Securing data collections may involve ensuring against corruption of content (integrity), safeguarding privacy (anonymity), or verifying users' identities (authentication) (Venugopal et al., 2006). Securing content against corruption is a matter of ensuring the fixity of the data object and is a responsibility of the data repository. Authentication—verifying the identities of those using a system or a dataset and determining the functions that the authenticated person is allowed to perform—is based on the role that a person has within the context of that data sharing system or a set of rules about the dataset itself. Personal identity authentication could be managed at the collection level, at the storage level, or at the home institution of the person: The collection could manage a control list of each person allowed to access the data (Rajasekar & Moore, 2008); a storage cloud could secure the data by requiring an encrypted signature as certificate of authorization (Geambasu et al., 2009); the home institution of an individual could authenticate the person and then pass a token to the collection as a certificate of authorization using a system such as Shibboleth (Scavo & Welch, 2007). Roles-based authorization defines a prescribed set of behaviors or functions that can be performed within a system such as resource discovery, resource acquisition, data upload, or metadata creation. These behaviors have associated polices that define the relationship between the authenticated person and the authorized behaviors (Jin & Ahn, 2006a). Within data collections, the behaviors are tied to specific data, creating a hybrid approach to authorization (Jin & Ahn, 2006b).

Human Infrastructure

We use this term to discuss many of the social, cultural, and ethical issues that arise around data sharing and how these are managed through policy and practice. Human infrastructure encompasses policy-related issues and scientific practice, although some of these ideas have been discussed elsewhere in this chapter as appropriate.

Policy

Policy on data sharing and use is a broad topic. Arzberger, Schroeder, Beaulieu, Bowker, Casey, Laaksonen, and colleagues (2004) articulate three domains that govern policy making and enforcement: the governmental, institutional, and cultural. The levels at which policy is made and enforced encompass national and international standards and agreements, institutional and other data repositories, guidelines at specific institutions where research data are generated and housed, and journal standards for publication of research data and results. In the U.S., for example, the National Institutes of Health (2003) requires grant applications of greater than $500,000 to submit a plan for data sharing. Many journals routinely require publishing researchers to submit their data to standardized repositories, complete with metadata (examples include the *Proceedings of the National Academy of Sciences* and *Molecular and Cellular Proteomics*, which has been requiring data submission since 2004). Professional societies such as the Microarray Gene Expression Data Society also promote data sharing by requiring researchers to submit their primary data to a public repository and provide a checklist to help achieve this goal. Such journals and societies have policies for ensuring privacy of the research data, including security mechanisms and de-identification of personal data.

Universities and other research institutions have developed a range of policies in the realm of data sharing in response to a variety of pressures. Institutional Review Boards (IRBs) in the U.S. and Research Ethics Boards (REBs) in the U.K. that govern human subjects research are a major influence. These entities place strictures on how data should be managed, stored, and shared to maximize benefit and minimize risk when human subjects are involved in research. These policies create incentives for data sharing but also introduce potential conflicts that inhibit it (Piwowar & Chapman, 2008).

Privacy

In the past, most data with highly personal information, primarily medical data, were simply not shared or were de-personalized by removing names and addresses (F. Berman et al., 2003). But even with de-personalized data, it is possible to identify individuals by triangulating multiple datasets. New techniques are being developed to de-indentify individuals in datasets through different automated anonymizing software tools including population-density-based Gaussian spatial blurring (Cassa, Grannis, Overhage, & Mandl, 2006) and the k-anonymization algorithm that ensures each record is indistinguishable from the others (Bayardo & Agrawal, 2005).

Data mining tools can be used to circumvent these operations. For example, a recent study found that some genomics data and research papers could be mined to reveal the identities of genetic disease patients even though data had been de-identified in genome-wide analysis studies (Kaye, Heeney, Hawkins, de Vries, & Boddington, 2009). Anonymization and informed consent are often used to protect the identity of research subjects, but both are problematic in the data sharing context. DNA, for instance, is a unique identifier; it is almost impossible to completely de-identify DNA and doing so would potentially make the research less useful. Informed consent protocols routinely take into account the uses of de-identified data but few consider the implications of aggregation for data sharing (Karp, Carlin, Cook-Deegan, Ford, Geller, Glass, et al., 2008).

Geographical information systems (GIS) provide another case of data-intensive technologies that illustrate some of the pitfalls associated with individual and demographic identification. Although individuals are not identifiable through GIS spatial coordinates, the potential for data mining and the aggregation of data may make sensitive data more visible. In particular, with aggregated GIS data, there is potential for racial profiling, redlining, and other potentially undesirable ways of segmenting social groups.

Ownership

Few financial rewards exist for sharing information; GIS layers are a potential commodity and thus create intellectual property dilemmas. A significant amount of GIS information is created by government agencies at local, state, and federal levels, which in the context of U.S. law and policy might suggest that GIS information should be freely shared because it is funded through public monies. However, many agencies are reluctant to share public data, knowing that private entities could potentially profit from public information while not sharing their own data. It is also unclear whether GIS data count as a public good in the same manner as other state-held resources. This creates concerns about how GIS should be used for commercial purposes.

Data sharing practices in science vary greatly. Intellectual property rights and the fair use of data remain problematic concepts for the sharing of scientific data. Because datasets are not formal publications or raw facts and are copyrighted but in the public domain (if generated with federal funds), they occupy a gray area in the arena of licensing and use restrictions and have not been governed by extant intellectual property regimes. Indeed, whether datasets are facts or publications is still contested in copyright law. One model from the Massachusetts Institute of Technology is the Science Commons, which takes a Creative Commons licensing approach to scientific data and indeed, uses the Creative Commons infrastructure. Scientists can use Science Commons to establish rights of attribution, sharing, and commercial/noncommercial use for datasets and other scientific data. Science Commons is not yet widely used or integrated into data repositories, although numerous projects exist as proof-of-concept, especially in the neurosciences.

Trust

Many factors affect the "quality" of data, which in turn influences how and when data are reused. One key element is the role of trust that researchers have in particular datasets. Extensive literature exists on the role of trust in data and its importance for data sharing, but there also has been a great deal of interest in the role of trust in the use of digital information, particularly in the context of digital libraries (Van House, 2002). The formal publication system eases some concerns through the process of peer review, as do the larger research collections with their vast resource-laden mechanisms for vetting data; trust in community-level collections, however, is not necessarily managed in the same way. For example, Van House, Butler, and Schiff (1998) describe two intermediate processes through which researchers in the environmental sciences decide whether to trust the quality of environmental datasets. First, these researchers take into account the scientific processes that were employed in creating the data. However, this condition, although necessary, is not sufficient. How data are collected and interpreted can be consciously or unconsciously biased by the creators, they argue. Thus the second criterion by which data trustworthiness is assessed is the personal and professional reputation of the individual, group, or organization that generated the dataset. Researchers often argue that they know how trustworthy data will be, based on the professional reputations of the creators (Shankar, 2007; Van House et al., 1998). These trust-building and credibility measures cannot be universally prescribed or formally built into digital data repositories; they are local, contingent, and fluid and are as much about the social conditions under which the data were generated as any qualities inherent in research design and method (Kelton, Fleischmann, & Wallace, 2008).

Local Practice Effects

The field of genomics (the characterization and sequencing of whole genomes of organisms) is one area that is widely cited as an exemplar of data sharing. Much of this has been driven by the need for large numbers of samples and declining costs and greater efficiencies of sequencing (Kaye et al., 2009). Funding agencies have made data sharing a requirement of financial support (Nelson, 2009; Schofield, Bubela, Weaver, Portilla, Brown, Hancock, et al., 2009). There are also extensive non-financial incentives for researchers to share data (Research

Information Network, 2008). Because the sequencing of a genome and its widespread acknowledgment by others generates credit for the sequencing laboratory or group, data sharing enhances reputation. Strong data description standards (with a limited and easily used metadata schema), limited data types, journal policies that require submission to repositories as a condition of publication, and a narrow scope of users (generally, other genetics researchers who are trained to use the data) further promote data sharing. Birnholtz and Bietz (2003) argue that genomics and similar disciplines where data sharing is relatively straightforward and routinized are characterized by low task uncertainty and the mutual interdependence of researchers. The relatively small community of genomics researchers agree on what the research problems are in the field, what kind of data are needed to address them, and the methods by which the data are produced; they rely on each other to provide such data. Few studies have been conducted in other disciplines, so it is not clear if this phenomenon is domain-specific.

Evaluation

Data repositories of all types are resource-intensive operations and represent substantial investments of time and money. It stands to reason that they require systematic evaluation for multiple reasons—the value of building the system, its usefulness and usability, importance to researchers, and other metrics. Some of these metrics are quantitative, others more interpretive. They represent the goals of different stakeholders in the data-sharing process. In short, evaluating the impact of data repositories and data sharing requires complex, extensive, often longitudinal study. Hilgartner and Brandt-Rauf (1994) argue that many studies of scientific practice have traditionally sidestepped data sharing as an explicit research problem.

However, this lacuna has since been addressed through numerous mixed-methods case studies of data access and use in cyberinfrastructure (Baker & Bowker, 2007; Karasti, Baker, & Halkola, 2005; Ribes & Finholt, 2007; Sonnenwald, Whitton, & Maglaughlin, 2008), scholarly communication in research collections (Palmer, 2005), and institutional repositories (Davis & Connolly, 2007). Many of these studies have been qualitative in nature and have emphasized local practices that emerge and shape the design and use of these resource-intensive infrastructures, often for the purpose of more effective design. Other recent turns include a call for more policy analysis, particularly with respect to institutional and systemic issues that influence practice (Olson, Zimmerman, & Bos, 2008). More comparative studies across disciplines and infrastructures are needed, as well as case histories of successful and unsuccessful data sharing.

The Future

Emerging technologies are being incorporated into infrastructures for sharing scientific data. Web 2.0 services are being built into generalized web services for e-science. RSS feeds (known as Really Simple Syndication or Rich Site Summary) can notify scientists of new data added to a database or of new data created by remote sensing equipment. Mash-ups, usually implemented as a client-side, data overlay service, can be more complex server-side services providing new methods of aggregating multiple sources of data into ad hoc applications (Fox, Guha, McMullen, Mustacoglu, Pierce, Topcu, et al., 2009; Geambasu et al., 2009). Web 2.0 services have been created to explore species distribution patterns, apply clustering algorithms, and integrate with GIS systems in a general workflow engine (Zhang, Altintas, Tao, Liu, Pennington, & Michener, 2006). Fox and colleagues (2009) are using Web 2.0 technologies to create small portable web services for database updates, data annotations, user management, and access rights. Infrastructure to create ubiquitous computing with transparent data exchange using wireless ad hoc peer-to-peer communications on smart phones and personal digital assistants (PDAs) is becoming widely available (Heinemann, Kangasharju, Lyardet, & Mühlhäuser, 2003). Building on these standards, systems to use ubiquitous computing infrastructure for collecting remote sensing data are being deployed (Chen & Kotz, 2001).

Web 2.0 is also being utilized in other ways, primarily by the user community. Contemporary science is influenced by competing impulses that permeate the daily work practices of scientists and the institutions in which they work. One such impulse is the need to share research results, data, and tools to promote greater impact of research, leverage scarce resources, conduct longitudinal studies, apply new analytical tools to existing datasets, and verify and refine the results of other researchers. Data sharing also has the potential to foster multidisciplinary research. The other, conflicting impulse has to do with concerns related to misuse of data, inappropriate or insufficient citation, or the desire to sequester data for the purposes of commercialization. In the scientific publication arena, these competing forces have engendered national and international discussions as well as a thriving open access movement (Willinsky, 2006). Proponents of open access argue that publishing in open access journals creates wider dissemination of results for other researchers and provides greater value to the general public, which funds most research in the U.S. Advocacy groups for greater taxpayer access to scientific research, librarians, and even national governments and the United Nations support open access. However, commercial publishers and other critics of open access have argued that there is little evidence of its merits. They contend that most people can access the literature they need, that open access would place undue burdens on researchers in some fields, and that it would not be economically viable.

Most recently, discussion has trickled down to the primary scientific data. As has been noted, although government agencies directly or indirectly sponsor a significant portion of basic scientific research, little research data is publicly accessible. Thus, the practice of science comes into conflict with its often-expressed ideals of openness, shared data, intellectual rigor, and verifiability. Advocacy groups and other stakeholders contend that open access to data promotes greater use of research data, not just by scientists but also by health care providers, individuals, and nonprofit organizations (Zuccala, 2009). However, contemporary science and its commercialization have been built upon the protection of data and records as forms of intellectual property that are closely held by the scientific community. In response to these challenges, scientists and organizations are building upon the open access movement to develop an approach to open research that respects intellectual property concerns. In the spirit of Free/Libre Open Source Software, many scientists are using portals, wikis, and blogs to share their workflows, datasets, and other preliminary research products.

A more radical approach is one in which all data and research are made publicly available from the outset:

> By [Open Notebook Science] I mean that there is a URL to a laboratory notebook that is freely available and indexed on common search engines. It does not necessarily have to look like a paper notebook but it is essential that all of the information available to the researchers to make their conclusions is equally available to the rest of the world. Basically, no insider information. (Bradley, 2006, para. 5)

This is different from open access science as discussed in the introduction, which emphasizes access to published journals through institutional repositories and other mechanisms, but builds upon a similar spirit of sharing. Although, for numerous reasons, Open Notebook Science is not yet widespread, it presents an intriguing new approach to scientific research with implications for data sharing, the development of institutional repositories, e-science and e-social science, cyberinfrastructure use, and national/international policy on data in science. Studying data sharing from the perspectives Open Notebook Science offers for collaboration, access, and ease of data management will be important to understanding current bottlenecks in access to data, verifiability, and the development and use of data repositories.

Lesk (2008) contends that a new professional field, data curation, needs to be created. Parsons and Duerr (2005) use the term data stewardship. Data curators or stewards would work with data creators to develop practices and skills to preserve data. Each scientific domain would not need to develop these in a vacuum but could use the data curator's professional skills in database design, digital forensics, and quality assurance. This new profession should have a reward system that demonstrates the value of the field including conferences, journals, academic credentials, and standing within their organization for the data curators and academic rewards for the scientists who deposit and preserve their data (Lesk, 2008; Research Information Network, 2008).

An important arena of ongoing discussion and research on data sharing is the development of sustainable funding models for data archiving. Understandably, costs vary widely based on data and file formats, required metadata, security needs for limiting access to sensitive or private data, and ramp-up costs for initiating a new repository (Beagrie, 2006). Ingest and initial archiving tasks are generally the most expensive; the maintenance of the archive over time may become less expensive with reduction in costs of memory and computing power. Lesk (2008) contends that the preservation, persistence, longevity, and management of data are all tightly coupled with access; funding for preservation and curation activities will be based on the perceived usefulness and accessibility of the data. This is not surprising. There is usually a direct relationship between the cost of metadata creation and the benefit to the user: Describing each item is more expensive than describing collections or groups of items but clearly more useful for data discovery (Duval, Hodgins, Sutton, & Weibel, 2002). Creating sustainable funding that does not respond to short-term pressures but, instead, is predicated upon long-term data need and use is challenging (Interagency Working Group on Digital Data, 2008). Career- and grant-related incentives to produce and develop sound data management plans are part of these challenges.

The 2009 award of the Nobel Prize in Economic Sciences to Eleanor Ostrom suggests another approach to distributing costs: the model of the commons. Ostrom's work demonstrates some of the failures of market-based approaches to governing public goods and highlights successes of information commons (Hess & Ostrom, 2009). Given the complex incentive problems we have already described and a globalized intellectual property regime that complicates data reuse, the self-archiving commons model is probably insufficient. However, positive incentives for self-archiving have been demonstrated to be useful in some domains such as microbiology (Dedeurwaerdere, Berleur, Nurminen, & Impagliazzo, 2009). Incentives include greater public exposure, faster publication times, and reduction of costs for publication and access. Case studies of sustainability and cost issues show that a single approach seldom works. Instead, hybrid strategies that incorporate in-kind support from host institutions, revenue generation, volunteer and community labor, cost-control mechanisms, and a long-term commitment to keeping resources accessible are essential to a successful model. Achieving balance is not simple (Maron, Smith, & Loy, 2009).

Conclusion

This exploration clearly suggests that there are many gaps in the various literatures that constitute research and practice in data sharing and no clear way of harmonizing what is known and what is not. Both practical and theoretical questions arise from the consideration of data sharing. On a practical level, numerous stakeholders are interested in making scientific data re-usable through the development and implementation of repositories; metadata schema; standardized vocabularies; and interfaces for relatively straightforward ingest, management, and access. Still more stakeholders are concerned about the policy implications of data sharing (or lack thereof) and are concerned with barriers to and incentives for doing so, the latter often implemented through normative measures and ethical training. And yet another group considers data sharing and access as forms of exchange that underpin and illuminate the daily workings of science as well as the broader political economy of this essential form of knowledge production. And of course, there are broad overlaps among these communities of interest.

Research has been global in nature for decades, but the ease with which data can move across national boundaries, the existence of competing (and often conflicting) legal regimes around its use and ownership, and the importance of preserving scientific data for longitudinal research mark this period of scientific research. The globalization of research is being fostered by and is in turn fostering greater research and policy making on e-science/digital infrastructures, legal and policy regimes, and calls for change in scientific practice. For these reasons, it is especially critical that research and development on data sharing be at the forefront of the consciousness of those who are most affected by it and have the most to gain or lose: policymakers, technologists, the public, and scientists themselves.

Acknowledgments

We would like to thank Heather Piwowar for sharing some of her bibliographic resources with us, Shannon Oltmann for her careful editing and thoughtful comments, the anonymous reviewers for their substantial input and help, and Katy Börner for suggesting this project to us in the first place.

References

Abrams, S. A. (2004). The role of format in digital preservation. *VINE, 34*(2), 49–55. Retrieved August 27, 2005, from www.emeraldinsight.com/10.1108/03055720410530997

Allan, R., Crouchley, R., & Ingram, C. (2009). *JISC information environment portal activity: Supporting the needs of e-research. Interim Report.* Daresbury, UK: Joint Information Steering Committee. Retrieved January 22, 2010, from epublicns03.esc.rl.ac.uk/bitstream/3692/interim.pdf

Altman, M., Andreev, L., Diggory, M., King, G., Sone, A., Verba, S., et al. (2001). A digital library for the dissemination and replication of quantitative social science research: The virtual data center. *Social Science Computer Review, 19*, 458–470.

Arenas, M., Kantere, V., Kementsietsidis, A., Kiringa, I., Miller, R. J., Mylopoulos, J., et al. (2003). The Hyperion project: From data integration to data coordination. *ACM SIGMOD Record, 32*(3), 53–58.

Arms, W. Y., Calimlim, M., & Walle, L. (2009). E-Science in practice: Lessons from the Cornell Web Lab. *D-Lib Magazine, 15*(5/6). Retrieved January 24, 2010, from www.dlib.org/dlib/may09/arms/05arms.html

Arzberger, P., Schroeder, P., Beaulieu, A., Bowker, G., Casey, K., Laaksonen, L., et al. (2004). Promoting access to public research data for scientific, economic, and social development. *Data Science Journal, 3*, 135–152.

Association of Research Libraries. (2006). *To stand the test of time: Long-term stewardship of digital datasets in science and engineering.* Arlington, VA: The Association.

Association of Research Libraries, Association of American Universities, Coalition for Networked Information, & National Association of State Universities and Land-Grant Colleges. (2009). *The university's role in the dissemination of research and scholarship.* Washington, DC: Association of Research Libraries.

Atkins, D. (2003). *A report from the U.S. National Science Foundation Blue Ribbon Panel on Cyberinfrastructure.* Arlington, VA: National Science Foundation, Directorate for Computer and Information Science and Engineering.

Baker, K. S., & Bowker, G. C. (2007). Information ecology: Open system environment for data, memories, and knowing. *Journal of Intelligent Information Systems, 29*(1), 127–144.

Baru, C., Moore, R., Rajasekar, A., & Wan, M. (1998, November/December). *The SDSC storage resource broker.* Paper presented at Conference of the Centre for Advanced Studies on Collaborative Research, Toronto, Ontario, Canada.

Bayardo, R. J., & Agrawal, R. (2005). Data privacy through optimal k-anonymization. *Proceedings of 21st International Conference on Data Engineering,* 217–228.

Beagrie, N. (2006). Digital curation for science, digital libraries, and individuals. *International Journal of Data Curation, 1*(1), 3–16.

Berman, F., Fox, G., & Hey, T. (2003). The grid: Past, present, future. In F. Berman, G. Fox, & T. Hey (Eds.), *Grid computing: Making the global infrastructure a reality* (pp. 9–50). Chichester, UK: Wiley.

Berman, H. M., Bhat, T. N., Bourne, P. E., Feng, Z., Gilliland, G., Weissig, H., et al. (2000). The Protein Data Bank and the challenge of structural genomics. *Nature Structural Biology, 7*, 957–959.

Berman, H. M., Henrick, K., & Nakamura, H. (2003). Announcing the worldwide Protein Data Bank. *Nature Structural Biology, 10*, 980.

Berman, H. M., Westbrook, J., Feng, Z., Gilliland, G., Bhat, T. N., Weissig, H., et al. (2002). The Protein Data Bank. *Nucleic Acids Research, 28*(1), 235–242.

Birnholtz, J., & Bietz, M. (2003, November). Data at work: Supporting sharing in science and engineering. *Proceedings of the 2003 International ACM SIGGROUP Conference on Supporting Group Work,* 339–348.

Boline, J., Lee, E. F., & Toga, A. W. (2008). Digital atlases as a framework for data sharing. *Frontiers in Neuroscience, 2*(1), 100–106.

Borgman, C. L. (2007). *Scholarship in the digital age: Information, infrastructure, and the internet.* Cambridge, MA: MIT Press.

Borgman, C. L., Wallis, J. C., Mayernik, M. S., & Pepe, A. (2007). Drowning in data: Digital library architecture to support scientific use of embedded sensor networks. *Proceedings of the 7th ACM / IEEE-CS Joint Conference on Digital Libraries*, 269–277.

Bose, R. (2002). A conceptual framework for composing and managing scientific data lineage. *Proceedings of the 14th International Conference on Scientific and Statistical Database Management.* Retrieved October 10, 2009, from dx.doi.org/10.1109/SSDM. 2002.1029701

Bose, R., & Frew, J. (2005). Lineage retrieval for scientific data processing: A survey. *ACM Computing Surveys, 37*(1), 1–28.

Bradley, J.-C. (2006). *Open notebook science.* Retrieved January 23, 2010, from drexel-coas-elearning.blogspot.com/2006/09/open-notebook-science.html

Brown, A. (2003). *Digital preservation guidance note 2: Selecting storage media for long-term preservation.* Kew, England: The National Archives of England, Wales and the United Kingdom.

Buneman, P., Khanna, S., & Tan, W. C. (2000). Data provenance: Some basic issues. In *Foundations of Software Technology and Theoretical Computer Science, 1974*, pp. 87–93.

Buyya, R., Yeo, C. S., & Venugopal, S. (2008). *Market-oriented cloud computing: Vision, hype, and reality for delivering IT services as computing utilities.* Paper presented at The 10th IEEE International Conference on High Performance Computing and Communications. Retrieved June 23, 2009, from arxiv.org/abs/0808.3558

Campbell, E. G., Clarridge, B. R., Gokhale, M., Birenbaum, L., Hilgartner, S., Holtzman, N. A., et al. (2002). Data withholding in academic genetics: Evidence from a national survey. *Journal of the American Medical Association, 287*(4), 473–480.

Cassa, C. A., Grannis, S. J., Overhage, J. M., & Mandl, K. D. (2006). A context-sensitive approach to anonymizing spatial surveillance data: Impact on outbreak detection. *Journal of the American Medical Informatics Association, 13*(2), 160–165.

Center for Research Libraries & Online Computer Library Center, Inc. (2007). *Trustworthy repositories audit and certification: Criteria and checklist.* Chicago: Center for Research Libraries.

Chaplin, M. 2004. A challenge to conservationists. *World Watch Magazine, 17*(6). Retrieved January 22, 2010, from www.worldwatch.org/node/565

Chen, G., & Kotz, D. (2001). Solar: Towards a flexible and scalable data-fusion infrastructure for ubiquitous computing. *Proceedings of the Workshop on Application Models and Programming Tools for Ubiquitous Computing at the Third International Conference on Ubiquitous Computing.* Retrieved January 22, 2010, from cmc.cs.dartmouth.edu/papers/ chen:solar.pdf

Chen, S. S. (2004). Digital preservation and workflow process. In *Digital libraries: International collaboration and cross-fertilization* (pp. 61–72). Berlin, Germany: Springer.

Cheung, K., Lashtabeg, A., Drennan, J., & Hunter, J. (2008). SCOPE: A scientific compound object publishing and editing system. *International Journal of Digital Curation, 3*(2). Retrieved January 22, 2010, from www.ijdc.net/index.php/ijdc/article/viewFile/84/55

Chin, G., & Lansing, C. (2004). Capturing and supporting contexts for scientific data sharing via the biological sciences collaboratory. *Proceedings of the 2004 ACM Conference on Computer Supported Cooperative Work*, 409–418.

Choudhary, A., Kandemir, M., No, J., Memik, G., Shen, X., Liao, W., et al. (2000). Data management for large-scale scientific computations in high performance distributed systems. *Cluster Computing, 3*(1), 45–60.

Consultative Committee for Space Data Systems. (2002). *Reference model for an open archival information system (OAIS), recommendation for space data system standards.* Washington, DC: The Committee.

Crow, R. (2002). *The case for institutional repositories: A SPARC position paper.* Washington, DC: Scholarly Publishing and Academic Resources Coalition.

Data Intensive Cyber Environments. (2009). *IRODS: Data grids, digital libraries, persistent archives, and real-time data systems.* Retrieved January 22, 2010, from www.irods.org

Davis, P. M., & Connolly, M. J. L. (2007). Institutional repositories: Evaluating the reasons for non-use of Cornell University's installation of DSpace. *D-Lib Magazine, 13*(3/4). Retrieved January 24, 2010, from www.dlib.org/dlib/march07/davis/03davis.html

Day, M. (2008). Toward distributed infrastructures for digital preservation: The roles of collaboration and trust. *International Journal of Digital Curation, 1*(3), 15–28.

Dedeurwaerdere, T., Berleur, J., Nurminen, M., & Impagliazzo, J. (2009). Databases, biological information and collective action. In J. Berleur, M. Nurminen, & J. Impagliazzo (Eds.), *Social informatics: An information society for all? In remembrance of Rob Kling* (pp. 159–169). New York: Springer.

Deutsche Initiative für Netzwerkinformation. (2007). *Electronic publishing: DINI-Certificate: document and publication services.* Retrieved January 22, 2010, from www.dini.de/english/dini-certificate

Dobratz, S., & Neuroth, H. (2004). Nestor: Network of expertise in long-term storage of digital resources: A digital preservation initiative for Germany. *D-Lib Magazine, 10*(4). Retrieved January 24, 2010, from www.dlib.org/dlib/april04/dobratz/04dobratz.html

Droegemeier, K. K., Gannon, D., Reed, D., Plale, B., Alameda, J., Baltzer, T., et al. (2005). Service-oriented environments for dynamically interacting with mesoscale weather. *Computing in Science & Engineering, 7*(6), 12–29.

DSpace. (2010). *Repository list.* Retrieved January 22, 2010, from www.dspace.org/whos-using-dspace/Repository-List.html

Duke, M., Day, M., Heery, R., Carr, L. A., & Coles, S. J. (2005, March). *Enhancing access to research data: The challenge of crystallography.* Paper presented at the 5th ACM/IEEE-CS Joint Conference on Digital Libraries, Denver, CO.

Duval, E., Hodgins, W., Sutton, S., & Weibel, S. L. (2002). Metadata principles and practicalities. *D-Lib Magazine, 8*(4). Retrieved January 22, 2010, from www.dlib.org/dlib/april02/weibel/04weibel.html

Eckersley, P., Egan, G., De Schutter, E., Yiyuan, T., Novak, M., Sebesta, V., et al. (2003). Neuroscience data and tool sharing. *Neuroinformatics, 1*(2), 149–165.

Fedora Commons. (n.d.) *eScience / eResearch.* Retrieved February 2, 2010, from www.fedora-commons.org/about/examples/escienceeresearch

Foster, I., Vockler, J., Wilde, M., & Zhao, Y. (2002, June). *The virtual data grid: A new model and architecture for data-intensive collaboration.* Paper presented at the Workshop on Data Provenance and Derivation, Chicago, IL. Retrieved October 10, 2009, from people.cs.uchicago.edu/~yongzh/papers/CIDR.VDG.submitted.pdf

Fox, G. C., Guha, R., McMullen, D. F., Mustacoglu, A. F., Pierce, M. E., Topcu, A. E., et al. (2009). Web 2.0 for grids and e-science. In F. Davoli, N. Meyer, R. Pugliese, & S.

Zappatore (Eds.), *Grid enabled remote instrumentation* (pp. 409–431). New York: Springer.

Galloway, P. (2004). Preservation of digital objects. *Annual Review of Information Science and Technology, 38*, 549–590.

Gardner, D., Goldberg, D., Grafstein, B., Robert, A., & Gardner, E. (2008). Terminology for neuroscience data discovery: Multi-tree syntax and investigator-derived semantics. *Neuroinformatics, 6*(3), 161–174.

Gardner, D., Toga, A., Ascoli, G., Beatty, J., Brinkley, J., Dale, A., et al. (2003). Towards effective and rewarding data sharing. *Neuroinformatics, 1*(3), 289–295.

Geambasu, R., Gribble, S. D., & Levy, H. M. (2009, June). *CloudViews: Communal data sharing in public clouds.* Paper presented at the HotCloud '09 Workshop, 2009 USENIX Annual Technical Conference, San Diego, CA. Retrieved June 12, 2009, from www.usenix.org/events/hotcloud09/tech/full_papers/geambasu.pdf

Geschwind, D. H. (2001). Sharing gene expression data: An array of options. *Nature Reviews Neuroscience, 2*, 435–438.

Gladney, H. M. (2004). Trustworthy 100-year digital objects: Evidence after every witness is dead. *ACM Transactions on Information Systems, 22*(3), 406–436.

Goslar, K., & Schill, A. (2004). Modeling contextual information using active data structures. In *Current Trends in Database Technology—EDBT 2004 Workshops* (pp. 325–334). Heidelberg, Germany: Springer.

Gray, J., Liu, D. T., Nieto-Santisteban, M., Szalay, A., DeWitt, D. J., & Heber, G. (2005). Scientific data management in the coming decade. *ACM SIGMOD Record, 34*(4), 34–41.

Green, A. G., & Gutmann, M. P. (2007). Building partnerships among social science researchers, institution-based repositories and domain specific data archives. *OCLC Systems & Services, 23*(1), 35–53.

Gruber, T. R. (1995). Toward principles for the design of ontologies used for knowledge sharing. *International Journal of Human-Computer Studies, 43*(4–5). Retrieved January 5, 2010, from tomgruber.org/writing/onto-design.htm

Hacker, T. J., & Wheeler, B. C. (2007). Making research cyberinfrastructure a strategic choice. *Educause Quarterly, 2007*(1), 21–29.

Hammond, T., Moritz, T., & Agosti, D. (2008). The conservation knowledge commons: Putting biodiversity data and information to work for conservation. *Proceedings of the Twelfth Biennial Conference of the International Association for the Study of Commons.* Retrieved November 15, 2009, from hdl.handle.net/10535/2132

Hank, C., & Davidson, J. (2009). International data curation education action (IDEA) working group: A report from the second workshop of the IDEA. *D-Lib Magazine, 15*(3/4). Retrieved January 24, 2010, from www.dlib.org/dlib/march09/hank/03hank.html

Harvard University Library. (2003). *Name resolution service: Introduction and use.* Cambridge, MA: The Library.

Hedstrom, M., & Montgomery, S. (1998). *Digital preservation needs and requirements in RLG member institutions.* Mountain View, CA: Research Libraries Group.

Heimbigner, D., & McLeod, D. (1985). A federated architecture for information management. *ACM Transactions on Information Systems, 3*(3), 253–278.

Heinemann, A., Kangasharju, J., Lyardet, F., & Mühlhäuser, M. (2003). iClouds?: Peer-to-peer information sharing in mobile environments. In H. Kosch, L. Böszörményi, & H. Hellwagner (Eds.), *Proceedings of the 9th International Euro-Par Conference* (pp. 1038–1045). Berlin, Germany: Springer.

Helly, J. J., Elvins, T. T., Sutton, D., & Martinez, D. (1999). A method for interoperable digital libraries and data repositories. *Future Generation Computer Systems, 16*(1), 21–28.

Helly, J. J., Elvins, T. T., Sutton, D., Martinez, D., Miller, S. E., Pickett, S., et al. (2002). Controlled publication of digital scientific data. *Communications of the ACM, 45*(5), 97–101.

Henricksen, K., Indulska, J., & Rakotonirainy, A. (2002). Modeling context information in pervasive computing systems. In F. Mattern & M. Naghshineh (Eds.), *Proceedings of the First International Conference on Pervasive Computing* (pp. 167–180). Berlin, Germany: Springer.

Hess, C., & Ostrom, E. (2007). *Understanding knowledge as a commons.* Cambridge, MA: MIT Press.

Hey, T., & Trefethen, A. E. (2002). The UK e-Science core programme and the grid. *Future Generation Computer Systems, 18*(8), 1017–1031.

Higgins, S. (2008). The DCC curation lifecycle model. *International Journal of Digital Curation, 1*(3), 134–140.

Hilgartner, S. (1995). Biomolecular databases: New communication regimes for biology? *Science Communication, 17*(2), 240–263.

Hilgartner, S., & Brandt-Rauf, S. (1994). Data access, ownership, and control: Toward empirical studies of access practices. *Science Communication, 15*(4), 355–372.

Interagency Working Group on Digital Data. (2009). *Harnessing the power of digital data for science and society*: Report of the Interagency Working Group on Digital Data to the Committee on Science of the National Science and Technology Council. Washington, DC: The Council.

Ives, Z. G., Halevy, A. Y., Mork, P., & Tatarinov, I. (2003). Piazza: Mediation and integration infrastructure for semantic web data. *Web Semantics, 1*(2), 155–175.

Ives, Z., Khandelwal, N., Kapur, A., & Cakir, M. (2005, January). *Orchestra: Rapid, collaborative sharing of dynamic data.* Paper presented at the Second Biannual Conference on Innovative Data Systems Research, Asilomar, CA. Retrieved June 12, 2009, from www.cidrdb.org/cidr2005/papers/P09.pdf

Jaiswal, A. R., Giles, C. L., Mitra, P., & Wang, J. Z. (2006, November). *An architecture for creating collaborative semantically capable scientific data sharing infrastructures.* Paper presented at the 8th Annual ACM International Workshop on Web Information and Data Management, Arlington, VA.

Jankowski, N. W. (2007). Exploring e-science: An introduction. *Journal of Computer-Mediated Communication, 12*(2, Article 10). Retrieved June 15, 2010, from jcmc.indiana.edu/vol12/issue2/jankowski.htm

Jin, J., & Ahn, G.-J. (2006a, June). *Role-based access management for ad-hoc collaborative sharing.* Paper presented at the Eleventh ACM Symposium on Access Control Models and Technologies, Lake Tahoe, CA. Retrieved June 6, 2009, from doi.acm.org/10.1145/1133058.1133086

Jin, J., & Ahn, G.-J. (2006b, November). *Towards secure information sharing and management in grid environments.* Paper presented at the 2006 International Conference on Collaborative Computing: Networking, Applications and Worksharing, Atlanta, GA. Retrieved April 29, 2009, from doi.ieeecomputersociety.org/10.1109/COLCOM.2006.361892

Karasti, H., Baker, K., & Halkola, E. (2005). Enriching the notion of data curation in e-science: Data managing and information infrastructuring in the long term ecological research (LTER) network. *Computer Supported Cooperative Work*, *15*(4), 321–358.

Karp, D., Carlin, S., Cook-Deegan, R., Ford, D., Geller, G., Glass, D., et al. (2008). Ethical and practical issues associated with aggregating databases. *PLoS Med*, *5*(9), e190.

Kaye, J., Heeney, C., Hawkins, N., de Vries, J., & Boddington, P. (2009). Data sharing in genomics: Re-shaping scientific practice. *Nature Reviews Genetics*, *10*, 331–335.

Kelton, K., Fleischmann, K. R., & Wallace, W. A. (2008). Trust in digital information. *Journal of the American Society for Information Science and Technology*, *59*(3), 363–374.

Kenney, A. R., McGovern, N. Y., Botticelli, P., Entlich, R., Lagoze, C., Payette, S., et al. (2002). Preservation risk management for web resources: Virtual remote control in Cornell's Project Prism. *D-Lib Magazine*, *8*(1). Retrieved January 22, 2010, from dlib.org/dlib/january02/kenney/01kenney.html

Kingsley, D. (2008, February). *Repositories, research and reporting: The conflict between institutional and disciplinary needs*. Paper presented at the VALA2008: Libraries, Technologies, and the Future Conference, Melbourne, Australia. Retrieved June 3, 2009, from www.valaconf.org.au/vala2008/papers2008/117_Kingsley_Final.pdf

Klump, J., Bertelmann, R., Brase, J., Diepenbroek, M., Grobe, H., Höck, H., et al. (2006). Data publication in the open access initiative. *Data Science Journal*, *5*, 79–83.

Koutrika, G. (2005). Heterogeneity in digital libraries: Two sides of the same coin. *DELOS Newsletter*, *3*. Retrieved April 3, 2009, from www.delos.info/index.php?option=com_content&task=view&id=411&Itemid=198

Kowalczyk, S. T. (2007). Digital preservation by design. In M. Raisinghani (Ed.), *Handbook of research on global information technology management in the digital economy* (pp. 405–431), New York: IGI Publishing.

Kunze, J. (2003, August). *Towards electronic persistence using ARK identifiers*. Paper presented at the Third European Conference on Digital Libraries Workshop on Web Archives, Trondheim, Norway. Retrieved October 6, 2009, from www.cdlib.org/inside/diglib/ark

Lagoze, C., Payette, S., Shin, E., & Wilper, C. (2005). Fedora: An architecture for complex objects and their relationships. *Journal of Digital Libraries*, *6*(2), 124–138. Retrieved October 5, 2009, from www.arxiv.org/abs/cs.DL/0501012

Lagoze, C., & Van De Sompel, H. (2007). Compound information objects: The OAI-ORE perspective. *Open Archives Initiative—Object Reuse and Exchange*. Retrieved October 5, 2009, from www.openarchives.org/ore/documents/CompoundObjects-200705.html

Lawrence, G. W., Kehoe, W. R., Rieger, O. Y., Walters, W. H., & Kenney, A. R. (2000). *Risk management of digital information: A file format investigation*. Washington, DC: Council on Library and Information Resources. Retrieved September 24, 2009, from www.clir.org/PUBS/reports/pub93/pub93.pdf

Lesk, M. (2008). Recycling information: Science through data mining. *International Journal of Digital Curation*, *3*(1), 154–157.

Lubell, J., Rachuri, S., & Mani, M. (2008). Sustaining engineering informatics: Towards methods and metrics for digital curation. *International Journal of Digital Curation*, *3*(2), 59–73.

Lynch, C. A. (2003). Institutional repositories: Essential infrastructure for scholarship in the digital age. *Libraries and the Academy*, *3*(2), 327–336.

Lyon, L. (2007). *Dealing with data: Roles, rights, responsibilities and relationships*. Bath, England: UKOLN.

Mann, R., Williams, R., Atkinson, M., Brodlie, K., Storkey, A., & Williams, C. (2002). Scientific data mining, integration, and visualization. *Technical Report UKeS-2002-06, National e-Science Centre*. Retrieved June 5, 2009, from citeseerx.ist.psu.edu/viewdoc/download?doi=10.1.1.8.6966&rep=rep1&type=pdf

Maron, N. L., Smith, K. K., & Loy, M. (2009). *Sustaining digital resources: An on-the-ground view of projects today: Ithaka case studies in sustainability*. Bristol, England: JISC. Retrieved November 17, 2009, from www.ithaka.org/ithaka-s-r/strategy/ithaka-case-studies-in-sustainability/report/SCA_Ithaka_SustainingDigitalResources_Report.pdf

Massachusetts Institute of Technology. (2004). *DSpace system documentation: Architecture*. Retrieved September 26, 2009, from dlib.ionio.gr/software/dspace-1.2.1-2-docs/architecture.html

McGovern, N. (2007). A digital decade: Where have we been and where are we going in digital preservation? *RLG DigiNews, 11*(1). Retrieved January 22, 2010, from hdl.handle.net/2027.42/60441

Michener, W. K. (2005). Meta-information concepts for ecological data management. *Ecological Informatics, 1*(1), 3–7.

Michener, W. K., Beach, J., Bowers, S., Downey, L., Jones, M., Ludaescher, B., et al. (2005). Data integration and workflow solutions for ecology. In B. Ludaescher & L. Raschid (Eds.), *Data integration in the life sciences* (pp. 321– 324). Berlin, Germany: Springer.

Moore, R. W. (2008). Towards a theory of digital preservation. *International Journal of Digital Curation, 1*(3), 63–75.

Moore, R. W., Baru, C., Rajasekar, A., Ludaescher, B., Marciano, R., Wan, M., et al. (2000a). Collection-based persistent digital archives: Part 1. *D-Lib Magazine, 6*(3). Retrieved January 24, 2010, from www.dlib.org/dlib/march00/moore/03moore-pt1.html

Moore, R. W., Baru, C., Rajasekar, A., Ludaescher, B., Marciano, R., Wan, M., et al. (2000b). Collection-based persistent digital archives: Part 2. *D-Lib Magazine, 6*(4). Retrieved January 24, 2010, from www.dlib.org/dlib/april00/moore/04moore-pt2.html

Moore, R. W., & Smith, M. (2007). Automated validation of trusted digital repository assessment criteria. *Journal of Digital Information, 8*(2). Retrieved January 10, 2010, from journals.tdl.org/jodi/rt/printerFriendly/198/181

Morris, R., & Truskowski, B. (2003). The evolution of storage systems. *IBM Systems Journal, 42*(2), 205–217.

Myers, J., Allison, T., Bittner, S., Didier, B., Frenklach, M., Green, W., et al. (2005). A collaborative informatics infrastructure for multi-scale science. *Cluster Computing, 8*(4), 244–253.

National Aeronautics and Space Administration. (1986). *Report of the EOS Data Panel on the Data and Information System. NASA TM-87777, Earth Observing System*, Vol. IIa. Washington, DC: The Administration. Retrieved January 22, 2010, from ntrs.nasa.gov/archive/nasa/casi.ntrs.nasa.gov/19860021622_1986021622.pdf

National Institutes of Health. (2003). *NIH data sharing policy and implementation guidance*. Retrieved June 6, 2009, from grants.nih.gov/grants/policy/data_sharing/data_sharing_guidance.htm

National Library of Medicine. (2009). The visible human project. Retrieved February 1, 2010, from www.nlm.nih.gov/research/visible/visible_human.html

Nelson, B. (2009). Data sharing: Empty archives. *Nature, 461*, 160–163.

Niu, J., & Hedstrom, M. (2008, October). *Documentation of social science data.* Paper presented at the Annual Meeting of the American Society for Information Science and Technology, Columbus, OH.

Olson, G. M., Zimmerman, A., & Bos, N. (2008). *Scientific collaboration on the internet.* Cambridge, MA: MIT Press.

Palmer, C. L. (2005). Scholarly work and the shaping of digital access. *Journal of the American Society of Information Science and Technology, 56*(11), 1140–1153.

Palmer, C. L., Cragin, M. H., & Hogan, T. P. (2004). Weak information work in scientific discovery. *Information Processing & Management, 43*(3), 808–820.

Parr, C. S., & Cummings, M. P. (2005). Data sharing in ecology and evolution: Why not? *Trends in Ecology & Evolution, 20*(7), 362–363.

Parsons, M. A., & Duerr, R. (2005). Designating user communities for scientific data: Challenges and solutions. *Data Science Journal, 4,* 31–38.

Pearson, D. (2002, June). *The grid: Requirements for establishing the provenance of derived data.* Paper presented at the Workshop on Data Provenance and Derivation, Chicago, IL. Retrieved October 6, 2006, from people.cs.uchicago.edu/~yongzh/papers/Provenance_ Requirements.doc

Pepe, A., Borgman, C. L., Wallis, J. C., & Mayernik, M. (2007, April). *Knitting a fabric of sensor data resources.* Paper presented at the International Conference on Information Processing in Sensor Networks. Cambridge, MA. Retrieved November 10, 2009, from polaris.gseis.ucla.edu/cborgman/pubs/pepe_ipsn_dsi_8.pdf

Piwowar, H. A., & Chapman, W. W. (2008). A review of journal policies for sharing research data. *Nature Precedings.* Retrieved January 22, 2010, from precedings.nature.com/ documents/1700/version/1

Plale, B., Ramachandran, R., & Tanner, S. (2006, January/February). *Data management support for adaptive analysis and prediction of the atmosphere in LEAD.* Paper presented at the 22nd Conference on Interactive Information Processing Systems for Meteorology, Oceanography, and Hydrology, Atlanta, GA.

Rajasekar, A. K., Marciano, R., & Moore, R. (1999, March). *Collection-based persistent archives.* Paper presented at the 16th IEEE Symposium on Mass Storage Systems, San Diego, CA. Retrieved January 22, 2010, from storageconference.org/STORAGE CONFERENCE/1999/papers/17rajase.pdf

Rajasekar, A. K., & Moore, R. W. (2008). Data and metadata collections for scientific applications. In B. Hertzberger, A. Hoekstra, & R. Williams (Eds.), *High-performance computing and networking* (pp. 72–80). Berlin: Springer.

Rajasekar, A. K., Wan, M., Moore, R. W., & Schroeder, W. (2004, June). *Data grid federation.* Paper presented at the International Conference on Parallel and Distributed Processing Techniques and Applications, Las Vegas, NV.

Rajasekar, A. K., Wan, M., Moore, R. W., & Schroeder, W. (2006). iRODS: Integrated rule-based data system. Retrieved January 22, 2010, from www.irods.org/pubs/DICE_irods-desc.pdf

Renear, A. H., Dolan, M., Trainor, K., & Cragin, M. (2009, October). *Towards a cross-disciplinary notion of data level in data curation.* Poster presented at the Annual Meeting of the American Society for Information Science and Technology, Vancouver, British Columbia, Canada. Retrieved January 22, 2010, from mail.asis.org/Conferences/AM09/ posters/103.pdf

Research Collaboratory for Structural Bioinformatics Protein Data Bank. (2009). *An information portal to biological macromolecular structures.* Retrieved June 15, 2009, from www.pdb.org

Research Information Network. (2008). *To share or not to share: Publication and quality assurance of research data outputs. A report commissioned by the Research Information Network.* London: Research Information Network. Retrieved January 22, 2010, from www.rin.ac.uk/our-work/data-management-and-curation/share-or-not-share-research-data-outputs

Rew, R., & Davis, G. (1990). Data management: NetCDF: An interface for scientific data access. *IEEE Computer Graphics and Applications, 10*(4), 76–82.

Ribes, D., & Finholt, T. A. (2007, November). *Tension across the scales: Planning infrastructure for the long term.* Paper presented at the International ACM Conference on Supporting Group Work, Sanibel Island, FL.

Ross, S., & McHugh, A. (2006). The role of evidence in establishing trust in repositories. *D-Lib Magazine, 12*(7/8). Retrieved January 24, 2010, from www.dlib.org/dlib/july06/ross/07ross.html

Ruusalepp, R. (2008). *Comparative study of international approaches to enabling the sharing of research data.* London: JISC. Retrieved November 15, 2009, from www.dcc.ac.uk/docs/publications/reports/Data_Sharing_Report.pdf

Saltz, J. (2002, October). *Data provenance.* Paper presented at the Workshop on Data Provenance/Derivation Workshop, Chicago, IL. Retrieved October 10, 2006, from people.cs.uchicago.edu/%7Eyongzh/papers/ProvenanceJS10-02.doc

Scavo, T., & Welch, V. (2007, November). *A grid authorization model for science gateways.* Paper presented at the Annual International Workshop on Grid Computing Environments, Reno, NV. Retrieved January 30, 2010, from library.rit.edu/oa journals/index.php/gce/article/view/99

Schindler, U., & Diepenbroek, M. (2008). Generic XML-based framework for metadata portals. *Computers & Geosciences, 34*(12), 1947–1955.

Schofield, P., Bubela, T., Weaver, T., Portilla, L., Brown, S., Hancock, J., et al. (2009). Post-publication sharing of data and tools. *Nature, 461*(7261), 171–173.

Schuchardt, K., Pancerella, C., Rahn, L. A., Didier, B., Kodeboyina, D., Leahy, D., et al. (2007). Portal-based knowledge environment for collaborative science. *Concurrency and Computation: Practice and Experience, 19*(12), 1703–1716.

Schwartz, C. (2000). Digital libraries: An overview. *Journal of Academic Librarianship, 26*(6), 385–393.

Semantic Counteroperability Community of Practice. (2008). Establish federated governance. Retrieved January 22, 2010, from semanticcommunity.wik.is/Best_Practices/Enterprise_Mashup:_A_Practical_Guide_to_Federal_Service_Oriented_Architecture/Section_4:_Keys_to_Federal_SOA_Implementation/4.1_Keys_to_Implementing_the_Service-Oriented_Enterprise/4.1.7_Establish_Federated_Governance

Shafer, K. E., Weibel, S. L., & Jul, E. (2001). The PURL project. *Journal of Library Administration, 34*(1), 123–125.

Shankar, K. (2007). Order from chaos: The poetics and pragmatics of scientific recordkeeping. *Journal of the American Society for Information Science and Technology, 58*(10), 1457–1466.

Shiffrin, R. M., & Börner, K. (2004). Mapping knowledge domains. *Proceedings of the National Academy of Sciences of the United States of America, 101*, 5183–5185.

Simmhan, Y., Plale, B., & Gannon, D. (2005). A survey of data provenance in e-science. *ACM SIGMOD Record, 34*(3), 31–36.

Simmhan, Y., Plale, B., & Gannon, D. (2006, September). *A performance evaluation of the Karma provenance framework for scientific workflows.* Paper presented at the International Conference on Web Service, Chicago, IL.

Smith, M., Barton, M., Bass, M., Branschofsky, M., McClellan, G., Stuve, D., et al. (2003). DSpace: An open source dynamic digital repository. *D-Lib Magazine, 9*(1). Retrieved January 22, 2010, from www.dlib.org/dlib/january03/smith/01smith.html

Sonnenwald, D. H., Whitton, M. C., & Maglaughlin, K. (2008). Evaluation of a scientific collaboratory system: Investigating a collaboratory's potential before deployment. In G. Olson, A. Zimmerman, & N. Bos. (Eds.), *Scientific collaboration on the internet* (pp. 171–194). Cambridge, MA: MIT Press.

Stanescu, A. (2005). Assessing the durability of formats in a digital preservation environment: The INFORM methodology. *OCLC Systems & Services, 21*(1), 61–81.

Steinhart, G. (2007). DataStaR: An institutional approach to research data curation. *IASSIST Quarterly, 31*(3–4), 34–39. Retrieved June 5, 2009, from hdl.handle.net/1813/12668

Toronto International Data Release Workshop. (2009). Prepublication data sharing. *Nature, 461*(10), 168.

Treloar, A., Groenewegen, D., & Harboe-Ree, C. (2007). The data curation continuum: Managing data objects in institutional repositories. *D-Lib Magazine, 13*(9). Retrieved June 6, 2009, from www.dlib.org/dlib/september07/treloar/09treloar.html

Treloar, A., & Wilkinson, R. (2008, December). *Rethinking metadata creation and management in a data-driven research world.* Paper presented at the Fourth International Conference on eScience, Indianapolis, IN.

U.S. National Science Board. (2005). *Long-lived digital data collections: Enabling research and education in the 21st century: Report of the National Science Board.* Arlington, VA: National Science Foundation.

U.S. Social Security Administration (2009). *Government information exchange glossary.* Retrieved June 5, 2009, from www.ssa.gov/gix/definitions.html

Van House, N. (2002). Digital libraries and practices of trust: Networked biodiversity information. *Social Epistemology, 16*(1), 99–114.

Van House, N., Butler, M., & Schiff, L. (1998). Cooperative knowledge work and practices of trust: Sharing environmental planning datasets. *Proceedings of the 1998 ACM Conference on Computer Supported Cooperative Work,* 335–343.

Vannier, M. W., Staab, E. V., & Clarke, L. P. (2003). Matching clinical and biological needs with emerging imaging technologies. *Proceedings of the IEEE, 91*(10), 1562–1573.

Venugopal, S., Buyya, R., & Ramamohanarao, K. (2006). A taxonomy of data grids for distributed data sharing, management, and processing. *ACM Computing Surveys, 38*(1). Retrieved April 21, 2009, from portal.acm.org/citation.cfm?id=1132952.1132955#

Vogeli, C., Yucel, R., Bendavid, E., Jones, L., Anderson, M., Louis, K. S., et al. (2006). Data withholding and the next generation of scientists: Results of a national survey. *Academy of Medicine, 81*(2), 128–136.

Wallis, J., Borgman, C., Mayernik, M., & Pepe, A. (2008). Moving archival practices upstream: An exploration of the life cycle of ecological sensing data in collaborative field research. *International Journal of Digital Curation, 1*(3), 114–126.

Waters, D., & Garrett, J. (1996). *Preserving digital information: Report of the task force on archiving of digital information*. Washington, DC: Commission on Preservation and Access and Research Libraries Group.

Weill, P., & Ross, J. W. (2004). *IT governance: How top performers manage IT decision rights for superior results*. Boston: Harvard Business School Press.

Westbrook, J., Feng, Z., Chen, L., Yang, H., & Berman, H. M. (2003). The Protein Data Bank and structural genomics. *Nucleic Acids Research, 31*(1), 489–491.

Westbrook, J., Ito, N., Nakamura, H., Henrick, K., & Berman, H. M. (2005). PDBML: The representation of archival macromolecular structure data in XML. *Structural Bioinformatics, 21*(7), 988–992.

Whyte, A., Job, D., Giles, S., & Lawrie, S. (2008). Meeting curation challenges in a neuroimaging group. *International Journal of Digital Curation, 3*(1), 171–181.

Willinsky, J. (2006). *The access principle: The case for open access to research and scholarship*. Cambridge, MA: MIT Press.

World Wide Web Consortium. (2001). *URIs, URLs, and URNs: Clarifications and recommendations 1.0. Report from the Joint W3C/IETF URI Planning Interest Group, W3C Note 21*. Retrieved October 6, 2006, from www.w3.org/TR/uri-clarification

Wright, D. J. (2009). Spatial data infrastructures for coastal environments. In X. Yang (Ed.), *Remote sensing and geospatial technologies for coastal ecosystem assessment and management* (pp. 91–112). Heidelberg, Germany: Springer.

Wroe, C., Goble, C., Greenwood, M., Lord, P., Miles, S., Papay, J., et al. (2004). Automating experiments using semantic data in a bioinformatics grid. *Intelligent Systems, 19*(1), 48–55.

Zhang, J., Altintas, I., Tao, J., Liu, X., Pennington, D. D., & Michener, W. K. (2006). Integrating data grid and web services for e-science applications: A case study of exploring species distributions. *Second IEEE International Conference on e-Science and Grid Computing*, 31–39.

Zimmerman, A. S. (2003). *Data sharing and secondary use of scientific data: Experiences of ecologists*. Unpublished doctoral dissertation, University of Michigan.

Zuccala, A. (2009). The layperson and open access. *Annual Review of Information Science and Technology, 43*, 359–396.

CHAPTER 7

Some Economic Aspects of the Scholarly Journal System

Donald W. King and Carol Tenopir
University of Tennessee, Knoxville, TN

Introduction

This chapter examines the economic aspects of the scholarly journal publishing system, particularly the economic consequences of technology and the introduction of alternative publishing models. Topics covered include the economic costs of the scholarly journal system, with special attention given to trends that affect economics. Library economics are examined, including consortia. A section on metrics and methods used, other than costs, includes a discussion of citation analysis and impact factors, including the pros and cons of these approaches. Open access (OA) is reviewed, including the positives and negatives of author-pays, self-archiving, and repository models. Adopting a systems approach to journals means examining the functions and activities of all participants in the scholarly journal system as they relate to economic factors. Participants include researchers (as authors, peer-reviewers, editors, and readers), publishers, libraries, intermediaries (e.g., consortia), and repositories. Several years ago the Association of Learned and Professional Society Publishers (ALPSP) made an award to the University of Pittsburgh to develop a retrievable database of references to the economics of scholarly journals. After entering nearly 2,000 citations the project stopped (due in part to Sally Morris's leaving ALPSP and Don King's leaving Pittsburgh). Further evidence of the abundance of literature on the subject is that Charles W. Bailey, Jr., publishes a periodic Scholarly Electronic Publishing Bibliography. The current version (77) brings the total entries to over 3,620 items (Bailey, 2009). This is obviously a topic of broad interest, particularly in light of the impact of electronic publishing and internet access on authors, publishers, libraries, other intermediaries, and readers. There has been much interest in international initiatives for new publishing models including open access, either through upfront payments by authors or their representatives, or author self-archiving to subject or institutional repositories. Because of the enormity of the literature, this review focuses on economic aspects of the participants in the scholarly journal system. Emphasis is placed on actual and potential economic consequences of technology and the introduction of alternative publishing models. Obviously the references in this chapter are incomplete, but serve as an attempt to provide an entrance to the literature.

Several major studies have explored the total cost of the national journal system (and its benefits) to determine the likely impact of open access and reliance on electronic-only publishing. These examine scholarly journal systems from the perspective of functions and activities performed and the participants who perform them. This approach serves as a framework for the present review. The relative costs of participants in the system have not changed much over the years or across countries.

Cost (in money and people's time) is a principal metric; different strengths and weaknesses of metrics and methods are emphasized here, however, because other metrics also have an enormous influence on participant decision, public policy, and how research is conducted. We review the cost associated with researcher activities (writing, editing, peer review, obtaining, reading, and self-archiving) because these costs dominate the overall system costs. The costs and pricing of traditional publishing are reviewed and compared with open access publishing models. Economics of libraries focuses on traditional print and electronic collection costs, use, and value, as well as the influence of consortia and licensing practices. We begin with an overview of the scholarly journal system's components and participants.

The Current Review

This review is based on a system approach involving researchers as authors, peer reviewers, editors (when not paid), and readers; publishers; libraries; intermediaries (e.g., consortia); and repositories. Each participant performs basic functions/activities that require resources such as people's time, systems, equipment, facilities, paper, and so on. One can think of the cost of resources as input necessary to perform the functions/activities.

The review begins with a section on the economics of the scholarly journal system by describing several studies that have estimated total costs of all participants and the functions/activities they perform. Some studies take a global perspective, others a national view, and one focuses on science. All have the objective of comparing a current system with alternative business models such as electronic-only publishing, open access via author-pays, or self-archiving with institutional repositories.

The total system cost is a sum of all resources employed by the participants, such as people's time. It does not include fees paid by authors or the purchase price paid by libraries or researchers for subscriptions because these are redundant in the system (i.e., the fees and subscription are not resources, but rather reflections of publishers' costs for their resources).

People's time is the dominant resource throughout the entire journal system, and it is led by researchers' time. Researchers' time is an important, but scarce, resource that they choose to use judiciously to perform research, teach, write, read, and so forth. They would not be willing to spend time writing and reading if they did not receive adequate value in return. For this reason, the second section emphasizes researchers' time in writing, reading, and donating their time to peer review and editing.

The section on publishing economics includes an overview of scholarly publishing trends that affect economics. Publishing costs include first copy costs (i.e., the resources involved in manuscript acceptance, peer review, editing, page composition, etc., and any non-article-related content). The first copy costs are important because they are essentially the same for subscription (print or electronic) and author-pays models. Also, the price necessary to recover costs depends on spreading these costs across a number of subscribers. Print subscription costs are also described. This section gives details of cost models, parameters that affect cost, examples of costs of print and electronic publishing, and comparative costs of subscription and open access models. Pricing of journals includes past trends, current pricing strategies, comparison of commercial and nonprofit pricing with alternative pricing strategies not yet attempted, and other publishing issues.

The next section is devoted to library economics (including consortia). A distinction is made between academic and special libraries because of their number (i.e., 3,772 academic and 9,066 special libraries in the U.S.) and the relative size of their journal collections. Particular attention is given to the cost of processing print and electronic journals, aspects of bundled "Big Deal" collections, and trends in library collection expenditures. The importance of consortia and licensing is discussed in addition to the economic advantages and disadvantages to libraries.

Another section focuses on economic metrics and methods other than cost. Particular attention is given to citation analysis and impact factors because they are often used to compare prices of commercial with nonprofit publishers and subscription with open access models. Citations are a proxy for use and impact factors sometimes are presented as a ratio of price and citations. Other methods and metrics include surveys of amount of reading time spent by readers, deep log analyses, server hits and downloads, and other means of counting use. The additional metrics include counts of the total number of journals and articles, as well as benefit, value, and return-on-investment analyses.

The final section, open access economics, discusses the economics associated with open access author-pays, self-archiving, and repository models. Some economic aspects of open access concepts are discussed. Author-pays issues are presented, author-pays fees given, and positive and negative assessments provided from an economic perspective. Self-archiving economic issues are given along with positive and negative aspects of this open access model. Finally, the economic costs of repositories are presented.

Past Reviews of the Literature

In 2006 Electronic Publishing Services, Ltd., in association with Charles Oppenheim (and funded by Research Information Network, Research Councils U.K. & dti), conducted an extensive review of scholarly journal economics in the U.K. The project analyzed data concerning scholarly journal publishing with a focus on: (1) journal market volume and value; (2) journal supply-side economics; (3) usage; (4) citations, impact factors, and their role; (5) disciplinary differences; and (6) cost and impact of alternative formal dissemination models. The report, consisting of 107 pages, addressed each topic by presenting key questions, the evidence, and gaps. An appendix (134 pages) reviewed sources of information such as directories and published research and rated them as to purpose of the publication, strength of design, author credentials, objectivity, and relevance to the U.K., among many such criteria. Some of the references are also covered here and some results of the project are included in this review.

Houghton, Steele, and Sheehan (2006) performed a national study of research communication costs and benefits (including scholarly journals among other communication media) for the Australian Department of Education, Science and Training. An appendix provides a literature review of the cost of scholarly communication, with topics including: (1) the research costs that enable production of articles, including writing and preparation, submission and revision, editorial and peer review activities, and reading; (2) the cost of all activities associated with publishing; (3) the cost of distribution including access to findings and library infrastructure; and (4) costs of research funding and management and the evaluation of research activities. Some findings and conclusions are covered in this review.

The Future of Academic Journals (Cope & Phillips, 2009) has 19 contributed chapters, several of which deal with economic aspects of the journal system. The first chapter (Cope & Kalantzis, 2009b, p. 13) discusses three disruptive factors that affect not only the form of the journal but also "the knowledge systems that the journal in its heritage form has supported." The first breaking point deals with changes in the business model and the challenge of developing economically sustainable publishing models. Another breaking point is the credibility of the peer-review system; the third is post-publication evaluation and the flawed nature of citation and impact analysis. Details of these issues are discussed in other sections of this review.

Brown and Boulderstone (2008) prepared a 340-page book on electronic publishing that provides an excellent review of that topic (although with an inadequate list of references). More importantly, it discusses how we arrived at the present situation and provides insights into the future of scholarly publication, the implication of drivers of change, and impact on system participants. Drivers of change include business models, research funding, technologies, data and datasets, e-science and cyberinfrastucture, the Semantic Web, mobile devices, archiving and preservation, and the Google generation. The authors provide a vision for scholarly communication and the future fates of publishers, libraries, and intermediaries.

Friedlander and Bessette (2003) prepared an extensive literature review on scientific journal publishing for the National Science Foundation (NSF; Eileen L. Collins, Project Director). In light of electronic publishing, the review sets out to characterize and evaluate the status of the scholarly literature concerning: issues, measuring impact, changes in researchers' behavior, implications for the underserved, and information security and privacy. Each topic yields numerous citations to relevant publications, a few of which are found in this review. Of particular interest are reviews concerning: electronic journal publishing; participants' (i.e., authors, readers, publishers, and libraries) issues and concerns; pricing and business models; professional analysis; peer review; archiving; econometric research; and citation-related metrics and methods. Not covered here are issues of intellectual property rights, security and privacy, and changes in research behavior.

Several previous *ARIST* chapters have dealt with different aspects of the economics of information throughout the years (Hindle & Raper, 1976; Lamberton, 1984; Mick, 1979; Spence, 1974; Wilson, 1972; and more recently, Braman, 2005). Although these reviews have some interesting general information on costs/benefits and methodologies, they do not deal specifically with the scholarly communication process. In a 1973 *ARIST* chapter on the economics of information, however, Cooper (1973, p. 9) discussed a study sampling 20 physics journals between 1959–1969, finding an "82 percent increase in number of issues, 147 percent increase in the number of pages published, 202 percent increase in subscription prices" during that time period. A discussion of the language sciences journal market in the same chapter states that both the demand for more pages to be published in these journals and the number of subscribers seemed to be growing without foreseeable surcease. In volume 17 of *ARIST*, Griffiths (1982) discussed some aspects of the value of journals and other information systems, products, and services. In a 1987 chapter on the economics of information, Repo (1987) very briefly reviewed the literature on cost-benefit analysis of journals.

Other relevant *ARIST* chapters that touch on economic aspects of scholarly communication include the following. In 1973, in a chapter on publication systems and services, Gannett (1973, p. 256) discussed whether the primary journal was "obsolescent." The impact of electronic forms was already being felt at the time, and he concluded that the journal in its traditional form had limited life in the future. In a 1983 chapter on the scholarly communication process, Hills (1983, p. 106) noted that "although many forms of academic publishing are desirable, they are not all necessarily economical," opining that "all of the alternatives to the scholarly journal ... result mainly from technical developments and economic pressures and not from dissatisfactions by scholars." Hills also discussed the economic impact of new technologies, from microform to databases, and discussed the role of photocopies in "making the separate paper the unit of communication between scientists," noting that "Publishers see photocopying as a threat to their existence" (p. 108). In a chapter on electronic journals and the internet, Kling and Callahan (2002, p. 127) discussed the economic crisis in scholarly publishing since the late 1980s with "the cost of scientific journals rising much faster than both inflation and library budgets." They also discussed the cost of producing ejournals and the pricing of them, concluding that ejournals have not proved as inexpensive to produce as was predicted. They cited an interesting example of an electronic journal, *Organic Letters*, which in 2002 was more expensive than its print edition. In his chapter on open access, Drott (2006) briefly discussed the rising price of journal subscription costs in relation to the declining costs of computing. In the most recent volume, Brown (2010) contributed a comprehensive review of the literature on how science communication has been influenced by e-publishing and collaborative e-communications.

King and Tenopir's (2001) *ARIST* chapter extensively discussed user behavior as it relates to using and reading scholarly literature. That chapter thoroughly reviewed the relevant previous *ARIST* chapters relating to the subject; therefore *ARIST* chapters on this topic prior to the 2001 chapter have not been included here unless they comment specifically on economic factors. This chapter also includes a discussion of price-demand relationships in scholarly publishing. Other *ARIST* chapters since 2001 that deal with different aspects of scholarly communication, but do not discuss economic factors, are by Borgman and Furner (2002, scholarly communication and bibliometrics), Kling and Callahan (2002, such communication as it relates to the internet), Bensman (2007, extensive discussion of the development and use of impact factors), and Nicolaisen (2007, citation analysis).

Although the time spent, direct costs, and indirect costs to authors and readers are economic issues and are therefore included in this review, the rich literature on reader behavior and the impact of ejournals on reading patterns is not covered here. For reviews of the behavioral literature see Tenopir, Hitchcock, and Pillow (2003), Rowlands (2007), Peek and Pomerantz (1998), and Bishop and Star (1996).

Overview of the Scholarly Journal System

Over the years there have been many descriptions and characterizations of the scholarly journal system. For example, Houghton, Rasmussen, Sheehan, Oppenheim, Morris, Creaser, and colleagues (2009) present examples including Coles (1993) who describes information and funding flows among system participants; Lin, Garvey, and Nelson (1970) show the flow of research findings through oral and written communication over time starting with research initiated up to book publication and subsequent citation; Cox (1998) also diagrams the exchange of information content among an expanded list of participants; Griffiths and King (1993) present a communication cycle of information used as a resource input to research and other work, which in turn leads to information as output; King, Lancaster, McDonald, Roderer, and Wood (1976) describe the early life cycle of science information through system functions; Tenopir and King (2000) provide a list of 15 system participants; and PIRA International (2003) presents content flow among participants.

The most comprehensive description of the scholarly journal system recently, however, is by Bjørk (2007). This model includes detailed activities of researchers, publishers, academics (as editors and reviewers), libraries, bibliographic services, readers, and practitioners who implement research results. The various versions of the model include 33 to 35 diagrams of particular functions and 103 to 113 activities. Each diagram has flow of input and output of activities. Houghton and colleagues (2009) present the model in detail and use it as a framework for their study in the U.K.

The scholarly publishing life cycle has been modeled in several studies over the years. In 2007, Bjørk updated the third description of the Scientific Publishing Life-Cycle Model (Bjørk & Hedlund, 2004). This version is the Scientific Communications Life-Cycle Model that builds on the Garvey model (Lin et al., 1970) that traces the flow of scientific discovery (i.e., information) through many communication means, with additions from Hurd (1996). Bjørk describes how technology developments have triggered changes in scientific communication in a broad sense and provides detailed descriptions of the flow among types of communication and functions and activities involved.

Scholarly Journal System Economics

Background

The overall scientific, technical, and medical (STM) market segment grew 10.3 percent in 2007; the "traditional" STM companies accounted for $14.9 billion and grew 11.2 percent (Outsell, Inc., 2008). However, fluctuating currency exchange rates may have inflated the growth calculations so that the traditional rate of increase might more likely be 7 percent. The Outsell report provides forecasts to 2011, key trends, a redefinition of the STM segment of the information industry market, growth from 2003 to 2007, and disruptive forces, among other informative suggestions. Disruptive forces include (1) the rise of Web 2.0, (2) the rise of the open repository, (3) the decline of primary content provision, (4) acceptability of alternative business models, and (5) macroeconomic volatility affecting STM niches.

In recent years several large-scale studies have examined the economic cost of entire scholarly journal systems. These studies focus primarily on the key participants in the system including R&D funders, authors, publishers, libraries, secondary services, repositories, and readers. One study was performed in Australia in 2006 (Houghton et al., 2006), two were performed in the U.K. (Cambridge Economic Policy

Associates, 2008;[1] Houghton et al., 2009[2]), and others under the guidance of Houghton in Denmark (Houghton, 2009a) and the Netherlands (Houghton, de Jonge, & van Oploo, 2009). Morris (2005) gives a secondary literature compilation of total system costs. The first study to examine the economic cost of scholarly journal systems was performed in 1977 in the U.S., under contract to the National Science Foundation (King, McDonald, & Roderer, 1981) and is presented here for comparative purposes.

The five sources of scholarly journal data are briefly described and costs given in national currencies with the proportion of total costs attributable to authorship, publishing activities (including peer review), access through libraries (and supporting secondary organizations), and reading. Also given are the principal parameters leading to the cost estimates, including national research funding, authors, articles, subscriptions, libraries, and amount of reading; these are all normalized by number of researchers and/or number of journals or articles. Each system study is then reviewed in detail. Some findings of these studies are reported throughout this review (e.g., cost of writing, reading).

The Australian Study

An Australian study (Houghton et al., 2006) was designed to examine the economic costs and benefits of research communication resulting from national research funding. In particular the study focused on three emerging models for communication and access:

- The "Big Deal," where institutional subscribers pay for access to online aggregations of titles through consortia or site licensing arrangements

- "Author-pays" publishing, where authors, or their employing or funding organizations, contribute to the costs of publishing

- Open access archives and repositories, where organizations support institutional repositories and/or subject archives

The study included other types of publications such as conference papers, book chapters, and research monographs, but journal article cost data are extracted here.

The total cost per journal of the scholarly journal system in Australia is as follows: writing (AUD 12,900); peer review (AUD 1,700); publishing (AUD 4,500); library acquisition (AUD 0.63), handling (AUD 1.10), and production (AUD 19,100); and reading (AUD 117,900) for a total of AUD 156,100. The benefit-to-cost ratio over 20 years for the modeled impacts of open access (assuming a 100 percent self-archiving compliance) to public sector research were found to be 51 (i.e., the benefits are 51 times greater than the costs).

The CEPA U.K./Global Study for RIN

The Cambridge Economic Policy Associates (CEPA) (2008) study for Research Information Network (RIN) examined the economic costs of electronic-only publishing, author-side publication fees, cash for peer review, and the consequences of increases in research funding. Economic cost data included total global costs; those attributable to U.K. expenditures are extracted for this review. The CEPA study was structured by a value chain of five components:

- Research production: The activities carried out by researchers to create a research article and to submit it for peer review and publication

- Publication: Peer review and editing of articles and composition into journals and distribution, as well as the activities required to transport copies of journals to libraries and other buyers

- Access: Activities carried out mainly by libraries

- Consumption: Researcher activities in identifying, searching for, and accessing articles

- Reading articles

Details are provided by type of costs (direct/indirect, fixed and variable, cash and non-cash donated); stage in value chain (publication, distribution, access); type of journals (traditional print [reader-pays] and open access [author-pays]); journal categories (popular hybrid, major discipline, niche); and libraries (RLUK-29 [large universities, national, etc.]; 38 old [chartered before Education Reforms Act 1992]; 51 new [chartered from 1992 to 2005]; HEC-32 [did not have formal status before 2005]; and 104 others, including special libraries).

Cambridge Economic Policy Associates (2008) finds that if 90 percent of journals are published as electronic journal only, the following cost reductions would occur: (1) £758 million global cost to libraries, (2) global publication and distribution costs of £318 million, and (3) U.K. libraries would save £23 million.

Cambridge Economic Policy Associates (2008) concluded that if 90 percent of all articles are made open access by an author-pays model, the savings would be £561 million split roughly evenly between publishers and libraries. However, the U.K.'s share of funding to meet the cost of publication, distribution, and access would rise from 5.2 to 7.0 percent because U.K. researchers are prolific writers.

The CEPA study assumes that unpaid (non-cash) costs of peer review undertaken largely by academics is £1.9 billion globally. If peer reviewers are paid by publishers, the funds would transfer to academics but increase subscription costs to universities globally by about £1.4 billion. For the U.K. this would be £53 million.

Cambridge Economic Policy Associates (2008) shows U.K. funding changes for several functions under two of their four scenarios. Each scenario is compared to the current base case cost per article (see Table 7.1).

The difference with publisher payment of cash for peer review is a negative cost of -£245. Detailed explanations are given as to how these changes take place. The base case and scenario vary in the proportion of publication format assumed (print and electronic, print only, and e-only) by type of journal business, model, and type of library.

CEPA finds that increases in research funding of 2.5 percent over ten years would result in a 28 percent increase in articles. The cost of publication and distribution would rise by £1.6 billion in real terms and U.K. libraries would increase expenditures by £38 million in real terms.

The U.K. Study for JISC by Houghton and Colleagues

A Joint Information Systems Committee (JISC) study was performed by two teams of researchers: (1) Information Science, LISU and Economics, Loughborough University headed by Charles Oppenheim and (2) Centre for Strategic Economic Studies, Victoria University headed by John Houghton (the lead on the Australian study). The project was partially motivated by a *U.K. Scholarly Journals Baseline Report* (Electronic Publishing Services, Ltd., 2006) which identified gaps and challenges in the U.K. scholarly journal system. The JISC study also included books as well as journals, but books are not covered here. It provides an economic comparison of subscription publishing, open access (author-pays) publishing, and self-archiving.

Houghton, Rasmussen, and colleagues (2009) summarize journal system cost results by the average cost per article in electronic-only format

Table 7.1 Comparison of cost per article of six scenarios with base cost and e-only and author-pays (Cambridge Economic Policy Associates, 2008)

	Scenario	
	E-only (£)	**Author-pays (£)**
Academic author-pays	-	+213
Academic subscriptions	-3	-105
Other subscriptions/revenue	-13	-32
Academic library access	-20	-28
Special library access	-6	-8
User donated search/print	+3	+3
Total	-39	+43

(for direct comparative purposes). They arrive at the following average costs: subscription-based (termed "toll access")—£8,296 per article; OA author-pays—£7,483; and OA self-archiving with overlay services (peer-review, editing, etc.) —£7,115. Therefore, OA author-pays would be £813 cheaper than "toll access" and OA self-archiving £1,180 cheaper.

In addition to the bottom-up analysis of detailed costs, they extend their analysis to include a top-down modeling of impacts on returns to R&D. Houghton and colleagues (2006) and Houghton and Sheehan (2006) discuss this modeling approach. An accessibility rationale establishes the proportion of research stock of knowledge that is in journals and how that proportion is affected by alternative publishing models. Another approach is the efficiency yielded by the alternative models. They then compare the costs and benefits of the publishing models, including journals and other forms of communication.

The Denmark and the Netherlands Studies

Houghton, Rasmussen, and colleagues (2009) followed up on studies done by Houghton and others in Australia (Houghton et al., 2006), the U.K. (Houghton, Rasmussen, et al., 2009), Denmark (Houghton, 2009a), and the Netherlands. The study focused on scholarly publishing as a system, with emphasis on scholarly journals, but including books as well. In the Netherlands study conducted in 2009 there were 44,116 FTE researchers, of whom 11,740 were researchers in higher education who were published. Total system costs are given for the nation and for higher education. Costs, benefits, and benefit/cost ratios are presented to compare open access alternatives against the subscription (called "toll access") system. The authors discuss the implications of the findings for funding, researchers, universities and research institutions, publishers and the publishing industry, research libraries, and government and central agencies. Houghton (2009b) gives some details as a comparison.

Houghton (2009b) summarizes and compares the national studies performed in the U.K., the Netherlands, and Denmark. Scholarly journal comparisons are made for the costs and benefits of three business models: subscription publishing, open access (author-pays), and open access (self-archiving with overlay services, i.e., peer review management, editing, production, and proofing).

The scholarly communication system costs per article (in Euros) are given for the three countries and three publishing models (Table 7.2).

Houghton provides logical reasons for the differences among the countries. A benefits model (see Houghton & Sheehan, 2009) showed that £78 million per annum returns to public sector R&D in the Netherlands, £40 million to Denmark, and £250 million to the U.K.

The U.S. Science Study

A 1977 NSF study of U.S. science journals was performed by King Research, Inc. (King et al., 1981) to examine the future of print vs.

Table 7.2 Comparison of the cost per article of three publishing models in the U.K., the Netherlands, and Denmark (Houghton, Rasmussen, et al., 2009)

	Country (EUR circa 2007)		
	U.K.	Netherlands	Denmark*
Subscription publishing	12,100	17,000	14,300
OA author-pays	10,900	15,900	13,500
Self-archiving with overlay	10,400	15,300	12,800
Interpreted from graph			

electronic journals and to provide some policy guidance concerning the future of science journals. To do this, it was necessary to examine the economic costs and technical feasibility of the entire science journal system. Detailed economic costs were obtained by surveying authors, reviewers, publishers, libraries, intermediary services, and readers. Costs were determined by listing detailed input, process, and output of 34 journal-related activities, establishing appropriate cost parameters and the cost of resources used to perform the activities. The study forecast that it would be 1997 before an electronic journal publishing system would be fully in place and accepted.

Authors spent an average of 82 hours processing and writing for a total of $689 million. Half of science articles had some form of author payment at an average of about $900 in current dollars. In 1977, average donated costs per journal were subject editor ($3,400) and reviewers ($17,600). Paid editors cost was $29,000. The first copy cost per article was $670 and average reproduction and distribution cost per subscription was under $10. The total was $629 million. Average library costs per subscription were: purchase ($96), maintenance ($31), storage ($6), and weeding ($1). Use cost was $2 per use and $20 for interlibrary lending and borrowing, for a total of $433 million. Intermediary costs totaled $152 million. Readers averaged 82 hours annually obtaining and reading articles for a total of $2.35 billion. Total cost of the scholarly journal system was $4.54 billion or about $16 billion in current dollars.

The number of authors, readers, publications, and libraries was updated in 1995 (Tenopir & King, 2000), resulting in total system costs of about $55 billion in 2007 dollars.

The Morris Summary of Costs

Morris (2005), formerly Chief Executive, ALPSP, and later Editor of *Learned Publishing*, summarized economic cost of the journal system. She describes six basic functions of the system and details activities for each function. Costs are then attributable to the various functions and activities with attribution for the sources of costs. Based on several secondary sources, she arrives at the following average cost per article in 2004 dollars: writing $6,700; donated refereeing $1,080, publishing $2,250 to $4,375, library $4,230, and reading $30,600 (Baldwin, 2004; Barschall, 1988; King, 2004; King, Aerni, Brody, Herbison, & Knapp, 2004a; Revill, 2002; Rowland, 2002; Schonfeld, King, Okerson, & Fenton, 2004; SQW Limited, 2004; Tenopir & King, 2000, 2002, 2004).

Comparison of Scholarly Journal System Studies

Five of the studies addressed the total cost of scholarly journal systems. Total costs must take into account the proportion of costs incurred by all types of system participants. Some of the studies are vague about certain costs and, therefore, some interpretations are made by the relevant authors. These estimates are shown in Table 7.3.

The difference in proportion due to publishing may vary among studies because it is not clear how much publishing is done in each country. CEPA assumed global publishing. The most important conclusion is that researchers' time dominates the overall cost of scholarly journal communication (it accounts for 79.5 percent, based on the average of the five studies). One possible confusion in the studies deals with editing. Some studies assume that all editors' time is donated. However, some editors are fulltime and most are paid at least an honorarium, which should be subtracted from the cost of what could be termed their "donated" time (see discussion of the science study for examples).

Researcher Economics

Because researcher time is a scarce and valuable resource to the journal system, this section deals with all activities involving that time including donated time of editing and peer review.

Reading

Cambridge Economic Policy Associates (2008) derives the cost of reading from two basic sets of data: number of researchers in universities and special libraries and annual amount of reading per researcher (based on Tenopir & King, 2002). These estimates are 258 annual readings for academics and 197 for those served by special libraries. These parameters yield a total system-wide cost of £74.7 billion subdivided as follows: £115.8b for research production (research and writing), £16.4b for publishing and distribution, £2.1b for access provision, £16.4b for user search and print, and £33.9b for reading.

Houghton, Rasmussen, and colleagues (2009) estimate article access and reading time and money based on secondary sources of data: number of readings per researcher per year (280), time spent reading (31 minutes per article), time spent searching and accessing articles (12.5 minutes), article requests per reading (1.4), time spent by authors obtaining permission (2 hours). The authors estimated the proportion of

Table 7.3   Proportion of national journal system costs by type of participant and study

	(Science)	Australia	U.K.	U.K.	General	
Participants	King et al., 1981	Houghton et al., 2006	Cambridge Econ Policy Associates, 2008	Houghton, Rasmussen, et al., 2009	Morris, 2005	Average of five authors
Authors	14.3	8.3	8.1	14	14.7	11.9
Donated reviewers & editors	2	1.1	5.9	4.8	1.6	3.1
Publishers	11.1	2.9	17.4	6.9	7.3	9.1
Libraries & intermediaries	12.2	12.1	8.1	15.1	9.3	11.4
Readers	60.4	75.5	60.5	59.2	67.1	64.5
Total	100	99.9	100	100	100	100

articles photocopied or printed (20 percent print, 69 percent electronic), with cost per printing and copying per page (5 pence) and time spent printing or copying an article (3 minutes). The total calculated U.K. cost was £665 million for writing, £23 million for permissions, £1.6 billion for reading, and £26 million for printing and copying. The sources of this information are Cambridge Economic Policy Associates (2008), Halliday and Oppenheim (1999), Tenopir and King (2000), and Society of College, National and University Libraries (2008).

Writing

Houghton, Rasmussen, and colleagues (2009) also examined the costs of performing research and communication in great detail. They arrived at an average of 95 hours to write an article and 4.5 hours per article for peer review; both estimates are based on works by Tenopir and King (2000) and King (2004). The authors estimated manuscript rejection and resubmission rates. They relied on industry consultants to provide time spent on editorial activities (20 days per year) and editorial boards (3/4 days per year). They also relied on calculations of and proportion of authors who are editors (8 percent) and/or serve on editorial boards (24 percent) based on Rowlands and Nicholas (2006).

Editing

Hedlund, Gustafsson, and Bjørk (2004) suggest that with OA several activities in the publishing value chain can be bypassed, thereby reducing costs and publication time. Here OA refers to parallel publishing from two perspectives: (1) survey respondent time of 163 median hours for five tasks and (2) 250 hours per year with approximation made by editors. The time spent processing the average article is 22 hours (10 hours for editorial review, 6 hours for peer review, 4 hours for technical editing, and 2 hours for placement of article). Editor time is considered relevant because many OA journals rely on volunteer time of editors. Cambridge Economic Policy Associates (2008) report that the time spent by editors on peer review is four hours with 2.5 reviewers per article (Tenopir & King, 2000).

Peer Review

Cope and Kalantzis (2009a) argue that in the journal system only representations of knowledge are being evaluated and that knowledge is what a scholar tells us. They discuss flaws in the review process, such as what the peer-review system purports to measure and why it is potentially disruptive. Davis, in a review of peer review submitted to the Scholarly Publishing Roundtable (2010), presented several studies that support the importance of peer review (e.g., King, Tenopir, & Clarke, 2006), his own views on its weaknesses, and the need to understand better whether peer review is ineffective or actually does what it purports to do.

Rowland (2002) prepared a thorough review of the peer-review process. He notes two components to peer-review costs: those of the editors and those of the reviewers themselves. There has been some confusion in reporting these costs; some writers apparently do not distinguish between donated and paid editor contributions, as well as reviewing and other editor duties. Rowland summarizes past aspects of editorial reviewing activities and concludes the cost is about $200 per submitted paper and $400 per published paper (Donovan, 1998; Halliday, & Oppenheim, 2000; Okerson & McDonnell, 1995; Page, Campbell, & Meadows, 1997; Rowland, 1996, Tenopir & King, 2000). In a survey of 2,165 reviewers, Ware (2009) observed that the respondents had taken about 24 days (elapsed time) to complete their most recent review. They spent an average of nine hours per review. King and colleagues (1981) surveyed authors on how much time they spent as reviewers in reviewing an article (i.e., 6.0 hours per accepted and 6.3 hours per rejected article). This estimate is apparently still accepted (Houghton, Rasmussen, et al., 2009; Morris, 2005). Rowland also reviewed suggested alternative mechanisms for peer review of electronic publications (Rowland, 1999; Weller, 2000; Williamson, 2002). Cambridge Economic Policy Associates (2008) report that the current U.K. contribution to peer review donated (non-cash) cost per article is £165 (£132 academic and £33 other reviewers).

Self-Archiving

Swan and Brown (2005) asked authors who self archive how long it took them and found the first time being much longer than subsequently reported (see Table 7.4).

Table 7.4 Time spent by authors to self archive (Swan & Brown, 2005)

	First (%)	Subsequent (%)
Done by someone else	11	12
A few minutes	30	52
Under an hour	36	23
1–2 hours	11	8
3–4 hours	5	2
More than a day	7	3

Carr and Harnad (2005) reported that it takes about ten minutes per paper to enter a self-archived article. They suggest that the number of co-authors should also be considered because the paper need be entered just once. They also emphasize that the researcher/author often delegates the task to a librarian, student, or assistant (see Swan & Brown, 2005). Based on past studies, Houghton, Rasmussen, and colleagues (2009) assume self-archiving (deposit to a repository) cost of authors time to be £9.35 per deposit.

Publishing Economics

Overview

Cox and Cox (2008) conducted the third survey of publishers in a series funded by ALPSP. A total of 203 publishers responded to the survey, of whom 54 percent published five or fewer journals and seven percent 100 or more titles. Information collected in the surveys included: new journals and branches, closures, and transfers; online-related information; pricing strategies; open access-related information; and licensing issues. General conclusions were that the online market is maturing (96.1 percent of STM and 86.5 percent of arts, humanities, and social science journals are accessible electronically); many publishers are separating print and electronic subscription pricing; licensing terms are becoming more generous; more publishers are offering an author-pays option; and publishers are concerned about articles in repositories.

Publishers indicate that they launched 1,463 new titles from 2003 to 2007, an average of 7.2 titles per publisher (Cox & Cox, 2008). The average increased over periods of four years: 5.3 titles per publication from 1999 to 2003 and 6.0 titles from 2001 to 2005. On the other hand, commercial publishers discontinued an average of 3.4 titles in 2005 and 7.0 in 2008; nonprofit publishers discontinued 0.32 to 5.9 titles in the same three-year period. The number of titles involved in mergers and/or transfers among publishers appears to be going down.

A survey of about 600 learned professional societies (118 responded) by Sage (2008) assessed their insight into and their understanding of the challenges facing them, including publishing. The authors conclude that editorial quality, supporting the dissemination of scholarly research, and supporting members are the core society focuses. Managing the move to online publishing is a priority for many societies and the same applies to new business models, including, but not exclusively, open access. They are concerned that these models be approached without damaging their financial stability.

Publisher Cost

King (2007) presents a review of the cost of journal publishing and a follow-up review of pricing and other means of charging for scholarly journals (King & Alvarado-Albertorio, 2008). The two reviews are separated because costs lead to prices and because there is confusion in the literature as to what is meant by cost because the term is often used when price is intended. For example, many refer to library *costs* when meaning the purchase price paid and where all processing costs are ignored. Impact factors are sometimes referred to as cost per citation, which is meant to be price per citation. The point is that comparison of journal prices of commercial and other publishers does not necessarily reflect the comparative first-copy cost of processing articles because the resulting price depends largely on circulation. That is, two journals can have exactly the same unit first-copy cost and distribution cost per subscription, but the price necessary to recover costs can reflect a ten-fold difference, depending on circulation.

Publishing costs involve direct and indirect fixed costs associated with first-copy costs and direct and indirect variable costs involving distribution of journals/articles; estimated costs for these factors are given in the review. Implications for librarians, OA author-side payment, the Big Deal, and electronic publishing are also discussed.

Comparisons of other costs of toll access (i.e., subscription) and OA publishing are shown in Table 7.5.

The CEPA authors estimate author fees charged to be about £1,525 for e-only OA publishing.

Parameters for estimating publishing costs include pages per article (12.4), articles per issue (10), issues per year (12), articles per title (120), non-article pages (14 percent), rejection rate (50 percent), subscriptions per title (1,200), management (20 percent), surplus profit (20 percent), and e-only relative to print (25 percent) (Houghton, Rasmussen, et al., 2009). These estimates are based, variously, on Cambridge Economic Policy Associates (2008), Bjørk (2007), King and Tenopir (2008), Waltham (2005), and Tenopir and King (2000). Some estimates are made by the JISC report authors. Detailed activity costs are also presented based on the parameters: publisher-side peer review (£344 per article), researcher donated peer-review (£630), editing and proofreading (£480), illustrations and graphics (£45), composition and typesetting (£335), and non-article processing (£100 per article).

Table 7.5 Comparison of cost per article of first copy activities by toll access vs. open access (Cambridge Economic Policy Associates, 2008)

	Toll Access	Open Access
Rights management	£50	£10
Author-side payment processing	-	£20
Marketing	£120	£40
Online hosting	£200	£100
Customer service	£50	£10
Sales administration	£100	-
Printing, inventory management	£150	-
Delivery and fulfillment	£120	£30

Houghton, Rasmussen, and colleagues (2009) go on to estimate costs per article by format and publishing model as shown in Table 7.6.

Very few studies provide publishers' circulation data (particularly distinguishing member or personal and institutional/library subscriptions). For example, the *Ulrich's* circulation data are unreliable, particularly those for commercial publishers. Thus, evidence of circulation from nine publishers (13 journals) provided by Waltham (2005) is welcome. From 2002 to 2004 total member subscribers (12 journals) dropped from 17,852 to 17,289 (-3 percent). Note that the average subscription per journal was 1,440 in 2004. Total institutional subscriptions of the 12 journals dropped even further, from 12,647 to 9,878 (-22 percent). The average is 823 subscriptions per journal, which has a significant impact on the price that must be charged to break even.

Using evidence of trends in the average number of print pages published per journal (9 journals) shows an increase of three percent from 2002 to 2004 (9.7 to 10.0 pages per article) (Waltham, 2005). The number of articles published increased 19 percent over that time. The total first-copy costs increased 11 percent over three years (including inflation). First-copy costs also depend on a number of factors such as number and type of special graphics (e.g., chemical compounds, mathematical equations, charts, photos, maps) and language of the text/author.

Tenopir and King (2009) indicate that the number of pages per article increased from 7.4 in 1975 to 13.3 in 2007, and articles per title increased from 72 in 1965 to 123 in 1995. First-copy costs also depend on a number of factors such as number and type of special graphics (e.g., chemical

Table 7.6 Cost per article for three publishing models and three formats (Houghton, Rasmussen, et al., 2009)

	Estimate (£)
Toll access	
Print-only	2,728
Dual-mode	3,247
E-only	2,337
OA author-pays	
Print-only	1,831
Dual-mode	2,003
E-only	1,524
OA self-archiving	
Peer review management	455
Editing and proofing	673
Hosting	132
Full-service	1,260

compounds, mathematical equations, charts, photos, maps), and language of the text/author.

Clarke (2007) presents a detailed description of publishing activities associated with the establishment of a journal, operations (submission-related, article-related, issue-related, generic), and infrastructure maintenance. These activities are described in detail and form publishing cost profiles. He then categorizes journals into nine types (e.g., an association with a single, hard-copy journal; a multi-journal commercial publisher applying conventional, subscription-based access) and gives estimates of the annual cost for each journal type and corresponding author-pays cost. He relies somewhat on the literature for cost estimates and discusses why some costs are not used or differ from other reported costs. He believes that the additional detail helps explain cost differences among the nine types of journals. For example, he claims commercial publishers have higher costs than not-for-profit associations, in part because of the additional functions they perform: in branding, customer relationship, management, and content protection.

Automation has allowed publishers to utilize online submission and review system capabilities. Cox and Cox (2008) point out that more publishers used such systems in 2008 compared with 2005 (up 6.4 percent). They show that online availability has increased substantially for science, technology, and medicine from 2003 to 2008 (82.6 percent to 96.1

percent of titles) and in arts, humanities, and social sciences (72.4 percent to 86.5 percent of titles). The proportions are slightly higher for commercial journals.

Subscription Pricing

Subscription prices have been the object of much attention. King and Alvarado-Albertorio (2008) review pricing and other means of charging for journals. They give trends of average prices from several sources dating back to 1960 for science journals. They also discuss pricing issues concerning electronic journals, bundling, alternatives to subscriptions, comparison of nonprofit and commercial journals, publisher surplus and profit, factors affecting prices, and open access as a solution to subscriptions. They attribute the past (pre-bundling) reasons library prices increased so much from 1975 to the 2000s to: (1) a spiraling effect of increasing prices, fewer subscribers, higher prices; (2) journals increased in size (articles and pages); (3) new journals tend to be niche journals with small audiences; (4) a move away from author-side payments meant that societies had to increase prices to maintain sufficient revenue; (5) the cost of publishing resources (e.g., labor) increased faster than inflation; and (6) many other factors such as fluctuating international exchange rates.

The pricing review article (King & Alvarado-Albertorio, 2008) points out that there are different ways of calculating average price that are not always made clear. That is, some reports calculate average price by averaging across titles (e.g., prices that are found in the *Library Journal* annual reports) and others calculate prices by averaging across distributed journals (e.g., the Association of Research Libraries [ARL] reports prices based on subscriptions in their member libraries). The latter average price is typically much less, depending on number of subscriptions included.

In their annual update of the journal pricing and publishing landscape, Van Orsdel and Born (2009) indicate that the recession (beginning in April 2009) is already playing havoc with the scholarly journal system. Publishers are being warned that double-digit cuts are expected in libraries while publishers must maintain prices, even at the inflation level. New features and products are likely to be ignored by libraries in an effort to keep prices down; the ARL suggests that worried publishers need to consult with member libraries about new publishing models that might keep them afloat.

Online journal publishers apply a range of pricing strategies (Cox & Cox, 2008). Examples in 2008, including trends from 2005 are: online only (44.4 percent of publishers, up 6.1 percent from 38.3 percent); free online with print (49.7 percent of publishers, down 12 percent); surcharge for online with print (24.1 percent of publishers, down 3.7 percent); discretionary for online only (33.2 percent of publishers, down slightly); discretionary for print only (9.1 percent of publishers, up 1.7 percent); customer size such as number of sites, fulltime equivalents, or

Carnegie classification (42.2 percent of publishers, up slightly); advance pay-per-view (4.3 percent of publishers, the same); and other (16.6 percent, up 11 percent). Provision of pay-per-view of downloaded articles increased from 65.1 percent of publishers in 2003 to 77.6 percent in 2008.

Bergstrom and Bergstrom (2006) examine 92 ecology journal prices to compare the effect of commercial and nonprofit publisher prices and citation rates on library subscriptions. For each journal entry they establish circulation (from OCLC), dollars per article, author fee (dollars per page) and total dollars per page. They conclude that the transition to online distribution has not affected basic pricing structure; commercial publishers charge several times as much per page, and price differences between type of publisher do not reflect an underlying difference in quality (citation rate and circulation are highly responsive to price differences).

Earlier, Bergstrom and Bergstrom (2004b) looked at differences in the cost per page and cost per citation of commercial and nonprofit publishers for six fields of science. Looking at implications of profit maximization and average-cost-pricing with electronic distribution when site licensing is employed, they conclude that the scientific community receives zero consumer surplus (consumer surplus is the difference in buyer value and what is paid). Therefore, the scientific community is worse off than it would be if subscriptions were sold only to individuals, and no better off than if the journal did not exist. With a society journal that seeks the largest possible circulation (and yet recovers costs), scientists will get greater total consumer surplus if universities purchase site licenses. The scientific community benefits from the site licenses rather than leaving individuals to purchase their own subscriptions.

McCabe, Nevo, and Rubinfeld (2006) examine alternative approaches to bundling journals and their effects on purchase price paid. The authors conjecture that "bundling can lead to higher prices. Indeed, recent practices of major publishers of bundling print and electronic journals can be seen as a form of price discrimination" (p. 27).

Over the years McCabe (2002, 2004, 2005) has studied nonprofit and commercial publishers and the consequences of publisher mergers. In effect, he has concluded that mergers between publishers contribute substantially to increases in price to libraries. He attributes this phenomenon to the market power of several commercial publishers and shows that prices are positively related to portfolio size, although he later adds that "we simulate the effects of mergers and find that the unlikely unilateral effect of a merger is to lower prices" (McCabe et al., 2006, p. 1). More recently he suggests that libraries are willing to pay more for high quality journals (determined by citation counts) and commercial publishers take advantage of this willingness.

Some aspects of McCabe's work are disputed by Duplantis, Haar, Silberman, Van Gieson, and Warren-Boulton (2005), who postulate that the relationship between mergers and price changes in the academic journal industry is poorly understood and that work to date (2005) does not provide a rationale for antitrust enforcement. One interesting observation is that publisher acquisitions might affect the prices of the acquiring publisher, as well as the acquired publisher. They give examples for five acquiring and nine acquired firms.

The U.K. Office of Fair Trading (2002) jumped into the commercial vs. nonprofit pricing debate by reporting examples of these trends and corresponding impact factor studies. However, they decided "for now it would not be appropriate for the OFT to intervene in the market, but the position will be kept under review" (p. 1).

Price Differentiation/Discrimination

Tiered pricing of journals established different prices based on characteristics of the subscribing institution. Hahn (2005) discusses the adoption of tiered pricing of journals and implications for library collections. She defines tiered pricing as "differential charges for both paper and electronic subscriptions to a journal based on the categorization of the subscribing institution" (p. 151) (see Varian [1996] for a full discussion of differential pricing). Basically, it means that small institutions (characterized in specific ways) are charged less than large ones. She describes 31 journals with tiered pricing (with 4 to 6 tiers) and price differentials ranging from 1.16 to 25.45 (i.e., highest price divided by lowest price). Four bases for tiered pricing are described: (1) Carnegie classes, (2) distribution of subscribers published online by the American Institute of Physics, (3) most subscriptions come from the top tier, and (4) most subscriptions come from the bottom tier. The issue is the extent to which low-tier prices affect revenue and the necessity for top-tier institutions to absorb higher prices. She finds that "when substantial numbers of subscribers are lower-tier institutions, institutions falling into the highest tier can experience staggering price increases" (p. 155). Furthermore, "if journals adopting tiered pricing succeed in maintaining or even increasing their subscriber base, they could set off a chain of events that result in decreased subscriptions for other titles and consequently smaller collections at research libraries" (p. 162). This sentiment is confirmed by Van Orsdel and Born (2009) noting the ARL warning that price discrimination will add more burdens to larger institutes in order to discount prices for smaller ones, which will not be acceptable and consortia that achieve this objective will also be condemned.

Effect of Interlibrary Loan

Interlibrary lending (ILL) and borrowing of copies of articles has been a long tradition among libraries. Libraries use ILL as an alternative to purchasing journals when the amount of use is not sufficient to warrant paying for subscriptions. Cost models show break-even points at which it is less expensive to borrow than to purchase (Kingma, 1996; Tenopir & King, 2000). Interlibrary lending continues to be heavily used in the

U.S.; in a survey of 822 U.S. academic libraries, 64 percent say they borrow electronic versions more now than five years ago and 41 percent borrow print versions more often (Griffiths & King, 2009a). However, Primary Research Group, Inc. (2008) found that interlibrary loans in the U.K. decreased from an average of 1,647 to 913 per library, perhaps reflecting the large increase in U.K. periodical collections (from 3,900 to 7,200).

The British Library charges £9.22 for an electronic loan and £10.40 for a hardcopy that is mailed. The Society of College, National and University Libraries (SCONUL) reports 674,000 interlibrary loans for higher education at a cost of £6.90 per ILL.

Pay-per-View

In a sense the pay-per-view (PPV) option, where downloads are paid for on an article-by-article basis, serves as a substitute for ILL (and document delivery). Harwood and Prior (2008) experimented with the two PPV models at ten universities in the U.K. and journals from five publishers. PPV rates for downloads ranged from £3.50 to £22 (about typical for interlibrary borrowing costs to libraries, but without the additional cost of lending to the journal system). For the PPV conversion to a recommended subscription model, once the cost of downloads reached the subscription price (plus a surcharge), the title would be converted to subscription (with no additional charges). This is what libraries should do with ILL, but they rarely do so because it is difficult to know the extent of use of journals (King, Harley, Earl-Novell, Arter, Lawrence, & Perciali, 2006). Harwood and Prior (2008) discuss important issues such as double counting, portable document format (PDF) vs. hypertext markup language (HTML) format (PDF generally preferred), archival rights, administration and payment, and role of subscription agents.

Since journals have become available electronically, some have proposed that articles be made available on a PPV basis (for examples of the PEAK experiment, see MacKie-Mason & Jankovich, 1997). Two new model proposals are "PPV converting to subscription," where institutions may have subscriptions but use PPV to access other titles and "Core plus Peripheral," where publishers provide access to all their titles and PPV is available to non-subscribed titles (Rightscom, 2005, reported by Harwood & Prior, 2008, p. 134).

Primary Research Group, Inc. (2008) indicated that the 45 libraries in their survey paid $421 on average for all the individual articles obtained ($520 for academic, $142 for non-academic libraries).

Other Publishing Issues

Phillips (2009) discusses business models in journal publishing. He emphasizes the financial aspects of publishing, including the long time required to recover the initial investment (see also Page et al., 1997;

Tenopir & King, 2000) and the risk of starting new journals, showing that of 1,925 new STM journals started in 2004, 1,850 were still active in 2007. He also mentions the necessary investment required for staff with new competencies, facilities, and systems, citing Elsevier's cost of about £200 million to establish Science Direct (Clarke, 2007). Morris (2009, p. 381) feels that current journals may not satisfy the following evolving needs of researchers: (1) increasing the speed of availability of articles, (2) a concern about the departure of a "version of record," (3) use of alternative communication modes, and (4) increased exposure of one's work among other researchers. She laments that small publishers may not be able to meet these needs due to inadequate financial resources; the average number of journals per publisher is 2.4 (1.8 when the top four are excluded).

A variety of other issues are of concern to the stakeholders in digital journal publishing. Nicholas, Huntington, Dobrowolski, and Rowlands (2006) speculate on a better method of marketing digital journals to consumers. Given the huge demand for scholarly articles, they suggest a market realignment in which consumers have a full and largely unfettered choice about what they purchase. However, such an approach must make sure consumers are responsible for their decision making. They could be given a certain number of download credits by the library (or similar agency) at the beginning of each term, with a different tariff for professors, postgraduates, and students. Such credits would be accepted by any scholarly journal vendor and the consumer would decide how to spend them.

Van Orsdel and Born (2009, p. 38) state that: "As economic times get harder, the rationale for Open Access becomes clearer," quoting Houghton, Rasmussen, and colleagues (2009) and their estimates of savings to U.K. libraries. Van Orsdel and Born discuss trends that may support OA, such as Springer acquiring BioMed Central and their agreement with the University of California (UC) libraries to experiment with a plan in which articles written by UC faculty would become OA upon publication and a PDF of the article deposited in eScholarship, the UC's digital repository. In the SCOAP3 experiment, libraries pay subscription fees into a common pool from which publishers of physics journals are paid, and journals will be free to all readers upon publication.

Hannay and Spencer (2007) present an innovative approach to communicating articles called Nature Precedings (precedings.nature.com), a preprint server that allows scientists to upload non-peer-reviewed (or pre-peer-reviewed) documents that can be discovered, downloaded, read, and cited by other researchers. It is like arXiv, but serves other fields and disciplines. It is designed to provide access to current activity and help balance publishing delays that impede progress. Readers can comment on and vote for contributions they consider noteworthy. When an article is published elsewhere in a peer-reviewed form, the authors and readers can provide links to the formal published article.

Advantages of online journal publishing include obviating the need for print distribution, accelerating peer review, reducing publishing costs, and permitting a range of alternative pricing policies (Shotton, 2009). Authors benefit from enhanced manuscript processing and less restriction on page limits. Readers gain from increased ease of access to online journals. Disadvantages include the additional cost and potential harmful author behavior in not exercising traditional and proven search and access activities. Readers need to cope with far more information than in the past. Shotton also lists shortcomings in PDF, digital object identifiers (DOIs), supplementary materials, mark-up data, and meta-data. In light of strengths and weaknesses of the current environment, he recommends semantic publishing: "anything that enhances the meaning of a published journal article, facilitates its automated discovery, enables it's [sic] linking to semantically related articles, provides access to data within the article in actionable form, or facilitates integration of data between papers" (p. 86). All of this should "increase the intrinsic value of journal articles" (p. 86). He goes on to indicate how the current system can evolve.

With only 49 percent of 45 libraries surveyed by Primary Research Group, Inc. (2008) familiar with the CLOCKSS (Controlled Lots of Copies Keep Stuff Safe) digital archiving program, general awareness of the importance of methods to archive digital journal articles is questionable.

Library Economics

Library expenditures account for about 11 percent of the total scholarly system cost (excluding purchase price paid because that is a redundant cost with publishing). They include costs of processing print and electronic journals as well as activities associated with use such as re-shelving, photocopying or downloaded printouts, library-related search support, and user training. The journal collection-related information is provided for academic libraries, special libraries, and consortia and licensing economics.

Academic Library Print and Electronic Collections

A much-needed cost analysis of alternative ways of dealing with academic print and electronic journal collections identifies the following: (1) the status quo, where libraries continue to receive, process, and bind and store journals; (2) storing materials at library storage facilities; (3) foregoing binding completely, storing in pamphlet boxes; (4) keeping materials on display shelves for a limited time and discarding them, and (5) sending materials directly from the publisher to a library storage facility (Cooper, 2006). Cooper not only presents costs for these alternatives, but also discusses the implications for readers and consideration of the extent to which titles are used.

Davies (2009, p. 214) suggests that "given the lead time to cancel subscriptions, book publishing has, in many cases, offered a much readier option to reduce spending, and it can be claimed that the bibliographic framework of scholarly research has significantly suffered." He emphasizes how libraries quickly adjusted to the new electronic environment by providing better services, encouraging open access journals and institutional repositories, as well as developing central open access funds (Cockerill, 2009); developing seamless electronic interfaces; and offering direct support to users.

Creaser, Maynard, and White (2006) provide ten-year trends of academic, government, and national libraries. They also examine trends in periodical prices (2004 to 2006) and U.K. data on library and information profession by occupation (1999–2000 and 2004–2005). Public library trends are also given. The trends in U.K. academic libraries (Old—incorporated before 1992, New—incorporated since 1992, and HE—all non-university institutions funded by HEFCs in the U.K.) are given in Table 7.7 for serials collection (change based on constant £).

The periodicals proportion of total expenditure increased from 16.7 percent to 18.4 percent over the five-year period.

The number of academic libraries in the U.K. increased from 778 to 846 (1999–2000 to 2004–2005) (Creaser et al., 2006). Journal acquisitions increased from 667,000 to 1,200,000 (+79.9 percent) or from 857 per library to 1,418 per library (+65.5 percent). It is clear that periodical/journal collections have increased substantially over the five years. In 2004–2005 nearly three-quarters of the collections were in electronic format (308 titles per library were print only, 162 print and electronic, 731 electronic only). During the five-year period visits increased only 1.6 percent, providing evidence that access to electronic journals may have an appreciable impact on in-person visits.

Primary Research Group, Inc. (2008) surveyed 45 academic and research libraries to determine their purchasing practices. These libraries represent a wide range of sizes, communities served, and geographic locations (including some from non-U.S. countries). Findings include spending, cancellations, and additions; spending by type of format; and opinions on the impact of open access journals, peer review, and the future of print journals. Average academic library expenditures were $847,000 in 2008–2009 and $280,000 for non-academic libraries. The average expenditures across all surveyed libraries were $131,000 for print-only (22.4 percent of journal expenditures), $310,000 for electronic-only (53.1 percent) and $143,000 for both printed and electronic (24.5 percent). Interestingly, 46 percent of subscriptions were in bundles of 50 or more titles (54 percent for academic, 24 percent for non-academic collections). The libraries averaged 145 subscription cancellations and 84 additions.

The ARL serials collection rose from 18,115 titles in 2003 to 36,812 in 2007–2008, or by about 103 percent (Kyrillidou & Bland, 2009). Kyrillidou (2006) reports a decline in the unit (purchase) cost per serial

Table 7.7 Trends in U.K. academic library collection statistics (Creaser et al., 2006)

	Year		
	1999–2000	2004–2005	Change (%)
Number of libraries	778	846	+8.7
Average total expenditures (£000)	£415	£521	+11.7
Average periodical expenditures (£000)	£69.1	£96.1	+39.1
Proportion (%) of titles (2001–2002 to 2004–2005)			
Print-only	39.3%	25.6%	-34.9
E-only	45.0%	60.9%	+35.3
Both	15.7%	13.5%	-14

in ARL libraries since 2000, when electronic subscriptions were officially included in serials purchased figures. In 2004–2005 the unit cost was $239 per title, but it has been on a declining trajectory over the past five years. However, she spells out the caveats of measuring unit costs in the current environment of replicated purchases of titles. Ultimately the trend line of publishing serial cost per subscription has been discontinued (Kyrillidou & Bland, 2009).

In 2007–2008 Griffiths and King (2009a) surveyed academic libraries in the U.S.; a total of 822 of 3,722 libraries responded. They averaged 7,380 unique periodical subscriptions or a projected 21.8 million total for all 3,772 libraries. Not all periodical subscriptions are scholarly journals, and unique titles do not include titles found multiple times across aggregated databases. The trend in academic library collection purchases from 2002–2003 to 2007–2008 is holding steady. The proportion of the collection in electronic format is substantial (60 percent of the library periodical collections are over 25 percent electronic and about 1 percent of libraries are all electronic). The trend in transitioning to electronic has stabilized from 2002–2003 to 2007–2008. Expenditures on electronic collections average $357,000 per academic library.

Research universities in the U.S. spent an average of $3.7 million for 10,000 academic journals (in 2002) plus $500,000 on processing and maintaining their collections, or $420 per title and $10.54 per article, assuming 40 articles per title (i.e., $9.23 publisher cost and $1.31 library cost). Shifting to digital publishing would save libraries about $0.80 per article (Getz, 2005b).

The Houghton, Rasmussen, and colleagues (2009) report to JISC combines four references to derive an estimate of the library costs of acquiring and handling scholarly journals (Halliday & Oppenheim, 1999; King, Aerni, Brody, Herbison, & Kohberger, 2004; Schonfeld et al., 2004; Society of College, National and University Libraries, 2008). The JISC

(Houghton, Rasmussen, et al., 2009) report also added costs of licensing negotiation, access and authentication control, and permission and copyright fees (Maynard & Davies, 2001). From these sources of evidence they reported the following costs:

- Print subscription: £132 per title, £0.111 per article

- Electronic-only subscription: £95 per title, £0.150 per article

- OA electronic-only: £20 per title, £0.170 per article

Summarizing the cost of 14 processing activities shows that processing print cost £112 per title, electronic £28, and OA (e-only) £20. Subscription content access and user costs are as follows: OA (e-only) is £20 per title and toll access ranges from £95 for e-only to £132 in print.

Special Library Print and Electronic Collections

There is some difficulty in establishing the number of special libraries in the U.K. Houghton and colleagues (2009) report three sources (Creaser et al., 2006; Spiller, Creaser, & Murphy, 1998; and Gale's *Directory of Special Libraries and Information Centers*). These estimates ranged from 1,650 to 4,000. Cambridge Economic Policy Associates (2008) used an estimate of 104 special libraries. According to Spiller and colleagues (1998), JISC reports that special libraries average about 220 serial subscriptions per library and LISU gives 97 journal titles per special library.

U.S. evidence is that 9,066 special libraries average 700 unique periodical subscriptions or a total of 6.3 million subscriptions (Griffiths & King, 2009b). The patterns of unique periodical titles are likely to be similar to academic library collections, suggesting that about 18 percent of scholarly journal subscriptions in the U.S. are from special libraries. In addition, some are found in public libraries. Special and public libraries would also benefit from the author-pays OA model.

Griffiths and King (2009b) report about 700 unique periodical titles per special library with the trend (2002–2003 to 2007–2008) somewhat down. However, the proportion of the periodicals collection that is electronic is appreciable (one-third of these libraries have over 25 percent of the collection in electronic format) and that trend is substantially up. The average expenditure for the electronic collection is $98,000 per library and trending up. There is a dramatic shift from books to electronic journals in U.S. special libraries.

Consortia and Licensing Economics

A historical review of library consortia (also variously called networks, cooperatives, and systems) by King and Xu (2002a) illustrates the ingenuity and generousness of the library community in developing consortia dating back to the 1960s. The number of consortia in the U.S.

dropped dramatically about 20 years ago when the federal government discontinued funding multi-type library networking. However, the evolution of electronic publishing reinvigorated library consortia to provide a range of electronic-journal-related services, particularly access to aggregated collections through site licenses.

A national survey of library networks, cooperatives, and consortia was conducted by the American Library Association funded by the Institute of Museum and Library Services (IMLS) (Davis, 2007). Three others were conducted in 1977–1978 (Eckert, 1982); 1985–1986 (King & Griffiths, 1987), and a 1997 survey by the U.S. Department of Commerce, Bureau of Census, for the National Center for Education Statistics (1997). One issue faced by all of these surveys is what constitutes a consortium; this is addressed in the report by Davis. The survey explored the characteristics of network participants, types of services provided, sources of revenue, expenditures, staffing, priorities, service jurisdiction, and so on. The average operating revenues were $2.69 million for the 145 respondents. Expenditures ranged from about $40,000 to $51 million.

The rapid growth of electronic-based consortia services is not unique to the U.S. and U.K. (Anglada & Comellas, 2002). Anglada and Comellas discuss the advantages and disadvantages of consortia-provided site licenses and argue for differential pricing based on several indicators of size of universities (see Hahn [2005] and Van Ordel & Born [2009] for arguments against differential pricing).

A survey of consortia (King & Xu, 2002b) showed some differences between U.S. and non-U.S. consortia. For example, those in the U.S. had much higher average budgets (i.e., $45 million vs. $640,000) but lower budgets per member ($52,000 vs. $64,000). At the time of the survey a higher proportion of non-U.S. consortia were providing electronic-related services (83 percent vs. 66 percent).

Key Perspectives, Ltd. (2002) conducted a library consortia and publisher study of the Big Deal. They concluded that most library consortia have formed only within the past five years and most publishers formed sales packages during the same time. Negotiations were often very time consuming. The Big Deal fulfilled its promise to make more information accessible to users but a large problem (at that time) was the unresolved issue of usage data provision.

Consortia licenses offer many advantages, Taylor-Roe (1997), Okerson (2000), Grimshaw (2000), and Friend (2002) note; disadvantages are also mentioned by Frazier (2001) and Friend (2002). Because licenses cover bundles of electronic journals, the unit cost per journal is reduced (Kyrillidou & Bland, 2008). On the other hand, some of the titles may not be relevant to users and, when a library enters into several licenses, there often is duplication of titles. Yet, evidence suggests that the expanded library collections have increased the number of article readings by faculty (Tenopir & King, 2000). Frazier (2001, online) says that Big Deal licenses "bundle the strongest with the weakest titles, the essential with the non-essential" and "the library cannot continue to receive the titles it most needs unless it continues to subscribe to the full package." Friend (2002) points out that different forms of purchasing deals are suitable for different libraries. Publishers benefit from licenses by expanding readings and citations to their journals, bringing greater and faster market penetration, and reducing promotional costs (Grimshaw, 2000; Inger, Kusma, & Allen, 2000).

Cox and Cox (2008) provide information about publisher and consortia arrangements. The 2003 to 2008 surveys suggest that commercial publishers are much more likely to make sales to consortia than not-for-profit publishers, perhaps because many not-for profits publish few journals and, therefore, have less incentive to work with consortia. There has been a shift to three-year agreements, with those for six years or more becoming obsolete, and the use of price caps is more widespread. Primary Research Group, Inc. (2008) reports that 48.4 percent of their journal spending is through consortia deals.

Bergstrom and Bergstrom (2004b) contend that university site licenses are beneficial to scholars when journals are published by nonprofit organizations so as to maximize subscriptions and recover average costs (i.e., the net benefits to the scientific community are larger than if sold only by subscriptions). The opposite is true when a journal is priced to maximize profits.

The problem with negotiations was ultimately resolved by the development of licensing procedures (e.g., Okerson, 1999) and COUNTER was created to deal with the usage issue (Shepherd, 2007). A study conducted by Nicholas and Huntington (2002) examined the consequences of licenses and the Big Deal through analysis of web log data. They used usage logs to discover changes occurring in information-seeking behavior.

In a controversial study, Sanville and Winters (1998) showed that the OhioLINK big deal arranged with Academic Press and Elsevier resulted in about 50 percent of downloads being for articles in journals not held in print in the libraries. Their findings were disputed by Davis (2002), who reexamined the OhioLINK data. Scigliano (2002) conducted a cost-benefit analysis in Canadian libraries that showed significant net savings for patrons through site licenses.

Economic Metrics and Methods

Much of the prior economic discussion focuses on cost; however, economic analyses of the scholarly journal system also depend on a variety of other metrics and methods. Economic metrics and methods are discussed in this review of scholarly journal economics because the various metrics play a major role in research, participant decisions, and policy making. Part of this discussion involves the strengths and weaknesses of metrics and methods. The approaches that seem to dominate much of the literature are citation analysis and impact factors. In addition to citations, other use metrics are also employed such as amount of time spent reading, downloads, and deep log analysis. Some strengths and weaknesses of these metrics are discussed. Other metrics are also presented and a general framework for relating metrics is given.

Citation Analysis and Impact Factors

Perhaps the most frequently employed method and metric are citation analysis and impact factors, respectively. Citation counts currently come from Thomson Reuter's Web of Science or Web of Knowledge, Elsevier's Scopus, CiteSeerX, and Google Scholar. Several studies have compared these methods. Cope and Kalantzis (2009a) express some concern with citation counts and impact factors in that they lack validity and reliability (citing Pellegrino, Chudowsky, & Glasov, 2001). Kostoff (1998), for example, provides an extensive examination of the many uses of citations and the problems with using citations for evaluating research. He questions the validity of citation counts when there are so many different reasons for citing articles. Citations do not measure the ultimate utility of knowledge (see also Quandt, 2003). They tend to value quantity over quality and devalue lightly cited articles, but low citation may be a function of potential audience size rather than intrinsic value (see also King & Tenopir, 2008).

Hundreds of studies dating back to the 1960s involve citation counts (see King et al., 1981), mostly using Institute for Scientific Information (ISI) data. Approaches to studying journal impact factors include the Eigenfactor (Bergstrom, 2007), which ranks journals; the h-index, which ranks scientific output within a discipline (Cronin & Meho, 2006; Glänzel, 2006; Hirsch, 2005); the y-factor, based on a combination of citations and PageRank algorithms (Bollen, Van de Sompel, Hagberg, & Chute, 2009); and others (Schreiber, 2008; Vorndran & Botte, 2008).

Many studies have employed impact factors to compare commercial and non-commercial publishing (e.g., Barschall, 1986, 1988; Bergstrom & Bergstrom, 2004a, 2006) and subscription and open access publishing models (e.g., Craig, 2006; Eysenbach, 2006; Hajjem, Harnad, & Gingras, 2005; Harnad & Brody, 2004; Hitchcock, 2006; Moed, 2007).

Craig and Ferguson (2009) also discuss alternative impact measures and compare three measures across ten journals: impact factor, Eigenfactor, and SCImago Journal Rank Indicator (based on Scopus data). The authors conclude that: "Whatever it is that each metric is measuring, it appears not to be the same thing" (pp. 182–188).

Harnad and Brody (2004) suggest that the way to test the impact of OA is not to compare the citation impact factors of OA and non-OA journals, but to compare the citation counts of individual OA and non-OA articles appearing in the same non-OA journals. They then present data to support their argument.

A comparison of citation counts for articles published in the *Journal of the American Society for Information Science and Technology* in 1985 and 2000 found that, for articles published in 2000, Google Scholar provided higher citation counts than either Web of Science or Scopus (the two are about the same) (Bauer & Bakkalbasi, 2005). For the 1985 articles, Web of Science provided the largest citation counts, but the results were not statistically significant.

One problem with citation counts and impact factors is that they can be measured only several years after publication. Brody and Harnad (2006) studied whether web usage statistics could be used to predict later citation impact. They found a significant and sizeable correlation (0.4) between the citations and download impact of articles in physics and mathematics. They believe the correlation could be even higher because they were unable to link the two observations automatically.

Pringle (2007) addresses some issues with regard to the Journal Impact Factor (JIF) and how it and other metrics can be applied in funding decisions, supporting library concerns, and measuring the value of journals for publishers. Nisonger (2004) discusses several aspects of impact factors. The criticisms include: (1) errors in the ISI database, (2) data not available for humanities and some science journals, (3) time lag between publication and use, (4) journal self-citations are included, (5) geographic bias, (6) cronyism, (7) both positive and negative citations counted, (8) not applicable to non-research journals, and (9) database of limited size. Nevertheless, Nisonger contends that it is a valid tool, if used appropriately, for journal collection management decisions.

One criticism of citation counts and impact factors is that they might not reflect the overall usage of journals or articles. Bollen and colleagues (2009) address the effects of community characteristics on assessments of scholarly impact from usage. Usage impact factor rankings are calculated from usage datasets of services of several universities in the California State University system. These rankings are compared with the ISI Impact Factor. The correlation appears to be stronger with larger communities of students and faculty.

According to Crossick (2007), citation analysis is a problem in the arts and humanities because Web of Knowledge does not offer sufficient coverage. In the 2001 Research Assessment Exercise (RAE), 52 percent of philosophy publications were in journals covered by Web of Knowledge; 40 percent of library and information management outputs were covered, and most other subjects had less than 30 percent coverage. Adams (2007) cites similar problems in science. Citation analysis may not be appropriate for all disciplines; for example, Vorndran and Botte (2008, p. 3) indicate that "the diversity of publication channels and strategies, as well as the national, cultural, and linguistic orientation of educational sciences create barriers which make it inappropriate to apply the citation analysis method on educational scholarly publications." Thus new indicators are needed. Cope and Kalantzis (2009a) state that only 76 percent of articles cited in the ecology literature support the claim being made for them and that only about 20 percent of cited papers are read (based on misprinted citations) (Todd & Ladle, 2008).

Craig and Ferguson (2009) feel that ranking journals, individuals, research groups, and institutions by the quality and quantity of their output in peer-reviewed articles is ill-advised for a number of reasons. There are substantial differences in communication modes among disciplines and in the coverage of citation databases. Review articles tend to be more frequently cited. The obsolescence of the literature means that older articles are less likely to be cited, making citation analysis suspect when conducted over short periods. Journals with a higher impact factor will attract more manuscripts.

Use Metrics and Methods

Most past studies (as early as the 1960s) that examined reading did so from the perspective of time spent reading (King & Tenopir, 2001). More recently, the amount of reading has been observed from surveys of researchers in universities, other settings, and association membership. Liu (2003) has observed growth in journal literature, using the number of pages produced per year as the key metric. Houghton, Steele, and Henty (2003) find that 82 percent of scholars surveyed in Australia are reading more articles. King, Boyce, Montgomery, and Tenopir (2003) also note an increase in reading, as do Tenopir, King, and Bush (2004) and Tenopir, King, Boyce, Grayson, and Zhang (2003). Boyce, King, Montgomery, and Tenopir (2004) examined how electronic journals have affected patterns of use, discussing how print has been displaced and the "significance of the shift from journals to separates" (Rowlands, 2007, p. 375). Some studies, however, have found that the advent of electronic journals has actually increased overall usage, including print usage (Siebenberg, Galbraith, & Brady, 2004). Other studies show that user behavior varies dramatically by reader discipline (Standing Committee for Research on Academic Libraries, 2008).

A 2003 report for the Council on Library and Information Resources (CLIR) looked at over 200 research publications published between 1995 and 2003 that focused on user studies of electronic library resources. Many research methods were used in these studies, "including observation, surveys, interviews, experiments, and transaction log analysis" (Tenopir, Hitchcock, et al., 2003, online). Rowlands (2007) updated this work in a comprehensive review.

Wang's (2001) *ARIST* chapter provides an extensive overview of the different methodologies available for user studies. Tenopir (2003, p. 14) also briefly reviews the history of user studies in information retrieval, describing how later studies fall into basically two categories: the "micro/holistic approach" and the "macro/longitudinal approach." Holistic studies seek to "develop models of the total process of human interaction with information systems" and longitudinal studies "often look at changing patterns over time to help predict the future" (p. 14). The two main methods of inquiry can be boiled down to "observing and asking" (p. 16). The article also notes that what people actually do is more telling than what they say they do or prefer and that "Well-designed human studies include both quantitative and qualitative data gathering and analysis" (p. 16).

Cope and Kalantzis (2009a) indicate that download metrics may be better than citation counts because they are proxies for reading for all purposes. However, downloads do not show that an article is actually read, that it is the one searched for, or whether researchers come back to the same article multiple times.

Nicholas, Huntington, and others at CIBER have conducted a number of studies using log analysis of actual use of electronic full-text databases. As of 2006 they had conducted studies of Blackwell Synergy, Science Direct, Emerald Insight, Oxford University Press (OUP), and OhioLINK. They demonstrated repeatedly that electronic journals are extensively used and that use has extended well beyond subscribers. For example, the Emerald Insight study showed that two-thirds of visitors are non-subscribers to journals (Nicholas, Huntington, & Watkinson, 2003).

Open access and search engines increased OUP journal downloads 213 percent in the space of one year (Nicholas & Huntington, 2006). The Synergy study showed that half a million people used the site, viewing about 5 million journal items during a single month (Nicholas, Huntington, & Watkinson, 2005). With the OhioLINK study (Nicholas, Huntington, Dobrowolski, et al., 2006; Nicholas, Huntington, & Jamali, 2006), 5,872 journals available in a month (October 2004) were surveyed and 5,193 were viewed when only articles were available (5,868 were viewed when content lists, abstracts, and articles were available). The usage of journals was highly skewed (4 percent were used once, 59 percent used 21 or more times). During this time, 319,000 full-text articles were viewed. The Science Direct study (Nicholas, Huntington, & Jamali, 2006) showed that shorter articles were viewed online but only the abstract was read. Nicholas and Huntington (2006) concluded that many more people are using electronic journals (than print journals in the past), many of these are occasional users, and open access caters to these users.

CIBER (Oxford University Press, 2006) studied one OUP journal, *Nucleic Acids Research*, to examine the impact of transferring to open access. The study sought to establish whether the change led to an increase in usage and reached the kinds of people that OA aspires to reach (i.e., those who could not afford subscriptions or who did not belong to institutions able to negotiate big deals). A 30-month deep log analysis showed that an increase of 140 percent in use was attributable to opening the site to search engines; the move to OA had only a small influence, increasing usage further (about 7 to 8 percent). There was an increase in new users, many from Eastern Europe. From January 2003 through June 2005 there were 1.5 million users and 7.5 million search sessions (including those by robots). The methods are discussed in great detail in the report.

Saxby (2006) provides another perspective on the study of *Nucleic Acids Research* reported by CIBER (Oxford University Press, 2006). Much of this report deals with current and past issues with the journal. Of interest here is their OA pricing policy. In 2006 charges were $950 per article for authors based at institutions with memberships in the journal and $1,900 for others.

More recently, CIBER (Nicholas, Rowlands, Huntington, Clark, & Jamali, 2009) surveyed readers for RIN to assess the use, value, and impact of electronic journals in ten universities and research institutions. The study combined data from 1,400 Science Direct and 61 Oxford journals and, using log analysis methods, correlated the database with library indicators and institutional information. Some findings are as follows:

- U.K. university researchers and students downloaded almost 102 million articles in 2006–2007 at a direct cost of £80 per download.

- In three years total use more than doubled.

- Use patterns vary appreciably among disciplines.

- There is a strong correlation between page views and articles published in institutions.

- Levels of usage are closely related to levels of expenditure and money is being spent efficiently at the U.K. level.

- There is a tentative link between electronic journal consumption and research outcomes.

Many studies of time spent and/or amount of reading of articles by professionals have been done. In the past libraries have relied on in-library counts of journals reshelved and/or articles photocopied as indicators of use. Bollen and colleagues (2009) point out the weaknesses in this method: (1) physical library visitors are unlikely to be representative of the community of library (and non-library) users, (2) journals can be taken from shelves for many reasons (by mistake and serendipitous curiosity), (3) reshelving provides no information on user interests or motivation, and (4) usage of individual articles cannot be determined.

Citation counts are sometimes used to draw conclusions about reading. In an exhaustive study using a database of over 34 million articles, Evans (2008, p. 395) found that, although actual numbers of citations are increasing, "as more journal issues came online, the articles referenced tended to be more recent, fewer journals and articles were cited, and more of those citations were to fewer journals and articles." Ironically, "Searching online is more efficient and following hyperlinks quickly puts researchers in touch with prevailing opinion, but this may accelerate consensus and narrow the range of findings and ideas built upon" (p. 395).

A growing number of studies examine total reading of journals or individual articles. King and colleagues (2006) reviewed the strengths and weaknesses of such methods and metrics:

- Citation to articles. It is relatively inexpensive when citation data are available. However, the act of citing involves a very small proportion of readers (see also King & Tenopir, 2001) and readings (see also Tenopir, King, Edwards, & Wu, 2009). One issue is the relationship of citation counts to actual reading. Tenopir, Love, Park, Wu, Kingma, and King (2010) show that for every article cited, many more are read. In fact, in eight universities worldwide, faculty members estimate reading more than twenty articles for each one they cite. These ratios were also observed in the 1970s (King et al., 1981).

- Electronic hits and downloads. They are inexpensive to observe in many venues. They may or may not capture actual reading, but they ignore reading from print versions (still extensive for personal subscriptions) and there are no means of assessing the outcome from reading. The same issues occur with log analysis unless observations are also conducted.

- Survey of total amount of reading divided by number of articles published. This expensive means depends on the ability to gain statistically valid estimates of a population of readers, average reading per professional, and an accurate number of articles published (adjusted by age of reading). This method has been used for the reading of science journals in the U.S. (King et al., 1981; Tenopir & King, 2000).

- Survey using tables of contents. This method involves sending journals' tables of contents to a relevant sample and asking whether each article is read. This method is relatively accurate and precise; and it overcomes some weaknesses of the other survey approaches. However, adjustments need to be made for projecting reading beyond the period of time the survey is in the field. Non-response and other kinds of survey bias may come into play. It is also relatively expensive. Examples include Garvey and Griffith (1963) for several fields of science; King, McDonald, and Olsen (1978) for worldwide cancer researchers; and Tenopir, King, Clarke, Kyoungsik, & Xiang (2007) for worldwide pediatricians.

Other Metrics and Methods

In the U.K., RAE is a formal assessment of the quantity and quality of research outputs by university faculty members. The primary purpose is to produce quality profiles of institutional research activity. Funding bodies will use this information to allocate their grant funding (RAE2008, 2008).

Adams (2007) provides a brief history of the RAE and potentially related bibliometric metrics. The RAE was designed to provide a more selective rationale for allocating funds based on expert ratings of research. The research selectivity exercise was first conducted in 1986 and has been repeated periodically since then. Critical data available to peer assessors are research outputs of faculty, including journal articles, books, chapters, conference proceedings, or even art or video. By the fifth such exercise some were questioning the cost and credibility of peer review, and the government began to look for "something a little harder, a little more quantitative, and a little more transparent" with bibliometrics as an option (Adams, 2007, p. 189).

Adams (2007) expressed some concern with bibliometrics, and his organization (Evidence, Ltd.) analyzed the impact of RAE2001 outputs in biology. He found a broad relationship between peer-reviewed RAE grade and bibliometric impact but also found considerable residual variance. He concluded that the design of valid metrics remains unclear and that researchers will need more relevant, sound information to enable them to make proper judgments.

Harnad (2009a) supports the idea of devising a rich and diverse battery of metrics of research productivity, performance, and impact (including citations, co-citations, downloads, tags, growth/decay metrics). However, he believes such metrics can be correlated and cross-validated with expert judgments such as those provided in the RAE. At issue is whether metrics can substitute for costly and time-consuming expert rankings in the retrospective assessment of published, peer-reviewed research for either submitted papers or research proposals.

Bjørk, Roos, and Lauri (2008) estimated the annual volume of peer-reviewed scholarly articles and the number available through open access as of 2006: about 1,350,000 articles in 23,750 journals. Of these, about 8.1 percent are OA author-pays articles and 11.3 percent are published articles, available as copies deposited in digital repositories or home pages (author self-archives); in total, 19.4 percent or 262,000 articles are OA. Bjørk and colleagues describe how these figures were established.

Mabe and Amin use data from *Ulrich's* to project the growth rate of journals at about 3.36 percent per year recently (1977 to about 2000) but down from 4.35 percent in the 1945 to 1977 era (Mabe, 2003; Mabe & Amin, 2001). Mabe and Amin (2001) suggest several reasons for the change over the years and show relationships among numbers of journals, articles, and scientists and engineers (from 1981 to 1995) with articles slightly outpacing both journals and scientists and engineers in the latter years.

Tenopir and King (2000) show a similar result from 1960 to 1995 for U.S. science journals and for journals worldwide. They also searched *Ulrich's* web in 2009 using Boolean searches from 2003 to 2008 to establish trends in different types and format of journals (Table 7.8) (Tenopir & King, 2009).

Table 7.8   Trend in number of journals (2003 and 2008) (Tenopir & King, 2009)

	2003	2008	5-year change (%)
Active (all)	175,639	219,774	25.1
Active AND online	33,393	56,885	70.4
Active AND academic/scholarly	39,565	61,620	55.7
Active AND refereed	23,231	24,059	3.6
Active AND academic/scholarly/refereed	17,649	23,973	35.8
Active AND online AND refereed	12,575	15,668	24.6

The numbers in the table row "active AND academic/scholarly AND refereed" are in line with Mabe (2003) and Bjørk and colleagues (2008). For the 1960 to 1995 trend, a *science journal* is defined as a primary vehicle for communicating information and research results, often employing peer review or refereeing processes to aid in screening and editorial control. U.S. science journals include publishers designated by *Ulrich's* as having a presence in the U.S. (although some are primarily located elsewhere). Results are shown in Table 7.9 (King et al., 1981; Tenopir & King, 2000):

The average page length of articles increased from 7.41 in 1965 to 13.35 in 2007. The ten-year trend in journal growth decreased from 1965 to 1975 (38.7 percent) to 1985 to 1995 (17.8 percent). However, growth in the number of articles over these periods fell much less, 62.7 percent and 52.5 percent respectively, perhaps reflecting the increase in article length.

Houghton and Sheehan (2009) present their method for calculating the returns to R&D of enhanced access to research outputs. In the case of Australia, they posit a potential 25 percent citation advantage from open access and calculate a 20 percent social return to publicly funded R&D or an AUD 165 million per annum in increased returns to government expenditures on R&D and AUD 111 million return to higher education expenditures on R&D. This economic approach has been applied in the U.K., the Netherlands, and Denmark (Houghton, 2009b).

It is difficult to compare alternative publishing models such as licenses, full-text databases, and open access through institutional repositories because of the many options available. Beckett and Inger (2006, p. 1) employ "conjoint analysis," which forces respondents to

Table 7.9 Trend in number of U.S. published journals and articles (1960–1995) (King et al., 1981; Tenopir & King, 2000)

Year	Number of Journals	Number of Articles	Articles/ Journals
1960	2,815	208,300	74
1965	3,010	217,400	72
1975	4,175	353,700	85
1985	5,750	546,000	95
1995	6,771	832,800	123

choose among levels of attributes of services. Attributes of articles that were considered in terms of their relative importance were quality (high, medium, low); cost (free, quarter price, half, and full); recency (available upon publication, 6, 12, 14 months after publication); reliability of access (high, average, less than average); version availability (final published article, accepted, peer reviewed and copy edited, only peer reviewed, author's original manuscript); and proportion of articles available (100 percent, 80 percent, 60 percent, 40 percent). A total of 424 respondents were asked to choose among these attributes and levels: for example, to choose between high quality or free (see discussion in the section on OA author-pays).

Research at Loughborough University LISU used several metrics involving trends in prices of biomedical and social science journals between 2000 and 2006 for eight commercial publishers and three university presses (White & Creaser, 2007). Trend analysis was performed using five basic metrics: median journal price, average and median price per page, median impact factor, and median price per point of impact factor. Correlation analyses were done on prices and number of pages per title, number of pages and price per page, and price and impact factor.

Productivity gains attributed to electronic journal publishing can be questioned depending on what is meant by productivity (Quandt, 2003): (1) a journal/article can be created with less labor or less total-factor involvement; (2) the content can be delivered to the end-user in a more efficient manner (faster, more convenient, etc.) and preserved for posterity in a more efficient manner; or (3) teaching, learning, and research become more productive (see Griffiths & King [1993] and Tenopir & King [2000] for examples). These questions have been addressed in different ways. Quandt discusses in great detail the advantages and disadvantages of electronic journals in the future and of alternative pricing structures.

Holmstrom (2004) explores examples of the cost per article reading (CPR) and suggests a way of calculating CPR from electronic downloads. He gives several illustrations of cost per use including: (1) extreme examples from the University of Wisconsin-Madison Libraries where cost per use ranges from $8.26 to $1,472.50 (*Journal value project*, 2005); (2) an analysis of licensing of *Annual Review Online* (Scigliano, 2002) where CPR ranges from $0.21 to $13.45; (3) after Drexel University transitioned to an almost entirely electronic journal collection, King and Montgomery (2002) estimated CPR to be $3.04; (4) Cox (2003) estimated CPR to be $7.28 for Emerald journals and $6.11 for the Institute of Physics Publishing. Holmstrom mentions that HighWire Press specifies article downloads as HTML *and* PDF, but implies that sometimes readers download HTML to PDF, which is double counting. He suggests adjusting by 25 percent. He calculates CPR for BioMed Central open access articles downloaded at the University of Helsinki. These cost $6,243 and received 2,126 uses, for a cost per use of $2.94. However, adjusting the 2,126 downloads by 25 percent reduces the figure to 1,594.5 readings per year and gives a $3.92 article CPR (i.e., university cost per articles read).

A telephone interview with 450 researchers and librarians identified gaps in then-current (2007) discovery services (Jubb, Look, & Sparks, 2007). Some findings for journal articles are: (1) users cannot always access articles they have discovered; (2) users tend to use very few services and for different purposes; (3) researchers use discovery services for a wide range of resources (e.g., articles, books, conference proceedings); (4) they also rely on peers and networks of colleagues; (5) blogs are not yet highly used; and (6) there is little difference by levels of experience but a difference among disciplines. Online backfiles of journals are too short and more specialist search engines are needed.

Value and Return-on-Investment

One suggested metric is the *value* of an information product or service. Machlup (1997) suggests an approach to assessing the value of scholarly journal articles:

1. Purchase or exchange value or what is paid for content in one's time and/or money

2. Use value or the favorable consequences of reading and using the information content

With journal system services or products peoples' time is often the greatest contribution to purchase value. In fact, as shown earlier, the journal systems cost is dominated by the time researchers spend identifying, obtaining, and reading article content. They would not spend that time, if the content was not worth it.

Quality is an attribute of information for which readers are willing to pay and which, in turn, leads to favorable consequences. Publishers contribute to quality through *value-added* processes such as selection, managing peer review, editing, and distribution platforms (Mabe & Amin, 2002; Rowlands & Nicholas, 2006).

Contingent valuation is an economic method used to assess benefits of non-priced goods and services (e.g., journals, libraries, and information services) by examining the implication of not having the good or service. One approach to contingent valuation is to ask readers to think back to the source of information read and where they would obtain the information if the source were not available. Some would not bother, but many would and, if so, they are asked about how much it would cost them in their time and money to use an alternative source. One can compare, as a ratio, the cost of using the alternative source to the one actually used. For example, with journals the ratio is 2.6 to one (King et al., 1981), with library journal collections about 2.9 to 3.3 to one (King, Tenopir, Choemprayong, & Wu, 2009; Tenopir & King, 2007), and 2.9 with special libraries (Griffiths & King, 1993).

In a sense, some of the scholarly journal system studies discussed earlier relied on the contingent valuation approach by comparing the current journal model with alternatives such as electronic-only publishing and OA (author-pays and self-archiving). Instead of ratios, the researchers make absolute cost number comparisons, such as that electronic-only publishing would save £X million over the current print subscription model (see Cambridge Economic Policy Associates, 2008; Houghton et al., 2006; Houghton, de Jonge, et al., 2009; Sheehan & Houghton, 2009).

Return-on-investment studies provide metrics for studying how investments in library ejournals bring returns to the institution. A study examining the use and outcomes of the University of Pittsburgh's print and electronic collections (King et al., 2004a) found that all readings by faculty and the current reader purchase cost (value) of using alternative sources other than library journal collection was $13.48 million. At the same time, the investment of cost to the University of Pittsburgh library collection was $3.43 million (King, Aerni, Brody, Herbison, & Knapp, 2004b). The net benefit of the collection was $10.05 million ($13.48 minus $3.43 million), so the ROI for the university library was 2.9 ($10.05/$3.43 million) (Tenopir & King, 2007).

Mezick's (2007) study demonstrated that library expenditures and the number of professional staff had a significant positive effect on student retention. Similarly, analyses (Jones, 2007) from publicly available online data from the National Center for Education Statistics showed that the top-ranked colleges (based on the 2004 *U.S. News & World Report* ranking) did indeed exhibit typically higher expenditures, greater book numbers, and higher staff numbers per student.

Holmstrom (2004) provides another approach to ROI, where return is measured by downloads and investment is the subscription fee. However, he is concerned that comparisons of traditional reader-pays publishing and OA using downloads need to take into account the downloads of a journal/article over time. He gives an example for Academic Press articles published in 1998 and gives the downloads of the articles for five years.

Research Information Network (2009) and Nicholas and colleagues (2009) analyzed past research on the use, value, and impact of electronic journals. One set of findings is that spending on ejournals is linked to more use and, in turn, better research outcomes: "more usage linked to the number of papers published, number of Ph.D. Awards, and income from research grants and contracts" (Research Information Network, 2009, online).

These ROI models focus primarily on cost savings rather than income generation. Prior to 2008, no methods offered a way to measure an academic library's role in generating grant income for the university. Consequently, researchers at the University of Illinois at Urbana-Champaign (UIUC) adapted an ROI method used in corporate libraries to the academic library environment, and conducted a pilot study to determine the ROI of the UIUC library (Luther, 2008). Tenopir and colleagues (2010) proposed that ROI value could be calculated through the relationship between the library and the grant income generated through its use.

General Metric Framework

Most of the metrics mentioned previously address specific situations and applications. King, Tenopir, Montgomery, and Aerni (2003) describe a framework that combines frequently used specific metrics into sets of derived metrics. The framework begins by establishing system measurement perspectives such as service provider (e.g., a library, publisher), user (e.g., reader), community served (e.g., a university, field of science), and all of society (e.g., national, global). Specific metrics can be established for each perspective. For example, *service provider* metrics include *input resources* (e.g., library staff, publisher editors) including their cost and attributes (e.g., competencies of staff) and *output* (e.g., number of journals processed in a library, articles published) with amount and attributes of output (e.g., electronic vs. print journals, quality of articles). A *derived metric* is the relationship of input and output such as cost per unit (of electronic vs. print journals, of cited articles-impact factor) or unit per cost (i.e., productivity).

Specific user metrics include amount of use (e.g., number of readings or downloads or citations as proxy metrics) and factors affecting use (e.g., ease/cost of use, available alternatives, purpose of use). *Effectiveness* is a derived metric relating use and service provider *output* (e.g., readings per journal processed in libraries, readings per article published). Another derived metric is *cost-effectiveness* which relates service provider *input* and *use* such as cost per use (cost of electronic vs. print journals processed per reading, publishing cost per reading, download, or citation).

Another specific metric is outcomes or consequences of using information (e.g., time saved, improved learning, productivity, quality of work, timeliness of work); effects on community goals (e.g., university teaching or research, society membership); and higher order effects. A derived metric is *impact*, which relates use to outcomes (e.g., number of readings resulting in reader time saved).

A final derived metric is *cost-benefit*, a sort of "accounting" of favorable outcomes (benefits) compared with unfavorable outcomes (costs) of some changes that might occur. For example, with library migration to electronic collections the benefits could be: reduced input costs, increased collection size, increased performance cost per title, increased reading, increased cost effectiveness (cost per reading), and favorable impact in time saved by readers. On the other hand, there are unfavorable outcomes (costs) such as the library cancelling some needed print journals. In this case the reduced input cost of processing these journals is a benefit, but this might result in a lower performance for processing print journals due to economies of scale; reading from the print collection is lost, meaning the reader might go elsewhere to obtain articles at a greater cost and outcomes could be diminished. King, Tenopir, and colleagues (2003) give examples of the framework from special and academic libraries (Griffiths & King, 1993; King et al., 2004b).

Open Access Economics

There is a great deal of interest in the provision of open access to scholarly research articles, either through publications in OA journals (sometimes funded by author-side payments) or by making copies of articles (often in a pre-publication version) available on author websites and in institutional or subject-based repositories. In the latter case, publisher policies sometimes require an embargo period of six or twelve months following publication before articles can be entered into or made available from repositories. Open access publishing can be defined in several ways (Houghton, Rasmussen, et al., 2009; Suber, 2006); AMERICAN-SCIENTIST-OPEN-ACCESS-FORUM@listserver/sigmaxi.org includes exhaustive discussions.

The ultimate objective of OA in any form is to make article content more widely available at less cost to the journal system with the result that the value of the information is enhanced because of its increased downstream use. In addition, OA brings an author's work to a potentially wider audience. Some attempts have been made to argue that OA benefits all system participants including funders, publishers, libraries, and readers. Houghton, Rasmussen, and colleagues (2009) succinctly clarify what is involved by quoting: "The key question is whether there are new opportunities and new models for scholarly publishing that would better serve researchers and better communicate and disseminate research findings" (Organisation for Economic Cooperation and Development, 2005, online).

There are, perhaps, hundreds of studies and reports of citation analysis and impact measures (in several forms) providing evidence that open access does improve article exposure. Some of this literature is presented here, although skeptics persist. Unfortunately, the entire body of relevant literature simply cannot be covered.

Davis, Lewenstein, Simon, Booth, & Connolly (2008) observed 1,619 articles from eleven journals to assess the effect of free access on article downloads and citations. They found that, in the first six months after publication, articles assigned to open access had 89 percent more full-text downloads, 42 percent more PDF downloads, and 23 percent more unique visitors (but fewer abstract downloads) than subscription access articles. Fifty-nine percent of open access articles were cited 9 to 12 months after publication compared with 63 percent of subscription access articles. The authors conclude that open access may reach more readers but offers no citation advantage in the first year of publication. Thus, the widely reported citation advantage from open access may be an artifact of other variables. Davis (2009b) also observed a trend from journals published in 2003 and 2007 that employ author-choice open-access models. There was a small (17 percent) increase in article citations and evidence to suggest that the open-access advantage declined by about seven percent per year from 32 percent in 2004 to 11 percent in 2007.

Regazzi (2004) discusses both author-pays open access and open access through author archives and institutional repositories. He suspects that most author-pays publishers (e.g., PLoS and BioMed Central) probably are not charging enough (in 2004) to cover their true costs. He suggests that commercial and other publishers are not against the concept of *free access* and mentions some publishers granting permission to self-archive, as well as Springer's announced "Open Choice," where authors can pay a fee from which the total revenue will be subtracted from subscription prices. He also argues that free access has always been available through interlibrary loan and in most public libraries that serve the entire public including scientists and other professionals (see also Griffiths & King [2008], which shows that 31 percent of public library use is educational and 14 percent is work-related, although not always related to scholarly communication).

Harnad (2009a, p. 128) gives an interesting evolution of open access. It starts with the Gutenberg era when what is termed a "toll booth" was erected between the document and the user; access was sold, with the publisher and author sharing the admission receipts. In the post-Gutenberg era of digital documents and online access, authors can now give away their writing, if they desire, although publishers and authors pretty much continue as they have in the past.

Authors have an incentive to maximize the use of their work and distribute free reprint copies of their articles (King et al. [1981] report that science authors averaged receiving 142 reprints or preprints from publishers, and they distributed 69 within the first year). This is done for many reasons including advancing their careers (see Bergstrom & Bergstrom, 2006). Author transfer of copyright to publishers that denies access to those who do not ultimately pay creates use barriers (which

Harnad [2009a, p. 129] calls a "Faustian bargain"). With digital documents and online access authors distribute their writing free (as with reprints) through email, self-archives online, and interoperable institutional repositories.

Harnad (2009c) claims that about 15 percent of the 2.5 million peer-reviewed articles published annually are made open access by authors. He believes that once all articles are made open access through author self-archiving, a question arises concerning the future of journal publishing, copyright, and peer review. He suggests that ultimately only peer review will survive. The cost of the process will include having an editor select the referees, adjudicate the referee reports and revisions, and manage online correspondence. This, he suggests, will lead author institutions to forego subscription fees for a peer review service fee per outgoing article, perhaps at one-third the current cost to the parent institutions.

Harnad (2009b) continues to believe that a universal green OA involving repositories will force a transition to gold OA author-pays, but refers to 1994 when he strongly advocated a universal green OA and was "convinced that the probability of universal green OA—spontaneous and unmandated—was so high in 1994 that it would be with us virtually overnight. Here we are, a decade and a half later, in 2009, and green OA is still only at about 15 percent, and only 39 of the planet's 10,000 universities have mandated green OA." A rare example of candor in our field!

Some funding agencies are mandating green open access (notably the U.S. National Institutes of Health and the U.K.'s Wellcome Trust) but the issue of mandates remains controversial. A 2010 report by the Scholarly Publishing Roundtable (2010, online) hosted by the U.S. House of Representatives, sought "to balance the need for increased access to scholarly articles with the need to preserve the essential functions of the scholarly publishing enterprise."

The Roundtable recommended green open access after an embargo period for final published articles that are products of U.S. federal grant funds. The members based their recommendation on five shared principles: (1) peer review is critical; (2) adaptable business models are necessary; (3) scholarly publications should be more accessible with improved functionality; (4) archiving and preservation are essential; and (5) research results need to be made available in ways that allow creative reuse and interoperation.

Bergstrom and Lavaty (2007) studied tables of contents for 33 economic journals and 16 political science journals in an attempt to find freely available online versions of each article. The most cited economic articles had 90 percent availability and less cited ones 50 percent availability. Only 30 percent of political science articles were freely available.

Stern (2005) raises some economic concerns with open access and claims that OA will result in far fewer commercial revenue sources and many lost academic library subscriptions. Libraries will be asked to cover the entire revenue base; it also means lost subsidies to support long-term archives, and would create a system more like HighWire, with reliance on annual subscriptions to support OA infrastructures. Therefore: (1) OA based on author-pays will reduce the number of subscriptions and problems with maintaining the existing revenue base, and (2) OA without author-pays will also reduce the number of subscribers.

The Kaufman-Wills Group, LLC (2005) surveyed society and other journal publishers and also conducted in-depth interviews with publishers to assess the then-current subscription and full open access environment. They received numerous revealing positive and negative statements about subscription-based access versus full open access; assumptions made about OA; economics of OA; and issues concerning editing, production, and subscriptions and licensing. Conclusions are: (1) it is too early (in 2005) to tell if full OA is a viable business model, (2) scholarly journal publishing is in an unprecedented mode, and (3) peer review and copy editing may be less rigorous with full open access journals.

OA Author-Pays (Gold)

Bergstrom and Bergstrom (2004a) describe the competitive nature of two publishing markets for readers and for authors. In subscription-based publishing the journal market is primarily for readers but journals must also compete for authors who want their articles published in prestigious journals. In the author-pays publishing model the primary market is for authors, with readers being important because authors wish to broaden their readership and increase citations to their work.

Shieber (2009) proposes an interesting twist to the author-pays model. He suggests that funding agencies and universities make a compact to ensure that all articles resulting from government funded research and all other articles written by university faculty or staff have author payment fees covered by them. His argument is this: "The crucial underwriters [of journal costs] are universities and funding agencies. Universities underwrite closed-access journals through the institutional subscriptions that they purchase. Funding agencies do so through the overhead charges that they provide to grantee institutions, a sizable (and specifically negotiated) fraction of which is applied to support the libraries and thereby subscription fees again. Because both universities and funding agencies are (directly or indirectly) underwriting journal subscriptions, both should be involved in underwriting article-processing fees for open-access journals as well" (online).

There are three conditions that must be met for the proposal to be successful:

- The processing fees must be non-fungible, that is, applicable only to open-access fees.

- The funds for processing fees from agencies should not come from the grant budget, but rather from a separate fund (e.g., from a new administration unit).

- Universities would commit funds for processing fees on behalf of all their authors including those reporting research not funded by grants.

Shieber then discusses ways to address issues such as placing potential caps on authors to prevent them from taking advantage of available funds for manuscript processing fees.

King (2010) goes even further, suggesting that the government fund the publishing of all science articles. This would have many advantages over other approaches even though it would add to the cost of funding articles that report government funded research. On the other hand, a significant number of scientists and medical practitioners do not have access to large library collections. Studies have shown that these professionals pay substantially more in their time and money to get needed information and often do not obtain it. King suggests that savings to professionals from 100 percent author payment is substantially higher than the additional cost to the government.

One important issue is whether commercial publishers can profitably participate in the author-pays model. Bergstrom and Bergstrom (2006) cite research which shows that the cost per page and cost per citation is much higher (as much as six times) for commercial journals than for nonprofit journals in six disciplines. They point out that buyers would not pay six times as much for cars because they can substitute one brand for another, but articles are different in that they are not substitutes for one another. Scientists seek not only the top articles to read, but also second and third rank articles as well. Thus, for a library, a second copy of a top journal is not a substitute for a second rank journal. Because of this feature of the market, commercial journals can survive even though their journals are less cost effective. Bergstrom and Bergstrom contend that the market for authors' inputs should be much more competitive because an author-pays journal that charges high fees is less likely to be competitive than one that charges low fees (if quality is considered equal). In this instance an author with two papers has no strong reason to publish one in each journal.

Bergstrom and Bergstrom also recognize that it is unlikely the entire market would switch to an author-pays scenario. They believe commercial publishers are unlikely to switch to the author-pays model because it would lead to greater competition and lower profits while societies will be reluctant if their surpluses have been particularly beneficial. Even so, they believe that the author-pays model can compete because evidence indicates that the model results in more citations than reader-pays and academic authors benefit in prestige and money from increased citations to their publications (e.g., for economists it was found that doubling one's citations increases one's salary 7 to 14 percent [Baser & Pena, 2003; Walker, 2004]). They do acknowledge, on the other hand, that increased readership will be in institutions that may be of less interest to authors. They conclude that internet access will favor the author-pays model depending on how much scholars care about broad distribution of their writings. Tenopir and King (2000) point out that three-quarters of science readings in the U.S. are in non-academic settings and are extremely valuable to these readers.

Rae and Rowland (2006) also examined the potential for commercial open access publishing under the gold road to open access (i.e., the publication of OA electronic journals on the basis of toll-free access to readers everywhere). The results are based on an interview with a publisher that experimented with OA, one that had not, and a consultant. They came to the same conclusion as Bergstrom and Bergstrom (2006) and Waltham (2006), namely that a viable OA model for commercial publishers has yet to be found and further experimentation with complex fees and models is needed.

One set of issues regarding author-pays is lack of funds to cover payments. Schroter, Tite, and Kassem (2006) studied 377 responding medical journal authors and found that a large proportion of published research is not extensively funded and that many funded researchers do not have access to financial support at the time their papers are accepted for publication. For example, only 25 percent could withdraw money from a grant at the time of paper acceptance and the grant was closed 45 percent of this time. The authors also mention that non-externally funded research was largely supported through departmental resources or conducted on one's own time. This problem could be resolved through grant and/or additional funding, but warrants acknowledgment by funders, researchers, and publishers. The Scholarly Publishing Roundtable (2010) cites Outsell, Inc. (2009) and Ware and Mabe (2009) as showing that subscription payments continue to dominate the publishing business model (90 percent of current titles) with author-payment models accounting for most of the remainder.

Funding of research comes from many sources. University of Pittsburgh scientists reported the following sources of funds for research leading to their last published article (King, 2004): the university itself (35 percent), government (33 percent), industry (25 percent), and foundations (7 percent). However, this did not include the medical faculty, which is heavily federally funded. SQW Ltd. (2004) produced a 24-page review of costs and business models in scientific research publishing for the Wellcome Trust. The document consists of discussions with senior individuals and a literature review. In particular, the review examines the cost and other implications of subscriber-pays and author-pays business models. The report presents examples of fixed (first copy) costs per article and variable costs per article and compares the costs of subscriber-pays and author-pays for good-to-high quality and medium-quality journals. Unfortunately, when comparing these costs it is assumed that all author-pays publishing costs involve electronic-only publishing, which is biased toward author-pays. Also, the existence of personal subscriptions is largely ignored. The review discusses market issues, publishers' objectives, open archives, effects on library costs, and revenue sources. It also addresses the issue of how to deal with those who cannot pay with the author-pays model.

Examinations of open access through author-pays nearly all assume electronic-only publishing of open access and include the reduction of print costs as a contribution to the comparison of OA author-pays vs. traditional publishing of reader-pays. However, there is no compelling reason why the author-pays model could not be exactly the same as traditional publishing in terms of print distribution and access. Print personal subscriptions are still much preferred by faculty and medical practitioners even though electronic versions are available (Tenopir, King, Clarke, Kyoungsik, & Xiang, 2007; Tenopir, King, Edwards, & Wu, 2009).

Nearly all discussions of the advantages of open access accomplished by author-side payment to publishers focus on increased use (i.e., citations) of article content. However, little has been said in the literature about the consequences on the flow of funds among the system participants (King, 2006). In essence, a pot of funds is currently exchanged among participants (funders, authors, publishers, libraries and intermediaries, and readers) and will dramatically change with the author-pays model. That is, the overall amount in the pot will change very little but flow among participants will change drastically. If the proven objective of this model is to broaden exposure and use, the transfer of funds should not matter. On the other hand, change should not be made to this model without recognizing all consequences.

Davis (2009a), in a review of access to scientific literature submitted to the Scholarly Publishing Roundtable, concludes that (1) access to the scientific literature is improving, (2) access is essentially a non-issue for researchers in developing countries, and (3) more research is needed to establish if free access to scientific information is making a difference in non-research contexts (e.g., teaching, medical practice, industry, and government policy making) and how scientific documents are transmitted in informal sharing via peer-to-peer networks. Houghton, Rasmussen, and colleagues (2009) describe funding flows relating to (1) research funding, (2) research performance, (3) scientific and scholarly publishing, and (4) the study and application of knowledge. Each aspect has a diagram with monetary and in-kind flows, and the authors describe the potential for change among the participants. Cambridge Economic Policy Associates (2008) acknowledges that there are winners and losers because some sectors have authors who publish more than others. In the U.K., CEPA estimates that libraries in higher education would benefit by £128 million, but the U.K.'s contributions to publication fees would amount to £213 million, and the U.K. share of funding globally (by either subscription or author-pays) would rise from 5.2 to 7.0 percent.

They point out that the main beneficiaries would be other institutions that currently purchase journal subscriptions but are not major producers of research outputs (i.e., articles). Others have also addressed the consequences of most authors being in the academy (King, 2006; Morris, 2005).

Both positive and negative assessments of author-pays publishing are often based on impact. Davis (2006) argues that causal comparisons of OA and non-OA article impact must meet three conditions: (1) covariance, (2) temporal order (the hypothesized cause must precede the effect), and (3) the rejection of alternative explanations. He then gives two types of explanations for the observed increased impact of OA articles. One is that articles are often duplicated in different journals. Studies in the 1960s found that a typical research grant produced an average of up to eight articles (Garvey & Gottfredson, 1975). This may hold true today. Thus, OA articles may have greater research impact but OA may not be the cause. Another explanation Davis suggests for increased impact is self-promotion.

McCabe and Snyder (2004) examine the reader-pays and author-pays business models, particularly to determine which is better for society as a whole. In the near term, emergence of electronic journals may increase the profitability of the reader-pays model, but the author-pays model gives publishers much less market power because author decisions to choose journals with the lowest submission fees put pressure on publishers to lower fees.

According to Waltham (2005), the average first copy cost per journal is £135,000 (i.e., £550 per article) and support costs £94,000 for a total fixed cost of £229,000. The average variable cost is £135,000 or about £60 per subscription (2,263 average subscriptions per journal). If all content costs are borne by institutional subscribers they would be charged £338 (i.e., £278 for content and £60 for access). Author-pays would be charged an average of about £550 per article (i.e., £135,000 divided by 246 articles) plus some contribution to support costs. Note that the first copy costs of these journals range from £221 to £841 per article.

Waltham (2005) suggests that to cover the average online-only costs for a ten-page article and deliver the average surplus (i.e., profit) to their societies, the OA author fee per article (in 2004) would need to be £1,166. Some 15.6 percent of the libraries Primary Research Group, Inc. (2008) surveyed had paid a publisher (author) fee on behalf of an author from their institution. The average fee was $1,168 (maximum $10,000). One-third of universities paid such a fee. After reviewing publishing costs, Cambridge Economic Policy Associates (2008) estimated author fees to be about £1,525 for e-only publishing.

Clarke (2007) states that the cost of producing an ejournal article is about $3,400 for commercial journal publishers compared to $730 for an open access journal. Cope and Kalantzis (2009a) suggest that 67 percent of journals allow some form of self-archiving in repositories given a color code by SHERPA ROMEO: green (can archive preprint and postprint), blue (can archive final drafts and post-refereeing), yellow (can archive pre-refereeing draft), and white (archiving not permitted).

Cox and Cox (2008) say that 34 percent of publishers in 2008 are using fees paid on manuscript submission either by themselves or in combination with fees paid upon publication of the article. Of publishers charging author-pays, 66.7 percent are levied at the time of publication, 5.5 percent at submission, and 27.8 percent both. In 2008, the range of publication fees was: under $500 (15 percent of those charging authors), $500 to $1,000 (20 percent), $1,000 to $2,000 (40 percent), and $2,000 to $3,000 (25 percent). Submission fees are much lower. Some publishers offer the option of author-payment but when they do, the per article fee is higher, ranging from under $500 (5 percent) to $3,000 or more (12 percent). Only 18 percent of publishers offer discounts on submission or publication fees to authors from institutions that already subscribe to the journal to which the paper is submitted.

Primary Research Group, Inc. (2008) asked 45 libraries if OA would affect journal prices; 25 percent said OA already had, 45 percent said it eventually would, and 30 percent that it wouldn't have an impact.

The Public Library of Science (2004) provides an early overview of their practices describing how publishing activities are performed and how they arrived at costs for published research articles. They report a cost of $1,070 per article including electronic manuscript processing of about $200. Butler (2006) describes some of the PLoS history up to 2006 and how they may have underestimated publishing costs (see Public Library of Science, 2004), which caused some financial difficulty. However, they increased their author fees and introduced a new pricing strategy in 2008 (Public Library of Science, 2009). Now PLoS appears to be in better shape and Morrison claims that it is projected to publish 4,300 articles in 2009 and 8,000 in 2010.

Outsell, Inc. (2008) believes that funding agencies will see open dissemination of research results to be a measure of success, challenging traditional impact factors that emphasize publication of results in what is termed a quality journal. This may disrupt pricing policies of academic publishers and force them into selling peer review services separate from production services. In summary, "this suggests scholarly publishing will ultimately shift to a hybrid service model, with different aspects of the publishing processes monetized separately, rather than together under the current umbrella subscription model. However, it also suggests the potential for value-added enterprise services. So a hybrid deal with a large institution might include repository provision, peer review services, institutional content collation, and performance measurement. Ultimately, subscription models will prevail, but will focus on service, not on access" (online).

One focus of the Cambridge Economic Policy Associates (2008) study was author-side publication fees. They conclude that if 90 percent of all articles are made open access upon payment by authors or their representatives there would be total savings in the global costs of publishing, distribution, and access of £561 million, split almost equally between publishers and libraries. There would also be additional savings assuming electronic-only publishing.

Houghton, de Jonge, and colleagues (2009) conclude that in the U.K. the average savings of OA author-pays publishing is £813 per article over traditional subscriptions and £1,180 per article with self-archiving with overlay services (e.g., peer review, editing). This translates to national U.K. savings of £213 million per annum for OA publishing. Furthermore, with 20 percent social return to publicly funded R&D, a five percent increase in accessibility and efficiency would generate the following per annum increased returns: (1) £172 million to public sector R&D, (2) £124 million to higher education, (3) £109 million to government R&D, and (4) around £33 million to research councils (RCUK) competitive grants funded R&D. Similar results were obtained in the Australian study (Houghton et al., 2006).

Craig, Plume, McVeigh, Pringle, and Amin (2007) suggest that claims made that open access has greater citation impact may be based on insufficient evidence in comparing OA and non-OA article citation differences. They caution that comparisons of groups of journals may introduce bias among disciplines because the journals in the group vary in their importance (Zitt, Ramanana-Rahary, & Bassecoulard, 2005). They also imply a selection bias, noting that citations have a long half-life that is not fully taken into account in comparisons and that the increasing number of citations may introduce bias. They maintain that insufficient evidence exists to conclude that OA provides authors with a citation advantage (citing Moed [2007] in support).

Waltham's (2005, 2006) in-depth survey of nine learned publishers explored the implications of open access (author-pays) on business and pricing models. She examined the publishing costs per article and per page, revenue trends, subscription trends, and article submissions within an OA model. The key requirements for society journals to be financially sustainable with the OA model are that it must: (1) cover costs, (2) return a modest surplus, and (3) archive existing content. However, she concludes that the OA model as currently construed is unlikely to meet all of these needs "because the reduced costs of eliminating print versions are less than the lost revenue" (Waltham, 2005, p. 3).

Publishers could make up for loss of revenue in various ways. For example, Willinsky (2003) provides evidence that nonprofit associations could make up the potential loss of revenue due to open access through cost savings and other sources of revenue. He analyzes savings through 13 stages involving authors, editors, reviewers, readers, and others.

Dominguez (2006) examined three open access author-pays models to see how the cost to CERN compares with the current cost of library purchases. The first model studied was that implemented by the Institute of Physics (IOP). She concluded that publication costs for CERN under the IOP model would be at least nine times higher than subscribing to a specific journal (*Journal of High Energy Physics*). The Springer Open Choice model (see also Regazzi, 2004) appears to be more than five times more expensive for the journal *Hyperfine Interactions,* and the PLoS author fees and/or membership model also has a much greater cost to CERN. Of course, this is with a very small sample and a very special environment. Dominguez does spell out general positive and negative aspects of open access to authors.

OA Self-Archiving (Green)

Swan and Brown (2005) surveyed about 1,300 respondents who typically self-archive. Conclusions at that time were: (1) more than half have self-archived at least one article during the past three years in an institutional (or departmental) repository (20 percent), a subject-based repository (12 percent), or personal or institutional website (27 percent). However, growth in use has largely been in the former two: (2) post-prints (peer-reviewed) are deposited more frequently than preprints, (3) awareness remains low (71 percent remain unaware), (4) time and difficulty invested are barriers to use, and (5) most (81 percent) would comply with an employer or funder mandate to participate.

Legislation was introduced in which the U.S. federal government would require work supported by the National Institutes of Health to be made available online and free within 12 months of publication. Ten university presses publicly support the idea of archiving and free release of published scholarly articles. However, the Association of American University Presses supports open access as long as funding or business models are established that will maintain the investment required to protect older materials and support new ones (Jaschik, 2009).

Recently, Sutherland (2009) decried OA and internet-accessible writing as undermining traditional scholarly communication but Adams (2009) maintained that Sutherland misunderstood the goals of the Open Access movement.

Open access through repositories can be made part of an array of digitizing efforts by libraries. For example, one new kind of service libraries are considering is publishing. Hahn (2008) reports that 44 percent of 80 responding ARL member libraries indicated they are delivering publishing services and another 21 percent are planning to do so. About 90 percent of the publishing libraries produce journals (131 established titles, 81 new titles, and 53 titles under development). This effort is considered an integral part of service evolution involving digital repository development, digitization projects, digital humanities initiatives, development of learning objects, and digital preservation activities.

Fisher (2008) contends that publishing cost savings achieved by open access should make this model economically viable and sustainable. He describes in detail activities leading to costs such as peer review and editorial management, emphasizing that "neither authors nor reviewers nor editors (in most cases) contribute directly to costs" (online). He presents a table with out-of-pocket costs under three conditions and standard costs vs. optional costs. From this he concludes that traditional publishing is $4,000 per article compared with about $60 for open-source-based publishing and if one reduces costs substantially, the question of who pays (author or reader) becomes irrelevant.

The arXiv database is often cited as an example of an institutional repository that has been successful over time (since 1991). Davis and Fromerth (2007) set out to demonstrate the effect on citations of articles held in the database. They observed from an analysis of 2,765 articles published in four math journals that articles deposited in the arXiv received 35 percent more citations on average or about 1.1 citations per article. However, there was little evidence to support a universal open access explanation and the deposited articles received 23 percent fewer downloads from the publishers' websites (or 10 fewer per article) in all but the two years after publication.

Gentil-Beccot, Mele, and Brookes (2009) provide recent evidence of the citation advantage of articles deposited in arXiv in high-energy physics (HEP). Their study set out to answer three important questions: (1) Is there an advantage for scientists to make their work available through repositories, often in preliminary form? They conclude that online access to preprints creates an immense advantage in HEP. (2) Is there an advantage to publishing in open access journals? Publication in open access journals presents no discernable difference. (3) Do scientists still read journals or do they use digital repositories? Some evidence suggests that HEP scientists seldom read journals, preferring preprints instead.

Getz (2005a) reports that research universities in the U.S. spend $3.7 million on average for 10,000 academic journals (in 2002) plus $500,000 in processing and maintaining, or $420 per title and $10.54 per article assuming 40 articles per title (i.e., $9.23 publisher cost and $1.31 library cost). He goes on to demonstrate that shifting to digital publishing would save libraries about $0.80 per article. He then compares arXiv cost of $4 per article to $10,000 per article for print journals with 1,000 library subscriptions. Open access would save $0.93 per article.

Antelman (2004) provides evidence that freely available articles have greater research impact in four disciplines. She concludes (p. 379) that "across a variety of disciplines, open-access articles have a greater impact than articles that are not freely available."

Authors' awareness of and attitudes toward institutional repositories will clearly have an effect on their success. Watson (2007) surveyed authors at Cranfield University and found that having institutional repositories should encourage authors to deposit their work.

Beckett and Inger (2006) describe a conjoint method to rank attribute importance of services: quality (24 percent), cost (19 percent), recency (18 percent), reliability (14 percent), version availability (13 percent), and proportion of articles available. Each attribute level is analyzed against the others (e.g., high quality [13 percent] is preferred over free cost [7 percent]). The authors conclude that "importance of acquiring high quality content is likely to override other factors" (p. 1).

There is some concern among libraries that self-archiving preprints and/or postprints by journal authors might negatively affect library collection sizes and services. Ware (2006) addressed this problem by surveying a self-selected sample of 340 librarians (survey funded by ALPSP). The study addressed reasons for journal cancellations and how self-archiving might lead to cancellations. The principal reasons given for cancellation are that (1) faculty no longer require the journal, (2) low usage, and (3) price. Well behind these three factors in terms of importance are availability of contents via open access and availability through aggregations. Those concerned about OA were asked why and responded with these points: (1) concerns about long-term availability of free archives, (2) concerns about the completeness and integrity of the archives, (3) faculty demand for what they view as the real journal, and (4) preprints and postprints not seen as adequate substitutes for the final journal articles. Of concern to publishers is that 53 percent say that availability of OA archives is an important or very important factor in determining cancellations. Morris (2007) examines publisher attitudes toward OA institutional repositories and concludes that some revenue will be lost, and if journals are damaged financially the value-added processes could be lost to readers. However, Pinfield (2007) examines whether OA repositories and peer-reviewed journals can coexist and concludes that they are not necessarily in competition.

Repository Economics

Shreeves (2009) reports that, as of February 2009, of 539 publishers surveyed, 63 percent allow some form of self-archiving and 51 percent allow the postprint to be deposited (SHERPA/RoMEO, 2008); OpenDOAR service reports 179 disciplinary repositories and 1,082 institutional or departmental repositories from around the world. Shreeves finds some evidence of the effects repositories have on journal publishing but that it is unclear if they might supplant or change the journal as we know it.

Cope and Kalantzis (2009a, p. 20) claim that open access disrupts the traditional economic market: "More and more academics are taking it upon themselves to do this, legally or illegally, with or without reference to the publishing agreements they have signed."

Several studies have examined author awareness and attitudes toward institutional repositories (Watson, 2007). Bailey (2010) maintains an extensive and ongoing bibliography on the literature. In anticipation of forthcoming needs to deposit electronic journals in national institutional repositories and archives, Fox (2002) presents some estimated unit costs (2005–2006) for preprint CD-ROMS (£84.69) and ebooks (£38.73). Preservation costs are also given, but are not included here. Two studies (Phillips, 2005; Willer, Buzina, Holub, Zajec, Milinovic, & Topolscak, 2008) analyzed the processing time necessary to

Table 7.10 Examples of repository set-up and running costs (Swan, 2008)

	Set-up costs	Running costs
MIT DSpace, U.S.	$2.4–$2.5 million	$285,000
National University of Ireland, Maynooth	€ 20,000	€ 30,000
Queens QSpace CARL, Canada	CAN $52,065	CAN $50,000
SHERPA, Nottingham, U.K.	£3,900	£33,900

archive web resources (e.g., journal articles). The total time (including gathering, quality assurance, archiving, and cataloging) ranged from about three to five hours per item.

DRIVER (Digital Repositories Infrastructure Vision for European Research) is a joint collaboration among ten European partners. Swan (2008) defines repository services, describes the value chain ranging from registration to preservation, sets forth a typology for repositories (i.e., institutional, public sponsors, community, subscription, and commercial models) and provides answers to the following questions: Who pays? Pays what? For what? To whom? And why? (based on Clarke, 2007). She gives several examples of the set-up and running costs for repositories (see Table 7.10).

Houghton, Rasmussen, and colleagues (2009) cite four sources that report institutional repository costs (Bailey, 2006; Houghton et al., 2006; Swan, 2008; Universities U.K., 2007). From these they estimate costs for a publication-focused institutional repository to be in the range of £45,000–£275,000. These direct costs exclude time of senior management.

Wheatley, Ayris, Davies, McLeod, and Shenton (2007) discuss an ongoing LIFE project, which details activities necessary to budget or cost digital preservation over the lifetime of materials including electronic journals. In a PowerPoint presentation, Kenney (2005) gives a detailed cost model for preserving digital assets involving arXiv, now located at Cornell University. The model details the cost of resources input, processes involved, and outputs, yielding total and unit costs. Hendley (1998) conducted an extensive study of the costs of digital preservation for JISC.

Conclusions

A system approach to the economics of scholarly journal publishing takes into account all of the functions and all of the stakeholders in this complex interrelated system. Researchers are essential to the system in their roles as readers, authors, peer reviewers, and editors. They, along with libraries and consortia, are the main users of the system. The largest component of how they pay for this use and access is their time.

Publishers are the other main participant. Each participant performs basic system functions/activities that require resources such as time, equipment, facilities, paper, and so on.

The relationships among these stakeholders, functions, and activities have a direct bearing on the economics of scholarly publishing. In addition to time spent, traditionally, subscription-based models from libraries to publishers paid for the direct costs of the system and the distribution of journals. There are alternative payment models, notably author-pays open access. Self-archiving of published articles has its own economics as well as an impact on the overall economics of the wider system.

A variety of metrics for evaluating the system and changes to the system, including cost-benefit, contingent valuation, and return on investment, are helping to inform our understanding of the future of the scholarly journal system. These metrics take into account all aspects of the system and how the functions and stakeholders interrelate. Changes to the system should be informed by these various metrics and by analyzing the full system components.

Acknowledgments

The authors wish to thank Regina Mays, University of Tennessee, and Etondi Tchwenko, University of North Carolina, for their extensive time and effort in preparing this chapter. We also wish to acknowledge Sally Morris, who, while Chief Executive of ALPSP, funded the effort to pull together an initial bibliography on the economics of scholarly journal publishing at the Sara Fine Institute, University of Pittsburgh, and Frances Alvarado-Albertorio, for gathering about 1,500 references.

Endnotes

1. Commissioned by the Research Information Network (RIN) in association with the Publishing Research Consortium (PRC), the Society of College, National, and University Libraries (SCONUL), and Research Libraries U.K. (RLUK).

2. Report to the Joint Information Systems Committee (JISC).

References

Adams, A. A. (2009, May 10). Those who criticise must understand what they are criticising. *a-cubed info (blog)*. Message posted to blog.a-cubed.info/index.php?

Adams, J. (2007). Bibliometrics, assessment and UK research. *Serials, 20*, 188–191.

Anglada, L., & Comellas, N. (2002). What's fair? Pricing models in the electronic era. *Library Management, 23*, 227–233.

Antelman, K. (2004). Do open-access articles have a greater research impact? *College & Research Libraries, 65*, 372–382.

Bailey, C. W. (2006). What is open access? In N. Jacobs (Ed.), *Open access: Key strategic, technical and economic aspects*. Oxford, UK: Chandos. Retrieved February 1, 2010, from www.digital-scholarship.org/cwb/WhatIsOA.htm

Bailey, C. W. (2009). *Scholarly electronic publishing bibliography*. Retrieved February 1, 2010, from www.digital-scholarship.org/sepb/sepb.html

Bailey, C. W. (2010). *Institutional repository bibliography*. Retrieved February 1, 2010, from digital-scholarship.org/irb/irb.html

Baldwin, C. (2004). *What do societies do with their publishing surpluses?* Worthing, UK: Association of Learned and Professional Society Publishers.

Barschall, H. H. (1986). The cost of physics journals. *Physics Today, 39*(12), 34–36.

Barschall, H. H. (1988). Cost-effectiveness of physics journals. *Physics Today, 41*(7), 56–59.

Baser, O., & Pena, E. (2003). The return of publications for academic faculty. *Economics Bulletin, 1*(1), 1–13.

Bauer, K., & Bakkalbasi, N. (2005). An examination of citation counts in a new scholarly communication environment. *D-Lib Magazine, 11*(9). Retrieved February 1, 2010, from dlib.org/dlib/september05/bauer/09bauer.html

Beckett, C., & Inger, S. (2006). *Self-archiving and journal subscriptions: Co-existence or competition?* London: Publishing Research Consortium.

Bensman, S. J. (2007). Garfield and the impact factor. *Annual Review of Information Science and Technology, 41*, 93–158.

Bergstrom, C. T. (2007). Eigenfactor: Measuring the value and prestige of scholarly journals. *College & Research Library News, 68*(5). Retrieved February 1, 2010, from www.ala.org/ala/mgrps/divs/acrl/publications/crlnews/backissues2007/may07/eigenfactor.cfm

Bergstrom, C. T., & Bergstrom, T. C. (2004a). Can "author pays" journals compete with "reader pays"? *Nature*, Web Focus: Access to the Literature. Retrieved February 1, 2010, from www.nature.com/nature/focus/accessdebate/22.html

Bergstrom, C. T., & Bergstrom, T. C. (2004b). The costs and benefits of library site licenses to academic journals. *Proceedings of the National Academy of Sciences, 101*, 897–902.

Bergstrom, C. T., & Bergstrom, T. C. (2006). The economics of ecology journals. *Frontiers in Ecology and the Environment, 4*, 488–495.

Bergstrom, T. C. (2001). Free labor for costly journals? *Journal of Economic Perspectives, 15*. Retrieved February 1, 2010, from www.econ.ucsb.edu/~tedb/Journals/jeprevised.pdf

Bergstrom, T. C., & Lavaty, R. (2007). *How often do economists self-archive?* Santa Barbara, CA: Department of Economics, University of California Santa Barbara (Paper 2007a). Retrieved February 1, 2010, from repositories.cdlib.org/ucsbecon/bergstrom/2007a

Bishop, A. P., & Star, S. L. (1996). Social informatics of digital library use and infrastructure. *Annual Review of Information Science and Technology, 31*, 301–401.

Bjørk, B.-C. (2007). A model of scientific communication as a global distributed information system. *Information Research, 12*(2), paper 307. Retrieved February 1, 2010, from informationr.net/ir/12-2/paper307.html

Bjørk, B.-C., & Hedlund, T. (2004). A formalised model of the scientific publication process. *Online Information Review, 28*(1), 8–21.

Bjørk, B.-C., Roos, A., & Lauri, M. (2008). Global annual volume of peer reviewed scholarly articles and the share available via different open access options. *Proceedings of the 12th International Conference on Electronic Publishing*. Retrieved February 12, 2010, from elpub.scix.net/data/works/att/178_elpub2008.content.pdf

Bollen, J., Van de Sompel, H., Hagberg, A., & Chute, R. (2009). A principal component analysis of 39 scientific impact measures. *PLoS ONE, 4*(6), e6022. Retrieved February 1, 2010, from dx.doi.org/10.1371/journal.pone.0006022

Borgman, C. L., & Furner, J. (2002). Scholarly communication and bibliometrics. *Annual Review of Information Science and Technology, 36,* 3–72.

Boyce, P., King, D. W., Montgomery, C., & Tenopir, C. (2004). How electronic journals are changing patterns of use. *The Serials Librarian, 46,* 121–141.

Braman, S. (2005). The micro- and macroeconomics of information. *Annual Review of Information Science and Technology, 40,* 3–52.

Brody, T., & Harnad, S. (2006). *Earlier web usage statistics as predictors of later citation impact.* Retrieved February 1, 2010, from eprints.ecs.soton.ac.uk/10713/01/timcorr.htm

Brown, C. (2010). Communication in the sciences. *Annual Review of Information Science and Technology, 44,* 287–316.

Brown, D. J., & Boulderstone, R. (2008). *The impact of electronic publishing: The future of publishers and librarians.* Mörlenbach, Germany: K.G. Saur.

Butler, D. (2006). Open-access journal hits rocky times. *Nature, 441*(914). Retrieved February 1, 2010, from www.nature.com/nature/journal/v441/n7096/full/441914a.html

Cambridge Economic Policy Associates. (2008). *Activities, costs and funding flows in the scholarly communications system in the UK.* London: Research Information Network.

Carr, L., & Harnad, S. (2005). *Keystroke economy: A study of the time and effort involved in self-archiving.* Southampton, UK: University of Southampton. Retrieved February 1, 2010, from eprints.ecs.soton.ac.uk/10688

Clarke, R. (2007). The cost profiles of alternative approaches to journal publishing. *First Monday, 12*(12). Retrieved February 1, 2010, from www.rogerclarke.com/EC/JP-CP.html

Cockerill, M. (2009). Why have a central open access fund? *CILIP Library & Information Update, 7*(3), 30.

Coles, B. R. (1993). *The scientific, technical and medical information system in the UK.* London: Royal Society.

Cooper, M. D. (1973). The economics of information. *Annual Review of Information Science and Technology, 8,* 5–40.

Cooper, M. D. (2006). The costs of providing electronic journal access and printed copies of journals to university users. *Library Quarterly, 76,* 323–351.

Cope, B., & Kalantzis, M. (2009a). Signs of epistemic disruption: Transformations in the knowledge system of the academic journal. *First Monday, 14*(4). Retrieved February 1, 2010, from www.uic.edu/htbin/cgiwrap/bin/ojs/index.php/fm/article/viewArticle/2309/2163

Cope, B., & Kalantzis, M. (2009b). Signs of epistemic disruption: Transformations in the knowledge system of the academic journal. In B. Cope & A. Phillips (Eds.), *The future of the academic journal* (pp. 13–61). Oxford, UK: Chandos.

Cope, B., & Phillips, A. (Eds.). (2009). *The future of the academic journal.* Oxford, UK: Chandos.

Cox, J. (1998). The changing economic model of scholarly publishing: Uncertainty, complexity and multi-media serials. *INSPEL, 32,* 69–78.

Cox, J. (2003). Value for money in electronic journals: A survey of the early evidence and some preliminary conclusions. *Serials Review, 29,* 83–88. doi:10.1016/S0098-7913(03)00041-8

Cox, J., & Cox, L. (2008). *Scholarly publishing practice: Academic journal publishers' policies and practices in online publishing (third survey)*. Brighton, UK: Association of Learned and Professional Society Publishers.

Craig, I. (2006). *The effect of self-archiving and open access on citations.* Oxford, UK: Blackwell Scientific Internal Report.

Craig, I. D., & Ferguson, L. (2009). Journals ranking and impact factors: How the performance of journals is measured. In B. Cope & A. Phillips (Eds.), *The future of the academic journal* (pp. 153–193). Oxford, UK: Chandos.

Craig, I. D., Plume, A. M., McVeigh, M. E., Pringle, J., & Amin, M. (2007). Do open access articles have greater citation impact? A critical review of the literature. *Journal of Informetrics, 1*, 239–248.

Creaser, C., Maynard, S., & White, S. (2006). *LISU annual library statistics 2006: Featuring trend analysis of UK public and academic libraries 1995–2005.* Leicestershire UK: Loughborough University.

Cronin, B., & Meho, L. (2006). Using the h-index to rank influential information scientists. *Journal of the American Society for Information Science and Technology, 57*, 1275–1278.

Crossick, G. (2007). Journals in the arts and humanities: Their role in evaluation. *Serials, 20*, 184–187.

Davies, J. E. (2009). Libraries and the future of the journal: Dodging the crossfire in the e-revolution, or leading the charge? In B. Cope & A. Phillips (Eds.), *The future of the academic journal* (pp. 214–223). Oxford, UK: Chandos.

Davis, D. (2007). *Library networks, cooperatives and consortia: A national survey.* Chicago: American Library Association.

Davis, P. M. (2002). Patterns in electronic journal usage: Challenging the composition of geographic consortia. *College & Research Libraries, 63*, 484–497.

Davis, P. M. (2006). Letter to the editor. *College & Research Libraries, 67*(2). Retrieved February 1, 2010, from www.ala.org/ala/mgrps/divs/acrl/publications/crljournal/2006/mar/mar06_ltr.cfm

Davis, P. M. (2009a). *Studies on access: A review.* Retrieved February 1, 2010, from arxiv.org/abs/0912.3953

Davis, P. M. (2009b). Author-choice open-access publishing in the biological and medical literature: A citation analysis. *Journal of the American Society for Information Science and Technology, 60*, 3–8.

Davis, P. M., & Fromerth, M. J. (2007). Does the arXiv lead to higher citations and reduced publisher downloads for mathematics articles? *Scientometrics, 71*(2). Retrieved February 1, 2010, from arxiv.org/pdf/cs.DL/0603056

Davis, P. M., Lewenstein, B. V., Simon, D. H., Booth, J. G., & Connolly, M. J. L. (2008). Open access publishing, article downloads, and citations: Randomized controlled trial. *BMJ, 337*(7665), 343–345.

Dominguez, M. (2006). Economics of open access publishing. *Serials, 19*, 52–60.

Donovan, B. (1998). The truth about peer review. *Learned Publishing, 11*, 179–184.

Drott, M. C. (2006). Open access. *Annual Review of Information Science and Technology, 40*, 79–109.

Duplantis, R. M., Haar, D. E., Silberman, S. D., Van Gieson, H., & Warren-Boulton, F. R. (2005). *Merger without markets: Do mergers among publishers of academic journals affect prices?* Washington, DC: Microeconomic Consulting and Research Associates, Inc.

Eckert, H. M. (1982). *Statistics of library networks and cooperative organizations. 1977–1987.* Washington, DC: National Center for Education Statistics, U.S. Department of Education.

Electronic Publishing Services, Ltd. (2006). *Market monitor: Legal, tax and regulatory (LTR) information: Market trends and industry performance.* New York: The Service.

Evans, J. A. (2008). Electronic publication and the narrowing of science and scholarship. *Science, 321,* 395–399.

Eysenbach, G. (2006). Citation advantage of open access articles. *PLoS Biology, 4*(5), e157. Retrieved February 1, 2010, from www.plosbiology.org/article/info%3Adoi%2F10.1371 %2Fjournal.pbio.0040157

Fisher, J. H. (2008). Scholarly publishing re-invented: Real costs and real freedoms. *Journal of Electronic Publishing, 11*(2). Retrieved February 1, 2010, from dx.doi.org/10.3998/ 3336451.0011.204

Fox, P. (2002). Archiving of electronic publications: Some thoughts on cost. *Learned Publishing, 15,* 3–5.

Frazier, K. (2001). The librarians' dilemma: Contemplating the costs of the "big deal." *D-Lib Magazine, 7*(3). Retrieved February 1, 2010, from www.dlib.org/dlib/march01/frazier/ 03frazier.html

Friedlander, A., & Bessette, R. S. (2003). *The implications of information technology for scientific journal publishing: A literature review.* Retrieved February 1, 2010, from www.nsf.gov/statistics/nsf03323/pdf/nsf03323.pdf

Friend, F. J. (2002). Library consortia in the electronic age. *Alexandria, 14*(1), 17–24.

Gannett, E. K. (1973). Primary publication systems and services. *Annual Review of Information Science and Technology, 8,* 243–275.

Garvey, W. D., & Gottfredson, S. D. (1975, October). *Scientific communication as an interactive social process.* Paper presented at the U.S./U.S.S.R Symposium, Yale University, New Haven, CT.

Garvey, W. D., & Griffith, B. C. (1963). *The American Psychological Association's project on scientific information exchange in psychology. Report no. 9.* Washington, DC: American Psychological Association.

Gentil-Beccot, A., Mele, S., & Brookes, T. C. (2009). *Citing and reading behaviours in high energy physics: How a community stopped worrying about journals and learned to love repositories.* Retrieved February 1, 2010, from www.arxiv.org/abs/0906.5418

Getz, M. (2005a). *Open scholarship and research universities* (Working paper 05-17). Nashville, TN: Department of Economics, Vanderbilt University. Retrieved February 1, 2010, from ideas.repec.org/p/van/wpaper/0517.html

Getz, M. (2005b). Open-source scholarly publishing in economic perspective. *Journal of Library Administration, 42*(1), 1–39.

Glänzel, W. (2006). On the opportunities and limitations of the H-index. *Science Forces, 1*(1), 10–11.

Griffiths, J.-M. (1982). The value of information and related systems, products, and services. *Annual Review of Information Science and Technology, 17,* 601–610.

Griffiths, J.-M., & King, D. W. (1993). *Special libraries: Increasing the information edge.* Washington, DC: Special Libraries Association.

Griffiths, J.-M., & King, D. W. (2008). *InterConnections: The IMLS national study of the use of libraries, museums, and the internet.* Washington, DC: Institute of Museum and Library Services. Retrieved February 1, 2010, from www.interconnectionsreport.org

Griffiths, J.-M., & King, D. W. (2009a). *A national study of the future of academic librarians in the workforce.* Washington, DC: Institute of Museum and Library Services. Retrieved February 1, 2010, from libraryworkforce.org/tiki-index.php

Griffiths, J.-M., & King, D. W. (2009b). *A national study of the future of special librarians in the workforce.* Washington, DC: Institute of Museum and Library Services. Retrieved February 1, 2010, from libraryworkforce.org/tiki-index.php

Grimshaw, S. (2000). Library consortia and publishers: Partnerships for the new millennium. *Assignation, 18,* 29–32.

Hahn, K. L. (2005). Tiered pricing: Implications for library collections. *portal: Libraries & the Academy, 5,* 151–163.

Hahn, K. L. (2008). *Research library publishing services: New options for university publishing.* Washington, DC: Association of Research Libraries.

Hajjem, C., Harnad, S., & Gingras, Y. (2005). Ten-year cross-disciplinary comparison on the growth of open access and how it increases research citation impact. *IEEE Data Engineering Bulletin, 28*(4), 39–47.

Halliday, L. L., & Oppenheim, C. (1999). *Economic models of the digital library.* Loughborough, UK: UKOLN. Retrieved February 12, 2010, from www.ukoln.ac.uk/services/elib/papers/ukoln/emod-diglib/final-report.pdf

Halliday, L. L., & Oppenheim, C. (2000). Comparison and evaluation of some economic models of digital-only journals. *Journal of Documentation, 56,* 660–673.

Hannay, T., & Spencer, H. (2007). Document sharing speeds up research. *Research Information, 33,* 25–26.

Harnad, S. (1994). *Scholarly journals at the crossroads: A subversive proposal for electronic publishing.* Washington, DC: Association of Research Libraries.

Harnad, S. (2009a). The post-Gutenberg open access journal. In B. Cope & A. Phillips (Eds.), *The future of the academic journal* (pp. 125–137). Oxford, UK: Chandos.

Harnad, S. (2009b, July 16). Reply to Anthony Watkins' entry. *Open Access Archivangelism Blog.* Retrieved February 1, 2010, from openaccess.eprints.org

Harnad, S. (2009c). Validating multiple metrics as substitutes for expert evaluation of research performance. *Nature, 457*(785). Retrieved February 1, 2010, from openaccess.eprints.org/index.php?/archives/508-quid.html

Harnad, S., & Brody, T. (2004). Comparing the impact of open access (OA) vs. non-OA articles in the same journals. *D-Lib Magazine, 10*(6). Retrieved February 1, 2010, from www.dlib.org/dlib/june04/harnad/06harnad.html

Harwood, P., & Prior, A. (2008). Testing usage-based ejournal pricing. *Learned Publishing, 21*(2), 133–139.

Hedlund, T., Gustafsson, T., & Björk, B.-C. (2004). The open access scientific journal: An empirical study. *Learned Publishing, 17,* 199–209.

Hendley, T. (1998). *Comparison of methods and costs of digital preservation* (British Library Research and Innovation Report 106). London: British Library Research and Innovation Centre.

Hills, P. J. (1983). The scholarly communication process. *Annual Review of Information Science and Technology, 18,* 99–125.

Hindle, A., & Raper, D. (1976). The economics of information. *Annual Review of Information Science and Technology, 11,* 27–54.

Hirsch, J. E. (2005). An index to quantify an individual's scientific research output. *Proceedings of the National Academy of Sciences of the United States of America, 102,* 16569–16572.

Hitchcock, S. (2006). *The effect of open access downloads ("hits") on citation impact: A bibliography of studies.* Retrieved February 1, 2010, from opcit.eprints.org/oacitation-biblio.html

Holmstrom, J. (2004). The cost per article reading of open access articles. *D-Lib Magazine, 10*(1). Retrieved February 1, 2010, from www.dlib.org/dlib/january04/holmstrom/01holmstrom.html

Houghton, J. W. (2009a). *Costs and benefits of alternative publishing models.* Copenhagen, Denmark: Danmarks Elektroniske Fag og Forskningsbibliotek.

Houghton, J. W. (2009b). *Open access—What are the economic benefits? A comparison of the United Kingdom, Netherlands and Denmark.* Melbourne, Australia: Victoria University.

Houghton, J. W., de Jonge, J., & van Oploo, M. (2009). *Costs and benefits of research communication: The Dutch situation.* Utrecht, The Netherlands: SURFfoundation.

Houghton, J. W., Rasmussen, B., Sheehan, P. J., Oppenheim, C., Morris, A., Creaser, C., et al. (2009). *Economic implications of alternative scholarly publishing models: Exploring the costs and benefits.* Report to the Joint Information Systems Committee. Melbourne, Australia: Victoria University & Loughborough University. Retrieved February 1, 2010, from www.jisc.ac.uk/publications/reports/2009/economicpublishingmodelsfinalreport.aspx

Houghton, J. W., & Sheehan, P. (2006). *The economic impact of enhanced access to research findings.* Melbourne, Australia: Centre for Strategic Economic Studies, Victoria University.

Houghton, J. W., & Sheehan, P. J. (2009). Estimating the potential impacts of open access to research findings. *Economic Analysis and Policy, 39*(1), 127–142.

Houghton, J. W., Steele, C., & Henty, M. (2003). *Changing research practices in the digital information and communication environment.* Canberra, Australia: Australian Department of Science, Education, and Training.

Houghton, J. W., Steele, C., & Sheehan, P. (2006). *Research communication costs in Australia: Emerging opportunities and benefits.* Retrieved February 1, 2010, from repositories.cdlib.org/ucsbecon/bergstrom/2004A

Hurd, J. M. (1996). Models of scientific communications systems. In S. Y. Crawford, J. M. Hurd, & A. C. Weller (Eds.), *From print to electronic: The transformation of scientific communication* (pp. 9–33). Medford, NJ: Information Today, Inc.

Inger, S., Kusma, T., & Allen, B. M. (2000). The pricing implications of site and consortia licensing into the next millennium. *Serials Librarian, 38,* 219–224.

Jaschik, J. (2009, June 4). Split over open access. *Inside Higher Ed.* Retrieved February 1, 2010, from www.insidehighered.com/news/2009/06/04/open

Jones, D. Y. (2007). How much do the "best" colleges spend on libraries? *College & Research Libraries, 68,* 343–351.

Journal value project. (2005). Retrieved June 19, 2010, from math.library.wisc.edu/reserves/JVP/JVP-SLA03.ppt

Jubb, M., Look, H., & Sparks, S. (2007). Researchers' use and perceptions of discovery services. *Learned Publishing, 20,* 147–153.

Kaufman-Wills Group, LLC. (2005). *The facts about open access: A study of the financial and non-financial effect of alternative business models for scholarly journals.* Brighton, UK: Association of Learned and Professional Society Publishers.

Kenney, A. R. (2005, July). *The Cornell experience: arXiv.org.* Paper presented at the DCC/DPC Workshop on Cost Models for Preserving Digital Assets, London.

Key Perspectives, Ltd. (2002). Library consortia research. In A. Pearce (Ed.), *The consortia site license: Is it a sustainable model?* (pp. 79–118). Oxford, UK: Ingenta Institute.

King, C. J., Harley, D., Earl-Novell, S., Arter, J., Lawrence, S., & Perciali, I. (2006). *Scholarly communication: Academic values and sustainable models.* Berkeley, CA: Center for Studies in Higher Education. University of California. Retrieved February 1, 2010, from cshe.berkeley.edu/publications/docs/scholarlycommreports.pdf

King, D. W. (2004). Should commercial publishers be involved in the model for open access through author payment? *D-Lib Magazine, 10*(6). Retrieved February 1, 2010, from www.dlib.org/dlib/june04/king/06king.html

King, D. W. (2006). Discussion of the bottom-up approach to examining economic impacts of open access: Annex III. In D. Prosser & J. Houghton (Eds.), *Roundtable on economic impacts of open access.* Washington, DC: Open Society Institute. Retrieved February 1, 2010, from www.cfses.com/documents/king.pdf

King, D. W. (2007). The cost of journal publishing: A literature review and commentary. *Learned Publishing, 20*, 85–106.

King, D. W. (2010). An approach to open access author payment. *D-Lib Magazine, 16*(3/4). Retrieved February 1, 2010, from www.dlib.org/dlib/march10/king/03king.html

King, D. W., Aerni, S., Brody, F., Herbison, M., & Knapp, A. (2004a). *Comparative costs of the University of Pittsburgh electronic and print library collections.* Pittsburgh, PA: The Sara Fine Institute for Interpersonal Behavior and Technology.

King, D. W., Aerni, S., Brody, F., Herbison, M., & Knapp, A. (2004b). *The use and outcomes of university library print and electronic collections.* Pittsburgh, PA: The Sara Fine Institute for Interpersonal Behavior and Technology.

King, D. W., Aerni, S., Brody, F., Herbison, M., & Kohberger, P. (2004). *A comparison of the cost of print and electronic journal collections.* Pittsburgh, PA: The Sara Fine Institute for Interpersonal Behavior and Technology.

King, D. W., & Alvarado-Albertorio, F. M. (2008). Pricing and other means of charging for scholarly journals: A literature review and commentary. *Learned Publishing, 21*, 248–272. Retrieved February 1, 2010, from dx.doi.org/10.1087/095315108X356680

King, D. W., Boyce, P. B., Montgomery, C. H., & Tenopir, C. (2003). Library economic metrics: Examples of the comparison of electronic and print journal collections and collection services. *Library Trends, 51*, 376–400. Retrieved February 1, 2010, from hdl.handle.net/2142/8476

King, D. W., & Griffiths, J.-M. (1987). *Survey of library networks and cooperative library organizations.* Washington, DC: King Research, Inc. for Office of Educational Research and Improvement, U.S. Department of Education.

King, D. W., Lancaster, F. W., McDonald, D. D., Roderer, N. K., & Wood, B. L. (1976). *Statistical indicators of scientific and technical information communication (1960–1980). Report to the National Science Foundation C-878* (GPO 083-000-00295-3). Washington, DC: King Research, Inc., Center for Quantitative Sciences.

King, D. W., McDonald, D. D., & Olsen, C. (1978). *A survey of readers, subscribers and authors of the Journal of the National Cancer Institute.* Available from the author.

King, D. W., McDonald, D. D., & Roderer, N. K. (1981). *Scientific journals in the United States: Their production, use, and economics.* Stroudsburg, PA: Academic Press.

King, D. W., & Montgomery, C. H. (2002). Comparing library and user related costs of print and electronic journal collections. *D-Lib Magazine, 8*(10). Retrieved February 1, 2010, from www.dlib.org/dlib/october02/montgomery/10montgomery.html

King, D. W., & Tenopir, C. (2001). Using and reading scholarly literature. *Annual Review of Information Science and Technology, 34,* 423–477.

King, D. W., & Tenopir, C. (2008). Scholarly journal and digital database pricing: Threat or opportunity? In J. K. MacKie-Mason & W. P. Lougee (Eds.), *Economics and usage of digital libraries: Byting the bullet.* Ann Arbor, MI: Scholarly Publishing Office, University of Michigan Library. Retrieved June 19, 2010, from quod.lib.umich.edu/cgi/t/text/text-idx?c=spobooks;idno=5621225.0001.001

King, D. W., Tenopir, C., Choemprayong, S., & Wu, L. (2009). Scholarly journal information-seeking and reading patterns of faculty at five U.S. universities. *Learned Publishing, 22,* 95–113.

King, D. W., Tenopir, C., & Clarke, M. (2006). Measuring total reading of journal articles. *D-Lib Magazine, 12*(10). Retrieved February 1, 2010, from www.dlib.org/dlib/october06/king/10king.html

King, D. W., Tenopir, C., Montgomery, C. H., & Aerni, S. E. (2003). Patterns of journal use by faculty at three diverse universities. *D-Lib Magazine, 9*(10). Retrieved February 1, 2010, from www.dlib.org/dlib/october03/king/10king.html

King, D. W., & Xu, H. (2002a). An appraisal of the consortium licensing model. In A. Pearce (Ed.), *The consortia site license: Is it a sustainable model?* (pp. 163–167). Oxford, UK: Ingenta Institute.

King, D. W., & Xu, H. (2002b). The role of library consortia in electronic journal services. In A. Pearce (Ed.), *The consortia site license: Is it a sustainable model?* (pp. 10–76). Oxford, UK: Ingenta Institute.

Kingma, B. (1996). *Economics of access versus ownership: The costs and benefits of access to scholarly articles via interlibrary loan and journal subscriptions.* New York: Haworth Press.

Kling, R., & Callahan, E. (2002). Electronic journals, the internet, and scholarly communication. *Annual Review of Information Science and Technology, 37,* 127–177.

Kostoff, R. N. (1998). The use and misuse of citation analysis in research evaluation. *Scientometrics, 43,* 27–43.

Kyrillidou, M. (2006). The impact of electronic publishing on tracking research library investments in serials. *ARL: A Bimonthly Report on Research Library Issues and Actions, 249,* 6–7.

Kyrillidou, M., & Bland, L. (2008). *ARL statistics: 2006–2007.* Washington, DC: Association of Research Libraries.

Kyrillidou, M., & Bland, L. (2009). *ARL statistics: 2007–2008.* Washington, DC: Association of Research Libraries.

Lamberton, D. M. (1984). The economics of information and organization. *Annual Review of Information Science and Technology, 19,* 3–30.

Lin, N., Garvey, W. D., & Nelson, C. E. (1970). A study of the communication structure of science. In C. E. Nelson & D. K. Pollock (Eds.), *Communication among scientists and engineers* (pp. 23–60). Lexington, MA: Heath Lexington Books.

Liu, Z. M. (2003). Trends in transforming scholarly communication and their implications. *Information Processing & Management, 39*, 889–898.

Luther, J. (2008). *University investment in the library: What's the return? A case study at the University of Illinois at Urbana-Champaign (white paper)*. San Diego, CA: Elsevier. Retrieved February 1, 2010, from libraryconnect.elsevier.com/whitepapers/0108/lcwp 010801.html

Mabe, M. (2003). Growth and number of journals. *Serials, 16*, 191–197.

Mabe, M., & Amin, M. (2001). Growth dynamics of scholarly and scientific journals. *Scientometrics, 51*, 147–162.

Mabe, M. A., & Amin, M. (2002). Dr Jekyll and Dr Hyde: Author-reader asymmetries in scholarly publishing. *Aslib Proceedings, 54*, 149–157.

Machlup, F. (1997). Uses, value, and benefits of knowledge. *Knowledge: Creation, Diffusion, and Utilization, 1*, 62–81.

MacKie-Mason, J. K., & Jankovich, A. L. L. (1997). PEAK: Pricing library access to knowledge. *Library Acquisitions, Practice, and Theory, 21*, 281–295.

Maynard, S., & Davies, J. E. (2001). *The cost of copyright compliance in further and higher education institutions*. Loughborough, UK: Loughborough University, LISU.

McCabe, M. J. (2002). Journal pricing and mergers: A portfolio approach. *American Economic Review, 92*, 259–269.

McCabe, M. J. (2004). Information goods and endogenous pricing strategies: The case of economic journals. *Economics Bulletin, 12*, 1–11. Retrieved June 19, 2010, from mccabe. people.si.umich.edu/EB.pdf

McCabe, M. J. (2005). Merging West and Thomson: Pro- or anti-competitive? *Law Library Journal, 97*(3), 4.

McCabe, M. J., Nevo, A., & Rubinfeld, D. L. (2006). *The pricing of academic journals*. Berkeley, CA: Berkeley Program in Law and Economics.

McCabe, M. J., & Snyder, C. M. (2004). The best business model for scholarly journals: An economist's perspective. *Nature, Web Focus: Access to the Literature*. Retrieved February 1, 2010, from www.nature.com/nature/focus/accessdebate

Mezick, E. M. (2007). Return on investment: Libraries and student retention. *Journal of Academic Librarianship, 33*, 561–566.

Mick, C. K. (1979). Cost analysis of information systems and services. *Annual Review of Information Science and Technology, 14*, 37–64.

Moed, H. F. (2007). *The effect of "open access" upon citation impact: An analysis of ArXiv's Condensed Matter Section*. Retrieved February 1, 2010, from www.citeulike.org/user/ janrito/article/1338912

Morris, S. (2005). The true costs of scholarly journal publishing. *Learned Publishing, 18*, 115–126.

Morris, S. (2007). Will the parasite kill the host? Are institutional repositories a fact of life— and does it matter? *Serials, 20*, 172–179.

Morris, S. (2009). The tiger in the corner: Will journals matter to tomorrow's scholars? In B. Cope & A. Phillips (Eds.), *The future of the academic journal* (pp. 379–385). Oxford, UK: Chandos.

National Center for Education Statistics. (1997). Library cooperatives survey: Fiscal year 1997. Washington, DC: Department of Education. National Center for Education Statistics.

Nicholas, D., & Huntington, P. (2002). Results and analysis from a pilot quantitative analysis of web log data. In A. Pearce (Ed.), *The consortia site license: Is it a sustainable model?* (pp. 187–215). Oxford, UK: Ingenta Institute.

Nicholas, D., & Huntington, P. (2006). Digital journals: Are they really used? *Interlending and Document Supply, 34,* 74–77.

Nicholas, D., Huntington, P., Dobrowolski, T., & Rowlands, I. (2006). Ideas on creating a consumer market for scholarly journals. *Learned Publishing, 19,* 245–249.

Nicholas, D., Huntington, P., & Jamali, H. R. (2006). *Obtaining rich use and user data on virtual scholars: A deep log analysis of ScienceDirect authors.* London: University College.

Nicholas, D., Huntington, P., Jamali, H. R., & Tenopir, C. (2006). OhioLINK: Ten years on: What deep log analysis tells us about the impact of Big Deals? *Journal of Documentation, 62,* 482–508.

Nicholas, D., Huntington, P., & Watkinson, A. (2003). Digital journals, big deals, and online searching behavior: A pilot study. *Aslib Proceedings, 55,* 84–109.

Nicholas, D., Huntington, P., & Watkinson, A. (2005). Scholarly journal usage: The results of deep log analysis. *Journal of Documentation, 61,* 248–280.

Nicholas, D., Rowlands, I., Huntington, P., Clark, D., & Jamali, H. R. (2009). *Ejournals: Their use, value and impact.* Retrieved February 1, 2010, from www.rin.ac.uk/use-ejournals

Nicolaisen, J. (2007). Citation analysis. *Annual Review of Information Science and Technology, 41,* 609–642.

Nisonger, T. E. (2004). The benefits and drawbacks of impact factor for journal collection management in libraries. *Serials Librarian, 47,* 57–75.

Okerson, A. S. (1999). The LIBLICENCE project and how it grows. *D-Lib Magazine, 5*(9). Retrieved February 1, 2010, from www.dlib.org/dlib/september99/okerson/09okerson.html

Okerson, A. S. (2000). *Strength in numbers: Library consortia in the electronic age.* Retrieved February 1, 2010, from www.library.yale.edu/~okerson/strength-numbers.html

Okerson, A. S., & McDonnell, J. J. (1995). *Scholarly journals at the crossroads: A subversive proposal for scholarly publishing.* Washington, DC: Association of Research Libraries.

Organisation for Economic Cooperation and Development. (2005). *Digital broadband content: Scientific publishing.* Paris: The Organisation. Retrieved February 1, 2010, from www.oecd.org/dataoecd/42/12/35393145.pdf

Outsell, Inc. (2008). *Scientific, technical & medical information: 2008 market forecast and trends report, volume 2.* Retrieved February 1, 2010, from www.outsellinc.com/store/products/772

Outsell, Inc. (2009). *An open access primer: Market size and trend.* Burlingame, CA: Outsell, Inc.

Oxford University Press. (2006). *Determining the impact of open access: A deep log analysis of Nucleic Acids Research.* London: University College London, Center for Publishing. Retrieved February 12, 2010, from www.homepages.ucl.ac.uk/~uczciro/nar.pdf

Page, G., Campbell, R., & Meadows, J. (1997). *Journal publishing.* Cambridge, UK: Cambridge University Press.

Peek, R. P., & Pomerantz, J. P. (1998). Electronic scholarly journal publishing. *Annual Review of Information Science and Technology, 33*, 321–356.

Pellegrino, J. W., Chudowsky, N., & Glasov, R. (2001). *Knowing what students know: The science and design of educational assessment.* Washington, DC: National Academies Press.

Phillips, A. (2009). Business models in journals publishing. In B. Cope & A. Phillips (Eds.), *The future of the academic journal* (pp. 83–103). Oxford, UK: Chandos.

Phillips, M. E. (2005). Selective archiving of web resources: A study of acquisition costs at the National Library of Australia. *RLG DigiNews, 9*(13). Retrieved February 1, 2010, from www.rlg.org/en/page.php?Page_ID320666#article0

Pinfield, S. (2007). Can open access repositories and peer-reviewed journals coexist? *Serials, 20*, 163–171.

PIRA International. (2003). *The EU publishing industry: An assessment of competitors.* Brussels, Belgium: European Commission.

Primary Research Group, Inc. (2008). *Survey of academic and research library journal purchasing practices.* Retrieved February 1, 2010, from www.researchandmarkets.com/reports/661631/the_survey_of_academic_and_research_library

Pringle, J. (2007). What impact? Whose value? Citation metrics in a work-flow perspective. *Serials, 20*, 192–198.

Public Library of Science. (2004). *Publishing open-access journals.* Retrieved February 1, 2010, from www.plos.org/downloads/oa_whitepaper.pdf

Public Library of Science. (2009). *Publication fees for PLoS journals.* Retrieved February 1, 2010, from www.plos.org/journals/pubfees.php

Quandt, R. E. (2003). Scholarly materials: Paper or digital? *Library Trends, 51*, 349. Retrieved February 1, 2010, from www.thefreelibrary.com/Scholarly+materials:+paper+or+digital%3F+%28Academic+Libraries%29-a0102270882

Rae, V., & Rowland, F. (2006). Is there a viable business model for commercial open access publishing? *Serials, 19*, 188–194.

RAE2008. (2008). Research assessment exercise: Quality profiles. Retrieved February 1, 2010, from www.rae.ac.uk/results

Regazzi, J. J. (2004). The shifting sands of open access publishing: A publisher's view. *Serials Review, 30*, 275–280.

Repo, A. J. (1987). Economics of information. *Annual Review of Information Science and Technology, 22*, 3–35.

Research Information Network. (2009). *Ejournals: Their use, value, and impact.* London: Research Information Network. Retrieved February 1, 2010, from informationr.net/ir/reviews/revs337.html

Revill, D. (2002). LISU annual library statistics 2001, featuring trend analysis of UK public and academic libraries 1990–2000. *New Library World, 103*(6), 236–238.

Rightscom. (2005). *Business models for journal content: Bristol report to JISC.* London: Joint Information Systems Committee. Retrieved March 8, 2010 from www.jisc.ac.uk/media/documents/events/2005/06/hugh_look.pdf

Rowland, F. (1996). The need for management of electronic journals. In R. P. Peek & G. B. Newby (Eds.), *Scholarly publishing: The electronic frontier* (pp. 243–250). Cambridge, MA: MIT Press.

Rowland, F. (1999). Electronic publishing: Non-commercial alternatives. *Learned Publishing, 12*, 209–217.

Rowland, F. (2002). The peer-review process. *Learned Publishing, 15*, 247–258.

Rowlands, I. (2007). Electronic journals and user behavior: A review of recent research. *Library & Information Science Research, 29*, 369–396. Retrieved February 1, 2010, from dx.doi.org/10.1016/j.lisr.2007.03.005

Rowlands, I., & Nicholas, D. (2006). The changing scholarly communication landscape: An international survey of senior researchers. *Learned Publishing, 19*, 31–55.

Sage. (2008). *Meeting the challenges: Societies and scholarly communication.* Thousand Oaks, CA: Sage.

Sanville, T., & Winters, B. (1998). A method out of madness: OhioLINK's collaborative response to the serials crisis. *Serials Librarian, 34*, 125–139.

Saxby, C. (2006). *NAR author and reader survey.* Oxford, UK: Oxford University Press.

Scholarly Publishing Roundtable. (2010). *Report and recommendations from the Scholarly Publishing Roundtable.* Retrieved February 1, 2010, from www.aau.edu/WorkArea/DownloadAsset.aspx?id.10044

Schonfeld, R. C., King, D. W., Okerson, A. S., & Fenton, G. E. (2004). *The non-subscription side of periodicals: Changes in library operations and costs between print and electronic journals.* Washington, DC: Council on Library and Information Resources. Retrieved February 1, 2010, from www.clir.org/pubs/reports/pub127/contents.html

Schreiber, M. (2008). An empirical investigation of the g-Index for 26 physicists in comparison with the h-Index, the A-Index and the R-Index. *Journal of the American Society for Information Science and Technology, 59*, 1513–1522.

Schroter, S., Tite, L., & Kassem, A. (2006). Financial support at the time of paper acceptance: A survey of three medical journals. *Learned Publishing, 19*, 291–297. Retrieved February 1, 2010, from www.ingentaconnect.com/content/alpsp/lp/2006/00000019/00000004/art00008

Scigliano, M. (2002). Consortium purchases: Case study for a cost-benefit analysis. *Journal of Academic Librarianship, 28*, 393–399.

Sheehan, P., & Houghton, J. (2009). Estimating the potential impacts of open access to research findings. *Economic Analysis and Policy, 39*(1). Retrieved February 1, 2010, from www.eap-journal.com.au/download.php?file.696

Shepherd, P. T. (2007). *Final report on the investigation into the feasibility of developing and implementing journal usage factors.* Oxon, UK: United Kingdom Serials Group. Retrieved March 11, 2010, from www.uksg.org/sites/uksg.org/files/FinalReportUsageFactorProject.pdf

SHERPA/RoMEO. (2008). *Publisher copyright policies & self-archiving.* Retrieved February 1, 2010, from www.sherpa.ac.uk/romeo

Shieber, S. M. (2009). Equity for open-access journal publishing. *PLoS Biology, 7*(8). Retrieved February 1, 2010, from www.plosbiology.org/article/info:doi%2F10.1371%2Fjournal.pbio.1000165

Shotton, D. (2009). Semantic publishing: The coming revolution in scientific journal publishing. *Learned Publishing, 22*, 85–94.

Shreeves, S. L. (2009). Cannot predict now: The role of repositories in the future of the journal. In B. Cope & A. Phillips (Eds.), *The future of the academic journal* (pp. 197–211). Oxford, UK: Chandos.

Siebenberg, T. R., Galbraith, B., & Brady, E. E. (2004). Print versus electronic journal use in three sci/tech disciplines: What's going on here? *College & Research Libraries, 65*, 427–438.

Society of College, National and University Libraries. (2008). *Statistics tables*. London: The Society.

Spence, A. M. (1974). An economist's view of information. *Annual Review of Information Science and Technology, 9*, 57–78.

Spiller, D., Creaser, C., & Murphy, A. (1998). *Libraries in the workplace*. Loughborough, UK: Loughborough University LISU.

SQW Limited. (2004). *Costs and business models in scientific research publishing: A report commissioned by the Wellcome Trust*. London: The Wellcome Trust. Retrieved February 1, 2010, from www.wellcome.ac.uk/stellent/groups/corporatesite/@policy_communications/documents/web_document/wtd003184.pdf

Standing Committee for Research on Academic Libraries. (2008). *SCREAL report: Results of a survey on information access and ejournal usage of researchers and graduate students*. Chiba, Japan: The Committee. Retrieved February 1, 2010, from www.screal.org/apache2-default/Publications/122308SCREAL_summary_eng.pdf

Stern, D. (2005, March 5). Open access or differential pricing for journals: The road best traveled? *Information Today, 29*(2). Retrieved February 1, 2010, from www.infotoday.com/online/mar05/Stern.shtml

Suber, P. (2006). *Open access overview*. Retrieved February 1, 2010, from www.earlham.edu/~peters/fos/overview.htm

Sutherland, K. (2009, April 30). Those who disseminate ideas must acknowledge the routes they travel. *Times Higher Education*. Retrieved February 1, 2010, from www.timeshighereducation.co.uk/story.asp?sectioncode.26&storycode.406309

Swan, A. (2008). The business of digital repositories. In K. Weenink, L. Waaijers, & K. van Godtsenhoven (Eds.), *A DRIVER's guide to European repositories*. Amsterdam: Amsterdam University Press. Retrieved February 1, 2010, from plip.eifl.net/eifl-oa/training/reading/business-digital/downloadFile/file/The_business_of_digital_repositories.pdf?nocache.1213643889.27

Swan, A., & Brown, S. (2005). *Open access self-archiving: An author study*. Truro, Cornwall: Key Perspectives Ltd.

Taylor-Roe, J. (1997). Consortia: What makes a negotiating unit? *Serials, 10*, 307–312.

Tenopir, C. (2003). Information metrics and user studies. *Aslib Proceedings, 55*(1), 13–17.

Tenopir, C., Hitchcock, B., & Pillow, A. (2003). *Use and users of electronic resources: An overview and analysis of recent research studies*. Washington, DC: Council on Library and Information Resources. Retrieved March 20, 2010, from www.clir.org/pubs/reports/pub120

Tenopir, C., & King, D. W. (2000). *Towards electronic journals: Realities for scientists, librarians, and publishers*. Washington, DC: Special Libraries Association.

Tenopir, C., & King, D. W. (2002). Reading behavior and electronic journals. *Learned Publishing, 15*, 259–265.

Tenopir, C., & King, D. W. (2004). *Communications patterns of engineers*. New York: Wiley.

Tenopir, C., & King, D. W. (2007). Perceptions of value and value beyond perceptions: Measuring the quality and value of journal article readings. *Serials, 20*, 199–207.

Tenopir, C., & King, D. W. (2009). The growth of journals publishing. In B. Cope & A. Phillips (Eds.), *The future of the academic journal* (pp. 105–123). Oxford, UK: Chandos.

Tenopir, C., King, D. W., Boyce, P., Grayson, M., & Zhang, Y. (2003). Patterns of journal use by scientists through three evolutionary phases. *D-Lib Magazine, 9*(5). Retrieved February 1, 2010, from www.dlib.org/dlib/may03/king/05king.html

Tenopir, C., King, D. W., & Bush, A. (2004). Medical faculty's use of print and electronic journals: Changes over time and in comparison with scientists. *Journal of the Medical Library Association, 92*, 233–241.

Tenopir, C., King, D. W., Clarke, M. T., Kyoungsik, N., & Xiang, Z. (2007). Journal reading patterns and preferences of pediatricians. *Journal of the Medical Library Association, 95*, 56–63.

Tenopir, C., & King, D. W., Edwards, S., & Wu, L. (2009). Electronic journals and changes in scholarly article seeking and reading patterns. *Aslib Proceedings, 61*, 5–32.

Tenopir, C., Love, A., Park, J., Wu, L., Kingma, B., & King, D. W. (2010). *Return on investment of the grant process in academic libraries*. San Diego, CA: Elsevier: Library Connect.

Todd, P. A., & Ladle, R. J. (2008). Citations: Poor practices by authors reduce their value. *Nature, 451*(244). Retrieved February 1, 2010, from doi:10.1038/451244b

U.K. Office of Fair Trading. (2002). *The market for scientific, technical, and medical journals: A statement by the Office of Fair Trading*. London: The Office.

Universities UK. (2007). *Policy briefing: Publishing research results: The challenges of open access*. London: Universities UK.

Van Orsdel, L. C., & Born, K. (2009). Reality bites. *Library Journal*, 36–40. Retrieved February 1, 2010, from www.libraryjournal.com/article/CA6651248.html

Varian, H. R. (1996). Differential pricing and efficiency. *First Monday*. Retrieved February 1, 2010, from 131.193.153.231/www/issues/issue2/different/index.html

Vorndran, A., & Botte, A. (2008). *An analysis and evaluation of existing methods and indicators for quality assessment of scientific publications*. Hamburg, Germany: European Educational Research Quality Indicators.

Walker, T. J. (2004). Open access by the article: An idea whose time has come? *Nature: Web Focus*. Retrieved February 1, 2010, from www.nature.com/nature/focus/accessdebate/13.html

Waltham, M. (2005). *JISC: Learned society open access business models*. Princeton, NJ. Retrieved February 1, 2010, from www.marywaltham.com/JISCReport.pdf

Waltham, M. (2006). Learned society business models and open access: Overview of a recent JISC-funded study. *Learned Publishing, 19*, 15–30.

Wang, P. (2001). Methodologies and methods for user behavior research. *Annual Review of Information Science and Technology, 34*, 53–99.

Ware, M. (2006). Open archives and their impact on journal cancellations. *Learned Publishing, 19*, 226–228.

Ware, M. (2009). *Peer review in scholarly journals: Perspectives of the scholarly community: An international study*. Bristol, UK: Publishing Research Consortium. Retrieved February 1, 2010, from www.publishingresearch.net/documents/PeerReviewFullPRC Report-final.pdf

Ware, M., & Mabe, M. (2009). *The STM report: An overview of scientific and scholarly journals publishing*. West Sussex, UK: International Association of Scientific, Technical and Medical Publishers. Retrieved February 1, 2010, from www.stm-assoc.org/2009_10_13_ Press_Release_The_STM_Report.pdf

Watson, S. (2007). Authors' attitudes to, and awareness and use of, a university institutional repository. *Serials, 20*, 225–230.

Weller, A. C. (2000). Editorial peer review for electronic journals: Current issues and emerging models. *Journal of the American Society for Information Science and Technology, 51*, 1328–1333.

Wheatley, P., Ayris, P., Davies, R., McLeod, R., & Shenton, H. (2007, October). *LIFE: Costing the digital preservation lifecycle*. Paper presented at the iPRES Annual Conference, Beijing, China.

White, S., & Creaser, C. (2007). *Trends in scholarly journal prices, 2000–2006*. Oxford, UK: Oxford University Press.

Willer, M., Buzina, T., Holub, K., Zajec, J., Milinovic, M., & Topolscak, N. (2008). Selective archiving of web resources: A study of processing costs. *Program: Electronic Library & Information Systems, 42*, 341–364.

Williamson, A. (2002, April). *What happens to peer review?* Paper presented at the ALPSP International Learned Journals Seminar, London. Retrieved February 1, 2010, from www.alpsp.org/wil120402.ppt

Willinsky, J. (2003). Scholarly associations and the economic viability of open access publishing. *Journal of Digital Information, 4*(2). Retrieved February 1, 2010, from journals.tdl.org/jodi/article/viewArticle/104

Wilson, J. H., Jr. (1972). Costs, budgeting, and economics of information processing. *Annual Review of Information Science and Technology, 7*, 39–67.

Zitt, M., Ramanana-Rahary, S., & Bassecoulard, E. (2005). Relativity of citation performance and excellence measures: From cross-field to cross-scale effects of field-normalisation. *Scientometrics, 63*, 373–401.

Technology
Trends

CHAPTER 8

Human–Computer Interaction

Jonathan Grudin
Microsoft Research, Redmond, WA

Preamble: History in a Time of Rapid Change

Efforts to define information science are hardy perennials. As the debate continues, hundreds of papers on the history of the field have appeared (see Burke's [2007] meta review). We are not sure what information science is, but we are getting a grip on its history.

There is greater consensus on the early history, from the antecedents of library and information science through the so-called "golden years" of the 1950s to the 1970s. Burke writes, "Hardly any publications have explored ... the science of information or the information business after the mid-1970s" (p. 19). In the late 1970s computer use began to dominate how many people create, manage, and use information, adding theoretical and organizational complexity.

As more information is represented digitally, human–computer interaction (HCI), broadly defined, becomes more central to information science. Reflecting this convergence, information schools have hired leading human–computer interaction researchers and initiated HCI programs and degree concentrations. Several such schools adopted simple names—school of information, faculty of information, information school—thereby sidestepping definitional disputes and shedding associations with library and information science. (Dropping "science" did not signal a renewed outreach to the humanities.)

Prior to this convergence, information science (or information) and its antecedents evolved apart from human–computer interaction and its antecedents. HCI developed as sub-disciplines in three fields: human factors, management information systems, and computer science. The three threads of HCI research mingled less than one might have expected. This survey covers the evolution of these four fields of research, with a view to understanding better the forces underlying the trajectories they have followed, forces that are still in play and thus will influence our future.

My focus is on the computer era. Other recent *ARIST* chapters that have dealt with aspects of human–computer interaction include Rogers's (2004) survey of HCI theory, Callahan's (2005) discussion of interface design and culture, and Ruthven's (2008) analysis of interactive information retrieval.

However, Burke (1994), Michael Buckland (1998), W. Boyd Rayward (1998), and others have shown that prior to the digital era, researchers, technology developers, and dreamers anticipated issues that are prominent today. My favorite illustration is H. G. Wells's 1905 proposal for a system built on index cards:

> These index cards might conceivably be transparent and so contrived as to give a photographic copy promptly whenever it was needed, and they could have an attachment into which would slip a ticket bearing the name of the locality in which the individual was last reported. A little army of attendants would be at work on this index day and night. ... An incessant stream of information would come, of births, of deaths, of arrivals at inns, of applications to post offices for letters, of tickets taken for long journeys, of criminal convictions, marriages, applications for public doles and the like. A filter of offices would sort the stream, and all day and all night for ever a swarm of clerks would go to and fro correcting this central register, and photographing copies of its entries for transmission to the subordinate local stations, in response to their inquiries. (Wells, 1905, online)

Would this human-powered Web 2.0 be a tool for social control or public information access? The image evokes the potential and the challenges of the coming information era.

Why Study the History of Human–Computer Interaction?

Information may have persistent qualities, but technologies fade away. For most of the computing era, interaction involved 80-column punch cards, paper tape, line editors, 1920-character displays, 1-megabyte diskettes, and other extinct species. Are the interaction issues of those times relevant today? No.

On the other hand, aspects of the psychology of human–computer interaction change more slowly, or not at all. Much of what was learned about perceptual, cognitive, social, and emotional processes in interacting with older technologies applies to emerging technologies. But there, history is of less interest than *what* was learned.

Nevertheless, the rapid pace of change strengthens some reasons for understanding aspects of the field's history:

1. Although several disciplines are engaged in human–computer interaction research and application, few people are exposed to more than one. By seeing how the others evolved, we can identify benefits in expanding our focus, as well as obstacles to doing so.

2. The recognition of past visionaries and innovators is part of building a community and inspiring future contributors, even when specific past achievements are difficult to appreciate today.

3. Some visions and prototypes were quickly converted to widespread application, others took decades, and some remain unrealized. By understanding the reasons for different outcomes, we might assess today's visions more realistically.

4. Crystal balls are notoriously unreliable, but anyone planning or managing a career in a rapidly changing field must consider the future. One thing is certain: It will not resemble the present. Our best chance to anticipate change is to find trajectories that extend from the past through the present.

This account is not an engineering history that emphasizes "firsts." It focuses on when technologies and practices became widely used, as reflected in the spread of systems and applications. This is often accompanied by disciplinary development, formalized in the growth of associations and research fields. More social history than conceptual history, this survey points to trends and trajectories that you might download into your crystal ball.

A central theme is the impact of successive waves of hardware innovation, "Moore's Law" broadly construed. This familiar phenomenon, unexamined in previous HCI histories, is essential to discussing disciplines and associations, which often sprang up around a new technology and withered or died when it was replaced. In addition, hardware costs had to drop for some applications to become practical. Conceptual histories pass over these factors. For example, graphical user interface concepts were invented early in the era of transistor-based computers. Conceptual development progressed slowly over the next half century. Only in the mid-1980s were widely available computers powerful enough to devote that much memory and processing to supporting interaction.

In terms of broad movements, the HCI threads within human factors, information systems, and computer science quickly expanded from narrow user bases to embrace broad constituencies. This is less true of technology use in information science and its predecessors. Until more recently the latter remained focused on narrower target audiences—librarians, document managers in business and government agencies, scientists and engineers, and other specialists. Nevertheless, the early history enables us to understand the developments in recent decades, when broad HCI concerns became significant in information studies.

An historical account is a perspective. It emphasizes some things while deemphasizing or omitting others. A history can be wrong in details but is never right in any final sense. Your questions and interests determine whether a perspective is useful to you.

Ron Baecker established a blueprint for intellectual histories of HCI in the opening chapters of the 1987 and 1995 editions of *Readings in Human–Computer Interaction* (Baecker & Buxton, 1987; Baecker, Grudin, Buxton, & Greenberg, 1995). Brian Shackel's (1997) account of European contributions and specialized essays by Brad Myers (1998) on HCI engineering history and Alan Blackwell (2006) on the history of metaphor in design added insights and references. Perlman, Green, and Wogalter (1995) provide a compendium of HCI papers that appeared in the human factors literature through 1994. Banker and Kaufmann (2004) cover HCI research within management information systems. Burke's (1998) chapter represents an example of a focused study of a digital effort within information science.

A wave of popular and scholarly books has addressed the history of personal computing, which is part of this account (e.g., Bardini, 2000; Hertzfeld, 2005; Hiltzik, 1999; Markoff, 2005). This chapter expands on Grudin's (2005, 2006, 2008) work. Historical topics are also present in the "Timelines" column of *ACM Interactions* from March 2006 through the present, including several of direct relevance to information science.

Few of the writers and editors listed here are trained historians. Many of us lived through much of the computing era as participants and witnesses, leaving us with rich insights and questionable objectivity. This account draws on extensive literature and hundreds of formal interviews and discussions, but we all have biases.

Acronyms: HCI, CHI, HF&E, IT, IS, LIS

Exploration of human–computer interaction literature is complicated by differences in how many simple terms are used. This is covered later in the chapter. Here I explain how several key disciplinary labels will be used. Unlike many authors, I use *human–computer interaction* broadly to cover work in several disciplines. *Computer–human interaction* (CHI) refers to one narrower focus, associated mainly with computer science, the Association for Computing Machinery Special Interest Group (ACM SIGCHI), and the latter's annual CHI conference. I use *human factors* (HF), *ergonomics*, and HF&E interchangeably—some writers define ergonomics a little more narrowly. The Human Factors Society (HFS) became the Human Factors and Ergonomics Society (HFES) in 1992. I use *information systems* (IS) to refer to the management discipline that has also been labeled data processing (DP) and management information systems (MIS). I follow common parlance in referring to organizational information systems specialists as "IT professionals (IT pros)." With IS taken, I do not abbreviate information studies or information science, but use LIS for *library and information science*.

Human–Tool Interaction and Information Processing at the Dawn of Computing

In the century prior to the first computers, advances in tool use and information processing technology initiated two fields of research that eventually contributed to human–computer interaction. One focused on making the human use of tools more efficient, the other on ways to represent and distribute information more effectively.

Origins of Human Factors

Frederick Taylor (1911) employed technologies and methods developed in the late 19th century—photography, moving pictures, and statistical analysis—to improve work practices. Time-and-motion studies were successful with assembly-line manufacturing and other manual tasks. In spite of the uneasiness with "Taylorism" reflected in Charlie Chaplin's popular satire *Modern Times*, science and engineering continued to pursue gains in efficiency.

The World Wars accelerated these efforts, matching people to jobs, training them, and then designing equipment and jobs to be more easily mastered. Engineering psychology was born during World War II after investigators found that simple flaws in the design of aircraft controls (Roscoe, 1997) and escape hatches (Dyson, 1979) led to aircraft losses and thousands of casualties. After the war, American aviation psychologists created the Human Factors Society. Two legacies of the conflict were respect for the potential of computing, based on its use in code-breaking, and enduring interest in behavioral requirements for design. For more on this period, see the books by Roscoe (1997) and Meister (1999, 2005).

Early tool use, whether by assembly-line workers or pilots, was not discretionary. If training was necessary, people were trained. One research goal was to reduce training time, but more important was to increase the speed and reliability of skilled performance.

Origins of the Focus on Information

As the cost of paper, printing, and transportation dropped in the late 19th and early 20th centuries, information dissemination and librarianship as a profession grew. Library associations formed in the U.S. and Great Britain in the 1870s. The Dewey Decimal System was developed the same decade. In the U.S., thousands of public libraries sprang up to serve local demand. They were poorly funded. In Europe, government-funded libraries appeared, often serving scientists and other specialized elites. This distinction had consequences that persisted through World War II, to the dawn of the computing era.

Librarianship

In the U.S., a pragmatic focus on library management and the training of thousands of librarians took precedence. There was no central funding for technology development, or for the needs of specialists in medicine, science, and the humanities. Public libraries were happy with the simple if inflexible Dewey Decimal system. Europe manifested more interest in technology and sophisticated information management, as reflected in the H. G. Wells quotation. Early in the 20th century, Belgian Paul Otlet obtained Melvil Dewey's permission to extend his classification system to enable the aggregation and linking of concepts in ways that foreshadowed tagging and hyperlinks—only after agreeing not to use it in English, an early example of legal constraint of technology use. Otlet's Universal Decimal Classification (UDC) is still used.

In the late 19th century, technologies and practices for compressing, distributing, and organizing information bloomed. In addition to the index card—a simple yet influential innovation—were Hollerith cards and electromechanical tabulation, celebrated steps toward computing that were heavily used to process information in industry. Typewriters and carbon paper facilitated information dissemination, as did the mimeograph machine, patented by Thomas Edison. Filing cabinets and folders—models for icons on computer displays much later—were important inventions that contributed to information management. Yates (1989) describes their impact on the management of organizations through the 1920s. Photography-based microform or microfilm, first developed in the 19th century, was the most efficient way to store information for a century.

Bibliography, Documentation, Documentalism

The American Library Association's (ALA) pragmatic focus meant that American research into technologies to advance indexing, cataloging, and retrieving information within or across libraries (called bibliography, documentation, or documentalism) formed a distinct thread outside the ALA. In Europe, research did not splinter: With a greater focus on scientific and specialized publishing in general, special libraries faced more sophisticated reader demands and a greater need to share resources; the creation in the U.K. of the Association for Special Libraries and Information Bureaux (Aslib) is a case in point. Different views of this history are forcefully presented in a discussion led by W. Boyd Rayward (1983) in Section 5 of Machlup and Mansfield's (1983) book; Burke (1994) presents a unified account.

Library Science

Over time, some American libraries engaged in limited scholarly work. The focus varied from technology innovation intended to support specialists in science and engineering to social science topics such as the history of publishing and typography. Then, in 1926, in a fateful move, the Carnegie Foundation endowed the Graduate Library School (GLS) at the University of Chicago to focus solely on research. For two decades Chicago was the only university granting the Ph.D. in library studies. The GLS included a laboratory for research on microphotography and social scientists who applied sophisticated statistical research methods (W. B. Rayward, personal communication, April 8, 2010), but its influential publications positioned library studies squarely in the humanities (Buckland, 1998). Professor Pierce Butler, whose interests included historical writing and typography, published *An Introduction to Library Science* (Butler, 1933). It became the major library research text for the next forty years. It did not mention information technologies in an era when Europeans and American documentalists were actively developing and exploring them. Studies of human-tool interaction were not part of the GLS program as conveyed by this book, and its prestige shaped the field until well into the computer era.

Specialist Use of Technology

Burke (2007, p. 15) summarized the early history, with its emphasis on training librarians and other specialists:

> Most information professionals ... were focusing on providing information to specialists as quickly as possible. The terms used by contemporary specialists appeared to be satisfactory for many indexing tasks and there seemed no need for systems based on comprehensive and intellectually pleasing classification schemes. The goal of creating tools useful to non-specialists was, at best, of secondary importance.

As noted earlier, this chapter focuses on when computer technologies came into non-specialist use. Only recently, with the web and declining digital storage costs, came the realization that each of us will soon be our own information manager, just as we are all now telephone operators. But we get ahead of our story. This section concludes with accounts of two individuals who, in different ways, shaped the history of information research.

Paul Otlet and the Mundaneum

Otlet envisioned a vast network of information organized on index cards and microfilm. Unlike his contemporary Wells, Otlet and his collaborators built it. Otlet had begun cataloging bibliographic references on index cards in the late 19th century and established a commercial research service around them. In 1919 the Belgian government provided additional financing and supported establishing a center, called the Mundaneum, in Brussels. By 1934, 15 million index cards and millions of images were collected and organized via Otlet's Universal Decimal Classification, which included a numerical formula that enabled items to be linked to others. Government funding was eventually cut off and the collection was damaged during World War II. Although the work was largely forgotten for half a century (for example, it was not cited in the 1980s by the developers of the metaphorically identical Xerox Notecards, an influential hypertext system), Rayward (1990) has shown that Otlet and collaborators such as the microphotography pioneer Robert Goldschmidt represented a significant thread of European research that was much less prominent in North America.

Technological innovation continued in Europe with the development of mechanical systems of remarkable ingenuity (Buckland, 2009). These included the use of photoreceptors to detect light passing through holes in index cards positioned to represent different terms, which enabled very rapid retrieval of items on specific topics. These innovations inspired little-known efforts by a well known American scientist and research manager, discussed next.

Vannevar Bush and Microfilm Machines

Massachusetts Institute of Technology (MIT) professor Vannevar Bush was one of the most influential American scientists. He advised Presidents Franklin Roosevelt and Harry Truman, served as Director of the Office of Scientific Research and Development, and was President of the Carnegie Institute. Bush is best known for a 1945 *Atlantic Monthly* essay titled "As We May Think." It described a hypothetical microfilm-based electromechanical information processing machine called the Memex. The Memex was to be a workstation that enabled professionals to index and retrieve documents or pictures quickly and to create hyper-text-like associations among them. This essay inspired computer engineers and computer scientists who contributed to computer graphics and human–computer interaction in the 1960s and 1970s.

The core of Bush's essay was written in the early 1930s. For over two decades, shrouded in secrecy, he devoted unprecedented resources to the design and construction of numerous machines comprising a subset of the Memex features. None was successful.

Microfilm—photographic miniaturization—had qualities that attracted Bush, as they had Otlet. Microfilm was light, easily transported, and easily copied (which paper documents were not: Xerox photocopiers did not appear until 1959). Microfilm was also the most efficient storage medium then available. Index codes placed on microfilm could be read by passing the film between light beams and photoreceptors. The moving picture industry had created tools for handling film and lowered the cost. Memory based on vacuum tubes would never be competitive. Magnetic memory, when it eventually arrived, was less versatile and far more expensive. It is easy to overlook the compelling case that existed for basing information systems on microfilm.

As recounted in Colin Burke's (1994) comprehensive book *Information and Secrecy: Vannevar Bush, Ultra, and the Other Memex,* Bush's machines failed because of overly ambitious compression and speed goals, patent ownership issues, and because Bush ignored librarians, documentalists, and decades of work on classification systems. American documentalists were active, albeit underfunded, prior to World War II. In 1937, the American Documentation Institute (ADI) formed, forerunner to today's American Society for Information Science and Technology (ASIST). Bush, an electrical engineer by training, did not work with them. He assumed that users could easily avoid problems arising from conflicting uses of terms, which was known to be false then and remains a key research challenge.

At times Bush considered libraries and the public as potential users, but his projects began with the Federal Bureau of Investigation (FBI) in mind, settled heavily on military uses for cryptography and information retrieval, and included a major Central Intelligence Agency (CIA) project. His machines cost far too much for librarians or library users to be plausible customers. These efforts might not belong in an account of broad technology deployments, were it not for Bush's influence. Through his academic and government positions, his writings, the vast resources he commandeered, and the scores of brilliant engineers diverted to his projects, Bush promoted his projects and exerted influence for two decades, well into the computer era that followed World War II.

Bush's (1945, online) vision emphasized the linking of information and discretionary use:

> associative indexing, the basic idea of which is a provision whereby any item may be caused at will to select immediately and automatically another. This is the essential feature of the Memex. ... Any item can be joined into numerous trails. ... New forms of encyclopedias will appear, ready made with a mesh of associative trails [which a user could extend].
>
> The lawyer has at his touch the associated opinions and decisions of his whole experience and of the experience of friends and authorities. The patent attorney has on call the millions of issued patents, with familiar trails to every point of his client's interest. The physician, puzzled by a patient's reactions, strikes the trail established in studying an earlier similar case and runs rapidly through analogous case histories, with side references to the classics for the pertinent anatomy and histology. The chemist, struggling with the synthesis of an organic compound, has all the chemical literature before him in his laboratory, with trails following the analogies of compounds and side trails to their physical and chemical behavior.
>
> The historian, with a vast chronological account of a people, parallels it with a skip trail which stops only on the salient items, and can follow at any time contemporary trails which lead him all over civilization at a particular epoch. There is a new profession of trail blazers, those who find

delight in the task of establishing useful trails through the enormous mass of the common record.

Bush knew that the Memex was not realistic. None of his many projects included designs for the "essential" associative linking. His inspirational account describes today's hands-on discretionary use of computers by professionals. But that was 50 years in the future and required technologies then undreamt of. Bush did not support the early use of computers, which were slow, bulky, and expensive, lacking the many qualities of microfilm.

1945–1955: Managing Vacuum Tubes

World War II changed everything. The unprecedented investment in science and technology during the war years revealed that huge sums could be directed to academic and industrial research that addressed national goals. Research expectations and strategies would never be the same. Sophisticated electronic computation machines built before and during World War II were designed for specific purposes, such as solving equations or breaking codes. Their limitations made clear the desirability of general-purpose computational devices. Extremely expensive cryptographic machines played a major part in winning the war, but each was designed to attack a specific encryption device; a new one was needed when the enemy changed machines. General purpose computers, more feasible as a consequence of war-time improvements in technologies such as vacuum tubes, eventually brought human–computer interaction into the foreground.

When engineers and mathematicians emerged from the military and government (and secret project rooms on university campuses), secrecy eroded. The Electronic Numeric Integrator and Calculator (ENIAC), arguably the first general-purpose computer, was begun in secret during the war but announced publicly as a "giant brain" when finished in 1946 (Berkeley, 1949). Its initial use, for calculations supporting hydrogen bomb development, was not publicized. Accounts of ENIAC dimensions vary, but it stood eight to ten feet high, occupied as many as 1,800 square feet, and consumed as much energy as a small town. It provided far less computation and memory than can be acquired for a few dollars, slipped into a pocket, and run on a small battery today.

Reducing operator burden was a key focus. Two major accomplishments were the reduction in the time to replace or reset vacuum tubes and the invention of stored-program computers that could be loaded from tape rather than by manually attaching cables and setting switches. These early human–computer interaction endeavors were straight post-war "knobs and dials" human factor/ergonomics efforts. Before long, one computer operator could do work that previously required a team.

Memory was inordinately expensive. The largest computers of the time had little of it. These computers were used for computation, not symbolic representation or information processing. Library schools continued to focus on librarianship, alongside some social science and historical research. Simple microfilm readers were used to assist in storing information as publication of scholarly and popular material soared.

Foundations for the emergence of information science were set. The war forged alliances among documentalists, electrical engineers, and mathematicians interested in communication and information management. Vannevar Bush's collaborators who were active after the war included Claude Shannon and Warren Weaver, co-authors in 1949 of the seminal work on information theory (then called communication theory) (Shannon & Weaver, 1949). Prominent American documentalist Ralph Shaw joined Bush's efforts. But libraries and librarians, where the GLS humanities orientation still dominated, were not involved. The divide was, if anything, greater: In the 1930s, the American Documentation Institute included librarians and support for systems spanning the humanities and science, but during and after the war its concerns became those of government and "Big Science" (Price, 1963).

Three Roles in Early Computing

Early computer projects employed people as managers, programmers, and operators. Managers oversaw design, development, and operation, specifying the programs to be written and distributing the output. Mathematicians, scientists, and engineers wrote the programs in concert with people skilled in mathematics who decomposed tasks into components the computer could manage (for ENIAC, a team of six women). A small army of operators was needed. Once a program was written, it might take days for people to load it by setting switches, dials, and cable connections. In spite of design innovations that boosted vacuum tube reliability, including operating them at lower than normal power and building in visible indicators of tube failure, ENIAC was down much of the time as people looked for and replaced tubes. Shopping carts full of vacuum tubes were reportedly wheeled around.

Eventually, each of these occupations—computer operation, management, and programming—became a major focus of HCI research, centered respectively in human factors, information systems, and computer science. Computers and our interaction with them evolved, but the research spectrum today reflects aspects of this early division of labor.

Grace Hopper, Liberating Computer Users

As computers became more reliable and capable, programming emerged as a central activity. The development of computer languages, compilers, and constructs such as subroutines can be seen as facilitating programmers' interfaces to computers. Grace Hopper, a pioneer in these areas, was unusually explicit about this, describing her goal as freeing mathematicians to do mathematics (mathematicians were the computer users of the 1940s and 1950s) (Hopper, 1952; see also Sammet, 1992). These words are echoed in today's usability goal of freeing users to do their work. Just as HCI professionals often complain of being marginalized by software developers, one could argue that Hopper's accomplishments are undervalued by computer scientists who focus on algorithms and operating systems.

1955–1965: Transistors, New Vistas

Early forecasts that the world would need few computers reflected the limitations of vacuum tubes. Solid-state computers, first available commercially in 1958, changed everything. Still used primarily for scientific and engineering tasks, they were reliable enough not to require a staff of computer engineers. The less computer-savvy operators overseeing them needed better interfaces. Although computers were too expensive and limited for wide use, researchers envisioned future possibilities that were previously unimaginable.

Supporting Operators: The First Systematic HCI Research

> In the beginning, the computer was so costly that it had to be kept gainfully occupied for every second; people were almost slaves to feed it. —Brian Shackel (1997, p. 977)

Almost all computer use of this period involved programs and data that were read in from cards or tape. Programs then ran without interruption until they terminated, along the way producing printed, punched, or tape output. This batch processing restricted human–computer interaction to basic operation, programming, and use of the output, of which only operation involved hands-on computer use.

Low-paid computer operators set switches; pushed buttons; read lights; loaded and burst printer paper; loaded and unloaded cards, magnetic tapes, and paper tapes; and so on. Teletypes supported direct interaction: commands typed by the operator interleaved with computer responses and status messages. Eventually, the paper that scrolled up one line at a time yielded to glass teletypes (tty's), also called visual display units (VDUs), terminals (VDTs), or cathode ray tubes (CRTs). They, too, scrolled operator commands and computer-generated messages, one line at a time. A monochrome terminal restricted to displaying alphanumeric characters cost $50,000 in today's dollars—expensive, but a small fraction of the cost of a computer. A large computer might have one such console, used only by the operator.

Improving the design of buttons, switches, and displays was a natural extension of human factors/ergonomics. Experts in this field authored the HCI papers. In 1959, British researcher Brian Shackel published the article, "Ergonomics for a Computer" (Shackel, 1959) followed in 1962 by "Ergonomics in the Design of a Large Digital Computer Console" (Shackel, 1962). These described the redesign of the consoles for the EMIac and EMIdec 2400 analog and digital computers. The latter was the largest computer at the time (Shackel, 1997).

In the U.S., the Human Factors Society formed in 1957 and focused on improving the efficiency of skilled performance, reducing errors in skilled performance, and training people to achieve skilled performance. Sid Smith's (1963) chapter "Man–Computer Information Transfer" marked the start of his career in the human factors of computing.

Visions and Demonstrations

As transistors replaced vacuum tubes, a wave of imaginative writing, conceptual innovation, and prototype building swept through the research community. Although some of the language now seems dated, notably the use of male generics, many of their key concepts resonate today.

J. C. R. Licklider at BBN and ARPA

Between 1960 and 1965, ideas and systems tied to the newly realized potential of computers poured out. Licklider, a psychologist, played a dual role. He wrote influential essays and backed highly influential research projects as a manager at Bolt Beranek and Newman (BBN) from 1957–1962 and as Director of the Information Processing Techniques Office (IPTO) of the Department of Defense Advanced Research Projects Agency (called ARPA and DARPA at different times) from 1962–1964.

BBN conducted extensive computer-related work funded by the government and employed dozens of influential researchers, including John Seely Brown, Richard Pew, and many who also worked at MIT (e.g., John McCarthy, Marvin Minsky, and Licklider himself). IPTO funding was crucial in launching computer science departments and establishing artificial intelligence as a field in the 1960s, in addition to its best-known accomplishment, giving birth to the internet.

In 1960, Licklider described *man-machine symbiosis*: "There are many man-machine systems. At present, however, there are no man-computer symbioses—answers are needed." The computer was "a fast information-retrieval and data-processing machine" destined to play a larger role: "One of the main aims of man-computer symbiosis is to bring the computing machine effectively into the formulative parts of technical problems" (Licklider, 1960, pp. 4–5).

This would require more rapid real-time interaction than batch systems supported. Licklider and Wes Clark (1962, p. 113) outlined the requirements of a system for "on-line man-computer communication." They identified capabilities that were ripe for development: time-sharing of a computer among many users; electronic input-output surfaces for the display and communication of symbolic and pictorial information; interactive, real-time support for programming and information processing; large-scale information storage and retrieval systems; and facilitation of human cooperation. They foresaw that other desirable technologies, such as speech recognition and natural language understanding, would be very difficult to achieve.

In a 1963 memorandum, Licklider addressed his ARPA colleagues as "the members and affiliates of the Intergalactic Computer Network," anticipating the internet that ARPA would be instrumental in developing (a copy of the memorandum is available at www.chick.net/wizards/memo.html) (Pew, 2003). His book *Libraries of the Future* summarized and expanded this vision (Licklider, 1965). Waldrop (2001) details Licklider's role in advancing computer science and HCI.

John McCarthy, Christopher Strachey, Wesley Clark

McCarthy and Strachey worked out details of time sharing, a crucial step in enabling interactive computing (Fano & Corbato, 1966). Apart from a small number of researchers using computers that were built with spare-no-expenses military funding, no one could use a computer interactively if exclusive access was required. Time sharing allowed several (and later dozens) of simultaneous users at terminals. Languages were developed to facilitate on-line control and programming of time-sharing systems (e.g., JOHNNIAC Open Shop System [JOSS] in 1964).

Clark was instrumental in building the TX-0 and TX-2 at MIT's Lincoln Labs to demonstrate time sharing and other innovative concepts. These machines, which cost on the order of $10 million, helped establish the Boston area as a center for computer research (all prices are in 2007 U.S. dollars). A CHI '05 panel focusing on this period, with Clark and Ivan Sutherland participating, can be viewed online (ePresence, 2006). The TX-2 was the most powerful and capable in the world at the time. It was less powerful than a smartphone is today.

Ivan Sutherland and Computer Graphics

Sutherland's (1963, online) doctoral dissertation, describing the Sketchpad system built on the TX-2 to make computers "more approachable," is arguably the most impressive and influential document in the history of HCI. (Alan Blackwell and Kerry Rodden have provided an edited version, available at www.cl.cam.ac.uk/TechReports/UCAM-CL-TR-574.pdf.) Sketchpad launched computer graphics, a field of research that would have a decisive impact on HCI twenty years later.

Sutherland demonstrated the iconic representations of constraints, the copying, moving, and deleting of hierarchically organized objects, and object-oriented programming concepts. He explored novel interaction techniques, such as picture construction using a light pen. He facilitated visualization by separating the coordinate system used to define a picture from the one used to display it, and demonstrated animated graphics, noting the potential for digitally rendered cartoons 20 years before *Toy Story*. His frank description of what did not work—when engineers found Sketchpad too limited for computer-assisted design (CAD) he called it a "big flop" —enabled others to make rapid progress (p. 97).

In 1964, his Ph.D. behind him, Sutherland succeeded Licklider as the director of IPTO. Among those whose work he then funded was Douglas Engelbart at the Stanford Research Institute.

Douglas Engelbart, Augmenting Human Intellect

In 1962, Engelbart published *A Conceptual Framework for the Augmentation of Man's Intellect*; over the next several years he built systems that made great strides toward realizing this vision (Engelbart, 1962). He also supported and inspired engineers and programmers who subsequently made major independent contributions.

Echoing Bush and Licklider, Engelbart saw the potential for computers to become congenial tools that people would choose to use interactively:

> By "augmenting human intellect" we mean increasing the capability of a man to approach a complex problem situation, to gain comprehension to suit his particular needs, and to derive solutions to the problems. ... By "complex situations" we include the professional problems of diplomats, executives, social scientists, life scientists, physical scientists, attorneys, designers ... We refer to a way of life in an integrated domain where hunches, cut-and-try, intangibles, and the human "feel for a situation" usefully co-exist with powerful concepts, streamlined terminology and notation, sophisticated methods, and highly-powered electronic aids. (Engelbart, 1962, online)

Engelbart used his ARPA funding to develop and integrate rapidly an extraordinary set of prototype applications into his NLS system. In doing so, he conceptualized and implemented the foundations of word processing, invented or refined input devices including the mouse and multikey control box, and made use of multi-display environments that integrated text, graphics, and video in windows. In 1968 these were demonstrated in a sensational 90-minute event at the Fall Joint Computer Conference in San Francisco (sloan.stanford.edu/MouseSite/1968Demo.html). The focal point for interactive systems research in the U.S. appeared to have moved from the East Coast to the West Coast.

Engelbart, an engineer, believed in careful human factors testing of systems to improve efficiency and reduce errors in skilled use, with concern for effects of fatigue and stress. He also emphasized training, feeling that people should be willing to tackle a difficult interface that delivered greater power once mastered. The relative importance of optimizing for skilled vs. initial use later became a source of contention and still surfaces in HCI discussions.

Ted Nelson's Vision of Interconnectedness

In 1960, while a graduate student in sociology, the inventor of the term *hypertext* founded Project Xanadu to create an easily used computer network. In 1965, he published a paper titled "A file structure for the complex, the changing and the indeterminate" (Nelson, 1965). Nelson continued to produce works (often self-published) with stirring calls for systems to democratize computing through a highly interconnected, extensible network of digital objects (e.g., Nelson, 1973). Xanadu was never fully realized. Nelson did not consider the early World Wide Web to be an adequate realization of his vision, but features of lightweight technologies such as weblogs, wikis, collaborative tagging, and search are enabling many of the activities he envisioned.

Nelson also foresaw the significance of intellectual property issues that would arise in digital domains. Although his solutions were again not fully implemented, they drew attention to the issues.

From Documentation to Information Science

This period saw the last major investments in microfilm and other pre-digital systems. The most ambitious were military and intelligence systems, including Vannevar Bush's final efforts (Burke, 1994). However, many documentalists recognized that declining memory costs would enable computation engines to become information processing machines. Conceptually, the evolution was relatively continuous, but at the institutional level changes were radical. New professions—mathematicians and engineers—were involved. New initiatives were launched, bearing few ties to contemporary librarianship or the humanities orientation of library schools. A new banner was needed.

Merriam Webster dates "information science" to 1960. Conferences at Georgia Institute of Technology in 1961 are credited with shifting the focus from information as a technology to that of an incipient science. In 1963, chemist-turned-documentalist Jason Farradane taught the first information science courses at City University, London. Chemistry as a profession had invested in organizing its literature systematically; another chemist-turned-documentalist, Allen Kent, was at the center of a major information science initiative at the University of Pittsburgh (Aspray, 1999). Preceding him at Pittsburgh, Anthony Debons, a psychologist and friend of J. C. R. Licklider, organized a series of North Atlantic Treaty Organization (NATO)-sponsored congresses in the early 1960s. Guided by Douglas Engelbart, these meetings centered on people, whose activities technology was to augment. In 1964 the Graduate Library School at the University of Pittsburgh became the Graduate School of Library and Information Sciences and Georgia Tech formed a School of Information Science, initially with one full-time faculty member.

Conclusion: Visions, Demos, and Widespread Use

Progress in HCI can be understood in terms of inspiring visions, conceptual advances that enabled aspects of the visions to be demonstrated in working prototypes, and the evolution of design and application. The engine, enabling visions to be realized and soon thereafter to be widely deployed, was the relentless hardware advances that produced devices millions of times more powerful than the far more expensive systems designed and used by the pioneers.

At the conceptual level, much of the basic foundation for today's graphical user interfaces was in place by 1965. However, it required individual use of a $10 million custom-built machine. Pew (2003, p. 3) describes the breakthrough 1960 Digital Equipment Corporation (DEC) PDP-1 as "truly a computer with which an individual could interact." The PDP-1 came with CRT display, keyboard, light pen, and paper tape reader. It cost about $1 million and had the capacity of a Radio Shack TRS 80 twenty years later. It required considerable technical and programming support. The PDP-1 was used by a few fortunate computer-savvy researchers.

Licklider's "man-computer symbiosis," Engelbart's "augmenting human intellect," and Nelson's (1973) "conceptual framework for man-machine everything" described a world that did not exist. It was a world in which attorneys, doctors, chemists, and designers chose to become hands-on users of computers. The reality, for some time to come, was that most hands-on use was routine, nondiscretionary operation. As for the visions, 40 years later some of the capabilities are taken for granted, some are just being realized, and others remain elusive.

1965–1980: HCI Before Personal Computing

Control Data Corporation launched the transistor-based 6000 series computers in 1964. In 1965, commercial computers based on integrated circuits arrived with the IBM System/360. These powerful systems, later called mainframes to distinguish them from minicomputers, brought computing into the business realm. Each of the three roles in computing—operation, management, programming—became a significant profession.

Operators interacted directly with computers to perform routine maintenance, load and run programs, handle printouts, and so on. As time-sharing spread, this hands-on category expanded to include data entry and other repetitive tasks.

Managers oversaw hardware acquisition, software development, operation, and routing and the use of output. They were usually not hands-on users, but people who relied on printed output and reports; they considered themselves computer users.

Apart from those working in research settings, programmers were rarely direct users until late in this period. Many flowcharted and wrote programs on paper forms. Keypunch operators then punched the program instructions onto cards. These were sent to computer centers for computer operators to run. Printouts and other output were picked up later. Many programmers would use computers directly when they could, but the cost of computer use generally dictated this efficient division of labor.

Human Factors and Ergonomics Embrace Computer Systems

In 1970, Brian Shackel founded the Human Sciences and Advanced Technology (HUSAT) Research Institute at Loughborough University in the U.K., devoted to ergonomics research emphasizing HCI. Sid Smith and other human factors engineers examined a range of input and output issues, notably the representation of information on displays (e.g., Smith, Farquhar, & Thomas, 1965); another early focus was computer-generated speech (Smith & Goodwin, 1970). In 1972, the Computer Systems Technical Group (CSTG) of the Human Factors Society formed; soon it was the largest technical group in the society.

Leading publications were the general journal *Human Factors* and, starting in 1969, the computer-focused *International Journal of Man-Machine Studies (IJMMS)*.

The first widely read HCI book was James Martin's 1973 *Design of Man-Computer Dialogues*. A comprehensive survey of interfaces for operation and data entry, it began with an arresting opening chapter that described a world in transition. Extrapolating from declining hardware prices, Martin (1973, pp. 3–4) wrote:

> The terminal or console operator, instead of being a peripheral consideration, will become the tail that wags the whole dog. ... The computer industry will be forced to become increasingly concerned with the usage of people, rather than with the computer's intestines.

In the mid-1970s, U.S. government agencies responsible for agriculture and social security initiated large-scale data processing system development efforts, described by Pew (2003). Although not successful, these efforts led to methodological innovation in the use of style guides, usability labs, prototyping, and task analysis.

In 1980, three significant HF&E books were published: two on VDT design (Cakir, Hart, & Stewart, 1980; Grandjean & Vigliani, 1980) and one general guideline (Damodaran, Simpson, & Wilson, 1980). German work on VDT standards, first released in 1981, provided an economic incentive to design for human capabilities by threatening to ban non-compliant products. Later that year a corresponding American National Standards Institute (ANSI) standards group formed for office and text systems.

Information Systems Addresses the Management of Computing

Beginning in 1967, the journal *Management Science* published a column titled "Information Systems in Management Science." Early definitions of IS included "an integrated man/machine system for providing information to support the operation, management, and decision-making functions in an organization" and "the effective design, delivery and use of information systems in organizations" (Davis, 1974; Keen, 1980; quoted by Zhang, Nah & Preece, 2004, p. 147). A historical survey of IS research (Banker & Kaufmann, 2004) identifies HCI as one of five major research streams and places its origin in Ackoff's (1967) paper describing challenges in handling computer-generated information.

Companies acquired expensive business computers to address major organizational concerns. At times the principal concern was to appear modern (Greenbaum, 1979), but when computers were used, managers could be chained to them almost as tightly as operator and data entry "slaves." That said, operator or end-user resistance to using a system was a major management concern. The sociotechnical approach to system design was one response; it educated representative workers in technology possibilities and involved them in design, in part to increase acceptance of the resulting system (Mumford, 1971).

Cognitive style, a major topic of early IS research, focused on difficulties that managers had communicating with computer-savvy employees. IS researchers published HCI articles in management journals and in the human factors-oriented *IJMMS*. The latter was rated the twenty-third most influential IS journal by Mylonopoulos and Theoharakis (2001, as amended in Grudin, 2005, p. 60 note 17).

Programming: Subject of Study, Source of Change

In the 1960s and 1970s, more than 1,000 research papers on variables affecting programming performance were published (Baecker & Buxton, 1987). Most viewed programming in isolation, independent of organizational context. Gerald Weinberg's landmark *The Psychology of Computer Programming* appeared in 1971 (Weinberg, 1971). Nine years later Ben Shneiderman (1980) published *Software Psychology* and the next year (1981) Beau Sheil reviewed studies of programming notation (conditionals, control flow, data types), practices (flowcharting, indenting, variable naming, commenting), and tasks (learning, coding, debugging).

Programmers changed their fields through invention. In 1970, Xerox Palo Alto Research Center (PARC) was founded to advance computer technology by developing new hardware, programming languages, and programming environments. It drew researchers and system builders from the labs of Engelbart and Sutherland. In 1971, Allen Newell of Carnegie Mellon University proposed a project to PARC, launched three years later: "Central to the activities of computing—programming, debugging, etc.—are tasks that appear to be within the scope of this emerging theory (a psychology of cognitive behavior)" (quoted by Card & Moran, 1986, p. 183).

Like HUSAT, also launched in 1970, PARC had a broad research charter. HUSAT focused on ergonomics, anchored in the tradition of nondiscretionary use, one component of which was the human factors of computing. PARC focused on computing, anchored in visions of discretionary use, one component of which was also the human factors of computing. Researchers at PARC and a few other places extended the primarily perceptual-motor focus of human factors to higher-level cognition. HUSAT, influenced by sociotechnical design, extended human factors by considering organizational factors.

Computer Science: A New Discipline

Computer science departments emerged in the mid-1960s. Some arose out of engineering. Computer graphics was a specialization of particular relevance to HCI; software engineering came later. Other computer science departments originated as applied mathematics, a background shared by many early artificial intelligence researchers.

Early machines capable of interesting work were very expensive. They were funded without regard to cost by branches of the military, for which technical success was the sole criterion (Norberg & O'Neill, 1996). ARPA under the direction of Licklider, Sutherland, and their successors played a major role. Reliance on massive funding meant that researchers were concentrated at a few centers, which bore little resemblance to the batch and time-shared environments of business computing. User needs also differed: The technically savvy hands-on users in research settings had less need for low-level interface enhancements.

The computer graphics and AI perspectives that developed in these centers differed from those of HCI researchers, who focused on less expensive systems that could be studied in many more settings. To these HCI researchers, hardware advances led to greater computing capability at a relatively fixed low price. Computer graphics and AI required processing power—hardware advances meant declining cost for a relatively fixed high level of computation. Only later could widely available machines support graphical interfaces and AI programming. Nevertheless, between 1965 and 1980 some computer science researchers focused on interaction, which was part of Ivan Sutherland's initial vision.

Computer Graphics: Realism and Interaction

In 1968 Sutherland joined David Evans to establish a hugely influential computer graphics lab at the University of Utah. The Utah computer science department was founded in 1965, in the first wave that emerged from mathematics and electrical engineering. The western migration continued as students from the lab, including Alan Kay and William Newman (and later Jim Blinn and Jim Clark), went to California. Most graphics systems were built on the DEC PDP-1 and PDP-7. These expensive machines—the list price of a high-resolution display alone was over $100,000 in today's dollars—were capable of multitasking, but a graphics program generally monopolized the processor.

In 1973, the Xerox Alto arrived, a powerful step toward realizing Alan Kay's vision of computation as a medium for personal computing (Kay & Goldberg, 1977). Too expensive to be widely used—the Alto never became a commercial product—and not powerful enough to support high-end graphics research, the Alto was produced in volume and supported graphical interfaces of the kind Engelbart had prototyped.

William Newman expressed the result this way: "Everything changed—the computer graphics community got interested in realism, I remained interested in interaction, and I eventually found myself doing HCI" (personal communication). Ron Baecker and Jim Foley were other graphics researchers whose focus shifted to broader interaction issues. Foley and Wallace (1974, p. 462) identified requirements for designing "interactive graphics systems whose aim is good symbiosis between man and machine"; 18 papers in the first SIGGRAPH conference that year had "interactive" or "interaction" in their titles.

At Xerox, Larry Tesler and Tim Mott recognized that the Alto could support a graphical interface accessible to untrained people, a significant step. By early 1974 they had developed the GYPSY text editor. GYPSY and Xerox's Bravo editor developed by Charles Simonyi preceded and influenced Microsoft Word (Hiltzik, 1999).

A distinct focus on interaction was highlighted in 1976, when SIGGRAPH sponsored a two-day workshop in Pittsburgh titled "User Oriented Design of Interactive Graphics Systems." Participants who were later active in CHI included Jim Foley, William Newman, Ron Baecker, John Bennett, Phyllis Reisner, and Tom Moran. J. C. R. Licklider and Nicholas Negroponte presented vision papers. The conference was managed by the chair of Pittsburgh's Computer Science Department and one participant was Anthony Debons, a key figure in building Pittsburgh's world-renowned information science program.

Perhaps UODIGS'76 marked the end of a visionary period, embodying an idea whose time had not quite yet come. Licklider (1976, p. 89) saw it clearly:

> Interactive computer graphics appears likely to be one of the main forces that will bring computers directly into the lives of very large numbers of people during the next two or three decades. Truly user-oriented graphics of sufficient power to be useful to large numbers of people has not been widely affordable, but it will soon become so, and, when it does, the appropriateness and quality of the products offered will to a large extent determine the future of computers as intellectual aids and partners of people.

UODIGS was not repeated. The 150-page proceedings was not cited. Not until 1981 was another user-oriented design conference held (*Proceedings of the Joint Conference on Easier and More Productive Use of Computer Systems*, 1981), after which they were held every year. Application was not quite at hand; most HCI research remained focused on interaction driven by commands, forms, and full-page menus.

Artificial Intelligence: Winter Follows Summer

In the late 1960s and early 1970s, AI burst onto the scene, promising to transform HCI. It did not go as expected. Logically, AI and HCI are closely related. What are intelligent machines for if not to interact with people? AI research has influenced HCI: speech recognition and natural language are perennial HCI topics; expert, knowledge-based, adaptive, and mixed-initiative systems have been tried, as have applications of production systems, neural nets, and fuzzy logic. Recently, human-robot interaction and machine learning have been attracting attention.

Although some AI features make their way into systems and applications, frequent predictions that more powerful machines would soon bring major AI technologies into widespread use were not borne out. Thus, AI did not come into focus in HCI, and AI researchers have shown limited interest in HCI.

To piece this together requires a brief review of the early history. The term *artificial intelligence* first appeared in a 1955 call by John McCarthy for a meeting on machine intelligence that was held in Dartmouth the next year. Also in 1956, Alan Turing's prescient essay, "Computing Machinery and Intelligence" attracted attention when reprinted in *The World of Mathematics*. (It was first published in 1950 [Turing, 1950], as were Claude Shannon's [1950] "Programming a Computer for Playing Chess" and Isaac Asimov's [1950] *I, Robot,* exploring his three laws of robotics.) Newell and Simon's (1956) logic theory machine appeared in 1956, after which they focused on developing a general problem solver. McCarthy invented the LISP programming language in 1958 (McCarthy, 1960).

Many AI pioneers were trained in mathematics and logic, where much is built from a few axioms and a small set of rules. Mathematics is considered a high form of intelligence, even by non-mathematicians. AI researchers anticipated that machines that operate logically and tirelessly would make great strides. The mathematicians overlooked the complexity and inconsistency that mark human beings and our social constructs. Early work on AI focused heavily on theorem-proving and on games and problems with a strong logical focus, such as Chess and Go. In 1988 McCarthy, who espoused predicate calculus as a foundation for AI, summed it up as follows:

> As suggested by the term "artificial intelligence" we weren't considering human behavior except as a clue to possible effective

ways of doing tasks. The only participants who studied human behavior were Newell and Simon. (The goal) was to get away from studying human behavior and consider the computer as a tool for solving certain classes of problems. Thus AI was created as a branch of computer science and not as a branch of psychology. (McCarthy, 1988, online)

Strong expectations for AI date back to its pre-dawn, when in the summer of 1949 Alan Turing was quoted in the *London Times*:

I do not see why [the computer] should not enter any one of the fields normally covered by the human intellect, and eventually compete on equal terms. I do not think you can even draw the line about sonnets, though the comparison is perhaps a little bit unfair because a sonnet written by a machine will be better appreciated by another machine. (Turing, 1949, online)

Licklider, a psychologist, saw that speech understanding was important to AI and difficult; he predicted that intelligent machines would appear in 15 to 500 years (Pew, 2003). As director of ARPA's Information Processing Techniques Office from 1962–1964, he initiated extensive support for computer science in general and AI in particular. MIT's Project Mac, founded in 1963 by Marvin Minsky and others, initially received $13M per year, rising to $24M in 1969. ARPA also sponsored the Artificial Intelligence Laboratory at Stanford Research Institute (SRI), AI research at SRI and Carnegie Mellon University (CMU), and Nicholas Negroponte's Machine Architecture Group at MIT. A dramatic early achievement, SRI's Shakey the Robot, was featured in 1970 articles in *Life* (Darrach, 1970) and *National Geographic* (White, 1970). Given a simple but non-trivial task, Shakey could apparently go to the desired location, scan and reason about the surroundings, and move objects as needed to accomplish the goal (for Shakey at work, see www.ai.sri.com/shakey).

In 1970, Negroponte outlined the case for machine intelligence:

People generally distrust the concept of machines that approach (and thus why not pass?) our own human intelligence. ... Why ask a machine to learn, to understand, to associate courses with goals, to be self-improving, to be ethical—in short, to be intelligent? (Negroponte, 1970, quoted by Baecker & Buxton, 1987, p. 50)

His answer to his own question was, "Because any design procedure, set of rules, or truism is tenuous, if not subversive, when used out of context or regardless of context" (p. 50). This insightful analysis, that it is risky to apply algorithms without understanding the situation at hand, led to a false inference: "It follows that a mechanism must recognize and understand the context before carrying out an operation" (p. 50).

A more tractable alternative is for the mechanism to be guided by humans who are cognizant of the context: Licklider's human-machine symbiosis. Ignoring this, Negroponte built a case for an ambitious research program:

> Therefore, a machine must be able to discern changes in meaning brought about by changes in context, hence, be intelligent. And to do this, it must have a sophisticated set of sensors, effectors, and processors to view the real world directly and indirectly. ... A paradigm for fruitful conversations must be machines that can speak and respond to a natural language. ... But, the tete-à-tete [sic] must be even more direct and fluid; it is gestures, smiles, and frowns that turn a conversation into a dialogue. ... Hand waving often carries as much meaning as text. Manner carries cultural information: the Arabs use their noses, the Japanese nod their heads. ...
>
> Imagine a machine that can follow your design methodology and at the same time discern and assimilate your conversational idiosyncrasies. This same machine, after observing your behavior, could build a predictive model of your conversational performance. Such a machine could then reinforce the dialogue by using the predictive model to respond to you in a manner that is in rhythm with your personal behavior and conversational idiosyncrasies. ... The dialogue would be so intimate—even exclusive—that only mutual persuasion and compromise would bring about ideas, ideas unrealizable by either conversant alone. No doubt, in such a symbiosis it would not be solely the human designer who would decide when the machine is relevant. (Negroponte, 1970, quoted by Baecker & Buxton, 1987, p. 50)

The same year, Negroponte's MIT colleague Minsky went further, as reported in *Life*:

> In from three to eight years we will have a machine with the general intelligence of an average human being. I mean a machine that will be able to read Shakespeare, grease a car, play office politics, tell a joke, have a fight. At that point the machine will begin to educate itself with fantastic speed. In a few months it will be at genius level and a few months after that its powers will be incalculable. (Darrach, 1970, p. 59)

Other AI researchers told Darrach (p. 59) that Minsky's timetable was ambitious: "'Give us 15 years' was a common remark—but all agreed that there would be such a machine and that it would precipitate the third Industrial Revolution, wipe out war and poverty and roll up centuries of growth in science, education and the arts."

Such predictions were common. In 1960, Nobel laureate and AI pioneer Herb Simon wrote, "Machines will be capable, within twenty years, of doing any work that a man can do" (Simon, 1960, p. 96). Five years later, I. J. Good (1965, p. 31), an Oxford mathematician, wrote, "the survival of man depends on the early construction of an ultra-intelligent machine" that "could design even better machines; there would then unquestionably be an 'intelligence explosion,' and the intelligence of man would be left far behind" (p. 33).

Responding to such calls, ARPA initiated major funding of speech recognition and natural language understanding in 1971. Five years later, disappointed with the progress, ARPA discontinued support for speech and language—for a while.

In Europe, a similar story unfolded. Through the 1960s, AI research expanded in Great Britain. A principal proponent was Turing's former colleague Donald Michie. Then in 1973, the Lighthill Report (Lighthill, 1973), which had been commissioned by the Science and Engineering Research Council, reached generally negative conclusions about the prospects for AI systems to scale up to address real-world problems. Almost all government funding was cut off.

The next decade is considered an AI winter, a recurrent season in which research funding is redirected away from AI due to disillusionment over unfulfilled promises.

Library Schools Embrace Information Science

The emphasis on technology in response to Sputnik had shown that the World War II "Big Science" research was not an anomaly. Aligning research and national priorities became a priority. Early information science, as well as studies of "human information behavior" initiated in the 1960s and 1970s, focused on support for scholarship and applications in science and engineering (Fidel, 2010).

Terminal-based computing costs declined. Concern about "information explosions" increased. With information science and technology unquestionably part of the future, the terms swept into use. The Pittsburgh and Georgia Institute of Technology programs flourished. Pittsburgh created the first information science Ph.D. program in the U.S. in 1970, focused on training information science scholars, and identifying humans "as the central factor in the development of an understanding of information phenomena" (Aspray, 1999, p. 12). The program balanced behavioral sciences (psychology, linguistics, communications) and technical grounding (automata theory, computer science). The emphasis shifted from behavior to technology over time. In 1973, Pittsburgh established the first information science department, and its program developed an extremely strong international reputation. Upon being awarded a major National Science Foundation (NSF) center grant in 1966, the Georgia Tech school expanded, and in 1970 became a Ph.D.-granting school rechristened Information and Computer Science.

In 1968, the American Documentation Institute became the American Society for Information Science; two years later the journal *American Documentation* became the *Journal of the American Society for Information Science*. In 1978 the ACM Special Interest Group on Information Retrieval (SIGIR) formed and launched an annual conference (titled "Information Storage and Retrieval" in this period), modeled on a 1971 conference. In 1984, the Association of American Library Schools somewhat belatedly embraced the i-word by renaming itself the Association for Library and Information Science Education (ALISE).

By 1980, schools at over a dozen universities had added *information* to their titles, many of them library school transitions. Delivery on the promise lagged, however. For example, from 1965 to 1972 the Ford and Carnegie Foundations, NSF, DARPA, and the American Newspaper Publishers Association invested over $30 million of today's dollars in MIT's Project Intrex (Burke, 1998). The largest non-military information research project of its time, Intrex was to be the library of the future. Online catalogs were to include up to 50 index fields per item, accessible on CRT displays, with full text of books and articles converted to microfilm and read via television displays. None of this proved feasible.

The ARPANET debuted in 1969, supporting email in 1971 and file-sharing in 1973. This spurred visions of a network society of the future (Hiltz & Turoff, 1978). As an aside, the technological optimism of AI and networking researchers of this era seems less insightful and nuanced than the view of E. M. Forster (1909), who in 1909 anticipated both developments in his story "The Machine Stops."

1980–1985: Discretionary Use Comes Into Focus

In 1980, most people in HF&E and IS were focused on the down-to-earth business of making efficient use of expensive mainframes. Almost unnoticed was the start of a major shift. Less expensive but highly capable minicomputers based on LSI technology enabled Digital Equipment Corporation, Wang Laboratories, and Data General to make inroads into the mainframe market. At the low end, home computers gained capability. Students and hobbyist programmers were drawn to these minis and micros, creating a population of hands-on discretionary users. There were limited trials of online library catalogs and electronic journal production.

Then, between 1981 and 1984, a flood of innovative and powerful computers was released: Xerox Star, IBM PC, Apple Lisa, Lisp machines from Symbolics and LMI (Lisp Machines, Inc.), workstations from Sun Microsystems and Silicon Graphics, and the Apple Macintosh. On January 1, 1984, AT&T's breakup into competing companies took effect. AT&T had the most employees and the most customers of any U.S. company. Neither its customers nor its employees had had much discretion in technology use, so AT&T and its Bell Laboratories division had focused on improving training and efficiency through human factors. Suddenly freed from a ban on entering the computer business while it had a monopoly on telephony, AT&T launched the ill-fated Unix PC in 1985. AT&T and the regional telephone operating companies now faced customers who had choices, and their HCI focus broadened accordingly (see Israelski & Lund, 2003).

In general, lower-priced computers created markets for shrinkwrap software; and for the first time, computer and software companies targeted significant numbers of non-technical hands-on users who received little or no formal training.

After twenty years, early visions were being realized. Non-programmers were choosing to use computers to do their work. The psychology of discretionary users was of particular interest to two groups: psychologists who liked to use computers and technology companies planning to sell to discretionary users. Result: Computer and telecommunication companies hired many experimental psychologists. Before describing this, I elaborate on the shift from non-discretionary operation to discretionary use of computers.

Discretion in Computer Use

Our lives are distributed along a continuum between the assembly line nightmare of *Modern Times* and utopian visions of completely empowered individuals. To use a technology or not to use it: Sometimes we have a choice, other times we do not. On the telephone, we may have to wrestle with speech recognition and routing systems. In contrast, home computer use may be largely discretionary. The workplace often lies in between: Technologies are recommended or prescribed, but we can ignore some injunctions, obtain exceptions, use some features but not others, and join with colleagues to press for changes in policy or availability.

For early computer builders, work was more a calling than a job, but operation required a staff to carry out essential if less interesting tasks. For the first half of the computing era, most hands-on use was by people given a mandate. Hardware innovation, more versatile software, and steady progress in understanding the psychology of users and tasks— and transferring that understanding to software developers—led to hands-on users with more choice in what they did and how they did it. Rising expectations played a role—people learned that software is flexible and expected it to be more congenial. Competition among vendors produced alternatives. Today there is more emphasis on marketing to consumers, more stress on user-friendliness.

Discretion is not all-or-none. No one must use a computer, but many jobs and pastimes require it. True, people can resist, sabotage, or quit the job. However, a clerk or systems administrator is in a different situation from someone using technology for leisure activity. For an airline reservation operator, computer use is mandatory. For a traveler booking a flight, computer use is discretionary. I explore effects of these differences.

The shift toward greater discretion was gradual. A quarter of a century ago, John Bennett (1979) predicted that discretionary use would lead to more emphasis on usability. The book *Human Interaction With Computers,* edited by Harold Smith and Thomas Green (1980) and published the following year, perched on a cusp. Jens Rasmussen's (1980) chapter, "The Human as a Systems Component," covered the nondiscretionary perspective. One-third of the book covered research on programming. The remainder addressed "non-specialist people," discretionary users who are not computer-savvy (Smith & Green, 1980, p. viii). The editors continued, "It's not enough just to establish what computer systems can and cannot do; we need to spend just as much effort establishing what people can *and want to do*" (emphasis in the original).

A decade later, Liam Bannon (1991, p. 25) noted broader implications of a shift "from human factors to human actors." The trajectory is not always toward choice. Discretion can be curtailed—for example, word processor use is now often a job requirement, not simply an alternative to using a typewriter. Even in an era of specialization, customization, and competition, the exercise of choice varies over time and across contexts.

Discretion is one factor of many, but an analysis of its role casts light on how HCI efforts differ and why they have remained distinct (Figure 8.1).

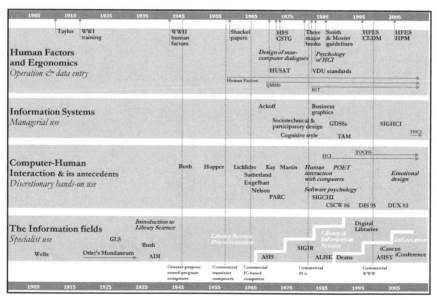

Figure 8.1 **Some of the HCI events and topics discussed. Acronym expansions are in the text.**

Minicomputers and Office Automation

Cabinet-sized computers that could support several people were available from the mid-1960s. Starting with the VAX 11/780, super-minis by the late 1970s supported integrated suites of productivity tools. In 1980, Digital Equipment Corporation, Data General, and Wang Laboratories were growth companies near Boston. Digital became the second largest computer company in the world.

A minicomputer could handle a database of moderate size or personal productivity tools used from terminals. For "dumb terminals," the central processor handled each keystroke; other minicomputer terminals had a processor that supported entering a screenful of data that was then sent as a batch to the central processor. These minis could provide a small group (or office) with file sharing, word processing, spreadsheets, email, and output devices. They were marketed as "office systems," "office automation systems," or "office information systems."

In 1980, the Stanford International Symposium on Office Automation launched a research field that was influential for a decade. Douglas Engelbart contributed two papers to the proceedings (Landau, Bair, & Siegman, 1982). The same year, the American Federation of Information Processing Societies (AFIPS, which was underwriting ACM and IEEE at the time) held the first of seven annual office automation conferences and product exhibitions. Also in 1980, ACM formed a Special Interest Group on Office Automation (SIGOA), which two years later launched the biennial Conference on Office Information System (COIS). In 1983 *ACM Transactions on Office Information Systems* (*TOIS*) emerged, one year after the independent journal *Office: Technology and People*.

Office information systems, which focused on the use of minicomputers, was positioned alongside management information systems, which focused on mainframes. Its scope was reflected in the charter of *TOIS*: database theory, artificial intelligence, behavioral studies, organizational theory, and communications. Minis were accessible database research tools; Digital's PDP series was a favorite of AI researchers; minis were familiar to behavioral researchers who used them to run and analyze experiments; and they became interactive computers of choice for many organizations. Computer-mediated communication was an intriguing new capability. Networking was still rare, but users at different terminals of a minicomputer could exchange email or chat in real time.

Researchers were discretionary computer users, but most office workers did not choose their tools. The term automation, challenging and exciting to the researchers, conjured up different images for office workers; some researchers preferred Engelbart's focus on augmentation rather than automation.

Papers in the SIGOA newsletter, COIS, and *TOIS* included technical work on database theory, a modest number of AI papers (the AI winter had not yet ended), decision support and computer-mediated communication papers from the IS community, and behavioral studies by researchers who later became active in CHI. IS papers were prevalent in the newsletter and technical papers in the journal. The journal was also a major outlet for behavioral studies before *HCI* started in 1985.

Although OA/OIS research was eventually absorbed by other fields, it led the way in identifying a range of important emerging issues, including hypertext, computer-mediated communication, and collaboration support more generally. Some OIS work was conceptually linked to the technical side of information science, notably in information retrieval and language processing.

The Formation of ACM SIGCHI

Major threads of HCI research arc illustrated in Figure 8.1: Human factors, information systems, and the research focused on discretionary hands-on use that became a significant force with the spread of microcomputers. In 1980, as IBM prepared to launch the PC, a groundswell of attention to computer user behavior was building. IBM had recently added software to hardware as a product focus. Several cognitive psychologists joined an IBM research group that included John Gould, who had engaged in human factors research since the late 1960s. They initiated empirical studies of programming and software design and use. Other psychologists leading recently formed HCI groups included Phil Barnard at the Medical Research Council Applied Psychology Unit in Cambridge, England; Tom Landauer at Bell Labs; Donald Norman at the University of California, San Diego; and John Whiteside at Digital Equipment Corp.

Xerox PARC and its CMU collaborators were particularly active, continuing work in several areas that proved to have singular influence. The 1981 Star, with its carefully designed graphical user interface, was not a commercial success (nor was a flurry of GUIs that followed, including the Apple Lisa), but it influenced researchers and developers—and of course the Macintosh.

Communications of the ACM created a "Human Aspects of Computing" department in 1980. The next year, Tom Moran edited a special issue of *Computing Surveys* on "The Psychology of the Computer User." Also in 1981, the ACM Special Interest Group on Social and Behavioral Science Computing (SIGSOC) extended its workshop to cover interactive software design and use. In 1982 a conference in Gaithersburg, Maryland on "Human Factors in Computing Systems" was unexpectedly well attended. Shortly afterward, SIGSOC shifted its focus to computer-human interaction and its name to SIGCHI (Borman, 1996).

In 1983, the first CHI conference drew more than 1,000 people. Half of the 58 papers were from the seven research labs just mentioned. Cognitive psychologists in industry dominated the program, although the Human Factors Society co-sponsored the conference and contributed the program chair Richard Pew, committee members Sid Smith, H. Rudy

Ramsay, and Paul Green, and several presenters. Brian Shackel and HFS president Robert Williges gave tutorials the first day.

The first profession to become discretionary hands-on users was computer programming, as paper coding sheets were discarded in favor of text editing at interactive terminals, PCs, and small minicomputers. Therefore, many early CHI papers, by Ruven Brooks, Bill Curtis, Thomas Green, Ben Shneiderman, and others, continued the psychology-of-programming research thread. IBM Watson researchers also contributed, as noted by John Thomas (personal communication, October 2003):

> One of the main themes of the early work was basically that we in IBM were afraid that the market for computing would be limited by the number of people who could program complex systems so we wanted to find ways for "non-programmers" to be able, essentially, to program.

Psychologists and studies of editing were so prevalent that Thomas Green remarked at the 1984 INTERACT Conference that "text editors are the white rats of HCI." As personal computing spread and the same methods were applied to studying other discretionary use, studies of programming gradually disappeared from HCI conferences.

CHI focused on novice use. Initial experience is particularly important to discretionary users and to the vendors developing software for them. Novice users are also a natural focus when studying new technologies and a critical focus when more people take up computing each year than did the year before.

Routinized heavy use was still widespread. Databases were used by airlines, banks, government agencies, and other organizations. This hands-on activity was rarely discretionary. Managers oversaw development and analyzed data, leaving data entry and information retrieval to people hired for those jobs. Improving skilled data handling was a human factors undertaking. CHI studies of database use were few—I count three over a decade, all focused on novice or casual use.

Fewer European companies produced mass-market software. European research favored in-house development and use. In his perceptive essay, Bannon (1991) urged that more attention be paid to discretionary use, yet criticized CHI's heavy emphasis on initial experiences, perhaps reflecting the European perspective. At Loughborough University, HUSAT focused on job design (the division of labor between people and systems) and collaborated with the Institute for Consumer Ergonomics, particularly on product safety. In 1984, Loughborough initiated an HCI graduate program drawing on human factors, industrial engineering, and computer science. The International Conference on Human–Computer Interaction (INTERACT), first held in London in 1984 and chaired by Shackel, drew HF&E and CHI researchers.

The early visionaries were not familiar to many of the CHI researchers who turned some of the visions into reality. The 633 references in the 58 papers presented at CHI '83 included many authored by cognitive scientists, but Bush, Sutherland, and Engelbart were not cited at all. Many computer scientists familiar with the early work entered CHI a few years later and the CHI psychologists eventually discovered and identified with these pioneers. Both groups were concerned with discretionary use. This conceptual continuity bestowed legitimacy on a young enterprise seeking to establish itself academically and professionally.

CHI and Human Factors Diverge

> Hard science, in the form of engineering, drives out soft science, in the form of human factors. —Newell and Card (1985, p. 212)

Between 1980 and 1985, researchers at Xerox PARC and CMU launched another influential research program. Card, Moran, and Newell (1980a, 1980b) introduced a "keystroke-level model for user performance time with interactive systems" (Card, Moran, & Newell, 1980b, p. 396), followed by the cognitive model GOMS—goals operators, methods, and selection rules—in their landmark book, *The Psychology of Human–Computer Interaction* (Card, Moran, & Newell, 1983).

This work was highly respected by the cognitive psychologists who made up much of CHI at the time. However, these models did not address discretionary, novice use. They focused on the repetitive expert use studied in human factors. In fact, GOMS was explicitly positioned in opposition to the stimulus-response bias of human factors research:

> Human factors specialists, ergonomists, and human engineers will find that we have synthesized ideas from modern cognitive psychology and artificial intelligence with the old methods of task analysis. ... The user is not an operator. He does not operate the computer, he communicates with it. (Card, Moran, & Newell, 1983, p. viii)

Newell and Card (1985, p. 221) noted that human factors had a role in design, but continued: "Classical human factors ... has all the earmarks of second-class status. (Our approach) avoids continuation of the classical human-factors role (by transforming) the psychology of the interface into a hard science."

In an email message sent in June 2004, Card wrote: "Human factors was the discipline we were trying to improve. ... I personally changed the (CHI conference) call in 1986 so as to emphasize computer science and reduce the emphasis on cognitive science, because I was afraid that it would just become human factors again."

Ultimately, human performance modeling drew a modest but fervent CHI following. Key goals of the modelers differed from those of practitioners and other researchers. "The central idea behind the model is that the time for an expert to do a task on an interactive system is determined by the time it takes to do the keystrokes," wrote Card, Moran, and Newell (1980b, p. 397). Modeling was extended to a range of cognitive processes but remained most useful in helping to design for nondiscretionary users, such as telephone operators engaged in repetitive tasks (e.g., Gray, John, Stuart, Lawrence, & Atwood, 1990). Its role in augmenting human intellect was unclear.

CHI and human factors moved apart, although "Human Factors in Computing Systems" remains the CHI conference subtitle. They were never closely integrated. Most of the cognitive psychologists had turned to HCI after earning their degrees and were unfamiliar with the human factors research literature. The Human Factors Society did not again cosponsor CHI and its researchers disappeared from the CHI program committee. Most CHI researchers who had published in the annual Human Factors conference and the *Human Factors* journal shifted to CHI, *Communications of the ACM,* and the journal *Human–Computer Interaction* established in 1985 by Moran and published by Erlbaum, a publisher of psychology books and journals.

The shift was reflected at IBM T.J. Watson Research Center. John Gould and Clayton Lewis (1983) authored a CHI '83 paper that nicely defined the CHI focus on user-centered, iterative design based on prototyping. Watson cognitive scientists helped shape CHI, but Gould's principal focus remained human factors; he served as HFS president four years later. Symbolically, in 1984, Watson's Human Factors Group faded away and a User Interface Institute emerged.

CHI researchers, wanting to be seen as doing "hard" science or engineering, adopted the terms "cognitive engineering" and "usability engineering." In the first paper presented at CHI '83, "Design Principles for Human–Computer Interfaces," Donald Norman (1983, p. 1) applied engineering techniques to discretionary use, creating what he called "user satisfaction functions" based on technical parameters. Only years later did CHI loosen its identification with engineering.

Workstations and Another AI Summer

High-end workstations from Apollo, Sun, and Silicon Graphics appeared between 1981 and 1984. Graphics researchers no longer had to congregate in heavily financed labs (notably MIT and Utah in the 1960s; MIT, New York Institute of Technology [NYIT], and PARC in the 1970s). These workstations were too expensive to reach a mass market, so graphics research that focused on photorealism and animation did not directly influence HCI more broadly.

The Xerox Star (formally named Office Workstation), Apple Lisa, and other commercial GUIs appeared; but when the first CHI conference was held in December 1983 none was succeeding. They cost too much or ran on processors that were too weak to exploit graphics effectively.

In 1981, Symbolics and LMI introduced their workstations optimized for the Lisp programming language favored by most AI researchers. The timing was fortuitous. In October of that year, a conference on Next Generation Technology was held in the National Chamber of Commerce auditorium in Tokyo; and in 1982 the Japanese government announced the establishment of the Institute for New Generation Computer Technology (ICOT) and its ten-year Fifth Generation project focused on AI. AI researchers in Europe and the U.S. sounded the alarm. Donald Michie at Edinburgh saw a threat to western computer technology, and Ed Feigenbaum from Stanford wrote:

> The Japanese are planning the miracle product. ... They're going to give the world the next generation—the Fifth Generation—of computers, and those machines are going to be intelligent. ... We stand, however, before a singularity, an event so unprecedented that predictions are almost silly. ... Who can say how universal access to machine intelligence— faster, deeper, better than human intelligence—will change science, economics, and warfare, and the whole intellectual and sociological development of mankind? (Feigenbaum & McCorduck, 1983, pp. 8–9, 287)

At the same time, parallel distributed processing or neural net models seized the attention of researchers and the media. Used to model a wide range of phenomena including signal detection, motor control, and semantic processing, neural nets represented conceptual and technical advances over earlier AI work on perceptrons. They were of particular interest because the new generation of minicomputers and workstations supported simulation experiments. Production systems, a computer-intensive AI modeling approach with a psychological foundation developed at CMU, also gained wider use in research.

These developments triggered an artificial intelligence gold rush. As with actual gold rushes, most of the money was made by those who outfitted and provisioned the prospectors, although generous government funding again flowed to AI researchers. The European ESPRIT and U.K. Alvey programs invested over $200M per year starting in 1984 (Oakley, 1990). In the U.S., funding for the DARPA Strategic Computing AI program alone, begun in 1983, rose to almost $400M in 1988 (Norberg & O'Neill, 1996). Investment in AI by 150 U.S. companies was estimated at about $2B in 1985 (Kao, 1998).

The unfulfilled promises of the past led to changes this time around. General problem solving was emphasized less, domain-specific problem solving was emphasized more. Terms such as *intelligent knowledge-based systems, knowledge engineering, expert systems, machine learning, language understanding, image understanding, neural nets,* and *robotics* were often favored over *AI.*

In 1983, Raj Reddy of CMU and Victor Zue of MIT criticized the mid-1970s abandonment of speech processing research, and soon funds were again plentiful (Norberg & O'Neill, 1996, p. 238). Johnson (1985) estimated that 800 corporate employees and 400 academics were working on natural language processing research in 1985. Commercial natural language understanding (NLU) interfaces to databases such as AI Corporation's Intellect and Microrim Clout appeared.

AI optimism is illustrated by two meticulously researched Ovum reports on speech and language processing (Engelien & McBryde, 1991; Johnson, 1985). In 1985, speech and language product "revenue" was $75 million, comprising mostly income from grants and investor capital. That year, Ovum projected that sales would reach $750 million by 1990 and $2.75 billion by 1995. In 1991, sales were under $90 million; but hope springs eternal, and Ovum forecast $490 million for 1995 and $3.6 billion for 2000.

U.S. corporations banded together, jointly funding the Microelectronics and Computer Technology Corporation (MCC). U.S. antitrust laws were relaxed to allow this cooperation. MCC embraced AI, reportedly becoming the leading customer for both Symbolics and LMI. MCC projects included two parallel NLU efforts, work on intelligent advising, and CYC (as in "encyclopedic," and later spelled Cyc), Douglas Lenat's ambitious project to build an encyclopedic common-sense knowledge base that other programs could consult. In 1984, Lenat predicted that by 1994 CYC would be intelligent enough to educate itself. Five years later CYC was reported to be on schedule and about to "spark a vastly greater renaissance in [machine learning]" (Lenat, 1989, p. 257).

Knowledge engineering involved human interaction. This could have brought AI closer to HCI, but AI researchers interested in representation and reasoning were frustrated by the difficulty of eliciting knowledge from experts. The latter non-discretionary activity created opportunities for HF&E, especially in Europe, where funding directives encouraged work that spanned technical and behavioral concerns. *International Journal of Man-Machine Studies* became a major outlet for both HF&E and AI research in the 1980s.

AI interaction with CHI was limited. CHI '83 and CHI '85 had sessions on speech and language, cognitive modeling, knowledge-based help, and knowledge elicitation; but in general, AI technologies did not succeed in the marketplace and were often directed at non-discretionary users. Before it disappeared, AI Corporation's primary customer for the database interface Intellect was the government. Few AI researchers and developers worried about interaction details. For example, they loved powerful tools such as EMACS and UNIX and forgot the painful weeks that were required to learn badly-designed command languages.

1985–1995: Graphical User Interfaces Succeed

> There will *never* be a mouse at the Ford Motor Company.
> —High-level acquisition manager (personal communication, 1985)

Graphical user interfaces were a disruptive revolution when they succeeded commercially, as were earlier shifts to stored programs and to interaction based on commands, full-screen forms, and full-screen menus. Some people were affected before others.

GUIs were particularly attractive to new users. Their success immediately affected the CHI field. However, only after Windows 3.0 succeeded in 1990 did GUIs influence the government agencies and business organizations that were the focus of HF&E and IS researchers. By 1990, the technology was better understood and less disruptive. The early 1990s also saw the maturation of local area networks and the internet, leading to a second transformation: computer-mediated communication and information sharing.

CHI Embraces Computer Science

Apple launched the Macintosh with a 1984 Super Bowl ad aimed at office work, but sales did not follow and in mid-1985 Apple was in trouble. Then Macs appeared with four times as much random access memory (RAM), sufficient to manage Aldus PageMaker, Adobe Postscript, the Apple LaserWriter, and Microsoft's Excel and Word for Macintosh as they were released. The more powerful Mac Plus arrived in January, 1986. Rescued by hardware and software advances, the Mac succeeded where the many commercial GUIs before it had not. It was popular with consumers and became the platform for desktop publishing.

Even within CHI, GUIs were initially controversial. They had disadvantages: an extra level of interface code increased development complexity and created reliability challenges; they consumed processor cycles and distanced users from the underlying system that, many believed, experienced users would eventually have to learn. Carroll and Mazur (1986) showed that GUIs confused and created problems for people familiar with existing interfaces. An influential essay on direct manipulation interfaces (Hutchins, Hollan, & Norman, 1986, p. 119) concluded, "It is too early to tell" how GUIs would fare. GUIs could well prove useful for novices, they wrote, but "we would not be surprised if experts are *slower* with Direct Manipulation systems than with command language systems" (p. 121). Because most prior HCI research had focused on expert use, this valid insight seemed significant. However, first-time use was critical in the rapidly expanding consumer market. Hardware and software advances overcame other difficulties. GUIs were here to stay.

The effects within CHI were dramatic. Active topics of research, including command naming, text editing, and the psychology of programming, were quickly abandoned. More technical topics such as user interface management systems became significant. At a higher level, psychology gave way to computer science as the driving force in interaction design.

Researchers had been engaged in establishing a comprehensive, theoretical, psychological framework based on formal experiments (Barnard, 1991; Carroll & Campbell, 1986; Long, 1989; Newell & Card, 1985). Such a framework was conceivable for constrained command- and form-based interaction, but could not be scaled up to design spaces that included color, sound, animation, and an endless variety of icons, menu designs, and window arrangements. The immediate mission was to identify the most pressing problems and satisfactory rather than optimal solutions. Rigorous experimentation, the principal skill of cognitive psychologists, gave way to quicker, less precise assessment methods. And to explore the dynamically evolving, unconstrained design space required software engineering expertise.

As a result, the late 1980s saw an influx of computer scientists into the CHI community. HCI entered the curricula of many computer science departments. Computer scientists working on interactive graphics saw CHI as a natural home, as did software engineers interested in interaction and some AI researchers working on speech recognition, language understanding, and expert systems. In 1994 ACM launched *Transactions on Computer-Human Interaction*. Some computer scientists brought with them knowledge of the early pioneering work that was unknown to many cognitive scientists.

Early PCs and Macs were not easily networked, but as local area networks spread, CHI's focus expanded to include collaboration support. This brought it into contact with efforts in MIS and office automation research.

Human Factors and Ergonomics Maintains a Non-Discretionary Use Focus

HF&E research continued to respond to the needs of government agencies, the military, aviation, and telecommunications. Government is the largest consumer of computing, with heavy use for census, tax, social security, health and welfare, power plant operation, air traffic control, ground control for space missions, military logistics text and voice processing for intelligence, and so on.

Most users in these settings are assigned technology. The focus is on skilled use. Small efficiency gains in individual transactions can yield large benefits over time. For routine data entry and other tasks, improvements that may not influence discretionary users can make a difference. After CHI formed, the Human Factors Society undertook a study to see how it would affect membership in its Computer Systems

Technical Group and found an unexpectedly small overlap (Richard Pew, personal communication, September 15, 2004).

Research funding in HF&E responded to governmental concerns and initiatives. Government agencies promoted the development of ergonomic standards, in part to help with the problem of defining system requirements for competitive bidding while remaining at arm's length from the potential developers who better understand technical possibilities. Compliance with standards could be specified in a contract.

In 1986, Sid Smith and Jane Mosier published the last of a series of government-sponsored interface guidelines (Smith & Mosier, 1986). Some 944 specific design guidelines were organized into sections titled Data Entry, Data Display, Data Transmission, Data Protection, Sequence Control, and User Guidance. The authors recognized that GUIs would expand the design space beyond the reach of an already cumbersome, comprehensive set of guidelines that did not cover icons, pull-down or pop-up menus, mice button assignments, sound, animation, and so on. Requirements definition shifted to specify predefined interface styles and design processes rather than features to be built from scratch.

DARPA's heavily funded Strategic Computing program set out to develop an Autonomous Land Vehicle, a Pilot's Associate, and a Battle Management system. All raised human factors research issues. These systems were to include interactive technologies such as speech recognition, language understanding, and heads-up displays. People might avoid these technologies when given a choice, but pilots, those guiding autonomous vehicles, and officers under stressful conditions might have no better alternative. Speech and language technologies might also have civilian uses: by translators and intelligence analysts, or when a telephone system provides no alternative, a disability limits keyboard use, or hands are otherwise occupied.

Information Systems Extends Its Range

Although graphical user interfaces were not quickly adopted by organizations, business graphics was important in a research field focused on managerial use. Remus (1984) contrasted tabular and graphic presentations, Benbasat and Dexter (1985) added color as another factor, and many studies followed. The concept of cognitive fit between task and tool was introduced in this context to explain apparently contradictory results in the literature (Vessey & Galletta, 1991). Studies considered online and paper presentation. In practice, color displays were rare in the 1980s; most managers dealt with printed reports.

Involvement of internal end-users in the development process was actively discussed, but rarely practiced outside of sociotechnical and participatory movements (Friedman, 1989). Hands-on managerial use was atypical, but it was central to group decision support systems research, which emerged from decision support systems and evolved into group support systems. Computer-supported meeting facility research was conducted in the mid-1980s in several laboratories (e.g., Begeman, Cook, Ellis, Graf, Rein, & Smith, 1986; Dennis, George, Jessup, Nunamaker, & Vogel, 1988; DeSanctis & Gallupe, 1987). Jay Nunamaker's group at the University of Arizona explored approaches to brainstorming, idea organizing, online voting, and other meeting activities (Nunamaker, Briggs, Mittleman, Vogel, & Balthazard, 1997). These systems were too expensive to be mass-market products—they were directed at decision makers, with key research in schools of management rather than computer science departments or software companies. This became a major IS contribution to Computer Supported Cooperative Work (CSCW).

The Technology Acceptance Model (TAM) introduced in F. D. Davis (1989) gave rise to considerable IS research. TAM focuses on perceived usefulness and perceived usability to improve "white collar performance" that is "often obstructed by users' unwillingness to accept and use available systems" (p. 319). "An element of uncertainty exists in the minds of decision makers with respect to the successful adoption," wrote Bagozzi, Davis, and Warshaw (1992, p. 664). This managerial view of individual behavior was influenced by Davis's exposure to some early CHI usability research.

High interest in TAM showed that the IS focus, in which hands-on use was primarily non-discretionary operation, data entry, and data retrieval, was shifting as hands-on use spread to white-collar workers who could refuse to play. Contrast IS with CHI: Consumers choose technologies that they perceive to be useful, so CHI assumes perceived utility and rarely considers utility at all. TAM researchers considered utility more important than usability. CHI focused on usability a decade before TAM, albeit more on measures of actual usability than measures of perceived usability. Perception was a secondary user satisfaction measure to CHI researchers, who believed (not entirely correctly) that measurable reduction in time, errors, questions, and training would, over time, translate into positive perceptions. Acceptance is not in the CHI vocabulary. A discretionary user chooses or adopts, rather than accepts.

The *Harvard Business Review* published "Usability: The New Dimension of Product Design" (March, 1994). In concluding that "user-centered design is still in its infancy," it made no mention of CHI (p. 149). The communities remained largely isolated.

Collaboration Support: OIS Gives Way to CSCW

In the late 1980s, three research communities focused on small-group communication and information sharing: (1) office automation/office information systems (discussed previously); (2) IS researchers focused on tools to support organizational decision making could apply them to group decision making more generally as computing costs declined; and (3) the proliferation of LAN networks encouraged some CHI researchers to move from individual productivity to a quest for so-called "killer apps" to support teams.

Although the OA/OIS field had led the way, it declined and largely disappeared in this period. The minicomputer, platform for most of OIS research, did not survive competition from PCs and workstations. The concept of "office" or group was problematic: organizations and individuals are persistent entities with goals and needs, but small groups often have ambiguous membership and shift in character as members join or depart. People with a need to communicate through technology often fall under different budgets, complicating technology acquisition decisions unless the technology is available organization-wide.

The rapid shift was reflected in terminology use. First, *automation* fell out of favor; in 1986, ACM SIGOA shifted to SIGOIS (Office Information Systems) and the annual AFIPS OA conferences ended. By 1991, the term *office* followed: *Transactions on Office Information Systems* became *Transactions on Information Systems*; *Office: Information and People* became *Information Technology and People*; "Conference on Office Information Systems" became "Conference on Organizational Communication Systems."

The AI summer, a contributor to the OA/OIS effort, ended when AI failed to meet expectations: Massive funding did not deliver a Pilot's Associate, an Autonomous Land Vehicle, or a Battle Management System for the military, or automated offices for enterprises. CHI conference sessions on language processing had diminished earlier, but sessions on modeling, adaptive interfaces, advising systems, and other uses of intelligence in interfaces increased through the late 1980s before declining in the 1990s. AI research did not disappear, but funding became scarce, employment opportunities dried up, and conference participation dropped off.

Building on a 1984 workshop (Greif, 1985), the 1986 Computer Supported Cooperative Work conference brought together researchers from diverse disciplines interested in issues of communication, information sharing, and coordination. Participants came primarily from IS, OIS, CHI, distributed AI, and anthropology. Four of thirteen CSCW program committee members and many papers were from schools of management, with similar numbers from OIS.

The field coalesced in 1988. *Computer-Supported Cooperative Work*, edited by Irene Greif (1988), was published, and SIGCHI sponsored the North American CSCW conference that would be held biennially. A European CSCW series (ECSCW) was initiated in 1989. With heavy participation from computer and software companies, North American CSCW had a small-group focus on networked individuals working on PCs, workstations, or minis, whether in an organization or linked by proliferating ARPANET, BITNET, or other networks. European participation was from academia and government agencies and focused on organizational users of technologies, as did the IS and OIS communities.

Scandinavian influences, described in the next section, influenced both camps.

Many IS researchers shifted participation to other conferences and a series of less selective bi-annual Groupware conferences that started in 1992. Their newsletter, *Groupware Report,* listed many relevant conferences but not CSCW. The Collaboration Technology track of HICSS (the annual Hawaii International Conference on System Sciences) became a major IS pre-journal publication arena, with some participating in the Organizational Computing Systems (1991–1995) and GROUP (1997–present) descendants of the Conference on Office Information Systems.

CSCW has been challenged by the pace of technology change. In 1985, supporting a small team was a technical challenge; ten years later, the web had arrived. Applications that provided awareness of the activity of distant collaborators was a celebrated achievement in the early 1990s; several years later, dark linings to the silver cloud arose in the form of privacy concerns and information overload. Major phenomena were identified—a productivity paradox in which IT investments were not returning benefits, health effects of internet use on young people—that were not visible in data collected and reported only a few years later. European CSCW had focused on development of IT in large organizations, which shifted to the use of commercial software. North American CSCW found that collaboration could not be supported one team at a time, that organizational context was important. With organizational behavior and theory thriving in other venues, CSCW welcomed ethnographers who studied technology use, a group marginalized in traditional anthropology departments.

CSCW remains a strong research area that has attracted a broad swath of HCI researchers. Content ranges from highly technical work to thick ethnographies of workplace activity, from studies of instant messaging (IM) dyads to scientific collaboratories involving the activities of hundreds of people dispersed in space and time.

Sociotechnical and Participatory Design

Pre-dating this period were experiments in employing design methods to involve systematically specific people who would interact with a resulting system, typically non-discretionary users of systems developed by a large enterprise for its own use. Sociotechnical design (Bjørn-Andersen & Hedberg, 1977; Mumford, 1976) took a managerial perspective, whereas participatory or cooperative design, rooted in the Danish trade union movement, focused on empowering the eventual users (Nygaard, 1977). These efforts became widely influential following the publication of the proceedings of a 1985 conference held in Aarhus, Denmark (Bjerknes, Ehn, & Kyng, 1987). Scandinavian influences also appeared in human factors (e.g., Rasmussen, 1986). The greatest resonance, though, was between Scandinavian and CHI researchers. In spite of cultural differences and differences in the contexts of development (in-house vs. commercial product) and use (non-discretionary vs. discretionary), they shared a focus on empowering hands-on users. They also, on balance, shared the perspective of a generation growing up in the 1960s, unlike the World War II generation that dominated HF&E and IS.

Library and Information Science: An Unfinished Transformation

Research universities have always supported prestigious professional schools, but the prestige of library schools declined as the training emphasis shifted to higher-paid IT and software engineering professions. Between 1978 and 1995, fifteen American library schools were closed (Cronin, 1995). Most of the survivors were rechristened Library and Information Science. Computer technology was unquestionably changing librarianship, requiring new curricula and faculty with different skills.

The changes did not go smoothly or as anticipated. Forced multidisciplinarity is never easy. Traditional library studies had largely dismissed technology, arguably a reasonable reaction to the cost and limitations of new technologies. But, in line with Moore's Law, costs decreased and many of the limitations disappeared with a speed that left little time to prepare. Young information scientists were not interested in absorbing a century of work on indexing, classifying, and providing access to complex information repositories; their eyes were fixed on a future in which many past lessons would not apply—and those that still applied would likely have to be relearned. The conflicts are exposed in a landmark 1983 collection, *The Study of Information: Interdisciplinary Messages* (Machlup & Mansfield, 1983). In the book, Rayward described the different views and argued that there had been some convergence. His essay is followed by commentaries attacking him from both sides.

In a series of meetings beginning in 1988, new deans at Pittsburgh, Syracuse, Drexel, and subsequently Rutgers discussed approaches to explaining and managing multidisciplinary endeavors. In spite of this progressive effort, Cronin (1995, p. 45) describes the library and information science camps as still very much at loggerheads and in a "deep professional malaise" that might require librarianship to be cut loose in favor of stronger ties to cognitive and computer science. In the early 1990s, a handful of universities dropped "library," becoming schools of information (see Figure 8.2). More would follow.

1995–2010: The Internet Era Arrives

How did the spread of the internet and emergence of the web affect the different HCI research threads? CHI researchers were relatively internet savvy. Although excited by the prospects, they took this change in

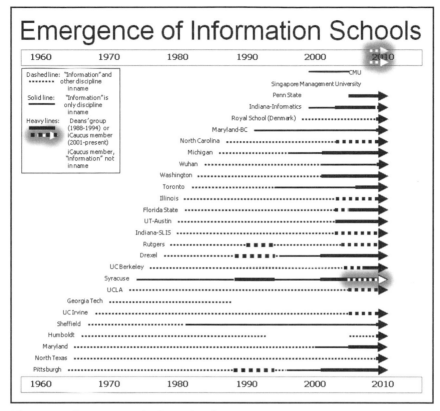

Figure 8.2 Emergence of Information Schools.

stride. Over time, the nature of research, development, and use evolved. The internet and web were not disruptive to human factors and ergonomics, either. The web was initially a return to a form-driven interface style; and for a few people it was a locus of routine work. However, the web had a seismic impact on information systems and information science, so this section begins there.

The Formation of AIS SIGHCI

Computer users in organizations were no longer almost slaves devoted to maximizing computer use—screen savers vied with Solitaire to be the main consumer of processor cycles. Embrace of the internet created more porous organizational boundaries. Employees downloaded free software such as instant messaging clients, music players, and weblog tools inside the firewall in spite of IT concerns about productivity and security. These are not the high-overhead applications of the past. Another change is that home use of software reduced employee patience with poor interactive software at work. In addition, managers who were hands-off users in the 1980s became late adopters in the 1990s, and are now hands-on early adopters of some technologies.

Significant as these changes are, the web had a more dramatic effect on IS research. Corporate IT departments had focused on internal operations; suddenly, organizations were creating web interfaces to external vendors and customers. Discretionary users! The internet bubble revealed that our understanding of these phenomena was limited, but online marketing, services, and business-to-business systems remained important when the bubble burst. The web became an essential business tool. In handling external customers IT professionals and IS researchers were in much the same place CHI had been 20 years earlier, whether they realized it or (most often) not.

In 2001, the Association for Information Systems (AIS) established the Special Interest Group in Human–Computer Interaction (SIGHCI). The founders defined HCI by citing 12 works by CHI researchers (Zhang et al., 2004, p. 148) and made it a priority to bridge to the CHI and the information science communities (Zhang, 2004). Although SIGHCI's charter includes a broad range of organizational issues, published work emphasizes interface design for ecommerce, online shopping, online behavior "especially in the internet era," and effects of web-based interfaces on attitudes and perceptions (p. 1). Eight of the first ten papers in SIGHCI-sponsored journal issues cover internet and web behavior.

In 2009, *AIS Transactions on Human–Computer Interaction* was launched. The shift from an organizational focus to the web and broader *end-user computing* is documented in an article appearing in it: Zhang, Li, Scialdone, and Carey's (2009) analysis of the IS literature related to HCI from 1990 to 2008.

The effort to bridge to CHI foundered, as had previous efforts between CHI and human factors, office information systems, and IS within CSCW. This will be discussed further.

Digital Libraries and the Evolution of LIS

By 1995, a wave of change had occurred (Figure 8.2). Digital technology was in the LIS curriculum. Familiarity with technology use was a prerequisite for librarianship. Overall, though, innovative research had not kept pace with professional training (Cronin, 1995).

Use of the internet grew exponentially, but in 1995 it was still a niche activity found mainly on campuses. In the mid-1990s, Gopher, a convenient system for downloading files from around the internet, attracted attention as a possible springboard for indexing distributed materials. Wells's (1938) "world brain" seemed within reach. Then the web hit, transforming all aspects of information—acquisition, management, access—at an accelerating pace. Between 1994 and 1999, two NSF/DARPA/NASA/National Library of Medicine/Library of Congress/National Endowment for the Humanities/FBI research initiatives on digital libraries awarded about $200M in today's dollars. This with other investments galvanized the research community.

By 2000 about ten schools (or equivalent units) had information as the sole discipline in their name; today it is twice that. In 2001, a new series of "deans meetings" formed, with original members Syracuse, Pittsburgh, and Drexel joined by Michigan, Berkeley, and the University of Washington, all of which are now information schools. In 2005, the first annual "iConference" drew participants from nineteen universities with information programs. The "iCaucus" now has 27 dues-paying university members. Some are transformed library schools, some had closer ties to information systems or computer science, and others formed recently. Collectively, they include HCI researchers from HF&E, IS, and CHI.

Within these schools, conflicts in academic cultures are addressed on a regular basis. The conference is not yet very visible. One could challenge the implication in Figure 8.2 that a shift from LIS to a field simply called "information" is well underway. Many faculty consider themselves to be "a researcher in {X} who is located in an information school," where X could be library science, HCI, CSCW, IS, communication, education, computer science, and perhaps others. It is too early to say how it will evolve. We can say that information has become, and will remain, a significant player in human–computer interaction.

Human Factors and Ergonomics Embraces Cognitive Approaches

In 1996, the Human Factors and Ergonomics Society formed a new technical group, Cognitive Engineering and Decision Making. It quickly became the largest technical group in the society. A decade earlier this would have been an unlikely development: Senior human factors researchers disliked cognitive approaches; it was in the CHI field that *cognitive engineering* was used in this sense (Norman, 1982, 1986).

Even more astonishing a decade earlier would have been the fact that in 2005, Human Performance Modeling was a new, thriving technical group in HFES, initiated by Wayne Gray and Dick Pew, CHI participants in the 1980s. Card, Moran, and Newell (1983) had introduced human performance modeling to reform the discipline of human factors from the outside. Work had continued, focused on expert performance (e.g., a special issue of *Human–Computer Interaction*, Vol. 12, Number 4, 1997). Today the reform effort has moved within human factors, still focused largely on non-discretionary use.

HF&E to a large degree shaped government funding of HCI. The U.S. National Science Foundation Interactive Systems Program—subsequently renamed Human–Computer Interaction—was described:

> The Interactive Systems Program considers scientific and engineering research oriented toward the enhancement of human–computer communications and interactions in all

modalities. These modalities include speech/language, sound, images and, in general, any single or multiple, sequential or concurrent, human–computer input, output, or action. (National Science Foundation, 1993, online)

One NSF HCI program manager reported that his proudest accomplishment was doubling the already ample funding for natural language understanding. Even after NSF established a separate Human Language and Communication Program in 2003, speech and language research continued to draw heavy funding support in the HCI and accessibility programs, and lighter support in AI and other NSF programs. Two subsequent NSF HCI program managers emphasized *direct brain interfaces* or *brain-computer interaction*, using brainwaves, implants, or other means. NSF program managers rarely attended CHI conferences, where there was little work on speech, language, or direct brain interaction. Whether or not these technologies prove useful, they will not appear soon in discretionary use situations in many homes or offices. A review committee noted that a random sample of NSF HCI grants included none by prominent CHI researchers (National Science Foundation, 2003).

Human factors research on computer use has dispersed. HCI issues now appear in most HFES technical groups, from telecommunications to medical systems, even as the Computer Systems Technical Group has declined in size.

CHI Evolves, Embraces Design

The steady flow of new hardware, software features, applications, and systems ensures that initial use and early adoption of digital technology is always present, important to technology producers, and generating new research issues. CHI has tracked this flow of innovation, generally picking up an innovation when it first attracts a wide audience.

As an application matures, use may become routine. Many people now must use email and word processing, for example. Such technologies receive less attention as CHI directs its gaze to discretionary use of the moment: instant messaging, blogging, collaboration technology, web design, ubiquitous computing, mobile computing, social computing, and so on. New technologies raised new issues, such as privacy, and encouraged new methods, such as ethnography. At a more abstract level CHI shows continuity: continued exploration of input devices, communication channels, information visualization techniques, and design methods.

The growing participation in an internet that steadily became more reliable and higher bandwidth through the mid-1990s increased the focus on real-time communication technologies and quasi-real-time technologies such as email. The web temporarily slowed this, however, by shifting attention to indirect interaction via static sites.

The web was like a new continent. First came explorers, posting flags here and there. Then came attempts at settlement, in the form of virtual worlds research and development. Few of these early pioneers survived; there was little to do in virtual worlds other than games and simulations. But more recently some people, primarily young people, shifted major portions of their work and play online, relying on online information sources, digital photo management, social software, digital documents, online shopping, multiplayer games, and so on. And this is reflected in CHI research topics.

The web curtailed research into self-contained personal productivity tools. In spite of high development and maintenance costs, representing knowledge in application software was appealing when external information resources were limited. With so much information available online today, including the ability to find knowledgeable people, static knowledge representation is less useful. In contrast, adaptive systems that build and maintain local knowledge can play a greater role. Steady progress in machine learning is influencing productivity tools—although implausible forecasts have not disappeared.

To the psychologists and computer scientists who formed CHI, interface design was a scientific and engineering undertaking. Focused on performance, they assumed that people eventually choose the most efficient alternatives. Because human discretion involves aesthetic preferences, and invites marketing and non-rational persuasion, this view could not be sustained when computing costs came down. But the engineering orientation held on longer in CHI than in SIGGRAPH, where aesthetic appeal motivated much research. CHI researchers labeled the study of enjoyment "funology" (Blythe, Monk, Overbeeke, & Wright, 2003, p. 1), lest someone think that the researchers were too relaxed about it.

Visual designers participated in graphical interface research early on. Aaron Marcus began working full time on computer graphics in the late 1960s. William Bowman's (1968) book *Graphic Communication* was a strong influence on the Xerox Star, for which the designer Norm Cox's icons were chosen (see Bewley, Roberts, Schroit, & Verplank, 1983). However, graphic design was usually seen as secondary (Evenson, 2005). In 1995, building on working group meetings at previous conferences, SIGCHI initiated Designing Interactive Systems (DIS), a biennial conference drawing a few visual designers and many systems designers. In 2003, SIGCHI, SIGGRAPH, and the American Institute of Graphic Arts (AIGA) initiated the Designing for User Experience (DUX) conference series that fully embraces visual and commercial design.

The evolution of CHI is reflected in the influential contributions of Donald Norman. A cognitive scientist who introduced the term *cognitive engineering,* he presented the first CHI '83 paper. It defined *user satisfaction functions* based on speed of use, ease of learning, required knowledge, and errors (Norman, 1983). His influential 1988 book *Psychology of Everyday Things (POET)* (Norman, 1988) focused on pragmatic usability. Its 1990 reissue as *Design of Everyday Things* reflected a field refocusing on invention. Fourteen years later he published *Emotional Design: Why We Love (or Hate) Everyday Things*, stressing the role of aesthetics in our response to objects (Norman, 2004).

Design's first cousin, marketing, has been poorly regarded in the CHI community (see Marcus, 2004). However, website design forces the issue. Site owners often wish to keep users on a site, whereas users may prefer to escape quickly. Consider supermarkets, where items that most shoppers want are positioned far apart, forcing people to traverse aisles so other products can beckon. CHI professionals usually align themselves with end-users, but when designing for a site owner, they face a stakeholder conflict. This was not true in the past: Designers of individual productivity tools had negligible conflict of interest with prospective customers. Marketing is likely to find a place in CHI because marketing is concerned primarily with identifying and fulfilling consumer needs.

Looking Back: Cultures and Bridges

In spite of a significant common focus and a dynamic environment with shifting alliances, the major threads of human–computer interaction research—HF&E, IS, LIS, and CHI—have not merged. They have not even interacted much, although not for lack of effort to build bridges. The Human Factors Society co-organized the first CHI conference. CSCW sought to link CHI and IS. AIS SIGHCI tried to engage with CHI.

Even within computer science, bridging proved difficult. Researchers interested in interaction left SIGGRAPH to join CHI rather than work to bridge the two. Twenty years later another opportunity arose as advanced graphics processing became available for use in design on standard platforms. The DUX conference series was cosponsored by the SIGS, but was discontinued after three meetings. In AI, SIGART and SIGCHI cosponsor the Intelligent User Interface series, but participation has remained outside mainstream HCI. We can identify some of the obstacles to greater interaction.

Discretion Is a Major Variable

HF&E and IS arose before discretionary hands-on use was widespread, whereas CHI made that its focus. HF&E and IS researchers examined organizational as well as technical issues; CHI generally avoided domain-dependent work. As a consequence, HF&E and IS researchers did share journals; for example, Benbasat and Dexter (1985) published in *Management Science* and cited five *Human Factors* articles. These three fields moved quickly to focus on general populations, whereas information science only slowly distanced itself from supporting specialists.

User motivation affects methods. HF&E and CHI were shaped by psychologists trained in experimental testing of hypotheses about behavior. Experimental subjects agree to follow instructions for an extrinsic reward. This is a good model for nondiscretionary use, but not for discretionary use. As a symbolic if cosmetic change, CHI researchers relabeled subjects to be *participants*, which sounds volitional. But they discovered that formal experimental studies were often overkill for their purposes, and that lab studies in general are more likely than ergonomics studies to require confirmation in real-world settings.

The same goals apply—fewer errors, faster performance, quicker learning, greater memorability, and being enjoyable—but the emphasis differs. For power plant operation, error reduction is key, performance enhancement is good, and other goals are less critical. For telephone order entry takers, performance is critical: testing an interface that could shave a few seconds from a repetitive operation requires a formal experiment.

In contrast, consumers often respond to visceral appeal and initial experience. In assessing designs for mass markets, catching obvious problems can be more significant than striving for an optimal solution. Less rigorous studies, such as discount usability or cognitive walkthroughs (Nielsen, 1989), can be enough, with more time-consuming qualitative approaches, such as contextual design or persona use (Beyer & Holtzblatt, 1998; Pruitt & Adlin, 2006), providing a deeper understanding of users when new circumstances arise. Unlike HF&E, CHI largely abandoned its roots in scientific theory and engineering. This did not impress HF&E researchers or theory-oriented IS researchers. The controversial psychological method of verbal reports, developed by Newell and Simon (1972), was applied to design by Clayton Lewis (1983; Lewis & Mack, 1982, p. 387) as "thinking-aloud." Perhaps the most widely used CHI method, it led some in the other fields to characterize CHI people as wanting to talk about their experiences instead of doing research.

Academic, Linguistic, and Generational Cultures

The traditional academic culture of the sciences is that conferences are venues for work in progress and journals are repositories for polished work. HF&E, IS, documentation, and library science all followed this practice. In contrast, CHI and other U.S. computer science disciplines shifted to conference proceedings as the final destination of most work. Outside the U.S., computer science retained more of a journal focus, arguably due to the absence of professional societies that archived conference proceedings (Grudin, in press). Information science is divided, drawing as it does on researchers from both camps. This circumstance impedes communication across disciplines and continents. Researchers in journal cultures chafe at CHI's rejection rates; CHI researchers are dismayed by the relatively unpolished work at other conferences.

CHI conferences are selective, accepting only about 20 percent of submissions. With a few exceptions, HF&E and IS conferences have acceptance rates of about 50 percent or more. On the other hand, CHI journals receive fewer submissions and have higher acceptance rates (see Grudin,

2005). Many CHI researchers report that journals are not relevant, and I estimate that as little as 10 percent of work in CHI-sponsored conferences reaches journal publication. In contrast, an IS track organizer for the Hawaii International Conference on System Sciences estimated that 80 percent of research there progressed to a journal (Jay Nunamaker, HICSS-38 presentation, January 2004).

A linguistic divide also set CHI apart. HF&E and IS used the term *operator*; in IS, *user* could be a manager who used printed computer output, not a hands-on *end-user*. Within CHI, *operator* was demeaning, *user* was always hands-on, and *end-user* seemed a superfluous affectation. In HF&E and IS, *task analysis* generally refers to an organizational decomposition of work, a broad analysis that can consider external factors; in CHI, it was a cognitive decomposition, such as breaking a text editing move operation into select, cut, select, paste. In IS, *implementation* meant deployment of a system in an organization; in CHI, it was a synonym for development. *System, application*, and *evaluation* also had markedly different connotations or denotations. Significant misunderstandings and rejections resulted from failure to recognize these distinctions.

Different perspectives and priorities were reflected in attitudes toward standards. Many HF&E researchers contributed to the development of standards, believing that standards contribute to efficiency and innovation. A view widespread in CHI was that standards inhibit innovation. There are elements of truth in both views, and positions may have converged as internet and web standards were tackled. However, the attitudes reflected the different demands of government contracting and commercial software development. Specifying adherence to standards is a useful tool for those preparing requests for proposals, but compliance with standards can make it more difficult for a product to differentiate itself.

A generational divide also existed. Many CHI researchers grew up in the 1960s and 1970s, and did not appreciate the prior generation's orientation toward military, government, and business systems, or the inability of HF&E and IS "man-machine interaction" researchers to adopt gender-neutral terminology (still occasionally occurring). Only in 1994 did *International Journal of Man-Machine Studies* become *International Journal of Human–Computer Studies*. Such differences affected enthusiasm for building bridges and exploring literatures.

Competition for resources was another factor. Computers of modest capability were extremely expensive for much of the time span we are considering. CHI was initially largely driven by the healthy tech industry; the other fields were more dependent on competing for government funding, which waxed and waned. Demand for researchers outstripped supply, as well. HCI tended to prosper in AI winters, starting with Sutherland's ability to use the TX-2 for the first graphics research when AI suffered its first setback and recurring with the emergence of major HCI labs during the severe AI winter of the late 1970s. Library schools laboring to create information science programs had to compete with computer science departments, some of which awarded faculty positions to graduates of master's programs due to the short supply.

Greater interdisciplinarity is intellectually seductive. More might be learned by looking over fences. But perhaps a better metaphor is the Big Bang—digital technology as an explosion dispersing effort in different directions, forming worlds that at some later date might discover one another and learn how to communicate, or might not.

Looking Forward: Trajectories

The future of human–computer interaction will be varied, dynamic, and full of surprises. Nevertheless, observations about the past and present state of the field may help us anticipate developments.

Discretion—Now You See It, Now You Don't

We exercise prerogative a great deal when buying online, more at home than at work, and not at all when confronted by a telephone answering system. We have more choice when young and healthy than when constrained by injury or aging. Software that was discretionary yesterday is indispensable today. The need to collaborate forces shared conventions.

Consider a hypothetical team that has worked together for twenty years. In 1990, one member still used a typewriter, others chose different word processors. All exchanged printed documents. One emphasized by underlining, another by *italicizing*, a third by **bolding**. In 2000, group members could share documents digitally—and thereby had to adopt the same word processor and forms of emphasis. Choice was curtailed; it could only be exercised collectively. Today, it often suffices to share documents in portable document format (PDF), so in 2010, the team can again use different word processors. Perhaps tomorrow I will be able to personalize my view, and see in italics what you see as bold.

Shackel (1997, p. 981) noted this progression under the heading "From Systems Design to Interface Usability and Back Again." Early designers focused at the system level; operators had to cope. When the PC merged the roles of operator, output user, and program provider, the focus shifted to the human interface and choice. Then individual users again became components in fully networked organizational systems. Discretion evaporates as to whether to use a technology that has become mission-critical, as email did for many people in the 1990s.

The converse also occurs. Employee discretion increases when one can download free software and demand capabilities enjoyed at home. Managers are less likely to mandate the use of a technology that they use and find burdensome. Even in the military, language processing systems appealed to military officers—until they themselves became hands-on users:

> Our military users ... generally flatly refuse to use any system that requires speech recognition. ... Over and over and over again, we were told "If we have to use speech, we will not take it. I don't even want to waste my time talking to you if it requires speech ..." I have seen generals come out of using, trying to use one of the speech-enabled systems looking really whipped. One really sad puppy, he said "OK, what's your system like, do I have to use speech?" He looked at me plaintively. And when I said "No," his face lit up, and he got so happy. (Forbus, 2003; see also Forbus, Usher, & Chapman, 2003)

As familiar applications become essential and security concerns curtail openness, one might expect discretion to recede. But Moore's Law (broadly construed), competition, and the ease of sharing bits may guarantee that a steady flow of unproven technologies will reach us.

Ubiquitous Computing, Invisible HCI?

Norman (1988, pp. 185–186) wrote of "the invisible computer of the future." Like motors, he speculated, computers would be present everywhere and visible nowhere. We interact with clocks, refrigerators, and cars. Each has a motor, but there is no human–motor interaction specialization. A decade later, at the height of the Y2K crisis and the internet bubble, computers were more visible than ever. We may always want a multipurpose display or two, but part of Norman's vision is materializing.

With computers embedded everywhere, concern with interaction is everywhere. Perhaps HCI itself will become invisible through omnipresence. As interaction with digital technology becomes part of everyone's research, the three major HCI fields are losing participation.

Human Factors and Ergonomics

David Meister, author of *The History of Human Factors and Ergonomics,* stresses the continuity of HF&E in the face of technology change:

> Outside of a few significant events, like the organization of HFS in 1957 or the publication of Proceedings of the annual meetings in 1972, there are no seminal occurrences ... no sharp discontinuities that are memorable. A scientific discipline like HF has only an intellectual history; one would hope to find major paradigm changes in orientation toward our human performance phenomena, but there are none, largely because the emergence of HF did not involve major changes from pre-World War II applied psychology. In an intellectual history, one has to look for major changes in thinking, and I

have not been able to discover any in HF. (personal communication, September 7, 2004)

Membership in the Computer Systems Technical Group of HFES has declined sharply; technology use is stressed in other technical groups, such as Cognitive Engineering and Decision Making, Communication, Human Performance Modeling, Internet, System Development, and Virtual Environment. Nor can Aging, Medical Systems, or other technical groups avoid "invisible computers."

Information Systems

As IS thrived during the Y2K crisis and internet bubble, other management school disciplines—finance, marketing, operations research, organizational behavior—become more technically savvy. When the bubble burst and enrollments declined, the IS niche was less well defined. The research issues remain significant, but this cuts two ways. With the standardization and outsourcing of IT functions, web portals and business-to-business attract more attention. These have economic and marketing elements, making it natural to outsource HCI functions to other management disciplines.

Computer–Human Interaction

This nomadic group started in psychology. It obtained a place at computer science banquets, often bestowed grudgingly. CHI, lacking a well defined academic niche, ties its identity to its conference. Participation peaked in 2001. Specialized conferences thrive. As technologies appear and attract a critical mass at an ever-increasing pace, researchers can start new conferences or blog their findings. For example, soon after the web emerged, WWW conferences included papers on HCI issues. Now there are conferences on ubiquitous, pervasive, accessible, and sustainable computing, agents, design, emerging technologies, and emerging markets. HCI is an invisible presence in each. High conference rejection rates and a new generational divide could accelerate this dispersion of effort.

Information

The first iConferences were marked by active discussion and disagreement about directions. Faculty from several disciplines worked to create pidgin languages. Since then, many assistant professors were hired and graduate students enlisted. Their initial jobs and primary identities are with Information. They are likely to creolize the pidgin languages.

Cronin (1995) proposed that information access, in terms of intellectual, physical, social, economic, and spatial/temporal factors, is the focus of the field. Information is acquired, through sensors, from human input, and flows and aggregates and is transformed over networks including the web. Information visualization is also critical, as is the information management that increasingly each of us must handle for ourselves, choosing what to keep locally, what to maintain in the cloud, and how to organize it and ensure its accessibility at a later time.

In speculating about the future, Cronin cites Wersig (1992, p. 215) who argued that concepts around information might function "like magnets or attractors, sucking the focus-oriented materials out of the disciplines and restructuring them within the information scientific framework." There is evidence for this in a migration of HCI faculty to information schools. On the other hand, the rise of specialized programs—biomedical informatics, social informatics, community informatics, information and communication technology for development (ICT4D) presents a countervailing force. Information, like HCI, could become invisible through ubiquity.

From talking with the younger generation, my sense is that the generals may still be arguing over directions, but the troops are starting to march. It is not clear where they will go. The annual conference is fragile; the generals are busy with other matters but reluctant to turn over command. In any case, in the long term, Information will be a major player in human–computer interaction. Design and Information are active HCI foci in 2010. Design activity is compensating for past neglect. Information is being reinvented.

Conclusion: The Next Generation

Until revoked, Moore's Law will ensure that digital landscapes will provide new forms of interaction to explore and new practices to improve. The first generation of computer researchers, designers, and users grew up without computers. The generation that followed used computers as students, entered workplaces, and changed the way technology was used. Now a generation has grown up with computers, game consoles, and cell phones. They absorbed an aesthetic of technology design while communicating with IM and text messaging. They are developing skills at searching, browsing, assessing, and synthesizing information. They use digital cameras and blog, acquire multimedia authoring talent and embrace social networking sites. They are entering workplaces, and everything will be changed once again.

However it comes to be defined and wherever it is studied, human–computer interaction will for some time be in its early days.

References

Ackoff, R. L. (1967). Management misinformation systems. *Management Science, 14*, B147–B156.

Asimov, I. (1950). *I, robot*. New York: Gnome Press.

Aspray, W. (1999). Command and control, documentation, and library science: The origins of information science at the University of Pittsburgh. *IEEE Annals of the History of Computing, 21*(4), 4–20.

Baecker, R., & Buxton, W. (1987). A historical and intellectual perspective. In R. Baecker & W. Buxton (Eds.), *Readings in human–computer interaction: A multidisciplinary approach* (pp. 41–54). San Francisco: Morgan Kaufmann.

Baecker, R., Grudin, J., Buxton, W., & Greenberg, S. (1995). A historical and intellectual perspective. In R. Baecker, J. Grudin, W. Buxton, & S. Greenberg (Eds.), *Readings in human–computer interaction: Toward the year 2000* (pp. 35–47). San Francisco: Morgan Kaufmann.

Bagozzi, R. P., Davis, F. D., & Warshaw, P. R. (1992). Development and test of a theory of technological learning and usage. *Human Relations, 45*(7), 660–686.

Banker, R. D., & Kaufmann, R. J. (2004). The evolution of research on information systems: A fiftieth-year survey of the literature in management science. *Management Science, 50*(3), 281–298.

Bannon, L. (1991). From human factors to human actors: The role of psychology and human–computer interaction studies in system design. In J. Greenbaum & M. Kyng (Eds.), *Design at work* (pp. 25–44). Hillsdale, NJ: Erlbaum.

Bardini, T. (2000). *Bootstrapping: Douglas Engelbart, coevolution, and the origins of personal computing.* Palo Alto, CA: Stanford University Press.

Barnard, P. (1991). Bridging between basic theories and the artifacts of human–computer interaction. In J. M. Carroll (Ed.), *Designing interaction: Psychology at the human–computer interface* (pp. 103–127). Cambridge, UK: Cambridge University Press.

Begeman, M., Cook, P., Ellis, C., Graf, M., Rein, G., & Smith, T. (1986). Project Nick: Meetings augmentation and analysis. *Proceedings of the ACM Conference on Computer-Supported Cooperative Work,* 1–6.

Benbasat, I., & Dexter, A. S. (1985). An experimental evaluation of graphical and color-enhanced information presentation. *Management Science, 31*(11), 1348–1364.

Bennett, J. L. (1979). The commercial impact of usability in interactive systems. In B. Shackel (Ed.), *Man-computer communication: Whence and whither?* Maidenhead, UK: Pergamon-Infotech.

Berkeley, E. C. (1949). *Giant brains or machines that think.* New York: Wiley.

Beyer, H., & Holtzblatt, K. (1998). *Contextual design: Defining customer-centered systems.* San Francisco, CA: Morgan Kaufmann.

Bewley, W. L., Roberts, T. L., Schroit, D., & Verplank, W. L. (1983). Human factors testing in the design of Xerox's 8010 "Star" office workstation. *Proceedings of the ACM CHI '83 Human Factors in Computing Systems Conference,* 72–77.

Bjerknes, G., Ehn, P., & Kyng, M. (Eds.). (1987). *Computers and democracy: A Scandinavian challenge.* Aldershot, UK: Avebury.

Bjørn-Andersen, N., & Hedberg, B. (1977). Design of information systems in an organizational perspective. In P. C. Nystrom & W. H. Starbuck (Eds.), *Prescriptive models of organizations* (pp. 125–142). Amsterdam: North-Holland.

Blackwell, A. (2006). The reification of metaphor as a design tool. *ACM Transactions on Computer-Human Interaction, 13*(4), 490–530.

Blythe, M. A., Monk, A. F., Overbeeke, K., & Wright, P. C. (Eds.). (2003). *Funology: From usability to user enjoyment.* New York: Kluwer.

Borman, L. (1996). SIGCHI: The early years. *SIGCHI Bulletin, 28*(1), 1–33.

Bowman, W. J. (1968). *Graphic communication.* New York: Wiley.

Buckland, M. K. (1998). Documentation, information science, and library science in the U.S.A. In T. B. Hahn & M. K. Buckland (Eds.), *Historical studies in information science* (pp. 159–172). Medford, NJ: Information Today, Inc.

Buckland, M. K. (2009). As we may recall: Four forgotten pioneers. *Interactions, 16*(6), 76–79.

Burke, C. (1994). *Information and secrecy: Vannevar Bush, Ultra, and the other Memex.* Metuchen, NJ: Scarecrow Press.

Burke, C. (1998). A rough road to the information highway: Project INTREX. In T. B. Hahn & M. K. Buckland (Eds.), *Historical studies in Information Science* (pp. 132–146). Medford, NJ: Information Today.

Burke, C. (2007). History of information science. *Annual Review of Information Science and Technology, 41,* 3–53.

Bush, V. (1945). As we may think. *The Atlantic Monthly, 176,* 101–108. Retrieved March 31, 2010, from www.theatlantic.com/magazine/archive/1969/12/as-we-may-think/3881

Butler, P. (1933). *An introduction to library science.* Chicago: University of Chicago Press.

Cakir, A., Hart, D. J., & Stewart, T. F. M. (1980). *Visual display terminals.* New York: Wiley.

Callahan, E. (2005). Interface design and culture. *Annual Review of Information Science and Technology, 39,* 257–310.

Card, S. K., & Moran, T. P. (1986). User technology: From pointing to pondering. *Proceedings of the Conference on the History of Personal Workstations,* 183–198.

Card, S. K., Moran, T. P., & Newell, A. (1980a). Computer text-editing: An information-processing analysis of a routine cognitive skill. *Cognitive Psychology, 12,* 396–410.

Card, S. K., Moran, T. P., & Newell, A. (1980b). Keystroke-level model for user performance time with interactive systems. *Communications of the ACM, 23*(7), 396–410.

Card, S. K., Moran, T. P., & Newell, A. (1983). *The psychology of human–computer interaction.* Mahwah, NJ: Erlbaum.

Carroll, J. M., & Campbell, R. L. (1986). Softening up hard science: Response to Newell and Card. *Human–Computer Interaction, 2*(3), 227–249.

Carroll, J. M., & Mazur, S. A. (1986). Lisa learning. *IEEE Computer, 19*(11), 35–49.

Cronin, B. (1995). Shibboleth and substance in North American library and information science education. *Libri, 45,* 45–63.

Damodaran, L., Simpson, A., & Wilson, P. (1980). *Designing systems for people.* Manchester, UK: NCC Publications.

Darrach, B. (1970, November 20). Meet Shaky: The first electronic person. *Life Magazine, 69*(21), 58B–68.

Davis, F. D. (1989). Perceived usefulness, perceived ease of use, and user acceptance of information technology. *MIS Quarterly, 13*(3), 319–339.

Davis, G. B. (1974). *Management information systems: Conceptual foundations, structure, and development.* New York: McGraw-Hill.

Dennis, A., George, J., Jessup, L., Nunamaker, J., & Vogel, D. (1988). Information technology to support electronic meetings. *MIS Quarterly, 12*(4), 591–624.

DeSanctis, G., & Gallupe, R. B. (1987). A foundation for the study of group decision support systems. *Management Science, 33,* 589–610.

Dyson, F. (1979). *Disturbing the universe.* New York: Harper & Row.

Engelbart, D. C. (1962). Augmenting human intellect: A conceptual framework (SRI Summary report AFOSR-3223). Republished in P. Howerton & D. Weeks (Eds.), *Vistas in information handling* (Vol. 1, pp. 1–29). Washington, DC: Spartan Books, 1963. Retrieved April 19, 2010, from www.dougengelbart.org/pubs/augment-3906.html

Engelien, B., & McBryde, R. (1991). *Natural language markets: Commercial strategies.* London: Ovum.

ePresence. (2006). *Early interactive graphics at Lincoln Labs.* Retrieved June 19, 2010, from epresence.kmdi.utoronto.ca/mediacontent/1/watch/197.aspx

Evenson, S. (2005, February). *Design and HCI highlights.* Paper presented at Human Computer Interaction Consortium Conference, Winter Park, Colorado.

Fano, R., & Corbato, F. (1966). Time-sharing on computers. *Scientific American, 214*(9), 129–140.

Feigenbaum, E. A., & McCorduck, P. (1983). *The fifth generation: Artificial intelligence and Japan's computer challenge to the world.* Reading, MA: Addison-Wesley.

Fidel, R. (2010). *Human information interaction: An ecological approach to information behavior.* Under review.

Foley, J. D., & Wallace, V. L. (1974). The art of natural graphic man-machine conversation. *Proceedings of the IEEE, 62*(4), 462–471.

Forbus, K. D. (2003, May 2). *Sketching for knowledge capture.* Lecture, Redmond, WA.

Forbus, K. D., Usher, J., & Chapman, V. (2003). Qualitative spatial reasoning about sketch maps. *Proceedings of the Innovative Applications of Artificial Intelligence Conference,* 85–92.

Forster, E. M. (1909, November). The machine stops. *Oxford and Cambridge Review, 8,* 83–122.

Friedman, A. (1989). *Computer systems development: History, organization and implementation.* New York: Wiley.

Good, I. J. (1965). Speculations concerning the first ultra-intelligent machine. *Advances in Computers, 6,* 31–88.

Gould, J. D., & Lewis, C. (1983). Designing for usability: Key principles and what designers think. *Proceedings of the ACM CHI '83 Human Factors in Computing Systems Conference,* 50–53.

Grandjean, E., & Vigliani, A. (1980). *Ergonomics aspects of visual display terminals.* London: Taylor and Francis.

Gray, W. D., John, B. E., Stuart, R., Lawrence, D., & Atwood, M. E. (1990). GOMS meets the phone company: Analytic modeling applied to real-world problems. *Proceedings of the Third International Conference on Human–Computer Interaction,* 29–34.

Greenbaum, J. (1979). *In the name of efficiency.* Philadelphia: Temple University Press.

Greif, I. (1985). Computer-supported cooperative groups: What are the issues? *Proceedings of the AFIPS Office Automation Conference,* 73–76.

Greif, I. (Ed.). (1988). *Computer-supported cooperative work: A book of readings.* San Mateo, CA: Morgan Kaufmann.

Grudin, J. (2005). Three faces of human–computer interaction. *IEEE Annals of the History of Computing, 27*(4), 46–62.

Grudin, J. (2006). Human factors, CHI, and MIS. In P. Zhang & D. Galletta (Eds.), *HCI in MIS (I): Foundations* (pp. 402–421). Armonk, NY: M.E. Sharpe.

Grudin, J. (2008). A moving target: The evolution of human–computer interaction. In A. Sears & J. Jacko (Eds.), *Handbook of human–computer interaction* (pp. 1–24). New York: CRC Press.

Grudin, J. (in press). Technology, conferences and community. *Communications of the ACM.*

Hertzfeld, A. (2005). *Revolution in the valley: The insanely great story of how the Mac was made.* Sebastapol, CA: O'Reilly Media.

Hiltz, S. R., & Turoff, M. (1978). *The network nation.* Reading, MA: Addison-Wesley.

Hiltzik, M. A. (1999). *Dealers of lightning: Xerox PARC and the dawn of the computer age.* New York: HarperCollins.

Hopper, G. (1952). The education of a computer. *Proceedings of ACM Conference*, reprinted in *Annals of the History of Computing, 9*(3–4), 271–281, 1987.

Hutchins, E. L., Hollan, J. D., & Norman, D. A. (1986). Direct manipulation interfaces. In D. A. Norman & S. W. Draper (Eds.), *User centered system design* (pp. 87–124). Mahwah, NJ: Erlbaum.

Israelski, E., & Lund, A. M. (2003). The evolution of human–computer interaction during the telecommunications revolution. In J. A. Jacko & A. Sears (Eds.), *The human–computer interaction handbook* (pp. 722–789). Mahwah, NJ: Erlbaum.

Johnson, T. (1985). *Natural language computing: The commercial applications.* London: Ovum.

Kao, E. (1998). *The history of AI.* Retrieved March 13, 2007, from www.generation5.org/content/1999/aihistory.asp

Kay, A., & Goldberg, A. (1977). Personal dynamic media. *IEEE Computer, 10*(3), 31–42.

Keen, P. G. W. (1980). MIS research: Reference disciplines and a cumulative tradition. *First International Conference on Information Systems*, 9–18.

Landau, R., Bair, J., & Siegman, J. (Eds.). (1982). *Emerging office systems.* Extended proceedings of the Stanford International Symposium on Office Automation, March 23–25, 1980. Norwood, NJ: Ablex.

Lenat, D. (1989). When will machines learn? *Machine Learning, 4*, 255–257.

Lewis, C. (1983, December). *The 'thinking aloud' method in interface evaluation.* Tutorial given at the ACM CHI '83 Human Factors in Computing Systems Conference, Boston, MA.

Lewis, C., & Mack, R. (1982). Learning to use a text processing system: Evidence from "thinking aloud" protocols. *Proceedings of the ACM CHI Human Factors in Computing Systems Conference*, 387–392.

Licklider, J. C. R. (1960). Man-computer symbiosis. *IRE Transactions of Human Factors in Electronics, 1*(1), 4–11.

Licklider, J. C. R. (1965). *Libraries of the future.* Cambridge, MA: MIT Press.

Licklider, J. C. R. (1976). User-oriented interactive computer graphics. *Proceedings of the SIGGRAPH Workshop on User-Oriented Design of Interactive Graphics Systems*, 89–96.

Licklider, J. C. R., & Clark, W. (1962). On-line man-computer communication. *AFIPS Conference Proceedings, 21*, 113–128.

Lighthill, J. (1973). Artificial intelligence: A general survey. In J. Lighthill, N. S. Sutherland, R. M. Needham, H. C. Longuet-Higgins, & D. Michie (Eds.), *Artificial intelligence: A paper symposium*. London: Science Research Council of Great Britain. Retrieved April 19, 2010, from www.chilton-computing.org.uk/inf/literature/reports/lighthill_report/p001.htm

Long, J. (1989). Cognitive ergonomics and human–computer interaction. In J. Long & A. Whitefield (Eds.), *Cognitive ergonomics and human–computer interaction* (pp. 4–34). Cambridge, UK: Cambridge University Press.

Machlup, F., & Mansfield, U. (Eds.). (1983). *The study of information: Interdisciplinary messages*. New York: Wiley.

March, A. (1994). Usability: The new dimension of product design. *Harvard Business Review, 72*(5), 144–149.

Marcus, A. (2004). Branding 101. *ACM Interactions, 11*(5), 14–21.

Markoff, J. (2005). *What the dormouse said: How the 60s counterculture shaped the personal computer*. London: Viking.

Martin, J. (1973). *Design of man-computer dialogues*. New York: Prentice-Hall.

McCarthy, J. (1960). Functions of symbolic expressions and their computation by machine, part 1. *Communications of the ACM, 3*(4), 184–195.

McCarthy, J. (1988). Review of the book *The question of artificial intelligence: Philosophical and sociological perspectives. Annals of the History of Computing, 10*(3), 224–229. Retrieved April 19, 2010, from www-formal.stanford.edu/jmc/reviews/bloomfield.pdf

Meister, D. (1999). *The history of human factors and ergonomics*. Mahwah, NJ: Erlbaum.

Meister, D. (2005). HFES history. *HFES 2005–2006 directory and yearbook*, 2–3.

Mumford, E. (1971). A comprehensive method for handling the human problems of computer introduction. *IFIP Congress*, 918–923.

Mumford, E. (1976). Toward the democratic design of work systems. *Personnel Management, 8*(9), 32–35.

Myers, B. A. (1998). A brief history of human computer interaction technology. *ACM Interactions, 5*(2), 44–54.

Mylonopoulos, N. A., & Theoharakis, V. (2001). Global perceptions of IS journals. *Communications of the ACM, 44*(9), 29–32.

National Science Foundation. (1993, January 13). *NSF 93-2: Interactive Systems Program description*. Washington, DC: The Foundation. Retrieved April 19, 2010, from www.nsf.gov/pubs/stis1993/nsf932/nsf932.txt

National Science Foundation. (2003, July 28). *NSF Committee of Visitors Report: Information and Intelligent Systems Division*. Washington, DC: The Foundation.

Negroponte, N. (1970). *The architecture machine: Towards a more humane environment*. Cambridge, MA: MIT Press.

Nelson, T. (1965). A file structure for the complex, the changing, and the indeterminate. *Proceedings of the ACM National Conference*, 84–100.

Nelson, T. (1973). A conceptual framework for man-machine everything. *Proceedings of the National Computer Conference*, M21–M26.

Newell, A., & Card, S. K. (1985). The prospects for psychological science in human–computer interaction. *Human–Computer Interaction, 1*(3), 209–242.

Newell, A., & Simon, H. A. (1956). The logic theory machine: A complex information processing system. *IRE Transactions on Information Theory, IT-2*, 61–79.

Newell, A., & Simon, H. A. (1972). *Human problem solving*. New York: Prentice-Hall.

Nielsen, J. (1989). Usability engineering at a discount. In G. Salvendy & M. J. Smith (Eds.), *Designing and using human–computer interfaces and knowledge based systems* (pp. 394–401). Amsterdam: Elsevier.

Norberg, A. L., & O'Neill, J. E. (1996). *Transforming computer technology: Information processing for the Pentagon, 1962–1986.* Baltimore: Johns Hopkins University Press.

Norman, D. A. (1982). Steps toward a cognitive engineering: Design rules based on analyses of human error. *Proceedings of the SIGCHI Conference on Human Factors in Computing Systems*, 378–382.

Norman, D. A. (1983). Design principles for human–computer interfaces. *Proceedings of the ACM CHI '83 Human Factors in Computing Systems Conference*, 1–10.

Norman, D. A. (1986). Cognitive engineering. In D. A. Norman & S. W. Draper (Eds.), *User centered system design* (pp. 31–61). Mahwah, NJ: Erlbaum.

Norman, D. A. (1988). *Psychology of everyday things.* New York: Basic Books.

Norman, D. A. (2004). *Emotional design: Why we love (or hate) everyday things.* New York: Basic Books.

Nunamaker, J., Briggs, R. O., Mittleman, D. D., Vogel, D. R., & Balthazard, P. A. (1997). Lessons from a dozen years of group support systems research: A discussion of lab and field findings. *Journal of Management Information Systems, 13*(3), 163–207.

Nygaard, K. (1977, July). *Trade union participation.* Paper presented at the CREST Conference on Management Information Systems. Stafford, England.

Oakley, B. W. (1990). Intelligent knowledge-based systems: AI in the U.K. In R. Kurzweil (Ed.), *The age of intelligent machines* (pp. 346–349). Cambridge, MA: MIT Press.

Perlman, G., Green, G. K., & Wogalter, M. S. (1995). *Human factors perspectives on human–computer interaction.* Santa Monica, CA: Human Factors and Ergonomics Society.

Pew, R. (2003). Evolution of human–computer interaction: From MEMEX to Bluetooth and beyond. In J. A. Jacko & A. Sears (Eds.), *The human–computer interaction handbook* (pp. 1–17). Mahwah, NJ: Erlbaum.

Price, D. J. D. (1963). *Little science, big science.* New York: Columbia University Press.

Proceedings of the Joint Conference on Easier and More Productive Use of Computer Systems. (1981). New York: ACM. (See portal.acm.org)

Pruitt, J., & Adlin, T. (2006). *The persona lifecycle: Keeping people in mind throughout product design.* San Francisco: Morgan Kaufmann.

Rasmussen, J. (1980). The human as a system component. In H. T. Smith & T. R. G. Green (Eds.), *Human interaction with computers* (pp. 67–96). London: Academic.

Rasmussen, J. (1986). *Information processing and human-machine interaction: An approach to cognitive engineering.* New York: North-Holland.

Rayward, W. B. (1983). Library and information sciences: Disciplinary differentiation, competition, and convergence. In F. Machlup & U. Mansfield (Eds.), *The study of information: Interdisciplinary messages* (pp. 343–363). New York: Wiley.

Rayward. W. B. (1990). *International organization and dissemination of knowledge: Selected essays of Paul Otlet.* Amsterdam: Elsevier.

Rayward. W. B. (1998). The history and historiography of information science: Some reflections. In T. B. Hahn & M. K. Buckland (Eds.), *Historical studies in information science* (pp. 22–33). Medford, NJ: Information Today, Inc.

Rayward, W. B. (2010). *Mundaneum: Archives of knowledge* (Occasional Paper No. 215). Urbana: University of Illinois Graduate School of Library and Information Science.

Remus, W. (1984). An empirical evaluation of the impact of graphical and tabular presentations on decision-making. *Management Science, 30*(5), 533–542.

Rogers, Y. (2004). New theoretical approaches for human–computer interaction. *Annual Review of Information Science and Technology, 38*, 87–143.

Roscoe, S. N. (1997). *The adolescence of engineering psychology.* Santa Monica, CA: Human Factors and Ergonomics Society.

Ruthven, I. (2008). Interactive information retrieval. *Annual Review of Information Science and Technology, 42*, 43–91.

Sammet, J. (1992). Farewell to Grace Hopper: End of an era! *Communications of the ACM, 35*(4), 128–131.

Shackel, B. (1959). Ergonomics for a computer. *Design, 120*, 36–39.

Shackel, B. (1962). Ergonomics in the design of a large digital computer console. *Ergonomics, 5*, 229–241.

Shackel, B. (1997). Human–computer interaction: Whence and whither? *Journal of the American Society for Information Science, 48*(11), 970–986.

Shannon, C. E. (1950). Programming a computer for playing chess. *Philosophical Magazine, 7*(41), 256–275.

Shannon, C. E., & Weaver, W. (1949). *The mathematical theory of communication.* Urbana: University of Illinois Press.

Sheil, B. A. (1981). The psychological study of programming. *ACM Computing Surveys, 13*(1), 101–120.

Shneiderman, B. (1980). *Software psychology: Human factors in computer and information systems.* Cambridge, MA: Winthrop.

Simon, H. A. (1960). *The new science of management decision.* New York: Harper.

Smith, H. T., & Green, T. R. G. (1980). *Human interaction with computers.* London: Academic.

Smith, S. L. (1963). Man-computer information transfer. In J. H. Howard (Ed.), *Electronic information display systems* (pp. 284–299). Washington, DC: Spartan Books.

Smith, S. L., Farquhar, B. B., & Thomas, D. W. (1965). Color coding in formatted displays. *Journal of Applied Psychology, 49*, 393–398.

Smith, S. L., & Goodwin, N. C. (1970). Computer-generated speech and man-computer interaction. *Human Factors, 12*, 215–223.

Smith, S. L., & Mosier, J. N. (1986). *Guidelines for designing user interface software* (ESD-TR-86-278). Bedford, MA: MITRE.

Sutherland, I. (1963). *Sketchpad: A man-machine graphical communication system.* Unpublished doctoral dissertation, Massachusetts Institute of Technology, Cambridge, MA. Retrieved April 19, 2010, from www.cl.cam.ac.uk/techreports/UCAM-CL-TR-574.pdf

Taylor, F. W. (1911). *The principles of scientific management.* New York: Harper.

Turing, A. (1949, June 11). Letter. *The Times (London).* Highlights presented in *The Computer Museum Report, 20*, Summer/Fall 1987. Retrieved March 30, 2010, from ed-thelen.org/comp-hist/TheCompMusRep/TCMR-V20.html

Turing, A. (1950). Computing machinery and intelligence. *Mind*, *49*, 433–460. Republished as "Can a machine think?" in J. R. Newman (Ed.), *The world of mathematics* (Vol. 4, pp. 2099–2123). Simon & Schuster, 1956.

Vessey, I., & Galletta, D. (1991). Cognitive fit: An empirical test of information acquisition. *Information Systems Research*, *2*(1), 63–84.

Waldrop, M. M. (2001). *The dream machine: J.C.R. Licklider and the revolution that made computing personal*. New York: Viking.

Weinberg, G. (1971). *The psychology of computer programming*. New York: Van Nostrand Reinhold.

Wells, H. G. (1905). *A modern utopia*. London: Jonathan Cape. Retrieved March 30, 2010, from www.gutenberg.org/etext/6424

Wells, H. G. (1938). *World brain*. London: Methuen.

Wersig, G. (1992). Information science and theory: A weaver bird's perspective. In P. Vakkari & B. Cronin (Eds.), *Conceptions of library and information science: Historical, empirical, and theoretical perspectives* (pp. 201–217). London: Taylor Graham.

White, P. T. (1970, November). Behold the computer revolution. *National Geographic*, *138*(5), 593–633.

Yates, J. (1989). *Control through communication: The rise of system in American management*. Baltimore, MD: Johns Hopkins University Press.

Zhang, P. (2004). AIS SIGHCI three-year report. *SIGHCI Newsletter*, *3*(1), 2–6.

Zhang, P., Nah, F. F.-H., & Preece, J. (2004). HCI studies in management information systems. *Behaviour & Information Technology*, *23*(3), 147–151.

Zhang, P., Li, N., Scialdone, M. J., & Carey, J. (2009). The intellectual advancement of human–computer interaction research: A critical assessment of the MIS literature. *Transactions on Human–Computer Interaction*, *1*(3), 55–107.

CHAPTER 9

The History of
Information Technology

Thomas Haigh
University of Wisconsin, Milwaukee, WI

Introduction

In many scholarly fields the new entrant must work carefully to discover a gap in the existing literature. When writing a doctoral dissertation on the novels of Nabokov or the plays of Sophocles, clearing intellectual space for new construction can be as difficult as finding space to erect a new building in central London. A search ensues for an untapped archive, an unrecognized nuance, or a theoretical framework able to demolish a sufficiently large body of existing work.

The history of information technology (IT) is not such a field. From the viewpoint of historians it is more like Chicago in the mid-nineteenth century (Cronon, 1991). Building space is plentiful. Natural resources are plentiful. Capital, infrastructure, and manpower are not. Boosters argue for its natural advantages and promise that one day a mighty settlement will rise there. Speculative development is proceeding rapidly and unevenly. But right now the settlers seem a little eccentric and the humble structures they have erected lack the scale and elegance of those in better developed regions. Development is uneven and streets fail to connect. The native inhabitants have their ideas about how things should be done, which sometimes causes friction with new arrivals. In a generation everything will be quite unrecognizable, but how?

This is a guide to the growing (if ramshackle) secondary literature in the history of information technology: monographs, edited volumes, and journal articles written to explore different aspects of computing from historical perspectives. Except as a frame in which to situate these secondary works, and reveal gaps in their coverage, I cannot attempt here to recount the substance of that history. My discussion is biased toward books rather than articles. Books are the primary unit of scholarly production for historians and few significant topics can be dealt with fully within the confines of a journal article. Material initially presented in article form often receives its mature presentation in monographs.

However, articles and unpublished dissertations are referenced when they provide material unavailable elsewhere.

Information Technology vs. Computing

In this chapter I consider digital computer technologies and their applications but neglect communication technologies (other than those used for computer communication) and all analog or non-electronic information technologies. This distinction reflects current segmentation in the world of historical specialists. The history of communications technology is still written and read primarily by a different community from the history of computer technology and has evolved its own questions (Aspray, 1994). The history of information science (Hahn & Buckland, 1998) has been written almost entirely within the information science discipline. Likewise library history (Wiegand & Davis, 1994), media history, and history of the book are all well developed fields written in different academic niches and progressing in almost complete isolation from the history of computer technology.

Fortunately, the difficulties and rewards of "information history" as a category to bridge some of these divides have already been considered expertly in a recent *ARIST* chapter (Black, 2006), as has the rapidly developing literature on the history of information science (Burke, 2007). These helpfully constrain my brief to the history of information technology. But even this is a problematic and potentially sprawling category. Treating information technology and computing as interchangeable concepts generally makes me a little uneasy, so let me explain my decision to do so here. Looking at its two constituent words would suggest that *information technology* should include everything from ancient clay tablets through scrolls and books to communication systems of all kinds, newspapers, street signs, libraries, encyclopedias, and any artifact used for educational purposes. And indeed one sometimes sees such expansive definitions in textbooks of library and information science. I pass no judgment on the inherent merit of such a definition in observing that outside this rather small community the phrase is almost never used in this way.

In fact, the great majority of references to *information technology* have always been concerned with computers, although the exact meaning has shifted over time (Kline, 2006). The phrase received its first prominent usage in a *Harvard Business Review* article (Haigh, 2001b; Leavitt & Whisler, 1958) intended to promote a technocratic vision for the future of business management. Its initial definition was as the conjunction of computers, operations research methods, and simulation techniques. Having failed initially to gain much traction (unlike related terms of a similar vintage such as information systems, information processing, and information science) it was revived in policy and economic circles in the 1970s with a new meaning. Information technology now described the expected convergence of the computing, media, and telecommunications industries (and their technologies), understood within the broader context of a wave of enthusiasm for the computer revolution, post-industrial society, information society (Webster, 1995), and other fashionable expressions of the belief that new electronic technologies were bringing a profound rupture with the past. As it spread broadly during the 1980s, IT increasingly lost its association with communications (and, alas, any vestigial connection to the idea of anybody actually being informed of anything) to become a new and more pretentious way of saying "computer." The final step in this process is the recent surge in references to "information and communication technologies" or ICTs, a coinage that makes sense only if one assumes that a technology can inform without communicating.

In the history of information technology, as in other areas defined through reference to "information," definitions are problematic and categories unstable. As Lionel Fairthorne (1965, p. 10) observed more than forty years ago, the word's appeal is often as "a linguistic convenience that saves you the trouble of thinking about what you are talking about." Valiant attempts have been made to create definitions of information (Capurro & Hjørland, 2003) broad enough to bolster the territorial ambitions of information science and coherent enough to be useful, but as an historian I am impressed more by the enduring lack of consensus around its actual meaning. Information, like other concepts such as progress, freedom, or democracy, has become ubiquitous because, not in spite, of its impressive degree of interpretative flexibility. Information has been seized upon by many different social groups, each of which has produced hybridized notions such as *information science*, *information worker*, and *information system*. Definitions of these terms attempt to demarcate boundaries (Gieryn, 1983) for the authority of particular specialist groups, and so are frequently contested and have evolved haphazardly over time. Such phrases are rarely taken to mean what one would expect by looking up their constituent words in a dictionary.

This is a particular problem for the historian because one is wary to frame one's work using analytical categories that embed the interests and assumptions of one or another group of the actors one is writing about. It is hard even to find a vocabulary to describe long term continuities of practice across these rhetorical ruptures. For example, I have sometimes described my own ongoing research project as "a history of information processing and its management in American business over the twentieth century," yet only in the 1960s would the idea that routine administrative systems involved "processing information" have begun to seem plausible to my historical actors. The emergence of information as a crucial building block of occupational identities and system-building discourse is an important part of what set the corporate computer staff of the 1960s apart from office managers of the 1920s. Yet the very act of framing my story as one about information and its manipulation tends to obscure this crucial rhetorical innovation.

My other source of ambivalence toward the title of this chapter is that "history of computing," rather than "history of information technology," has traditionally been the phrase more widely adopted by specialists in the field. This is probably a result of the naming of the field's primary journal *Annals of the History of Computing* back in the 1970s, which in turn reflected its sponsorship by the American Federation of Information Processing Societies (AFIPS), a now defunct professional umbrella group that had adopted *computing* as an identity bridging the interests of its constituent societies in mathematical calculation, computer science, business data processing, and so on. Computing, however, has come to sound a little vulgar and old fashioned next to information technology, and so several name changes have taken place in recent years. The Charles Babbage Foundation recently became the IT History Society, and the Charles Babbage Institute, the field's leading research center, now bills itself as a "Center for the History of Information Technology" (www.cbi.umn.edu). So it seems inevitable that the history of computing will eventually complete its rebranding as the history of information technology.[1] This may in time facilitate more interaction between specialists in the history of computing and those working on other aspects of information history.

Origins of the History of Information Technology

The computer's history has been told for as long as there have been computers. Historian Michael S. Mahoney (1990, online) observed, in this context, that "nothing is really unprecedented. Faced with a new situation, people liken it to familiar ones and shape their responses on the basis of the perceived similarities." The search for precedent is also a search for a narrative. Humans make sense of the world by telling stories to themselves and each other (Weick, 1995), and so to understand and explain the first electronic computers it was necessary to package them inside a story.

One sees this most strikingly in Edmund Callis Berkeley's (1949) classic book *Giant Brains, or Machines that Think*. This was the first popular treatment of the new technology, providing an introduction to the hitherto obscure world of computing to a generation of impressionable youngsters. He described computers of the 1940s, such as the Electronic Numerical Integrator and Calculator (ENIAC), the Massachusetts Institute of Technology's (MIT) differential analyzer, and the series of machines built by Harvard and Bell Labs in some detail. Berkeley made an unconventional choice in building his story. The most obvious understanding of the early computer was as a calculating machine, literally as something performing computations. For decades to come these inventions were usually understood, for example, by Goldstein (1972) and Williams (1985), as a natural evolution of earlier calculating devices such as the hand cranked calculators widely used in business.

Berkeley, however, downplayed this understanding of the computer. He (Berkeley, 1949, p. vii) called the computer a giant brain not because it could think but because it "can handle information with great skill and great speed." This sense-making narrative was much more novel at the time, although it has since become a cliché. In this context the digital computer was precedented by earlier machines and systems for handling information, such as nerve cells, cave paintings, beads on strings, and human language (pp. 10–13). But, in "a deep break from the past" it could transfer "information from one part of the machine to another [with] flexible control over the sequence of its operation" (p. 5). In other words, it could execute a program. This framing led Berkeley to an exceptionally bold set of predictions as to the future impact of computer technology, which he forecasted "will take a load off men's minds as great as the load that printing took off men's writing" (p. vii) thanks to the perfection of capabilities such as automatic transcription and translation, machine vision, economic simulation, weather prediction, and even computerized psychotherapy. After making a preemptive strike on anti-computer prejudice as a disease in need of treatment he concluded that we should get ready to "welcome the robot machine as our deliverer from the long hard chores of many centuries" (p. 208).

One particular strand of computing history was heavily researched and exhaustively argued during the early 1970s. The inventors of the ENIAC eventually received a patent and its holder was seeking hundreds of millions of dollars in licensing fees from the other major computer companies. Several years of legal action centered on the circumstances and timing of their work and its relationship to prior art, documented in a trial transcript of more than twenty thousand pages. No other historical topic has ever assumed a similar practical urgency for the computer industry. Academic historians are not particularly concerned with assigning firsts but this question has continued to resonate elsewhere (Bucks, 2003). Even today, if one looks up the reviews on Amazon.com for a general history of computing, many of the reviews will invariably focus on whether the author answers this question "correctly." Partisans for the German contender Konrad Zuse or Iowa's oft-forgotten John Atanasoff are quick to lash out with one star reviews at those who slight the contributions of their idols. Historians try to sidestep such problems by employing long strings of hyphenated adjectives, so that a particular machine might hypothetically be described not as "the first computer" but as "the first large-scale general-purpose stored-program digital electronic computer to enter regular operation."

The history of computing emerged as an area of scholarly research during the 1970s. The pioneering generation of computer industry leaders and academic computer specialists started to develop an interest in preserving the history of their cohort's accomplishments in the face of milestone anniversaries, encroaching mortality, and a sense that the heritage of their communities was at risk. In the late 1960s and early 1970s this was reflected in a set of conference sessions organized by the

Association for Computing Machinery (ACM) and a major investment (Carlson, 1986) made by AFIPS to support a Smithsonian program of oral histories (Tropp, 1980) with pioneers from the earliest days of electronic computing. The late 1970s saw the launch of two ventures that have provided the field's institutional backbone for three decades now: the journal *Annals of the History of Computing* (Galler, 2004) and the Charles Babbage Institute (Aspray, 2007; Norberg, 2001). Chartered by the newly created Charles Babbage Foundation and supported financially by AFIPS, the latter found a previous home at the University of Minnesota, along with an endowed chair and the Tomash dissertation fellowship. Several computer museums were established with local support, most notably the Computer Museum in Boston.

Computer scientists and other pioneers were, during this period, the main suppliers and consumers of historical work. Bernie Galler (Akera, 2008), the founding editor of *Annals of the History of Computing,* was famous for his work on timesharing operating systems. Paul Armer, formerly head of numerical analysis at the RAND Corporation, headed the Charles Babbage Foundation. The most important early edited volume on the history of computing (Metropolis, Howlett, & Rota, 1980) was prepared by members of the Los Alamos scientific computing staff. The first textbook for the history of computing, *The Computer from Pascal to von Neumann* (Goldstein, 1972), was a mixture of historical research and memoir from a close collaborator of von Neumann.

The past three decades have seen a steady shift of activity away from retired participants and toward younger scholars with graduate training in history or science studies. This appears to be a common pattern in the historical study of scientific, technical, and professional fields. A few senior historians, such as I. Bernard Cohen of Harvard University, developed interests in the field, but most new entrants were graduate students. Indeed the list of winners of the Tomash dissertation fellowship (Yost, 2001) offered by the Charles Babbage Institute also serves as a register for most of those who have gone on to do important work in the area. Today the editorial board of *IEEE Annals of the History of Computing* is dominated by Ph.D. historians, including (for the first time) the editor-in-chief. Research practices in the field usually follow the humanities model: individual researchers, lots of archival work, rare and tiny grants, and primary publication in monographs. Some grants of appreciable size have been received to support historical projects run by professional societies or experiments with use of web communities to capture historical memory.

This shift has been associated with a gradual evolution in the kinds of research being undertaken. Much historical writing done by computer specialists has been far more than simple memoir, and many works by pioneers involved significant research in journals and archives to give balance to their accounts, solve mysteries, and verify facts. But historical work carried out by members of a field inevitably has a different character from work performed by outsiders. Scholars have long distinguished between *internalism* and *externalism* as approaches toward the history of scientific and technical fields.[2] The primary difference concerns the ways in which historical work is framed and the implicit research questions guiding the historian. Internalist work is typically written within the conceptual framework of the specialist community involved. It focuses on important discoveries or inventions, fitting specific episodes into a trajectory of development and (almost invariably) progress. Its insights are directed at an assumed readership within the discipline. Externalist work is explicitly concerned with integrating developments within a particular specialized field with broader historical trajectories, such as major political, social, or economic shifts (for example, the Cold War or Industrial Revolution). This involves reinterpreting the history of a community according to a set of perspectives and concerns that might be very different from those held by the historical actors themselves. The work of trained historians, particularly those without advanced training in information technology, will naturally be oriented toward questions of interest to other historians and so is more often associated with the externalist approach. Of course, one can write good and bad history from either perspective.

Not all changes since the 1970s have been positive. Changes in the computer industry have eliminated many of the early sources of support for historical work. Today's leading computer companies have short-term cultures, downplay corporate philanthropy, keep few accessible archives, and sponsor almost no historical projects. AFIPS collapsed and the IEEE Computer Society took over publication of *Annals of the History of Computing*, providing it a stable home since 1992. Interest in historical projects still waxes and wanes among the professional societies, but with a preponderance of waning. However in recent years the Association for Computing Machinery has supported an ACM History Committee. Its main achievement to date is arranging for the archiving of the society's records. The Computer Museum folded as DEC ran into trouble; much of its collection made its way to California where it formed the core holdings of a new Computer History Museum in the heart of Silicon Valley. So far the museum has built excellent connections with computer industry executives and technology enthusiasts but has had few interactions with historians.

In contrast, interest in information technology within scholarly associations such as the Business History Conference, the Society for Social Studies of Science, the History of Science Society, and (especially) the Society for the History of Technology has been rising consistently, albeit from a very low base. The latter includes a thriving specialist group, the Special Interest Group for Computers, Information and Society (SIG-CIS). The field is also becoming much more international, with major projects underway in many European countries. It is increasingly interdisciplinary. Scholars usually approach topics in the history of information technology from within the perspectives of historical sub-disciplines (business, labor, social, technology, economic, or science) and frame their contributions within these literatures rather than primarily as a contribution to the history of information technology. This brings diversity, but it does slow the development of a canon, common research agenda, or a shared core set of concerns.

The institutional affiliation of scholars in the field is similarly diverse. Few history departments or science studies programs have actively sought to hire in the history of IT, but many scholars trained in this area have found academic employment in schools of information, business, communication, or (outside the U.S.) computer science. This presents opportunities for interdisciplinary collaboration and outreach to professional communities, but also threatens them with institutional marginality and reduces opportunities to teach or supervise new generations of specialists in the history of information technology.

Bibliographic Guides and Reviews

One can chart the developments by looking at the images of the field presented in introductory articles, review articles, and manifestos over the years. The earliest articles such as that by May (1980) were aimed at giving computer scientists a general idea of historical methods and concerns. The same task has been attempted frequently over the years, recently by Haigh (2004a). Two major articles of the 1980s (Aspray, 1984; Mahoney, 1988) captured the field as credentialed historians were first beginning to make their mark. Aspray sketched its institutional development and categorized major early works; Mahoney (p. 115) glided rapidly over existing work in the field ("historians stand before the daunting complexity of a subject that has grown exponentially in size and variety, looking not so much like an uncharted ocean as like a trackless jungle. We pace on the edge, pondering where to cut in ...") to discuss research questions from better developed areas of the history of technology that might profitably be applied to computing. Both bemoaned the many gaps in topics and approaches. Reviews (Aspray, 1994; Mahoney, 1996) from the same authors published in the 1990s followed a similar pattern. William Aspray (1994) acknowledged gaps (particularly the study of applications and software) but also noted rapid growth in the field, new activity internationally, and a number of promising studies underway. Mahoney (1996, p. 772) again stressed conceptual poverty: "we have lots of answers but very few questions, lots of stories but no history, lots of things to do but no sense of how to do them or in what order. Simply put, we don't yet know what the history of computing is really about." Shortly after becoming director of the Charles Babbage Institute, Tom Misa (2007) surveyed the literature from the viewpoint of a historian of technology, noting a reluctance to engage with the part computer technology has actually played in reshaping society. The regular "Think Piece" opinion column in *IEEE Annals of the History of Computing* can be counted on to feature an historian proposing to call on the community to adopt one or another perspective from more mature historical communities (comparative history, social history, memory studies, etc.).

Much has changed over thirty years, but the message that our challenges are great, our concerns parochial, and our methods mostly inadequate has been a constant. Following this tradition, I have found myself composing many variations on the same sentence (indeed so many that I edited most out). This sentence informs the reader that the existing literature on a particular aspect of the history of information technology is, at best, full of holes and that most of the obvious topics have been utterly neglected. It is generally followed with the sad caution that even those episodes that have been explored have usually been examined from a rather narrow perspective that ignores issues of general importance to historians.

James Cortada (1996a, 1996b) has been the field's most prolific assembler of annotated bibliographies, addressing the history of computing with particular reference to business history. He has also cataloged sources on the history of computer applications (Cortada, 1996a). Another survey examines sources for scientific computing (Yost, 2002). Such guides are perhaps less widely used within the history of information technology than in other fields because the vast array of accessible sources for recent decades means that no guide can aim to cover all, or even a significant fraction, of them. Cortada (1990) and Bruemmer (1987) surveyed archival sources. Both works are conspicuously dated, but still useful for locating personal papers or collections held at institutions one would not otherwise think to examine. Books about the history of computing are surveyed with useful summaries in work by Sterling (2003); Sterling and Grier (2003) cover books relevant to the history of software (most of them classics rather than secondary sources). Haigh (2004b) provides annotations for selected secondary sources of various kinds, including web sites.

Synthetic Histories

Many overviews of the history of computing have been produced over the years. Your starting point should be *Computer: A History of the Information Machine* (Campbell-Kelly & Aspray, 1996). Created with the support of the Sloan Foundation, it is written by two of the field's most prominent scholars but intended to be accessible to a general audience. Unlike earlier synthetic accounts, it shows the computer as a tool designed to tackle specific applications, going back into history to explore its relationship to earlier office machines, communication technologies, and calculating aids. It mixes the business history of computer firms with the development of key computing technologies. Paul Ceruzzi's (1998) *A History of Modern Computing* makes a good complement to *Computer*. Ceruzzi's book has less to say about applications, and skips the digital computer's forebears completely to launch the story in the mid-1940s. Ceruzzi provides more detail on the architectural development of computers and better coverage of the minicomputer, which he argues for persuasively as the source of today's personal computing technologies. His book focuses more on technical history and has a somewhat more episodic structure. A more recent summary, intended to be accessible to high school students, is by Swedin (2005). Several older and journalistic overviews exist, but you will find little cause to consult them.

As historical work necessarily takes place sometime after the events concerned we can trace the spread of computer technology in the changing narratives of the history of computing. The lag appears to be two or three decades. Early work focused on the computer as an experimental calculating machine and situated it as an evolution of earlier calculating machines. By the 1990s scholars began to explore its administrative use and situate it in the context of earlier technologies such as punched card machines and typewriters. *Computer* echoes this perspective. On its publication the book's most novel feature was its insistence on the computer as primarily a tool for administrative coordination rather than scientific calculation. (In other words its framing had caught up with the world of the 1960s, rather than remaining in the 1940s.) Although accessible, it is not simplistic and nicely summarizes and connects key insights and stories from the secondary literature as it had developed to the early 1990s.

All three books include coverage of personal computing and the internet (particularly in their revised second editions) but this is in part a concession to commercial realities. The state of the secondary literature permitted well documented and analytical coverage of events up to the early 1970s, at which point a notable shift in tone and source material occurs. Falling back on conventional wisdom, their authors summarize key events celebrated in popular histories.

Computer works particularly well as a proxy for the strengths and weaknesses of the historical literature in the early 1990s. One of its most striking features is the centrality of the ENIAC to its narrative structure. The earliest chapters consider a whole range of technologies, from file cabinets to telegraphs, used in a range of settings. The middle part of the book abruptly shifts to look in detail at ENIAC and a handful of other early experimental machines built during the 1940s in government, academic, and corporate research labs to automate routine calculation. Then the narrative follows digital computers back out into the world as commercial goods. It charts their growing capabilities through three distinct generations of mainframes (culminating in the IBM System 360 range of the 1960s), the evolution of software, the minicomputer industry of the 1970s, and the growing importance of personal computers in the 1980s. This gives the story a distinctive, hourglass shape with ENIAC as the tiny isthmus linking these two worlds. It is what sociologists of scientific knowledge have called an "obligatory passage point" (Callon, 1986, p. 205) in the history of information technology. ENIAC took that role quite literally in the *Information Age* exhibit shown at the Smithsonian from 1990 to circa 2005. A spacious hall of early information technologies narrowed to a small passageway, in which visitors walked through a partial reconstruction of the machine before emerging into the computer age.

I have argued elsewhere (Haigh, 2001a) that this kind of structure yields a peculiar picture. Understanding the history of information technology does indeed involve looking at the replacement of one technology by another and its use within particular applications. But the most satisfactory way to do this would be to focus on a single social sphere (school, office, hospital, library) and examine changes in the type, use, cultural understanding, and management of the information technologies found there over a particular period. A one-volume history of computer technology or the computer hardware industry would be hefty but conceptually unproblematic, but a one volume synthetic history that takes the use, work, and social dimensions of information technology seriously is probably impossible given the proliferation of computer technology in recent decades. Think of the precursor technologies one would have to integrate. Computers (whether free standing or embedded in consumer electronics) have replaced record players, Walkmen, analog television receivers, and video cassette recorders. Books, newspapers, and conventional telephones now appear endangered. In the office, computers have replaced typewriters, adding machines, bookkeeping and billing machines, duplicating machines, letters, memos, and carbon paper. File cabinets are vanishing, and in recent years the amount of paper used in American offices has finally begun to diminish. Computer networks are central to every kind of business operation and play an increasingly vital role in our social lives and personal communication. Databases, automatic data capture, modeling, and statistical analysis capabilities have transformed practice in almost every area of science. Even the game of solitaire has been remade as a shuffling of mice rather than of playing cards.

As computers are used in more and more ways in more and more social contexts, the challenge to synthesis becomes more and more serious. Mahoney (2005) expressed a similar idea, more elegantly, when he suggested that we should recognize that there is not a single "history of computing" but multiple histories. Furthermore even the technologies themselves will have been literally and metaphorically reconstructed to fit the context at which one is looking. So he titled his article "The Histories of Computing(s)."

Computer Technologies

The abacus is several thousand years old. It was followed by a long series of increasingly complex technologies for counting, adding, and calculating. However, I have neither the space nor the expertise to explore in any detail the literature on calculating devices before the electronic computer, a topic worthy of its own lengthy review. These devices loomed large in early overviews of the computer, including Williams's (1985) comprehensive and well illustrated book; but as the field has developed, their history has come to seem more distinct. This is probably because fewer people today think of the computer as primarily a device for calculation. As its range of applications has grown, so too has the diversity of its precursors. The primary literature on calculating machines is surveyed in a comprehensive and well illustrated catalog of publications issued before 1955 (Tomash and Williams, 2008). Major museums, including the Smithsonian, the Science Museum in London (Pugh & Baxandall, 1975), and the Deutsches Museum, have extensive collections of the machines themselves and have played an important part in documenting and preserving their history. I am aware of no comprehensive overview of the recent secondary literature on the topic.

The most famous early devices, and those most clearly related to programmable computers, are Charles Babbage's (1791–1871) Difference Engine and Analytical Engine. Neither machine was constructed in his lifetime. Babbage's work was omitted entirely from Berkeley's (1949) seminal popular discussion of computing; his failed efforts to build calculating engines having long since slipped from public memory. Within a few years, however, Babbage enjoyed a dramatic surge in his posthumous reputation and was pressed into service as the forgotten inventor of the programmable general purpose computer. The Difference Engine has since been built according to Babbage's plans and can be seen at the Science Museum in London. Its story is told with some zest, along with that of Babbage himself, by the project's leader (Swade, 2001). Other difference engines were attempted in Sweden (Lindgren, 1990). The Analytical Engine was intended to store and run programs, but Babbage never finished its design, let alone its construction. Babbage has been the subject of several biographies, most notable being that by Hyman (1982). Ada Lovelace (daughter of the famous Lord Byron) wrote a tutorial describing the analytical engine. She has thus been adopted as a rallying point for women in computing and herself received many biographies, of which Stein's (1985) is the least overheated. The letters and papers of both have been published. Babbage is perhaps the only topic in the history of information technology one might plausibly describe as over studied.

The edited volume *Computing Before Computers* (Aspray, 1990a) surveys technologies used for calculation from the abacus through Babbage's uncompleted calculating engines to punched card machines and electro mechanical calculators of the 1940s. One of its main contributors, Ceruzzi (1983) provides a more detailed exploration of the key computing projects of the 1940s, looking at the electro-mechanical automatic calculators built by research groups in Germany, Harvard, and Bell Labs as well as the University of Pennsylvania's iconic ENIAC project. The electronic, non-programmable Atanasoff-Berry Computer, constructed at Iowa State University, has also received attention (Bucks, 1988). Early digital computers were built specifically to handle numerical mathematical calculations. Analog mechanical and electronic computers were a separate genre of machine, used to solve differential equations, model electrical power networks, and simulate flight paths. Although analog computers are generally dismissed merely as precursors to their digital cousins, James Small (2001) has shown that they remained widely used into the 1960s and supported a thriving network of specialized suppliers and users.

Although scholars and participants have devoted articles (Burks & Burks, 1981) and chapters to ENIAC, the only full length study of the project is journalistic (McCartney, 1999). Stern (1981) presents a thorough discussion of the machine and its immediate legacy. For a long time it was considered to be the first fully operational programmable electronic computer. In recent decades, however, this title has been claimed by the wartime British Colossus project (Copeland, 2004, 2006). Excessive state secrecy meant that its creators had to wait for more than three decades to reveal its capabilities (Randell, 1980).

The first stored program, electronic, digital computers have also been relatively well covered. Although ENIAC was a high speed electronic computer it did not, as originally constructed, read programs into memory. Configuring it for a new problem involved turning knobs and rewiring patch boards. In contrast, stored program computers treat the program as another kind of data to be loaded into memory for execution. The fundamental design behind modern digital computers is often called *von Neumann architecture*, after celebrated mathematician John von Neumann (1993), whose "First Draft of a Report on the EDVAC" inspired many early computer projects. Aspray (1990b) used von Neumann's contributions during the 1940s and 1950s to computer design, numerical analysis, computing theory, and several other areas as a window into the broader history of computing and applied mathematics during this period.

Many computer-building projects sprang up during the late 1940s. These are given thorough summary in the chapters assembled for Rojas and Hashagen (2000). The first two stored program computers to become operational were British: a proof-of-concept test system at the University of Manchester and the more powerful Electronic Delay Storage Automatic Calculator (EDSAC) built by a team at Cambridge University. Manchester's efforts, which gave rise to a tradition of large-scale computer development that endured into the 1970s, were profiled by Lavington (1998) and reexamined by Anderson (e.g., 2007) in a series of publications. The most comprehensive overview of the EDSAC project remains the autobiography of its leader (Wilkes, 1985), although Campbell-Kelly (1998) has probed the early development of programming practices around the machine.

Electromechanical punched card machines, which will be discussed in the context of the computer industry and their application to administrative work, are in many ways the most direct technological ancestors of early commercial computers. The most obviously important computer hardware technologies from the 1960s onward are the transistor and the silicon chip. These stories lead us toward the history of electronic engineering and the business history of the electronics industry. Readable, well researched overviews exist of the history of solid state electronics (Riordan & Hoddeson, 1997) and the integrated circuit (Reid, 2001). Two books combining the structural development of the industry with technical innovations and manufacturing processes are particularly relevant. *To The Digital Age* (Bassett, 2002) tells the story of the development of MOS transistors, their integration onto silicon chips, and the creation of the microprocessor. It uses interviews and archival documents to discuss the contributions of Fairchild, IBM, and Intel. Bassett makes a particular effort to trace the transfer of ideas between firms, and to tie the dramatically different fortunes of IBM and Intel in turning research into products to their different cultures and internal organizations. Christophe Lecuyer's *Making Silicon Valley* (Lecuyer, 2006) documents the rise of the region's industry, looking particularly at the role of military demand and the distinctive network organization of small, specialized producers that sprang up there. Biographies cover leading figures in the most famous dynasty within the industry. William Shockley (Shurkin, 2006) was a brilliant crank who invented the transistor and founded Shockley Semiconductor. He proved an abysmal manager, and soon his star employees Robert Noyce (Berlin, 2006) and Gordon E. Moore (creator of an eponymous "Law") left to found Fairchild Semiconductor and, when that became stale, Intel Corporation. Intel established the market for memory chips, built the first microprocessor, and under the leadership of Andrew Grove (Tedlow, 2007) came to dominate the market for personal computer processor chips.

Away from this sliver of history one finds very few histories of computer technologies after the 1950s. Nothing much has been written on computer manufacturing techniques. Components and peripherals have fared little better, but two articles (Tomash & Cohen, 1991a, 1991b) cover the early history of printers and Pugh's (1984) book pays particular attention to IBM's early memory technologies. No overall history of computer networking technologies has been attempted, although we do have a popular history of fiber optics (Hecht, 1999). The reader looking for a clearly written, accessible, and thoughtful overview of the story of the vacuum tube (the basic building block of computer logic in the 1950s), the microprocessor (as opposed to chips in general), disk storage, computer graphics, supercomputers, minicomputers, operating systems, computer communications, computer architecture, or virtually any other aspect of computer science or computer technology will have to wait.

Almost nothing scholarly has been written on the personal computer industry and its products; the origins of personal and interactive computing technologies, however, have received more attention. Until the mid-1970s it was rarely economical to provide individuals with their own computers. But many aspects of today's computing experience were already available on an experimental basis in the 1960s, including interactive communication and access to shared network resources. Science journalist Mitch Waldrop (2001) bit off a big chunk of this history in his book *The Dream Machine*. He focused on J. C. R. Licklider, a psychology professor at the Massachusetts Institute of Technology, who developed a distinctive vision of "man-computer symbiosis" in which people worked interactively with computers to solve problems (Licklider, 1960, p. 4). Intended for non-specialists, the book sprawls across much of the history of interactive computing, which provides context but blunts the narrative. As the founding director of the Information Processing Techniques Office (IPTO) (Kita, 2003) within the U.S. Government's Advanced Projects Research Agency, Licklider had great personal latitude to fund work in this direction, underwriting crucial research on interactive computing and laying the foundations for the experimental ARPANET (seed of the internet). As well as its now legendary work in support of networking, the U.S. Department of Defense's Advanced Research Projects Agency (ARPA) supported fundamental research advances in several areas of computer science including operating systems, computer graphics, and artificial intelligence. This story has been told by Nordberg and O'Neil (1996). As an official history, the book is well sourced but rather careful in its conclusions. Between the lines, however, one glimpses a fascinating story of an incestuous and dynamic research culture quite oblivious to today's worries about research ethics and conflicts of interest.

One of the recipients of IPTO's largess during the 1960s was Douglas Engelbart's lab at the Stanford Research Institute (Bardini, 2000). Engelbart was an enthusiastic advocate of the power of interactive computers to support daily activities. By 1968 his group had already invented the mouse and, in a famous technology demonstration at the Joint Computer Conference, demonstrated a mouse-controlled hypertext system with a text editor able to display information in multiple windows and collapse outline headings into a reshufflable hierarchy.

Researchers from Engelbart's lab went on to fill key positions in Xerox's Palo Alto Research Center (PARC), which opened in 1970. Over the next decade its research teams invented many of the fundamental technologies behind the graphical workstations of the 1980s and personal computers of the 1990s, including laser printers, Ethernet, the graphical user interface, what-you-see-is-what-you-get editing (displaying editable text with the actual fonts, sizes, and formatting it will have when printed), computer paint programs, and graphical environments for object-oriented programming. PARC achieved notoriety as the source of many of the breakthrough ideas commercialized in Apple's Lisa and Macintosh computers and as an example in the business literature of a company that failed to reap the economic benefits of its technological triumphs (Smith & Alexander, 1989). Michael A. Hiltzik (1999) has provided the most nuanced telling of the PARC story, using interviews with participants and extending the narrative into the firm's commercial product efforts of the early 1980s. Xerox's Star workstation was intended to put powerful, networked, personal computers with big screens and graphical capabilities on the desks of managers, professionals, and secretaries.

Hiltzik observes that Xerox recouped its investments in the lab many times over even though it never became a dominant force in personal computing. The story has also been told by its participants (Goldberg, 1988). The Star failed commercially, but the 1980s did see the emergence of a specialized market for powerful graphical workstations costing tens of thousands of dollars. Firms in this industry played an important role in creating the technologies of today's personal computers, but have so far received no historical attention other than a journalistic book on Sun Microsystems (Southwick, 1999).

Software technologies have suffered a similar neglect, even though the history of the software industry is relatively well documented. Articles, usually by computer scientists or pioneers, have discussed aspects of the history of specific software systems. Best developed is the history of programming languages (Sammet, 1969), where a series of three conferences held over the decades by the ACM's Special Interest Group on Programming Languages has yielded a series of carefully researched, well edited, technical histories authored by the creators of major programming languages (Bergin & Gibson, 1996; Wexelblat, 1981). Journalist Steve Lohr (2001) produced an accessible and well researched popular history of the topic. Historical efforts have also been made within the software engineering community (Broy & Denert, 2002). Coverage of other areas is at best patchy. The history of formal methods, attempts to prove the correctness of programs mathematically to a logical specification or reason mathematically about their behavior, has been explored by sociologist of science Donald MacKenzie (2001) and one of its key practitioners (Jones, 2003).

Computer technologies have also been explored by some economic historians. Economic history has increasingly diverged from business history and is largely conducted within the discipline of economics. Authors thus tend to focus on specific technologies as test cases for larger theories, meaning that the same handful of topics such as the QWERTY keyboard layout and its putative inferiority to alternative designs are debated from a variety of theoretical perspectives (David, 1985).

Computer Science

The first university departments of computer science and accompanying degree programs were created in the 1960s. Computing research had originally been an interdisciplinary venture, carried out by people from varied backgrounds who stumbled into computer projects or found work in computing centers (Aspray, 2000). The push to establish study of the computer and its associated technologies as an autonomous scientific discipline passed a series of milestones, from the establishment of the Association for Computing Machinery in 1947 through the gradual growth of research and teaching in the field during the late 1950s and early 1960s to the chartering of the first department of computer science at Purdue in 1962 (Rice & Rosen, 1994) and the first awarding of a Ph.D.

in computer science to Richard Wexelblat at the University of Pennsylvania in 1965. In 1986 the National Science Foundation (NSF) established its Directorate for Computing and Information Science and Engineering (Harsha, 2004), funding computing research on the basis of its contribution to computer science rather than, as in the 1960s and early 1970s, supporting computing facilities as means to the ends of other disciplines (Aspray & Williams, 1994). Undergraduate enrollment rose rapidly, peaking (until the dot.com boom made computer science briefly fashionable again) with forty-two thousand graduating students in 1986 (Fiegener, 2008). Computer science accounted for four percent of all bachelor's degrees granted in the U.S. that year.

There are two main ways to approach this history. The first is to study the institutions of computer science. The major professional societies, leading academic departments, mightiest corporate research labs, and key funding bodies all deserve in-depth analysis. One might also hope for the creation of synthetic histories that weave together these different strands to show their interrelationship. So far we have only a few bits and pieces of the overall picture. Aspray has published seminal articles on the history of early computing departments (Aspray, 2000) and the University of Pittsburgh's information science program (Aspray, 1999). The history of the Association for Computing Machinery appears as a subsidiary theme in the work of several scholars (Haigh, Kaplan, & Seib, 2007) and has been sketched by several insiders. The recent transfer of the Association's records to the Charles Babbage Institute is likely to spur additional work in this area. Little has been written about the history of other associations such as the IEEE Computer Society (and its precursors) and the Society for Industrial and Applied Mathematics. The history of computer science funding agencies is relatively well developed, mainly because government bodies sometimes commission their own histories. A lengthy article covers the early history of NSF funding for computer science (Aspray & Williams, 1994); books on ARPA's support for key computing technologies (Norberg & O'Neill, 1996) and the Strategic Computing Initiative of the 1990s (Roland & Shiman, 2002) round out the picture. The latter began as an authorized history but was completed independently and gives a fascinating and well conceptualized account of the interplay of politics, empire-building administrators, and grant-hungry researchers. Corporate labs have been much less well documented, with the exception of the Xerox PARC facility, which looms large in histories of personal computing.

The other main approach is to look at the evolving content of computer science research. This might be tackled as an exercise in intellectual history in the manner of traditional internalist history of science, looking at the rise and fall of schools of thought and the succession of key problems and areas of interest. This requires the researcher to develop a high degree of expertise in the discipline as understood during the time period in question, and so in many fields work of this kind is more often tackled by members of the discipline in question rather than by

Ph.D. historians. One might also imagine more externalist histories of computer science, in which shifts in the style or content of research are explained with reference to politics, funding priorities, or attempts to legitimate the discipline as academically respectable.

Computer science has not, as a discipline, made a significant commitment to history and historical material is almost entirely absent from the curriculum. This contrasts with many professional fields such as business, medicine, and indeed librarianship where historical research and teaching has traditionally taken place within the discipline (although even there it is increasingly losing ground). Several computing researchers of the pioneer generation made significant early contributions to the history of computing; younger faculty members, however, generally cannot afford to devote time to such a marginal topic. No Ph.D. historian has ever been hired to a computer science faculty in the U.S. Michael Mahoney (1997, 2002) was the only historian to attempt a broad intellectual history of theoretical computer science; although his effort yielded some suggestive and intellectually intimidating articles, he did not produce a monograph on the topic.

The biography is an important genre within the history of science. Only mathematician and computing theory pioneer Alan Turing has so far received much attention here, most notably in the monumental biography *Alan Turing: The Enigma of Intelligence* (Hodges, 1983). In popular culture Turing has been computer science's breakout hit as genius, oppressed homosexual, and war-winning code breaker. Grace Hopper, who led important early work on programming languages in the 1950s before becoming a manager of computing projects for the U.S. Navy, is the poster lady for women in computing and has been profiled in two biographies (Beyer, 2009; Williams, 2004). In contrast, the best known academic computer scientists such as Richard Hamming, Marvin Minsky, Edsger Dijkstra, Donald E. Knuth, and C. A. R. Hoare are yet to receive full length biographies.

Business Histories: Mainframes and Minicomputer Producers

The development of the computer industry up to the early 1970s is, along with the development of early one-off computers, one of the best documented corners of the history of information technology. The computer industry features prominently in recent overviews of the history of computing and has received a focused summary (Yost, 2005a). *Before the Computer* (Cortada, 1993) puts the industry into its historical context, showing the extent to which the mainframe computer industry grew out of the earlier office machine industry. Norberg (1990) also showed the importance of punched-card machine companies to scientific computing practice even before the development of electronic computers.

Until the 1980s the global computer industry was dominated by IBM, which maintained a market share of around 75 percent and enjoyed a similar share of the books devoted to the computer business. Dozens of books by journalists and popular writers cover IBM's early history; they recycle a fairly small pool of incidents and anecdotes. Early accounts (Bedlen & Bedlen, 1962) focused on the charismatic autocrat Thomas J. Watson who led the firm (and its precursor) from 1914 to the 1950s. Watson's gift for self-promotion ensured that he was famous as a business visionary and friend of presidents long before his company reached the top echelons of American business. Watson's complex relationship with his son and successor, Thomas Watson, Jr. and other family members has provided grist for more recent work (Tedlow, 2003).

Two books on IBM stand out. Emerson W. Pugh (1994), a former IBM insider, has written a careful and thoughtful overview of the firm's development, based on archival sources, which goes beyond anecdotes to expose relationships between IBM's market positions, technologies, and internal dynamics. Watson's autobiography (Watson & Petre, 1990) is a model of its kind; it skillfully interweaves his personal story with the development of the firm. More recently, scholars have begun to put Watson's management style into broader historical contexts, such as the development of the American industrial style of welfare capitalism (Stebenne, 2005). Drawing on business theory, the firm's success has been explained in terms of its development of organizational capabilities appropriate to market needs (Usselman, 1993).

Anyone interested in the rest of the industry will find rather slim pickings in the current academic literature. In fact there are only two scholarly monographs devoted to individual companies other than IBM. One is the award winning *ICL: A Technical and Business History* (Campbell-Kelly, 1989). The scope of the book is broader than one might suppose, as ICL was created by government order in the 1960s as an amalgamation of almost the entire British computer industry. Arthur Norberg (2005) followed this with an examination of two of the first startup companies in the industry (The Eckert-Mauchley Computer Company and Engineering Research Associates) and their merger as the foundation of Univac, the number two player in the early computer industry.

National Cash Register was an important force in the computing market but its history has been told primarily as an adjunct to IBM's because Watson Sr. got his start in the office machine business there. The only full-length published history is a memoir credited to a former executive (Allyn, 1967), which says almost nothing about the computer era.[3] General Electric's years in the mainframe business provide a sad tale told so far only by its participants (Lee, 1995; Lee & Snively, 2000; Oldfield, 1996). Almost nothing has been written about the post-War history of calculating machine giant Burroughs, which carved out a respectable niche in the computer industry. Similarly, no overall histories have been produced of the role of Xerox, RCA, or Honeywell in the mainframe markets of the 1960s and 1970s, or of the history of Univac after the 1950s. I am unaware of any major English language histories of European or Asian computer companies. Shane Greenstein has looked at the economic history of a number of aspects of computing, including the mainframe market (Greenstein & Wade, 1998).

Control Data Corporation pioneered the market for scientific supercomputers and dominated it during the 1960s. The firm's extensive archives are at the Charles Babbage Institute but have so far seen minimal use, so those interested in the firm will find little more than a retrospective musing on its management secrets (Price, 2005). Its star designer, Seymour Cray, went on to achieve fame through two eponymous companies that built the world's fastest computers during the 1970s and 1980s. A typically breathless journalistic account, *The Supermen* (Murray, 1997), tells this story, as does a scholarly article (Elzen & MacKenzie, 1994).

Digital Equipment Corporation (DEC) grew from a specialized producer of laboratory control equipment to pioneer the market for minicomputers in the 1960s, diversifying into mainframes and office computers in the 1970s. By the 1980s it was second only to IBM in the global computer market, with a thriving network of research and development centers. DEC's story was sketched in a nicely produced and relentlessly upbeat corporate history written by its then archivist (Pearson, 1992) and a hagiographic biography of its founder (Harrar & Rifkin, 1988). A more recent book written by former employees focused on its "legacies" (Schein, 2003, p. 1); some of its early history was documented in a self-published memoir (Ornstein, 2002) and a coffee table book of pictures (Earls, 2004). Its main rival in the minicomputer business, Data General, received a wonderfully vivid bottom-up portrait in *The Soul of a New Machine* (Kidder, 1981) but its history remains undocumented.

Work so far on the history of the computer industry gives a reasonably good sense of its important products and technologies and of the strategies used by some of its key firms. Future research should address limitations of perspective as well as extend coverage to companies and national industries so far neglected. We have little sense of what it was like to work in these firms as anything other than an engineer or executive. Nothing has been written about manufacturing processes, production engineering, or assembly line work. And, although computer firms became emblems of the new high technology economy by the 1960s and had been pioneering the personnel policies of what has been termed welfare capitalism since the 1920s, no major studies of the industry have yet explored its role as the model for a new kind of industrial culture.

Business Histories: Personal Computing

The early history of the personal computer industry is another topic so far untouched by scholars. *Fire in the Valley*, in its first edition (Freiberger & Swaine, 1984), gave a fresh and immediate account of the industry's idiosyncratic origins and the travails of briefly successful firms during the 1970s. A revised edition adds coverage of later events but the new material is patchy and dilutes the original's charm. Events of the 1980s are covered best in *Accidental Empires* (Cringely, 1992). Written by the gossip columnist of a computer newspaper, the book provides the expected scuttlebutt on the personalities of industry celebrities such as Bill Gates and Steve Jobs alongside the development of crucial products such as the Apple II, Lotus 1-2-3, PostScript, and IBM PC-compatible BIOS. But it is also unexpectedly thoughtful, convincingly linking their foibles to the structural development of the hardware and software industries and providing some exceptionally clear analysis of the nature of platform-based competition. Its PBS television adaptation preserved some of these qualities.

The idea of computers as tools for some kind of personal liberation, nurtured by Licklider and Engelbart during the 1960s, was also channeled into the early development of the personal computer. A cluster of new technologies including RAM chips, microprocessors, and floppy disk drives made it possible for electronics hobbyists to design and build cheap computers using readily available components. The more entrepreneurial of these hobbyists founded companies to sell peripherals, software, and preassembled computers to their fellow enthusiasts. The freshest and most influential account of this movement was given by technology journalist Steven Levy (1984) in his wonderfully observed book *Hackers*. John Markoff (2005), also a journalist, retraced much of the same ground in his more recent *What the Dormouse Said* but the book suffers in comparison from a meandering narrative and his failure to conceptualize the counterculture clearly.

One company founded by computing hobbyists, Apple Computer, had become the dominant force in the American personal computer industry by the end of the 1970s. In spite of subsequent travails, it endures today as one of the world's most successful technology companies. As with Microsoft, space does not permit anything like a full listing of the many books journalists have written about this company, its corporate culture, and its mercurial leader Steve Jobs. Some are more interesting and more reliable than others, but none is particularly ambitious intellectually or does much to frame the personalities, triumphs, and mishaps of the company in a broader context. Readers interested in its earlier history and the introduction of the Macintosh will find *The Little Kingdom* (Moritz, 1984) indispensable. Levy's (1994) account of the development of the Macintosh, *Insanely Great*, is not a patch on his earlier book *Hackers* but was informed by input from within the design team. One key member of that team offers his own recollections in a blog-turned-book (Hertzfeld, 2004). Hatchet jobs are also plentiful and the firm's stumbles and oddities give their authors much material to work with. The best supported is a memoir by the ill-fated Gil Amelio, who briefly led the company during its mid-1990s nadir (Amelio & Simon, 1998). This chronicle of disaster and frustration exerts a certain uneasy fascination. Apple's corporate archives are now available for scholarly use at

Stanford University, so one can at least hope that some brave historian will soon delve into this material in search of less familiar stories.

No other personal computer company has inspired anything like the same outpouring of material. At one time or another Atari (Cohen, 1984), Texas Instruments, and Radio Shack (Kornfeld, 1983) held significant chunks of the American home computer market but none seems to have received significant historical attention. Commodore, which produced the best selling computer model of all time (the Commodore 64), has been largely ignored by historians and journalists alike because its breakthrough hit was an inexpensive machine for home use. Bagnall (2005) has redressed this. His lengthy and unashamedly partisan tome was self-published and could have used an editor, but its scope and depth of research make it the most ambitious history to date of a home computer company. It captures the flavor of the era and culture of the company as well as many details of its technical accomplishments. The first substantial work on the history of personal computing is now arriving in dissertation form from a new generation of scholars (Lean, 2008; Veraart, 2008).

In 1981 IBM released its personal computer (Chposky & Leonsis, 1988), rapidly establishing market dominance and setting a powerful de facto standard for the industry just as it had previously done for mainframe computers. But by the 1990s the personal computer industry had evolved to a quite different structure. It became a complex ecosystem in which Microsoft and Intel held strategic power over two key components of the overall system, personal computer "manufacturers" did little more than screw together, market, and support commodity computers built from a dozen or so major components, and these components were designed by anonymous, specialized firms in places such as Korea and Taiwan. There was a standard design, but it was neither imposed by a single company nor defined by a formal process. This will surely make for a shelf full of fascinating histories, but so far we have only a provocative sketch (Sumner, 2008). Firms such as Dell did no actual engineering and so will need to be analyzed in rather different ways from earlier computer companies (Dell & Freedman, 1999).

Those curious about the development of handheld computers will find that Kaplan's (1994) memoir of the ill-fated tablet computing pioneer GO Corporation provides a fascinating picture of the Silicon Valley venture capital and startup company rituals of the early 1990s and of the challenges faced in competing directly with Microsoft in this era. The pen computing concept eventually took off with the Palm Pilot, a geek icon during the internet boom years of the late 1990s. Its story is cleanly but blandly recounted by Butler and Pogue (2002). Cell phones have developed over the past decade into versatile computing platforms, but no history yet covers this.

How will the stories historians eventually tell about the personal computer differ from those already spun by journalists and enthusiasts? A look at the development of corresponding literatures in other fields suggests four important areas. First, historians are likely to broaden the narrative beyond Silicon Valley and the handful of other firms (such as Microsoft) included in popular accounts. Personal computers, and home computers, spread around the U.S. and around the world in a process that cannot be fully understood without a much bigger canvas. Second, historians will be interested in the users of personal computer technologies as well as their producers. In this case the two categories can be rather porous anyway, as enthusiasts built peripherals or wrote programs, thus using one kind of technology to create another. Users created their own meanings and applications for standard technologies such as the Apple II, transforming it into an educational tool, piece of lab equipment, games console, or financial workstation. Third, historians will be interested in the web of social groups and communities that sprang up around the new technologies: user groups, specialist dealers, newsletters, bulletin boards, and so on. These networks have been probed for other technologies of the era (Greenberg, 2008) but not yet for the personal computer. Finally, historians will not be satisfied to explain the personal computer's rise as the inevitable consequence of the geeky genius of its creators. They will look at the social and economic context of the late 1970s and early 1980s, particularly the power of notions such as the "post industrial society" (Bell, 1974) and "microelectronic revolution" (Forrester, 1981) and the symbolic position of computer technology as counterbalance to the crumbling of traditional industries in the face of Asian competition.

Business Histories: Software Producers

In one sense the software industry can be traced back to the 1950s, as early computer users often hired specialized firms to assist with programming work or provide other computer-related services. For example, much of the work on the very first administrative computing application in the U.S., a payroll system for General Electric's appliance plant in Louisville, Kentucky, was handled by members of the accounting firm Arthur Andersen. New firms such as the Systems Development Corporation sprang up at about the same time to handle system development chores for the burgeoning array of Cold War computer systems. The term *software* gained currency in the early 1960s (Haigh, 2002), originally to describe everything beyond the hardware itself that a computer manufacturer would supply with a machine (programs, documentation, services, etc). Only in the late 1960s, however, did a market develop for what we would today think of as software: standardized computer programs licensed to many customers and flexible enough to be configured to match their needs without being reprogrammed. Pioneering firms of the late 1960s focused primarily on systems software tools such as utilities for programmers. The market for applications programs, such as standard payroll and accounting packages, followed a little later. By the late 1970s the mainframe software industry was well established, and a decade later the fast growing personal computer industry was producing its own stars.

The earliest software companies such as the Systems Development Corporation (Baum, 1981) and Informatics General received book-length histories in the 1980s. The latter was the world's largest independent software company for much of the 1960s and 1970s, beginning as a contractor on government projects but diversifying into other areas (Bauer, 1996). Its Mark IV software package was the first packaged software to reach ten million dollars in cumulative sales (Postley, 1998). The firm commissioned a thorough and professionally produced history (Forman, 1984). Issued just as the company was being broken up, it is impossible to buy but can easily be obtained via interlibrary loan.

Martin Campbell-Kelly (2007a) has surveyed the development of historical work on software. By the late 1990s historians of information technology were uncomfortably aware that very little work to date had addressed any aspect of the history of software. A conference in Paderborn, Germany led to a book intended to showcase promising approaches, record debates, and lay out some kind of research agenda for studying software (Hashagen, Keil-Slawik, & Norberg, 2002). This is still the best starting point for this topic.

Recent work has provided relatively good coverage of the structural evolution of the packaged software industry. Campbell-Kelly's (2003) implausibly titled *From Airline Reservations to Sonic the Hedgehog* is the outstanding contribution here, tracing the development of the software industry from consulting and services firms through the mainframe era and on into the mass market merchandising of the personal computer software industry. He strives to provide coverage of the major companies and market niches in rough proportion to their economic importance, inserting anecdotes and capsule biographies to enliven a narrative driven by statistics and market share reports. Mowery (1995) explores the economic history of the software industry; Yost's (2005b) survey gives particular attention to the services side of the industry.

Campbell-Kelly's book is focused on the structure of the software industry and, because of its broad scope, can say little about the development of software technologies, user experiences, or the evolution of particular kinds of computer program. These topics require more tightly focused historical studies, some which are beginning to appear in article form, as usual with a lag of twenty to thirty years.

The Software History SIG of the Computer History Museum (formerly the Software History Center) has been active in preserving the history of the early software industry. A series of workshops addressing different aspects of its history has been held from 2002 onward, including oral history interviews and roundtable discussions transcribed and placed online (Johnson, 2003). This work has been showcased in a special issue of *IEEE Annals of the History of Computing* (2001) and a series of subsequent articles in the same venue. Three special issues of this journal, edited by Burton Grad of the Software History SIG, have addressed key software genres. Campbell-Kelly (2007b) himself has written about the development of spreadsheet programs, anchoring a special issue on the topic. Tim Bergin and I have carried out a similar role in issues on the early development of word processing (Bergin, 2006a, 2006b; Haigh, 2006) and database management systems (Bergin & Haigh, 2009; Haigh, 2009). These issues also featured articles by participants, including the authors of important programs such as VisiCalc and WordStar and the leaders of companies that developed and published them.

In the absence of scholarly histories one turns as always to memoirs and books by business journalists. One could fill a fairly hefty bookcase using nothing but books on Bill Gates and Microsoft. But doing so would be a mistake because most retread the same worn anecdotes. Of the biographies, the early *HardDrive* (Wallace, 1992) is among the freshest, covering the company's origins and its many troubled products of the 1980s. Its sketch of Gates as a brilliant, pathologically competitive, and socially maladjusted man-boy crystallized his public image. The more recently updated *Gates* (Manes & Andrews, 2002) covers developments through the late 1990s. By this point Gates's story and that of his firm were diverging, as Gates married, mellowed, and shifted his attentions to philanthropy while Microsoft hunkered down into a more bureaucratic and conservative phase of its existence. Michael Cusumano's (1995) book *Microsoft Secrets* was among the first to consider the firm as more than just a backdrop for Gates, digging into its corporate culture, marketing, and project management practices during its rise to industry dominance. Today's Windows products are based not on the ancient code base of MS-DOS and Windows 3.0 but on Windows NT, designed in the early 1990s by minicomputer operating system specialist David Cutler as an industrial strength alternative. Its creation was recorded by journalist G. Pascal Zachary (1994). Around the same time Microsoft made a major expansion into multimedia publishing, adding CD-ROM products such as the *Expedia* encyclopedia. Fred Moody (1995) spent a year embedded in a multimedia product team; his book gives a vivid look at the firm's evolving culture and efforts to blend programming and creative content development. The company's next big challenge, the internet, prompted serious internal divides and some fundamental shifts in strategy and organization. David Bank (2001), a reporter for the *Wall Street Journal*, presented a well researched and readable account of this traumatic era in *Breaking Windows*.

Other major software firms of the personal computer era such as Novell, Lotus, Borland, and Ashton-Tate have left remarkably little coverage of this kind. The main exceptions to date are a memoir by an executive of the business responsible for the once-ubiquitous WordPerfect (Peterson, 1994) and a tell-all memoir cum business advice book from an entrepreneur who developed the FrontPage web editing software and sold his firm to Microsoft (Ferguson, 1999). Enterprise software firms work outside the direct experience of most people, so although today's business software giants such as Oracle and SAP are almost as large as Microsoft, and more strategically important to the operation of the economy, they have received nothing like the same attention. Oracle is at least blessed with Larry Ellison, whose widely reported wealth, arrogance, and love of expensive things have caught the attention of several biographers. Of these *Softwar* (Symonds & Ellison, 2003) offers the best coverage of the firm's culture and technologies and, in a novel twist, is footnoted with asides from Ellison himself. The book has about one hundred pages of company history and several times that volume of badly dated, celebrity-style profiling of Ellison's personal life and blow-by-blow reportage of industry politics circa 2000. Oracle's onetime competitor in the database management systems business, Informix, is the subject of a memoir dealing largely with the circumstances that sent its chief executive to prison (Martin, 2005). SAP, provider of the world's most successful suite of administrative applications, enjoys an uninspired journalistic profile (Meissner, 2000) and a solid scholarly article (Leimbach, 2008).

National and International Stories

American scholars tend to view the history of information technology as a fundamentally American narrative. The U.S. is the only country with a sufficiently central role in most areas of information technology that a coherent (if skewed) overall history of computing can, and often has, been written with minimal reference to the world outside its borders. A few Englishmen force their way into the narrative: Charles Babbage, Alan Turing, the teams behind the Manchester Mark 1 and the EDSAC, the LEO group that pioneered administrative computing, and Tim Berners-Lee. Konrad Zuse flies the flag for Germany. Jacquard's automatic loom earns France a paragraph somewhere in an early chapter. But these can be dismissed in passing as brilliant figures whose seminal technical accomplishments quickly passed into the hands of Americans for practical exploitation. The history of personal computing, in particular, is told by Americans entirely without reference to the existence of a world beyond the oceans, or in most cases beyond the Valley.

Historians based in the U.S. have therefore been much less likely than those working in other countries to attempt to isolate peculiarities of their own national experience or relate the development of information technology industries to the influence of government policy. One exception is Flamm's (1988) account of the early history of the computer industry and its technologies, with close attention to the sources and influence of state funding. Another is by Chandler and Cortada (2000), an edited volume exploring the application of information technology (including older systems such as mail delivery) within American society. The chapters dealing with earlier developments are, unfortunately for our purposes, noticeably stronger than those addressing the computer era. Coopey (2004) presents policy perspectives, mostly on the relationship of governmental actions to the development of national computer industries.

Scholars in other countries have tended to focus on national narratives, generally framed with perceived differences between local developments and those in America. To date the U.K., Germany, France, Japan, Canada, the Netherlands, the former U.S.S.R., and the Nordic countries have the best developed historical literatures. Histories of national computing, unfortunately for the monoglot, tend to be written in national languages. Historians have largely resisted the trend among scientists of publishing primarily in English, perhaps because of the richer vocabulary required. My discussion here is confined to English-language publication.

Few companies had large enough national markets to support a fully developed indigenous computer industry; therefore, national narratives tend to focus on quite short historical periods and follow a similar course whether the country in question is the U.K., France, the Netherlands, Canada, the former U.S.S.R., or Czechoslovakia. Resourceful teams working at national scientific institutes produce experimental computers. Local firms enjoy some success in producing machines based on indigenous designs, but at some point in the 1960s are either driven out of business, acquired by American companies, or merged into state-sponsored national champions intended to enjoy economies of scale. Researchers in academic and corporate centers continue to do great work but the benefits of their breakthroughs are largely appropriated by foreign firms. Yet local IT companies continue to thrive in particular niches, such as business software or embedded system design. National computing stories thus tend to have a rather melancholy tone, in which flurries of success are followed by painful declines and squandered opportunities. IBM and other American firms have thus been seen as the enemy, a kind of wave that eventually sweeps away local capabilities. Recent work has begun to complicate this picture, looking at the place of local branches of American firms within national computing cultures and challenging the idea of IBM as a monolithic and alien force (Medina, 2008; Schlombs, 2008). Asian countries may, of course, have different national master narratives of computing in which they become involved later but, in many cases, enjoy considerable success with the development of hardware and electronics.

Many works on aspects of the British experience are discussed elsewhere in this chapter. Computer technology occupies a fairly prominent place in British collective memory, as an exemplar of national decline in which the spectacular innovations of the 1940s somehow entitled Britain to a dominant role in the international computer industry that was then squandered through the incompetence of business and government leaders. This idea receives its clearest examination by Hendry (1990). However this "declinist" tendency in British twentieth century historiography has itself been critiqued recently as a skewed perspective based on myths held during the period and the hangover of empire (Tomlinson, 2009, p. 227).

John Vardalas (2001) has produced a fascinating and multifaceted examination of Canadian computing. It covers topics from the first academic use of computing in Canada, through military electronic projects, to civilian applications in business. His integration of these different perspectives and situation of the Canadian story in an international perspective makes this the best developed national story to date.

Soviet computing has been treated in two major English-language publications. One (Gerovitch, 2002) is focused on cybernetics, which came late to the Soviet world but endured as a rubric for computer applications long after it lapsed into eccentric marginality in the West. Gerovitch focuses on the relationship of Soviet science and its discourse to politics and its institutions. The other (Malinovsky & Fitzpatrick, 2006) is an edited translation of historical and autobiographical work by Boris N. Malinovsky, whose career ran from a junior role on the very first Soviet computer project, through designing important minicomputers in the 1960s for industrial control and scientific applications, to work on early personal computers in the 1970s and 1980s. Soviet computing has also been explored in a number of articles, generally focused on specific early projects, such as Ichikawa's (2006) and Crowe and Goodman's (1994).

A significant amount has been published on the history of French computing, although this does not include an English language overview of the national story. The best starting point is a series of special issues of *IEEE Annals of the History of Computing* edited by Pierre E. Mounier-Kuhn in 1989 and 1990.[4] These include coverage of inventors, companies, computers, and institutions. Mounier-Kuhn has continued to write prolifically on many aspects of the history of computing in France.

The Dutch literature is also well developed. Its national story follows the usual pattern, including seminal research at the Mathematisch Centrum, commercialized by the plucky but doomed firm Electrologica (de Wit, 1997). Computer building efforts by electronics giant Philips were also unsuccessful. However, the Netherlands also has an exceptionally well developed literature on the use of computers by government and industry, such as work by van den Ende (1995) and de Wit (1997). This includes recent work on personal computing (Veraart, 2008)—a topic so far neglected by American scholars. I have been unable to find an English language overview of computing in Germany, although several focused articles have been published including those in a July 2004 special issue of *IEEE Annals of the History of Computing* devoted to the IBM Boeblingen Laboratory.

The Nordic countries have also generated a disproportionately diverse literature on the history of information technology, produced by scholars from a range of disciplinary backgrounds. The best introduction is by Bubenko, Impagliazzo, and Solvberg (2005), based on a 2003 conference. This work, too, blends concern with the traditional stories of pioneers and early machines with a refreshing interest in issues of computer use, personal computing, and professional identity (Vehvilainen, 1999). A second volume recently appeared (Impagliazzo, Järvi, & Paju, 2009). Paju (2008) explores Finland's national story, together with a survey of the relevant literature. Lundin (2009) recently concluded a large scale Swedish project to document the national history of computer use, including a novel focus on the experiences of ordinary computer users.

Not much is written in English and easily accessible on the history of information technology in Japan. Takahasi (1996) gives an overview of the early computer industry. A recent special issue (Nandasara & Mikami, 2009) has explored the evolution of computer support for Asian languages, a fascinating example of the barriers posed by local culture to the diffusion of information technology and the huge amount of work necessary to reconfigure supposedly universal devices. Discussion of Latin America is more sparse still; Medina (2006) explores the special role of computer networks and cybernetics to the economic plans of Chile's Allende government.

International and comparative studies remain quite rare. Chandler (Chandler, Hikino, & Nordenflycht, 2001) has considered the history of the computer industry from a comparative international perspective; Cortada (2004) has sketched some of the issues involved in international computing history. In the context of European technology policy, some attention has been paid to the failed international consortium Unidata intended to unify Europe's leading mainframe producers in the 1970s (Kranakis, 2004).

A promising collaborative project is currently underway in the area. During the 1960s the Soviet Union launched a massive project across the Council for Mutual Economic Assistance (COMECON) countries to replace existing mainframe designs with a new, compatible architecture copied from IBM's System 360 range. This history is currently being explored from several national and international perspectives.

Networking Technologies and Applications

The rise of computer networks and applications, in particular the World Wide Web, inspired a hunt for historical precedents. A great deal has been written about engineer and science policy pioneer Vannevar Bush (1945) and his magazine article describing an imaginary machine known as the Memex (see Grudin's chapter in the present volume). This was to be a desk equipped with a screen, a camera, and an enormous microfilm storage capacity. Users could retrieve existing articles and construct "associative trails" linking related items (p. 107). The Memex would never have been practical with the specific technologies Bush proposed, but his vision of an extensible network of links tying together a huge database of text and graphics was a major influence on later work (Nyce & Kahn, 1991). Unusually for a non-existent machine, the Memex has spawned an intimidatingly large body of literature, including the unusual honor of its own *ARIST* chapter (Houston & Harmon, 2007), the existence of which relieves me of the need to attempt a full reckoning here. The Memex, like Babbage, is one of those few topics in the history of information technology about which more research is not urgently needed. Other scholars have mooted similar grand projects as antecedents of the World Wide Web; Campbell-Kelly (Campbell-Kelly & Aspray, 1996) is partial to the idea of a "world brain" proposed by H. G. Wells (1938), a concept explored in more detail by Boyd Rayward (1999). Rayward (1998) has also analyzed Paul Otlet's efforts to catalog and cross reference the world's knowledge as a precursor of hypertext.

The modern concept of hypertext, as a set of active links embedded in electronic text, can be traced to Ted Nelson who built a reputation as a brilliant but idiosyncratic computer visionary. Nelson invented the concept of hypertext in the early 1960s and used a book entitled *Computer Lib / Dream Machines* (Nelson, 1974) to promote his planned electronic publishing systems as the foundation for new kinds of artistic creativity. Nelson struggled for years, and with the assistance of several companies and groups of supporters, to deliver his long promised Xanadu system. In the meantime the World Wide Web created a real global hypertext network, although one that failed to support many of Nelson's original concepts. No historian has yet tackled this story, although Wolf (1995) sketched the Xanadu's tortuous progression in a memorable article in *Wired Magazine*.

The internet's underlying technical structure evolved from ARPANET, a network constructed in the late 1960s and early 1970s for the use of computing researchers funded by the American military research agency ARPA. This was the first large-scale network designed around packet switching technology, in which data were bundled into small packets for separate routing over the network rather than being sent over a dedicated electrical circuit from source to destination as had been the practice with the telephone system and earlier computer networks. In *Inventing the Internet*, Abbate (1999) explores the development of the ARPANET and its evolution into the early, non-commercial incarnation of the internet. Concise but clear and well researched, the book outlines the technical and institutional stories. Its treatment of network users is particularly revealing, illuminating the coevolution of infrastructure and applications. Abbate demonstrates that email, rather than the intended application of logging into remote computers, emerged as the driving force behind the network's success. A chapter in Norberg and O'Neill's (1996) book is devoted to the institutional story of ARPA's support for this and other networking initiatives. The other full length history of the internet, *Where Wizards Stay Up Late* (Hafner & Lyon, 1998), is readable and somewhat more thoughtful than one might expect from its title but focuses more on personalities and anecdotes than context or analysis.

Historians have also uncovered two European networks constructed in the 1970s around packet switching technology. A British national network was proposed by Donald Davies prior to the creation of ARPANET but was initially realized with only one computer, which unfortunately limited its impact (Campbell-Kelly, 1988). Davies also invented the term packet switching. The French Cyclades network was built in the early 1970s and introduced several important advances. In contrast, the Soviet Union did not build a national network in spite, or as one historian has argued because, of its political commitment to cybernetic central control of the economy (Gerovitch, 2008).

A range of other networks served various niche groups. Usenet (later UUCPNET) was developed in 1979 for users of Unix-based computers. It employed a system of automatic file transfers to synchronize files and pass messages between computers. This powered the popular system of Usenet Newsgroups, which by the early 1990s had transitioned to the internet. BITNET linked American universities of the 1980s, primarily those using IBM mainframes. LISTSERV software for the maintenance of email discussion and announcement lists was pioneered on BITNET (Grier & Campbell, 2000). Hobbyists created thousands of amateur bulletin board servers, which were linked to provide email and file exchange capabilities via FidoNet. These systems have slipped rapidly from general awareness, but almost nothing has been published so far on their history. Online database publishing has its own separate history, explored with remarkable detail and comprehensiveness in its infancy during the 1960s and early 1970s by Bourne and Hahn (2003).

A number of commercial networks sprang up during the 1980s. The best documented of these was the WELL (Hafner, 1995) a rather highbrow system tied to *Whole Earth Catalog* founder Stewart Brand. Technology writer Howard Rheingold (1993) used his experiences on the WELL to popularize the idea of the virtual community in his influential book of the same name. Its history is explored by Fred Turner (2006) in his book on Brand and his projects.

In contrast, the leading commercial networks of the period have seen little attention. In the late 1970s and early 1980s a wave of enthusiasm for videotext systems swept the western world. These combined cheap terminals, slow modems, and chunky displays (often via a standard television set) to offer affordable access to computer networks. Videotext was intended to provide the masses with online shopping, stock trading, reference materials, email, and entertainment. Dozens of national and commercial systems were launched and widely ignored by their putative users. Only in France, where France Telecom stopped printing telephone directories and gave away its unique Minitel terminals instead, did this push to bring ordinary people online succeed. No general history of videotext has yet been written, although Fletcher (2002) examined Minitel's success.

The failure of videotext was followed from the mid-1980s by the gradual success of a less ambitious set of services, aimed at the niche market of personal computer enthusiasts and small business users. They included BIX (the Byte Information eXchange), Compuserve, GEnie, and

Prodigy. These services provided database access, technical support forums, file downloads, games, and other services. AOL, which originated as a set of specialized services aimed at users of particular computer models, grew rapidly in the 1990s to become the biggest of these online services as its frenetic marketing activities succeeded in bringing a mass audience online. This topic, too, has been neglected by historians, although AOL was the subject of a number of books by business journalists drawn by its meteoric rise and audacious takeover of media giant Time Warner. Of these the gushingly titled *aol.com: How Steve Case Beat Bill Gates, Nailed the Netheads, and Made Millions in the War for the Web* (Swisher, 1998) provides the most thorough history of the industry's development.

By the end of the 1990s the internet had unexpectedly supplanted these proprietary networks. Abbate (2010) discusses the initial commercialization of internet infrastructure and Greenstein (2001a, 2001b) recounts the emergence of the commercial internet access industry. This abrupt transition of the internet from academic backwater to universal infrastructure has tended to make people forget that most networking experts of the early 1990s, including many of those running the internet itself, believed that the future lay with a quite different set of network protocols. Conceptual work from the 1970s led to the development of the Open Systems Interconnection seven-layer model and a massive international standards effort to develop universal protocols for applications such as file transfer and email within this framework. This story has received some historical attention (Abbate, 1999; Russell, 2006) but lacks a definitive account.

The World Wide Web originated in the early 1990s as a simple application based on the existing infrastructure of the internet's applications and protocols. Like other developments of the 1980s and 1990s, this falls into a kind of historiographic dead zone in which it is sufficiently remote for journalists and policy scholars to have moved on but not yet far enough removed to attract the attention of many historians. We do have two histories of the web, both based on insider accounts. Tim Berners-Lee, the web's inventor, partnered with a journalist to produce *Weaving the Web* (Berners-Lee & Fischetti, 1999), a light but vivid memoir of its origins. Robert Cailliau, a former colleague of Berners-Lee at the European Organization for Nuclear Research (CERN) and a key early supporter of the project, has presented a broader and deeper account of the web's origins (Gillies & Cailliau, 2000) including a revealing summary of the lab's internal functioning and a detailed history of the first few years of web browser and server development outside CERN. Other internet applications and their associated protocols (email, news, file transfer, and the like) have received little historical analysis with exception of a single article (Frana, 2004) on the short-lived Gopher system.

The commercialization of the web browser and its rapid development during the so-called browser wars between Netscape and Microsoft in the late 1990s received some thoughtful attention at the time

(Cusumano & Yoffie, 1998), particularly in the context of the government's antitrust action against Microsoft (1998–2001). The latter loomed large as an apparently epoch-defining event, as testified to by business journalist Ken Auletta's (2001) choice of the title *World War 3.0*, but slipped quickly from public awareness in the light of subsequent world events and the Bush administration's decision to impose only token penalties on Microsoft. My own work (Haigh, 2008a) sets the commercialization of web browser, server, and email technology into a broader historical context, sketching connections between the shaping of internet technologies in the academic environment and their unexpected commercial success. This appeared in the recent book *The Internet and American Business* (Aspray & Ceruzzi, 2008). Authors, mostly historians of information technology, were charged with examining different aspects of the rapid embrace of the internet by business. Chapters focus on topics from the growth of online pornography to the rise of online travel agents. Tackling the history of such recent events carries undeniable risks, and the book's exclusive focus on the U.S. has incurred criticism, but the volume is likely to provide a useful and sometimes provocative foundation for future work on these topics.

The dot.com businesses of the late 1990s inspired many dozens of hastily written books lauding their vision, the inexperience of their youthful founders, and their ability to raise and spend large quantities of venture capital. Some of these turned into cautionary tales of failure and excess even as they were being written. But volumes devoted to short-lived firms such as CDNow and boo.com are not really contributions to the historical literature, and even enduring companies such as Amazon were profiled too hastily and too early in their history to provide much insight. The flavor of the age is preserved with charm, confusion, and hubris intact in books by Lewis (2000), Reid (1997), and Wolff (1998). Cassidy (2002) provides a more cynical perspective, from the immediate aftermath of the crash. Meanwhile, the success of Google has inspired several new journalistic histories of the search engine and portal industry (Battelle, 2005; Stross, 2008; Vise & Malseed, 2005) and my own analytical overview (Haigh, 2008b). We do not yet have much historical distance on this era and are too bound up in supporting or critiquing ideas advanced at the time to begin to put it into context. However, work is underway to analyze more systematically the success and failure of early internet firms (Goldfarb, Kirsch, & Miller, 2007).

Information Technology in Use—Why Study Applications?

The most convincing claim that can be made for the importance of information technology history is the importance of information technology in modern society. Computer technologies have, admittedly, had less influence on the fabric of life in America than early twentieth- and late nineteenth-century innovations such as automobiles, electric light, domestic refrigerators, air conditioning, or telephones. If we compare

1960 to 2010 we see that Americans still live in cities, drive around, purchase preserved food from supermarkets, watch moving pictures on screens, and talk for business and pleasure over long distances. Historians are instinctively skeptical of any kind of deterministic reasoning about the *impact* of technology on society, and the history of technology tells us that it is more common for technologies to adjust themselves to fit existing social practices and institutions than the reverse. Indeed we have been told since the late 1940s that computer technology will unleash some kind of social revolution, evidence of which often seemed lacking. Yet information technology has already played an important role in reshaping many aspects of daily life and new applications and modes of use are being invented all the time.

Much early work in the field followed a heroic model in explaining and celebrating particular technological accomplishments. David Alan Grier (2003, p. 95) has called, without apparent irony, for the development of "The Great Machine Theory of History." But studying information technology itself cannot tell us how or why it has been used to change the world, as Tom Misa (2007) pointed out in an argumentative survey of the existing literature. Neither will studying the hardware or software industries, however fascinating the stories we uncover. These constitute only a tiny part of the economy. We can understand the importance of information technology to society only by studying it in use.

The study of users and use (Oudshoorn & Pinch, 2003) has emerged over the past decade or two as a central concern within the history of technology and the allied field of science and technology studies. An earlier focus on machines, their inventors, and the companies that produced them has shifted appreciably toward the people who used them. Historians of technology have tended to treat use and consumption as interchangeable, looking at technologies adopted and used directly by individuals (Cowan, 1987). A parallel movement in the business literature on innovation and technological change has explored the role of organizations as users of technology (Yates, 2006) and the part played by users in developing new applications of technology (Von Hippel, 2005).

The next three sections survey historical work on the use of information technology in science, administration, and embedded control systems. Literature on other application areas is sparse indeed. An enormous amount has been written about the use of computers in schools and universities, but I am aware of no significant historical work on the topic. Computer use in libraries was the subject of two special issues of *IEEE Annals of the History of Computing* (Graham & Rayward, 2002). Domestic computer use has been the topic of some interesting sociological and anthropological work, such as Lally's (2002), but is yet to be explored from an historical perspective. Similarly, a truly vast ethnographic and social scientific literature has grown up on use of the internet and other online systems (e.g., Turkle, 1995), but nobody has attempted to reconstruct the history of networks from the user perspective.

Applications in Science

The electronic computer was invented as a tool for scientific and engineering calculation. Although its main market shifted during the 1950s to business administration, computer technology went on to transform the practice of science in one discipline after another. Without computers it would be quite impossible to crunch the vast quantities of data captured in particle physics experiments, map genomes, or perform the statistical analyses expected in many fields of social science.

Grier's (2006) highly readable recent book looks at the human and institutional stories of large-scale mathematical calculation from the nineteenth century to the immediate aftermath of the Second World War. Its title, *When Computers Were Human*, indicates that the term originally described a person who performed computations. Only later did people begin to talk about "automatic computers" or "electronic computers." The institutional history of scientific calculation in Britain has also been explored (Croarken, 1990), and an edited volume (Campbell-Kelly, Croarken, Flood, & Robson, 2003) looked specifically at the history of mathematical tables, the preparation of which motivated funding for several important projects including Babbage's work and the ENIAC. Jen Light (1999) has explored gendered labor in the ENIAC project, showing that many programming tasks were carried out by women whose work was erased from media reports.

Electronic computers carried out calculations thousands of times faster than human computers with mechanical aids. A few institutional studies have been made of key users of computer technology for large-scale calculation and simulation. These have focused on computer use in the national research labs of the Atomic Energy Commission (Seidel, 1998), particularly Los Alamos (Fitzpatrick, 1999; MacKenzie, 1991) and Argonne national laboratories (Yood, 2005). The most ambitious book on early scientific computing is *Calculating a Natural World* (Akera, 2006), covering the ENIAC project and computing efforts at the National Bureau of Standards, MIT, IBM, and the University of Michigan. Akera (2006, pp. 13–22) mixes historical genres such as biography, business history, and the institutional history of science to chart the interdisciplinary "ecology of knowledge" within which early computing practices sprang up.

Computers needed to be programmed, which turned out to be a lot harder and more time-consuming than anyone had expected. Most of the scientific and technical calculations to which computers were applied involved calculating numerical approximations rather than manipulating algebraic symbols to achieve an exact solution. Existing mathematical methods, however, had been designed within the constraints of human mathematical labor. Harnessing the growing power of the digital computer thus demanded the creation of whole new families of mathematical methods and the development of new kinds of theory (particularly error analysis) and tacit knowledge. Numerical analysis emerged (Nash, 1990) as an important and growing field of research, and a new community (Cowell, 1984) developed from the 1960s on around the production of high quality mathematical software. The history of mathematical software was addressed in a recent series of oral history interviews by the Society for Industrial and Applied Mathematics and is a fertile topic for future work by historians of computing.

Historians of science, unlike scientists, have been woefully slow to take computer technology seriously. There are a few exceptions to this general neglect. I. Bernard Cohen, a Harvard historian of science and one of the discipline's American pioneers, took an interest in the work of Harvard computing pioneer Howard Aiken (Cohen, 1999), seeing him as a modern inventor on a par with historical subjects such as Ben Franklin. Peter Galison, a leading historian of physics, has drawn attention to the importance of studying the technologies of scientific instruments and their coevolution with theory and practice. His work includes discussion of the computer as a device for data reduction and simulation, and of the evolving position of computer specialists within the social world of science (Galison, 1997). Historians of science have been drawn to the colorful and briefly fashionable world of cybernetics (Bowker, 1993; Heims, 1991), looking particularly at connections between information theory, computing, and genetics (Kay, 2000). The computer's importance to weather forecasting and climate research has received some historical attention (Edwards, 2000; Harper, 2008), as has the introduction of computers into biological research (Hagen, 2001; November, 2006). More work will surely follow. As historians turn to the late twentieth and early twenty-first centuries they will find it hard to tell the story of any discipline without covering the influence of technological change on its laboratory practice, publication patterns, methods of collaboration, or analytical habits.

Applications in Administrative Work and Business

From the mid-1950s onward the main market for computers has been in the world of business and government administration. The same was true of their most direct technological ancestors, punched-card machines. Punched-card machines were originally invented for use in tabulating the U.S. census. Their creator, Herman Hollerith, founded the business that became IBM. The origins of the punched-card business were thus reasonably well covered in the voluminous literature on IBM and its international counterparts. Until recently, however, we knew much less about the capabilities of the machines themselves or the applications for which they were used.

Work by JoAnne Yates and Lars Heide has done a great deal to address these gaps. Heide (2009) examines the development of punched-card technology through the Second Word War in the U.S., France, Germany, and Britain. Looking for evidence of the factors that shaped the development and adoption of the technology, he explores not only the business history of punched-card machine companies but also the role of key governmental applications, such as Social Security in the U.S. and a national registry in France. Yates (2005) focuses on a single American industry: life insurance. Using several detailed case studies she demonstrates the important role of user companies in influencing, and sometimes pioneering, the addition of new technological capabilities. Her work is also notable for its recognition of technological adoption as something that takes place by an entire industry, guided by trade associations and informal networks, rather than by isolated firms. She follows the story through to the 1960s, documenting the gradual transition from punched-card machines to electronic computers.

In 1954, General Electric became the first American company to computerize an administrative job when it began to use a Univac computer to issue payroll checks to some of the workers at its Louisville, Kentucky, appliance plant (Osborn, 1954). However, somewhat less predictably, it was not the world's first business to do so. This honor goes to Lyons, a British company best known for its nationwide chain of teashops. So keen were business systems experts within this company to apply the power of the computer to their administrative chores that they built their own computer, modeled on Cambridge University's EDSAC, rather than wait for one to be available commercially. It entered service in late 1951. This gave rise to LEO Computers, a computer hardware and systems implementation company that enjoyed reasonable commercial success into the 1960s. The quirkiness of this story has ensured it significant popular attention (Bird, 1994), most recently in a well told account that properly situates the story in the broader context of administrative systems work (Ferry, 2003). The most detailed account of the LEO story was given by the participants themselves (Caminer, Aris, Hermon, & Land, 1996).

Yates's work on the insurance industry provides the only extended treatment of the use of information technology in a single American industry. Bernardo Batiz-Lazo and his colleagues have written a number of papers (Batiz-Lazo, 2009; Batiz-Lazo & Billings, 2007; Batiz-Lazo & Boyns, 2004) about the co-evolution of information technology and business operations in the banking industry, which collectively provide similar insights for another corner of the financial world. Other English language studies of computer use elsewhere include an examination of computerization in three Dutch institutions (de Wit, 1994), of an early airline reservation system (McKenney, Copeland, & Mason, 1995), in the British Railway Clearing House (Campbell-Kelly, 1994), in the banking industry, and in various corners of the British government (Agar, 2003). The latter is an ambitious and sprawling work, positing connections between the organization and culture of the civil service and the particular uses it made of information technologies and techniques of administrative systematization. A recent article (Peeters, 2009) and dissertation (Kahl, 2007) explore the early use and development of systems for materials requirements processing (precursors to today's integrated enterprise software suites).

Until the 1970s there was no significant market for prepackaged application software (Haigh, 2002). Any company installing a computer also had to assemble a team of systems analysts and application programmers to create or extensively modify each of the programs it planned to run. This was true even of very common applications such as payroll, inventory management, or accounting. For this reason the history of administrative computer use is also, for its first few decades, largely congruent with the history of administrative application development. Each new computer installation was accompanied by a data processing department, home to teams of well paid specialists whose number and variety increased inexorably along with the department's budget. Data processing evolved as a set of practices, a new institution whose place on the corporate organization chart remained in flux, and a cluster of new occupational identities (Haigh, 2001a). Friedman and Cornford (1989) give a careful overview of the history of system development practices, intertwining organizational and technological developments.

Very little has been published about the social history or labor practices of information technology, with the work of computer operators and data entry clerks shrouded in particular obscurity. A recent dissertation (Hicks, 2009) looks at data processing workers within the British government. Campbell-Kelly produced a series of three highly detailed technical studies of programming practices around the very first British computers, summarized in a single report (Campbell-Kelly, 1982), but nothing has been attempted for the later period. I have presented the genesis of the idea of the management information system as an episode in the social history of corporate America, driven by the aspirations of the self-proclaimed "systems men" (Haigh, 2001b, p. 15). The rhetoric surrounding computer programming in the 1960s has received some historical attention (Ensmenger, 2003) and the experience of system development work has been vividly captured in a memoir (Ullman, 1997).

To call this coverage of administrative computing patchy would be to greatly exaggerate its comprehensiveness. A dearth of secondary accounts has not, however, been enough to deflect the boundless energies of James W. Cortada. A prolific author of works on the history and management of information technology in business, Cortada is also an IBM executive. His three volume opus *The Digital Hand* chronicles the use of computers in manufacturing, transport, and retail industries (Cortada, 2003); service and communication industries (Cortada, 2006); and the public sector (Cortada, 2007). Each section examines the introduction of successive waves of computer technology with a focus on the applications and technologies most distinctively associated with the industry in question. These chapters will provide valuable starting points for future historians and Cortada's voluminous footnotes are an impressive resource.

Applications in Embedded and Control Systems

Historical attention has been focused primarily on computers that look like computers. The computer has had several paradigmatic forms over time (Atkinson, 1998). In the 1940s and early 1950s this meant ramshackle looking complexes of wires, switches, and electronic components arranged in metal frames. In the late 1950s and 1960s it meant complexes of smooth metal boxes, elegantly arranged with wires hidden under raised flooring and an array of printers, disk drives, and particularly the iconic banks of spinning tape drives. The minicomputer, which came into its stride in the late 1960s, was a smaller box with a generous selection of switches and flashing lights. And the personal computer, with which historians are just starting to get involved, tended to look like a typewriter or piece of consumer electronics but remained a self-contained box coupled with a screen and a selection of other, smaller, peripheral boxes.

But since the 1970s most computers have not looked like this at all. The microprocessor, core of the personal computer, was originally invented for use in a pocket calculator (Aspray, 1997). It shrank the core capabilities of a programmable digital computer onto a single chip. Coupling it with a small amount of memory and control programs burned onto a ROM chip made it an affordable and flexible automatic control system for equipment of all kinds. By the 1980s these camouflaged computers, known as embedded systems, were standard equipment inside cars, microwave ovens, digital watches, washing machines, automated teller machines (ATMs), home heating control boxes, video game consoles, and video cassette recorders. Without them more recent consumer products such as the cell phone and iPod would have been impossible. Some luxury cars now contain more than a hundred microprocessors.

The microprocessor made embedded computer control systems cheap and tiny; but in fact they have a long history in applications with large budgets or specialized needs. Indeed, the devices to be called computers were not free-standing boxes but the control mechanisms used to guide torpedoes, control antiaircraft guns, and so on from the 1930s onward (Mindell, 2002). David Mindell's book *Between Human and Machine* explores the gradual development of automatic control technologies over the first half of the twentieth century. Subtly undermining the claims of cybernetics to have achieved a revolution during and just after the Second World War, he credits a variety of specialized engineering communities with incremental advances based on local practices.

The single most important project for the development of computer technology was the development of the SAGE air defense network in the 1950s. This began as an effort at MIT to develop a high speed digital computer, Whirlwind. Whirlwind and SAGE pioneered a number of key technologies, among them real-time computer operation, networking, graphics, core memory, complex systems software, and light guns (a kind of precursor of the mouse). They have been profiled in two detailed technical histories

(Redmond & Smith, 1980, 2000) and given a lively portrait as artifacts of Cold War military thinking in *The Closed World* (Edwards, 1996). The latter is one of the few books on the history of information technology to win wide recognition among members of the science studies community.

The computers built for SAGE were the most powerful of their day and physically the largest ever constructed (275 tons each). Other military applications required smaller, portable computers (Ceruzzi, 1989). Computers guided missiles (at first from the ground, later inside the missile itself) and were built into planes for navigation and weapons control. Applications such as the Minuteman I and II missiles drove fundamental advances in the use and packaging of electronics, creating a need for small, reliable, and modularized components.

In the 1960s the space program played an important role in boosting the development of rugged, miniaturized computer systems including the Apollo guidance computer used in its command module and landing craft. In his book on this topic (Mindell, 2008), as in his earlier work, Mindell stresses the engineering of systems including both human and machine elements. The U.S. National Aeronautics and Space Administration (NASA) has a well developed program of high quality commissioned histories, meaning that many aspects of its technical and institutional history are well documented. Perhaps the most relevant is Tomayko's (2000) history of NASA's successful push to transfer computer control technologies to aircraft.

Programmable computers also found early application in industrial control (Stout & Williams, 1995). They were particularly well suited to continuous flow industries, such as oil and chemical processing. Although the automatic factory was a potent concept in political debate and popular culture from the 1950s onward, little has so far been written on its history with the exception of David Noble's (1984) provocative *Forces of Production*. Noble, writing from a Marxist perspective heavily influenced by the work of 1970s labor theorist Harry Braverman, surveyed the development of automatic machine tools in the context of the Cold War. He argued that the ideological desire of business managers and computer researchers to replace skilled and potentially troublesome workers with machines had pushed the development of this technology in a dehumanizing and inefficient direction. The book is undeniably a polemic, but Noble's determination to ground technical history in its broadest possible social context and illustrate the effect of technical choices on the experience of ordinary people reminds us of just how narrowly focused most other work in this area has been and of how useful the historical study of information technology might be in understanding the direction of society over recent decades.

Studies of more recent embedded systems are conspicuous by their absence. There have been a couple of studies of the cell phone but these have paid little attention to the status of handsets as special purpose computers. Historians of recorded music, film, and popular culture have yet to get to grips with the influence of computer-based media such as digital video discs (DVDs), MPEG-1 Audio Layer 3 (MP3) files, and iPods. Nobody has yet told the story of the computerization of cars; even the pocket calculator (received in the 1970s as an icon of the microelectronic revolution to come) has failed to attract a scholarly history. However Greg Downey (2008) has recently looked at the evolution of television closed captioning (made possible by microcomputers and embedded chips) from the perspective of labor and political history.

Videogames have attracted a thriving industry of scholars from cultural studies, economics, and anthropology; but, in spite of a respectable industry producing coffee table books and memoirs devoted to classic video games, historical research on this topic is only just beginning to appear. The most notable book to date is *Racing the Beam* (Montfort & Bogost, 2009), which draws on concepts from the field of science and technology studies to explore the influence of technological choices made in the design of the seminal and charmingly primitive Atari VCS game console (released 1977) on the subsequent evolution of game design and programming practice in the home videogame industry that grew up around it.

Future of the History of Information Technology

The history of information technology has until recently been a rather obscure subfield falling mostly within the history of technology. During the last few years it has become much more visible in history of technology journals and conferences and is beginning to assume greater prominence within business history and the history of science. But most work in the area continues to reflect the mindset and concerns of technical specialists rather than the concerns of academic historians. Its questions and methods are at best unconcerned with academic fashion and at worst antediluvian. Class, race, and gender emerged several decades ago as the central analytical categories in social history but rarely surface in historical discussion of information technologies. Neither have what have been called the "linguistic turn" of the 1970s or the "cultural turn" of the 1980s, inescapable in the humanities, been taken very often. Histories of information technology have rarely considered representative experiences, social changes, or the influence of information technologies on different kinds of work. To be blunt, outsiders from more mature historical subfields are likely to find the bulk of existing scholarship narrow, dry, obsessed with details, under conceptualized, and disconnected from broader intellectual currents.

This is already beginning to change, driven by the growing and changing importance of information technology in the world itself. Computers have, as discussed previously, become a kind of universal technology. They have (whether in recognizable forms or embedded within digital appliances) replaced many of the technologies formerly ubiquitous in everyday life. For the relatively small band of scholars who identify primarily as historians of computing or of information technology, this poses challenges and opportunities. As the history of the early twenty-first century is written, nobody telling the story of any genre of popular music, any industry, any company, any scientific discipline, or any form of communication will be able to tell the story fully without paying some attention to information technology. And yet it is neither realistic nor desirable to imagine that fifty years hence most historians will call themselves historians of information technology. What does that mean for the history of information technology? Must it become the history of everything? If so who will write it and what can we do with it?

The obvious parallel is with the history of the book (which is, after all, an information technology in the literal sense). Historians, literary scholars, and other humanities researchers write about books and their authors all the time. Yet the book itself is often taken for granted. "History of the book" has emerged as an interdisciplinary field probing the materiality of culture. It cuts across established fields of studies and historical narratives to rediscover the evolution of book technology and its relationship to reading practices, publishing industries, and intellectual history.

Perhaps the history of information technology may one day win recognition as a similarly interdisciplinary endeavor, an intellectual space for people interested in the relationship between the internal characteristics of computer technology and its applications and interpretations in many different fields. Attention to information technology will likewise provide novel or subversive ways to reinterpret historical causality, upend assumptions about high and low cultures, and expose the role of technological change in unexpected places. With historical distance the cultural power and slippery appeal of ideas such as *information revolution* and *the digital* will make them attractive frames in which to understand much of the late twentieth century. But the biggest challenge will be for those few historians, among whose number I count myself, who care deeply about information technology as technology, savoring arcane knowledge of Turing machines, network protocols, and long dead mainframes. It will not be enough to dive deep into the internals of these devices and tell their stories. We must resurface from our excursions holding insights packaged in such a way as to be useful and comprehensible to the many, many historians who will be studying the process by which one or another field of human endeavor was fundamentally restructured around the capabilities of these protean devices.

Acknowledgments

I wrote much of this chapter as a fellow in the Center for 21st Century Studies of the University of Wisconsin Milwaukee during the 2008–2009 academic year. Thanks for close reading of drafts and insightful comments to William Aspray, Paul Ceruzzi, Peggy Kidwell, Ed Benoit, Petri Paju, Chigusa Kita, and the anonymous reviewers.

Endnotes

1. This transition is not entirely unproblematic. "Computing" has its own conceptual limitations as it literally refers to the act of calculation. This was the original task of computers but has become something of a misnomer given the rapid development of their capabilities and applications. But it retains two advantages over information technology. It is more descriptive of the kinds of technology that are actually being considered. And it describes an activity, albeit one performed with technology, rather than the technology itself. "History of Information Technology," like "History of the Computer" puts the emphasis on the obsolete widgets and doodads themselves rather than their associated applications, work practices, cultural meanings, and influence on the world.

2. In actuality scholars have tended to back away from the idea that this is a simple dichotomy and seek more nuanced or hybrid approaches. One problem is that "internal" and "external" are often expressed not just with reference to a specific identifiable community but with reference to science as a whole, and modern work in science studies challenges the whole idea of science as something with a definable inside or outside. However, the idea of a split in approaches is still a useful one in this context.

3. A four volume history of NCR was prepared and given to employees on the occasion of the firm's 100th anniversary in 1994. The third volume, *NCR: 1952–1984: The Computer Age*, apparently deals with this topic.

4. This encompassed the whole of volume 11, issue 4, and several articles in each issue of volume 12.

References

Abbate, J. (1999). *Inventing the internet*. Cambridge, MA: MIT Press.

Abbate, J. (2010). Privatizing the internet: Competing visions and chaotic events, 1987–1995. *IEEE Annals of the History of Computing, 32*(1), 10–22.

Agar, J. (2003). *The government machine: A revolutionary history of the computer*. Cambridge, MA: MIT Press.

Akera, A. (2006). *Calculating a natural world: Scientists, engineers, and computers during the rise of U.S. cold war research*. Cambridge, MA: MIT Press.

Akera, A. (2008). The life and work of Bernard A. Galler (1928–2006). *IEEE Annals of the History of Computing, 30*(1), 4–14.

Allyn, S. C. (1967). *My half century at NCR*. New York: McGraw-Hill.

Amelio, G., & Simon, W. L. (1998). *On the firing line: My 500 days at Apple*. New York: Harper Business.

Anderson, D. P. (2007). Patrick Blackett: Physicist, radical, and chief architect of the Manchester computing phenomenon. *IEEE Annals of the History of Computing, 29*(3), 82–85.

Aspray, W. (1984). Literature and institutions in the history of computing. *Isis, 75*(1), 162–170.

Aspray, W. (Ed.). (1990a). *Computing before computers*. Ames: Iowa State University Press.

Aspray, W. (1990b). *John von Neumann and the origins of modern computing*. Cambridge, MA: MIT Press.

Aspray, W. (1994). The history of computing within the history of information technology. *History and Technology, 11*, 7–19.

Aspray, W. (1997). The Intel 4004 microprocessor: What constituted innovation. *IEEE Annals of the History of Computing, 19*(3), 4–15.

Aspray, W. (1999). Command and control, documentation, and library science: The origins of information science at the University of Pittsburgh. *IEEE Annals of the History of Computing, 21*(4), 4–20.

Aspray, W. (2000). Was early entry a competitive advantage? US universities that entered computing in the 1940s. *IEEE Annals of the History of Computing, 22*(3), 42–87.

Aspray, W. (2007). Leadership in computing history: Arthur Norberg and the Charles Babbage Institute. *IEEE Annals of the History of Computing, 29*(4), 16–26.

Aspray, W., & Ceruzzi, P. (Eds.). (2008). *The internet and American business*. Cambridge, MA: MIT Press.

Aspray, W., & Williams, B. O. (1994). Arming American scientists: NSF and the provision of scientific computing facilities for universities, 1950–73. *IEEE Annals of the History of Computing, 16*(4), 60–74.

Atkinson, P. (1998). Computer memories: The history of computer form. *History and Technology, 15*, 89–120.

Auletta, K. (2001). *World War 3.0: Microsoft and its enemies*. New York: Random House.

Bagnall, B. (2005). *On the edge: The spectacular rise and fall of Commodore*. Winnipeg, Manitoba: Variant Press.

Bank, D. (2001). *Breaking Windows: How Bill Gates fumbled the future of Microsoft*. New York: The Free Press.

Bardini, T. (2000). *Bootstrapping: Douglas Engelbart, coevolution, and the origins of personal computing*. Stanford, CA: Stanford University Press.

Bassett, R. K. (2002). *To the digital age: Research labs, start-up companies, and the rise of MOS technology*. Baltimore: Johns Hopkins University Press.

Batiz-Lazo, B. (2009). Emergence and evolution of proprietary ATM networks in the UK. *Business History, 51*(1), 1–27.

Batiz-Lazo, B., & Billings, M. (2007). Banking on change: Information systems and echnologies in UK High Street banking 1919–1969. *Financial History Review, 14*(2), 177–205.

Batiz-Lazo, B., & Boyns, T. (2004). The business and financial history of automation and technological change in 20th century banking. *Accounting Business and Financial History Journal, 14*(3), 225–232.

Battelle, J. (2005). *The search: How Google and its rivals rewrote the rules of business and transformed our culture*. New York: Portfolio.

Bauer, W. F. (1996). Informatics: An early software company. *IEEE Annals of the History of Computing, 18*(2), 70–76.

Baum, C. (1981). *The system builders: The story of SDC*. Santa Monica, CA: System Development Corporation.

Bedlen, T. G., & Bedlen, M. R. (1962). *The lengthening shadow: The life of Thomas J. Watson*. Boston: Little, Brown.

Bell, D. (1974). *The coming of post-industrial society: A venture in social forecasting*. New York: Harper Colophon.

Bergin, T. J. (2006a). The origins of word processing software for personal computers: 1976–1985. *IEEE Annals of the History of Computing, 28*(4), 32–47.

Bergin, T. J. (2006b). The proliferation and consolidation of word processing software: 1985–1995. *IEEE Annals of the History of Computing, 28*(4), 48–63.

Bergin, T. J., & Gibson, R. G. (Eds.). (1996). *History of programming languages II.* New York: ACM Press.

Bergin, T. J., & Haigh, T. (2009). The commercialization of data base management software 1969–85. *IEEE Annals of the History of Computing, 31*(4), 26–41.

Berkeley, E. C. (1949). *Giant brains or machines that think.* New York: Wiley.

Berlin, L. (2006). *The man behind the microchip: Robert Noyce and the invention of Silicon Valley.* New York: Oxford University Press.

Berners-Lee, T., & Fischetti, M. (1999). *Weaving the web: The original design and ultimate destiny of the World Wide Web by its inventor.* San Francisco: Harper.

Beyer, K. W. (2009). *Grace Hopper and the invention of the information age.* Cambridge, MA: MIT Press.

Bird, P. (1994). *LEO: The first business computer.* Wokingham, UK: Hasler.

Black, A. (2006). Information history. *Annual Review of Information Science and Technology, 40*, 441–473.

Bourne, C. P., & Hahn, T. B. (2003). *A history of online information services: 1963–1976.* Cambridge, MA: MIT Press.

Bowker, G. (1993). How to be universal: Some cybernetic strategies. *Social Studies of Science, 23*, 107–127.

Broy, M., & Denert, E. (Eds.). (2002). *Software pioneers: Contributions to software engineering.* Berlin: Springer-Verlag.

Bruemmer, B. H. (1987). *Resources for the history of computing.* Minneapolis, MN: Charles Babbage Institute.

Bubenko, J., Impagliazzo, J., & Solvberg, A. (Eds.). (2005). *History of Nordic computing.* New York: Springer.

Bucks, A. R. (2003). *Who invented the computer? The legal battle that changed computing history.* Amherst, NY: Prometheus Books.

Bucks, A. W. (1988). *The first electronic computer: The Atanasoff story.* Ann Arbor: University of Michigan Press.

Burke, C. (2007). History of information science. *Annual Review of Information Science and Technology, 41*, 3–53.

Burks, A. W., & Burks, A. R. (1981). The ENIAC: The first general-purpose electronic computer. *Annals of the History of Computing, 3*(4), 310–389.

Bush, V. (1945). As we may think. *Atlantic Monthly, 176*(1), 101–108.

Butler, A., & Pogue, D. (2002). *Piloting Palm: The inside story of Palm, Handspring and the birth of the billion dollar handheld industry.* New York: John Wiley.

Callon, M. (1986). Some elements of a sociology of translation: Domestication of the scallops and the fishermen of St. Brieuc Bay. In J. Law (Ed.), *Power, action and belief: A new sociology of knowledge?* (pp. 196–223). New York: Routledge.

Caminer, D., Aris, J., Hermon, P., & Land, F. (Eds.). (1996). *User driven innovation: The world's first business computer.* London: McGraw-Hill.

Campbell-Kelly, M. (1982). The development of computer programming in Britain (1945–1955). *Annals of the History of Computing, 4*(2), 121–139.

Campbell-Kelly, M. (1988). Data communications at the National Physical Laboratory (1965–1975). *Annals of the History of Computing, 9*(1), 221–247.

Campbell-Kelly, M. (1989). *ICL: A technical and business history.* New York: Oxford University Press.

Campbell-Kelly, M. (1994). The railway clearing house and Victorian data processing. In L. Bud-Frierman (Ed.), *Information acumen: The understanding and use of knowledge in modern business.* London: Routledge.

Campbell-Kelly, M. (1998). Programming the EDSAC: Early programming activity at the University of Cambridge. *IEEE Annals of the History of Computing, 20*(4), 46–67.

Campbell-Kelly, M. (2003). *From airline reservations to Sonic the Hedgehog: A history of the software industry.* Cambridge, MA: MIT Press.

Campbell-Kelly, M. (2007a). The history of the history of software. *IEEE Annals of the History of Computing, 29*(4), 40–51.

Campbell-Kelly, M. (2007b). Number crunching without programming: The evolution of spreadsheet usability. *IEEE Annals of the History of Computing, 29*(3), 6–19.

Campbell-Kelly, M., & Aspray, W. (1996). *Computer: A history of the information machine.* New York: Basic Books.

Campbell-Kelly, M., Croarken, M., Flood, R., & Robson, E. (Eds.). (2003). *The history of mathematical tables: From Sumer to spreadsheets.* Oxford, UK: Oxford University Press.

Capurro, R., & Hjørland, B. (2003). The concept of information. *Annual Review of Information Science and Technology, 37,* 343–411.

Carlson, W. M. (1986). Why AFIPS invested in history. *Annals of the History of Computing, 8*(3), 270–274.

Cassidy, J. (2002). *Dot.Con: How America lost its mind and money in the internet era.* New York: HarperCollins.

Ceruzzi, P. E. (1983). *Reckoners: The prehistory of the digital computer, from relays to the stored program concept, 1935–1945.* Westport, CT: Greenwood Press.

Ceruzzi, P. E. (1989). *Beyond the limits: Flight enters the computer age.* Cambridge, MA: MIT Press.

Ceruzzi, P. E. (1998). *A history of modern computing.* Cambridge, MA: MIT Press.

Chandler, A. D., & Cortada, J. W. (Eds.). (2000). *A nation transformed by information: How information has shaped the United States from colonial times to the present.* New York: Oxford University Press.

Chandler, A. D., Hikino, T., & Nordenflycht, A. V. (2001). *Inventing the electronic century: The epic story of the consumer electronics and computer industries.* New York: Free Press.

Chposky, J., & Leonsis, T. (1988). *Blue magic: the people, power, and politics behind the IBM personal computer.* New York: Facts on File.

Cohen, I. B. (1999). *Howard Aiken: Portrait of a computer pioneer.* Cambridge, MA: MIT Press.

Cohen, S. (1984). *Zap: The rise and fall of Atari.* New York: McGraw Hill.

Coopey, R. (Ed.). (2004). *Information technology policy: An international history.* Oxford, UK: Oxford University Press.

Copeland, B. J. (2004). Colossus: Its origins and originators. *IEEE Annals of the History of Computing, 26*(4), 38–45.

Copeland, J. (2006). *Colossus: The first electronic computer*. New York: Oxford University Press.

Cortada, J. W. (1990). *Archives of data-processing history: A guide to major U.S. collections*. New York: Greenwood Press.

Cortada, J. W. (1993). *Before the computer: IBM, Burroughs and Remington Rand and the industry they created, 1865–1956*. Princeton, NJ: Princeton University Press.

Cortada, J. W. (1996a). *A bibliographic guide to the history of computer applications, 1950–1990*. Westport, CT: Greenwood Press.

Cortada, J. W. (1996b). *Second bibliographic guide to the history of computing, computers, and the information processing industry*. Westport, CT: Greenwood Press.

Cortada, J. W. (2003). *The digital hand: How computers changed the work of American manufacturing, transportation, and retail industries*. Oxford, UK: Oxford University Press.

Cortada, J. W. (2004). How did computing go global: The need for an answer and a research agenda. *IEEE Annals of the History of Computing, 26*(1), 53–58.

Cortada, J. W. (2006). *The digital hand, volume 2: How computers changed the work of American financial, telecommunications, media, and entertainment industries*. Oxford, UK: Oxford University Press.

Cortada, J. W. (2007). *The digital hand, volume 3: How computers changed the work of American public sector industries*. Oxford, UK: Oxford University Press.

Cowan, R. S. (1987). The consumption junction: A proposal for research strategies in the sociology of technology. In W. E. Bijker, T. Pinch, & T. P. Hughes (Eds.), *The social construction of technological systems* (pp. 261–280). Cambridge, MA: MIT Press.

Cowell, W. (Ed.). (1984). *Sources and development of mathematical software*. New York: Prentice-Hall.

Cringely, R. X. (1992). *Accidental empires: How the boys of Silicon Valley make their millions, battle foreign competition, and still can't get a date*. Reading, MA: Addison-Wesley.

Croarken, M. (1990). *Early scientific computing in Britain*. Oxford, UK: Clarendon Press.

Cronon, W. (1991). *Nature's metropolis: Chicago and the great west*. New York: Norton.

Crowe, G. D., & Goodman, S. E. (1994). S.A. Lebedev and the birth of Soviet computing. *IEEE Annals of the History of Computing, 16*(1), 4–24.

Cusumano, M. A. (1995). *Microsoft secrets: How the world's most powerful software company creates technology, shapes markets, and manages people*. New York: Free Press.

Cusumano, M. A., & Yoffie, D. B. (1998). *Competing on internet time*. New York: Free Press.

David, P. A. (1985). Clio and the economics of QWERTY. *American Economic Review, 75*(2), 332–337.

de Wit, D. (1994). *The shaping of automation: A historical analysis of the interaction between technology and organization, 1950–1985*. Hilversum, The Netherlands: Verloren.

de Wit, D. (1997). The construction of the Dutch computer industry: The organizational shaping of technology. *Business History, 39*(3), 81–104.

Dell, M., & Freedman, C. (1999). *Direct from Dell*. New York: Harper Business.

Downey, G. J. (2008). *Closed captioning: Subtitling, stenography, and the digital convergence of text with television*. Baltimore: Johns Hopkins University Press.

Earls, A. R. (2004). *Digital Equipment Corporation*. Portsmouth, NH: Arcadia Publishing.

Edwards, P. N. (1996). *The closed world: Computers and the politics of discourse in Cold War America*. Cambridge, MA: MIT Press.

Edwards, P. N. (2000). The world in a machine: Origins and impacts of early computerized global systems models. In A. C. Hughes & T. P. Hughes (Eds.), *Systems, experts, and computers: The systems approach in management and engineering, World War II and after* (pp. 221–253). Cambridge, MA: MIT Press.

Elzen, B., & MacKenzie, D. (1994). The social limits of speed: The development and use of supercomputers. *Annals of the History of Computing, 16*(1), 46–61.

Ensmenger, N. L. (2003). Letting the "computer boys" take over: Technology and the politics of organizational transformation. *International Review of Social History, 48*(Supplement), 153–180.

Fairthorne, R. A. (1965). "Use" and "mention" in the information sciences. In L. B. Heleprin, B. E. Markuson, & F. L. Goodman (Eds.), *Proceedings of the Symposium on Education for Information Science* (pp. 9–12). Washington, DC: Spartan Books.

Ferguson, C. H. (1999). *High stakes, no prisoners: A winner's tale of greed and glory in the internet wars*. New York: Times Business.

Ferry, G. (2003). *A computer called LEO: Lyons Tea Shops and the world's first office computer*. London: Fourth Estate.

Fiegener, M. K. (2008). *S&E Degrees: 1996–2006* (Detailed statistical tables. NSF 08–321). Washington, DC: National Science Foundation.

Fitzpatrick, A. (1999). *Igniting the light elements: The Los Alamos Thermonuclear Weapon Project, 1942–1952* (LA-13577-T). Los Alamos, NM: Los Alamos National Laboratory.

Flamm, K. (1988). *Creating the computer: Government, industry, and high technology*. Washington, DC: Brookings Institution.

Fletcher, A. L. (2002). France enters the computer age: A political history of Minitel. *History and Technology, 18*(2), 103–117.

Forman, R. L. (1984). *Fulfilling the computer's promise: The history of informatics, 1962–1982*. Woodland Hills, CA: Informatics General Corporation.

Forrester, T. (1981). *The microelectronics revolution*. Cambridge, MA: MIT Press.

Frana, P. L. (2004). Before the web there was Gopher. *IEEE Annals of the History of Computing, 26*(1), 20–41.

Freiberger, P., & Swaine, M. (1984). *Fire in the valley: The making of the personal computer*. Berkeley, CA: Osborne/McGraw-Hill.

Friedman, A. L., & Cornford, D. S. (1989). *Computer systems development: History, organization and implementation*. New York: Wiley.

Galison, P. (1997). *Image and logic: A material culture of microphysics*. Chicago: University of Chicago Press.

Galler, B. A. (2004). Annals: How the first issue came to be. *IEEE Annals of the History of Computing, 26*(1), 4–7.

Gerovitch, S. (2002). *From newspeak to cyberspeak: A history of Soviet cybernetics*. Cambridge, MA: MIT Press.

Gerovitch, S. (2008). InterNyet: Why the Soviet Union did not build a nationwide computer network. *History and Technology, 24*(4), 335–350.

Gieryn, T. F. (1983). Boundary-work and the demarcation of science from non-science: Strains and interests in professional ideologies of scientists. *American Sociological Review, 48*, 781–795.

Gillies, J., & Cailliau, R. (2000). *How the web was born: The story of the World Wide Web*. Oxford, UK: Oxford University Press.

Goldberg, A. (Ed.). (1988). *A history of personal workstations*. New York: Addison-Wesley/ACM.

Goldfarb, B. D., Kirsch, D. A., & Miller, D. A. (2007). Was there too little entry during the dot com era? *Journal of Financial Economics, 86*(1), 100–144.

Goldstein, H. H. (1972). *The computer from Pascal to von Neumann*. Princeton, NJ: Princeton University Press.

Graham, R., & Rayward, W. B. (Eds.). (2002). Computer applications in libraries [Special issues]. *IEEE Annals of the History of Computing, 24*, 2–3.

Greenberg, J. M. (2008). *From Betamax to Blockbuster: Video stores and the invention of movies on video*. Cambridge, MA: MIT Press.

Greenstein, S. (2001a). Commercialization of the internet: The interaction of public policy and private actions. In A. Jaffe, J. Lerner, & S. Stern (Eds.), *Innovation, policy, and the economy* (pp. 151–186). Cambridge, MA: MIT Press.

Greenstein, S. (2001b). Technological mediation and commercial development in the early internet access market. *California Management Review, 43*(2), 75–79.

Greenstein, S., & Wade, J. (1998). The product life cycle in the commercial mainframe computer market, 1968–1983. *Rand Journal of Economics, 29*(4), 772–789.

Grier, D. A. (2003). The great machine theory of history. *IEEE Annals of the History of Computing, 25*(3), 95–96.

Grier, D. A. (2006). *When computers were human*. Princeton, NJ: Princeton University Press.

Grier, D. A., & Campbell, M. (2000). A social history of Bitnet and Listserv, 1985–1991. *IEEE Annals of the History of Computing, 22*(2), 32–41.

Hafner, K. (1995, May). The epic saga of the Well: The world's most influential online community (and it's not AOL). *Wired Magazine, 5*, 98–142.

Hafner, K., & Lyon, M. (1998). *Where wizards stay up late: The origins of the internet*. New York: Touchstone Books.

Hagen, J. B. (2001). The introduction of computers into systematic research in the United States during the 1960s. *Studies in the History and Philosophy of Biological and Biomedical Sciences, 32*(2), 291–314.

Hahn, T. B., & Buckland, M. (Eds.). (1998). *Historical studies in information science*. Medford, NJ: Information Today, Inc.

Haigh, T. (2001a). The chromium-plated tabulator: Institutionalizing an electronic revolution, 1954–1958. *IEEE Annals of the History of Computing, 23*(4), 75–104.

Haigh, T. (2001b). Inventing information systems: The systems men and the computer, 1950–1968. *Business History Review, 75*(1), 15–61.

Haigh, T. (2002). Software in the 1960s as concept, service, and product. *IEEE Annals of the History of Computing, 24*(1), 5–13.

Haigh, T. (2004a). The history of computing: An introduction for the computer scientist. In W. Aspray & A. Akera (Eds.), *Using history to teach computer science and related disciplines* (pp. 5–26). Washington, DC: Computing Research Association.

Haigh, T. (2004b). Key resources in the history of computing. In W. Aspray & A. Akera (Eds.), *Using history to teach computer science and related disciplines* (pp. 279–293). Washington, DC: Computing Research Association.

Haigh, T. (2006). Remembering the office of the future: The origins of word processing and office automation. *IEEE Annals of the History of Computing, 28*(4), 6–31.

Haigh, T. (2008a). Protocols for profit: Web and email technologies as product and infrastructure. In W. Aspray & P. Ceruzzi (Eds.), *The internet and American business* (pp. 105–158). Cambridge, MA: MIT Press.

Haigh, T. (2008b). The web's missing links: Search engines and portals. In W. Aspray & P. Ceruzzi (Eds.), *The internet and American business* (pp. 159–200). Cambridge, MA: MIT Press.

Haigh, T. (2009). How data got its base: Generalized information storage software in the 1950s and 60s. *IEEE Annals of the History of Computing, 31*(4), 6–25.

Haigh, T., Kaplan, E., & Seib, C. (2007). Sources for ACM history: What, where, why. *Communications of the ACM, 50*(5), 36–41.

Harper, K. C. (2008). *Weather by the numbers: The genesis of modern meteorology.* Cambridge, MA: MIT Press.

Harrar, G., & Rifkin, G. (1988). *The ultimate entrepreneur: The story of Ken Olsen and Digital Equipment Corporation.* Chicago: Contemporary Books.

Harsha, P. (2004). IT research and development funding. In W. Aspray (Ed.), *Chasing Moore's law: Information technology policy in the United States.* Raleigh, NC: SciTech Publishing.

Hashagen, U., Keil-Slawik, R., & Norberg, A. L. (Eds.). (2002). *Mapping the history of computing: Software issues.* New York: Springer-Verlag.

Hecht, J. (1999). *City of light: The story of fiber optics.* New York: Oxford University Press.

Heide, L. (2009). *Punched-card systems and the early information explosion, 1880–1945.* Baltimore: Johns Hopkins University Press.

Heims, S. J. (1991). *The cybernetics group.* Cambridge, MA: MIT Press.

Hendry, J. (1990). *Innovating for failure: Government policy and the early British computer industry.* Cambridge, MA: MIT Press.

Hertzfeld, A. (2004). *Revolution in the valley: The insanely great story of how the Mac was made.* Sevastapol, CA: O'Reilly.

Hicks, M. (2009). *Compiling inequalities: Office computerization in the British civil service and nationalized industries, 1940–1979.* Durham, NC: Duke University Press.

Hiltzik, M. (1999). *Dealers of lightning: Xerox PARC and the dawn of the computer age.* New York: Harper Business.

Hodges, A. (1983). *Alan Turing: The enigma of intelligence.* New York: Simon and Schuster.

Houston, R. D., & Harmon, G. (2007). Vannevar Bush and Memex. *Annual Review of Information Science and Technology, 41*, 55–91.

Hyman, A. (1982). *Charles Babbage: Pioneer of the computer.* Princeton, NJ: Princeton University Press.

Ichikawa, H. (2006). Strela-1, the first Soviet computer: Political success and technological failure. *IEEE Annals of the History of Computing, 28*(3), 18–31.

Impagliazzo, J., Järvi, T., & Paju, P. (2009). *History of Nordic computing 2* (IFIP AICT 303). Berlin: Springer.

Johnson, L. (Ed.). (2003). *ADAPSO reunion transcript: May 2–4, 2002.* Bloomington, IN: 1st Books.

Jones, C. B. (2003). The early search for tractable ways of reasoning about programs. *IEEE Annals of the History of Computing, 25*(2), 26–49.

Kahl, S. J. (2007). *Considering the customer: Determinants and impact of using technology on industry evolution*. Cambridge, MA: MIT Press.

Kaplan, J. (1994). *Startup: A Silicon Valley adventure*. Boston: Houghton Mifflin.

Kay, L. E. (2000). *Who wrote the book of life: A history of the genetic code*. Stanford, CA: Stanford University Press.

Kidder, T. (1981). *The soul of a new machine*. Boston: Little, Brown.

Kita, C. I. (2003). JCR Licklider's vision for the IPTO. *IEEE Annals of the History of Computing, 25*(3), 62–77.

Kline, R. (2006). Cybernetics, management science, and technology policy: The emergence of "information technology" as a keyword. *Technology and Culture, 47*(3), 513–535.

Kornfeld, L. (1983). *To catch a mouse make a noise like a cheese*. New York: Prentice-Hall.

Kranakis, E. (2004). Politics, business, and European information technology policy: From the Treaty of Rome to Unidata, 1958–1975. In R. Coopey (Ed.), *Information technology policy: An international history* (pp. 209–246). New York: Oxford University Press.

Lally, E. (2002). *At home with computers*. New York: Berg.

Lavington, S. (1998). *A history of Manchester Computers*. Swindon, UK: The British Computer Society.

Lean, T. (2008). *The making of the micro: Producers, mediators, users and the development of popular microcomputing in Britain (1980–1989)*. Manchester, UK: University of Manchester.

Leavitt, H. J., & Whisler, T. L. (1958). Management in the 1980s. *Harvard Business Review, 36*(6), 41–48.

Lecuyer, C. (2006). *Making Silicon Valley: Innovation and the growth of high tech, 1930–70*. Cambridge, MA: MIT Press.

Lee, J. A. N. (1995). The rise and fall of the General Electric Corporation Computer Department. *IEEE Annals of the History of Computing, 17*(4), 24–45.

Lee, J. A. N., & Snively, G. E. (2000). The rise and sale of the General Electric Computer Department: A further look. *IEEE Annals of the History of Computing, 22*(2), 53–60.

Leimbach, T. (2008). The SAP story: Evolution of SAP within the German software industry. *IEEE Annals of the History of Computing, 30*(4), 60–76.

Levy, S. (1984). *Hackers: The heroes of the digital revolution*. Garden City, NY: Anchor Press/Doubleday.

Levy, S. (1994). *Insanely great: The life and times of Macintosh, the computer that changed everything*. New York: Viking.

Lewis, M. (2000). *The new new thing*. New York: W. W. Norton.

Licklider, J. C. R. (1960, March). Man-computer symbiosis. *IRE Transactions on Human Factors in Electronics, 1*, 4–11.

Light, J. S. (1999). When computers were women. *Technology and Culture, 40*(3), 455–483.

Lindgren, M. (1990). *Glory and failure: The difference engines of Johann Muller, Charles Babbage, and Georg and Edvard Scheutz*. Cambridge, MA: MIT Press.

Lohr, S. (2001). *Go to: The story of the math majors, bridge players, engineers, chess wizards, maverick scientists and iconoclasts: The programmers who created the software revolution*. New York: Basic Books.

Lundin, P. (2009). *Documenting the use of computers in Swedish society between 1950 and 1980. Final report on the Project "From Computing Machines to IT."* (Working Papers from the Division of History of Science and Technology, TRITA/HST 2009/1). Stockholm, Sweden: The Division.

MacKenzie, D. (1991). The influence of Los Alamos and Livermore National Laboratories on the development of supercomputing. *Annals of the History of Computing, 13*(2), 179–291.

MacKenzie, D. (2001). *Mechanizing proof.* Cambridge, MA: MIT Press.

Mahoney, M. S. (1988). The history of computing in the history of technology. *Annals of the History of Computing, 10*(2), 113–125.

Mahoney, M. S. (1990). The roots of software engineering. *CWI Quarterly, 3*(4), 325–334. Retrieved April 17, 2010, from www.princeton.edu/~hos/mike/articles/sweroots.pdf

Mahoney, M. S. (1996). Issues in the history of computing. In T. J. Bergin & R. G. Gibson (Eds.), *History of programming languages II* (pp. 772–781). New York: ACM Press.

Mahoney, M. S. (1997). Computer science: The search for a mathematical theory. In J. Krige & D. Pestre (Eds.), *Science in the 20th century.* Amsterdam: Harwood Academic.

Mahoney, M. S. (2002). Software as science: Science as software. In U. Hashagen, R. Keil-Slawik, & A. L. Norberg (Eds.), *Mapping the history of computing: Software issues* (pp. 25–48). New York: Springer-Verlag.

Mahoney, M. S. (2005). The histories of computing(s). *Interdisciplinary Science Review, 30*(2), 119–135.

Malinovsky, B., & Fitzpatrick, A. (2006). *Pioneers of Soviet computing.* Retrieved June 19, 2010, from www.sigcis.org/files/malinovsky2010.pdf

Manes, S., & Andrews, P. (2002). *Gates: How Microsoft's mogul reinvented an industry—and made himself the richest man in America.* New York: Touchstone.

Markoff, J. (2005). *What the doormouse said: How the 60s counterculture shaped the personal computer industry.* New York: Viking.

Martin, S. W. (2005). *The real story of Informix Software and Phil White: Lessons in business and leadership for the executive team.* Rancho Santa Margarita, CA: Sand Hill Publishing.

May, K. O. (1980). Historiography: A perspective for computer scientists. In N. Metropolis, J. Howlett, & G.-C. Rota (Eds.), *A history of computing in the twentieth century: A collection of papers* (pp. 11–20). New York: Academic Press.

McCartney, S. (1999). *ENIAC: The triumphs and tragedies of the world's first computer.* New York: Walker & Co.

McKenney, J. L., Copeland, D. C., & Mason, R. O. (1995). *Waves of change: Business evolution through information technology.* Boston: Harvard Business School Press.

Medina, E. (2006). Designing freedom, regulating a nation: Socialist cybernetics in Allende's Chile. *Journal of Latin American Studies, 38*(3), 571–606.

Medina, E. (2008). Big blue in the bottomless pit: The early years of IBM Chile. *IEEE Annals of the History of Computing, 30*(4), 26–41.

Meissner, G. (2000). *SAP: Inside the secret software power.* New York: McGraw-Hill.

Metropolis, N., Howlett, J., & Rota, G.-C. (Eds.). (1980). *A history of computing in the twentieth century: A collection of papers.* New York: Academic Press.

Mindell, D. (2008). *Digital Apollo: Human and machine in spaceflight.* Cambridge, MA: MIT Press.

Mindell, D. A. (2002). *Between human and machine: Feedback, control, and computing before cybernetics.* Baltimore: Johns Hopkins University Press.

Misa, T. J. (2007). Understanding "how computing changed the world." *IEEE Annals of the History of Computing, 29*(4), 52–63.

Montfort, N., & Bogost, I. (2009). *Racing the beam: The Atari video computer system.* Cambridge, MA: MIT Press.

Moody, F. (1995). *I sing the body electronic: A year with Microsoft on the electronic frontier.* New York: Penguin Books.

Moritz, M. (1984). *The little kingdom: The private story of Apple Computer.* New York: William Morrow.

Mowery, D. (Ed.). (1995). *The international computer software industry: A comparative study of industry evolution and structure.* New York: Oxford University Press.

Murray, C. F. (1997). *The supermen: The story of Seymour Cray and the technical wizards behind the supercomputer.* New York: Wiley.

Nandasara, S. T., & Mikami, Y. (Eds.). (2009). Asian language processing: History and perspective [Special Issue]. *IEEE Annals of the History of Computing, 31*(1).

Nash, S. G. (Ed.). (1990). *A history of scientific computing.* New York: ACM Press.

Nelson, T. H. (1974). *Computer lib/dream machines.* Peterborough, NY: Bits Inc.

Noble, D. F. (1984). *Forces of production: A social history of industrial automation.* New York: Knopf.

Norberg, A. L. (1990). High-technology calculation in the early 20th century: Punched card machinery in business and government. *Technology and Culture, 31*(4), 753–779.

Norberg, A. L. (2001). A perspective on the history of the Charles Babbage Institute and the Charles Babbage Foundation. *IEEE Annals of the History of Computing, 23*(4), 12–23.

Norberg, A. L. (2005). *Computers and commerce: A study of technology and management at Eckert-Mauchly Computer Company, Engineering Research Associates, and Remington Rand, 1946–1957.* Cambridge, MA: MIT Press.

Norberg, A. L., & O'Neill, J. E. (1996). *Transforming computer technology: Information processing for the Pentagon, 1962–1986.* Baltimore: Johns Hopkins University Press.

November, J. (2006). *Digitizing life: The introduction of computers to biology and medicine.* Princeton, NJ: Princeton University Press.

Nyce, J. M., & Kahn, P. (Eds.). (1991). *From Memex to hypertext: Vannevar Bush and the mind's machine.* New York: Academic Press, Inc.

Oldfield, H. R. (1996). *King of the seven dwarfs: General Electric's ambiguous challenge to the computer industry.* Los Alamitos, CA: IEEE Computer Society Press.

Ornstein, S. (2002). *Computing in the middle ages: A view from the trenches 1955–1983.* Bloomington, IN: AuthorHouse.

Osborn, R. F. (1954). GE and UNIVAC: Harnessing the high-speed computer. *Harvard Business Review, 32*(4), 99–107.

Oudshoorn, N., & Pinch, T. (2003). *How users matter: The co-construction of users and technology.* Cambridge, MA: MIT Press.

Paju, P. (2008). National projects and international users: Finland and early European computerization. *IEEE Annals of the History of Computing, 30*(4), 77–91.

Pearson, J. P. (1992). *Digital at work.* Burlington, MA: Digital Press.

Peeters, J. (2009). Early MRP systems at Royal Philips Electronics in the 1960s and 1970s. *IEEE Annals of the History of Computing, 31*(2), 56–69.

Peterson, W. E. (1994). *Almost perfect: How a bunch of regular guys built WordPerfect Corporation*. Rocklin, CA: Prima Publishing.

Postley, J. A. (1998). Mark IV: Evolution of the software product, a memoir. *IEEE Annals of the History of Computing, 20*(1), 43–50.

Price, R. M. (2005). *The eye for innovation*. New Haven, CT: Yale University Press.

Pugh, E. W. (1984). *Memories that shaped an industry: Decisions leading to IBM System/360*. Cambridge, MA: MIT Press.

Pugh, E. W. (1994). *Building IBM: Shaping an industry and its technologies*. Cambridge, MA: MIT Press.

Pugh, J., & Baxandall, D. (1975). *Calculating machines and instruments: Catalogue of the collections in the Science Museum*. London: The Museum.

Randell, B. (1980). The Colossus. In N. Metropolis, J. Howlett, & G.-C. Rota (Eds.), *A history of computing in the twentieth century: A collection of papers* (pp. 47–92). New York: Academic Press.

Rayward, W. B. (1998). Visions of Xanadu: Paul Otlet (1868–1944) and hypertext. In T. B. Hahn & M. Buckland (Eds.), *Historical studies in information science* (pp. 65–80). Medford, NJ: Information Today, Inc.

Rayward, W. B. (1999). H.G. Wells's idea of a world brain: A critical re-assessment. *Journal of the American Society for Information Science, 50*, 557–579.

Redmond, K. C., & Smith, T. M. (1980). *Project Whirlwind: The history of a pioneering computer*. Bedford, MA: Digital Press.

Redmond, K. C., & Smith, T. M. (2000). *From WHIRLWIND to MITRE: The R&D story of the SAGE air defense computer*. Cambridge, MA: MIT Press.

Reid, R. H. (1997). *Architects of the web: 1,000 days that built the future of business*. New York: Wiley.

Reid, T. R. (2001). *The chip: How two Americans invented the microchip and launched a revolution*. New York: Random House.

Rheingold, H. (1993). *The virtual community: Homesteading on the electronic frontier*. Reading, MA: Addison-Wesley.

Rice, J. R., & Rosen, S. (1994). The origins of computer science at Purdue University. In R. DeMillo & J. R. Rice (Eds.), *Studies in computer science: In honor of Samuel D. Conte*. New York: Plenum.

Riordan, M., & Hoddeson, L. (1997). *Crystal fire*. New York: W. W. Norton.

Rojas, R., & Hashagen, U. (Eds.). (2000). *The first computers: History and architectures*. Cambridge, MA: MIT Press.

Roland, A., & Shiman, P. (2002). *Strategic computing: DARPA and the quest for machine intelligence*. Cambridge, MA: MIT Press.

Russell, A. L. (2006). "Rough consensus and running code" and the internet-OSI standards war. *IEEE Annals of the History of Computing, 28*(3), 48–61.

Sammet, J. E. (1969). *Programming languages: History and fundamentals*. Englewood Cliffs, NJ: Prentice Hall.

Schein, E. H. (2003). *DEC is dead, long live DEC: The lasting legacy of Digital Equipment Corporation*. San Francisco: Berrett-Koehler.

Schlombs, C. (2008). Engineering international expansion: IBM and Remington Rand in European computer markets. *IEEE Annals of the History of Computing, 30*(4), 42–58.

Seidel, R. W. (1998). "Crunching numbers": Computers and physical research in the AEC Laboratories. *History and Technology*, *15*, 31–68.

Shurkin, J. N. (2006). *Broken genius: The rise and fall of William Shockley, creator of the electronic age*. New York: Palgrave Macmillan.

Small, J. S. (2001). *The analogue alternative: The electronic analogue computer in Britain and the USA, 1930–1975*. New York: Routledge.

Smith, D. K., & Alexander, R. C. (1989). *Fumbling the future: How Xerox invented, then ignored, the first personal computer*. New York: HarperCollins.

Southwick, K. (1999). *High noon: The inside story of Scott McNealy and the rise of Sun Microsystems*. New York: Wiley.

Stebenne, D. L. (2005). IBM's "new deal": Employment policies of the International Business Machines Corporation, 1933–1956. *Journal of The Historical Society*, *5*(1), 47–77.

Stein, D. (1985). *Ada: A life and legacy*. Cambridge, MA: MIT Press.

Sterling, C., & Grier, D. A. (2003). Histories of computer programming and software: From ALGOL to Windows XP. *Communication Booknotes Quarterly*, *34*(3), 151–167.

Sterling, C. H. (2003). Histories of computers: From Aiken to Zuse. *Communication Booknotes Quarterly*, *33*(4), 221–242.

Stern, N. B. (1981). *From ENIAC to UNIVAC: An appraisal of the Eckert-Mauchly Computers*. Bedford, MA: Digital Press.

Stout, T. M., & Williams, T. J. (1995). Pioneering work in the field of computer process control. *IEEE Annals of the History of Computing*, *17*(1), 6–18.

Stross, R. (2008). *Planet Google: One company's audacious plan to organize everything we know*. New York: Free Press.

Sumner, J. (2008). Standard and compatibility: The rise of the PC computing platform. In J. Sumner & G. J. N. Gooday (Eds.), *By whose standards? Standardization, stability and uniformity in the history of information and electrical technologies* (pp. 101–127). London: Continuum.

Swade, D. (2001). *The difference engine: Charles Babbage and the quest to build the first computer*. New York: Viking Penguin.

Swedin, E. G. (2005). *Computers: The life story of a technology*. Westport, CT: Greenwood.

Swisher, K. (1998). *aol.com: How Steve Case beat Bill Gates, nailed the netheads, and made millions in the war for the web*. New York: Random House.

Symonds, M., & Ellison, L. (2003). *Softwar: An intimate portrait of Larry Ellison and Oracle*. New York: Simon & Schuster.

Takahasi, S. (1996). A brief history of the Japanese computer industry before 1985. *IEEE Annals of the History of Computing*, *18*(1), 76–79.

Tedlow, R. S. (2003). *The Watson dynasty: The fiery reign and troubled legacy of IBM's founding father and son*. New York: Harper Business.

Tedlow, R. S. (2007). *Andy Grove: The life and times of an American business icon*. New York: Portfolio.

Tomash, E., & Cohen, A. A. (1991a). Marks on paper: Part 1: A historical survey of computer output printing. *Annals of the History of Computing*, *13*(1), 63–79.

Tomash, E., & Cohen, A. A. (1991b). Marks on paper: Part 2: A historical survey of computer output printing. *Annals of the History of Computing*, *13*(2), 203–222.

Tomash, E., & Williams, M. R. (2008). *The Erwin Tomash Library on the History of Computing: An annotated and illustrated catalog.* Minneapolis, MN: Charles Babbage Institute. Retrieved April 17, 2010, from www.cbi.umn.edu/hostedpublications/Tomash/index.htm

Tomayko, J. E. (2000). *Computers take flight: A history of NASA's pioneering digital fly-by-wire project.* Washington, DC: NASA History Office.

Tomlinson, J. (2009). Thrice denied: "Declinism" as a recurrent theme in British history in the long twentieth century. *Twentieth Century British History, 20*(2), 227–251.

Tropp, H. S. (1980). The Smithsonian Computer History Project and some personal recollections. In N. Metropolis, J. Howlett & G.-C. Rota (Eds.), *A history of computing in the twentieth century: A collection of papers* (pp. 115–124). New York: Academic Press.

Turkle, S. (1995). *Life on the screen: Identity in the age of the internet.* New York: Simon and Schuster.

Turner, F. (2006). *From counterculture to cyberculture: Stewart Brand, the Whole Earth Network, and the rise of digital utopianism.* Chicago: University of Chicago Press.

Ullman, E. (1997). *Close to the machine: Technophilia and its discontents.* San Francisco, CA: City Lights Books.

Usselman, S. (1993). IBM and its imitators: Organizational capabilities and the emergence of the international computer industry. *Business History Review, 22*(1), 1–35.

van den Ende, J. (1995). Computers and industrial organization: Early sources of "just in time" production in the Dutch steel industry. *IEEE Annals of the History of Computing, 17*(2), 22–32.

Vardalas, J. (2001). *The computer revolution in Canada: Building national technological competence.* Cambridge, MA: MIT Press.

Vehvilainen, M. (1999). Gender and computing in retrospect: The case of Finland. *IEEE Annals of the History of Computing, 21*(2), 44–51.

Veraart, F. (2008). Basicode: Co-producing a microcomputer Esperanto. In J. Sumner & G. J. N. Gooday (Eds.), *By whose standards? Standardization, stability and uniformity in the history of information and electrical technologies* (pp. 129–148). London: Continuum.

Vise, D. A., & Malseed, M. (2005). *The Google story.* New York: Delacorte.

Von Hippel, E. (2005). *Democratizing innovation.* Cambridge, MA: MIT Press.

von Neumann, J. (1993). First draft of a report on the EDVAC. *IEEE Annals of the History of Computing, 15*(4), 27–75.

Waldrop, M. (2001). *The dream machine: JCR Licklider and the revolution that made computing personal.* New York: Viking Press.

Wallace, J. (1992). *Hard drive: Bill Gates and the making of the Microsoft empire.* New York: Wiley.

Watson, T., Jr., & Petre, P. (1990). *Father, son & co.: My life at IBM and beyond.* New York: Bantam.

Webster, F. (1995). *Theories of the information society.* New York: Routledge.

Weick, K. E. (1995). *Sensemaking in organizations.* Thousand Oaks, CA: Sage.

Wells, H. G. (1938). *The world brain.* London: Methuen.

Wexelblat, R. L. (Ed.). (1981). *History of programming languages.* New York: Academic Press.

Wiegand, W. A., & Davis, D. G. (Eds.). (1994). *Encyclopedia of library history*. New York: Routledge.

Wilkes, M. (1985). *Memories of a computer pioneer*. Cambridge, MA: MIT Press.

Williams, K. B. (2004). *Grace Hopper: Admiral of the cyber sea*. Annapolis, MD: US Naval Institute Press.

Williams, M. R. (1985). *A history of computing technology*. Englewood Cliffs, NJ: Prentice-Hall.

Wolf, G. (1995, June). The curse of Xanadu. *Wired Magazine, 3*, 137–202.

Wolff, M. (1998). *Burn rate: How I survived the gold rush years on the internet*. New York: Simon & Schuster.

Yates, J. (2005). *Structuring the information age*. Baltimore: Johns Hopkins University Press.

Yates, J. (2006). How business enterprises use technology: Extending the demand-side turn. *Enterprise and Society, 7*(3), 422–455.

Yood, C. N. (2005). *Argonne National Laboratory and the emergence of computer and computational science, 1946–1992*. Unpublished doctoral dissertation, Pennsylvania State University, University Park.

Yost, J. R. (2001). CBI/Tomash Fellowship: Sponsoring a generation of scholars in information processing. *IEEE Annals of the History of Computing, 23*(4), 24–28.

Yost, J. R. (2002). *A bibliographic guide to resources in scientific computing, 1945–1975*. Westport, CT: Greenwood Press.

Yost, J. R. (2005a). *The computer industry*. Westport, CT: Greenwood Press.

Yost, J. R. (2005b). Maximization and marginalization: A brief examination of the history of historiography of the US computer services industry. *Enterprises et Histoire, 40*, 87–101.

Zachary, G. P. (1994). *Show stopper!: The breakneck race to create Windows NT and the next generation at Microsoft*. New York: Free Press.

CHAPTER 10

Online Social Movements

Noriko Hara and Bi-Yun Huang
Indiana University, Bloomington, IN

Introduction

The emergence of "e-movements" and new forms of "e-protest" and "e-activism" (Earl & Schussman, 2003, p. 162) has signified the importance of the internet as an organizational and mobilization vehicle for those engaged in social change. Social and political scientists have widely studied social movements for a number of years, including the use of information and communication technologies (ICTs) to support these movements. Historically, technology has constructively influenced social movements; perhaps most compelling is the use of the printing press by European social movements in the late eighteenth century (Tarrow, 1998). With the press, social movement organizers were able to distribute their ideas widely and better coordinate their activities. More recently, radio, television, telephones, direct mailings, fax machines, and email have commonly been used to disseminate information as well as mobilize a mass (Lievrouw, 2006; McCarthy & Zald, 1977; Porta & Diani, 1999).

In a similar vein, the array of new ICTs associated with the internet (e.g., websites, streaming videos, blogs, voice-over-IP, and social networking sites) has assisted numerous contemporary social movements. For example, although so-called activists have traditionally been the primary participants in social movements, today citizens who may not consider themselves activists are participating in online mobilization (e.g., Hara, 2008). Because of the wide use of the internet, social movements are finding ways to reach the general public. Bennett (2003) has reported that some social movements have taken advantage of ICTs to reach wider audiences faster, with lower costs than traditional methods. More recently, social networking sites such as MySpace, Facebook, and Twitter have played influential roles in political mobilization (Greengard, 2009; Gueorguieva, 2008). These technologies began to provide powerful means to organize forces—whether to fight against corporations (Shirky, 2008) or to coordinate international protests (Pérez, 2008).

Traditional social campaigns have resorted to activities such as public demonstrations, street theater, sit-ins, and protests to wrestle with power holders and opponents. The internet has altered this dynamic by electronically advertising a movement's views, goals, and tactics, publicizing information on the movement's activities, and linking like-minded individuals and groups transnationally. Global mobilizing forces and advocacy networks have assisted dozens of social activist groups to expand their networks worldwide (e.g., Arquilla & Ronfeldt, 2001; Gillan, 2009; Kahn & Kellner, 2004).

In this chapter, we use the following anchor definition: "The term *online social movements* refers to the adoption and use by social movements and community activists of new information and communication technologies (ICTs), such as the internet and the World Wide Web" (Loader, 2003, p. 1319, emphasis in the original). This includes both social movements that use ICTs as well as social movements that take place (exclusively) on the internet. Online social movements are a small but important area for research in information science and related fields due to the emerging roles of ICTs. Although this review does not attempt to be comprehensive, it hopes to offer some insights into the literature of online social movements, which is spread across a number of disciplines. The review begins with the definition of social movements and introduces prominent theories used to study online social movements. Subsequently, we present an overview of discussions regarding ICTs' influence on social movements. Next, we focus on five uses of ICTs to facilitate social movements: ICTs as resources, ICTs as framing devices, ICTs to support collective identity, ICTs as mobilization tools, and ICTs as spaces for social movements. Then, we discuss the opportunities and threats that online social movements provide, as well as how researchers explicitly theorize ICTs' influence on social movements. Finally, possible future directions are considered.

Social Movements

Sociologists and political scientists have studied the topic of social movements for decades. Various definitions of social movements exist; several of the more relevant are reviewed in this section.

Some authors have emphasized the transformation of a society; others have emphasized networks, collective identity, and mobilization. According to McCarthy and Zald (1977, pp. 1217–1218), a social movement is "a set of opinions and beliefs in a population which represents preferences for changing some elements of the social structure and/or reward distribution of a society." Castells (1997, p. 3) characterized social movements as being "purposive collective actions whose outcome, in victory as in defeat, transforms the values and institutions of society." Porta and Diani (1999, p. 16) defined social movements as "(1) informal networks, based on (2) shared beliefs and solidarity, which mobilize about (3) conflictual issues, through (4) the frequent use of various forms of protests." Diani (2000, p. 387) later refined the definition as "networks of informal relationships between a multiplicity of individuals and organizations, who share a distinctive collective identity, and mobilize resources on conflictual issues."

As these definitions demonstrate, the main goal of social movements is to seek social change and alter the relations of power. Different schools vary in their emphases. For example, theorists of resource mobilization, McCarthy and Zald (1977), take an organizational perspective focusing on factors of organization and resources. New social movement theorists, such as Castells (1997) and Diani (2000), see collective identity, networks, and life values as being crucial to contemporary movements. New social movements differ from traditional ones because they are less concerned with economic issues and emphasize instead group or collective identity, values, and lifestyles.

Because the goal of this review is to explore the relationship between a social movement and ICTs, Diani's (2000) definition of social movements is the most relevant to adopt. As his definition illustrated, computer-mediated communication (CMC) has the potential to influence some primary dimensions of social movements such as the actors (individuals and organizations) and the movement's collective identity, networks, and resources. Diani's definition stresses that within the process of pursuing a new social order, social activists find themselves by constructing their own meaning, which is premised upon the movement's capacity to create communication and connections among its actors.

A number of studies that investigate online social movements apply traditional social movement theories; it is thus useful to discuss these theories here. Although the literature on social movements is vast, contemporary social movement theory can be categorized into four frameworks as Diani (1992), Hess, Breyman, Campbell, and Martin (2008), and Sawyer and Tapia (2007) suggest: resource mobilization theory, frame analysis, political process theory, and new social movement theory.

Resource mobilization theory, as represented by the work of McCarthy and Zald (1977), views social movements as rational and organized activities, unlike earlier work that considered social movements as irrational behaviors (e.g., Olson, 1965). The main concern is to maximize both tangible and intangible resources within social movement organizations. Examples of resources include money, facilities, labor, land, technical expertise, means of communication, legitimacy, organizing and special skills, supporter loyalty, interpersonal ties, solidarity, common awareness, moral commitment, and authority (Freeman, 1979; Gamson, 1990; Jenkins, 1981; McCarthy & Zald, 1977; Tilly, 1978). The focus is on how to run social movement organizations effectively; ICTs can be seen as resources or means to maximize other resources.

Frame analysis examines how social movement organizations facilitate the development of collective cognitive understandings (i.e., collective action frames) to justify their activities and encourage wider participation. Frames enable individuals "to locate, perceive, identify, and label" events within their life space or the world at large (Goffman, 1974, p. 21). Collective action frames have been widely used to examine traditional (face-to-face) social movements. McAdam (1994) argues that collective action frames serve as cultural resources analogous to the material resources deployed by social activists to achieve their goals. Benford and Snow (2000, p. 614) define collective action frames as "action-oriented sets of beliefs and meanings that inspire and legitimate the activities and campaigns of a social movement organization." Their review of the literature on framing processes and social movements indicates that this theoretical framework has been increasingly used over the years in studies of social movements. ICTs can help disseminate frames for social movements so that they can be easily reached by the general public and assist the development of collective identity.

Political process theory argues that the failure or success of social movements depends on political opportunity structures—the broad social, economic, and political dynamics that shape opportunities and constraints for mobilization (Tarrow, 1998; Tilly, 1978). For political process theorists, the organizational perspective of resource mobilization theory is too static and emphasizes formal organization while ignoring network and political opportunity structures. Whereas resource mobilization theory conceptualizes resources internal to social movement organizations, political process theory includes discussions about opportunities and challenges put forth by authorities and political structures, which are external to movements (Tarrow, 1998). McAdam (1996, p. 27) synthesized the political opportunity structure along four main dimensions: "(a) The relative openness or closure of the institutionalized political system; (b) The stability or instability of that broad set of elite alignments that typically under-gird a polity; (c) The presence or absence of elite allies; and (d) The state's capacity and propensity for repression." As an example of elite alignments, the U.S. Supreme Court ruling in *Brown v. Board of Education* and Presidents Kennedy's and Johnson's statements about civil rights positively influenced civil rights movements (Meyer, 2004). When considering ICT use in social movements, even in repressive regimes, governments have limited capacity to control the internet compared to traditional media. This creates opportunities for social movements to take action in the form of cyberhacktivism[1] or cyberactivism (Denning, 2001), as in the "Twitter Revolution" (Berman, 2009, online) following the 2009 Iranian presidential election.

New social movement (NSM) theory advocates the values of identity, equality, direct participation, democracy, plurality, and difference. Melucci (1989) observed that a movement is a way for individuals to act collectively, where people with many different viewpoints and goals work together in a relatively stable fashion. For Melucci (1996, p. 84), contemporary movements arise from the construction of collective identity, an interactive process that addresses "the question of how a collective becomes a collective." NSM is primarily associated with Western European scholars, who developed it in the 1960s as a critique of the limits of resource mobilization theory. Instead of focusing on the traditional social movement of classes, the cultural version of the NSM theory examines collective action based on other identities such as gender, ethnicity, and sexuality. Scholars of the new social movement perspective consider peace, lesbian/gay, feminist, ecological, community, and youth movements to be new social movements that emerged in opposition to growing threats to personal autonomy (Castells, 1997; Cohen, 1985; Melucci, 1985, 1988, 1989; Offe, 1985; Touraine, 1981). ICTs have the potential to provide more opportunities for participation and foster collective identities (Diani, 2000).

These theoretical frameworks are undoubtedly useful in research on online social movements, and a number of studies has applied traditional social movement frameworks to online environments. Studies of online social movements have used resource mobilization (e.g., Clark & Themudo, 2006; Cronauer, 2004; Hara & Estrada, 2005; Hsu, 2003; Huang, 2009; Pudrovska & Ferree, 2004) and new social movement theories (e.g., Hsu, 2003; Huang, 2009; Ma, 2007; Nip, 2004; Pudrovska & Ferree, 2004; Wall, 2007), whereas few studies have used frames (e.g., Clark & Themudo, 2006; Hara & Shachaf, 2008; H. S. Park, 2002; Pudrovska & Ferree, 2004) or political process theory (Clark & Themudo, 2006; Cronauer, 2004; Pickerill, 2001; Pudrovska & Ferree, 2004). Table 10.1 presents a summary of studies and their use of theoretical frameworks. The studies listed

Table 10.1   Summary of studies and their use of theoretical frameworks

Authors	Movement	Theoretical Frameworks
Clark & Themudo (2006)	Anti-globalization movement	Resource mobilization (RM) Framing theory Political process theory
Pickerill (2001)	Environmental movement	Political process theory RM New social movement (NSM)
Pudrovska & Ferree (2004)	Women's movement	Political process theory NSM Framing theory
Riemer (2003)	Social activism (anti-mine)	Framing theory RM
Cheta (2004)	Disability movement	Social constructionist
Cronauer (2004)	Social activism (anti-globalization)	RM Political process theory NSM Framing theory
Hara & Estrada (2005)	Social activism	RM
Hara & Shachaf (2008)	Peace movement	Framing theory
Huang (2009)	Religious movement (Falun Gong)	RM NSM
Hsu (2003)	Broadcasting reform movement	RM NSM
Ma (2007)	Pro-democracy movement	NSM
Nip (2004)	Lesbian movement	NSM
H. S. Park (2002)	Anti-Communication Decency Act of 1999	Framing theory
Wall (2007)	Social activism (anti-WTO)	NSM

demonstrate the types of frameworks that have been used in research on online social movements. The next section discusses perceptions of ICT's influence on social movements.

Researchers use a mixture of social movement theories as frameworks to investigate online social movements. Myers (1994, 2002) specifically pointed out that using resource mobilization and new social movement theories would serve as a solid framework to explore social movements' internet usages:

> Not only can the researchers use data from activists' computers to examine resource mobilization processes, such as attempts to gather and allocate collective resources, plan strategies, and perpetuate the movement, but she or he can also observe processes related to the formation of collective identities and solidarity. (Myers, 2002, p. 125)

Do ICTs Make a Difference in Social Movements?

A series of articles questions whether ICTs make a difference in social movements and, if so, in what ways. These articles can be categorized into three positions: equalization thesis, normalization thesis, and undecided.

Some authors, especially in early literature about online activism (e.g., Arquilla & Ronfeldt, 2001; Castells, Fernandez-Ardevol, Qiu, & Sey, 2007, Danitz & Strobel, 1999; Kahn & Kellner, 2004), support an equalization thesis whose argument is that online tools will distribute power relatively equally, particularly in terms of access to and dissemination of information. In this view, technologies are a significant factor in driving change. For example, Nah, Veenstra, and Shah (2006) examined how news consumption (TV, newspaper, and web) and political discussions affected political participation, both online and face-to-face. Their 2003 study used survey data at a time when the majority of the U.S. population supported the Iraq War. The results indicated that using web news had a positive and significant relationship with political discussions in general and that both face-to-face and online discussions were closely related to political participation. Interestingly, TV news viewing had a significant negative relationship with political participation. In other words, the more people watched TV news, the less likely they were to engage politically. Nah and colleagues (2006) conclude that the internet is a pivotal resource for political participation in the context of anti-war activism.

The utopian vision of a new technology (Kling, 1994) fits with the equalization thesis; the internet improves democracy, offering both internal and external ways for citizens to participate in political decision-making processes. Internally, some applications of the internet could potentially raise civil awareness of political decision-making processes; externally it is possible to provide a channel for citizens to make their voices heard by using online forums or sending email messages. The internet's interactive nature is the feature most expected to expand the role of citizens from passive message consumers to active message creators. In sum, the logic of the equalization thesis is similar to the perspective of technological determinism (Webster, 2006).

On the other hand, according to the *normalization* thesis, the internet has certain limits when it comes to reshaping social movements. This thesis states that online social movements are mere reflections of offline environments and will fail to overcome the existing social structure (Stromer-Galley, 2000). Traditional media are accessible to ordinary people; the influence of the internet, however, depends on its accessibility and the willingness of individuals to search for information on websites (Norris, 2001; van Dijk & Hacker, 2003). Some scholars argue that information inequalities exist in digital communication. Castells (1999, p. 403) notes that "the information age does not have to be the age of stepped-up inequality, polarization and social exclusion. But for the moment it is." Although cost is a concern when purchasing equipment, researchers have observed that online participation does not depend solely on the availability of cheap computer equipment. Kling (1999) warned users that the actual purchase price of a computer includes the price of software, maintenance, peripherals, and in institutional settings, training, planning, and administration are also part of the total cost of ownership. In addition to the affordability of access to computer networks, other factors influence information inequality, such as differences in knowledge and skills in using computers, attitudes toward using them, training, gender, income, race/ethnicity, age, location, governmental controls or limited use of the internet (Fox, 2004; National Telecommunications and Information Administration, 2000a, 2000b, 2002, 2007; Rainie, Reddy, & Bell, 2004; Spender, 1995; Spooner, 2003; Warschauer, 2002).

Finally, there is a position that does not answer yes or no to the question of whether ICTs make a difference. The social informatics approach serves as a needed corrective and an antidote to naive technological determinism. Although not denying that technologies have social effects, the focus, rather, is on the social forces that give rise to particular uses of technologies that follow existing social hierarchies (Kling, Rosenbaum, & Sawyer, 2005; Shirky, 2008). In addition, some early studies of online social movements (e.g., Zelwietro, 1998) concluded that the penetration rate of the internet was not high enough to make claims about effects. Zelwietro examined four environmental organizations that used the internet to support their activities. Although he found some differences between online and offline groups, he concluded that further investigation was necessary because the internet had not been adopted widely enough.

Thus, the internet alone can hardly create a new social order. For example, based on an historical analysis, Garrett and Edwards (2007) went beyond the cliché that the internet made an impact on the South African anti-apartheid movement. They noted that previous research on online social movements tended to take a technologically determinist perspective and presented an analysis that incorporated interactions among users, organizations, and the internet. The consideration of social processes surrounding the internet should include much more than one-sided generalizations. This is the general premise on which the current chapter is based.

Although there is some dissent, many scholars agree that ICTs do influence social movements to some extent. In the next section, we discuss how ICTs facilitate or impede social movements.

How Do ICTs Facilitate or Impede Social Movements?

We categorize ICTs for social movements into the following five uses: ICTs as resources, ICTs to support collective identity, ICTs as framing devices, ICTs as mobilization tools, and ICTs as spaces. The first four categories are manifested in the literature and based on the major social movement theories—ICTs as resources (resource mobilization); as framing devices (framing theory); as collective identity support (new social movement theory); and as mobilization tools (resource mobilization, new social movement theory, political process theory). The last category is about social movements that exist solely online. In other words, ICTs provide spaces in which social activists can assemble for communication, interaction, and goal-oriented action.

ICTs as Resources

Resource mobilization theory pays attention to tangible resources, such as labor, money, and means of communication, as well as intangible resources, such as interpersonal ties, solidarity, and moral engagement, that social movement organizations are capable of mobilizing (McCarthy & Zald, 1977; Porta & Diani, 1999). Furthermore, as Hess and colleagues (2008, p. 474) noted, "science and technology are viewed as one of many potential resources that a movement can access." Thus, ICTs can be seen as resources or means to capitalize on other resources such as money, time, and materials.

First, as resources, ICTs allow social movement organizations to have control and legitimacy over content disseminated through the internet (Garrett, 2006). Almeida and Lichbach (2003) examined the reporting of worldwide protests for the World Trade Organization (WTO) and found that activists' own websites had the most accumulative reporting of the protest events. Even international news organizations did not report extensively on the protest events. This is attributed in part to the fact that news organizations tend to cover sensational (e.g., violent and large) protests more than civil and peaceful protests (Oliver & Maney, 2000). Almeida and Lichbach's (2003) study illustrated how the internet offered alternative means for activist organizations to disseminate information without relying on mass media, because the reporting in traditional mass media is predisposed to certain perspectives (Lievrouw, 2006; Webster, 2006).

Second, ICTs have been used to capitalize on resources for social movements. Hara and Estrada (2005, p. 507) identified four types of virtual resources: "knowledge, credibility (access to credible information), interpersonal interactions (sociability), and identity support (validation of personal identity and group identity)" and analyzed how the internet may support grassroots organizations in mobilization. They studied an online grassroots activist group called MoveOn.org and discussed how the organization took advantage of the internet. MoveOn.org utilized the internet to disseminate information about the issues, as well as ways to involve supporters in activities. In addition, they contended, online discussion forums were used to facilitate interpersonal interactions, and as a result, a sense of community was fostered through continuous communication.

Internet use has been considered a cost-effective medium for many activist groups that do not have sufficient financial resources for their political actions (Leizerov, 2000). Scholars (Cronauer, 2004; Kobrin, 1998) note the potential for internet technology to reduce and shift the resources necessary for online and offline mobilization. Thus, internet use can maximize "money" (or other forms of capital) that makes a movement viable. In Porter's (2003) study of the Falun Gong religious movement, some interviewees noted that the internet was crucial to the movement, especially because of the low cost of access and use. Similarly, Carty (2002) emphasized that inexpensive internet access made it possible for the anti-Nike campaign's activists to disseminate information and coordinate activities across the world, which is important for grassroots movements operating with limited budgets.

Regarding financial advantages, the internet provides a means to raise funds for campaigns. An anti-mine campaign in Crandon, Wisconsin, provides an example (Riemer, 2003). A website, Nashville Under Siege, was created to support the town of Nashville, where a portion of the Crandon mine was to be located. The website helped the town gain financial support from external parties as it publicized its cause. Support of the Free Tibet movement provides another example of online fund-raising. One of the more prominent sites to support Tibetan independence, the Tibet Fund (www.tibetfund.org), was developed to finance pro-Tibetan activities. This fund-raising website provides detailed information to potential donors about how the funds will be used; a mechanism for making a contribution online is available on the website (Chase & Mulvenon, 2002).

ICTs as Framing Devices

Another use of ICTs for social movements is to help shape the "collective action frame" by supporting movements in framing their activities to promote participation by the general public (Benford & Snow, 2000,

p. 612). Oliver and Johnston's (2000) characteristics of frame analysis suggest a way to focus on the representations of frames to understand how ICTs are utilized. Oliver and Johnston defined frames in terms of how individuals perceive phenomena as "individual cognitive structures" (p. 41). Although individually developed, frames have the potential to grow into resonated entities when united and eventually to become collective frames. These become pivotal elements in supporting collective action and can be observed by examining representations of frames. For example, peace movement websites are snapshots of representations of collective action frames (Hara & Shachaf, 2008). Although frames can be analyzed as a snapshot of a stable cognitive framework, some studies have examined processes of developing frames (e.g., see the discussion of the frame alight process examined by Snow, Rochford, Worden, & Benford, 1986).

Collective action frames do not emerge spontaneously, but rather require processes of integration whereby individual frames of a movement are organized into a coherent and collective frame. Such integration enables collective action. Snow and colleagues (1986, p. 464) explained "frame alignment processes" as the processes necessary to link individual interpretations of a movement to the frame provided by social movement organizations. They further elaborate and explain four types of frame alignment processes: frame bridging, frame amplification, frame extension, and frame transformation. Snow and colleagues (1986, p. 467) described frame bridging as making a link between "two or more ideologically congruent but structurally unconnected frames regarding a particular issue or problem," which is primarily executed by disseminating information through social networks, mass media, and other means. Frame amplification refers to strengthening a frame that supports a certain issue. Frame extension describes efforts to expand an existing frame to increase the number of supporters and participants. Finally, frame transformation occurs when the original framing is a misfit, which requires social movement organizations to readjust their frames. Snow and colleagues' frame alignment process is useful when analyzing the use of the internet as a communication tool for social movements.

H. S. Park's (2002) case study of the Electronic Frontier Foundation's online campaign was one of the first to demonstrate that the frame alignment process conceptualized in traditional social movements was applicable to online social movements. Although the entire framing alignment processes can be facilitated through ICTs, frame bridging is best facilitated through new technologies according to Snow and colleagues (1986). This is attributed to the fact that these technologies allow social movement organizations to promote their own agendas. Like other researchers (e.g., Kahn & Kellner, 2004; H. S. Park, 2002), Hara and Estrada (2005) have shown how ICTs, such as email, websites, and blogs, have helped mobilize not only hardcore activists, but also socially conscious lay people. In the past, social movement organizations had limited means to promote their activities and ideologies, relying for the most part on the news media. The framing of social movements' activities by the news media was sometimes inconsistent with the organizations' framing (e.g., Gamson, Croteau, Hoynes, & Sasson, 1992).

Similarly, Owens and Palmer (2003) examined the successful use of web communication by anarchists during the 1999 protests against the WTO. Although they found that activists had a tight network presence online prior to 1999, the network was not strongly connected outside of its own organization, especially to mainstream networks. After a radical anarchist group, Black Bloc, used violence for the protests, their activities triggered negative news coverage. Soon after, a website called Infoshop not only covered some stories about the WTO protests but also explained and justified Black Bloc's activities. For the protests against the International Monetary Fund/World Bank in Washington DC, Infoshop posted Black Bloc's intentions before the events and recruited participants. The website attracted many visitors. Owens and Palmer contend that the availability of the anarchists' perspective online caused the news coverage to become more favorable. In this sense, the anarchists were able to frame their activities by using websites. With the use of ICTs, organizations now have a more effective way to reach the general public and better frame their message.

Framing could be a useful strategy to provide a rhetoric of identity for recruiting new participants and to reinforce solidarity among members of social movements (Polletta & Jasper, 2001). Hunt, Benford, and Snow (1994) also made connections between framing and identity construction processes. Similar to frames, collective identity provides a framework to "make sense of the social world" (Polletta & Jasper, 2001, p. 298). How ICTs are used to foster collective identity and solidarity is discussed in the next section.

ICTs to Support Collective Identity and Solidarity

Social movement theorists classify identity as follows: "individual identity, collective identity, and public identity" (Laraña, Johnston, & Gusfield, 1994, pp. 11–12). Individual identity consists of "wholly personal traits that … are internalized and imported to social movement participation as idiosyncratic biographies" (p. 15). Collective identity consists of the "agreed upon definition of membership, boundaries, and activities for the group" (p. 15). Public identity "captures the influence that the external public has on the way social movement adherents think about themselves" (p. 18).

Among those identities, collective identity is most discussed by social movement scholars because it "goes to the core of social movement formation" and is a driving force for movement participation (Stryker, Owens, & White, 2000, p. 18). Scholars have argued for the importance of understanding collective identity in the study of social movements. As discussed previously, collective identity is a core concept of NSMs.

Melucci (1989) conjectured that all social movements have an identity dimension; collective identity is represented in the movement and the movement is a process within which collective identity finds realization. Melucci (1995, p. 48) stated that people take action for "the possibility of recognizing themselves and being recognized as subjects of their action."

Collective identity is an important outcome of social movement mobilization because, according to Peteet (2000, p. 184), "the very form of identity used as a mobilizing frame can be transformed during the course of social movement participation." In addition, identity helps to define the realms of action and possibility. Melucci (1995, p. 43) states that "individuals acting collectively ... define in cognitive terms the field of possibilities and limits they perceive while at the same time activating their relationships so as to give sense to their 'being together' and to the goals they pursue."

The internet could be considered a useful tool to support processes of collective identity construction (Jones, 1998; Miller & Slater, 2000; Nakamura, 2002; Smith & Kollock, 1999) but some studies (e.g., Cronauer, 2004; Nip, 2004; Wall, 2007) did not find that the internet successfully or fully supported the development of collective identity. E. Park (2002, p. 19), who takes the former position, observed: "The formation of collective identity is easier due to the internet's ability to put people with similar grievances in disparate geographical area[s] [together] ... also the diffusion of collective identity is faster and easier."

Through communication, a collective identity can be fostered to mobilize participants for social movements. CMC may also have the potential to help cross-movement (e.g., anti-Iraq War movement [Gillan, 2009]; global anti-mine campaign [Riemer, 2003]) or cross-culture interaction, enabling the sharing of ideas and perhaps fostering feelings of solidarity. Electronic communication can act as a new means by which like-minded individuals are able to connect to each other, help form a united consciousness, and mobilize participation around a specific issue (Schwartz, 1998).

Research in internet use by contemporary social movements demonstrates that the internet has the capability to foster construction of collective identity and solidarity among movement members. For example, in 1999 three privacy advocacy groups launched an online protest to fight Intel's intention to include a processor serial number (PSN) in the Pentium III processor that would enable websites to verify a user's identity (Leizerov, 2000). In response, privacy advocacy groups developed a website (www.bigbrotherinside.org) to present relevant information for the campaign and provide links to many sympathetic international news articles, as well as coordinate the public actions of these privacy advocates. The privacy advocacy groups successfully forced Intel to stop using the PSN in Pentium III processors in 2000. Leizerov (2000, p. 476) posited that "the combination of similar demographics, heightened political awareness, and the pursuit of a common value shared by the group (privacy, for instance) clearly identifies such individuals as a group even if in an online campaign those individuals are usually unaware of one another." This case shows that the internet can facilitate the formation of collective identity.

As far as Taylor and Whittier's (1992) three components of collective identity (a sense of "we," a consciousness, an oppositional culture) are concerned, participants in the anti-Intel campaign clearly demonstrated that they shared a common consciousness about their goal (intent to protect privacy) and had an oppositional culture in terms of fighting against Intel. In spite of Leizerov's position, there is no clear evidence to judge whether the individuals shared a sense of "we" or solidarity in the anti-Intel protest. Nonetheless, the sense of being a group may be indicated, broadly by the participants' pursuit of a common value—privacy.

For instance, a sense of solidarity is evident in the anti-Nike campaign. This campaign against sweatshops has received much attention and several studies have investigated its characteristics. The campaign began when MIT graduate student Jonah Peretti ordered personalized shoes labeled with the word "sweatshop" through the Nike Corporation (McCaughey & Ayers, 2003). The request was denied and email exchanges between Peretti and Nike were widely circulated online. Micheletti, Stolle, Nishikawa, and Wright (2004) analyzed online messages that expressed support for the anti-Nike protest. The study found the capability for building the sense of "we," or solidarity, in these online messages. This is one of the collective identity components Taylor and Whittier (1992) proposed. In addition, Carty (2002, p. 134) discussed "globalized identity politics" in her case study of the anti-Nike campaign. The internet was used to link geographically dispersed, multi-identity groups that formed a singular globalized identity under the label of "working group on Nike" (p. 134). Similarly, Micheletti and colleagues (2004) found that identity is naturally constructed in an invisible discourse space. The users identified Nike as "you," the oppressed worker as "they" and the consumer as "we." Furthermore, Bullert (2000) argued that in the anti-Nike campaign, without the internet and email to transmit information across national boundaries and access to receive the information, it would have been impossible to create the sense of "we."

One way of producing a feeling of solidarity is to use verbal encouragement. Thus, the text-based internet serves as an ideal medium for exchanging inspiring words. For example, a worker in Indonesia posted a letter on the United Students Against Sweatshops listserv to support the striking workers in Mexico (both produced goods for Nike). Indonesian workers provided encouragement by stating that "after eight years of strikes, Indonesian workers successfully attained the right to form an independent union that has resulted in a number of additional benefits" (Carty, 2002, pp. 137–138). Moreover, the listserv was used to coordinate "National Days of Action" on two occasions, which also served as acts of solidarity in support of the workers' needs (p. 138).

In Pickerill's (2001) environmental social movement study, activists used CMC to boost morale and solidarity by communicating with other activists who showed support or were involved in environmental activism. Interviewees from Green Student Network, Friends of the Earth UK, Lyminge Forest, and McSpotlight agree that internet use may inspire activists. Similarly, the fostering of feelings of solidarity frequently occurs in women's movements online (e.g., Kennedy, 2000; Onosaka, 2003; Pini, Brown, & Previte, 2004).

Nip (2004) studied the identity-building capacity of the internet in a lesbian movement by examining the Queer Sisters bulletin board. His study showed examples of solidarity and a less successful example regarding the internet's capability to foster collective identity. Nip investigated the three elements of collective identity in social movements conceptualized by Taylor and Whittier (1992): a sense of "we," a consciousness, and an oppositional culture. The participants' internet use successfully led to a sense of "we" and an oppositional culture. However, the data failed to show collective consciousness among participants.

Nip (2004) argued that the absence of a collective consciousness among participants related to the bulletin board's lack of resources and organizational goals: The bulletin board became a service platform rather than a tool for cultivating consciousness. In a similar vein, Cronauer (2004) lent support to Nip's analysis in her examination of two email lists. She found that a list was not an effective tool for building collective identity, although collective identity is crucial to collective action. Online hostilities, anonymous postings, and preferences for face-to-face contact were cited as reasons for this failure.

Wall (2007) also demonstrated that the internet does not necessarily facilitate collective identity development. Based on a study of three email lists that supported the Seattle World Trade Organization (WTO) protests, Wall concluded that these email lists had diverse ways of communicating collective identities; although all three were opposing WTO, some were more successful than the others. All three were not particularly effective in supporting articulation of collective identities.

Although some cases (e.g., Cronauer, 2004; Nip, 2004; Wall, 2007) revealed that social movements had limited success in using the internet for the formation of collective identity and solidarity due to negative postings, different preferences of internet uses, and a weak organizational capability, the internet still forges a certain level of collective identity among social movement activists and assists movement activities. To sum up, the internet is acknowledged by various scholars (e.g., Carty, 2002; Diani, 2000; Huang, 2009; Leizerov, 2000; Ma, 2007; Micheletti et al., 2004; Pickerill, 2001) as an effective tool for fostering collective identity and solidarity. Most empirical studies illustrate that the internet, especially the use of the text-based tools in which it is easy for groups' members to express their verbal encouragement to movement participants, aids in the formation of these two elements.

Constructed collective identity and solidarity increase the possibility of success for social movements.

ICTs as Mobilization Tools

According to Tilly (1978, p. 69), "mobilization is the process by which a group goes from being a passive collection of individuals to an active participant in public life." Klandermans (1984, p. 586) identified two different processes. First, *consensus mobilization* refers to "a process through which a social movement tries to obtain support for its viewpoints. Consensus mobilization bears resemblance to the spread of generalized belief." Secondly, *action mobilization* is a process of motivating people to participate (Klandermans, 1984). Marden (1978) and Klandermans (2004) both caution that consensus mobilization does not necessarily lead to action mobilization, but action mobilization cannot occur without consensus mobilization.

Mobilization intertwines with matters such as the effectiveness of communication, the influence of social networks, barriers, and the perceived costs and benefits of participation, all of which are affected by the use of the internet. The technology affordances provided by the web not only offer information about campaigns, but also allow social movement organizations to coordinate their efforts online (Diani, 2000). For example, the internet allows social movement activists to take direct control of mobilizing media (e.g., Almeida & Lichbach, 2003). More importantly, technologies such as email, blogs, wikis, and websites allow organizers of online movements to combine the advantages of one-to-one and communication media. A key feature of the internet is its ability to reach a number of diverse groups quickly, affordably, and at the same time. The internet also offers the possibility for people to reply to social activists, responding with email that includes questions, elaborations, and personal contributions.

Cronauer (2004) examined two email lists used by activists to oppose globalization summits, using the concepts of consensus mobilization and action mobilization to investigate how effective the lists were for mobilizing subscribers. The findings indicate that neither list posted much information about group views, aims, or tactics unless the subscribers had personal contact with other anti-globalization activists. Hence, list subscribers could not learn much about the groups if they were not involved in offline activities. The results further revealed that in the case of consensus mobilization, the most mobilized, most supportive subscribers to both lists were those who had extensive personal contact with other activists for similar causes. These results illustrate how important established social movement actors are in creating consensus mobilization.

However, sometimes ICTs do not necessarily assist mobilization, especially action mobilization. Cronauer (2004) found that the majority of online participants were not involved in the offline organizing of groups and did not attend events the groups organized. In both lists, female participants appeared to be the least facilitated because they did not have much personal contact with other subscribers and were turned away by negative movement dynamics (e.g., hostile messages and agnostic debate). Participants who had prior experience with activism and knew other participants from past activities were most likely to be mobilized into action.

Perhaps one of the best known mobilizations on the internet was the anti-Multilateral Agreement on Investment (MAI) campaign. The agreement was a draft international treaty sponsored by the Organisation for Economic Co-operation and Development (OECD), comprised of 29 wealthy nations. The MAI's objective was to promote greater trade liberalization in investments among its members. In February 1997, an early draft of the agreement was leaked to *Public Citizen* and posted on the web. As a result, 600 organizations in 70 countries, including Amnesty International, AFL–CIO, Sierra Club, the Malaysia-based Third World Network, United Steelworkers of America, and Western Governors' Association, began to express strong opposition to the treaty (Kobrin, 1998). The MAI was criticized for promoting corporate power at the expense of national sovereignty, the environment, and labor rights. The anti-MAI protest lasted until the negotiations were canceled in October 1998.

Assisted by the internet, the anti-MAI activists were able to launch a successful trans-national protest. Warkentin and Mingst (2000) also emphasize the importance of the internet to anti-MAI campaigns. They found that information and analysis about MAI, produced by protesting non-government organizations, was linked via their websites. Deibert (2000) found that the internet was used in three distinct ways by the anti-MAI activists: (1) publicizing, sharing, and distributing information; (2) binding together individuals and organizations around the world participating in the protest; and (3) contributing to influence politicians and decision makers.

The anti-MAI campaign illustrated that the internet helped activist groups influence global policy making. It also showed how collaborative mobilization can happen with simple email lists and websites—especially how one key document posted on the internet made a significant impact on mobilization.

The internet can also be used as a mobilizing tool to raise public awareness, as demonstrated by the Canadian Women's Internet Association, which campaigned to raise public awareness about violence against women. In November 1996, the campaign began with a website (www.mistress-of-my-domain.com/candle/candle.html) and a striking image of a glowing candle that could be taken by people to their own webpages and used as a link back to the Vigil website to create "The Annual Candlelight Vigil Across the Internet." The campaign lasted ten days and marked the anniversary of the deaths of 14 female engineering students at Montreal's Ecole Polytechnique in 1989. During the ten days, approximately 12,000 people visited the webpage from fifty countries. The site received over 500 email messages (Sayers, 1998).

The power of the internet to aid social movement mobilization was also illustrated by the case of Falun Gong practitioners' organized protest against the Chinese Communist Party. On April 25, 1999, Falun Gong practitioners from various provinces assembled in front of a Chinese Communist Party leadership compound, participated in a peaceful protest against state repression of their activities, and asked for freedom of religious belief. Falun Gong supporters communicated with each other via email, mobile phones, and face-to-face contact in order to spread word of the massive demonstration quickly (Hurley & Charleton, 2005; Lin, 2001; Yu, 2004).

On a smaller scale, some social networking sites, such as Facebook and MySpace, facilitate collective action (e.g., Gueorguieva, 2008). Collective action describes the joint activity of a group of individuals to pursue the public good through voting, lobbying, or demonstrating, which occurs on different social bases (class, ethnic group, or gender), and is oriented toward achieving a variety of goals (e.g., material resources, new laws, or new positions) (Hechter, Friedman, & Appelbaum, 1982).

Gueorguieva (2008) discussed the influence of MySpace and YouTube on the 2006 U.S. midterm election. In addition to using these online tools for capitalizing on resources, such as fund raising and information dissemination, Gueorguieva showed that they were also used for consensus mobilization. For example, less well known candidates were able to reach out to voters due to the relatively low cost associated with YouTube; and citizens circulated inappropriate comments by politicians through YouTube—as in the case of Republican Senator George Allen who used a "racial slur" (p. 292) during a campaign appearance.

In addition to political campaigns, Nisbet and Kotcher (2009) discussed the use of social networking sites to facilitate climate change campaigns. They examined an attempt to work through online opinion leaders to recruit ten million activists to support activities. A Facebook application was launched to recruit supporters and raise money, although this initiative resulted in rather disappointing outcomes. Nisbet and Kotcher identified noteworthy disadvantages of using online media to recruit opinion leaders.

The internet could help social movements expand (Kobrin, 1998), reach the general public to support consensus mobilization (Sayers, 1998), and assist action mobilization, although action mobilization probably is the most difficult, as noted earlier (Cronauer, 2004; Nisbet & Kotcher, in press).

ICTs as Spaces

ICTs have provided spaces for social movements to exist and undertake their activities. For example, Denning (1999, 2001) identified three broad categories of online activism: cyberactivism, cyberhacktivism, and cyberterrorism. Online activism usually is non-disruptive and legal and focuses on coordination, information transmission, and communication (McCaughey & Ayers, 2003; Vegh, 2003). The aforementioned example of the anti-Nike campaign (e.g., Kidd, 2003) took place entirely online. Similarly, some users of MyBO (an internet platform for candidate Obama) voiced dissent on its social networking tools (Kreiss, 2009). "During the summer of 2008 activists created a MyBO group called 'Get FISA Right' (Foreign Intelligence Surveillance Act)" (Kreiss, 2009, p. 16) to oppose Obama's changing position on warrantless surveillance. This attracted over 15,000 members as a result of publicity on blogs, Facebook, and other media. Although Obama did not change his position on the bill, he issued a statement to the group to clarify his position.

Hacktivism's main goal is to be disruptive, but usually not damaging, and may or may not be illegal. Hacktivism is a term created by the fusion of "hacking" and "activism." Neeley (2000, p. 30) believes that "hacktivists are a special breed of hackers and crackers who attempt to call attention to an issue with a virtual call to arms using intrusion ... or creating technology to advance a political or social cause." A well-known and widely cited web sit-in was the pro-Zapatista movement's use of the Electronic Disturbance Theater (EDT). After the 1997 massacre of indigenous Mexicans in the city of Chiapas, the EDT (a U.S.-based group comprised of four activists) determined to take action and draw attention to the struggles of the Mexican Zapatistas through the practice of "electronic civil disobedience," a phrase coined by Critical Art Ensemble (CAE) (Meikle, 2002, p. 25). The EDT developed a software program, FloodNet, which is a web-based Java applet that repeatedly sends browser reload commands. Their technical activism aimed to flood the websites of Mexican and U.S. governments and financial institutions in Mexico City until the overload shut down the servers. Its larger purpose was to produce a "simulated threat" (Wray, 2000, p. 442), drawing attention to the Zapatista cause.

Collin (1997, p. 15) coined the term "Cyberterrorism." In contrast to hacktivism, cyberterrorism involves more aggressive action rather than a simple attempt to call attention to a cause. The term refers to an act, or acts, of terrorism carried out through the use of computing technology. For example, several Estonian websites were attacked by (presumed) Russian hackers in May, 2007. Users experienced a flood of distributed denial of service attacks, which forced many government, media, and banking websites to close down (Bloomfield, 2007).

These three types of online activism use ICTs as spaces for their existence. In the next section, we show how ICTs can provide opportunities and/or threats to online social movements.

Opportunities and Threats to Online Social Movements

As discussed in the previous section, ICTs offer various means to support or constrain social movements. By adopting ICTs, social movements gain new opportunities, such as wider dissemination of information at lower cost, while having to deal with some threats, such as surveillance. Garrett's (2006) outstanding literature review on social movements synthesized how ICTs facilitate mobilization in three ways. First, as many scholars assert, ICTs help reduce the cost of distributing information, as well as the cost of participation. ICTs offer an inexpensive means to disseminate information via activist organizations' websites (Almeida & Lichbach, 2003), Indymedia.org (Kidd, 2003; Lievrouw, 2006), and the blogosphere (Kahn & Kellner, 2004) without filtering. Second, Garrett (2006) identified the promotion of collective identity and the idea that participants are a part of larger community concerns as advantages of ICTs. This collective identity becomes a driving force to mobilize participants for collective action. Third, intertwined with the promotion of collective identity, Garrett (citing Diani, 2000) mentioned that ICTs foster community development: "new ICTs provide the largely passive support base with a low-intensity forum for issue-based communication" (Garrett, 2006, p. 206).

Although the internet can provide opportunities such as these, a few social movement researchers caution against undue optimism. Balka (1993) and Cronauer (2004) have shown that anonymous messages result in antagonistic behavior and uncomfortable feelings when posted to the lists and questioned the reliability of previously posted messages. Others are skeptical about the development of stable and long-lasting movements in the future. McAdam, Tilly, and Tarrow (1996) point out that the improved capacity for transnational communication will not automatically lead to global social movements. They believe that new virtual contacts on the internet cannot substitute for meaningful social networks. Etzioni and Etzioni (1999) are also skeptical about virtual contacts being equal to in-person contacts. In addition, Pini and colleagues' (2004) study indicates that face-to-face contact is more powerful and effective than e-lobbying in working with politicians. In a study of six environmental groups, Pickerill (2001) found that online lobbying was not very effective.

Diani (2000) contends that virtual interactions may be unable to construct permanent relations due to the lack of trust, and that surveillance or censorship may worsen mutual trust between internet users. The threat of surveillance may decrease internet users' motivation to participate online or even seek out online information (Cronauer, 2004). This concern is more common in non-democratic countries such as Burma (Danitz & Strobel, 1999) or China. According to Yang (2003), protest in China is less likely because of state sanctions, as witnessed in the Tiananmen Square massacre (Zuo & Benford, 1995).

Another possible limitation of online social movements is that, although it is relatively easy to have online discussions about issues, taking action, especially offline, requires effort. Byrne (2007) examined the potential for using a black social networking site (SNS) to assist political mobilization. The study found that, although participants in the black SNS engaged in discussions about racially relevant issues, the discussions (e.g., serious concerns about Hurricane Katrina) did not lead to action. Byrne contends that using online communities to build a foundation for civic engagement requires a specifically articulated purpose for mobilization. In fact, this finding was similar to Nip's (2004) earlier study of the Queer Sisters bulletin board—discussion does not necessarily lead to political action.

Another problem with media such as SNSs for mobilization is that people tend to self-select the sources from which they receive information (Gueorguieva, 2008). Although a wide range of choices is available through the internet and satellite television, this does not necessarily mean that people are exposed to diverse perspectives. On the contrary, they have channeled themselves into a narrow set of self-selected views (Sunstein, 2009). As Castells (2000, p. 370, original emphasis) stated eloquently, "while the media have become globally interconnected, and programs and messages circulate in the global network, *we are now living in a global village, but in customized cottages globally produced and locally distributed.*" While acknowledging the opportunities that ICTs offer, the concerns raised by social movement researchers may temper utopianism and help develop more effective applications of ICTs in support of social change.

Emerging Theories of Online Social Movements

So far, we have dealt with online social movements within the framework of traditional social movement theories. Although the traditional theories provide useful perspectives, they do not address specifically how ICTs have an impact on social movements. In the realm of science and technology studies, Callon (e.g., 1986), Law (e.g., 1987), and Latour (e.g., 1987, p. 84), changed the way we perceive the impact of "actants," including ICTs, by explicitly conceptualizing non-human actants. In a similar vein, some scholars have identified novel characteristics of internet-enabled social movements and proposed promising theoretical frameworks to investigate such phenomena.

Edwards (2004), for example, examined how the internet supports organizational infrastructure in the context of the Dutch women's movement. He proposed a model illustrating that internet use can be explained by the interaction of three factors within the context of a given political opportunity structure: the first of these, organizational characteristics, includes: (a) the goal orientation of the organization, (b) the function that the organization wants to achieve within the movement, and (c) the internal structure of the organization. Based on these three characteristics, an organization decides to use appropriate actions (including ICT use) to achieve its goals. His second factor, availability of resources, refers to the low costs of building a website, which then has further uses such as providing rich content related to movements. The third factor, the organization's perceptions of opportunities of the internet, refers to the range of potential internet uses to facilitate the functioning of the organization. Edwards's model shows how organizations develop their uses of the internet based on these three criteria. He argues that internet usage is expected to have an impact on three dimensions within social movements.

Huang (2009) extended Edwards's conceptual scheme by incorporating additional elements to be considered for internet-enabled social movements. Her framework in a study of a religious movement illustrated that internet use can be explained by the interaction of five factors: organizational characteristics, repertoires of online activism, the formation of collective identity, perception of political opportunities, and perception of available internet resources. Internet usage may influence a movement's capability to deal with actors (individuals and virtual organizations), networks, collective identity/solidarity, resources, mobilization, and opportunities offered by the internet. Both Edwards's and Huang's models were based on traditional social movement theories but emphasized the roles of ICTs in the frameworks.

In contrast to these scholars who use existing social movement theories with an emphasis on the roles of ICT, Bennett (2003) suggests that the internet can be beneficial to resource-poor organizations that do not traditionally have access to mass media outlets. He further observes that a characteristic of online activism is ideological thinness—the low threshold to engagement in any specific form of online activism means more opportunities to join multiple organizations. For example, membership in ICT-driven collective actions is unlike traditional membership with dues; it tends to be less committed and more flexible (Chadwick, 2007). To be a part of an activist movement, all one has to do is register with an email address. This creates a situation in which an individual's commitment to specific activism may be weak due to multiple commitments to different causes, but the experiences that individuals gain from various activities may be enriched because they can participate in a range of actions.

Bennett and Toft (2009) argue that we need to examine narrative processes separately from frames and framing; and that by investigating how narratives spread and develop, we can focus on how personal networks are formed and how narratives travel through such networks. Through the use of ICTs, including social networking tools, "the idea of narratives as networking devices offers a useful mechanism for understanding how individuals and organizations actually construct social ties" (Bennett & Toft, 2009, p. 259). Again, their conceptualization explicitly includes the effect of ICTs.

Similarly, Bimber, Flanagin, and Stohl (2005) contend that the traditional theory of collective action needs to be reexamined in a context where ICTs play a major role. First, they argue that the classic dilemma of public goods and free riding needs to be reconsidered in the context of ICT-facilitated collective action. The successful growth of Wikipedia (Nov, 2007) is an example. In other words, due to the massive participation of users, free riding is no longer an issue (Anthony, Smith, & Williamson, 2009). This is a departure from traditional social movement theories. Second, they point out how the grassroots nature of ICTs (including email, instant messaging, and websites) can be useful for mobilizing collective action. One of their compelling arguments is to conceptualize collective action as a boundary crossing from "a private domain of interest and action to a public one" (Bimber et al., 2005, p. 377). To be more precise, ICTs can help bridge public and private spheres much more fluidly than could be done when ICTs were not readily available. Bimber and colleagues used the blogosphere as an example to illustrate the blurring of public and private spaces, noting that many blogs publish personal journals in public space. Individuals can easily express support for or opposition to a specific movement on the internet. The porous nature of boundaries is one of the differences of ICT-facilitated collective action from traditional modes. This conceptualization is a first step toward examining collective action facilitated by ICTs.

Hara (2008) examined Bimber and colleagues' (2005) theorization that the internet makes boundary crossings less demanding. She studied an online grassroots activist group, MoveOn.org, and examined members whose activity levels differed (a passive online participant; active online participants; and active offline participants). This group used a hybrid of online and offline mobilization to achieve social change. The study found Bimber and colleagues' conceptualization applicable to MoveOn members who are either passive or active online without offline participation. However, MoveOn members who are active offline bear a resemblance to traditional social movement participants. This case study highlights the fact that ICT-facilitated collective actions not only take place online, but also are undertaken offline. Thus, we ought to better conceptualize the hybrid nature of offline collective action facilitated through online activities.

Instead of treating ICT-driven social movements as a different species, Garrett and Edwards's (2007) historical analysis of the antiapartheid movement in South Africa presented a more complex and holistic picture of ICTs embedded in context. They identified four factors that interplay between ICTs and social movements: ongoing technological innovation, user practices, technical competence, and organizational routines. These factors match the three levels proposed by Mantovani (1996) to describe the levels at which actors interact with the environment. The first level represents social context where we produce and comply with social norms. The second level depicts how we interpret situations in everyday life. The third level is about how we interact with environments through artifacts. Garrett and Edwards (2007) and Mantovani (1996) caution that we fail to understand the complexity of the phenomenon by not recognizing the interactions of factors and levels. Finally, Garrett and Edwards emphasize the contextual nature of ICT use in social movements and the importance of socio-technical analysis.

Another notable development is a framework called "computerization movements" (Iacono & Kling, 2001, p. 93; Kling & Iacono, 1994). Computerization movements are "a kind of movement whose advocates focus on computer-based systems as instruments to bring about a new social order" (Kling & Iacono, 1994, online). The focus is specific social movements that are driven by core technologies (see Elliott & Kramer [2008] and Hara & Rosenbaum [2008] for more discussion on the topic). One of the useful ideas in computerization movements is *technological action frames*, which is based on the concept of *technological frames* drawn from the field of science and technology studies (e.g., Bijker, 2001). "Technological frames" elucidates the idea that different social groups perceive a given technology differently. People's beliefs about technologies drive or impede computerization movements. Computerization movements are specifically social movements motivated by technologies.

Although pure online social movements (in which all the activities take place online) may have distinct characteristics, we need to examine online social movements carefully and consider the possibility of hybrid (online and offline) social movements. One type of ICT, the internet, certainly assists social movements in various ways, by capitalizing resources, accelerating coordination for mobilization, and sometimes fostering collective identity among members of the movement. Nevertheless, some hybrid social movements are not radically different from offline social movements at present. This is in line with the social informatics notion that ICTs do not bring about radical social change and that "there are usually important continuities in social life in addition to the discontinuities" (Kling et al., 2005, p. 28).

Future Directions and Conclusions

Many interesting cases examining ICTs' roles in mobilizing grassroots activities have emerged in recent years, but research in this area appears to be still in its infancy, primarily focusing on a limited number of case studies, such as the anti-WTO movement (e.g., Kahn & Kellner, 2004), Zapatista movement (e.g., Arquilla & Ronfeldt, 2001), Indymedia (e.g., Kidd, 2003; Pickard, 2006; Pickerill, 2007), and anti-Nike campaigns (e.g., Carty, 2002; Micheletti et al., 2004). To date, these case studies have principally paid attention to internet use. Few have investigated mobile devices and other technologies that, in many cases, are more inclusively utilized to mobilize people. Cases such as the SARS crisis in China in 2003 (Castells et al., 2007) and the April 10 Mobilization in 2006 by undocumented immigrants in the U.S. saw the use of cell phones strengthen ties among participants; yet these movements appear to be abrupt surges of mobilization, not sustainable for a long period of time.

Another interesting study (Paulos, Honicky, & Hooker, 2008) reported the use of mobile sensors to encourage citizens to participate in data collection pertaining to air quality in Accra, Ghana. The study describes the development of a new mobile phone that includes an air quality sensor. This type of mobile device use has a potential for developing a sense of community among activists in the long term, although it has yet to be proven. Studies of these innovative technologies should enhance existing theoretical frameworks.

In terms of novel internet applications, mobilization through social networking sites will likely increase. Social media such as Facebook or Twitter do provide a means to connect with others and organize collective action with relative ease. Facebook has more than 400 million active users and is one of the most popular websites in the world (Facebook, 2010). Several articles have described the success of the Obama campaign in the 2008 U.S. presidential election in mobilizing voters through Facebook (e.g., Talbot, 2008). Sanson (2008, p. 168), in particular, discussed the effective use of "microtargeting"—marketing a candidate by using targeted ads for profiled populations—for the youth vote by the Obama campaign. Another successful example was the massive protests against the Revolutionary Armed Forces in Columbia, internationally organized by Facebook (Pérez, 2008). Iranian protesters' use of Twitter in response to the presidential election in 2009 attracted much media attention; some called it the "Twitter Revolution" (Berman, 2009, online). Schectman (2009), however, reported that people who resided outside Iran, not Iranians, were the primary users of Twitter in this case.

As the development of internet applications continues, movement organizers need to consider taking advantage of the internet's many innovative features to organize and mobilize activities rather than relying solely on informational yet passive webpages and simple email communication. Thus, social movements that utilize Web 2.0 technologies could possibly flourish. Smith, Costello, and Brecher (2009) suggest that social movements 2.0 have advantages in: facilitating group formation, amplifying scale, increasing interactivity, reducing hierarchies, and having access to easy-to-use tools. Nonetheless, it is still uncertain how useful Web 2.0 technologies will be to social movements.

Future studies may shed additional light on the diverse strategies used by ICT-driven movements, including the frame alignment processes that these movements undergo. In this review, we discussed five ways in which ICTs can be used to support or impede social movements within the traditional frameworks: ICTs as resources, ICTs to support collective identity, ICTs as framing devices, ICTs as mobilization tools, and ICTs as spaces for social movement. Although traditional social movement theories are informative, current theoretical frameworks that explicitly address ICT-driven mobilization are scarce. Some researchers, such as Bimber and colleagues (2005), Bennett (2003), and Bennett and Toft (2009), attempt to address this lacuna. However, a disconnect between traditional theories about social movements and emerging ICT-driven social movements is evident. As Garrett (2006) suggests, it would be fruitful to combine multiple methods to understand ICT-driven phenomena.

In conclusion, there is no doubt that various social movements will take advantage of emerging technologies and that ICT use to support movement activities will continue to grow. In this sense, more empirical studies are needed. At the same time, the focus of research should not be solely on technologies. We need an integrated view that bridges the online and offline worlds. Although social movement theories have been applied to the internet, these theories were developed in pre-online times. As such, we need a better framework to conceptualize the interactions among ICTs, social movement actors, and their environments. Using a social informatics perspective, we hope that empirical studies will be synthesized and utilized to develop further theoretical understanding of online social movements.

Acknowledgments

The authors would like to thank Jenny Pickerill and the anonymous reviewers.

Endnote

1. Innovative software was developed to execute a range of internet-based attacks, such as denial of service, computer break-ins, and domain name system attacks. These attacks help activists challenge and further counteract an authority's repressive actions.

References

Almeida, P. D., & Lichbach, M. I. (2003). To the internet, from the internet: Comparative media coverage of transnational protests. *Mobilization, 8*(3), 249–272.

Anthony, D., Smith, S. W., & Williamson, T. (2009). Reputation and reliability in collective goods: The case of the online encyclopedia Wikipedia. *Rationality & Society, 21*, 263–306.

Arquilla, J., & Ronfeldt, D. (2001). Emergence and influence of the Zapatista social netwar. In D. Ronfeldt & J. Arquilla (Eds.), *Networks and netwars: The future of terror, crime, and militancy* (pp. 171–199). Santa Monica, CA: Rand.

Balka, E. (1993). *Women's access to online discussions about feminism*. Retrieved May 27, 2009, from feminism.eserver.org/gender/cyberspace/feminist-use-of-cyberspace.txt/document_view

Benford, R. D., & Snow, D. A. (2000). Framing processes and social movements: An overview and assessment. *Annual Review of Sociology, 26*, 611–639.

Bennett, W. L. (2003). Communicating global activism: Strengths and vulnerabilities of networked politics. *Information, Communication & Society, 6*(2), 143–168.

Bennett, W. L., & Toft, A. (2009). Identity, technology, and narratives: Transnational activism and social networks. In A. Chadwick & P. N. Howard (Eds.), *Routledge handbook of internet politics* (pp. 246–260). London: Routledge.

Berman, A. (2009, June 15). Iran's Twitter revolution. *The Nation.* Retrieved July 9, 2009, from www.thenation.com/blogs/notion/443634

Bijker, W. E. (2001). Social construction of technology. In N. J. Smelser & P. B. Baltes (Eds.), *International encyclopaedia of the social and behavioral sciences* (Vol. 23, pp. 15522–15527). Oxford, UK: Elsevier Science.

Bimber, B., Flanagin, A. J., & Stohl, C. (2005). Reconceptualizing collective action in the contemporary media environment. *Communication Theory, 15*(4), 365–388.

Bloomfield, A. (2007, May 18). Estonia calls for NATO cyber-terrorism strategy. Retrieved February 9, 2010, from www.telegraph.co.uk/news/worldnews/1551963/Estonia-calls-for-Nato-cyber-terrorism-strategy.html

Bullert, B. (2000). *Strategic public relations, sweatshops, and the making of a global movement.* Working Paper# 2000–14. Cambridge, MA: The Joan Shorenstein Center on the Press, Politics and Public Policy. Harvard University. Retrieved June 30, 2009, from www.hks.harvard.edu/presspol/publications/papers/working_papers/2000_14_bullert.pdf

Byrne, D. N. (2007). Public discourse, community concerns, and civic engagement: Exploring Black social networking traditions on BlackPlanet.com. *Journal of Computer-Mediated Communication, 13*(1), 319–340.

Callon, M. (1986). Some elements of a sociology of translation: Domestication of the scallops and the fishermen of St. Brieuc Bay. In J. Law (Ed.), *Power, action and belief* (pp. 196–233). London: Routledge & Kegan Paul.

Carty, V. (2002). Technology and counter-hegemonic movements: The case of Nike corporation. *Social Movement Studies, 1*(2), 129–146.

Castells, M. (1997). *The power of identity.* New York: Blackwell.

Castells, M. (1999). An introduction to the information age. In H. Mackay & T. O'Sullivan (Eds.), *The media reader: Continuity and transformation* (pp. 398–410). London: Sage.

Castells, M. (2000). The rise of the network society (2nd ed.). New York: Blackwell.

Castells, M., Fernandez-Ardevol, M., Qiu, J. L., & Sey, A. (2007). *Mobile communication and society: A global perspective.* Cambridge, MA: MIT Press.

Chadwick, A. (2007). Digital network repertoires and organizational hybridity. *Political Communication, 24*(3), 283–301.

Chase, M., & Mulvenon, J. (2002). *You've got dissent!: Chinese dissident use of the internet and Beijing's counter-strategies.* Santa Monica, CA: Rand.

Cheta. (2004). Dis@bled people, ICTs and a new age of activism: A Portuguese accessibility special interest group study. In W. van de Donk, B. D. Loader, P. G. Nihon, & D. Rucht (Eds.), *Cyberprotest: New media, citizens and social movements* (pp. 207–232). New York: Routledge.

Clark, J. D., & Themudo, N. S. (2006). Linking the web and the street: Internet-based "dot-causes" and the "anti-globalization." *World Development, 34*(1), 50–74.

Cohen, J. (1985). Strategy or identity: New theoretical paradigms and contemporary social movements. *Social Research, 52,* 663–716.

Collin, B. (1997, March). The future of cyberterrorism. *Crime and Justice International*, *13*(2), 15–18.

Cronauer, K. (2004). *Activism and the internet: A socio-political analysis of how the use of electronic mailing lists affects mobilization in social movement organizations.* Unpublished doctoral dissertation, University of British Columbia, Vancouver.

Danitz, T., & Strobel, W. P. (1999). The internet's impact on activism: The case of Burma. *Studies in Conflict and Terrorism*, *22*(3), 257–269.

Deibert, R. (2000). International plug 'n play? Citizen activism, the internet, and global public policy. *International Studies Perspectives*, *1*, 255–272.

Denning, D. (1999). *Information warfare and security*. Boston: Addison-Wesley.

Denning, D. (2001). Activism, hacktivism, and cyberterrorism: The internet as a tool for influencing foreign policy. In J. Arquilla & D. Ronfeldt (Eds.), *Networks and netwars* (pp. 239–288). Santa Monica, CA: Rand.

Diani, M. (1992). The concept of social movement. *Sociological Review*, *40*, 1–25.

Diani, M. (2000). Social movement networks: Virtual and real. *Information, Communication and Society*, *3*(3), 386–401.

Earl, J., & Schussman, A. (2003). The new site of activism: Online organization, movement entrepreneurs, and the changing location of social movement decision making. *Research in Social Movement, Conflict and Change*, *24*, 155–187.

Edwards, A. (2004). The Dutch women's movement online: Internet and the organizational infrastructure of a social movement. In W. van de Donk, B. D. Loader, P. G. Nihon, & D. Rucht (Eds.), *Cyberprotest: New media, citizens and social movements* (pp. 183–206). London: Routledge.

Elliott, M. S., & Kraemer, K. L. (Eds.) (2008). *Computerization movements and technology diffusion: From mainframes to ubiquitous computing*. Medford, NJ: Information Today, Inc.

Etzioni, A., & Etzioni, O. (1999). Face-to-face and computer-mediated communities: A comparative analysis. *The Information Society*, *15*, 241–248.

Facebook. (2010). *Press room: Statistics*. Retrieved March 12, 2010, from www.facebook.com/press/info.php?statistics

Fox, S. (2004). *Older Americans and the internet*. Washington, DC: Pew Internet & American Life Project. Retrieved June 17, 2009, from www.pewinternet.org/~/media//Files/Reports/2004/PIP_Seniors_Online_2004.pdf.pdf

Freeman, J. (1979). Resource mobilization and strategy: A model for analyzing social movement organization actions. In M. N. Zald & J. D. McCarthy (Eds.), *Dynamics of social movement* (pp. 167–189). Cambridge, MA: Winthrop.

Gamson, W. A. (1990). *The strategy of social protest*. Belmont, CA: Wadsworth Publishing.

Gamson, W. A., Croteau, D., Hoynes, W., & Sasson, T. (1992). Media images and the social construction of reality. *Annual Review of Sociology*, *18*, 373–393.

Garrett, R. K. (2006). Protest in an information society: A review of literature on social movements and new ICTs. *Information, Communication & Society*, *9*(2), 202–224.

Garrett, R. K., & Edwards, P. N. (2007). Revolutionary secrets: Technology's role in the South African anti-apartheid movement. *Social Science Computer Review*, *25*(1), 13–26.

Gillan, K. (2009). The UK anti-war movement online: Uses and limitations of internet technologies for contemporary activism. *Information, Communication & Society*, *12*(1), 25–43.

Goffman, E. (1974). *Frame analysis*. New York: Harper.

Greengard, S. (2009). The first internet president. *Communications of the ACM, 52*(2), 16–18.

Gueorguieva, V. (2008). Voters, MySpace, and YouTube: The impact of alternative communication channels on the 2006 election cycle and beyond. *Social Science Computer Review, 26*(3), 288–300.

Hara, N. (2008). Internet use for political mobilization: Voices of the participants. *First Monday, 13*(7). Retrieved May 20, 2009, from www.uic.edu/htbin/cgiwrap/bin/ojs/index.php/fm/article/view/2123/1976

Hara, N., & Estrada, Z. C. (2005). Analyzing the mobilization of grassroots activities via the internet: A case study. *Journal of Information Science, 31*(6), 503–514.

Hara, N., & Rosenbaum, H. (2008). Revising the conceptualization of computerization movements. *The Information Society, 24*(4), 229–245.

Hara, N., & Shachaf, P. (2008). Online peace movement organizations: A comparative analysis. In I. Chen & T. Kidd (Eds.), *Social information technology: Connection society and cultural issues* (pp. 52–67). Hershey, PA: Idea Group.

Hechter, M., Friedman, D., & Appelbaum, M. (1982). A theory of ethnic collective action. *International Migration Review, 16*(2), 412–434.

Hess, D., Breyman, S., Campbell, N., & Martin, B. (2008). Science, technology and social movements. In E. J. Hackett, O. Amsterdamska, M. Lynch, & J. Wajcman (Eds.), *The handbook of science and technology studies* (3rd ed.) (pp. 273–498). Cambridge, MA: MIT Press.

Hsu, C. (2003, May). *The internet and social movements: An exploratory study of a Taiwanese virtual mobilization*. Paper presented at the Annual Meeting of the International Communication Association, San Diego, CA.

Huang, B. (2009). *Analyzing a social movement's use of internet: Resource mobilization, new social movement theories and the case of Falun Gong*. Unpublished doctoral dissertation, Indiana University.

Hunt, S., Benford, R., & Snow, D. (1994). Identity fields: Framing processes and the social construction of movement identities. In E. Laraña, H. Johnston, & J. R. Gusfield (Eds.), *New social movements: From ideology to identity* (pp. 185–208). Philadelphia: Temple University Press.

Hurley, B., & Charleton, D. (2005). *April 25: Not just a significant day on the Australian calendar*. Retrieved February 20, 2005, from www.fofg.org

Iacono, S., & Kling, R. (2001). Computerization movements: The rise of the internet and distant forms of work. In J. Yates & J. Van Maanen (Eds.), *Information technology and organizational transformation: History, rhetoric, and practice* (pp. 93–136). Thousand Oaks, CA: Sage.

Jenkins, J. C. (1981). Sociopolitical movements. In S. Long (Ed.), *The handbook of political behavior* (Vol. 4, pp. 81–153). New York: Plenum Press.

Jones, S. (1998). *Cybersociety 2.0 revisiting computer-mediated communication and community*. Thousand Oaks: Sage.

Kahn, R., & Kellner, D. (2004). New media and internet activism: From the "Battle of Seattle" to blogging. *New Media and Society, 6*(1), 87–95.

Kennedy, T. (2000). Women and the internet: An exploratory study of feminist experiences in cyberspace. *Cyberpsychology and Behavior, 2*(5), 707–719.

Kidd, D. (2003). Indymedia.org: A new communications commons. In M. McCaughey & M. D. Ayers (Eds.), *Cyberactivism: Online activism in theory and practice* (pp. 47–70). London: Routledge.

Klandermans, B. (1984). Mobilization and participation: Social psychological expansions of resource mobilization theory. *American Sociological Review, 49*, 583–600.

Klandermans, B. (2004). The demand and supply of participation: Social psychological correlates of participation in a social movement. In D. A. Snow, S. Soule, & H. Kriesi (Eds.), *Blackwell Companion to Social Movements* (pp. 360–379). Oxford, UK: Blackwell.

Kling, R. (1994). Reading "all about" computerization: How genre conventions shape nonfiction social analysis. *The Information Society, 10*(3), 147–172.

Kling, R. (1999). Can the next-generation internet effectively support ordinary citizens? *The Information Society, 15*(1), 57–64.

Kling, R., & Iacono, S. (1994). Computerization movements and the mobilization of support for computerization. In L. Starr (Ed.), *Ecologies of knowledge*. Albany, NY: SUNY Press. Retrieved February 10, 2010, from rkcsi.indiana.edu/archive/kling/pubs/MOBIL94C. htm

Kling, R., Rosenbaum, H., & Sawyer. S. (2005). *Understanding and communicating social informatics: A framework for studying and teaching the human contexts of information and communication technologies*. Medford, NJ: Information Today, Inc.

Kobrin, S. (1998). The MAI and the clash of globalization. *Foreign Policy, 112*, 97–109.

Kreiss, D. (2009, October). *The whole world is networking: Crafting networked politics from Howard Dean to Barack Obama*. Paper presented at the Society for Social Studies of Science Annual Meeting, Washington, DC.

Laraña, E., Johnston, H., & Gusfield, J. R. (Eds.). (1994). *New social movements: From ideology to identity*. Philadelphia: Temple University Press.

Latour, B. (1987). *Science in action: How to follow scientists and engineers through society*. Cambridge, MA: Harvard University Press.

Law, J. (1987). Technology and heterogeneous engineering: The case of Portuguese expansion. In W. E. Bijker, T. P. Hughes, & T. J. Pinch (Eds.), *The social construction of technology systems: New directions in the sociology and history of technology* (pp. 111–134). Cambridge, MA: MIT Press.

Leizerov, S. (2000). Privacy advocacy group versus Intel: A case study of how social movements are tactically using the internet to fight corporations. *Social Science Computer Review, 18*(4), 461–483.

Lievrouw, L. A. (2006). Oppositional and activist new media: Remediation, reconfiguration, participation. *Proceedings of the Participatory Design Conference: Expanding Boundaries in Design*, 115–124. Retrieved June 12, 2009, from polaris.gseis.ucla.edu/l lievrou/LievrouwPDC06Rev2.pdf

Lin, N. (2001). *Social capital: A theory of social structure and action*. Cambridge, UK: Cambridge University Press.

Loader, B. D. (2003). Social movements online. In K. Christensen & D. Levinson (Eds.), *Encyclopedia of community: From the village to the virtual world* (pp. 1319–1320). Thousand Oaks, CA: Sage.

Ma, L. (2007). Cyberactivism: Internet gratifications, collective identity and political participation. *Asian Communication Research, 4*(1), 25–42.

Mantovani, G. (1996). Social context in HCI: A new framework for mental models, cooperation, and communication. *Cognitive Science, 20*, 237–269.

Marden, M. L. (1978). The proliferation of a social movement, ideology and individual incentives in the contemporary feminist movement. In L. Kriesberg (Ed.), *Research in social movement, conflict and change* (Vol. 1, pp. 179–196). Greenwich, CT: JAI.

McAdam, D. (1994). Culture and social movements. In E. Laraña, H. Johnston & J. R. Gusfield (Eds.), *New social movements: From idealogy to identity* (pp. 36–57). Philadelphia: Temple University Press.

McAdam, D. (1996). Political opportunities: Conceptual origins, current problems, future directions. In D. McAdam, J. D. McCarthy, & M. N. Zald (Eds.), *Comparative perspectives on social movements: Political opportunities, mobilizing structures, and cultural framings* (pp. 23–40). Cambridge, UK: Cambridge University Press.

McAdam, D., Tilly, C., & Tarrow, C. (1996). To map contentious politics. *Mobilization, 1,* 17–34.

McCarthy, J. D., & Zald, M. N. (1977). Resource mobilization and social movements: A partial theory. *American Journal of Sociology, 82,* 1212–1239.

McCaughey, M., & Ayers, M. D. (Eds.). (2003). *Cyberactivism: Online activism in theory and practice.* New York: Routledge.

Meikle, G. (2002). *Future active: Media activism and the internet.* New York: Routledge.

Melucci, A. (1985). The symbolic challenge of contemporary social movements. *Social Research, 52*(4), 789–816.

Melucci, A. (1988). Social movements and the democratization of everyday life. In J. Keane (Ed.), *Civil society and the state: New European perspectives* (pp. 245–261). London: Verso.

Melucci, A. (1989). *Nomads of the present.* Philadelphia: Temple University Press.

Melucci, A. (1995). The process of collective identity. In H. Johnston & B. Klandermans (Eds.), *Social movements and culture* (pp. 41–63). Minneapolis: University of Minnesota Press.

Melucci, A. (1996). *Changing codes: Collective action in the information age.* Cambridge, UK: Cambridge University Press.

Meyer, D. S. (2004). Protest and political opportunities. *Annual Review of Sociology, 30,* 125–145.

Micheletti, M., Stolle, D., Nishikawa, L., & Wright, M. (2004, August). *A case of discursive political consumerism: The Nike email exchange.* Paper presented at the 2nd International Seminar on Political Consumerism, Oslo, Norway.

Miller, D., & Slater, D. (2000). *The internet: An ethnographic approach.* New York: Berg.

Myers, D. (1994). Communication technology and social movements: Contributions of computer networks to activism. *Social Science Computer Review, 12,* 250–260.

Myers, D. (2002). Social activism through computer networks. In O. V. Burton (Ed.), *Computing in the social sciences and humanities* (pp. 124–137). Urbana: University of Illinois Press.

Nah, S., Veenstra, A. S., & Shah, D. V. (2006). The internet and anti-war activism: A case study of information, expression, and action. *Journal of Computer-Mediated Communication, 12,* 230–247.

Nakamura, L. (2002). *Cybertypes: Race, ethnicity, and identity on the internet.* New York: Routledge.

National Telecommunications and Information Administration. (2000a). *National Telecommunications and Information Administration Annual Report 2000.* Washington,

DC: The Administration. Retrieved June 8, 2009, from www.ntia.doc.gov/ntiahome/annualrpt/2001/2000annrpt.htm

National Telecommunications and Information Administration. (2000b). *Falling through the net: Toward digital inclusion.* Washington, DC: The Administration. Retrieved June 8, 2009, from www.ntia.doc.gov/ntiahome/fttn00/contents00.html

National Telecommunications and Information Administration. (2002). *A nation online: How Americans are expanding their use of the internet.* Washington, DC: The Administration. Retrieved June 15, 2009, from www.ntia.doc.gov/ntiahome/dn/html/toc.htm

National Telecommunications and Information Administration. (2007). *Households using the internet in and outside the home, by selected characteristics: Total, urban, rural, and central city.* Washington, DC: The Administration. Retrieved June 15, 2009, from www.ntia.doc.gov/reports/2008/Table_HouseholdInternet2007.pdf

Neeley, D. (2000). Hacktivism or vandalism? *Security Management, 44*(2), 30.

Nip, J. (2004). The queer sisters and its electronic bulletin board: A study of the internet for social movement mobilization. *Information, Communication & Society, 7*(1), 23–49.

Nisbet, M. C., & Kotcher, J. E. (2009). A two-step flow of influence? Opinion-leader campaigns on climate change. *Science Communication 30*(3), 328–354.

Nisbet, M. C., & Kotcher, J. E. (in press). A two-step flow of influence? Opinion-leader campaigns on climate change. *Science Communication.*

Norris, P. (2001). *Digital divide: Civic engagement, information poverty, and the internet worldwide.* Cambridge, UK: Cambridge University Press.

Nov, O. (2007). What motivates Wikipedians? *Communications of the ACM, 50*(11), 60–64.

Offe, C. (1985). New social movements: Challenging the boundaries of institutional politics. *Social Research, 52*(4), 817–868.

Oliver, P. E., & Johnston, H. (2000). What a good idea! Frames and ideologies in social movement research. *Mobilization, 5*(1), 37–54.

Oliver, P. E., & Maney, G. M. (2000). Political processes and local newspaper coverage of protest events: From selection bias to triadic interactions. *American Journal of Sociology, 106*(2), 463–505.

Olson, M. (1965). *The logic of collective action: Public goods and the theory of groups.* Cambridge, MA: Harvard University Press.

Onosaka, J. (2003). Opening a Pandora's box: The cyber activism of Japanese women. In K. C. Ho, R. Kluver, & K. C. Yang (Eds.), *Asia.Com: Asia encounters the internet* (pp. 211–227). New York: Routledge.

Owens, L., & Palmer, L. K. (2003). Making the news: Anarchist counter-public relations on the World Wide Web. *Critical Studies in Media Communication, 20*(4), 335–361.

Park, E. (2002). *"Net" profit of the nonprofits.* Unpublished doctoral dissertation, Cornell University Press.

Park, H. S. (2002). Case study: Public consensus building on the internet. *Cyber Psychology and Behavior, 5*(3), 233–239.

Paulos, E., Honicky, R. J., & Hooker, B. (2008). Citizen science: Enabling participatory urbanism. In M. Roth (Ed.), *Handbook of research on urban informatics: The practice and promise of the real-time city* (pp. 414–436). Hershey, PA: Information Science Reference, IGI Global.

Pérez, M. C. (2008, February 8). Facebook brings protests to Columbia. *New York Times.* Retrieved June 14, 2009, from www.nytimes.com/2008/02/08/business/worldbusiness/08iht-protest11.html?_r=1

Peteet, J. (2000). Refugees, resistance, and identity. In J. Guidry, M. Kennedy, & M. N. Zald (Eds.), *Globalization and social movements* (pp. 183–209). Ann Arbor: University of Michigan Press.

Pickard, V. W. (2006). United yet autonomous: Indymedia and the struggle to sustain a radical democratic network. *Media, Culture, and Society, 8*(3), 315–336.

Pickerill, J. (2001). *Weaving a green web? Environmental activists' use of computer mediated communication in Britain.* Unpublished doctoral dissertation, University of Newcastle upon Tyne.

Pickerill, J. (2007). "Autonomy online": Indymedia and practices of alter-globalisation. *Environment and Planning A, 39,* 2668–2684.

Pini, B., Brown, K., & Previte, H. (2004). Politics and identity in cyberspace: A case study of Australian women in agriculture online. *Information, Communication and Society, 7*(2), 167–194.

Polletta, F., & Jasper, J. M. (2001). Collective identity and social movements. *Annual Review of Sociology, 27,* 283–305.

Porta, D. D., & Diani, M. (1999). *Social movements: An introduction.* Oxford, UK: Blackwell Publishing.

Porter, N. (2003). *Falun Gong in the United States: An ethnographic study.* Parkland: University of South Florida.

Pudrovska, T., & Ferree, M. M. (2004). Global activism in virtual space. The European women's lobby in the network of transnational women's NGOs on the web. *Social Politics, 11*(1), 117–143.

Rainie, L., Reddy, P., & Bell, P. (2004). *Rural areas and the internet.* Washington, DC: Pew Internet & American Life Project. Retrieved March 7, 2010, from www.pewinternet.org/Reports/2004/Rural-Areas-and-the-Internet.aspx

Riemer, J. (2003). Grass-roots power through internet technology: The case of the Crandon mine. *Society and Natural Resources, 16,* 853–868.

Sanson, A. (2008). Facebook and youth mobilization in the 2008 presidential election. *Gnovis Journal, 8*(3), 152–174.

Sawyer, S., & Tapia, A. (2007). From findings to theories: Institutionalizing social informatics. *The Information Society, 23*(4), 263–275.

Sayers, T. (1998). *Cyberfeminism in Canada: Women, women's organizations, the women's movement and internet technology.* Unpublished doctoral dissertation, Queen's University, Kingston, Ontario, Canada.

Schectman, J. (2009, June 17). Iran's Twitter revolution? Maybe not yet. *Business Week.* Retrieved July 9, 2009, from www.businessweek.com/technology/content/jun2009/tc20090617_803990.htm

Schwartz, E. (1998). An internet resource for neighborhoods. In R. Tsagarousianou, D. Tambini, & C. Bryan (Eds.), *Cyberdemocracy: Technology, cities and civic networks* (pp. 110–124). London: Routledge.

Shirky, C. (2008). *Here comes everybody. The power of organizing without organizations.* New York: Penguin Books.

Smith, B., Costello, T., & Brecher, J. (2009, January 15). Social movements 2.0. *The Nation*. Retrieved June 20, 2010, from www.thenation.com/article/social-movements-20

Smith, M., & Kollock, P. (1999). *Communities in cyberspace*. New York: Routledge.

Snow, D. A., Rochford, B., Worden, S. K., & Benford, R. D. (1986). Frame alignment processes, micromobilization, and movement participation. *American Sociological Review*, *51*(4), 464–481.

Spender, D. (1995). *Nattering on the net: Women, power and cyberspace*. Victoria, Australia: Spinefex.

Spooner, T. (2003). *Internet use by region in the United States*. Washington, DC: Pew Internet & American Life Project. Retrieved March 19, 2010, from www.pewinternet.org/Reports/2003/Internet-Use-by-Region-in-the-US.aspx

Stromer-Galley, J. (2000). On-line interaction and why candidates avoid it. *Journal of Communication*, *50*(4), 111–132.

Stryker, S., Owens, T. J., & White, R. W. (2000). *Identity, self, and social movements*. Minneapolis: University of Minnesota Press.

Sunstein, C. R. (2009). *Republic.com. 2.0*. Princeton, NJ: Princeton University Press.

Talbot, D. (2008, September/October). How Obama really did it. *Technology Review*. Retrieved June 14, 2009, from www.technologyreview.com/web/21222

Tarrow, S. (1998). *Power in movement: Social movements and contentious politics* (2nd ed.). Cambridge, UK: Cambridge University Press.

Taylor, V., & Whittier, E. (1992). Collective identity in social movement communities: Lesbian feminist mobilization. In A. Morris & C. McClurg Mueller (Eds.), *Frontiers in social movement theory* (pp. 104–129). New Haven, CT: Yale University Press.

Tilly, C. (1978). *From mobilization to revolution*. London: Addison-Wesley.

Touraine, A. (1981). *The voice and the eye: An analysis of social movements*. Cambridge, UK: Cambridge University Press.

van Dijk, J., & Hacker, K. (2003). The digital divide as a complex and dynamic phenomenon. *The Information Society*, *19*, 315–326.

Vegh, S. (2003). Classifying forms of online activism. In M. McCaughey & M. D. Ayers (Eds.), *Cyberactivism: Online activism in theory and practice* (pp. 71–95). New York: Routledge.

Wall, M. A. (2007). Social movements and email: Expressions of online identity in the globalization protests. *New Media and Society*, *9*(2), 258–277.

Warkentin, C., & Mingst, K. (2000). International institutions, state, and global civil society in the age of the World Wide Web. *Global Governance*, *6*(2), 237–256.

Warschauer, M. (2002). Reconceptualizing the digital divide. *First Monday*, *7*(7). Retrieved March 15, 2005, from www.firstmonday.org/issues/issue7_7/warschauer

Webster, F. (2006). *Theories of information society*. London: Routledge.

Wray, S. (2000). Electronic civil disobedience and the World Wide Web of hacktivism: A mapping of extraparliamentarian. In D. Alberts & D. Papp (Eds.), *Information age anthology: National security implications of the information age* (Vol. 2, pp. 431–456). Retrieved March 22, 2010 from www.dodccrp.org/files/Alberts_Anthology_ II.pdf

Yang, G. (2003). The internet and the rise of a transnational Chinese cultural sphere. *Media, Culture and Society*, *25*(4), 469–490.

Yu, H. (2004, June–July). *The new living-room war: Media campaigns and Falun Gong.* Paper presented at the 15th Biennial Conference of the Asian Studies Association of Australia, Canberra.

Zelwietro, J. (1998). The politicization of environmental organizations through the internet. *The Information Society, 14,* 45–56.

Zuo, J., & Benford, R. D. (1995). Mobilization processes and the 1989 Chinese democracy movement. *Sociological Quarterly, 36,* 131–156.

Public Policy

CHAPTER 11

Toward a Functional Understanding of Fair Use in U.S. Copyright Law

Tomas A. Lipinski
University of Wisconsin-Milwaukee, WI

Introduction

The relevance and importance of fair use in copyright law continue to increase with each passing year. This is so for several reasons. The first reason is based upon the interplay between the rights granted to owners and the exceptions granted to users by the copyright law as codified in title 17 of the United States Code. (Subsequent statutory references are to sections of this title.) The rights are in the form of limited monopoly, in that not all conceivable uses of a work fall within the purview of the copyright owner. The rights that are granted to owners by section 106 are nonetheless in the form of exclusive rights: the exclusive right to reproduce the work, the exclusive right to make public displays and performances of the work, the exclusive right to control the creation of derivative works, and the exclusive right to make a public distribution of the work. Limitations on these exclusive rights are granted to users in subsequent sections of the copyright law. However, the specific limitations on the exclusive rights granted to users in sections 108 through 122 are becoming less and less useful. By design these provisions often apply to specific categories of works, specific users, and specific uses. Fair use (section 107), in contrast, applies across the array of uses; it may limit any of the owner's exclusive rights and apply to any category of work. In the digital world, most if not all use implies reproduction in conjunction with some other use; scanning as a prerequisite to some other use, a use that implicates one or more of the remaining exclusive rights of the copyright owner such as display or performance. In a world of increasing digitization, these provisions become more outdated and are in need of reform, such as section 108. The situation worsens when revised; the rights granted are conditioned upon elaborate and unwieldy requirements such as those found in the amendment of section 110(2) in 2002. Moreover, recent Congressional activity demonstrates an affinity for "solving" a "problem" not by expanding the rights of users through use of an affirmative defense such as that offered by sections 107 through 122, but by the alternative solution of offering users a limitation on the remedies available to copyright owners should the use be found infringing. Examples are sections 512, which created safe harbor monetary damage limitation for online service providers, or the pending solution to the problem of orphan works in proposed section 514. As the unattractiveness of the limitation-on-the-remedies approach increases, the attractiveness and necessity of fair use increase.

A second reason fair use is important relates to the duration of copyright. It could be argued, to borrow from cosmology, that the public domain is in a steady state, neither expanding nor shrinking. The 1998 extension of copyright duration, for works still under protection at that time, provided them another twenty years of copyright life. As a result, published works have ceased entering the public domain and will not do so again until the stroke of midnight in 2018, when works published in 1923 will finally fall into the public domain. To make matters worse, it could be argued that the recent copyright law creates a negative dynamic with the restoration of copyright protection for qualifying foreign works under section 104A. As a result, the corpus of unprotected works may not be growing adequately as time progresses, leading to increased use of works still under protection.

In spite of these factors, analysis of the recent fair use case law reveals several encouraging trends that also contribute to increased dependence upon section 107. Significantly, many court decisions on fair use are rendered in disputes between two commercial entities or with the defendant user otherwise deemed to be making a commercial use of the work. This should be encouraging for the nonprofit user of protected works; if fair use can apply in these circumstances it should be equally, if not more, applicable when a similar use occurs in a noncommercial setting. Of course, the difficulty lies in distinguishing a true noncommercial use from a commercial use; a use by a nonprofit entity or an individual in a non-transactional setting may still be deemed commercial by a court, as will be discussed. Courts have nonetheless concluded that when a transformative use is made, the first factor as well as the overall analysis of factors can nonetheless favor fair use.

More significant is the importance of a transformative use within the first factor and again in the overall analysis of fair use. Dominance of this element exists in two distinct senses. First, there is dominance within the particular fair use factor to which the commercial/transformative inquiry applies, that is, the first factor. Second, there is dominance in the sense of the impact that a transformative use may have upon two of the remaining three fair use factors in the overall analysis.

Two sources of documents are key in discussing fair use: Primary sources are the case law that reveals how courts have interpreted and applied the four statutory factors; secondary literature reveals how commentators have discussed the courts' interpretations and applications of the four statutory factors. Few secondary sources have attempted a comprehensive qualitative or quantitative review or analysis. This chapter is one of the few comprehensive, at least in terms of recent cases, qualitative treatments. Beebe (2008) provides a recent and also comprehensive quantitative analysis. He surveyed all reported fair use cases from the effective date of the codification of the concept in 1978 through 2005. Beebe's statistical analysis includes "fair use win rates" (p. 575), "*interfactor* analysis" (p. 582) of the four fair use factors, and "intrafactor analysis" (p. 594) through both correlation and regression analysis and confirms to some extent this author's observation of the importance of the first and fourth factors in a fair use analysis. Beebe's word count analysis demonstrates that, for the most part, judges decide the factors independently of the overall fair use determination. Critics of fair use have long complained that analysis is too often outcome-determinative (Beebe [p. 588] adopts the concept of "stampeding" to describe this occurrence), whereby judges first determine what the overall result should be (a fair use or not a fair use) then manipulate each factor toward this target. This chapter focuses on the case law and includes secondary sources as examples. In the author's view there is little substitute for reviewing the case law; statistical studies confirm what a synthetic review might otherwise yield. One drawback of purely statistical analysis is that older cases are weighted equivalent to newer cases; thus, the nuance of the evolving nature of fair use may not be fully captured: The oldest case and its factors or subfactors are treated as if they are as significant as the newest. Nonetheless, Beebe, as with the work of Landes and Posner (2003) on copyright issues such as duration, serves as a fine example of quantitative applications to broader policy concepts in copyright law. Nimmer (2008, Chapter 8) provides a qualitative study of 60 cases; he uses a modified four-factor test (productive, published or factual, wholesale use, loss of revenue) that results in a reinterpretation of several courts' conclusions regarding particular factors. A useful table (pp. 363–374) presents his analysis.

Numerous articles and monographs discussing fair use have been published in the library and information science (LIS) literature and of course in the legal literature. Several recent examples from the law reviews are included, but so-called case notes or other articles focusing on a particular case are not. Many of the LIS offerings do not focus on fair use alone but include other copyright issues and so are not referenced here unless the discussion of fair use is of some useful depth or in the author's opinion of significant merit. Still others begin well, but end poorly. For example, "the Council of Editors of Learned Journals asked two experts in the area of publishing and copyright law to update editors and publishers about issue of copyright and fair use facing us in the digital age" (Spoo, 2002, p. 125), yet the article spends two pages discussing fair use, and the majority of the discussion is focused on the impact of the then recent *New York Times Co. v. Tasini* (2001) decision, not a fair use case. One explanation is that some commentators appear to use the concept of fair use to describe a general sense of access under the copyright law. For example, in discussing the challenges to copyright developments and reform in the 1990s, Gasaway (1997) discusses section 108 (the library and archive provision) and section 109 (codification of the first doctrine) but does not discuss fair use, making the title of the article a bit of a misnomer.

As with the legal literature, many LIS or related offerings appear prompted by a particular case or a cluster of cases and discuss how a recent court decision has an impact on our understanding of fair use or the impact related copyright legislation may have on fair use. For example, Trosow (2001) discusses university course-pack creation in the aftermath of *Basic Books, Inc. Kinko's v. Graphics Corp.* (1991) and *Princeton University Press v. Michigan Document Services* (1996) and argues that the market factor should not include lost revenues for article reproduction. These cases and *American Geophysical Union v. Texaco, Inc.* (1994) were the focus of two detailed and critical discussions by Wiant (1997) and Patterson (1997, who called the cases "dangerous nonsense," p. 352) in a collection of chapters edited by Gasaway. Lawrence and Timberg (1989) provide a similar and useful collection but it is also somewhat dated, with over twenty years of case law extant since its publication. These discussions are likewise wanting—the focus is decidedly singular—and, except for those discussing the most recent cases, often suffer from a lack of currency as well. For example, Band (2007a) reviews three cases, *Blanch v. Koons* (2006), *Perfect 10 v. Amazon.com, Inc.* (2007), and *Bill Graham Archives v. Dorling Kindersley Ltd.* (2006) ("This paper will not offer a comprehensive analysis of the current state of fair use in the educational context" [Band, 2007a, p. 2]), and posits that the application of fair use in educational contexts is robust and refutes those that offer a dim or shrinking view, although he admits that "fair use decisions are highly fact specific" (p. 12). Metcalfe, Diaz, and Wagoner (2003) discuss a wider array of cases and reevaluate the precedent in light of an innovative four frame analysis (academic, technological, social, and market). This author would argue that the four frames exist within fair use analysis either as factors or sub-factors, and singling out any individual factor or sub-factor may distort overall fair use analysis. Metcalfe and colleagues (2003, p. 202) conclude "that courts favor the Market Frame" in deciding fair use cases. Others, such as Patry (1995), provide comprehensive treatment discussing all reported cases but the fifteen years of case law since its publication relegates the resource to a decidedly historical value. Still, Patry includes an important discussion of the historical development of fair use prior to codification as well as the legislative history surrounding the codification. Rupp-Serrano (1997) discusses the potential impact of what would ultimately become part of the 1998 amendments to the copyright act, offers a synthetic assessment within broader policy concerns and goals, but likewise discusses little if any actual case law.

In other instances, fair use was the focus of the article; yet the discussion was not of sufficient depth either in terms of descriptive synthesis or analytic assessment to be of enduring value, with many articles offering little more than a recounting of the four fair use factors. This is not to say that such articles are without merit. For example, Dames (2005) offers an accurate summary of the four factors but discusses no actual cases. Schragis (2001) also mentions several cases and the impact of more recent copyright legislation but offers little synthesis or explanation. Heller (2004, pp. 35–57) is a more satisfying contribution, and the work is exemplar of the books on copyright that include a chapter on fair use. Hoffman (2001) applies fair use to more recent topics such as linking and framing. Lipinski (2005) discusses the four factors and sub-factors as well as a number of cases and applies them to various distance education scenarios.

Examples exist of bibliographic approaches to fair use (Becker, 2003; Pressman, 2008; Rivera-Morales, 1999; Schlosser, 2006), including several in *ARIST* (Keplinger, 1980), but these are woefully out of date (see also Beard, 1974; Weil, 1975). Keplinger's chapter discusses the 1976 Copyright Act (new at that time) and the role of the U.S. National Commission on New Technological Uses of Copyrighted Works (1978) (CONTU) in the development of that legislation, although with little discussion of fair use and the actual law.

In recent years numerous authors have examined fair use in light of existing and developing practices. In the academic setting reserves, including e-reserves and the delivery of service or documents, often dominate the review (Austin & Taylor, 2003; Crews, 1993, 1999; Melamut, 2000; Melamut, Thibodeau, & Albright, 2000; Ou, 2003). If an "answer" is sought, the literature is quite lacking. True, fair use analysis is "fact" dependent. Melamut and colleagues, for example, merely discuss the four factors and various approaches (limited, involved, pay-per-use, or license) in designing reserve policies without actually applying the four factors to several varying scenarios. In corporate or other for-profit settings discussion is dominated by consideration of *American Geophysical Union v. Texaco, Inc.* (1994), a leading decision (see, e.g., Heller, 2002). Another theme in the literature is criticism of (or at times adherence to, see, e.g., Sinofsky, 1984) so-called fair use guidelines that were an inheritance of the CONTU and later Conference on Fair Use (CONFU) (1998) processes.

Blind dedication to the parameters of fair use set out in the guidelines becomes more problematic with each passing year. This frustration was expressed in a series of articles in a 1999 issue of the *Journal of the American Society for Information Science* (Buttler, 1999; Frazier, 1999; Gasaway, 1999; Levering, 1999). Whether the CONTU or CONFU guidelines provided an accurate guess of the contours of fair use through articulation of so-called safe harbor portion limitations at the time the various guidelines were created is beyond the scope of this chapter; suffice it to say that the case law marches on while the guidelines remain, accurate or inaccurate, time capsules.

A number of web-based resources exist but have not generally been subject to peer review. An example is the report published by the

Brennan Center for Justice at the New York University School of Law (Hines & Beckles, 2005), which discusses trademark fair use as well as copyright fair use. Although there is some discussion of the case law related to cultural expression (discussed in the "Social Commentary in Art and Literature, Parody in Entertainment, Advertisement, and Consumer Products" section of this chapter), the discussion is more in the way of example rather than detailed description or synthesis across cases. A number of scenarios that did not result in litigation are described as well. Through 320 online surveys, 17 telephone interviews, and review of 320 "cease and desist" requests, the report demonstrates that many fair users either misunderstand fair use or are intimidated by property owners through various communications to forego further use in instances where fair use might have justified the use. Fair use operates as an affirmative defense to a claim of copyright infringement; for example, fair use can be a legal response to an initial pleading of infringement. Yet, it is interesting to note that a recent district court held that an essential step in the initial section 512 process, requiring copyright owners assert a good faith belief that the content is infringing before requesting that online intermediaries either take down or disable access to alleged infringing content, is an assessment by the owner of fair use: "the owner must evaluate whether the material makes fair use of the copyright" (*Lenz v. Universal Music Corp.*, 2008, p. 1154). This assessment must be made before the copyright owner communicates his or her good faith allegation that the use is indeed infringing and requests the content be taken down or access to it disabled. As a result, the need for copyright owners as well as copyright users to understand fair use is essential.

Method

This chapter consists of a descriptive review of the U.S. case law of fair use since the codification of that doctrine in the 1976 Copyright Act. The population of cases consists of decisions indexed under section 107 of the United States Code Annotated. The population of total cases decided since the effective date of the 1976 Copyright Act (January 1, 1978) was limited by including the three Supreme Court decisions rendered since that date but excluding all other cases except those with decision dates since 1997 (1998–early 2009, roughly a ten year period). The primary discussion focuses on those cases positive of fair use, that is, where a finding of fair use was made by the court. Those cases where fair use was not found (the use was infringing) are referenced for purposes of comparison and contrast. Earlier cases are referenced also for the sake of comparison where appropriate but may not be discussed in detail. The list of possible cases was drawn from a Westlaw search of the United States Code Annotated in January of 2009, with a supplemental search for more recent cases performed in May of 2009.

This chapter begins with a brief review of the four fair use factors and how courts apply each, including sub-factors within each factor as well as the interrelationships among the four factors and sub-factors within each factor. Cases predating the time frame are included in order to demonstrate how courts generally view application of the four factors. Next, three Supreme Court decisions regarding fair use are discussed. The significant portion of the chapter discussing the case law categorizes fair uses by the sort of transformative use made of the work or the tool or product created with the work in conjunction with similar works, such as an index of images or reference guide to a series of literary works.

Focus upon the interrelationship of the four factors and revelation of the dominance of a transformative use results in an alternative "functional" approach to understanding fair use as opposed to a traditional weighing or balancing of the four factors or an over-emphasis of the "how much" question. Selected district and circuit court decisions within the time frame are discussed and organized according to this functional use, in contrast to an analysis based upon the category of copyrighted work, for example. Building on Beebe's (2008) work, Samuelson (2009, p. 2543) also offers a qualitative review of cases "into policy-relevant clusters" that is also, as is this chapter, functional in organization in order to "provide courts [and others] with a more useful and nuanced tool kit for dealing with the plethora of plausible fair uses than can be achieved merely by focusing on the four factors set forth in the statute." The hope is that this organization of cases encourages the reader to understand better the sorts of uses that are fair and how a future use might be altered or adjusted to make it more likely for a court to conclude the use is fair. Reference to earlier cases further demonstrates the evolution of the functional approach over time within the courts.

The (Policy) Goal of Fair Use

The overall goal of copyright law is to achieve balance; to offer an incentive to create, but allow society to access the new creation in sufficient aspect. As explained by the Supreme Court in the first case decided under the 1976 codification of fair use: "The monopoly privileges that Congress may authorize are neither unlimited nor primarily designed to provide a special private benefit. Rather, the limited grant is a means by which an important public purpose may be achieved. It is intended to motivate the creative activity of authors and inventors by the provision of a special reward, and *to allow the public access* to the products of their genius after the limited period of exclusive control has expired" (*Sony Corporation of America v. Universal City Studios, Inc.*, 1984, p. 429, emphasis added). This sentiment echoed earlier pre-1976 case law as well: "The immediate effect of our copyright law is to secure a fair return for an 'author's' creative labor. But the ultimate aim is, by this incentive, to stimulate artistic creativity for the *general public good*" (*Twentieth Century Music Corp. v. Aiken*, 1975, p. 156, emphasis added).

It could be said that access to the work during the term of its protection is also an element of the formula, in that access to new creations may encourage others to make similar investment in creative endeavors in addition to the obvious access to and use of the work that is allowed under the copyright, that is, only those uses indicated in section 106 are within the exclusive purview of the copyright owner. "The purpose of federal copyright protection is to *benefit the public* by encouraging works in which it is interested. To induce individuals to undertake the personal sacrifices necessary to create such works, federal copyright law extends to the authors of such works a limited monopoly to reap the rewards of their endeavors" (*Baltimore Orioles, Inc. v. Major League Baseball Players Association*, 1986, p. 678, emphasis added). Likewise, the goal of fair use is to facilitate access and use during the duration of copyright protection; its goal is to effect this balance in day-to-day settings. "From the infancy of copyright protection, some opportunity for fair use of copyrighted materials has been thought necessary to fulfill copyright's very purpose, 'to promote the Progress of Science and useful Arts'" (*Campbell v. Acuff-Rose Music*, 1994, pp. 1335–1336, quoting the "copyright" clause of the U.S. Constitution, Article I, Section 8, Clause 8). The importance of fair use to future creators was underscored in *New Kids on the Block v. News America Pub., Inc.* (1992, p. 308, at n. 6): "Sound policies underlie the fair use defense. The copyright holder has a property interest in preventing others from reaping the fruits of his labor, not in preventing the authors and thinkers of the future from making use of, or building upon, his advances. The process of creation is often an incremental one, and advances building on past developments are far more common than radical new concepts." A concomitant constitutional concept of free speech, including the right to speak, to receive (or have access to) the speech of others, as well as the right to read are also balanced by the concept of fair use. As explained by the Supreme Court in a case involving the constitutionality of the 1998 copyright term extension legislation, "in addition to spurring the creation and publication of new expression, copyright law contains built-in First Amendment accommodations" (*Eldred v. Ashcroft*, 2003, p. 219). What are the accommodations? The "fair use defense allows the public to use not only facts and ideas contained in a copyrighted work, but also expression itself in certain circumstances" (*Eldred v. Ashcroft*, 2003, p. 219). However, fair use is not without limits. In the first case to address squarely the limits of fair use through the use of the technical protection measures under section 1201, the Second Circuit observed rather cryptically: "One example is that of a school child who wishes to copy images from a DVD movie to insert into the student's documentary film. We know of no authority for the proposition that fair use, as protected by the Copyright Act, much less the Constitution, guarantees copying by the optimum method or in the identical format of the original. ... Fair use has never been held to be a guarantee of access to copyrighted material in order to copy it by the fair user's preferred technique or in the format of the original"

(*Universal City Studios, Inc. v. Corley*, 2001, p. 459). At least once the courts have skewed the delicate balance. Through decisions in *Salinger v. Random House, Inc.* (1987) and *Wright v. Warner Books* (1990), the Second Circuit gave excessive weight to the second factor (nature of the work) when the work was unpublished (both cases involved correspondence and other unpublished content of two famous authors; the cases are discussed in detail later in the chapter). Congress rebuffed this imbalance by adding the following sentence to the end of section 107: "The fact that a work is unpublished shall not itself bar a finding of fair use if such finding is made upon consideration of all the above factors." As explained by the House Report, "by adding the following new sentence at the end of that section ... this sentence has a narrow, but important purpose: to reiterate Congress's intention in codifying fair use that in evaluating a claim of fair use, including claims involving unpublished works, the courts are to examine all four statutory factors set forth in section 107, as well as any other factors deemed relevant in the court's discretion" (U.S. Congress, House of Representatives, 1992, p. 9).

Fair Use Factors: An Overview

Fair use operates as a form of privilege in law, to undertake what otherwise in its absence would be an infringing use of content protected by copyright. Fair use is therefore an affirmative defense to a claim of copyright infringement. Fair use is also an equitable doctrine. As such, courts refuse to establish bright line tests, with section 107 providing the minimum number and character of factors a court must consider when determining whether, on the whole, the use should be deemed fair. These factors are not exclusive, but courts are not aggressive in creating additional ones, or at least not applying additional factors in all instances. The presence of good or bad faith on the part of the users is often an additional factor, although some courts have used this concept as a sub-factor within the first factor. Although the four statutory factors may appear somewhat vague, several points can nonetheless be made concerning each of them. In addition, courts in a given case proceed through the four factors and each factor's sub-part in a rather systematic ad seriatim fashion, typically going through each factor and its sub-part in statutory order and coming to a determination as to whether a particular factor favors fair use, keeping tally of the factors that favor and those that do not favor fair use and how strongly or weakly the factor leans, finally reviewing the tally sheet and arriving at the judicial result. Fair use evaluation, whether by court, jury, or a potential user, is fact-dependent. Furthermore, many judicial pronouncements come to the reader with a particular procedural posture in terms of the law, that is, in conjunction with a motion for summary judgment that the use is fair or that the use is not fair, for dismissal of the complaint alleging infringement, or for an injunction to stop the alleged infringing use or appeal of such motion by an appellate court. The facts of the dispute have not been vetted in the context of a trial. Rather, a typical standard is for judges to review the facts as alleged in the complaint and in the most favorable light to the non-moving party.

There are four fair use factors: (1) the purpose and character of the use, including whether such use is of a commercial nature or is for nonprofit educational purposes, (2) the nature of the copyrighted work, (3) the amount and substantiality of the portion used in relation to the copyrighted work as a whole, and (4) the effect of the use upon the potential market for or value of the copyrighted work. These four factors are prefaced by a statutory preamble that lists a number of possible fair uses: "Notwithstanding the provisions of sections 106 and 106A, the fair use of a copyrighted work, including such use by reproduction in copies or phonorecords or by any other means specified by that section, for purposes such as criticism, comment, news reporting, teaching (including multiple copies for classroom use), scholarship, or research, is not an infringement of copyright." However, a categorical determination, such as, all uses in "teaching" are fair uses, is rejected by the very next sentence. Any such consideration must instead be based upon all four fair factors: "In determining whether the use made of a work in any particular case is a fair use the factors to be considered shall include ..." A final sentence of section 107, as has been discussed, reflects an amendment necessitated by a federal circuit court decision (*Salinger v. Random House, Inc.*, 1987) that suggested that use of an unpublished work could never be a fair use. "The fact that a work is unpublished shall not itself bar a finding of fair use if such finding is made upon consideration of all the above factors." Evaluation of any particular circumstances must therefore involve recourse to all four factors and each factor's various sub-parts.

First Factor: The Purpose and Character of the Use

The first factor considers the purpose and character of the use and by command of the statute inquires whether the use is "commercial [in] nature or is for nonprofit educational purposes" (section 107). Courts have had little opportunity to discuss the contours of what constitutes "nonprofit educational purposes" but do consider whether a use is commercial or noncommercial, with the former weighing against a finding of fair use. However, a commercial use may be offset, so to speak, by a use that is transformative. Non-transformative uses tend to supersede the original work or operate as a market substitute, thus do not favor fair use. Transformative uses have the opposite effect. As Judge Posner explained, fair use promotes uses that are complementary but not those that are substitutive: "We may say that copying that is complementary to the copyrighted work (in the sense that nails are complements of hammers) is fair use, but copying that is a substitute for the copyrighted work (in the sense that nails are substitutes for pegs or screws), or for derivative works from the copyrighted work ... is not fair use" (*Ty, Inc.*

v. Publication International Ltd., 2002, p. 517). Applying this concept Posner concluded in a subsequent opinion that "music downloaded for free from the internet is a close substitute for purchased music; many people are bound to keep the downloaded files without buying originals" (*BMG Music v. Gonzalez*, 2005, p. 890). Courts inquire whether "the new work merely supersede[s] the objects of the original creation, or instead adds something new, with a further purpose or different character, altering the first with new expression, meaning, or message; it asks, in other words, whether and to what extent the new work is transformative" (*Campbell v. Acuff-Rose Music*, 1994, p. 579).

Transformative uses are preferred: "The more transformative the new work, the less will be the significance of other factors such as the commercial aspect of the use that may weigh against a finding of fair use" (*Campbell v. Acuff-Rose Music*, 1994, p. 579). The "transformation" must be more than a mere reproduction into another medium. "Courts have been reluctant to find fair use when an original work is merely retransmitted in a different medium" (*Kelly v. Arriba Soft Corp.*, 2003, p. 819). This does not mean that use in the same format cannot ever be transformative; it can if its function is different, but that mere shift of format alone will not satisfy the transformative inquiry. In determining that space-shift copying from CD format to MP3 file was not transformative, the court commented that the space shifting argument "is simply another way of saying that the unauthorized copies are being retransmitted in another medium—an insufficient basis for any legitimate claim of transformation" (*UMG Recordings, Inc. vs. MP3.com, Inc.*, 2000, p. 351). In contrast, creating a commercial thumbnail index of pictures on a website is not a superseding use for the original images and more important is transformative: "Arriba's search engine functions as a tool to help index and improve access to images on the internet and their related websites … users are unlikely to enlarge the thumbnails and use them for artistic purposes because the thumbnails are of much lower-resolutions that the originals; any enlargement results in a significant loss of clarity of the image, making them inappropriate as display material" (*Kelly v. Arriba Soft Corp.*, 2003, p. 818). The format and context of the images remained the same in *Kelly v. Arriba Soft Corp.*—digital images of objects searchable and viewable in a web-based environment, as opposed to, say, a photograph in a magazine that is then scanned to make an appliqué for a T-shirt design, moving from paper to cotton fabric.

In spite of these cases there is support for multiple and non-transformative educational copying within the statute, as the Supreme Court acknowledged: "The obvious statutory exception to this focus on transformative uses is the straight reproduction of multiple copies for classroom distribution" (*Campbell v. Acuff-Rose Music*, 1994, p. 579, n. 11). This might suggest that the transformative test of the first fair use factor will not be as stringently applied to the educational setting. There is no case squarely posing or answering this question, but if so it would lend support for the seemingly non-transformative use of scanning text into a campus e-reserve system or scanning text into a collection of readings, such as a course-pack.

Still, the other three factors must be considered. This is the challenge of fair use assessments as the Supreme Court cautions against reading any sort of bright-line test into the first prong of analysis: "The language of the statute makes clear that the commercial or nonprofit educational purpose of a work is only one element of the first factor enquiry into its purpose and character ... the mere fact that a use is educational and not for profit does not insulate it from a finding of infringement, any more than the commercial character of a use bars a finding of fairness" (*Campbell v. Acuff-Rose Music*, 1994, p. 579). Recent case law focuses on commercial exploitation as opposed to the mere commercial nature of the use—use of the work without paying the customary price. For example, in the much publicized P-2-P file sharing decision, the Ninth Circuit concluded that the purpose and character of the use by individuals who participated in the sharing of music through Napster technology was indeed commercial. The court explained that "direct economic benefit is not required to demonstrate a commercial use. Rather, repeated and exploitative copying of copyrighted works, even if the copies are not offered for sale, may constitute a commercial use. ... In the record before us, commercial use is demonstrated by a showing that repeated and exploitative unauthorized copies of copyrighted works were made to save the expense of purchasing authorized copies" (*A&M Records, Inc. v. Napster, Inc.*, 2001, p. 1015). In a decision involving a nonprofit religious organization, the Ninth Circuit added that a use is "commercial" where the user nonetheless "profited" because the "production and distribution of copies [to] its membership grew to some seven thousand members ... it gained an 'advantage' or 'benefit' from its distribution and use ... without having to account to the copyright holder" (*Worldwide Church of God v. Philadelphia Church of God, Inc.*, 2000, p. 1118).

Finally, recent decisions demonstrate that courts will consider whether good or bad faith is demonstrated by the circumstances leading up to the alleged infringing use of the work as well as circumstances after litigation commences. One court observed that "defendants' efforts to contact the plaintiff and inform her of their plan to use her show are evidence of defendants' good faith effort to initially seek her informed consent" (*Kane v. Comedy Partners*, 2003, p. *7). The opposite is not true, as a failure to seek permission is not evidence of bad faith. "We are aware of no controlling authority to the effect that the failure to seek permission for copying, in itself, constitutes bad faith" (*Blanch v. Koons*, 2006, p. 256). Likewise, in *Lennon v. Premise Media Corp.* (2008, p. 325), the fact that the defendants failed to seek permission for use of the song "Imagine" in a motion picture when the permission was sought and granted for other songs in the film did not evince bad faith. However, bad faith was observed where: "Even after this lawsuit was filed, the Defendant continued to use course materials that duplicated portions of the Plaintiff's copyrighted work. ... The Defendant's failure to take any action to cease infringing the Plaintiff's copyright and its apparent misrepresentations in claiming that it would remedy the infringement satisfy the Court that it acted willfully and in bad faith" (*Greaver v. National Association of Corporate Directors*, 1997, p. *7).

The bad-faith or good-faith sub-factor alone cannot override, for example, a use that is commercial and non-transformative: "Even if we were to credit the district court's good-faith finding ... its existence here would not outweigh the commercial and superseding nature of defendants' use" (*Peter Letterese and Associates, Inc. v. World Institute of Scientology Enterprises, Inc.*, 2008, p. 1312, n. 27). However, a transformative use can outweigh evidence of bad faith: "We find that even if the bad faith subfactor weighs in plaintiffs' favor, the first factor still favors defendants in light of the transformative nature of the secondary use as criticism" (*NXIVM Corp. v. Ross Institute*, 2004, p. 479). Courts appear to be using the sub-factor as a double check on the overall weighing of the first factor. For example, in *Field v. Google, Inc.*, the court observed: "Comparing Field's conduct with Google's provides further weight to the scales in favor of a finding of fair use" (2006, p. 1123).

Second Factor: The Nature of the Work

The second fair use factor considers the nature of the work. Although many sub-factors, such as age and price of the work, could be hypothesized, courts focus on two sub-factors when determining whether and the degree to which the nature of the work favors or disfavors a fair use. (As with other factors, in a particular circumstance the factor may be neutral, neither favoring nor disfavoring fair use.) The first sub-factor assesses the publication status of the work. Fair use favors less the use of unpublished works or, said another way, courts tend to be more protective of unpublished works. This occurs for two reasons. First, the historical context of copyright reveals the right of "first publication" as a significant right of the copyright holder. Second, because copyright is an economic right, in the circumstance of an unpublished work the copyright holder has not yet experienced the benefit of the marketplace. The right to this benefit is the copyright holder's. Having an unpublished work reproduced and distributed to the public may spoil the market, usurping the right of the copyright holder to benefit from it.

The concept of first publication is embodied in the exclusive right of the copyright owner under section 106(3): The owner of a copyright has the exclusive right "to distribute copies or phonorecords of the copyrighted work to the public by sale or other transfer of ownership, or by rental, lease, or lending." Although public distribution is not defined other than in the grant of right in section 106(3), publication is defined in section 101: "'Publication' is the distribution of copies or phonorecords of a work to the public by sale or other transfer of ownership, or by rental, lease, or lending." Although not identical, the concepts are akin to one another, with the public distribution right inclusive of the publication right, that is, the right of public distribution includes the right to make public distribution of the work through publication but also includes the right to make a public distribution of unpublished works. An example of the latter would be a library or archive's public distribution through circulation of a collection of personal correspondence or personal photographs of historical significance. Neither set of works is published but remains available for use by patrons in the special collections room of the library or archive or to another library or archive through a period of limited loan. This use or loan would be a public distribution, but such distribution does not change the publication status of the work; the letters and the photos remain unpublished. (It should be noted that fair use is not needed for the library or archive to use the works in this way because section 109 allows for the public distribution of these works as long as the copy of the work, in this case the original items, is lawfully made.)

Consider *Estate of Martin Luther King, Jr. v. CBS, Inc.* (1999) where the Eleventh Circuit concluded that King's "I Have a Dream" speech, made from the steps of the Lincoln Memorial on the Mall in Washington, D.C., heard by thousands, and broadcast to thousands more was not a publication, although numerous distributions of copies of the speech have been made over the years. Several cases involving the use of previously unpublished letters, memoirs or other writings of famous individuals are discussed in detail later in this chapter. Using the King speech as well as other documentary film cases, High (2009, pp. 754–756) "argues that the fair use right should be broader in works of historical significance." For example, in *Salinger v. Random House, Inc.* (1987), the Second Circuit concluded that use of unpublished letters of recluse author J. D. Salinger was not a fair use, but a subsequent district court within the same circuit later concluded that use of published material as well as paraphrasing of unpublished material in a biography of expatriate Richard Wright was a fair use (*Wright v. Warner Books*, 1990). The difference being that the more extensive Salinger excerpts captured the creative nature of his writing style in addition to the fact that Salinger was quite protective of his privacy, intending to keep his letters undisclosed during his lifetime. In contrast there was evidence that Wright's widow, as the copyright holder, had sold some of her husband's unpublished writings in the past.

A second "nature of the work" sub-factor attempts to determine whether the work, based on its creative content, falls on the "thick" or the "thin" end of a protection continuum. Courts have placed scientific and technical information, journal literature from the hard sciences such as chemistry or physics, for example, on the far end of copyright protection, or so-called "thin" copyright, and poetry or works of fiction on the opposite end. This is not to say that such works merit less copyright protection and should not be taken as a slight against authors of those works. Courts rather focus on the factual nature of "thin" work, such as, "I mixed these two chemicals together at a certain temperature and this is what I got" or "when asked x, 39 percent of the respondents said y." For example, in *American Geophysical Union v. Texaco, Inc.* (1994, p. 925), the scientific journal articles photocopied were "essentially factual in nature" but the chapter excerpts from various social science and humanities monographs used to compile the course packs in *Princeton University Press v. Michigan Document Services* (1996, p. 1389) were "creative material." In both cases the overall use was deemed not fair. Likewise, the nature of the newspaper articles posted to an electronic bulletin board in *Los Angeles Times v. Free Republic* (2000, p. *55) was "predominantly factual" and although the "defendants' fair use claim is stronger than it would be had the works been purely fictional" the use overall did not favor a finding of fair use.

Facts and figures are not protected by copyright whatsoever and could be said to fall off the end of the thin side of the continuum altogether. Copyright protection can exist for a compilation of unprotected facts and figures such as a database. Section 101 defines a compilation as "a work formed by the collection and assembling of preexisting materials or of data that are selected, coordinated, or arranged in such a way that the resulting work as a whole constitutes an original work of authorship." As a result, courts tend to find fair use in the access and use of protected content when that content is mixed or commingled with unprotected elements and the use is an intermediate step in the access of the unprotected content. For example, the Seventh Circuit, consistent with reverse engineering computer program cases such as *Sega Enterprises Ltd. v. Accolade, Inc.* (1992), *Atari Games Corp. v. Nintendo of America, Inc.* (1992), and *Sony Computer Entertainment, Inc. v. Connectix Corp.* (2000) and data extraction cases such as *Ticketmaster, Corp. v. Tickets.com* (2000), stated that "if the only way WIREdata could obtain public-domain data about properties in Wisconsin would be by copying the data in the municipalities' databases as embedded in Market Drive, so that it would be copying the compilation and not just the compiled data only because the data and the format in which they were organized could not be disentangled, it would be privileged to make such a copy, and likewise the municipalities" (*Assessment Technologies of WI, LLC. v. Wiredata, Inc.*, 2003, p. 645).

Recent cases have considered the second factor of lesser significance when the use is transformative. As will be discussed, this serves to underscore the importance of getting the fair use analysis off on the proper copyright footing, so to speak. In making a transformative use of a pre-existing photograph in a new work of neo-Pop or appropriation art, the second circuit commented that "'Silk Sandals' is a creative work, although, it does not follow that the second fair-use factor, even if it somewhat favors Blanch, has significant implications for our overall fair-use analysis ... the second fair-use factor has limited weight in our analysis because Koons used Blanch's work in a transformative manner to comment on her image's social and aesthetic meaning rather than to exploit its creative virtues" (*Blanch v. Koons*, 2006, p. 257). Similarly, the concert posters used to illustrate a book about the music group the Grateful Dead "even though … creative works, which are a core concern of copyright protection, the second factor has limited weight in our analysis because the purpose of DK's use was to emphasize the images' historical rather than creative value" (*Bill Graham Archives v. Dorling Kindersley Ltd.*, 2006, pp. 612–613).

Third Factor: The Amount and Substantiality of the Portion Used in Relation to the Work as a Whole

In the third factor courts make not only a quantitative but also a qualitative assessment. Determining the amount of the use is accomplished by examining the work as a whole and comparing to this the amount actually used. In an early case concluding that the new analysis of excerpts of interviews from one monograph in another was a fair use, the Second Circuit recounted the calculation made by the district court: "The first essay in 'Rachel Weeping' was approximately 37,000 words long, and about 7,000 of these were direct quotations from the interviews in 'Pregnant by Mistake.' Burtchaell's book contains 325 pages of text, and the title essay filled 60 pages. The district court found that Rachel Weeping [the alleged infringing second book written by Burchaell] includes 4.3 percent of the words in Pregnant by Mistake [the alleged, infringed first book]" (*Maxtone-Graham v. Burtchaell*, 1986, p. 1257). Notice that the court does not compare the amount taken from the first book with the overall length of the second. This sort of reverse proportionality is typically not undertaken by courts in fair use analysis, although courts on occasion have at least hinted at this assessment: "The [alleged, infringed concert poster] images constitute an inconsequential portion of *Illustrated Trip* [the alleged infringing second work] … the book is 480 pages long, while the BGA images appear on only seven pages" (*Bill Graham Archives v. Dorling Kindersley Ltd.*, 2006, p. 611).

A second assessment is made to determine if the user nonetheless takes a substantial portion of the work in another sense: Although the proportion of the amount of the work used is small, does the use nonetheless appropriate the most significant part of the work, its essence, or as courts have deemed it, the "heart" of the work? In the same dispute over the interview excerpts the Second Circuit commented that it could not be "said that Burtchaell [author of the second book] took the heart of Pregnant by Mistake, because Maxtone-Graham's [author of the first book] book consists of narratives by 17 women, and has no identifiable core that could be appropriated" (*Maxtone-Graham v. Burtchaell*, 1986, p. 1263). This inquiry is made because if the heart is taken, it is akin to a wholesale taking that appropriates the creative core of the work, such as revealing the surprise ending in the trailer for a movie (*Video Pipeline, Inc. v. Buena Vista Home Entertainment, Inc.*, 2004, p. 201), the signature guitar or bass line in a popular song (*Campbell v. Acuff-Rose Music*, 1994, p. 569), or a controversial political decision explained in one's memoirs (*Harper & Row Publishers, Inc. v. Nation Enterprises*, 1985). As will be discussed in greater detail, the third factor is also related to the next factor, the market impact of effect. Courts are concerned that at some point market substitution will occur. If a user takes—reproduces, performs, displays, etc.—the entire work there is no need to purchase a copy or pay for access to an exhibition of the work. When the heart of the work is taken there is likewise no need, for example, to watch the movie because plot twists in M. Night Shyamalan stories such as *The Sixth Sense* (Bruce Willis's character is also dead, thus a ghost too) or *The Village* (the compound lies within a gated nature preserve in contemporary, not historic, New England) is revealed (oops!), or purchase a copy of President Ford's memoirs just to read his explanation of the Nixon pardon.

In either assessment courts are concerned that using too much of the work will undermine the need for the original. As the Eleventh Circuit commented in *Peter Letterese and Associates, Inc. v. World Institute of Scientology Enterprises, Inc.* (2008, p. 1315), using headings and subheadings from one book in course outlines based on the book could "hardly" be imagined to "have a substitution effect on the market for *Big League Sales* or derivative works. ... Quantitatively, the amount of verbatim copying or paraphrasing appears to be a small portion of *Big League Sales.*" However, the court added that "the incorporation of the sales drills ... adds flesh to the organizational bones and renders the whole of defendants' copying substantial enough that demand for the book or derivative works might be reduced. Thus, the amount and substantiality of the portion used slightly favors PL&A" (p. 1315). This two-pronged assessment prevents the analysis from reducing the third factor to a quantifiable "how much is too much?" or "how much can I use?" test. However, recent cases underscore aversion to a simplistic, numeric approach often sought by users, especially teachers and librarians. Indeed, attempts to quantify fair use persist and may do more harm than good. For example, the Electronic Frontier Foundation's (2009, online) *Fair Use Principles for User Generated Video Content* offers a take-down standard triggered when "nearly the entirety (e.g., 90 percent or more) of the challenged content is comprised of a single copyrighted work." This is a problematic standard for two reasons. First, depending on the case, taking 90 percent may be too much or it may be too little; 100 percent taking could be justified in some circumstances, as discussed later in this chapter. Second, the focus of the query (the proportion of the work infringed to the infringing work) is uncommon among court discussions, ("the challenged content is comprised of a single copyrighted work") (Electronic Frontier Foundation, 2009, p. 2). Moreover, the focus on a single work is strange in that an infringing use might take 100 percent from two or more sources but with the user adding an equal amount of original content. Thus, two or more complete works (100 percent of each work) are used but the infringed work or works never represent more than 50 percent of the challenged content. This use would fall outside the EFF guidelines although surely there are circumstances where this would not be a fair use. This reverse proportionality misses the primary focus of the query: What is the proportion of the infringed work taken? Does it constitute an impermissible amount either in terms of an actual quantitative amount (in fraction or percentage) or in terms of a conceptual taking of the heart (qualitatively) of the work?

Courts are less concerned with "how much?" but are more concerned with whether the amount (quantitative) or substantiality (qualitative) is reasonable in light of the good purpose (read "criticism, comment, news reporting, teaching [including multiple copies for classroom use], scholarship, or research" or otherwise transforming) of the use of the work made by the defendant. Each of the concert posters might be needed in their entirety for the timeline in the *Illustrated Trip* to be effective (*Bill Graham Archives v. Dorling Kindersley Ltd.*, 2006) or the signature guitar or bass line might be needed in a parody of the Roy Orbison "Pretty Woman" by the musical group Two Live Crew in order to conjure the spoofed song in the mind of the listener (*Campbell v. Acuff-Rose Music*, 1994). "The inquiry is whether the amount taken is reasonable in light of the purpose of the use and the likelihood of market substitution" (*Peter Letterese and Associates, Inc. v. World Institute of Scientology Enterprises, Inc.*, 2008, p. 1314, n. 30). The fair user takes (quantitatively or qualitatively) only as much as is necessary. For example, in making "commentary on the social and aesthetic consequences of mass media" the Second Circuit observed that in the artist's "choice to extract the legs, feet, and sandals in 'Silk Sandals' from their background, we find his statement that he copied only that portion of the image necessary to evoke 'a certain style of mass communication' ... weighs distinctly in Koons's favor" (*Blanch v. Koons*, 2006, p. 253 and p. 258). Likewise, in *NXIVM Corp. v. Ross Institute* (2004, p. 481), the court observed that "in order to do the research and analysis necessary to support their critical commentary, it was reasonably necessary for defendants to quote liberally from NXIVM's manual."

Decisions also indicate that for many users this may require using the work in its entirety or appropriating the heart or substantiality of the work. In these circumstances the third factor becomes less significant, contributes little to the overall analysis, or in the words of some courts may be "neutral" in counting the plus and minus or balls and strikes that each factor contributes to the overall assessment of fair use. Examples of the sorts of works where use of the work in its entirety was neutral, inapplicable, or otherwise did not weigh against a finding of fair use include evaluation, indexing, or some other transformative use of visual objects such as photographs, posters, or images of sculptural works, such as the indexing and caching of photographs in *Perfect 10 v. Amazon.com, Inc.* (2007) and *Field v. Google, Inc.* (2006), respectively, use of posters to "provide a visual context for the accompanying text" in a documentary book in *Bill Graham Archives v. Dorling Kindersley Ltd.* (2006, p. 613), or use of photographs of Beanie Babies in a collector's guide in *Ty, Inc. v. Publication International Ltd.* (2002, see, p. 522: "no one, we imagine, wants a photograph of part of a Beanie Baby").

There may be times when using a literary work (text) in its entirety may be just as necessary. "In this case, it is clear that iParadigms uses the entirety of the original works [student papers]. In order to be successful in its plagiarism detection services, it must" (*A.V. v. iParadigms, Ltd.*, 2008, p. 483). The context is paramount in assessing whether using the work in its entirety is necessary in the view of the court. "Both the book review and the collectors' guide are critical and evaluative ... copyright does not confer a legal right to control public evaluation of the copyrighted work" (*Ty, Inc. v. Publication International Ltd.*, 2002, p. 521). Both uses are complementary, according to Judge Posner, the difference being that although the collector's guide requires complete photographs of each Beanie Baby evaluated, the book reviewer need not include the entire text in his or her review but can produce good criticism with a few quotes alone: "were a book reviewer to quote the entire book in his review, or so much of the book as to make the review a substitute for the book itself, he would be cutting into the publisher's market, and the defense of fair use would fail" (p. 516). In contrast, a photograph of a Beanie Baby is an unlikely substitute for the actual three-dimensional object. Copyright law does not protect against the market fallout (or, to use Posner's phrase, a "negative complement" [p. 518]) that a scathing book review or a poor evaluation in a guidebook may effect, that is, fewer people buy the book to read or purchase the Beanie Baby to collect. Judge Posner rhetorically observed that although criticism (in a case of standardized tests) is a good purpose as far as fair use is concerned, using the entire test to accomplish that purpose is not: "Granted that he had to quote some of the test questions in order to substantiate his criticisms, why entire tests? Does he think all the questions in all six tests bad? He does not say. What purpose is served by quoting the good questions? Again, no answer" (*Chicago Board of Education v. Substance, Inc.*, 2003, pp. 629–630).

Finally, a quantitative or qualitative taking may not weigh against fair use in parody cases. In the dispute over the Roy Orbison excerpt, the Supreme Court (*Campbell v. Acuff-Rose Music*, 1994, p. 588) recognized that in order to have a successful parody, the heart was needed to "'conjure up' at least enough of the original work to make the object of its critical wit," the Orbison melody, accomplished unmistakably by incorporating the opening signature guitar riff into the backing track. These cases demonstrate several concepts in fair use. First, even a small taking can weigh against fair use in the proper circumstances, underscoring again the point that there is no bright-line test as to the third factor. Parody is an acceptable form of fair use, even if by necessity it means the creative heart of the work is used. These considerations again stress that working through the four factors is less about keeping score and more about the interrelationships among the four factors.

Fourth Factor: The Effect of the Use Upon the Potential Market for or Value of the Work

When assessing the market impact or effect upon the value of the work, again, several considerations are required. First, the concept of market is not singular; for example, lost revenue because a reproduction of the work was made instead of purchasing an additional copy. It is necessary to assess the impact the use may have on future primary markets and secondary (reprint) as well as derivative markets. The decision to enter a new market, for example, release the first season of a popular television or cable series on DVD, is the copyright holder's, as is the right to develop derivative markets, such as a video game based on a blockbuster movie or vice versa. For example, one primary market for a musical work or sound recording before P-2-P file sharing technologies and the internet was a CD, and before that, a vinyl disk. At the time of the Napster litigation, obtaining music through the internet was an example of a future primary market, which of course is now realized through iTunes and similar entities: "We, therefore, conclude that the district court made sound findings related to Napster's deleterious effect on the present and future digital download market" (*A&M Records, Inc. v. Napster, Inc.*, 2001, p. 1017). A secondary market (akin to a reprint market for books) for a musical recording might be its use in a motion picture sound track or arguably a snippet as a cell phone ringtone. A derivative market for a musical work might be the use of the melody with new words in an advertising jingle or as the basis for a one-act play.

These concepts are reflected in a recent controversy involving a print version of the popular web-based *Harry Potter Lexicon*. No one would argue that publication of a reader's guide is a substitute for reading the original *Harry Potter* as there is "no plausible basis to conclude that publication of the Lexicon would impair sales of the *Harry Potter* novels" (*Warner Brothers Entertainment, Inc. v. RDR Books*, 2008, p. 550). However, the publication of the planned guide might impair the market for Rowling's two companion books (*Quidditch through the Ages* and *Fantastic Beasts & Where to Find Them*): "publication of the Lexicon could harm sales of ... companion books. Unless they sought to enjoy the companion books for their entertainment value alone, consumers who purchased the Lexicon would have scant incentive to purchase either of Rowling's companion books ... information ... in these short works has been incorporated into the Lexicon almost wholesale" (p. 550). However, the "Lexicon" was not a derivative work: "By condensing, synthesizing, and reorganizing the preexisting material in an A-to-Z reference guide, the Lexicon does not recast the material in another medium to retell the story of *Harry Potter* [as a theatrical staging off-Broadway would do for example], but instead gives the copyrighted material another purpose. ... Under these circumstances, and because the Lexicon does not fall under any example of derivative works listed in the statute, Plaintiffs have failed to show that the Lexicon is a derivative work" (p. 539).

Section 101 defines a derivative work as "a work based upon one or more preexisting works, such as a translation, musical arrangement, dramatization, fictionalization, motion picture version, sound recording, art reproduction, abridgment, condensation, or any other form in which a work may be recast, transformed, or adapted."

A recent circuit court decision explained further the goal of the fourth factor: "The adverse effect with which fair use is primarily concerned is that of market substitution. Uses which are complementary, on the other hand, are more likely to be found fair because most authors would not want those uses to be impeded by a license requirement" (*Peter Letterese and Associates, Inc. v. World Institute of Scientology Enterprises, Inc.*, 2008, pp. 1315–1316). In other words, the need to seek permission through a license agreement is not necessary because complementary works are not derivative but "contribute" to the market or demand for the original work. The Seventh Circuit, speaking through Judge Posner, would also include negative complementary uses as well in the acceptable range of uses that contribute but do not affect the market. An example of a negative complementary use is a book review. "Book reviews and parodies are merely examples of types of work that quote or otherwise copy from copyrighted works yet constitute fair use because they are complements of (although sometimes negative complements, as in the case of a devastating book review) rather than substitutes for the copyrighted original" (*Ty, Inc. v. Publication International Ltd.*, 2002, p. 518).

Book reviews are not substitutes for reading the actual book even if a bad book review might otherwise harm the market for the book. The meaning of market "effect" under section 107 may not be the same as its literal or ordinary meaning. The "effect" or harm to the "market" as a result of such uses is not a concern of the copyright law: "That the fair use, being transformative, might well harm, or even destroy, the market for the original is of no concern to us so long as the harm stems from the force of the criticism offered" (*NXIVM Corp. v. Ross Institute*, 2004, p. 482). This is because uses such as criticism, which includes reviews and evaluative collector's guides, are not derivative of the original but rather are reactive to it and serve as complements. An episode guide to a television series, however, is derivative. "The Book [*Welcome to Twin Peaks: A Complete Guide to Who's Who and What's What*] contains a substantial amount of material from the teleplays, transformed from one medium into another" (*Twin Peaks Productions, Inc. v. Publications International Ltd.*, 1993, p. 1373). The problem for the publisher of the "detailed report of the [*Twin Peaks* television series] plots" was that in the eyes of the Second Circuit "the abridgment serves no transformative function and elaborates in detail far beyond what is required to serve any legitimate purpose" (p. 1375 and p. 1376). A transforming and non-derivative contrast would be including brief plot summaries in order to make a scholarly review of the plotlines from a psycho-analytical perspective. The Supreme Court observed that there is a "distinction between potentially remediable displacement and unremediable disparagement ... reflected in the rule that there is no protectable market for criticism ... no derivative market for critical works" (*Campbell v. Acuff-Rose Music*, 1994, p. 592). The Second Circuit echoed and broadened the concept: "a copyright holder cannot prevent others from entering fair use markets merely 'by developing or licensing a market for parody, news reporting, educational or other transformative uses of its own creative work'" (*Bill Graham Archives v. Dorling Kindersley Ltd.*, 2006, pp. 614–615, quoting *Castle Rock Entertainment, Inc. v. Carol Publishing Group*, 1998, p. 146, n. 11).

A true, derivative market does implicate the fourth fair use factor. Courts distinguish between aspects of the market for the original work and markets for derivative works, which the copyright owner might also develop. "In finding that defendants' course materials actually contributed to the market for the book, the district court overlooked the crucial fact that the control of derivative works is part of a copyright owner's bundle of rights. The course materials may be complementary to the book, but they may also be market substitutes for derivative works of the book" (*Peter Letterese and Associates, Inc. v. World Institute of Scientology Enterprises, Inc.*, 2008, 1318, n. 55). In other words, the "course materials" here might interfere with an accompanying workbook that the author might choose to develop. The point is that although a textbook author might logically develop a companion workbook (which would be derivative of the textbook) an author does not typically submit a review or make parody of his or her own creation. Of course some uses might have an impact on the market for the original (such as a bad review of the textbook) as well as any derivatives the author might choose to develop (such as a bad review of a workbook or quiz book). The trivia book based on the popular *Seinfeld* television series entered this market, affecting a right of the copyright owner: "Although Castle Rock has evidenced little if any interest in exploiting this market for derivative works based on *Seinfeld*, such as by creating and publishing *Seinfeld* trivia books (or at least trivia books that endeavor to 'satisfy' the 'between-episode cravings' of *Seinfeld* lovers), the copyright law must respect that creative and economic choice" *Castle Rock Entertainment, Inc. v. Carol Publishing Group*, 1998, pp. 145–146).

The decision to enter additional markets, whether primary, secondary or derivative, rests with the copyright owner. However, impact upon the derivative market must reflect a reasonable possibility. "What is necessary is a showing by a preponderance of the evidence that some meaningful likelihood of future harm exists" (*Sony Corporation of America v. Universal City Studios, Inc.*, 1984, p. 451). As the Second Circuit observed in finding that the partial use of a photograph in a collage was fair, there was an absence of a derivative market: "We have sometimes found that the fourth factor favors the plaintiff even in the absence of evidence that the plaintiff has tapped, or even intends to tap, a derivative market. ... But nothing in the record here suggests that there was a derivative market for Blanch to tap into that is in any way related to

Koons's use of her work, even if she dearly wanted to" *Blanch v. Koons*, 2006, p. 258, n. 9).

Although a movie trailer is derivative of the motion picture that it previews, the issue in *Video Pipeline, Inc. v. Buena Vista Home Entertainment, Inc.* (2003, pp. 202–203, quoting *Campbell v. Acuff-Rose Music*, 1994, p. 591) was not the impact the defendant's trailers might have on the primary market for motion pictures by giving away too much of the plot but that the trailers developed by an online retailer competed in the derivative market for movie trailers, which Disney also entered by producing its own trailers: "We have already determined that the clip previews lack transformative quality and that, though the clips are copies taken directly from the original full-length films rather than from the trailers, display of the clip previews would substitute for the derivative works. As a result, the clips, if Video Pipeline continues to stream them over the internet, will 'serve ... as a market replacement' for the trailers, 'making it likely that cognizable market harm to the [derivative trailers] will occur.'"

In *American Geophysical Union v. Texaco, Inc.* (1994), the market harm was the key to a decision against the user-corporation. The researchers copied journal articles but not entire journal issues, which are protected as a collective work. (Section 101 defines a collective work as "a work, such as a periodical issue, anthology, or encyclopedia, in which a number of contributions, constituting separate and independent works in themselves, are assembled into a collective whole.") The court looked not only at the loss of potential "sales of additional journal subscriptions, back issues and back volumes" (*American Geophysical Union v. Texaco, Inc.*, 1994, pp. 927–929) but also potential "licensing revenues and fees" from individual articles (pp. 929–931). The secondary market for offprints or reprints was already established through clearinghouses such as the Copyright Clearance Center. However, it is unclear whether the secondary market must be well established or at least developing or have only the potential to develop before it will be considered to have suffered from impact. In *Ringgold v. Black Entertainment Television, Inc., Home Box Office, Inc.* (1997, p. 81, quoting *Campbell v. Acuff-Rose Music*, 1994, p. 590), the use of a poster of the story quilt as a set decoration on a popular television show was evaluated: "The fourth factor will favor her [the artist Faith Ringgold] if she can show a 'traditional, reasonable, or likely to be developed' market for licensing her work as set decoration." However, a copyright holder "is simply not entitled to licensing fees for uses of her work that otherwise qualify as fair uses" (*Kane v. Comedy Partners*, 2003, p. *6).

Finally, courts assess not only the market effect but the impact the use may have on the value of the work. For example, in *Chicago Board of Education v. Substance, Inc.* (2003), there was no evidence that the school district was planning to sell the standardized tests it created, but the publishing of complete tests by critics of standardized testing meant the questions could not be used in the future. There was no actual market to usurp, but the fourth factor nonetheless weighed against a finding of fair use because the use destroyed "the value of the test" (p. 630) just the same. Such use if widespread would have an impact on the future "value of the copyrighted work" as much as lost sales would in a transactional market: "If ever a 'floodgates' argument had persuasive force, therefore, it is in this case. ... The board will never be able to use the same question twice, and after a few years of Schmidtian tactics [Schmidt published the Substance, Inc. newsletter in which the tests appeared] there will be such difficulty in inventing new questions without restructuring the curriculum that the board will have to abandon standardized testing" (pp. 630–631).

Maximizing a Functional Approach through Control of the Fair Use Factors

When applying the four fair use factors to a particular set of circumstances it is important to understand which factors are under the control of the user and which are not, that is, which factors are internal and which are external in a sense to the scenario in question. The first (purpose and character of the use) and the third (amount and substantiality of the use) factors are under the control of the user. Although some users may not desire to take responsibility for their decisions under these two factors (an educator might say "in order to adequately prepare to *teach* my class I *had* to copy the *entire* workbook") the reality is that a choice under these two factors remains. The user can indeed decide what purpose to make of the work and how much of the work to take in making that use. True, the user may not be pleased with the available choices of what purposes and what amounts and substantiality courts through interpretation of section 107 have deemed indicative of fair use, but choices remain nonetheless. As these two factors are subject to the choice of the user, understanding what "purposes" and what "amounts and substantialities" in a particular scenario favor fair use in the view of the courts and which do not is the premier task of fair use analysis.

The remaining two factors, the second (the nature of the work) and the fourth (the effect on the potential market for or value for the work) are in essence external factors that cannot be changed. The work is what it is (its nature). As has been discussed, and according to the courts, its publication status is either published or unpublished and its creative constitution, so to speak, is placed upon the thin to thick continuum. The market or potential market for the work is also either extant or not; the use will either harm the "market for or value of" the work or it will not. Courts look to reasonable as opposed to hypothetical markets and so users can to some extent make this prediction as well. As with the nature of the work inquiry, the user has little control over this factor, although anticipating how courts will construe unfavorable market harm is somewhat challenging because the cases reveal a consistent but evolving pattern of considerations.

The implication for the fair user is that, because two factors remain under user control and the doctrine of fair use is an equitable doctrine, in most cases where the user adjusts these two factors to favor fair use, a court is likely to decide that the use overall is fair. Moreover, where both factors (purpose and amount) favor fair use there is less likelihood that there is a negative impact on the market. The fourth factor, though external, is then also dependent upon the first and third factors. As a result, the argument could be made that the fourth factor, at least as far as the impact the user "chooses" to make upon the extant "market for or value of" the work, is nonetheless also under the control of the user. In other words, although the market or potential market (primary, secondary, or derivative) or value of the work being what it is, is either extant or not, the user can control his or her use to limit the negative impact upon that market or potential market or value of the work.

A final consideration of the importance of fair use is derived from the impact a reasonable but ultimately unsuccessful use (in terms of the fair use analysis) can have in litigation or the threat of it. Under section 504(c)(2), a court must remit (foreclose) an award of statutory damages where "an infringer believed and had reasonable grounds for believing that his or her use of the copyrighted work was a fair use under section 107, if the infringer was: an employee or agent of a nonprofit educational institution, library, or archives acting within the scope of his or her employment who, or such institution, library, or archives itself, which infringed by reproducing the work in copies or phonorecords." This provision is part of the so-called innocent infringer rules. The advantage of the nonprofit statutory damage remission provision is its continued application in cases where the infringed work is published with proper notice. So an infringing reproduction of a work made with a reasonable but erroneous belief that the use was fair will limit the plaintiff's remedy to actual damages or injunctive relief and attorneys' fees and costs but not statutory damages including rewards for willful infringement. Moreover, because award of attorneys' fees and costs is discretionary with the court, in a situation qualifying for innocent infringement status a court may see fit to award minimal fees and costs. The application of the nonprofit innocent infringer provision can be a powerful disincentive to a plaintiff when considering whether to commence litigation.

Relationships Among the Four Factors: The "Domino" Effect of a Good Purpose

Establishing that the first factor favors fair use or a least does not disfavor a finding of fair use (i.e., the factor is neutral) is of paramount importance for several reasons related to the relationships between the first and the third and the first and fourth factors. This is reflected in recent case law, which is paving the way for the ascendancy of the first factor. This is not to suggest that the first factor should be weighed more heavily than the others, but underscores the importance of having the use under review in a given set of facts be a "good" purpose in terms of the first fair use factor—the character and nature of the use. As has been discussed, courts ask whether the amount or substantiality of the taking is limited to as much as is necessary to accomplish a "good" purpose. Fair users take only as much as is necessary. In some cases this may be the entire work, in other cases far less. The amount of this necessity cannot be answered without the context of the immediate circumstances, and so the third factor is dependent upon or is sympathetic to the first factor and cannot be reduced to any bright-line "how-much" test. Fair use remains a fact-intensive assessment, but with practice it need not be time-consuming.

When examining the first factor, a commercial purpose will disfavor fair use. The Supreme Court has indicated that such a conclusion makes the overall use presumptively unfair (*Sony Corporation of America v. Universal City Studios, Inc.*, 1984, p. 450). The absence of commerciality, however, merely eliminates "the presumption of unfairness" (*Worldwide Church of God v. Philadelphia Church of God, Inc.*, 2000, p. 1117). If a use is deemed commercial, the court will inquire whether the use is nonetheless transformative and, depending on the degree of transformation, this factor overall can still favor fair use. When the overall assessment of the first factor favors a finding of fair use, the burden is on the plaintiff copyright holder to demonstrate market harm or decline in value, that is, that the use, if widespread, would undermine the market for or value of the work. On the other hand, when the first factor disfavors a finding of fair use, the defendant user has the burden of demonstrating that the use does not have an impact on the relevant markets or affect the value of the work: "Actual present harm need not be shown; such a requirement would leave the copyright holder with no defense against predictable damage. Nor is it necessary to show with certainty that future harm will result. What is necessary is a showing by a preponderance of the evidence that *some* meaningful likelihood of future harm exists. If the intended use is for commercial gain, that likelihood may be presumed. But if it is for a noncommercial purpose, the likelihood must be demonstrated" (*Sony Corporation of America v. Universal City Studios, Inc.*, 1984, pp. 450–451).

A second relationship between the first and fourth factors relates to the impact of a good purpose on the market. A good purpose is unlikely to have deleterious impact on the market. This is so because good purposes are either non-commercial—uses which by definition do not affect the market—or if commercial are nonetheless transformative. A transformative use cannot have an impact on the market for the original work. A transformative use—as opposed to a superseding or substitutive use—does not supplant the market for the original or its derivative. It is critical that users understand whether uses are transformative.

Finally, limiting the amount and substantiality of a work to that which is reasonably necessary to accomplish or execute that good purpose is paramount. After discussing three significant Supreme Court fair use decisions, the remaining and significant portion of this chapter reviews what sorts of undertakings constitute transforming uses and how those uses function to affect the overall assessment of fair use in a given set of facts.

The Supreme Court and Fair Use

Since the concept of fair use was codified in the 1976 Copyright Act, the Supreme Court has had few occasions on which to discuss fair use. The three significant cases are *Sony Corp. of America v. Universal City Studios, Inc.* (1984); *Harper & Row Publishers, Inc. v. Nation Enterprises* (1985); and *Campbell v. Acuff-Rose Music, Inc.* (1994). It is important to understand not only the facts and the result but the reasoning on which the Supreme Court held the uses to be fair or not.

In *Sony Corp. of America v. Universal City Studios, Inc.*, the Supreme Court concluded that time-shifting by home viewers of broadcast television programming for later viewing—a use which "enlarges the television viewing audience" because such use "enables viewers to see programs they otherwise would miss because they are not at home, are occupied with other tasks, or are viewing a program on another station at the time of a broadcast that they desire to watch"—was a fair use (*Sony Corp. of America v. Universal City Studios, Inc.*, 1984, p. 421 and p. 423). Because some creators of television programming relied on the time-shifted audience, the Supreme Court was reticent to offer a remedy to the few creators who did object to this practice: "a finding of contributory infringement would inevitably frustrate the interests of broadcasters in reaching the portion of their audience that is available only through time-shifting" (p. 446).

> The *Sony* decision is often misinterpreted to mean that all home reproduction of television, cable, satellite programming, and so on is a fair use or that any reproduction of other works in the home such as CDs, CD-ROMs, DVDs is also a fair use (or worse that all personal copying is fair use!). Support for this is not evident in the Supreme Court's opinion. Understanding the rationale underlying the decision offers additional clarification. For example, library building (the keeping of the recordings for an extended time period or in a permanent collection at home) was not a use included within the *Sony* holding nor was the recording of programs without commercials. Judge Posner explained: Sony's Betamax video recorder was used for three principal purposes, as Sony was well aware (a fourth, playing home movies, involved no copying). The first, which the majority opinion emphasized, was time shifting, that is, recording a television program that was being shown at a time inconvenient for the owner of the Betamax for later watching at a

convenient time. The second was "library building," that is, making copies of programs to retain permanently. The third was skipping commercials by taping a program before watching it and then, while watching the tape, using the fast-forward button on the recorder to skip over the commercials. The first use the Court held was a fair use (and hence not infringing) because it enlarged the audience for the program. The copying involved in the second and third uses was unquestionably infringing to the extent that the programs copied were under copyright and the taping of them was not authorized by the copyright owners—but not all fell in either category. Subject to this qualification, building a library of taped programs was infringing because it was the equivalent of borrowing a copyrighted book from a public library, making a copy of it for one's personal library, then returning the original to the public library. The third use, commercial-skipping, amounted to creating an unauthorized derivative work, namely a commercial-free copy that would reduce the copyright owner's income from his original program, since 'free' television programs are financed by the purchase of commercials by advertisers. (*In Re Aimster Copyright Litigation*, 2003, pp. 647–648, citation omitted)

Understanding why such other uses were not fair depends upon the rationale offered by the Supreme Court that revolved around the economics of television production and the impact that off-air taping for later viewing would have or not have on that market. The economic incentive for production of the creative works in question—free broadcast television programs and to a lesser extent theatrical motion pictures that are later shown on free broadcast television—are the revenues garnered from sponsors who underwrite the programming by purchasing time slots in which to air commercials for their products or services. This is why the two other scenarios (library building and recording without commercials) were rejected as fair or at least not brought within off-air taping use that was deemed fair. Library building may interfere with the competing owner's market for pre-recorded versions or programming. Similarly, commercial skipping deprives the sponsor of the opportunity at least to present its message to viewers who remain in the room during the commercial break, or forget to fast-forward during playback. Of course, there is no way advertisers can ensure that even with a live broadcast to a live viewer the commercials will reach the viewer. The viewer may, for example, get up and leave the room to get a beverage or take a telephone call, remain in the room but turn down the sound, be distracted by a crying child or annoying spouse. But advertisers know this and factor such audience diminution into their calculations of cost and benefit. A program recorded including commercials will at least initially pose the same opportunity for the advertising pitch to reach the potential next customer-viewer. With a time-shifted but commercial-inclusive recording, there is a potential that the program coupled with the advertisement might reach a wider audience. The Supreme Court was able to conclude, based upon these considerations, that the incentive to create television programming remains in place even if some of the consumption of the programming occurs through a time-shifted point of access.

A year later, in *Harper & Row Publishers, Inc. v. Nation Enterprises* (1985), the Supreme Court concluded that the publication by *The Nation* magazine of an excerpt from former President Ford's soon to be published memoirs was not a fair use: "For the reasons set forth below, we find that this use of the copyrighted manuscript, even stripped to the verbatim quotes conceded by *The Nation* to be copyrightable expression, was not a fair use within the meaning of the Copyright Act" (p. 549). *The Nation* article at the center of the controversy was timed to scoop an article scheduled shortly to appear in *Time* magazine. As a result, *Time* cancelled its contract with Harper & Row regarding the pre-publication teaser of a 7,500 word excerpt from the memoirs of former President Ford. *The Nation* article related to one of the most controversial aspects of the Ford Administration, the pardon of former President Nixon.

The Supreme Court again had occasion to apply the four fair use factors and began the discussion with an important statement of policy regarding the copyright law: "Copyright is intended to increase and not to impede the harvest of knowledge" (*Harper & Row Publishers, Inc. v. Nation Enterprises*, 1985, p. 545). The Supreme Court suggested that if one took too much of a fact-based work, such as an autobiography, memoir, or interview account of life episodes, that the copyright in the work as a whole would be infringed (p. 548). The complicating element was not the factual nature of the work in question, which would tend to favor fair use, but its unpublished status, which would interfere with the historical right of first publication. "Under ordinary circumstances, the author's right to control the first public appearance of his undisseminated expression will outweigh a claim of fair use" (p. 555). The context of one serial scooping the story out from under its competitor convinced the Supreme Court that the circumstances did not warrant a turn-back of that presumption against fair use.

As in *Sony Corp. of America v. Universal City Studios, Inc.*, the larger implications of the Supreme Court's ruling on the impact of future creation was paramount. If the court decided that the scooping of a memoir by another publisher was fair use, the ruling "would expand fair use to effectively destroy any expectation of copyright protection in the work of a public figure. Absent such protection, there would be little incentive to create or profit in financing such memoirs, and the public would be denied an important source of significant historical information" (*Harper & Row Publishers, Inc. v. Nation Enterprises*, 1985, p. 557). The Supreme Court concluded that the first factor did not favor fair use. Rather than being motivated by news reporting alone, *The Nation* "actively sought to exploit the headline value" of the content, as "the crux of the profit/nonprofit distinction is not whether the sole motive of the use is monetary gain but whether the user stands to profit from exploitation of the copyrighted material without paying the customary price" (p. 561). The purpose of the use was to scoop a competitor, the nature of this scoop resulting in a commercial advantage without paying the customary price, as *The Nation* could have bid with other magazines, as did *Time*, for the right to publish an excerpt of the Ford memoirs.

The second factor also weighed against fair use as "the scope of fair use is narrower with respect to unpublished works" (*Harper & Row Publishers, Inc. v. Nation Enterprises*, 1985, p. 564). In discussing the third fair use factor, the Supreme Court commented that the portion taken, although small, constituted the "key role in the infringing work" (p. 566), which appears to imply a reverse qualitative or proportionality approach although it is clear that this amount represented the "heart" of the infringed work as well! In discussing the final factor, the Supreme Court observed the fourth factor "is undoubtedly the single most important element of fair use" (p. 566). In so doing the Court commented on the shift of burden that occurs when the nature of the use is commercial: "Similarly, once a copyright holder establishes with reasonable probability the existence of a causal connection between the infringement and a loss of revenue, the burden properly shifts to the infringer to show that this damage would have occurred had there been no taking of copyrighted expression" (p. 568). In addition, the "inquiry must take account not only of harm to the original but also of harm to the market for derivative works" (p. 568). Here the "derivative market" of the Ford memoir was "the market for prepublication excerpts" in which *The Nation* "directly competed" (p. 568).

The most recent Supreme Court decision involving fair use is well over a decade old. In *Campbell v. Acuff-Rose Music, Inc.* (1994, p. 572), the Supreme Court "h[e]ld that a parody's commercial character is only one element to be weighed in a fair use inquiry, and that insufficient consideration was given to the nature of parody in weighing the degree of copying" by the appellate court. The controversy arose when the rap group Two Live Crew desired to use a few select notes from the Roy Orbison song "Pretty Woman," the song's signature guitar riff, in a new recording. If Two Live Crew merely desired to record a cover version of the song, statutory licensing would have been available, but that provision of the copyright law requires that the musical work not be altered. Parodies do not qualify for the so-called mechanical licensing privilege. The group's request for permission was rejected by the copyright holder. Undaunted, Two Live Crew proceeded with its recording of Big Hairy Woman using the signature riff from Orbison's song throughout. The Supreme Court again proceeded to discuss the four fair use factors in relation to the facts.

The two sub-factors of the first fair use factor—transformation and commerciality—operate on a somewhat sliding scale: "the more transformative the new work, the less will be the significance of other factors, like commercialism, that may weigh against a finding of fair use" (*Campbell v. Acuff-Rose Music, Inc.*, 1994, p. 579). Fair use cares little whether the parody, satire, review, or critique is well done, rather, the main question is "whether a parodic character may reasonably be perceived. Whether, going beyond that, parody is in good taste or bad does not and should not matter to fair use" (p. 581). The Supreme Court concluded that the first factor favored a finding of fair use.

The second factor "calls for recognition that some works are closer to the core of intended copyright protection than others, with the consequence that fair use is more difficult to establish when the former works are copied" (*Campbell v. Acuff-Rose Music, Inc.*, 1994, p. 586). The Supreme Court concluded, as did both the district and appellate courts, that the nature of the work allegedly infringed is creative. The Court quipped that "this fact, however, is not much help in this case, or ever likely to help much in separating the fair use sheep from the infringing goats in a parody case, since parodies almost invariably copy publicly known, expressive works" (p. 586).

The third factor is closely related to the first. Questions such as "how much is too much?" or, in the context of the present case, whether the "heart" of the work is taken, matter little. What matters is whether the parodist takes more than is necessary to accomplish his or her task. The amount necessary for parody may indeed be the heart, in that the parodist must conjure in the mind of the viewer of the "bastard" work, its "legitimate" parent. This may require taking the very essence of the work, the "original's most distinctive or memorable features, which the parodist can be sure the audience will know" (*Campbell v. Acuff-Rose Music, Inc.*, 1994, p. 588). However, a parodist, like any user, can take too much: "Once enough has been taken to assure identification, how much more is reasonable will depend, say, on the extent to which the song's overriding purpose and character is to parody the original or, in contrast, the likelihood that the parody may serve as a market substitute for the original" (p. 588). In figuring how much is too much there is no bright line; everything depends, as the Supreme Court admonished, on the "context." The Court sidestepped this inquiry by remanding the case back to the lower court to make this assessment in the new light of its 1994 opinion.

In discussing the fourth factor, the Supreme Court again emphasized the consideration of both the original and derivative markets—for "rap derivatives" or other versions of "Pretty Woman." The Supreme Court distinguished this market impact, which the copyright law protects, from the market result that might be wrought because of the new content such as a parody, critique, or review: "when a lethal parody, like a scathing theater review, kills demand for the original, it does not produce a harm cognizable under the Copyright Act. ... The market for potential derivative uses includes only those that creators of original works would in general develop or license others to develop" (*Campbell v. Acuff-Rose Music, Inc.*, 1994, pp. 591–592). This may be an obvious but significant statement, in that one seldom critiques or parodies one's own work. The copyright law does not recognize critical or evaluative works, such as parody, satire, or review, as derivative. Therefore, the exclusive right of the copyright owner is not implicated.

Toward a Functional Approach to Fair Use

The discussion of cases in the remainder of the chapter is organized into three broad clusters of transformative functions: creation, access, and (for lack of a better word) reflection. The creation function includes scholarship, preparation of outlines, illustration, example, or documentation, including news reporting or other current event coverage. The access function relates to tools such as guides and indexes but includes archiving, preservation, and extraction that assist others in locating content or serve as an intermediary step in the access or use of content. Finally, the "reflective" function encompasses social commentary in art and literature, including criticism, parody in entertainment, advertisement, and consumer products.

Scholarship (Textbooks, Analysis of Interviews and Other Primary Data, Biographies), Preparation of Outlines and Training Materials, Illustration, Example, or Documentation

Use is often fair with the creation of new knowledge or, in the terms of the copyright law, when a new work of authorship results and when this knowledge creation is related to education or learning. Fair use can exist whether the work is the product of the academic, independent author, not-for-profit organization, or corporate enterprise, even if based upon pre-existing protected work. Section 107, the fair use statute, in its preamble to the list of four fair use factors, cues users to productive "purposes" related to "teaching (including multiple copies for classroom use), and scholarship" and the case law confirms these purposes as sound. In this way fair use provides the legal breathing space necessary for the creation of new works, an overriding goal of the copyright law. Again, fair use analysis is fact-dependent, and comparing the cases dispositive of fair use within the broad notion of "creation" with those where the use was found unfair can signal users to scenarios or circumstances where for example, too much (third factor) was taken or where the market or value (fourth factor) was negatively affected.

Scholarship: Textbooks, Analysis of Interviews and Other Primary Data, Biographies

In a case from the early 1990s, a district court concluded that the inclusion of pre-existing material, a "love scale," in a college level social psychology textbook was a fair use. The first factor favored fair use because it was not superseding of the original work, rather, the textbook "presents the Love Scale in a productive and scholarly manner, and is circulated within an educational setting for the purposes of teaching and higher learning" (*Rubin v. Brooks/Cole Pub. Co.*, 1993, p. 916). The second factor also favored fair use because the test or self-rating exercise, one of many in the textbook, although creative in design, was "significantly outweighed by the Love Scale's scientific nature and the scientific nature of its reproduction" (p. 919). In discussing the third factor, the court observed that although all of the Love Scale was taken, it was reasonable and necessary to do so under the circumstances: "Full reproduction of the Love Scale provided a productive enhancement to his discussion of Rubin's work which could not have been fully accomplished had he used only a few sample items" (p. 920). As a result, the third factor only "slightly" favored the copyright holder. In discussing market impact the district court did not view the use of the Love Scale in the textbook as interfering with either (1) uses of the scale that original creator Rubin might, for example, license in an issue of a poplar magazine or (2) in competing textbooks that Rubin or others might write. "There is simply no credible evidence that even widespread use of the Love Scale in comprehensive college textbooks, at least in the manner of Brooks/Cole's use, creates a meaningful likelihood of harm to those markets" (p. 921). Nonetheless the court concluded that some "meaningful likelihood of harm exists" and therefore the market effect factor—the most important factor—points just a tad in Rubin's favor (p. 922). Nonetheless, the court concluded the overall analysis weighed in favor of fair use. Notice that because the first factor favored fair use, the legal burden was on Rubin, the creator of the love scale, to proffer evidence of market harm; although the market factor favored the copyright owner, albeit in the words of the court "just a tad," the other three factors were sufficient to constitute an overall finding of fair use.

The use of interviews published in a previous monograph was the subject of the dispute in *Maxtone-Graham v. Burtchaell* (1986). Burtchaell used the same original source material recounted in *Pregnant by Mistake*, authored by Maxtone-Graham, in the first essay in his book *Rachel Weeping* but gave the interviews a different interpretation in order to forward his pro-life stance. Although Burtchaell's book was commercial, the "educational elements of *Rachel Weeping* far outweigh the commercial aspects of the book" (p. 1262). The reinterpretation of the interviewees' comments was transformative and, in considering the opposite perspective, did not substitute for the original "case" made in *Pregnant by Mistake*. In an important recognition of the value of the "interview" as source material and fuel for new works, the court concluded that the second factor favored fair use: "the interview is an invaluable source of material for social scientists, and later use of verbatim quotations within reason is both foreseeable and desirable" (p. 1264). Consider and contrast a hypothetical situation where one simply includes previously published articles in an anthology or reader on a particular topic. Both the nature and treatment of the source material are different: There is no new analysis or production of new content. As to the amount, use of 4.3 percent of the words in *Pregnant by Mistake* by Burchaell was "not incompatible with a finding of fair use" (p. 1257) nor did it take the heart of the work: "since Maxtone-Graham's book consists of narratives by 17 women, and has no identifiable core that could be appropriated" (p. 1263). Because the two books in question present opposite positions of the abortion debate it would be "unthinkable" in the court's word to find any evidence of negative impact through market substitution (p. 1264).

Reflect upon the policy considerations within the copyright law demonstrated by this case. First, copyright law is not designed to protect what might be called industrious collection. Consider the scholar who took the time to collect what is essentially factual material. Inquiries such as "What is your favorite childhood memory?" or "Tell me about the time you first broke your arm" or "How did you feel about the death of your son?" prompt the interview subject to recount events. There might be sympathy with the initial researcher that the content "belongs" to the collector, (i.e., a legal finding that interview content is protected by content [see discussion of *Craft v. Kobler*, 1987]. If there is an ownership right it would arguably lie with the interview subject, the "creator" of the comment). Second, a holding that re-use by subsequent scholars is not a fair use would mean in essence that a case such as *Maxtone-Graham* could prevent others from making a further use of the content collected, whether to expand on its analysis or critique or offer an alternative analysis. Think of such content as the raw material or natural resource of intellectual activity, a part of the information well or commons from which all may draw or graze. Without fair use, further scholarship on the topic would be impeded. This is not an interest the copyright law is designed to further, rather, the opposite is true. Concepts such as fair use are designed to preserve a certain intellectual breathing space.

Critique or criticism is a good purpose. More important, the effect that criticism such as a scathing book review may have on the demand for the work does not constitute market impact in the eyes of the copyright law. This was demonstrated in *NXIVM Corp. v. Ross Institute* (2004) where the defendants made a critical and fair use review of a life-skills seminar. "It is plain that, as a general matter, criticisms of a seminar or organization cannot substitute for the seminar or organization itself or hijack its market. If criticisms on defendants' websites kill the demand for plaintiffs' service, that is the price that, under the First Amendment, must be paid in the open marketplace for ideas" (p. 482). The second factor favored the plaintiff because the seminar material was not previously published. However, the third factor favored the defendants: "in order to do the research and analysis necessary to support their critical commentary, it was reasonably necessary for defendants to quote liberally from NXIVM's manual (p. 481). The fourth factor likewise favored the use, as market harm is not considered relevant under the copyright law where "the harm stems from the force of the criticism offered" (p. 482).

Contrast the reasonable amount taken (and ultimately fair use) to make criticism of the training program in *NXIVM Corp. v. Ross Institute* (2004) (or the interviews in the *Maxtone-Graham v. Burtchaell* decision) with the unreasonable amount taken (and overall an unfair use) to critique the use of standardized testing in *Chicago Board of Education v. Substance, Inc.* (2003). Judge Posner, writing for the Seventh Circuit, offered insights into the application of each of the four factors. Although criticism is a good purpose, the amount taken must be reasonable in relation to need. Judge Posner believed that publishing complete tests as did Schmidt, the editor of the *Substance* newsletter where the tests appeared, was more than necessary to accomplish the good purpose of criticism. Worse, the use of a complete test had an impact on the "value of" the work. The "tests are expressive works that are not costlessly created, and the costs are greater and so the incentive to create the tests diminished if the tests cannot be reused" (*Chicago Board of Education v. Substance, Inc.*, 2003, p. 627). Observe also Judge Posner's concern with the impact of such use upon the future incentive to create; an overriding goal of the copyright law is to promote the creation of new works. This is true in cases where as here the copyright owner never intended to sell the infringed work, so there are no lost revenues and profits to calculate. "Harm" can be demonstrated by a negative impact of the use upon the value of the work to the copyright owner and not by market impact alone. Rather than engaging in systematic criticism of the tests, Judge Posner observed that Schmidt's goal was simply to end the use of such testing altogether. "So if Schmidt can publish six tests, other dissenters can each publish six other tests, and in no time all 44 will be published. The board will never be able to use the same question twice, and after a few years of Schmidtian tactics there will be such difficulty ... it is goodbye to standardized tests in the Chicago public school system" (pp. 630–631).

Sundeman v. Seajay Society, Inc. (1998) also demonstrates the evolving relationship between the first and third factors. Here Pulitzer prize winning (*The Yearling*) author Marjorie Kinnan Rawlings's unpublished first manuscript (*Blood of My Blood*) was reproduced in its entirety. The Seajay Society, Inc. "made one whole copy of *Blood of My Blood* for Dr. Anne Blythe. ... Seajay also made a partial copy [six pages short of a complete copy] of the manuscript which it sent to the Rare Books Room at the University of Florida Library. ... In April of 1988, Blythe orally presented her critical analysis of *Blood of My Blood* to a symposium of the Marjorie Kinnan Rawlings Society at the University of Florida. ... In the presentation, Blythe quoted approximately 2,464 words from the text of *Blood of My Blood*, or four to six percent of the total text" (p. 199). The complete copy, the near complete copy, and the quotation and paraphrase in the conference paper and presentation were the subject of an eventual claim of infringement that arose out of a convoluted story of possession and current ownership of Rawlings's estate, including her

correspondence and manuscripts. The lower court concluded the reproductions fell within fair use. The plaintiffs disagreed and this appeal followed. In applying the first factor, the appellate court observed: "While
it does quote from and paraphrase substantially *Blood of My Blood*, its
purpose is to criticize and comment on Ms. Rawlings's earliest work.
Thus, Blythe's transformative paper fits within several of the permissi-
ble uses enumerated in § 107; it has productive uses as criticism, comment, scholarship, and literary research" (pp. 202–203).

The court also found that each of the events of reproduction favored a
good and transformative purpose. The complete copy was made in order
to facilitate Blythe's research and to preserve the fragile, seventy-year-
old original manuscript. The near complete copy was made for the
library in order to authenticate the Blythe copy, should the need arise in
the future, and to assess its worthiness for publication, again at some
point in the future. The paraphrase and quoting occurred in the course
of scholarship. Even though publication of the Blythe commentary might
have resulted in some economic benefit to Blythe, this was not the sole
motivation. Moreover, the paper was never published because permission was never received from the copyright owner (*Sundeman v. Seajay
Society, Inc.*, 1998, p. 203). This fact also contributed to a conclusion that
the defendants did not intend to usurp the copyright owner's right of
first publication. "All of these purposes serve the public benefit and aid
in the development of the arts" (pp. 202–204). This resulted in the court
concluding that the first factor "heavily favored" a finding of fair use (p.
204). The court again discussed the unpublished nature of the manuscript from which the reproductions were made. "Thus, we hold that
while the unpublished nature of Blood of My Blood weighs against a
finding of fair use, the allegedly infringing copies have not stripped from
the Foundation its right to determine whether or not to publish
Rawlings' first work at all" (p. 205). In addition, because the work was
creative the second factor weighed against a finding of fair use.

In discussing the third factor, the court made a significant observation regarding the use of even small portions of a work for purposes of
scholarship, criticism, and comment and the qualitative or "heart of the
work" assessment: "Obviously, the quoted material is of significant
value, or it would not have been quoted. All quoted material is of significant value, but it cannot be said to be the 'heart of the work' or the fair
use doctrine would be destroyed. ... If all quoted material were deemed
significant enough to preclude a fair use just because it was significant
enough to be quoted, no one could ever quote copyrighted material without fear of being sued for infringement" (*Sundeman v. Seajay Society,
Inc.*, 1998, p. 205). In discussing the quantitative portion taken—complete, near complete, and paraphrase and quoting—the court observed:
"In order for Blythe to perform her scholarly criticism of the novel, she
obviously needed access to either the original or an entire copy.
Similarly, in order for the Library to authenticate *Blood of My Blood* as
being Rawlings's work, to determine whether the work was worthy for

publication, and to obtain the necessary permission from the copyright holder, it too needed either the original or a nearly complete copy. It would severely restrict scholarly pursuit, and inhibit the purposes of the Copyright Act, if a fragile original could not be copied to facilitate literary criticism. Thus, we find that the amount and substantiality of the portion of *Blood of My Blood* copied for Blythe and the Library did not exceed the amount necessary to accomplish these legitimate purposes" (p. 206). The court concluded that both qualitative and quantitative takings were "substantial" (p. 206) yet necessary to accomplish the intended good purposes.

This good purpose of criticism and comment also suggested a lack of market harm. "As we held then, Blythe's paper was transformative; it did not amount to mere duplication of the original, and did not have the purpose or effect of supplanting the copyrighted work. It did not serve as a market replacement for Blood of My Blood, rather it served as a criticism of and comment about Blood of My Blood." (*Sundeman v. Seajay Society, Inc.*, 1998, p. 207). The court also observed that comment or criticism is not derivative, thus no impact on the derivative markets for the work such as a screenplay. The court concluded that the four factors when taken together favor a finding of fair use.

The case is also important in demonstrating that "research" and "scholarship" is within the statutory (section 107) "good" purpose, and in this context may justify taking the entire work. The scholar cannot pore adequately over a text if limited to in-house special collections use only or to reproduction of excerpts made upon initial review. In addition, purposes of preservation and authentication were also viewed as a justification for a complete or near complete copy.

Use of Source Material in Biographies

Use of excerpts from the work of author Richard Wright was also a fair use in *Wright v. Warner Books* (1990). Although the publication of Richard Wright's *Daemonic Genius* was intended to be a commercial enterprise (whether such use is of a commercial nature or is for non-profit educational purposes), the overall nature of the endeavor to create a new work, a biography, tipped the first factor in favor of fair use. "There is a strong presumption that if the allegedly infringing work is a biography, factor one favors the biographer" (p. 108). Regarding the second factor, although some of the works were unpublished letters, journal entries, and essays of author Wright, the court contrasted this use with that found infringing in *Salinger v. Random House, Inc.* (1987): "First, she has paraphrased, rather than directly quoted, Wright's work. And second, the paraphrasing by and large involves straightforward factual reportage. Although *Salinger*, too, concerned paraphrasing but nonetheless concluded with a finding of infringement, there the Second Circuit confronted attempts not merely to paraphrase factual data but also—and significantly—to adopt creative expression that was distinctly personal" (*Wright v. Warner Books*, 1990, p. 110). As a result, the second factor also favored a finding of fair use. The third factor likewise favored the defendant because the passages used were quite small, "no more than 1 percent. ... Moreover, the passages quoted or paraphrased cannot reasonably be seen to represent anything like the central portion of former President Ford's memoir" (*Wright v. Warner Books*, 1990, p. 112, referring to *Harper & Row Publishers, Inc. v. Nation Enterprises*, 1985). In assessing the fourth factor the court observed that the insignificance of the excerpts used could not harm the market either for those works already published (novels and autobiographical works) or those unpublished such as the essay "1 Choose Exile." As a result, the fourth factor also favored a fair use.

Distinguish the fair use of unpublished works in *Wright v. Warner Books* (1990) from the unfair use of unpublished letters in *Salinger v. Random House, Inc.* (1987). In the Wright case, his writings were used to established factual occurrences in his life whereas the more extensive use of J.D. Salinger's letters captured his style of writing. Although the first factor favored fair use, the court nonetheless admonished: "The copier is not at liberty to avoid 'pedestrian' reportage by appropriating his subject's literary devices" (*Salinger v. Random House, Inc.*, 1987, p. 97). Because the letters were unpublished, the second factor weighed against a finding of fair use. The use of unpublished letters was far more extensive than in *Wright v. Warner Books* (1990): "Of these 44 letters, the Hamilton biography copies (with some use of quotation or close paraphrase) protected sequences constituting at least one-third of 17 letters and at least 10 percent of 42 letters. ... The taking is significant not only from a quantitative standpoint but from a qualitative one as well ... are at least an important ingredient of the book as it now stands. To a large extent, they make the book worth reading. The letters are quoted or paraphrased on at least 40 percent of the book's 192 pages" (*Salinger v. Random House, Inc.*, 1987, pp. 98–99). This latter comment is also an example of an atypical observation of the significance of the work infringed to the infringing work, a sort of reverse-proportionality. As the amount was so extensive the court concluded that the fourth factor weighed slightly against fair use because "some impairment of the market seems likely. The biography copies virtually all of the most interesting passages of the letters, including several highly expressive insights about writing and literary criticism" (*Salinger v. Random House, Inc.*, 1987, p. 99). Recall, the result in *Salinger v. Random House, Inc.* prompted Congress to amend section 107 regarding the necessity of assessing all four factors regardless of publication status. As a result, the case may be of less significance today. Moreover, the case arose against the context of Salinger's reclusiveness, demonstrated through efforts to keep his personal papers private until his death.

Taking too much, even in a biography, is the death knell of fair use. This was evident in a dispute involving a biography of composer Igor Stravinsky. The plaintiff "was a member of the Stravinsky household and became virtually an adoptive son to the Maestro and Mrs.

Stravinsky. Craft is the author or co-author of approximately 15 copyrighted books on Stravinsky" (*Craft v. Kobler*, 1987, p. 121). In an instructive statement the court demarcated the acceptable from the unacceptable when using factual source material: "When a biographer or historian, using a copyrighted work as a source, takes historical information from it, he does not infringe the copyright. The law does not recognize private ownership of historical information. ... [T]he copyright law does not protect research [but may protect the products of that research]. Notwithstanding that enormous effort and great expense may have been required to discover factual information, it may, nonetheless, be freely taken from the original writer's copyrighted work and republished at will. ... [T]here is no doubt a large amount of factual information about Stravinsky that Kobler acquired from the extensive Craft-Stravinsky literature. Such takings, however, do not constitute infringement" (p. 123). Moreover, the court observed that at times verbatim quotation is necessary to demonstrate the style or manner of the quoted material. However, the use is "far too numerous and with too little instructional justification to support the conclusion of fair use ... without restraint throughout the book to describe and comment on the events and personages of Stravinsky's life" (p. 129). The court also pointed to the fact that quotes from the Craft books constituted 3 percent of the Kobler biography and "that they are the liveliest and most entertaining part of the biography" (p. 129). As a result of the extensive inclusion of Stravinsky's colorful recounting of his life events in the Kobler book, the book could indeed compete in the marketplace of the Craft inventory of Stravinsky titles. The ruling did not mean that Kobler could not write and publish a biography of Stravinsky but that the current version simply took too much, the product of Kobler's effort "may require revisions reducing the use of Stravinsky's prose" (p. 130). In the eyes of the court, taking a more satisfactory amount realigns the third factor in favor of fair use and it may also solve another problem; taking less would mean that Kobler would have to add more of his own content, adding to the "instructional justification" missing from his current attempt. These two elements would work to lessen the substitutive market impact, thus the fourth factor would then also align with fair use.

Cases involving use of material in less than flattering biographies have arisen over controversial personalities such as L. Ron Hubbard and Jack E. Robinson. In *New Era Publications International, ApS v. Carol Publishing Group* (1990, p. 156), the court, in finding that the first factor favored fair use, reiterated that "biographies and critical biographies in particular" are within the reach of fair use. The second factor also favored fair use because Hubbard's writing—opinions on a variety of topics such as the nature of an interview—"are more properly viewed as factual or informational" (p. 157). In discussing the third factor, the court concluded that it would not be unfair to use "a minuscule amount of 25 of the 48 works that appellee claimed were infringed, 5–6 percent of 12 other works and 8 percent or more of 11 works, each of the 11 being only a few pages in length" (p. 158). The court rejected a reverse proportionality standard proposed by the plaintiff (the work used in relation to the work produced) that 2.7 percent of the biography consisted of Hubbard's words. The court was finally skeptical of the negative impact the book might have on the authorized biography planned by the plaintiffs: "potential customers for the authorized favorable biography of Hubbard in the future will [not] be deterred from buying because the author's unfavorable biography quotes from Hubbard's works. ... [T]he book 'might stimulate further interest' in the authorized biography" (*New Era Publications International, ApS v. Carol Publishing Group*, 1990, pp. 159–160, quoting *Maxtone-Graham v. Burtchaell*, 1986, p. 1264).

Two years prior, the church engaged in a failed attempt to enjoin future distribution of another biography of Hubbard, entitled *Bare-Faced Messiah* (*New Era Publications International, ApS v. Henry Holt and Co., Inc.*, 1988). The trial court had "no difficulty concluding that this is one of those special circumstances in which the interests of free speech overwhelmingly exceed the plaintiff's interest in an injunction. As a practical matter, an injunction would kill this informative book. As the book is already in print, the expense and waste involved in republishing after deleting infringing material would be prohibitive. The injury to freedom of speech would be significant. The public would be deprived of an interesting and valuable historical study. No significant copyright interest would be served by an injunction. I conclude, notwithstanding some small degree of infringement, that a permanent injunction should be denied" (p. 1528). Again consider the impact in terms of copyright policy that would be wrought by an opposite conclusion. If the negative complement of a critical biography and the deleterious impact on future sales of a more favorable or "authorized" biography would be a relevant element of the fourth factor (effect on the market), or if the subject or other party in interest could "own" the facts, figures, and events relating to the life of a person, then a biopic subject (or other person of interest) could use the copyright law to stifle debate, commentary, interpretation, or re-interpretation. This result would be counterproductive to the goals that the copyright law seeks to promote and moreover accommodate other rights such as free speech.

In contrast to these two cases and in a similar vein to the "too much" taking found in the Stravinsky biography (*Craft v. Kobler*, 1987), extensive use and reliance in a biography on content taken from an earlier biography of Pan Am founder Jack E. Robinson was found not to be fair use in *Robinson v. Random House, Inc.* (1995). The court observed that in spite of the factual nature of biographies ("common use of certain scenes, locations, phrases or characters"), by "copying 25–30 percent of the Daley book verbatim or through close paraphrase; as hundreds of passages were taken wholesale from the earlier work" the second book captured the protected expression of the first author (p. 839). Moreover, by borrowing an amount that the court believed by conservative estimate constituted nearly a third of the book undermined any transformative purpose. The amount taken was simply too large to fall within fair use: "Robinson appropriated the essence of the Daley book, the heart of what made the Daley book worth reading, albeit in an abridged form" (p. 842). Even though the first book was out of print, the court concluded that the Robinson book competes with the Daley book in "market niches" in which Daley expressed interest: "Daley has presented uncontradicted evidence that a version of the Daley Book is currently being marketed in an audio tape version and that Daley has had discussions regarding the use of an updated version of his book in conjunction with a documentary project" (p. 843). As the purpose was a "good" one in terms of fair use, the plaintiff nonetheless met the legal burden of proof and demonstrated more than a mere possibility of harm to the secondary (audio book) or derivative (revised edition) market. The court had little trouble in concluding the extensive and competing use of the material from the previous book was not fair.

Preparation of Outlines and Training Materials

Reproduction and distribution by spin-off religious group Philadelphia Church of God (PCG) of an out-of-print text authored by Worldwide Church of God (WCG) leader Herbert W. Armstrong entitled *Mystery of the Ages* (*MOA*) for training and education purposes was not a fair use in a more recent Ninth Circuit decision (*Worldwide Church of God v. Philadelphia Church of God, Inc.*, 2000). PCG intended to use *MOA* as part of its training materials but did not necessarily produce training materials based upon it. The case is included here for purposes of contrast. The first factor favored the plaintiffs. PCG is obviously a nonprofit organization, so the focus of the commerciality sub-factor ("whether such use is of a commercial nature or is for nonprofit educational purposes") is not inquiry into the character of the user but whether the user stands to gain from the use without payment of the customary price. With this test the court found that the PCG nonetheless profited by making copies of *MOA* in its entirety available to each of its thousands of church members without cost and without any additional content that might offer new interpretation, render new application, or be otherwise transformative. The second factor also weighed against fair use: "While it may be viewed as 'factual' by readers who share Armstrong's religious beliefs, the creativity, imagination and originality embodied in *MOA* tilt the scale against fair use" (p. 1118). The third factor likewise weighed against fair use: "PCG uses the *MOA* as a central element of its members' religious observance; a reasonable person would expect PCG to pay WCG for the right to copy and distribute *MOA* created by WCG with its resources" (pp. 1118–1119). The fourth factor also did not favor fair use. In considering not only the market impact but also the impact of the use on the value of the work, the court observed the necessity of protecting the unique value of the work to WCG as well as other institutions so situated: "Religious, educational and other public interest institutions would suffer if their publications invested with an institution's reputation and goodwill could be freely appropriated by anyone" (p. 1119). As in *Robinson v. Random House, Inc.* (1995), the out-of-print status of the work did not lessen the negative impact upon the market for the work because the fourth factor looks to not only existing markets but also potential or future markets. WCG was intending to publish a revised version of the *MOA*. In addition, copyright law recognizes an owner's right to change his or her mind—in this case to decide at a later date to republish or revise the *MOA*, or not. The court concluded the use was not fair, with the first three factors leaning against fair use and the fourth "at worst, neutral" (p. 1120).

Likewise in a case involving the book *Big League Sales* written by a former church member now represented by Peter Letterese and Associates (PL&A), the use of the book to make general training materials by the Church of Scientology Institute (CSI) was not a fair use. The court first determined that the course outlines were not derivative of the book (*Peter Letterese and Associates, Inc. v. World Institute of Scientology Enterprises, Inc.*, 2008, p. 1300). This is important for educators because it means that constructing a course outline from an adopted textbook does not implicate the derivative right of the textbook's copyright holder. Rather, such works are complements. Proceeding to fair use analysis, the court found the first factor not to favor fair use because the "course materials do not reshape the instructional purpose or character of the book, or cast the book in a different light through a new meaning, message, or expression" (p. 1311). Although the book was out of print, it was the author's decision to withdraw it from the marketplace, not lack of demand or interest. The economic viability of the book remained, so market harm could still be demonstrated even though the book was not available in the marketplace. The second factor was "neutral" as "the semi-factual nature of *Big League Sales* neither expands nor constricts the scope of the fair use defense" (p. 1314). Incorporation of the headings, subheadings, and sales drills from the original book into the training materials prepared by the church "slightly favors" the plaintiffs in assessing the third factor (p. 1315). Even though no companion course outline or study guide was planned by the plaintiffs, the court did not view the value of the original book as "zero" and concluded that the "unrestricted and widespread dissemination of the Sales Course ... may well usurp the potential market for Big League Sales and derivative works" in the future (pp. 1317–1318).

Also under discussion by the court were advanced course materials used by CSI for internal management training purposes that did not rely on the original book to the same extent and consisted "exclusively of writings by L. Ron Hubbard" (*Peter Letterese and Associates, Inc. v. World Institute of Scientology Enterprises, Inc.*, 2008, p. 1318). Because "derivative works developed by PL&A (or developed by others pursuant to a license) would not be utilized by CSI, because they would not derive from Hubbard's writings ... registrars and officers would not study such texts ... PL&A's derivative works would not be market substitutes for

CSI's courses, and vice versa" (pp. 1318–1319). As a result, there was no likelihood of market substitution and the use of the content from *Big League Sales* in internal church training materials was a fair use.

A similar result was reached in two decisions where disputes arose after the plaintiff in each case became aware that the defendants continued using content after the initial training and development relationship of the plaintiff with the defendant ended. Neither use was found to be fair. In the first case the plaintiff was contracted by the defendant to develop and present the materials for the defendant. The court observed that "twenty-three pages in the Defendant's new course manual consists of material that duplicates almost exactly the material in nineteen of the pages in the Plaintiff's copyrighted materials" (*Greaver v. National Association of Corporate Directors*, 1997, p. *2). In light of these facts, the district court found the first factor did not favor fair use because the use was commercial, that is, "the defendant stood to gain by not having to invest its own time and energy" in new course development (p. *5). Although the plaintiff's manual contained unprotected (derived also from pre-existing sources) as well as protected content, the wholesale use of the manual captured the protected content as well. Nor did the third factor favor fair use because the defendant copied "word-for-word … a substantial number of the entire outlines" (p. *6). The fourth factor also did not favor fair use because the use of the plaintiff's manuals in this way "directly impaired his ability to market his manual for his own use" (p. *6).

Similarly, in *SCQuARE Intern., Ltd. v. BBDO Atlanta, Inc.* (2006, p. 1354) the defendant initially hired the plaintiff—a "company that operates training programs to teach problem solving and communication skills"—to offer a series of internal development seminars. The defendant later developed its own set of training programs based on the plaintiff's detailed training manual. The first factor weighed against a finding of fair use because the defendant's use was commercial; the new manuals were not transformative so there was greater likelihood of "supplanting plaintiff's copyrighted work in the marketplace" (p. 1363). The second factor also weighed against fair use because the "SCQuARE Manual is neither a derivative work nor a factual compilation" (p. 1363). The third factor was neutral because the quantitative taking was a "relatively small" rendering of materials that would amount to about a half-hour presentation condensed from the plaintiff's original 24- to 26-hour session, although the condensation took the "very essence" of the original (p. 1364). Because the manuals accomplish the same training, the court concluded that the "unrestricted and widespread dissemination of defendant's condensed version of the SCQuARE Manual would undoubtedly impair the marketability of plaintiff's training program, which is expensive and lengthy" (p. 1365).

In a somewhat related scenario, a district court concluded the defendant's composition of how-to materials not to be a fair use. Here the how-to was a series of *Idea Books* and CD-ROM products that explained how to construct scrapbooks from a variety of sources, including the plaintiff's pre-made thematic sheets of stickers, such as camping and day at the beach. Some of the how-to explanation included reproductions of the stickers themselves. The district court focused not only on the stickers, but also on the idea books (derivative of the stickers) the plaintiff also published; the idea books recast (and reproduced) the stickers in various vignettes as examples of how to use its own products. The defendants argued that its books "not only promote the purchase of the Plaintiff's product, but also offer, for purchase, a differently appearing product, as they are not simply selling a sheet of Plaintiff's thematically united stickers, but a product which displays the stickers so as to portray a scenic portrayal" (*Antioch Co. v. Scrapbook Borders, Inc.*, 2003, p. 989). The court, like others before it, focused upon the derivative/transformative determination: "Here, we find that the Defendants' Idea Books are derivative works of the Plaintiff's stickers, as they are essentially a recasting of the stickers, in a compilation. ... [T]he Defendants' books might still be transformative, which would still qualify as a fair use. However, we are unable to find that the Defendants' use is transformative or, if it is, it is only inappreciably so" (pp. 990–991). As a result, the court concluded that the first factor weighed heavily against the defendants, the educational, how-to nature of the books incorporating the stickers does not override the decidedly commercial use. The second factor also weighed against fair use: "While pictorial in appearance, the stickers are not mere photographs, but are artistic renditions, which capture the creativity of their designer" (p. 994). Because the first factor weighed against fair use, the assessment of whether the amount taken was reasonable in light of a good purpose was not made; rather, the court inquired whether the use was so great that market substitution occurred. The court concluded in the affirmative, explaining: "While not every one of the Defendants' borders contains the whole complement of stickers covered under any one copyright, a great number of them use all, or the majority of, the stickers covered under a single copyright. ... [T]he quantity of the Plaintiff's stickers, which were used by the Defendants, is sufficiently substantial to elevate the Defendants' Idea Books as a market substitute for the Plaintiff's own idea books" (p. 996). In addition, the court reasoned that the heart was taken because the use was "in the exact manner for which they were intended to be used" (p. 996). The fourth factor involved consideration of both the primary market for stickers and the derivative market for how to use those stickers. Although the former market experienced "little adverse impact" and perhaps an uplift ("as promotional to the sale of the stickers") the derivative, how-to market "buyer is unlikely to purchase the Plaintiff's idea book, since he or she has already purchased one from the Defendants. As a consequence, we conclude that this factor weighs heavily in favor of a finding that the Defendants' use was not fair" (p. 997). As a result the overall use of the stickers was deemed not fair.

Two companies were at odds in *Gulfstream Aerospace Corp. v. Camp Systems International, Inc.* (2006). Gulfstream manufactures corporate jet aircraft and published maintenance manuals to accompany its planes. Camp Systems provides maintenance services for aircraft of all sorts. As Gulfstream refused to sell its manuals to Camp Systems—the typical way in which manuals were obtained by Camp Systems—Camp Systems "resorted to borrowing [per its subscription agreement with its Gulfstream owning clients] the manuals from the aircraft owners and loading parts of them onto Camp's systems" (p. 1372). When service is due on a client's aircraft, Camp Systems "sends them copies of the relevant pages from the Gulfstream manual" (p. 1373). Because the manuals were used by Camp Systems for their intended use, as instructional maintenance guides, the purpose was not transformative and the first factor weighed against a finding of fair use. The second factor, however, favored Camp Systems because the manuals were so-called "thin" (very near to uncreative and unprotected factual material) copyright: "The manuals contain mostly procedures, lists of systems, and detailed methods of operations" (p. 1378). Although the manuals were not used in their entirety, the taking was nonetheless "significant ... from both a quantitative and a qualitative standpoint ... 2,200 out of the more than 12,000 total pages in the Gulfstream manuals" (p. 1379). The court noted that this amount would count against Camp Systems "as strongly as it would" if all 12,000 pages were use, although it might nonetheless still be a fair use overall. In discussing the fourth factor, the court admitted that the reproduction and use of the manuals by Camp Stream cuts into the maintenance services also provided by Gulfstream; the service market, however, is not a derivative market of the manuals but a derivative market of aircraft manufacture. "Therefore, this fourth fair use factor weighs heavily in favor of Camp, for copyright law does not mean to protect an 'author' such as Gulfstream on these facts, where Gulfstream's desire for copyright protection has nothing to do with needing an incentive to create its manuals. Rather, what Gulfstream seeks here is to use its claimed copyright in its manuals to gain a judicially-enforced monopoly in maintenance-tracking services for Gulfstream aircraft" (p. 1380). The court concluded that the use of the manual was a fair use.

With little discussion of the four factors, the wholesale copying of a translation was deemed not fair use in *Merkos L'Inyonei Chinuch, Inc. v. Otsar Sifrei Lubavitch, Inc.* (2002). The Second Circuit reviewed a preliminary injunction issued by the district court that prevented the defendant "from disseminating a new version of Siddur Tehillat Hashem, a prayerbook widely used within the Lubavitch movement of Hasidic Judaism" (p. 96). In discussing the irreparable harm standard used in reviewing preliminary injunctions, the court made comment that also relates to an element of the fourth fair use factor: "Since Otsar sells essentially the same product as Merkos to the same market, it will obviously suffer considerable loss if Otsar disseminates its prayerbook, because each sale of an Otsar prayerbook probably results in one less sale of the Merkos' prayerbook" (pp. 96–97). The court also commented upon the creative nature of the translation: "The translation process requires exercise of careful literary and scholarly judgment" (p. 97). The plaintiff claimed that "Otsar's new version of the prayerbook violates Merkos' copyright in the original Siddur Tehillat Hashem by copying verbatim Rabbi Nissen Mangel's English translation of the Hebrew prayers, which appears in Merkos' Siddur Tehillat Hashem" (p. 96). The court concluded that on balance the four factors favored the plaintiff and against a finding of fair use "the third and fourth factors overwhelmingly favor Merkos, because Otsar has copied the entire Mangel translation and used it for a purpose identical to Merkos' use" (pp. 98–99).

Illustration, Example, or Documentation

Although not necessarily a scholarly work, fair use was found in the use of images of several concert posters to help illustrate a timeline in a documentary-style book of the popular rock band the Grateful Dead. The first factor favored fair use. Although the book *Grateful Dead: The Illustrated Trip* was a commercial work, the Second Circuit found that the "use of each image is transformatively different from the original expressive purpose" because the original posters were meant for purposes of "artistic expression and promotion" whereas here the reduced images appearing in the timeline were used "as historical artifacts to document and represent" the actual concert events (*Bill Graham Archives v. Dorling Kindersley Ltd.*, 2006, p. 609). Even though the works were creative, the court found the second factor to be of limited weight because use of the posters (and tickets) was not dependent upon the posters' creative but historical value. Similarly, the third factor "did not weigh against fair use" even though the images were used "in their entirety," in that the defendant took care to ensure that each image only "displayed the minimal image size and quality necessary" (p. 613). The plaintiff showed evidence of previous authorized re-publication of its posters in return for a license fee but the court did not view that as a justification of market harm. "Since DK's use of BGA's images falls within a transformative market, BGA does not suffer market harm due to the loss of license fees" (p. 615). If such a showing would be allowed to tip the fourth factor in favor of the plaintiff, then virtually every unauthorized use would have an impact on the market in the eyes of copyright plaintiffs because every owner would likely prefer that all uses be compensated through a license fee. Yet, as the Supreme Court and lower courts have pointed out, this would result in circular argument: "since you (the defendant) did not license the use from me you have deprived me (the plaintiff) of revenue that in turn results in market harm therefore the fourth factor should weigh against a finding of fair use." Courts, however, are careful to point out that transformative or complementary uses are fair uses that do *not* have impact upon the market in the eyes of the copyright law, therefore there can be no lost revenue from a use when a license fee is not needed to justify the use in the first instance.

Two cases involving the use of pre-existing works, one in an informational public television program and another in a documentary film, both resulted in findings of fair use. In *Higgins v. Detroit Educational Television Foundation* (1998), the defendant used two excerpts from the musical work "Under the Gun" in a 5-minute feature segment of a 28-minute, teen-targeted public television program entitled *Club Connect.* The court found the first factor favored fair use because the purpose was "non-profit, teaching" and "transformative" because the gangster rap tune was used as background music during a segment decrying gang violence (pp. 705–706). Although the work was creative in nature, the second factor did not weigh heavily in the plaintiff's favor. The third factor also favored fair use because the amount taken was small, 35 seconds of a three minute and 35 second song, or 16 percent of the work. Finally, the fourth factor also favored a finding of fair use because the use of the clip in the informational program "does not have any effect on the potential market for 'Under the Gun' ... use of two very short musical excerpts, without lyrics, of a recording of the song as background music in an educational video—cannot be said to be a substitution for the musical composition" (p. 709).

Similarly, a transformative and fair use was made of an excerpt of the John Lennon song "Imagine" in the film "EXPELLED: No Intelligence Allowed," a documentary forwarding support for the concept of intelligent design. The film juxtaposed 15 seconds of melody and 10 words from the lyrics of the chorus, relating Lennon's view of a better world to the filmmaker's impression of what the world without religion would become. In discussing the first factor the court acknowledged the commercial nature of the use, the film having grossed over 7 million dollars, "however, the movie's use of Imagine is highly transformative and not merely exploitative ... [of] broader public interest by stimulating debate on an issue of current political concern" (*Lennon v. Premise Media Corp.,* 2008, p. 322). The transformative nature was accomplished by juxtaposing the music and lyrics with stock footage from the Cold War that, in the court's view, offered a critique on the future of a world without religion. Like the photograph in *Blanch v. Koons* (2006), "defendants here use a portion of Imagine as 'fodder' for social commentary, altering it to further their distinct purpose" (*Lennon v. Premise Media Corp.,* 2008, p. 323). As with the use in *Bill Graham Archives v. Dorling Kindersley Ltd.* (2006), the excerpt constituted an insignificant portion (.27 percent) of the film. As a result, the transformative nature weighed strongly in favor of fair use. Such determinations are not without criticism in the legal literature. In spite of caution by commentators, courts have embraced such uses as transformative and fair. Henslee (2009, p. 697) argues that "allowing filmmakers to state that the images synchronized with a song are commenting on the naiveté of the song is ripe for abuse." The court admitted the creative nature of the work but, quoting *Blanch v. Koons* (2006), observed that the second factor has "limited weight, ... It thus weighs against a finding of fair use, but not strongly" (*Lennon v.*

Premise Media Corp., 2008, p. 325). The quantitative amount taken favored the defendant because the amount was reasonable in order to offer a critique of the utopian opinion expressed by several lines of the song: that the world would be better off without religion. Qualitatively, the plaintiffs attempted to demonstrate that the "Imagine" theme in lyrics and melody appears throughout the song for a total of 87 seconds or 48.8 percent of the song, arguably taking the heart of the work. Assuming this was true, the court nonetheless discounted the qualitative taking because the repetitive structure of the song requires that most all excerpts would include this sequence. Second, in situations of criticism or comment, such as the use of the signature guitar riff from "Pretty Woman" in *Campbell v. Acuff-Rose Music* (1994), the social commentator, like the parodist, needs to take a portion that references the heart of the work. As a result, both quantitative and qualitative assessments favor a finding of fair use. Comparing the market in *Bill Graham Archives v. Dorling Kindersley Ltd.* (2006) to the present case, the court observed that, although clips of the song have been used in other films such as *The Killing Fields,* the market impact in both cases occurred in a transformative market as distinguished from the primary or derivative market for the work: "Here, similarly, defendants copied plaintiffs' work for a transformative purpose, and plaintiffs have proffered no evidence to date that permitting defendants to use a fifteen-second portion of the song for a transformative purpose will usurp the market for licensing the song for traditional uses. Accordingly, this factor does not weigh strongly, if at all, against fair use" (p. 327).

In *Hofheinz v. AMC Productions, Inc.* (2001), a convoluted sequence of failed negotiations over the right to license clips of several films in a documentary about pioneer monster and teen genre movie studio American International Pictures (AIP) entitled "It Conquered the World! The Story of American International Pictures" led to an eventual court battle. Setting aside discussion of the express and implied license issues, the district court concluded that the use of the clips and other artifacts would likely be fair use. Even though the documentary was made as a commercial undertaking, the use was transformative and did "not merely purport to supersede the original works at issue, but to create a new copyrightable documentary ... a biographer is permitted to quote his subject, so too a documentary about two filmmakers should be permitted to sparingly show clips of the subjects' works ... and a handful of photographs depicting the late Nicholson" (pp. 137–138). Because the material in question was creative, the second factor "slightly favors" the plaintiff. The documentary used only clips from the studio's films, with some as short as 10 seconds and others as long as 54 seconds. Quantitatively this amount was small. The clips did not take the heart of the work but rather illustrated "the progression of AIP from its inception through its eventual demise, noting its evolution from monster genre films such as I Was a Teenage Werewolf to films glorifying the rebellious youth of the 1950s and '60s such as Beach Blanket Bingo and

Bikini Beach Party and, finally, attempting to create films that captured the experimental drug age and anti-war sentiment of the late 1960s and early '70s in films like The Wild Angels and The Trip" (pp. 139–140). The fourth factor also favored a finding of fair use, with the court observing that the documentary may even increase demand for the original films and "make more people aware of the influence that AIP had in developing the 'B' movie genre" (p. 140).

Contrast these two cases dispositive of fair use with the negative result (in terms of fair use) in *Video Pipeline, Inc. v. Buena Vista Home Entertainment, Inc.* (2003). The dispute involved the use of movie excerpts to construct competing movie trailers. The court focused on the defendant's clips in comparison to the trailers Disney had itself prepared of its own movies. In this light the Third Circuit observed that "given the shared character and purpose of the clip previews and the trailers (so that the clips will likely serve as a substitute for the trailers) and the absence of creative ingenuity in the creation of the clips, the first factor strongly weighs against fair use in this case" (p. 201). Because the source of the trailers, films such as *Pretty Woman* and *Fantasia,* constitute "paradigms of creative, non-factual expression," the second factor also weighed against a finding of fair use. The clips or trailers tended to be a minute or two in length, so the quantitative aspect of the third factor favored a fair use. The qualitative aspect did as well, in that the clips did not give away the heart of the movie and were taken from only the first half of the movies (concluding plot revelations or summations were not revealed). In considering the fourth factor, the court not only examined the impact on the original full length motion pictures but also assessed the impact on the derivative market for trailers in which Disney participated: "In light of Video Pipeline's commercial use of the clip previews and Disney's use of its trailers as described by the record evidence, we easily conclude that there is a sufficient market for, or other value in, movie previews such that the use of an infringing work could have a harmful effect cognizable under the fourth factor" (p. 202).

The "recast" of a motion picture into a cleaner, more family friendly version minus its objectionable elements—naughty words deleted, nudity either deleted or shaded out—was not a fair use in *Clean Flicks of Colorado, LLC v. Soderbergh* (2006). The first factor did not favor fair use because the use was commercial and there was "nothing transformative about the edited copies" (p. 1241). The second and third factors also favored the copyright holder in that the motion pictures were creative and "copied in almost their entirety for non-transformative use" (p. 1241). Although clean versions of the films might appeal to a new family-friendly market, the decision to enter that market is the copyright holder's: "More than merely a matter of marketing; it is a question of what audience the copyright owner wants to reach" (p. 1242). This case demonstrates that such derivative abridgment or recasting is a right of the copyright owner. In response to the decision, Congress enacted The Family Movie Act of 2005, creating a statutory exemption for companies that encode so-called objectionable content flags into motion pictures. Observe, however, that there is no actual edited reproduction of films either by such companies or the home viewer. Rather, a viewing of a "clean" version of the film is accomplished through the performing technology. When the work is "perform[ed] in or transmitted to that household for private home viewing" (17 U.S.C. § 110(11)) on an enabled machine the embedded flag signals the machine to skip the objectionable segment. The films appear edited but in reality the copy of the film is the original film in its entirety.

Compare two district cases involving the same vitamin company and the use of advertising designs in order to make information regarding the product more accessible and in turn increase sales of the product. In the first case, the use was deemed fair, and in the second, the use was not fair. In *S&L Vitamins, Inc., v. Australian Gold, Inc.* (2007), the use of small, low-resolution images of another company's products (Australian Gold), including the label design and artwork, was not transformative because both parties used the design and artwork to market the same products. Although the labels are creative, this factor weighed slightly in favor of the copyright owner. Regarding the third factor, the court observed: "Although S&L used the entire work, such use was reasonable in light of the purpose—to sell the Products. AG's artwork is not easily severable, like a literary piece, video or song" (p. 215). Discussing the fourth factor, the court identified the market as that of the vitamins in contrast to a market for the artwork on the labels of the vitamin bottles. As a result, this factor favored S&L's use in marketing the Australian Gold products. The court proceed to summarize the overall weighing of the four factors: "On balance, with two factors weighing in favor of S&L's use and two factors, albeit one only slightly, weighing against S&L's use ... this claim is not the typical copyright infringement claim ... S&L puts photographs of AG's Products, including AG's copyrighted artwork, on its website in order to sell AG's Products at a discounted price. ... Considering the statutory factors ... the Court finds that the 'copyright law's objective to promote the Progress of Science and useful Arts' would not be undermined by S&L's conduct. ... As such, the Court finds that S&L has engaged in fair use of AG's copyrighted artwork" (p. 215).

Another district court came to the opposite conclusion regarding similar circumstances. The district court in Arizona also concluded that the commercial use of the design renderings was "minimally transformative at best." Although the "electronic renderings at issue in this case were created by Designer Skin's graphic designer ... fundamentally creative in nature ... the renderings were not created for any aesthetic or educational purpose but for the functional purpose of selling products ... because of the clearly creative nature of the work, this factor weighs slightly against fair use" (*Designer Skin, LLC v. S&L Vitamins, Inc.*, 2008, p. 824). Because the entire design was used, the third factor weighed against fair use. The court identified the proper market: "The relevant market is ... the electronic images themselves. Designer Skin seems to concede that there is no market for these images" (pp. 824–825). As a result there was no harm to this market. "Nonetheless, with three factors weighing against fair use (although two only slightly) and only one weighing in favor of it (albeit the most important one), the Court finds that copying the electronic renderings from Designer Skin's website and pasting them on S & L Vitamins' own sites for the purpose of selling Designer Skin's products is not protected by the fair use doctrine" (p. 825). Both courts found the use to be commercial and not transformative, the second factor to weigh only slightly in the plaintiffs' favor, and little evidence of an independent market for the artwork found on vitamin bottles. The difference appears to be that in the first case the court characterized the amount taken as reasonable in light of the functional purpose of advertising.

In vacating a district court order for preliminary injunction against the defendant the Ninth Circuit implied that, depending on the particular circumstances, use of a screen shot to advertise a compatible competing product could be fair use. The first factor favored fair use because "comparative advertising redounds greatly to the purchasing public's benefit with very little corresponding loss to the integrity of Sony's copyrighted material" (*Sony Computer Entertainment America, Inc. v. Bleem, LLC*, 2000, p. 1027). Although the video game as a whole might be creative, the court indicated that a screen shot is an "inanimate sliver" of the game and so the second factor favors neither party (p. 1028). The third factor favored fair use in that a screen shot is 1/30 of a second's worth of the video game. The fourth factor also favored a finding of fair use. The use of several screen shots in Bleem's advertisements did not impair the value of screen shots. Consistent with other decisions, the appellate court distinguished harm to the market for the product from harm to the market for copyright aspects of the product. The former is not within the remedy of the copyright law: "If sales of Sony consoles drop, it will be due to the Bleem emulator's technical superiority over the PlayStation console, not because Bleem used screen shots to illustrate that comparison" (p. 1029).

News Reporting and Current Event Coverage

Several cases demonstrate that use of protected material, such as photographs and film clips, for purposes of documentation in news reporting and related current event coverage is often a fair use. Courts are careful to preserve the delicate balance of interests in these cases. The subject of the content is obviously factual, which would weigh in favor of fair use. This is supported by a First Amendment interest in news reporting. Yet property interests must also be recognized in order to preserve the incentive to capture newsworthy information and images. In *Nunez v. Caribbean International News Corp.* (2000), the First Circuit concluded that fair use applied to a newspaper that published photographs of a Miss Puerto Rico contestant in conjunction with a news story about her qualifications. The photographs were originally intended as part of her modeling portfolio, but once a scandal erupted over her prior conduct, the use of "the photographs in conjunction with editorial commentary" was deemed transformative and tipped the first factor in favor of fair use (p. 23). Although photographs can be creative, the court concluded the second factor was neutral in that "the photographs were not artistic representations designed primarily to express Nunez's ideas, emotions, or feelings, but instead a publicity attempt to highlight Giraud's abilities as a potential model" (p. 23). Although the photographs were used in their entirety, the court observed that "to copy any less than that would have made the picture useless to the story" (p. 24). In other words, the amount taken was reasonable in light of the purpose; therefore the third factor was of "little consequence" in the overall assessment of fair use (p. 24). In assessing the fourth factor, the court looked to the market for the specific photographs but also questioned "whether wide-scale reproduction of professional photographs in newspapers (for similar purposes) would in general affect the market for such photography" (pp. 24–25). As the specific photographs were distributed for free and were not created originally as news or scoops but as head shots of Giraud, there would be no disincentive message sent to Nunez, or other photographers for that matter. True, another market for the photographs—as news items—might exist and "El Vocero's use of the photograph without permission essentially destroys this market. There is no evidence, however, that such a market ever existed in this case" (p. 25). Looking at the lack of market harm from another perspective, the question becomes whether allowing such uses by newspapers will destroy the incentive of professional photographers to create such works in the future. If so, such a result would promote neither the public policy behind the fair use exception, nor the copyright law in general, to encourage the creation of new works. If the result of such uses is to leave unaffected the incentive to create such works—photographers will continue to undertake modeling shoots even though some headshots might end up on the front page of the local newspaper—then the public interest is served and use can be deemed fair. In other words, Nunez and other professional modeling photographers will continue to offer services, create new photographs of hopeful models, and earn a living from such work even though it is possible that some of the subjects of future photographs may likewise end up on the front pages as news.

Contrast the result in *Fitzgerald v. CBS Broadcasting, Inc.* (2007), where the use of one of the few known images of famous gangster Stephen Flemmi was not a fair use. The original shot was scooped by an independent photojournalist years before, capturing Flemmi as he was being transferred from a police vehicle. Years after the shots of Flemmi were taken, he again became a news item when another gangster, John Martorano, was due to be sentenced. "That day, CBS-4 reporter Christina Hager and video editor Scott Erdman prepared a news report on the sentencing. Erdman found the unpurged image of Flemmi on the pitch reel, cropped out the part of the photo showing the officers accompanying

Flemmi, and used an exposure of the cropped image on the 11:00 news that evening on CBS-4. The report was broadcast again at 1:35 AM on June 25, and probably three times more, at 5:00 AM and 6:00 AM on CBS-4, and at 7:00 AM on UPN-38 that same day. The photograph was also posted on the CBS-4 website from June 25 to June 29" (p. 181). The court concluded that the first factor did not favor fair use, with the use falling "somewhere between" *Nunez v. Caribbean International News Corp.* (2000) and *Los Angeles News Service v. KCAL-TV Channel 9* (1997), because the use was commercial and the cropping into the new story was not transformative. The second factor weighed in favor of fair use because the photographs were factual in nature. The photograph was not used in its entirety but cropping down to the Flemmi image alone nonetheless took the heart of the work. Even though the third factor was "balanced between fair use and infringement ... overall significance of this factor to the fair use determination is minor" (*Fitzgerald v. CBS Broadcasting, Inc.*, 2007, p. 189). When the purpose for creating the photograph in the first instance is to document or scoop an event, as news, then similar use of the photograph, as news, can have an impact upon the incentive structure to create such works in the first place. Fitzgerald was a freelance photojournalist and his livelihood depended on revenue from use of his scoop photos as news. Concluding that such subsequent uses would be fair undermines the purpose of the copyright law, which is to foster the creation of more works. The court considered this broader impact that unrestricted use of news photographs would have on the market for the creation of similar images by other photojournalists: "CBS's use of the photographs is paradigmatic of the only market the photographs could reasonably have: licensing to media outfits. There is no significant demand for 8 x 10 glossies of Flemmi sold directly to the public [or distributed for free as part of a modeling portfolio in *Nunez v. Caribbean International News Corp.* (2000)]. ... It is hard to imagine that freelance photojournalists would continue to seek out and capture difficult to achieve pictures if they could not expect to collect any licensing fees. This is exactly the kind of situation that copyright is meant to impact—where unrestricted use would likely dry up the source" (*Fitzgerald v. CBS Broadcasting, Inc.*, 2007, p. 189).

In a similar vein, contrast two cases with opposite results in terms of fair use concerning the same clip of news film. In a dispute arising over the use of video footage of the Reginald Denny beating during riots spawned by the Rodney King verdict, the Ninth Circuit concluded that the grant of summary judgment in favor of the defendants based on fair use was improper. The court implied that news reporting was not the sole purpose: "The fact that KCAL used LANS's copyrighted footage free of charge, rather than paying LANS or someone else for the footage, or investing in its own helicopter and crew to obtain the footage itself, at least raises an inference that its articulated purpose of reporting the news was mixed with the actual purpose of doing so by using the best version—whether or not it meant riding LANS's (or some other station's) copyrighted coattails" (*Los Angeles News Service v. KCAL-TV Channel 9*, 1997, p. 1121). The addition of a voice-over by a KCAL-TV Channel 9 reporter did not transform the use into anything new. The factual nature of the clip of the Denny beating and rioting after the Rodney King decision weighs in favor of fair use. Although of short duration, in comparison to the entire footage shot by LANS of the riots, the clip of rioters pulling Denny from his truck and savagely beating him "was all that mattered" (p. 1122). Addressing the fourth factor, the court observed that the facts may defy traditional classification, or "niche," as there typically is not a wide secondary market for news clips (p. 1122). The circumstances revealed that there was at least a market for KCAL-TV's use of the clip because LANS refused it a license when first approached. Although the use of the "copyrighted tape was arguably in the public interest ... KCAL's use was commercial and came in the wake of LANS's refusal of a license ... it is not obvious that there was no impact on the market for first publication rights as KCAL itself requested a license. There is no dispute that KCAL used the heart of the tape. Under these circumstances, we cannot say that fair use is the only reasonable conclusion a trier of fact could reach in this case" (p. 1123).

Compare the result in *Los Angeles News Service v. CBS Broadcasting, Inc.* (2002), where the Ninth Circuit examined use of a few seconds of the same clip several years later but in a somewhat different context removed from reportage and "concluded that each factor, particularly the nature of the copyrighted work, weighs in favor of fair use except the substantiality of the use, which we treat as neutral. Accordingly, we agree with the district court that CourtTV's use was protected, and we affirm the grant of summary judgment in its favor" (*Los Angeles News Service v. CBS Broadcasting, Inc.*, 2002, p. 942). KCAL-TV Channel 9 used the clip as news, but CourtTV used it in a promotional montage juxtaposed with trial testimony of the assailants accused of the beating. Although the first factor weighed weakly in favor of fair use, the second factor favored fair use because the clip was information, factual, and news. "We do not gainsay the importance of the frames that CourtTV used—if not the heart, they amount at least to a ventricle—but we think that this factor weighs less in LANS's favor than in the previous cases involving the Denny video. Indeed, weighing the brevity of the portion copied against its significance, this factor appears neutral" (p. 941). The market for news reporting visuals is different from the market for court room drama representations, therefore the court could not conclude that use of the clip would have an impact on the market through substitution: "Court TV was not competing with LANS to show riot coverage, or even breaking news of the same general type; the courtroom setting is, after all, singularly unsuited to helicopter coverage" (p. 942).

Fair use was also found in the use by *The Globe* of segments from a television program in *National Association of Government Employees/ International Brotherhood of Police Officers v. BUCI* (2000). Although the plaintiffs claimed the purpose was to discredit the plaintiffs rather than for news reporting, the court observed that no evidence was offered to forward that claim. The fact that the comments in question were informational, made during an interview that had already aired, and used "a relatively small and qualitatively insubstantial portion [three sentences of four pages of transcripts] of the copyrighted work favors a fair-use finding" (p. 129). As a result, the second and third factors favored a finding of fair use. The fourth factor was neutral, again for lack of evidence but also because "any negative impact must result from the alleged act of copyright infringement, not merely from a disparaging remark" (p. 129). The news reporting cases involving photographs and clips indicate that when the subsequent use is for the same purpose (as news or scoop) the use is not fair if the incentive to create such works in the future is jeopardized. The cases also demonstrate that the nature of the images is often factual, either favoring fair use or of little significance. Moreover, in the case of photographs the entire image may be necessary but still not weigh against a finding of fair use.

A number of good purposes regarding the creation of new content include textbooks or other learning tools such as outlines and training material; use or re-evaluation of interviews and other primary sources in the biographies; and illustration, example, or documentation including news reporting or other current event coverage.

The lesson of these cases is tri-fold. First, the amount or substantiality of the portion used should be no more than is necessary in order to make a transforming use; this may represent the entire work in cases involving photographs or other images. Moreover, the nature of the work, even where "thick" or creative, is a less significant factor in the overall fair use analysis when a transformative purpose is present. Second, uses such as critique and evaluation are complementary and do not implicate the exclusive right of the copyright owner to make derivative works. Third, complementary and transformative uses tend not to have an impact on the market for, or value of, the work.

Access Tools Such as Guides and Indexes, Including Archiving and Extraction of Unprotected Elements

New works such as guides and indexes—including archiving, preservation, and data extraction that assist others locating content or serve as an intermediary step in the access or use of content—are also functional uses. The goal is to provide access to other works, not to supersede the work itself. By design such uses are not superseding or substitutive, but complementary. Such uses are often fair but must be distinguished from uses that exploit the value of the original or otherwise supersede the market for the original. Another lesson, consistent with the theme of this chapter, is that an entire taking matters little if use of the work in its entirety is necessary in order to make the access tool or index useful. This may be the case with indexes of visual objects. These cases were often cited by commentators (and by Google, Inc.) in support of the necessity of full-text reproduction of literary works, such as books, in order to make an effective search tool. In the normal course of their work educators, librarians, archivists, and other information professionals compile pathfinders or other search and subject guides; annotated bibliographies; book, product, and resources reviews; and similar advisory services.

The publication of photographs of Beanie Babies in two distinct contexts was the focus of the Seventh Circuit discussion in *Ty, Inc. v. Publication International Ltd.* (2002). The first context was as a source of entertainment in titles such as *For the Love of Beanie Babies* aimed at a child audience; the second context was informational in a *Beanie Babies Collector's Guide*. The decision, written by Judge Posner, engaged in an elaborate discussion of complementary and substitutive goods in the context of derivative works; for example, photographs of sculptural works such as Beanie Babies (quoted earlier in this chapter). It was clear that a photographic representation of a Beanie Baby is not a substitute for the original soft sculptural work itself: "No one who wants a Beanie Baby, whether a young child who wants to play with it or an adult (or older child) who wants to collect Beanie Babies, would be tempted to substitute a photograph" (pp. 518–519). Although not actually discussing the four fair use factors, Posner nonetheless made several observations intended for the district court to consider upon remand, insights that may guide other users in the construction of reviews and evaluative tools. Such products serve a valuable purpose, especially in light of Ty, Inc.'s practice of licensing only "authorized" guides to publishers, allowing Ty, Inc. to control the text of such guides, and, more oddly, to include on those licensed guides a statement to the effect that the guide was not associated with Ty, Inc. even though Ty, Inc. could vet the text at its discretion. "Indeed, a collectors' guide is very much like a book review, which is a guide to a book and which no one supposes is a derivative work. Both the book review and the collectors' guide are critical and evaluative as well as purely informational; and ownership of a copyright does not confer a legal right to control public evaluation of the copyrighted work" (pp. 520–521). Guides, reviews, and evaluative tools are not derivative of the works that form the basis of the guide, review, or evaluation; rather, the reader may recall, such works are complements of the work. The court focused on the use of the derivative photographs (a photograph is derivative of the protected work it represents) in a non-derivative work, a collector's guide, and assessed whether the amount, a full photograph of each Beanie Baby, was justified. Judge Poser explored the limits of the copyright holder's exclusive right in light of possible anti-competitive effects from exercise of those rights: "How could a competitor forbidden to publish photos of the complete line compete? And if it couldn't compete, the result would be to deliver into Ty's hands a monopoly of Beanie Baby collectors' guides … if Beanie Babies collectors guides are indeed a complement to Beanie Babies (and they are), and Ty has a monopoly of Beanie Babies (and it does), Ty can get a second monopoly profit by taking over the guides market" (p. 521). This case demonstrates the broader economic considerations that underlie copyright and fair use. Copyright law strives to protect the incentive to create, but it also dissuades protection of monopolistic control over facts or other fair uses. Again, without discussing the four fair use factors per se, Posner summarized the issue: "The question is whether it would be unreasonable to conclude, with reference to one or more of the enjoined publications, such as the *Beanie Babies Collector's Guide*, that the use of the photos is a fair use because it is the only way to prepare a collectors' guide" (p. 522). Again, the presence of necessity, in the use of the work in its entirety (a photograph of an entire Beanie Baby), is often a crucial factor in determining the impact of the third factor upon the overall assessment of fair use. In discussing two previous cases, Judge Posner distinguished between the detailed episode guide to the television series *Twin Peaks* held not to be a fair use in *Twin Peaks Productions, Inc. v. Publications International Ltd.* (1993) and the similarly unfair use of a trivia book based on the television series *Seinfeld* in *Castle Rock Entertainment, Inc. v. Carol Publishing Group* (1998).

Although not a "guide" per se but a supplement to a television series, the publication of the *Seinfeld* trivia book entitled *The Seinfeld Aptitude Test (SAT)* was deemed not fair in *Castle Rock Entertainment, Inc. v. Carol Publishing Group* (1998). In discussing the four fair use factors, the Second Circuit concluded that the first factor did not favor fair use because the transformative purpose was "slight to non-existent [because] the work as a whole, drawn directly from the *Seinfeld* episodes without substantial alteration, is far less transformative than other works we have held not to constitute fair use" (p. 143). The *Seinfeld* series, being a work of fiction, was creative so the second factor also favored the plaintiffs. The third factor also weighed against fair use, although the court discussed it little other than to note the 643 questions included in the *SAT* stressed the non-transformative and entertainment purpose of the book. Nor did the fourth factor favor fair use. Although the trivia book may or may not be a substitute for watching the series, the book did enter the derivative market for products based on the original work, the television series: "Because The SAT borrows exclusively from *Seinfeld* and not from any other television or entertainment programs, The SAT is likely to fill a market niche that Castle Rock would in general develop" (p. 143).

Similarly, the episode guide in *Twin Peaks Productions, Inc. v. Publications International Ltd.* (1993) was also held not to be a fair use. The first factor again weighed against a finding of fair use. The problem for the compilers of the episode guide was that too much was taken, which lessened the transformative purpose that guides generally serve, while at the same time making it more likely to substitute for the original: "Use of the protected expression in the teleplays consists primarily of summarizing in great detail the plots of the first eight episodes. ... [I]t is not uncommon for works serving a fair use purpose to give at least a brief indication of the plot. ... Detailed report of the plots goes far beyond merely identifying their basic outline for the transformative purposes of comment or criticism. What PIL has done is simply to recount for its readers precisely the plot details of each teleplay" (p. 1375). The second factor weighed against a finding of fair use because the television series was creative. In order to make fair comment, some of the original must be taken but the creators of the episode guide took too much: "What PIL lifted was plainly substantial in relation to the copyrighted works as a whole" (p. 1377). Although the court hypothesized that the episode guide could be a substitute for the actual series, by filling in the blanks if an episode was missed by a viewer, the more significant market harm occurred to the derivative market in that creators of television series would be expected to produce such guides. As a result the fourth factor also weighed against a finding of fair use.

The most recent decision involving guide books involved the publication of a print version of the *Harry Potter Lexicon*. The lesson of the case is that an evaluative work, such as a collector's guide, or as here an index—an alphabetic and encyclopedic lexicon to a multi-volume fictional book series—can be a good purpose as long as the work does not take too much. The lesson of the relationship between the first and third factors is also underscored. A good purpose will diminish as more of the original is taken, reducing the transformative nature while likely also increasing the substitutive nature of the new work. In *Warner Brothers Entertainment, Inc. v. RDR Books* (2008), the publication of *The Lexicon: An Unauthorized Guide to Harry Potter Fiction and Related Material* was found to be an unfair use. The court observed that such multi-volume fiction "works lend themselves to companion guides or reference works because they reveal an elaborate imaginary world over thousands of pages, involving many characters, creatures, and magical objects that appear and reappear across thousands of pages" (p. 526). Alphabetic and encyclopedic guides do not recast the content of the original in any creative way or recast "the material in another medium to retell the story," so the product is not derivative. "Plaintiffs have failed to show that the Lexicon is a derivative work" (p. 539). The court applied the four fair use factors to two sets of books, the original *Harry Potter* series and the companion books Rawlings also wrote. Although the "practical purpose of making information about the intricate world of Harry Potter readily accessible to readers in a reference guide" is transformative of the series, the purpose with respect to the companion works is so to a "much lesser" extent (p. 541). The second factor clearly weighed against a finding of fair use: "Such highly imaginative and creative fictional works are close to the core of copyright protection, particularly where the character of the secondary work is not entirely transformative ... the second factor favors Plaintiffs" (p. 549). Most problematic and key to the overall conclusion against fair use was the court's view that too much was taken. The *Lexicon* was too detailed; as more and more was taken its informational and "good" transformative purpose lessened and its entertaining "bad" substitutive effect increased. The court was reluctant to establish any bright-line test of how much was too much: "While it is difficult to draw the line at each entry that takes more than is reasonably necessary from the *Harry Potter* series to serve its purposes ... the *Lexicon* disturbs the balance and takes more than is reasonably necessary to create a reference guide. In these instances, the *Lexicon* appears to retell parts of the storyline rather than report fictional facts and where to find them" (p. 549). Regarding the shorter companion books, the assessment "presents an easier determination. The *Lexicon* takes wholesale from these short books" (pp. 548–549). In considering the fourth factor, the court observed that use of the *Lexicon* alone by a reader would impair not the market for the actual series books themselves but "publication of the *Lexicon* could harm sales of ... two companion books. Unless they sought to enjoy the companion books for their entertainment value alone, consumers who purchased the Lexicon would have scant incentive to purchase either of Rowling's companion books ... information ... in these short works has been incorporated into the *Lexicon* almost wholesale" (p. 550). The court summarized its analysis: "The fair-use factors, weighed together in light of the purposes of copyright law, fail to support the defense of fair use in this case. The first factor ... is not consistently transformative. Without drawing a line at the amount of copyrighted material that is reasonably necessary to create an A-to-Z reference guide, many portions of the *Lexicon* take more of the copyrighted works than is reasonably necessary in relation to the *Lexicon*'s purpose. Thus, in balancing the first and third factors, the balance is tipped against a finding of fair use. The creative nature of the copyrighted works and the harm to the market for Rowling's companion books weigh in favor of Plaintiffs" (p. 550). The lesson again is well taken: Guide books can be fair use when informational in purpose, rather than entertainment oriented, and when the amount of the work used is limited to a reasonable portion necessary to make an effective evaluation. Band (2007a, p. 2) also comments favorably upon the decision even if the use was not fair: "The decision leaves ample room for the creation of reference guides to literary works, even when the works do not contain scholarly criticism or analysis." Using the opinion as a blueprint, the author Steve Vander Ark published a revised version in 2009 under the title *The Lexicon: An Unauthorized Guide to Harry Potter Fiction and Related Material*.

The first case to address indexing in the internet context concluded that use of a search engine crawler to compile a database of images that appeared to searchers as thumbnails was a fair use. Clicking on the thumbnail allowed the searcher access a larger version of the image. Arriba created its thumbnails by copying images from other websites; the full size images were created by use of in-line linking and other techniques that displayed but did not reproduce the images. In applying fair use to the reproduction issue alone, the Ninth Circuit observed that even though the use was commercial, the reduced size of the 35 images by the photographer Kelly made the use unlikely to be superseding; moreover, the use was transformative: "This case involves more than merely a retransmission of Kelly's images in a different medium. Arriba's use of the images serves a different function than Kelly's use—improving access to information on the internet versus artistic expression" (*Kelly v. Arriba Soft Corp.*, 2003, p. 819). The court admitted that Kelly's photographs were creative but that their published nature (posted on the internet) weighed only "slightly in favor" of Kelly. The third factor "neither weighs for nor against either party" because it was reasonable and necessary "to copy the entire image to allow users to recognize the image and decide whether to pursue more information about the image or the originating website. If Arriba only copied part of the image, it would be more difficult to identify it, thereby reducing the usefulness of the visual search engine" (p. 820). In discussing the fourth factor the court observed that there is less chance of market substitution where a transformative use is made of the work. Moreover, the low resolution of the thumbnails ensured that anyone who desired the full-sized image for its aesthetic value would need to obtain the image from the Kelly website.

Archiving, Preservation, and Extraction

In two cases assessing the caching and archiving of webpages by Google, Inc., courts commented on the public benefit of such practices and concluded that fair use applied in both cases. In *Perfect 10 v. Amazon.com, Inc.* (2007) the Ninth Circuit concluded that the reproduction of thumbnail images by Google, Inc. as part of its search system to locate images on the World Wide Web was a fair use, although the court indicated that secondary liability might still be present when Google, Inc. provides access to infringing images that others have posted: "Google could be held contributorily liable if it had knowledge that infringing Perfect 10 images were available using its search engine, could take simple measures to prevent further damage to Perfect 10's copyrighted works, and failed to take such steps" (p. 1172). The individuals who scanned and posted the "centerfolds" would be the primary infringers: "Perfect 10 alleges that third parties directly infringed its images in three ways. First, Perfect 10 claims that third-party websites directly infringed its copyright by reproducing, displaying, and distributing unauthorized copies of Perfect 10's images. Google does not dispute this claim on appeal" (p. 1169). Secondary liability, either vicarious or contributory, is predicated on the existence of primary liability on the part of a third party. Vicarious liability is based on the relationship between the primary infringer and the intermediary or third party. A typical example is the employer-employee relationship, where the employer is vicariously liable for the primary infringement of its employees, such as a school district and its teachers. If a teacher reproduces unauthorized copies of a workbook to distribute to a class, the teacher would be the primary infringer and the school district the vicarious infringer. Contributory liability is based upon the conduct of a third party toward the direct infringer where, with knowledge or a reason to know of the infringing result, the third party somehow substantially contributes, causes, or induces the person to engage in infringing conduct. An example might be where, instead of making the copies of the protected workbook for the class, the teacher orders students to go to the library where the workbook is on reserve, check out the workbook, and "make a copy of the workbook and bring it to class next week, you can't pass this course without it." Given the nature of the K-12 teacher-student relationship, a court might well conclude that substantial contribution is present.

In contrast to the primary liability of third-party websites in posting the images that Google, Inc.'s search engines cache and archive, the court discussed the application of fair use as defense to the primary liability resulting from the reproduction of the Perfect 10 images, that is, reproduction performed by Google, Inc. as part of its cache and archive processes. In discussing Google, Inc.'s primary liability and fair use, the court observed the transformative purpose and value of search engine practices: "We conclude that the significantly transformative nature of Google's search engine, particularly in light of its public benefit, outweighs Google's superseding and commercial uses of the thumbnails in this case" (p. 1168). Although the images in question were creative, the second factor "weighed only slightly in favor of the photographer" (p. 1167). As with other image cases and citing its own precedent in *Kelly v. Arriba Soft Corp.* (2003), the appellate court agreed with the district court that the third factor favored neither party. Although the district court weighed the fourth factor in favor of Perfect 10 because downloading thumbnail images for use on cell phones was a potential market— Google, Inc.'s thumbnails could be a market substitute for the thumbnails cell phone users might want to purchase from Perfect 10— the Ninth Circuit concluded that the "potential harm to Perfect 10's market remains hypothetical. We conclude that this factor favors neither party" (*Perfect 10 v. Amazon.com, Inc.*, 2007, p. 1168).

In *Field v. Google, Inc.* (2006) Google, Inc.'s caching practices were also at issue. The district court again observed the good purpose behind efforts such as archiving or caching: "The fact that the owners of billions of webpages choose to permit these links to remain is further evidence that they do not view Google's cache as a substitute for their own pages. Because Google serves different and socially important purposes in offering access to copyrighted works through 'cached' links and does not merely supersede the objectives of the original creations, the Court concludes that Google's alleged copying and distribution of Field's webpages containing copyrighted works was transformative" (p. 1119). Field failed to exercise the do-not-cache protocol when creating his website by including the robots.txt file that would have prevented the Google, Inc. system from caching his website along with images it contained. The court found this indicative of bad faith: Field crying wolf for the very acts that he sought to encourage or at least could have easily prevented by inclusion of the file command. This also tipped the first factor in favor of fair use. Even if the photographs at issue in this case, like those in *Kelly v. Arriba Soft Corp.* (2003), are creative, the second factor weighs "only slightly in Field's favor" (*Field v. Google, Inc.*, 2006, p. 1120). Although Google, Inc. caches the complete image, "no more of the works than is necessary" is taken, and as in other cases of photographs, the third fair use factor was neutral (p. 1121). Field failed to introduce any evidence of market harm or the value of his photographs: "Field makes the works available to the public for free in their entirety, and admits that he has never received compensation from selling or licensing them" (p. 1121). As a result the use was fair.

The public benefit of large-scale archiving, search, and retrieval processes was again evident in a case involving not images but literary works—the texts of student papers. The full-text reproduction and storage was again necessary in order for the TurnItIn database to prevent plagiarism effectively. The court concluded that the first factor favored a finding of fair use because the use "was completely unrelated to expressive content and was instead aimed at detecting and discouraging plagiarism" (*A.V. v. iParadigms, Ltd.*, 2009, p. 640). The court observed that a transformative use need not alter the original; the function rather than form is paramount: "The use of a copyrighted work need not alter or augment the work to be transformative in nature. Rather, it can be transformative in function or purpose without altering or actually adding to the original work" (p. 639). Thatcher (2009) presents a recent and brief but insightful rebuttal of this interpretation of "transformative." When discussing the second fair use factor, the court observed that although the student papers were unpublished, the use of the papers in the TurnItIn database did nothing to impede the right of first publication, and even though the papers were creative, the use "was not related to the creative core of the works" (*A.V. v. iParadigms, Ltd.*, 2009, p. 641). Although complete reproduction of the student papers occurred, the circuit court found no error in the district court's finding that "iParadigms uses the entirety of the original works. In order to be successful in its plagiarism detection services, it must" (p. 483). In commenting on the fourth factor, the court acknowledged that the market for the papers as fodder for future plagiarists might be affected: Once in the system, the student-author would be prevented from offering his or her paper for sale on one of the buy-a-term-paper websites. "There is a market for students who wish to purchase such works and submit them as their own for academic credit ... archiving of such papers on the TurnItIn website might well impair the marketability of such works to student buyers intending to submit works they did not author without being identified as plagiarists" (p. 643). Without decrying the use of papers in this way, the court simply found no evidence of actual or probable harm to this market, rather the allegation of harm was no more than "unfounded speculation" (p. 645). The appellate court confirmed the district court's finding of fair use.

The value of archived screenshots from a prior iteration of the plaintiff's website, which was at one time public and had since been removed but was now stored by the Internet Archive, was acknowledged in *Healthcare Advocates, Inc. v. Harding, Earley, Follmer & Frailey* (2007). Healthcare Advocates, Inc. was the plaintiff in underlying litigation with a competing patient service entity regarding trademark and trade secret violations; Harding, Earley, Follner, and Frailey were attorneys for the defendant in that case. Healthcare Advocates, Inc. did not want the Harding law firm to use the previous website material against it because it might disprove its allegation of infringement. Healthcare Advocates, Inc. turned to the copyright law in order to thwart the pretrial discovery process that attempted "to see what Healthcare Advocates' public website looked like prior" to its current state, that is, what information was available to the public on its website at the particular time the defendants in the underlying litigation accessed and relied upon it. In accessing the stored websites through use of the Wayback Machine, none of the screen shots were saved "onto their computer hard drives" of the law firm (p. 630). In an odd but related corollary to this litigation, Healthcare Advocates, Inc. used the robots.txt file to prevent the archiving of its website. Unfortunately, it added this protocol to its website after a number of versions were cached by the Internet Archive. This would have prevented a new searcher from accessing any content, including those prior to its do-not-cache command, according to the procedures that the Internet Archive had in place at that time. Worse, on the day that the Harding law firm searched for an earlier version of the Healthcare Advocates, Inc. "the servers which checked for robots.txt files and blocked the images were malfunctioning. Internet Archive's servers did not respect the robots.txt file on Healthcare Advocates' live website. Thus, the Harding firm was able to view and print copies of archived screenshots of Healthcare Advocates' website stored in Internet Archive's database" (p. 632). Healthcare Advocates, Inc. commenced the present litigation thereafter, alleging among other things copyright infringement by the Harding law firm through its "viewing and printing copies of the archived images of the Healthcare Advocates' webpages, by unknowingly saving copies of these webpages in temporary files known as caches, and by distributing the images to their co-counsel in the Underlying Litigation" (p. 633). Harding responded by claiming fair use and the district court agreed. The court saw the purpose behind the law firm's viewing and printing the archived images of the public website to favor fair use necessitated by "an attempt to defend their client against a charge of copyright infringement" (p. 637). The website was "primarily a marketing tool" and "advertising" for the medical group; therefore, the "nature of these works was predominately informational" (p. 638). The second factor also favored fair use. Although the law firm "copied everything," the use was reasonable and "necessary" because the screenshots were used to "defend their clients against copyright and trademark infringement claims ... the firm had a duty to preserve relevant evidence. They fulfilled that duty by printing copies. Therefore, the substantiality of the portion used does not militate against a finding of fair use" (p. 638). The fact that the screenshots represented examples of webpages that were no longer used "suggested that the worth [of the webpages] is negligible" (p. 639). The court also observed that "copies of the images may exist all over the world" (p. 639). As a result, the fourth factor also favored a finding of fair use. The website or other internet archive cases do not stand for the proposition that any archive is a fair use. A consistent factor in these cases is the public or comprehensive but singular source these repositories represent. In most of the cases the act of caching, cache-linking, archiving, or full-text searching and retrieval does not allow the user to obtain a copy of the work in its original state. Although Google, Inc. offered thumbnails, this being arguably a "bad," non-transformative reproduction of each image used, the court rather explained the necessity of using the entire unaltered work in order to facilitate the operation of the finding tool, access point, verification service, or some other sort of location or authority control.

Of course, the next logical case would be text indexing, which to some extent is present in the *A.V. v. iParadigms, Ltd.* (2009) and *Healthcare Advocates, Inc. v. Harding, Earley, Follmer & Frailey* (2007), but on a cosmic scale, involving every book in a particular library. This scenario should sound familiar given the various iterations of the Google Book and Library projects. Numerous commentators in both the LIS (Baksik, 2006) and legal (Band, 2007b; Hanratty, 2005; Thatcher, 2006) literatures have contributed to the assessment of whether fair use would be extended by the courts to include such initiatives. Band forwards a fair use defense; Thatcher decries extending fair use to Google Book or Google-esque settings; and Hanratty falls somewhere in the middle, concluding that such use is not fair but it would be in the publishers' best interest to acquiesce and embrace a new market model for the access and distribution of protected works. One clear impact of the settlement is that although no precedential legal opinion was rendered in the matter, the actual application of fair use to the Google, Inc. projects and the implication such a ruling might have had for other practices, such as e-reserve and online course management practices, remain relegated to the musing of academics and other interested parties.

Contrast these positive cases, in terms of fair use, with the substitutive unfair use of content in the following two cases. The reproduction of six sets of construction photographs in arbitration proceedings was deemed not fair in *Images Audio Visual Productions, Inc. v. Perini Building Co., Inc.* (2000). "These six sets, totaling approximately 1,830 copies, were intended for distribution to the three arbitrators, the witnesses, and each side's counsel" (p. 1078). The alleged infringement arose because the defendant repeatedly rejected the plaintiff's price quotes for the copying as exorbitant, so the defendant had a local copy shop make the copies instead. Unlike the transformative use of the website archiving cases, here there was nothing transformative or preservative in the photocopying. Although the defendant attempted to use a "litigation" exception similar to the *Healthcare Advocates, Inc. v. Harding, Earley, Follmer & Frailey* (2007) case, the court was unreceptive because the plaintiff was hired specifically to create a visual history of the defendant's construction site, should a dispute such as this arise. Moreover, that contract set the price for additional reprints of the plaintiff's work product. Because the copies were used for the same purpose as the original photographs were intended, "as a pictorial record of Defendant's progress on the Soaring Eagle construction project," there is no transformative use (*Images Audio Visual Productions, Inc. v. Perini Building Co., Inc.*, 2000, p. 1081). The first factor weighed heavily in favor of the plaintiff. The court found the photographs creative in that the visual archive of the construction progress "captured the various stages of the project in a way that no other form of evidence could. This is precisely the creative insight provided by a professional photographer, whether he is shooting a construction site or a natural scene" (p. 1085). The court also pointed to the defendant's desire to use the photographic record as evidence supporting the conclusion that the "photos lie more at the creative than at the functional end of the spectrum of copyrighted works" (p. 1085). The third factor also weighed against fair use because 287 of the 305 photographs were used in their entirety, including color copies of some as well. An existing contract identified the market for or value of the photographs, that is, what a set of the images would cost should a dispute occur and copies of the photographic record of the construction site serve as evidence in arbitrating that dispute; the court therefore concluded that the "unauthorized reproduction of Plaintiff's photos substantially impaired one of the intended markets for the works. Moreover, such unauthorized reproduction, were it to become more widespread, would severely jeopardize the potential market for works intended for use in litigation"—the market image for documentation services (p. 1086).

A similar result of non-transformative, unfair use of a subscription-based work was found in *Lowry's Reports, Inc. v. Legg Mason, Inc.* (2003). The publication at the center of the infringement dispute was a daily and weekly newsletter entitled *Lowry's New York Stock Exchange Market Trend Analysis* that consisted of "original and proprietary technical analysis of the stock market. Each issue includes unique statistics, comparative graphs, charts, and commentary" (*Lowry's Reports, Inc. v. Legg Mason, Inc.*, 2003, p. 742). According to the complaint "since at least 1993 Legg Mason [has] been reproducing and distributing throughout the company each daily and weekly version of Lowry's New York Stock Exchange Market Trend Analysis via facsimile, and since at least August 29, 2000 via its company-wide intranet" (*Lowry's Reports, Inc. v. Legg Mason, Inc.*, 2001, para 17). The defendant admitted this use was infringing but argued that the "more limited paper—and email—copying within its research department" was fair use (*Lowry's Reports, Inc. v. Legg Mason, Inc.*, 2003, p. 748). The court had little difficulty in determining that the purpose and character of this use also "weighs heavily against Legg Mason ... use thus exploited the Reports for the commercial benefit of Legg Mason, at the price of a single subscription" (p. 748). The nature of the work also weighed against the defendant, although the reports consisted of factual information in addition to creative content. The court, relying on the legislative history, indicated that the scope of the fair use privilege for newsletters and other ephemeral publications is narrower. Because the newsletters were reproduced in their entirety to advance the business of Legg Mason without due payment to Lowry's, the third factor also "weighs more heavily against Legg Mason" (pp. 748–749). As a result, the harm to the primary subscription market was obvious: "To the extent the six or more copies represented additional, potential subscriptions, the copying within the research department diminished Lowry's market ... perfect clones ... substituted for additional subscription copies, whose cost Legg Mason thereby avoided" (p. 749). The court concluded that use of the newsletter in this fashion was not fair.

Personal Archiving as a "Bad" Substitutive Purpose

Contrast also website, internet, and other functional archiving, search, and retrieval reproduction with the substitutive copying of personal "library building," such as downloading music or recording content from television, cable, or other broadcasts that courts have deemed not to be a fair use, that is, copying in lieu of purchasing the work. The unique and public nature of the undertakings in the previous cases might be contrasted with a series of cases involving use of P-2-P or other mechanisms that allow individuals to create and access the archive or library for personal use. Like the personal library-building of television programs not included in the *Sony Corporation of America v. Universal City Studios, Inc.* (1984), fair use holding, uploading or downloading from websites that allow individuals to duplicate a library or archive of recordings for personal use, has consistently been held not to be a fair use. *UMG Recordings v. MP3.com, Inc.* (2000) was the earliest case to apply the four fair use factors to a commercial entity that made available a library of recordings for download. MP3.com, Inc. "purchased tens of thousands of popular CDs in which plaintiffs held the copyrights, and, without authorization, copied their recordings onto its computer servers so as to be able to replay the recordings for its subscribers ... Subscriber[s] can access via the internet from a computer anywhere in the world the copy of plaintiffs' recording made by defendant. Thus, although the defendant seeks to portray its service as the 'functional equivalent' of storing its subscribers' CDs, in actuality defendant is replaying for the subscribers converted versions of the recordings it copied, without authorization, from plaintiffs' copyrighted CDs" (p. 350). Under the first factor the court did not view the change in format from CD to MP3 file to be transformative: "simply repackages those recordings to facilitate their transmission through another medium.

While such services may be innovative, they are not transformative" (p. 351). The second factor also did not favor fair use because the musical recordings of popular songs, "far removed from the more factual or descriptive work were creative in nature" (p. 351). The third factor also did not favor fair use because the entire recording was used. In discussing the fourth factor, the court rejected the argument that making musical recordings available in this format will actually help rather than harm the market. The rationale "but I'm really helping the market" is seldom accepted by courts: "Any allegedly positive impact of defendant's activities on plaintiffs' prior market in no way frees defendant to usurp a further market that directly derives from reproduction of the plaintiffs' copyrighted works ... a copyrighterholder's 'exclusive' rights ... include the right, within broad limits, to curb the development of such a derivative market by refusing to license a copyrighted work or by doing so only on terms the copyright owner finds acceptable" (p. 352).

In a seminal downloading case, the Ninth Circuit concluded that file sharing of musical recordings through the Napster, Inc. system was not fair use. Even though the file-sharing exchanges did not occur in the presence of an actual commercial transaction, the first factor did not favor fair use: "Direct economic benefit is not required to demonstrate a commercial use. Rather, repeated and exploitative copying of copyrighted works, even if the copies are not offered for sale, may constitute a commercial use" (*A&M Records, Inc. v. Napster, Inc.*, 2001, p. 1015). As in *UMG Recordings v. MP3.com, Inc.* (2000), the court found the nature of the works to be creative and the use of each song in its entirety weighed both the second and third factors against fair use. The fourth factor, again emphasizing the right of the copyright holder and future market entry, favored the plaintiffs: "We, therefore, conclude that the district court made sound findings related to Napster's deleterious effect on the present and future digital download market. ... Lack of harm to an established market cannot deprive the copyright holder of the right to develop alternative markets. ... Having digital downloads available for free on the Napster system necessarily harms the copyright holders' attempts to charge for the same downloads" (*A&M Records, Inc. v. Napster, Inc.*, 2001, p. 1017).

Use and distribution of P-2-P systems similar to Napster have met with the same fate in the courts. In *In Re Aimster Copyright Litigation* (2003), Judge Posner did not discuss the four fair use factors because the focus of the litigation was on the intermediary—the supplier of the file sharing technology—under a theory of contributory infringement. However, the court did discuss in great detail how the use deemed fair by the Supreme Court in *Sony Corporation of America v. Universal City Studios, Inc.* (1984) differed from the use at issue in various file swapping systems; the comment appears to accept that the file swappers were not engaging in a fair use under the existing precedent: "If the music is copyrighted, such swapping, which involves making and transmitting a digital copy of the music, infringes copyright. The swappers, who are ignorant or more commonly disdainful of copyright and in any event discount the likelihood of being sued or prosecuted for copyright infringement, are the direct infringers" (*In Re Aimster Copyright Litigation*, 2003, p. 645). The implications of these cases for library e-reserve or campus course management practices do not bode well for fair use, in that the extensive population of such systems at a given institution in a given year across its curricula and given the numbers of students in each class that access, download, print, or otherwise copy content would likely number in the hundreds if not thousands of articles. A court might well reason that such availability, if made without proper permission through license to a subscription database, for example, would, to repeat the quote from the Ninth Circuit in the Napster litigation, constitute "repeated and exploitative copying of copyrighted works" (*A&M Records, Inc. v. Napster, Inc.*, 2001, p. 1017).

In discussing the file sharing system developed by Grokster, Ltd., the Supreme Court also focused on a theory of contributory infringement and not a detailed fair use analysis. The Supreme Court held that "one who distributes a device with the object of promoting its use to infringe copyright, as shown by clear expression or other affirmative steps taken to foster infringement, is liable for the resulting acts of infringement by third parties" (*Metro-Goldwyn-Mayer Studios Inc. v. Grokster, Ltd.*, 2005, p. 918). Even the district court in the litigation observed that: "Furthermore, it is undisputed that at least some of the individuals who use Defendants' software are engaged in direct copyright infringement of Plaintiffs' copyrighted works" (*Metro-Goldwyn-Mayer Studios Inc. v. Grokster, Ltd.*, 2003, p. 1034). The Supreme Court likewise commented upon the record developed in the lower courts regarding the inapplicability of fair use in vacating and remanding the decision back to the lower courts: "Here, there has been no finding of any fair use and little beyond anecdotal evidence of noninfringing uses. In finding the Grokster and StreamCast software products capable of substantial noninfringing uses, the District Court and the Court of Appeals appear to have relied largely on declarations submitted by the defendants" (*Metro-Goldwyn-Mayer Studios Inc. v. Grokster, Ltd.*, 2005, p. 945). It is typical for defendants to allege circumstances supportive of fair use, but the lower court used the defendants' own assertions to find the tune swapping infringing. It is likely that if the case were to come before the Supreme Court in the posture of fair use, and unless other evidence were introduced, the Supreme Court would conclude that such conduct is infringing and unsupported by a defense of fair use.

In a slight twist, the Seventh Circuit rejected the argument that downloading in order to determine whether to purchase the work (a "try-before-you-buy" sort of defense) constitutes a fair use in *BMG Music v. Gonzalez* (2005). This court did not view the case as one of library building, which would be a substitute for purchase. Judge Posner again made similar comments on the commercial character of the personal use in file sharing scenarios: "Gonzalez was not engaged in a nonprofit use; she downloaded (and kept) entire copyrighted songs," foregoing payment of the customary price, thus the use was commercial and did not favor a fair use (p. 890). The second and third factors also did not favor a fair use because the songs were creative and the entire song was taken. The court questioned why, if the purpose was to sample or taste the song, the entire recording was sampled and in 30 cases complete copies were retained. Moreover, authorized places on the internet exist where a user could listen to a snippet without employing file sharing systems to download a copy of the work. Again in assessing the fourth factor the court looked beyond the scope of the immediate or primary market alone: "Gonzalez proceeds as if the authors' only interest were in selling compact discs containing collections of works. Not so" (p. 891). The court made clear that the secondary market for sales of musical recordings in downloadable file format was affected as well and, like other courts before it, rejected the "but I'm really helping the market" rationale: "downloading on a try-before-you-buy basis is good advertising ... expanding the value of their inventory. The Supreme Court thought otherwise in *Grokster*. ... Music downloaded for free from the internet is a close substitute for purchased music; many people are bound to keep the downloaded files without buying originals. That is exactly what Gonzalez did for at least 30 songs" (p. 890).

The use of recorded music in karaoke systems is also not a fair use. The defendant argued that the purpose was educational—learning to sing songs—and so dispositive of fair use: "Plaintiff's contention that its karaoke device is a teaching tool for the customer or that it assists parents in regulating the music to which their children listen is immaterial because a fair use analysis focuses on the use of the infringing party, not on the consumer" (*Leadsinger, Inc. v. BMG Music Publishing*, 2005, pp. 1196–1197). It could be added that the use the customers make of the product in their homes with family and friends does not implicate the exclusive rights of the copyright owner of the musical work or sound recording because the performance of the musical work or display of song lyrics would not be a public performance or even a display, and the exclusive right of the copyright owner in a performance does not extend to a sound recording unless by means of a digital audio transmission. The court focused on the use the maker of the karaoke machine made of the works because this was a case of direct infringement: "The purpose and character of use, establish that the purpose behind Plaintiff's device is so that Plaintiff can market and sell the device and receive revenue. As has been discussed, the customer's use of the product is irrelevant" (p. 1197). The second and third factors weighed against fair use because the works were creative in nature and the amount taken represented the entire work in that the machine "displays the lyrics in their entirety" (p. 1197). Although it had insufficient information upon which to discuss the fourth factor, the court nonetheless concluded "that there is no support for a finding that Plaintiff's device is protected from liability under the fair use doctrine" (p. 1197).

In a very recent decision, a New York district court concluded that selling music previews (clips) as ring tones for the cell phone market was not a fair use (*U.S. v. American Society of Composers, Authors and Publishers*, 2009). The uses made of the musical works was not transformative "but rather serve only to facilitate applicant's sales of ringtones and ringback tones from applicant's website and wireless device application" (p. 425). The second factor also weighed against fair use because the music covered under the license from ASCAP is creative. Only a clip is used, but the court nonetheless concluded that the "expressive value" of the music was copied and "that expressive value constitutes the previews in their entirety" (p. 431). The court recognized that people choose a part of the song for a particular reason, whether as their general ringtone or to identify specific callers by individual ringback or incoming call tones. By using the previews without paying the licensing fee, the defendant avoids paying the customary price. The court also found that ASCAP demonstrated the existence of a market for preview and other short segments of its music: "Nineteen companies pay ASCAP for the right to deliver short segments of ASCAP music to their customers ... markets are 'traditional' and 'reasonable' markets for derivative works of original ASCAP music ... the party arguing for fair use here, has the burden of proving that its use of ASCAP music will not harm these markets ... [and] failed to meet this burden. Therefore, from ASCAP's standpoint, at worst, this factor is neutral" (pp. 432–433). In related and recent litigation, the same district court concluded that a retail wireless service provider does not need a public performance license for musical compositions when it provides ringtones to its customers. The use of the ring tone by cell phone customers was not infringing; there could thus be no secondary liability on the part of the service provider, not because the customer use was fair but because a statutory exemption for public performances of nondramatic musical works exists under section 110(4): "In sum, customers do not play ringtones with any expectation of profit. The playing of a ringtone by any Verizon customers in public is thus exempt under 17 U.S.C. § 110(4) and does not require them to obtain a public performance license" (*In re Cellco Partnership*, 2009, p. *8).

Extraction of Unprotected Content from Mixed Works

Reproduction or other use of a protected work in order to extract the unprotected elements contained within it is a fair use of the protected material even though the protected content is reproduced in its entirety. The rationale of courts allowing such reproduction is based, as in other cases including 100 percent takings, on a sort of necessity argument. Here, however, such reasoning is bolstered by the fact that the reproduction is an intermediate step and no further use is made of the protected work once the unprotected elements have been accessed. The policy implications of the opposite result are also at play. If a copyright owner could prevent access and use of public domain content by simply mingling or mixing that content with protected content, then leverage given the copyright owner over unprotected content would skew the balance that the copyright law seeks to achieve between owners and users. If this were not a fair use, copyright owners could make less accessible public domain content (including facts, works for which the copyright is expired, and works designated by law to be in the public domain such as works of the federal government under section 105) simply by jumbling together protected and unprotected works. These cases do not offer carte blanche use of the underlying protected work, but they do support fair use of the protected work by reproduction limited to the intermediate copying necessary in order to extract the unprotected elements and leaving untouched for further use the protected elements of the mixed or merged work.

A number of cases demonstrating this principle involved the reproduction of computer programs in order to extract the unprotected elements (routine sequences of code) through some form of reverse engineering. In a case of first impression, the Ninth Circuit concluded that the intermediate copying by the defendant was a fair use: "Because, in the case before us, disassembly is the only means of gaining access to those unprotected aspects of the program, and because Accolade has a legitimate interest in gaining such access (in order to determine how to make its cartridges compatible with the Genesis console), we agree with Accolade" (*Sega Enterprises Ltd. v. Accolade, Inc.*, 1992, p. 1520). In considering the first factor, the court observed that although the goal was to develop a marketable product, thus commercial, the public benefit garnered from compatible gaming programs, as more works are created so the "harvest of knowledge" is made more abundant, is: "an increase in the number of independently designed video game programs offered for use with the Genesis console" (p. 1523). Because of their functional nature, video game programs cannot be examined without copying; the court therefore assigned "a lower degree of protection than more traditional literary works" and concluded that the second factor also favored fair use (p. 1526). Although the third factor favored Sega Enterprises, Ltd., in that the entire program was copied, the court concluded that the factor was of "very little weight" (p. 1527). In concluding that the fourth factor favored fair use, the court admitted that some market impact ("minor economic loss") is apparent because a gamer would not buy both Accolade's "Mike Ditka Power Football" and Sega's "Joe Montana Football"; however, "an attempt to monopolize the market by making it impossible for others to compete runs counter to the statutory purpose of promoting creative expression and cannot constitute a strong equitable basis for resisting the invocation of the fair use doctrine" (pp. 1523–1524).

Decided the same year, reverse engineering was not fair in *Atari Games Corp. v. Nintendo of America, Inc.* (1992). The Federal Circuit nonetheless recognized that the application of the fair use doctrine to reverse engineering of a computer program was possible: "The fair use reproduction of a computer program must not exceed what is necessary to understand the unprotected elements of the work" (p. 843). However, other circumstances suggested the use was unfair in this instance. "Reverse engineering, untainted by the purloined copy of the 10NES program and necessary to understand 10NES, is a fair use" (p. 843). Unfortunately for Atari it did not use an "untainted" copy, so under these circumstances fair use did not apply: "Atari's attorney applied to the Copyright Office for a reproduction of the 10NES program. ... Atari falsely alleged that it was a present defendant in a case in the Northern District of California" (p. 846). This was not true and as a result in the eyes of the court was "not in authorized possession of the Copyright Office copy of 10NES, [so] any copying or derivative copying of 10NES source code from the Copyright Office does not qualify as a fair use" (p. 843).

In *Sony Computer Entertainment, Inc. v. Connectix Corp.* (2000), the Ninth Circuit concluded "under the facts of this case and our precedent, Connectix's intermediate copying and use of Sony's copyrighted BIOS was a fair use for the purpose of gaining access to the unprotected elements of Sony's software" (p. 602). The court discussed various options, such as complete disassembly and emulation; the former, urged by Sony Computer Entertainment, Inc., would have been less efficient but result in fewer copies of the program being made. The court rejected this standard and concluded the emulation was "necessary" under the holding of *Sega Enterprises Ltd. v. Accolade, Inc.* (1992), thus was also fair use: "More important, the rule urged by Sony would require that a software engineer, faced with two engineering solutions that each require intermediate copying of protected and unprotected material, often follow the least efficient solution. ... Such an approach would erect an artificial hurdle in the way of the public's access to the ideas contained within copyrighted software programs" (p. 605). As a result the court found the creation of the Virtual Game Station product "modestly transformative. The product creates a new platform, the personal computer, on which consumers can play games designed for the Sony PlayStation" (p. 606). The court also observed that the purpose of compatibility is a "legitimate one under the first factor of the fair use analysis" (p. 607). The second factor weighed in favor of Connectix Corp. because the elements of the program were functional and not creative. If Sony Computer Entertainment, Inc. desired monopolistic protection over these elements as well, the court suggested that the patent law would be the better vehicle of protection, there being no similar concept of fair use in the U.S. patent law. Although the third factor weighed against Connectix Corp. in that the entire program was copied repeated times, the court concluded that this factor was of very little weight. Although it is obvious that a compatible product might have an impact on the market for authorized players, "Sony understandably seeks control over the market for devices that play games Sony produces or licenses. The copyright law, however, does not confer such a monopoly" (p. 607).

In *Evolution, Inc. v. SunTrust Bank* (2004) a district court concluded that the defendants' use of the plaintiff's source code to create QTR.exe, ABCNotes, and LNSNotes was, as a matter of law, fair use. With little discussion of the four factors but stating that the "first, third, and fourth" factors favored a finding of fair use, the court, relying on both *Sega Enterprises Ltd. v. Accolade, Inc.* (1992) and *Assessment Technologies of WI, LLC. v. Wiredata, Inc.* (2003), observed: "In the present case, defendants copied portions of plaintiff's source code in order to write the QTR.exe, ABCNotes, and LNSNotes computer programs, which extracted defendants' own data from plaintiff's program. Defendants' situation is factually similar to that described by the *WIREdata* court, in that the present defendants wished to access and extract uncopyrightable data that was embedded in a copyrighted computer program" (*Evolution, Inc. v. SunTrust Bank*, 2004, p. 956). Contrast these cases to the result in *DSC Communications Corp. v. Pulse Communications, Inc.* (1999) where the Federal Circuit distinguished copying to understand how a program worked from copying in the normal operation of the program, the latter not a fair use: "Rather than being part of an attempt at reverse engineering, the copying appears to have been done after Pulsecom had determined how the system functioned and merely to demonstrate the interchangeability of the Pulsecom POTS cards with those made and sold by DSC" (p. 1363).

Although not a fair use case per se, the principle that some elements of a computer program are too fundamental to warrant copyright protection was made clear in *Lexmark International, Inc. v. Static Control Components, Inc.* (2004), a case involving the application of anti-circumvention rules under section 1201, rules that apply only if the content subject to the control is protected by copyright. The court made the following observation regarding the computer program the company employed to ensure that only authorized toner cartridges could be used in its copiers: "Generally speaking, 'lock-out' codes fall on the functional-idea rather than the original-expression side of the copyright line. ... To the extent compatibility requires that a particular code sequence be included in the component device to permit its use, the merger and scènes à faire doctrines generally preclude the code sequence from obtaining protection" (p. 536). Even if the code was protected, the court indicated that the purpose of compatibility or interoperability can be a fair use. The appellate court disagreed with the district's application of the first and fourth factors, the district court concluding that the fair use defense did not apply. The Sixth Circuit observed that "SCC's chip uses the Toner Loading Program for a different purpose, one unrelated to copyright protection. Rather than using the Toner Loading Program to calculate toner levels, the SMARTEK chip uses the content of the Toner Loading Program's data bytes as input to the checksum operation and to permit printer functionality" (p. 544). According to the appellate court the fourth factor might also favor fair use: "Here, the district court focused on the wrong market: It focused not on the value or marketability of the Toner Loading Program, but on Lexmark's market for its toner cartridges ... but that is not the sort of market or value copyright law protects. ... Lexmark has not introduced any evidence showing that an independent market exists for a program as elementary as its Toner Loading Program, and we doubt at any rate that the SMARTEK chip could have displaced any value in *this* market" (p. 545, emphasis in the original).

Although this was neither a fair use nor a reverse engineering case, Judge Posner had the opportunity to comment on the extraction of public domain (real property tax assessment information) contained in a database used by a county government for which the operating software was proprietary. The company that developed the software wanted to prevent access to the data the system collected by a competing database company. "Similarly, if the only way WIREdata could obtain public-domain data about properties in Wisconsin would be by copying the data in the municipalities' databases as embedded in Market Drive, so that it would be copying the compilation and not just the compiled data only because the data and the format in which they were organized could not be disentangled, it would be privileged to make such a copy, and likewise the municipalities" (*Assessment Technologies of WI, LLC. v. Wiredata, Inc.*, 2003, p. 645).

Two years later, a district court relying on *Assessment Technologies of WI, LLC. v. Wiredata, Inc.* (2003) acknowledged that copying a database in order to extract unprotected elements would be a fair use. Without assessing the four fair use factors, the court commented that it was not "convinced, however, that Madison copied the TCS database to extract its raw data. ... The intended use of the ProvideC copy of the TCS database was to, among other things, run reports. ... Because the court cannot find Madison copied the TCS database to extract its raw data and there is a question as to whether Madison copied the database in order to take advantage of the TCS data structure, the copyrighted element of the program, the court declines to find that Madison's creation of ProvideC is fair use as a matter of law" (*Madison River Management Co. v. Business Management Software Corp.*, 2005, p. 537). Similarly, in *DSMC, Inc. v. Convera Corp.* (2007, p. 71), the court concluded that a "dispute between two companies involved in the migration of National Geographic film footage onto a searchable internet website" fell outside the scope of *Assessment Technologies of WI, LLC. v. Wiredata, Inc.* (2003). Without discussing the four fair use factors, the district court rejected Convera Corp.'s argument that "any alleged intermediate copying of the database schema in order to write scripts to migrate the NGTL data into Convera's Screening Room product was fair use under the copyright laws" (*DSMC, Inc. v. Convera Corp.*, 2007, p. 83). The evidence suggested the compatibility or interoperability was the purpose behind the copying. "The email evidence and internal documents from Convera discussed above suggest that Convera not only wanted to extract raw data but also wanted to create a product similar to DMAS that contained many of the same features as DMAS," placing Convera in a "very different posture" from the parties in either *Assessment Technologies of WI, LLC. v. Wiredata, Inc.* (2003) or *Sega Enterprises Ltd. v. Accolade, Inc.* (1992) (*DSMC, Inc. v. Convera Corp.*, 2007, p. 83).

The reproduction-extraction concept has been applied in the internet context regarding the extraction of unprotected content (concert event information such as performer, date, venue, or ticket price) located on a website. Citing *Sony Computer Entertainment, Inc. v. Connectix Corp.* (2000), the district court applied the extraction through reverse engineering computer program concept to webpages: "Reverse engineering to get at unprotected functional elements is not the same process as used here but the analogy seems to apply. The copy is not used competitively. It is destroyed after its limited function is done. It is used only to facilitate obtaining non-protectable data—here the basic factual data. It may not be the only way of obtaining that data (i.e., a thousand scriveners with pencil and paper could do the job given time), but it is the most efficient way, not held to be an impediment in Connectix" (*Ticketmaster, Corp. v. Tickets.com*, 2000, pp. *12–*13). Here the court implied that even if an alternative means of access is available, such as visiting the website and cutting and pasting all the unprotected data piece by piece, it need not be sought first, that is, reproduction then extraction need not be the last resort before it is allowed but is fair use when it is the most efficient means available.

The cases discussed in the cluster of functions promoting "access" to protected works include the creation of guides, assessments, and other aids. These extend to archiving, caching, and similar reproductions whereby protected content is then stored and later subject to search and retrieval. The lessons from these cases should be familiar to readers of this chapter. Protected works incorporated into these access tools may be reproduced in their entirety if that amount is necessary in order to make the tool effective. So far many of the cases positive of fair use have occurred in unique or singular settings and leave unanswered the question of whether, for example, every public library in America could scan and make searchable the full text of its collections. As in the extraction cases, reproduction of the works in question in their entirety did not prevent numerous courts from concluding that such use was fair use. However, those circumstances appear limited to cases in which the protected content was either housed or comingled with unprotected elements, the ultimate target of the reproduction, with no further use made of the protected elements. In addition, development of future compatible and arguably competing products was a theme in several cases. Courts stressed the limits of the copyright in not providing a monopoly (rather, copyright is couched as a limited monopoly) and also acknowledged the public benefit that such tools provide users of protected content through enhanced access capabilities. The broader policy implication of these fair uses is paramount in many of the decisions.

Social Commentary in Art and Literature, Parody in Entertainment, Advertisement, and Consumer Products

Several cases demonstrate that even where the work is created with some intention of profit, if an element of social commentary, cultural critique, or similar transformative use is present in addition to some parody of the work itself, the use is fair. This is in contrast to parody where the butt of the joke is limited to the work in question and not the broader societal implications of the commentary or critique. Often the factual circumstances reflect a mix of both spoof of the original and a broader social purpose. These cases might be clustered under a broad umbrella of *reflection*. Finally, the reflection function encompasses social commentary in art and literature but is not limited to parody or critique in entertainment, advertisement, and consumer products.

Social Commentary in Art and Literature

The presentation of commentary and critique in the context of visual art or literature by artists and authors is at the core of the creative process, reflecting their surroundings through a creative prism. Although use often falls within the broad sweep of fair use, it must make some discernable commentary, critique, or parody of the original in the context of a broader societal reflection rather than merely appropriate the original work or make comment on society in general.

After a series of cases concluding that the use of fictional characters and other iconic images as the basis for his sculptural subjects was not fair use, artist Jeff Koons succeeded in stumbling upon an artistic technique and result that the Second Circuit believed indeed achieved a fair use. Previous cases involved, for example, his sculptural casting of the famous "string of puppies" photograph where a couple sits on a sofa trying to contain on their laps a large number of puppies and of the Odie character from the "Garfield the Cat" comic strip. Courts doubted that his mere translating of a photograph and a comic strip image into a three-dimensional sculpture necessarily accomplished any particular act of criticism or social commentary on the underlying works on which the sculptures were based, nor was the rendering particularly transformative, and the work was certainly derivative. Koons "belongs to the school of American artists who believe the mass production of commodities and media images has caused a deterioration in the quality of society, and this artistic tradition of which he is a member proposes through incorporating these images into works of art to comment critically both on the incorporated object and the political and economic system that created it" (*Rogers v. Koons*, 1992, p. 309). However, the problem for Koons in the "string of puppies" litigation was that although the critique, satire, or parody may be "of modern society, the copied work must be, at least in part, an object of the parody, otherwise there would be no need to conjure up the original work" (p. 310). As a result, the first factor did not favor Koons. The second factor also weighed against fair use because the photograph was creative in nature. The entire photograph was taken as well. Finally, the court observed the impact that Koons's use would have on the market for derivative works: "Here there is simply nothing in the record to support a view that Koons produced 'String of Puppies' for anything other than sale as high-priced art. Hence, the likelihood of future harm to Rogers' photograph is presumed, and plaintiff's market for his work has been prejudiced" (p. 312). In *United Feature Syndicate, Inc. v. Koons* (1993, pp. 383–384), the court similarly commented that "the 'Wild Boy and Puppy' sculpture cannot qualify as a parody or satire because, as in *Rogers* [*v. Koons* (1992)], the sculpture is, at best, a parody of society at large, rather than a parody of the copyrighted 'Odie' character."

Koons persevered both with his art and his attorney's bills and finally achieved a fair use in *Blanch v. Koons* (2006), where he incorporated a part of a photograph from a fashion magazine into a collage painting. Unlike the previous cases involving Koons, the use of only a portion of the pre-existing work shifted the third factor in his favor: "In light of Koons's choice to extract the legs, feet, and sandals in 'Silk Sandals' from their background, we find his statement that he copied only that portion of the image necessary to evoke 'a certain style of mass communication' ... weighs distinctly in Koons's favor" (p. 258). By juxtaposing the portion taken with his original contribution, the purpose of critique or parody of the original could be realized: "Koons is ... using Blanch's image as fodder for his commentary on the social and aesthetic consequences of mass media ... in the furtherance of distinct creative or communicative objectives, the use is transformative" (p. 253). The first factor shifted as well and strongly favored fair use. Although the photograph Koons appropriated was creative, "the second fair-use factor has limited weight in our analysis because Koons used Blanch's work in a transformative manner to comment on her image's social and aesthetic meaning rather than to exploit its creative virtues" (p. 257). Because the plaintiff failed to produce any evidence of derivative markets, the fourth factor also favored Koons.

Popular classics of American literature are not beyond the reach of transformative satiric fair uses. A retelling of the classic *Gone with the Wind* (GWTW) from the perspective of one of the slaves in *The Wind Done Gone* (TWDG) was at the center of litigation in *Suntrust Bank v. Houghton Mifflin Co.* (2001). The Eleventh circuit found the recasting of the story as transformative parody outweighed the commercial aspect of the use: "TWDG is more than an abstract, pure fictional work. It is principally and purposefully a critical statement that seeks to rebut and destroy the perspective, judgments, and mythology of GWTW. Randall's literary goal is to explode the romantic, idealized portrait of the antebellum South during and after the Civil War" (p. 1270). In order to make the parody work, some elements of the target must be appropriated but the court was unable at this point in the proceedings to "determine in any conclusive way" whether the amount used was reasonable. The second factor was also of little help because this "factor is given little weight in parody cases" (p. 1271). Once the "good" purpose of the first factor is established, the burden is on the copyright holder to demonstrate market harm through substitution in either primary or derivative markets. The court found "that Suntrust's evidence falls far short of establishing that TWDG or others like it will act as market substitutes for GWTW or will significantly harm its derivatives. Accordingly, the fourth fair use factor weighs in favor of TWDG" (p. 1276).

Parody was not present in a contrasting, earlier case. In *Dr. Seuss Enterprises, L.P. v. Penguin Books USA, Inc.* (1996), a use of the accoutrements and other particulars of the Dr. Seuss character and story *The Cat in the Hat* in *The Cat NOT in the Hat: A Parody* by Dr. Juice was not a fair use parody of the O. J. Simpson trial. The court observed the value of parody: "Parody is regarded as a form of social and literary criticism, having a socially significant value as free speech under the First Amendment" (p. 1400). However, the problem for the defendant was that the spoof was not of Dr. Seuss but of the events surrounding the Simpson trial. The book used the creative and stylistic elements of Dr. Seuss and in particular *The Cat in the Hat* to opine on the injustice of the verdict: "These stanzas and the illustrations simply retell the Simpson tale. Although *The Cat NOT in the Hat!* does broadly mimic Dr. Seuss' characteristic style, it does not hold his style up to ridicule. …While Simpson is depicted 13 times in the Cat's distinctively scrunched and somewhat shabby red and white stove-pipe hat, the substance and content of *The Cat in the Hat* is not conjured up by the focus on the Brown-Goldman murders or the O.J. Simpson trial" (p. 1401). The "creativity, imagination and originality" of the Dr. Seuss classic likewise favored the plaintiff (p. 1402). The use of Seuss's cat character and its signature stove pipe hat on the front, back, and in the text took the "highly expressive core" of the work (p. 1402). As a result the second and third factors also did not favor fair use. Finally, without a transformative use, the possibility of "market substitution is at least more certain, and market harm may be more readily inferred" where the use is non-transformative and commercial" (p. 1400).

In a recent case involving a sequel to the *Catcher in the Rye* entitled *60 Years* the New York district court did not view this revisiting as parody because it did not attempt to comment on the original story, plot, or character. "*60 Years,* however, contains no reasonably discernable rejoinder or specific criticism of any character or theme of *Catcher*" (*Salinger v. Colting*, 2009, p. *5). In fact, reviews, press releases, and other evidence indicated that Colting designed his work as a straightforward sequel, not parody. "In fact, it can be argued that the contrast between Holden's authentic but critical and rebellious nature and his tendency toward depressive alienation is one of the key themes of Catcher. … It is hardly parodic to repeat that same exercise in contrast, just because society and the characters have aged" (p. *6). Sequels, as opposed to a retelling through satire or parody as with *The Wind Done Gone*, are derivative or at least reproductive of the fictional characters of the original. After legal proceedings commenced Colting began to argue that the new work served as a criticism of Salinger: "The ratio of the borrowed to the novel elements is quite high, and its transformative character is diminished ... while there is some non-parodic transformative element in *60 Years* with regard to its use of the Salinger character to criticize the author J. D. Salinger, its effect is diminished ... and the determination of whether it constitutes fair use will depend heavily on the remaining factors" (p. *9). The creative nature of the Salinger book placed the work within the core of protected expression, so the second factor weighed against a finding of fair use. Although criticism of Salinger himself could be a "good" purpose, the relationship with the third factor is again important. Like the author of *The Harry Potter Lexicon*, Colting took too much: "Defendants have taken well more from *Catcher,* in both substance and style, than is necessary for the alleged transformative purpose of criticizing Salinger and his attitudes and behavior. Most notably, Defendants have utilized the character of Holden Caulfield, reanimated as the elderly Mr. C, as the primary protagonist of *60 Years*" (p. *10). *60 Years* contained other similarities, as the work "depends upon similar and sometimes nearly identical supporting characters, settings, tone, and plot devices to create a narrative that largely mirrors that of *Catcher*" (p. *11). It is true that Salinger-the-author appears as a character in the Colting novel. However, critique of Salinger could have been made without placing him as a character in a sequel to his own book along with Caulfield and other characters. As a result, the court concluded: "Because Defendants have taken much more from Salinger's copyrighted works than is necessary to serve their alleged critical purpose ["Salinger as an object of criticism or ridicule"], the third factor weighs heavily against a finding of fair use" (p. *14). Because the court characterized the Colting novel as a sequel, the derivative rights and so, too, derivative markets are affected. The court observed that the right to enter derivative markets belongs to the copyright owner. Even if Salinger chooses not to enter the market—Salinger for years denounced writing a sequel—the court observed that the copyright law allows an author to change his or her mind. The reality that fans of the original book might need to speculate no longer what the future would have in store for Holden Caulfield if such derivative sequels were allowed does not outweigh the fact that this speculation is also part of the author's artistic vision as well. This speculation and the right to refuse license or allow derivatives can "sometimes act as an incentive to the creation of originals" because such a decision would free Salinger, as it would any author in a similar position, to turn his or her creative energies to new projects and the creation of new characters and stories (p. *15). Again, this would achieve the goal of the copyright law. As a result, the court concluded that "because it is likely that the publishing of *60 Years* would harm the potential market for sequels or other derivative works based upon *Catcher,* the fourth factor weighs, albeit only slightly, against fair use" (p. *15). Finally, the court concluded that Salinger was likely to prevail on his copyright claim and so enjoined the further publication and distribution of the work.

Parody in Entertainment

Spoofs of characters from popular culture are fair use fodder for the comedian and artist alike. Fair use is often found, although the use is commercial—the program or product is not eleemosynary in nature but is designed for broadcast to or purchase by the consuming public and with revenues and profits generated as a part of those processes. The parodist in *Burnett v. Twentieth Century Fox Film Corp.* (2007, pp. 965–966) "borrows heavily from popular culture ... routinely puts cartoon versions of celebrities in awkward, ridiculous, and absurd situations in order to lampoon and parody those public figures and to poke fun at society's general fascination with celebrity and pop culture." The dispute arose when a segment of the "Family Guy" television show used comedian Carol Burnett's maid and mop character "Charwoman" placed in an adult entertainment store; one "Family Guy" character comments "'You know, when she tugged her ear at the end of that show, she was really saying goodnight to her mom.' Another friend responds, 'I wonder what she tugged to say goodnight to her dad,'" finishing with a comic's explanation, 'Oh!'" (p. 965). Burnett argued that use was not parody, but the court disagreed: "It is immaterial whether the target of Family Guy's 'crude joke' was Burnett, the Carol Burnett Show, the Charwoman, Carol's Theme Music or all four. ... A parodic character may reasonably be perceived in the Family Guy's use of the Charwoman ... in an awkward, ridiculous, crude, and absurd situation in order to lampoon and parody her as a public figure" (pp. 966–968). Consistent with other parody cases, the court observed that the creative nature of the work "does not accord great weight here" (p. 969). The third factor also favored a finding of fair use because the Burnett character, theme music, and jokes run "approximately eighteen seconds" taking "just enough" to be recognizable (pp. 970–971). Burnett argued to no avail that the unsavory use of the Charwoman character would harm the good will and reputation of the work. In response the court discussed the important role of "destructive parodies" in social and literary criticism, although the effect may be to "discourage or discredit" an original author (*Burnett v. Twentieth Century Fox Film Corp.*, 2007, pp. 970–971, citing *Fisher v. Dees*, 1986, p. 436). The court concluded that the four factors strongly favored a finding of fair use.

A more recent case also involving *Family Guy* concerned parody. Although there is wide leeway given to such parodic uses, McCrann (2009) argues that musical parodies should be presumptively fair. The court found that the segment "I Need a Jew" was a parody of the Academy Award-winning iconic Disney tune from the motion picture *Pinocchio*, "When You Wish Upon A Star" (see *Bourne v. Twentieth Century Fox Film Corp.*, 2009, pp. 504–507, also discussing the distinction between parody and satire). "The Court's finding is further supported by Defendants' proffered evidence that the song in the Episode makes an additional comment, or 'inside joke', about the 'widespread belief' that Walt Disney was anti-Semitic" (p. 507). The court also observed that even if the joke failed, it can nonetheless qualify as parody. "Therefore, even if Defendants intended to make an 'inside joke' about Walt Disney's alleged anti-Semitism but that joke failed, it can still support a finding of fair use if its 'parodic character can be reasonably perceived'" (*Bourne v. Twentieth Century Fox Film Corp.*, 2009, p. 507, quoting *Campbell v. Acuff-Rose Music*, 1994, pp. 582–583). As a result, the court had little difficulty concluding that the altered melody and new lyrics of the original song constituted a transformative use with the first factor "weigh[ing] in favor of a finding of fair use" (*Bourne v. Twentieth Century Fox Film Corp.*, 2009, p. 509). Again quoting *Campbell v. Acuff-Rose Music* (1994), the court observed that although the original song fell within the core of expressive works, the second factor (nature of the work) was of little help "in separating the fair use sheep from the infringing goats in a parody case" (*Bourne v. Twentieth Century Fox Film Corp.*, 2009, p. 509, quoting *Campbell v. Acuff-Rose Music*, 1994, p. 586). A theme of this chapter, and reiterated in the parody case law here, is the link that exists between the third "how much?" factor and the first factor. Courts consider whether the user takes only as much as is necessary to accomplish the transformative use. In parody cases that amount is just enough to conjure the original. In this case testimony regarding the creative process of "I Need a Jew" revealed that several notes from an earlier version of the tune were changed to make the illusion to "When You Wish Upon A Star" more clear in the ears of the audience: "The internal, creative dispute over how much of the original to use demonstrates that Defendants were concerned about taking just enough of the original to make their point clear" (*Bourne v. Twentieth Century Fox Film Corp.*, 2009, p. 510). Because they stayed within the "just enough" limits, the third factor also favored the defendants. In discussing the market factor, the court rejected a loss of licensing revenue as well as a harm-by-association argument. Market suppression or destruction is not a concern of the fourth factor; rather the concern is market usurpation. "Plaintiff argues for a reading of the fourth factor that would swallow the rule entirely. All uses of copyrighted work under a fair use rationale deprive the owner of licensing fees. If a parody of the original work would usurp the market for licensing other comedic uses of the original work, then all parodies would fail under this prong of the analysis" (p. 510). In aggregate analysis, the court concluded that use to be fair because "factors one, three, and four each weigh heavily in Defendants' favor" (p. 510).

Fair use was also found when another popular cable television program, *The Daily Show,* spoofed the banality of a public access television program known as The "Sandy Kane Blew Comedy Show," in which Kane "sings, dances, and delivers explicit jokes while wearing little to no clothing" (*Kane v. Comedy Partners*, 2003, p. *1). The court did not see parody here, only ridicule, the belittling falling still comfortably within the umbrella of criticism or comment the statute commands: "unlike a parody, the use of plaintiff's clip in this case did not involve an altered imitation of a famous work but the presentation of an obscure, original work in a mocking context. The only similarity between a parody and the work at issue in this case is the element of ridicule ... crux of the show, which airs on Comedy Central, concerns itself with ridicule. Virtually any clip appearing on this show is implicitly accompanied by a comment on its absurdity" (p. *4). As in the parody cases, the second factor "is without much force." The third factor favored the defendant in that the two-second clip was "only one-tenth of one percent of plaintiff's television show" (p. *5). The court also observed that it did not matter that the clip was used over and over again, because the statutory factor commands focus on the amount and portion in relation to the original work, not to the work created with the original. Any qualitative "heart" assessment is less useful to the court in situations of parody. In discussing the fourth factor, the court made the following assessment: "Where the secondary work serves a fundamentally different function ... there is little risk that the secondary work will supplant the original. ... [T]he fourth factor does not take into account any diminished interest in the original work that results from the force of the critique ... it cannot be credibly argued that defendants' use of two seconds of plaintiff's show ... would have the effect of siphoning away demand for her comedy routine" (p. *6).

Use of several lines of the opening melody and lyrics to the bucolic song "What a Wonderful World" to introduce the rap song "The Forest" portraying a quite different world weighed "heavily in favor" of fair use in *Abilene Music, Inc., et al. v. Sony Music Entertainment, Inc., et al.* (2003, p. 94). "Here, the overall message of 'The Forest' is that the world is corrupted and ridden with crime and drugs. In the process of making that point, 'The Forest' sets up a contrast between the assertedly delusional innocence of mainstream culture and the purportedly more realistic viewpoint of the rapper" (p. 91). More important, the "alteration of the tone, lyrics and musical features of 'Wonderful World' makes clear that the song itself is a target of parodic criticism, and that the creators of 'The Forest' are not merely using the original song as an ironic or satirical device to comment on what they view as a less than wonderful world" (p. 92). In contrast, the uses of the same song in the movies *12 Monkeys* and *Good Morning Vietnam* were not parodies of the song, but broader and contrasting social commentaries alone of the "the real or imagined worlds depicted by the filmmakers" (p. 92). Once again, the second factor was of little help to the court; the work, although creative, was not used to capture this aspect of the original, that is, the song is not used for its creative attribute or effect. The song takes no more of the original than "absolutely necessary" because "every part of the original that is used in the parody is modified, in word, melody or style," and after the opening, the song is not used again (p. 93). Although the court appeared willing to entertain the notion that use of "What a Wonderful World" in derivative music markets, a reggae cover of the song by UB40 for example, might have an impact on this market, such was not the case here because "The Forest" is not a hip-hop or other genre version of "What a Wonderful World" but uses a musical genre to mock the sentiment of the original, therefore "it could not possibly supplant the market for non-parody hip-hop versions of 'Wonderful World'" (p. 94). Finally, the court commented on the effect that holding this use and similar uses not to be fair would have on the goals of the copyright law: "Disallowing this use of Wonderful World would contravene copyright's purpose of allowing new works to acknowledge influence and react to what has gone before, and would allow copyright owners to quash parodies and other forms of transformation and comment of which they do not approve" (p. 94).

Parody in Advertisements

Advertising is another commercial environment where parody is found and where that parody is also fair use. The famous Annie Leibovitz *Vanity Fair* cover shot of a pregnant and nude Demi Moore "evocative of Botticelli's Birth of Venus" in the "Due This March" promotional advertisements for the motion picture *Naked Gun 33 and 1/3: The Final Insult* was deemed a fair use. Here Paramount did not use the original photograph but "commissioned another photograph to be taken of a nude, pregnant woman, similarly posed ... to ensure that the photograph resembled in meticulous detail the one taken by Leibovitz ... digitally enhanced by a computer to make the skin tone and shape of the body more closely match those of Moore ... final step was to superimpose on the model's body a photograph of Nielsen's face, with his jaw and eyes positioned roughly at the same angle as Moore's, but with her serious look replaced by Nielsen's mischievous smirk" (*Leibovitz v. Paramount Pictures Corp.*, 1998, pp. 111–112). In identifying the element of parody present the court found significant the fact that the Leibovitz photograph itself drew from a famous painting. "A photographer posing a well known actress in a manner that calls to mind a well known painting must expect, or at least tolerate, a parodist's deflating ridicule" (pp. 114–115). The new rendering in the *Naked Gun* ads might be seen to insult the pretentiousness of the cover photo or to comment upon its extolling of the beauty of the pregnant female body. Although the work was creative, the weight of second factor was "slight" in this case. Some aspects of the painting or photograph are in the public domain ("basic pose of a nude, pregnant body and the position of the hands"); other elements are not: "Leibovitz is entitled to protection for such artistic elements as the particular lighting, the resulting skin tone of the subject, and the camera angle that she selected" (p. 116). Important statements are made by the court in its remaining assessment that relate to the theme of this chapter and underscore the value of a "good" purpose. Even though the amount taken was "extensive" the court concluded the third factor to be of "little, if any weight … use so long as the first and fourth factors favor the parodist" (p. 116). Second, the loss of license revenue from a fair use parody of the work is not part of the derivative market and need not be considered. Even though Leibovitz licenses use of her photographs, there is no market harm in parody because "she is not entitled to a licensing fee for a work that otherwise qualifies for the fair use defense as a parody" (p. 117). Other cases discussed in this chapter have stressed this point; transformative uses such as parody or criticism do not trigger derivative rights or market assessments and as such are not those markets copyright owners generally enter. A user need not otherwise consider lost licensing revenue in the evaluation of the fourth factor if the use is otherwise fair because doing so would be to engage in circular reasoning and would swallow whole the four factor analysis: The owner would then be able to demonstrate market harm in every instance where a user fails to pay a license fee or otherwise compensate the owner. This would surely defeat the point and purpose of fair use.

Political commentary can also constitute parody. Use of the phrase and format of MasterCard's Priceless Advertisements ("There are some things money can't buy. For everything else there's MasterCard") in the Ralph Nader presidential campaign was a fair use parody. The "ad included a sequential display of a series of items showing the price of each ('grilled tenderloin for fund-raiser; $1,000 a plate,' 'campaign ads filled with half-truths: $10 million,' 'promises to special interest groups: over $100 billion'). The advertisement ends with a phrase identifying a priceless intangible that cannot be purchased ('finding out the truth: priceless. There are some things that money can't buy')" (*MasterCard International, Inc. v. Nader 2000 Primary Committee, Inc.*, 2004, p. *1). The court observed the dual purpose of the ad: to get across Nader's own message but also to parody MasterCard. Although the jab of the parody may be "subtle rather than obvious" it is nonetheless sufficient (suggesting a reasonably perceived standard). Although the ad may be clever and creative, the court commented that the second factor "is without much force in most cases and its relevance here is slight" (p. *14). In order to make the parody successful, enough of the original must be taken "to assure that the viewer will be reminded of the ad that it borrows from" (p. *14). Because the purpose of the Nader political ad was entirely different from the message of the original MasterCard priceless advertisements, there could be no substitution effect in the marketplace.

In contrast, fair use was not found where the defendant photographed a clothing model wearing the plaintiff's protected works (fashion eyewear) to use in a series of advertisements (*Davis v. The Gap, Inc.*, 2001). The first factor did not favor fair use because the court found "nothing transformative about the Gap's presentation of Davis's copyrighted work. The ad shows Davis's Onoculii being worn as eye jewelry in the manner it was made to be worn—looking much like an ad Davis himself might have sponsored for his copyrighted design" (p. 174). Moreover, the use was in an advertisement, "the outer limit of commercialism" (p. 175).

The second factor also did not favor fair use because the fashion glasses were "in the nature of an artistic creation." Recall that copyright law protects sculptural works, including Beanie Babies. Section 101 states that "'Pictorial, graphic, and sculptural works' include two-dimensional and three-dimensional works of fine, graphic, and applied art. ... Such works shall include works of artistic craftsmanship insofar as their form but not their mechanical or utilitarian aspects are concerned; the design of a useful article ... shall be considered a pictorial, graphic, or sculptural work only if, and only to the extent that, such design incorporates pictorial, graphic, or sculptural features that can be identified separately from, and are capable of existing independently of, the utilitarian aspects of the article." In the view of the court the advertisement took a significant portion of the protected work: "the Gap's ad presents a head-on full view of Davis's piece, centered and prominently featured. The Gap cannot benefit from the third factor" (p. 175). Contrasting the harm from a "devastating" (fair use) book review the court distinguished the exploitative use here and the harm it wrought: "Gap's use is not transformative. It supersedes. By taking for free Davis's design for its ad, the Gap avoided paying 'the customary price' Davis was entitled to charge for the use of his design. Davis suffered market harm through his loss of the royalty revenue to which he was reasonably entitled in the circumstances, as well as through the diminution of his opportunity to license to others who might regard Davis's design as preempted by the Gap's ad. In our view, all the fair use factors favor Davis" (p. 176).

The use of unpublished photographs in the Microsoft Windows 2000 "the old rules of business no longer apply" advertisement campaign was at the center of the dispute in *Fournier v. Erickson* (2003). Fournier was the photographer of an original set of images for the ad campaign. Microsoft, Inc. stuck with the concept for the campaign but used another photographer for the final shots. Although the court did not analyze each factor in detail or come to any conclusion as to whether the use was fair, it nonetheless observed: "The Court recognizes the merit in Fournier's claims that the first, second, and fourth fair use factors weigh in his favor because defendants' photograph was used for commercial purposes with minimal, if any, artistic or intellectual value beyond that of the original work ... photographs were unpublished ... for commercial exploitation. ... Defendants' photograph has displaced Fournier's principal opportunity for commercial exploitation" (pp. 335–336). (One of the legal issues before the court was the request of Fournier to preclude the defendant-photographers from asserting the fair use defense in later proceedings.) As unresolved issues remained relating to the amount of creative elements in the Fournier photographs, access to the photographs, and similarity between both parties' sets of photographs, the request (in legal parlance, a "motion") was denied because "these types of questions, present a question of fact properly deferred to a jury" (p. 336). These issues persisted due to the complicating facts of the case; Fournier was given some instruction as to the composition of the photographs—a man dressed casually in a sea of business-suited commuters. Another free-lance photographer's photographs were eventually used in the campaign and Fournier claimed foul (*Fournier v. Erickson*, 2002, pp. 292–293). As a result, no conclusion regarding the fair use of the photographs could be made, but assuming the photographs were creative, and the defendant has access and took the protected element of the photographs at issue, it is likely the court would conclude the use was not fair.

Parody in Consumer Products

Although it might be expected that parody in entertainment and even radio or television advertisements would be fair use, several cases demonstrate that even if the parody results in a new consumer, good fair use may still apply where the butt of the joke is a recognized cultural symbol, or artifact. For example, in *Mattel, Inc. v. Pitt* (2002), the defendant sold a repainted and re-costumed Barbie Doll as a "Dungeon Doll." The defendant's website, www.dungeondolls.com, featured images of dungeon Barbie dolls in sexually explicit poses. The defendant argued fair use based on the purported "comment" on the "sexual nature of Barbie through her use of customized Barbie figurines in sadomasochistic costume and/or storylines" (p. 322). The court agreed and observed the lesser significance of the second factor given the "patently transformative character" of the use (p. 322). "In a critical comment or parody analysis, however, this factor, even if weighing in favor of plaintiff, assumes less importance than the other three factors" (p. 323). Although the defendant used the entire doll (Barbie Dolls are protected under copyright law as sculptural works), the court appeared to view this factor also as of lesser importance. In a transformative use any amount taken poses little chance for substitute. The fourth factor also favored the fair use, as to both primary and derivative markets: "The dolls do not appear to pose any danger of usurping demand for Barbie dolls in the children's toys market. The sale or display of 'adult' dolls does not appear to be a use Mattel would likely develop or license others to develop" (p. 324).

Parody of kitsch pillars of culture such as professional wrestling was a fair use in *World Wrestling Federation Entertainment Inc. v. Big Dog Holdings, Inc.* (2003), where the defendant developed a line of consumer products including clothing—the Big Dog Brand—with graphics mocking the pomp and posturing of various well-known professional wrestlers such as The Rock, Stone Cold Steve Austin, and the Undertaker. The court got the joke: "A visual examination of the graphics themselves is evidence of the humor, ridicule, and/or comment on the over-hyped world of professional wrestling. The graphics depict dogs in wrestling garb, with beards and goatees, one dog wearing an earring, with tattoos, wearing leather jackets and vests, wearing sunglasses, smashing each other with chairs, and in fact, wrestling" (p. 427). This commenting or criticizing was sufficient to tip the first factor in favor of fair use. Although the second factor favored the plaintiff, the court offered its own social commentary on the creativity present in the world of professional wrestling: "The court certainly questions the originality and creativity of the WWE characters and storylines. The good guys against the bad guys certainly precedes the establishment of professional wrestling. ... We are not talking about the literary works of Victor Hugo. ... [T]he second factor favors WWE, but only minimally" (p. 428). Consistent with other cases of parody and social commentary, the "third factor carries very little, if any, weight against fair use when the first and fourth factors favor the parodist" (p. 429). In order for parody to be successful, that is, deemed to be parody by a court, the use must be transformative; and because the use is transformative it cannot operate as a substitute or replace the market. As a result, the copyright owner cannot claim loss of licensing revenue to evidence market harm because the copyright holder "is not entitled to a licensing fee for a work that otherwise qualifies for the fair use defense as a parody" (p. 430).

Similarly in *Louis Vuitton Malletier S.A. v. Haute Diggity Dog, LLC* (2006), the mocking and mimicking of high-brow fashion and luxury goods in a series of canine chew toys and dog beds suggestive of famous product lines such as Chewnel # 5, Dog Perignon, Chewy Vuiton, and Sniffany & Co. was a fair use. Regarding the first factor the court concluded that the use was a parody. Again, the insignificance ("less important factor") of the second factor in cases of parody was observed: "this Court will not address the nature of the copyrighted work, other than to acknowledge that it is a creative design" (p. 507). The "obvious wordplay" in the "chewy Vuiton" product as well as the use of the superimposed "C" and "V" was necessary as in previous cases, to conjure the original: "The parody is not possible unless the logo and name are similar to those of Plaintiff, and therefore such parody constitutes a fair use in this respect" (p. 507). Consistent with other cases discussed in this chapter, the market or parody market is not one that copyright holders generally enter with respect to their own works. Moreover, the pet owner market is not one that the copyright holder exploits, even though the plaintiff "does sell some pet items, but not toys or beds, and only in a limited, high-end market" (p. 507). There was no evidence of market crossover for the similar products Louis Vuitton Malletier produces so there could be no market harm. This factor also favored fair use.

In cases of parody and criticism fair use provides a robust breathing space for comment. Whether this results in a new work of art, literature, or song, part of a segment on a television or cable show, part of a new clever advertising campaign or consumer product, fair use accommodates the creative spirit to a considerable extent. In the fair use analysis of these cases the nature of the work used is frequently creative. The work's nature is often a driving force behind the defendant's choice or target of that work or category of work as the subject of parody, criticism, comment, or ridicule. Courts find this factor of little weight. Moreover, the third factor is also deemed less significant either in quantity—the entire work must be taken—or in quality—the heart of the work is necessary to conjure up the original in order to signal the target and effect of the parody or critique. Finally, market impact is also less likely because parody, criticism, comment, or ridicule of a work is not a use the copyright owner typically makes.

Toward the Future of and Threats to Fair Use (DRM and Licensing)

Where does the second quarter century after its codification leave the concept of fair use? Its importance is paramount for reasons already stated and its scope widespread, as demonstrated by the cases assembled herein. Further, the concept is evolving and perhaps maturing, away from infancy, in the use of guidelines, for example, and other reductionist approaches. The numerous cases discussed in this chapter demonstrate that fair use is available for a number of undertakings important to a vibrant knowledge society. An underlying goal of the copyright law is to provide fertile ground and encouragement for the creation of additional works. Benefits of this knowledge creation can be observed in a number of fair activities, such as scholarship, including biographical compositions; education, such as preparation of outlines; use of existing works to offer illustration, example, or documentation, including news reporting; creation of access tools such as guides and indexes; archiving and preservation of existing works and extraction of unprotected content from various sources; and social comment or critique in art and literature, including parody for pure entertainment and even in advertisements and consumer products. Moreover, most cases occurred in commercial settings. This circumstance notwithstanding, where a transforming use was made of the work, this "good" purpose had an impact on the remaining factors, often resulting in an overall conclusion by the court that the use was indeed a fair one. In terms of the amount and substantiality taken, often a use to be a successful transformation by necessity requires that the entire work be used or that a taking of the heart of the work is necessary in order to conjure the original. It could be argued that based on many of the cases discussed in this chapter the answer to the "how much?" question is least important or helpful to the remaining factors of assessment. Finally, a transformative use is unlikely to affect the market because there is no substitutive effect from the use. Uses that a copyright owner would or could by logic or nature develop or enter implicate derivative rights and therefore derivative markets, but not all uses fall into this category; parody and critical inquiry are examples. As a result, parody, as well as a criticism such as a simple book review or more elaborate guide to the literature, is transformative but is also not derivative. Such works are not substitutes but are enhancements or, as some courts have phrased it, complements. As a result, there is robust intellectual space within the copyright law for such uses that contribute to the improvement of new works and increase access to existing ones.

The true and better answer to the age-old question *how much can I take?* comes from the case law: *take only as much as is necessary to accomplish your good purpose.* That amount may be dependent upon the circumstances of each situation and includes the purpose to which the work is put. Understanding "good" purposes has been a major focus of this chapter. At the same time, the horizon may not be as bright if other developments are allowed to close the intellectual space or restrict movement within that intellectual space that fair use provides. It is beyond the scope of this chapter to detail such threats, but two concerns may nonetheless be identified. The first is the threat to fair use from use of technological protection measures (TPMs) by copyright owners, especially in circumstances where the circumvention of the TPM is prohibited by statute (e.g., section 1201(a)(1)) or where the sharing of circumvention information may also be prohibited (e.g., sections 1201(a)(2) and 1201(b)). For a thorough explanation of these provisions, see Lipinski (2006). The second threat is licensing: To be more precise, the loss of fair use and other privileges of use that the copyright law would otherwise grant when a user or an intermediary of the user, such as a public library or educational institution, enters into an agreement with the copyright owner or supplier of the work. The license agreement, a binding contract that by its terms limits fair use and other privileges, can shrink the intellectual space of the licensee or its constituents. In an educational setting the college or university would be the licensee and the students its constituents.

As Sharp (2002, p. 44) summarizes, the early disputes litigated under the Digital Millenium Copyright Act (DMCA; section 1201) over access to protected digital content "foretell troubled days for educational fair use." Russell (2003, p. 33) discusses problems with digital rights management (DRM), including privacy and rights of access. Three cases are demonstrative of this threat. In the first appellate decision to apply section 1201 and pit fair use and free speech concepts squarely against the rights of copyright owners under the section, the copyright owners came out ahead. The Second Circuit offered the following observation of these competing interests and the fair use rights that nonetheless still exist in a world of content subject to TPM: "One example is that of a school child who wishes to copy images from a DVD movie to insert into the student's documentary film. We know of no authority for the proposition that fair use, as protected by the Copyright Act, much less the Constitution, guarantees copying by the optimum method or in the identical format of the original. Although the Appellants insisted at oral argument that they should not be relegated to a 'horse and buggy' technique in making fair use of DVD movies, [footnote omitted] the DMCA does not impose even an arguable limitation on the opportunity to make a variety of traditional fair uses of DVD movies, such as commenting on their content, quoting excerpts from their screenplays, and even recording portions of the video images and sounds on film or tape by pointing a camera, a camcorder, or a microphone at a monitor as it displays the DVD movie.

The fact that the resulting copy will not be as perfect or as manipulable as a digital copy obtained by having direct access to the DVD movie in its digital form, provides no basis for a claim of unconstitutional limitation of fair use" (*Universal City Studios, Inc. v. Corley*, 2001, p. 459). A similar sentiment was expressed by a district court on the opposite side of the country: "Thus to the extent the DMCA impacts a lawful purchaser's 'right' to make a backup copy, or to space shift that copy to another computer, the limited impairment of that one right does not significantly compromise or impair the First Amendment rights of users so as to render the DMCA unconstitutionally overbroad" (*United States v. Elcom Ltd.*, 2002, p. 1135). The district court also suggested the sort of mechanics involved in making fair use of protected content now subject to TPM: "For example, nothing in the DMCA prevents anyone from *quoting from a work or comparing texts for the purpose of study or criticism*. It may be that from a technological perspective, the fair user may find it more difficult to do so—*quoting may have to occur the old fashioned way, by hand or by re-typing*, rather than by 'cutting and pasting' from existing digital media. Nevertheless, the fair use is still available" (p. 1131, emphasis added). The same district court made a similar pronouncement two years later in *321 Studios v. Metro Goldwyn Mayer Studios, Inc.* (2004, p. 1102, emphasis added): "*Fair use is still possible under the DMCA*, although such copying will not be as easy, as exact, or as digitally manipulable as plaintiff desires." Although fair use is still possible, of course, the efficiency of the use is compromised. The content is digital, yet the use suggested by all three cases is analog. A compounding problem is that as access and use controls (section 1201 prohibits only circumvention of access TPMs, but prohibits trafficking in either access or use TPMs) merge, it can be argued that an access control in essence controls use as well. In any space that may exist within the statutory structure, circumventing a use control is not prohibited, because copyright owners "may be closing the token crack in the fair use window completely as they merge access and rights controls" (Conley, 2009, p. 316). This is also why section 1201(a)(1)(D) contains a three-year cycle of an administrative de novo rule-making that allows for exemption from the prohibition on circumventing an access TPM or control where "noninfringing uses by persons who are users of a copyrighted work are, or are likely to be, adversely affected" (17 U.S.C. § 1201(a)(1)(D)). Sharp (2002, p. 43) observes in a telling criticism that "the Librarian of Congress becomes the Fair Use Czar under the DMCA." Whether courts continue a cautious application of section 1201, legislative reform offers some relief, or future cycles of rule-making continue to expand the number of useful exemptions is a question only time will answer. Henderson, Spinello, and Lipinski (2007) review these related developments.

A second threat to fair use or other use rights granted under the copyright law is posed by license terms that control access to protected content, such as control access to databases, websites, and installation of software programs. Although some commentators propose legislative address of restrictive contract terms (Baker, 2009), most courts recognize the validity of license agreements in various forms, and so-called shrink wrap, click-wrap, web or browse wrap plus new iterations such as click-to-enter websites can be enforceable (Casamiquela, 2002; Nimmer & Dodd, 2008). This legal position reflects the deference by the courts to an underlying policy of American commerce: the freedom to contract, even when that contract might not be in our better interest. So the agreement can alter what would be the result in the absence of the agreement—what would exist under the copyright law (or other law for that matter). A leading decision standing for the proposition of the supremacy of contract over copyright is *ProCD Inc. v. Zeidenberg* (1996, p. 1454), where the Seventh Circuit, Judge Easterbrook writing, observed: "A copyright is a right against the world. Contracts, by contrast, generally affect only their parties; strangers may do as they please, so contracts do not create 'exclusive rights.'" A similar comment was made by the Federal Circuit and stands for the general proposition that one can contract away rights which would otherwise exist, including privileges of use under the copyright law: "Parties to a contract may limit their right to take action they previously had been free to take" (*Universal Gym Equipment, Inc. v. ERWA Exercise Equipment Ltd.*, 1987, p. 1550). The result may be better or it may be worse in terms of use rights, obligations, conditions, and limitations. The threat that licensing poses to fair use is limited only by the savvy of users in the agreements signed, clicked, and so forth, or to which the user or intermediary assents. In spite of the increased use of both TPM and licenses to control access to content, fair use offers many applications, as this chapter has demonstrated. Users will continue to push the envelope of uses and courts for the most part will make evaluation in light of the balance of rights among both owners and users.

References: Case Law

321 Studios v. Metro Goldwyn Mayer Studios, Inc., 307 F. Supp. 2d 1085 (N.D. Cal. 2004).

A&M Records, Inc. v. Napster, Inc., 239 F.3d. 1004 (9th Cir. 2001).

Abilene Music, Inc., et al. v. Sony Music Entertainment, Inc., et al., 320 F. Supp. 2d 84 (S.D.N.Y. 2003).

American Geophysical Union, et al. v. Texaco, Inc., 60 F.3d 913 (2d Cir. 1994).

Antioch Co. v. Scrapbook Borders, Inc., 291 F.Supp.2d 980 (D. Minn. 2003).

Assessment Technologies of WI, LLC. v. Wiredata, Inc., 350 F.3d 640 (7th Cir. 2003).

Atari Games Corp. v. Nintendo of America, Inc., 975 F.2d 832 (Fed Cir. 1992).

A.V. v. iParadigms, Ltd., 544 F.Supp.2d 473 (E.D. Va. 2008), aff'd in part, rev'd in part, 562 F.3d 630 (4th Cir. 2009).

A.V. v. iParadigms, Ltd., 562 F.3d 630 (4th Cir. 2009).

Baltimore Orioles, Inc. v. Major League Baseball Players Association, 805 F.2d 663 (7th Cir. 1986).

Basic Books, Inc. Kinko's v. Graphics Corp., 758 F. Supp. 1522 (S.D.N.Y. 1991).

Bill Graham Archives v. Dorling Kindersley Ltd., 448 F.3d 605 (2d Cir. 2006).

Blanch v. Koons, 467 F.3d 244 (2d Cir. 2006).

BMG Music v. Gonzalez, 430 F.3d 888 (7th Cir. 2005).

Bourne v. Twentieth Century Fox Film Corp., 602 F.Supp.2d 499 (S.D.N.Y. 2009).

Burnett v. Twentieth Century Fox Film Corp., 491 F.Supp.2d 962 (C.D. Cal. 2007).

Campbell v. Acuff-Rose Music, 510 U.S. 569 (1994).

Castle Rock Entertainment, Inc. v. Carol Publishing Group, 150 F.3d 132 (2d Cir. 1998).

Chicago Board of Education v. Substance, Inc., 354 F.3d 624 (7th Cir. 2003), cert. denied 543 U.S. 816 (2004).

Clean Flicks of Colorado, LLC v. Soderbergh, 433 F.Supp.2d 1236 (D. Colo., 2006).

Craft v. Kobler, 667 F. Supp. 120 (S.D.N.Y. 1987).

Davis v. The Gap, Inc., 246 F.3d 152 (2d Cir. 2001).

Designer Skin, LLC v. S&L Vitamins, Inc., 560 F.Supp.2d 811 (D. Ariz. 2008).

Dr. Seuss Enterprises, L.P. v. Penguin Books USA, Inc., 109 F.3d 1394 (9th Cir. 1996), cert. dismissed, 521 U.S. 1146 (1997).

DSC Communications Corp. v. Pulse Communications, Inc., 170 F.3d 1354 (Fed. Cir. 1999), cert. denied 528 U.S. 923 (1999).

DSMC, Inc. v. Convera Corp., 479 F.Supp.2d 68 (D.D.C. 2007).

Eldred v. Ashcroft, 537 U.S. 186 (2003).

Estate of Martin Luther King, Jr. v. CBS, Inc., 194 F.3d 1121 (11th 1999).

Evolution, Inc. v. SunTrust Bank, 342 F.Supp.2d 943 (D. Kan. 2004).

Field v. Google, Inc., 412 F.Supp.2d 1106 (D. Nev. 2006).

Fisher v. Dees, 794 F.2d 432 (9th Cir. 1986).

Fitzgerald v. CBS Broadcasting, Inc., 491 F.Supp.2d 177 (D. Mass. 2007).

Fournier v. Erickson, 202 F.Supp.2d 290 (S.D.N.Y. 2002).

Fournier v. Erickson, 242 F.Supp.2d 318 (S.D.N.Y. 2003).

Greaver v. National Association of Corporate Directors, 1997 WL 34605245 (D.D.C., 1997) (unpublished).

Gulfstream Aerospace Corp. v. Camp Systems International, Inc., 428 F.Supp.2d 1369 (S.D. Ga. 2006).

Harper & Row Publishers, Inc. v. Nation Enterprises, 471 U.S. 539 (1985).

Healthcare Advocates, Inc. v. Harding, Earley, Follmer & Frailey, 497 F.Supp.2d 627 (E.D. Pa. 2007).

Higgins v. Detroit Educational Television Foundation, 4 F.Supp.2d 701 (E.D. Mich. 1998).

Hofheinz v. AMC Productions, Inc., 147 F.Supp.2d 127 (E.D.N.Y. 2001).

Images Audio Visual Productions, Inc. v. Perini Building Co., Inc., 91 F.Supp.2d 1075 (E.D. Mich. 2000).

In Re Aimster Copyright Litigation, 334 F.3d 643 (7th Cir. 2003).

In re Cellco Partnership, 2009 WL 3294861 (S.D.N.Y. 2009).

Kane v. Comedy Partners, 2003 WL 22383387 (S.D.N.Y. 2003) (unpublished), affirmed 98 Fed.Appx. 73, 2004 WL 1234062 (2d Cir. 2004).

Kelly v. Arriba Soft Corp., 336 F.3d 811 (9th Cir. 2003).

Leadsinger, Inc. v. BMG Music Publishing, 429 F.Supp.2d 1190 (C.D. Cal. 2005).

Leibovitz v. Paramount Pictures Corp., 137 F.3d 109 (2d Cir. 1998).

Lennon v. Premise Media Corp., 556 F.Supp.2d 310 (S.D.N.Y. 2008).

Lenz v. Universal Music Corp., 572 F. Supp. 2d 1150 (N.D. Cal. 2008).

Lexmark International, Inc. v. Static Control Components, Inc., 387 F. 3d 522 (6th Cir. 2004).

Los Angeles News Service v. CBS Broadcasting, Inc., 305 F.3d 924 (9th Cir. 2002), as amended and superseded 313 F.3d 1093 (9th Cir. 2002).

Los Angeles News Service v. KCAL-TV Channel 9, 108 F.3d 1119 (9th Cir. 1997).

Los Angeles Times v. Free Republic, 29 Media L. Rep. 1028 (C.D. Cal. 2000).

Louis Vuitton Malletier S.A. v. Haute Diggity Dog, LLC, 464 F.Supp.2d 495 (E.D. Va. 2006).

Lowry's Reports, Inc. v. Legg Mason, Inc., 271 F.Supp.2d 737 (D. Md. 2003).

Lowry's Reports, Inc. v. Legg Mason, Inc., Complaint, 2001 WL 34898871 (No. 01CV3898, Dec. 18, 2001).

Madison River Management Co. v. Business Management Software Corp., 387 F.Supp.2d 521 (M.D.N.C. 2005).

MasterCard International, Inc. v. Nader 2000 Primary Committee, Inc., 2004 WL 434404 (S.D.N.Y. 2004) (unpublished).

Mattel, Inc. v. Pitt, 229 F.Supp.2d 315 (S.D.N.Y. 2002).

Maxtone-Graham v. Burtchaell, 803 F.2d 1253 (2d Cir. 1986), cert. denied 481 U.S. 1059 (1987).

Merkos L'Inyonei Chinuch, Inc. v. Otsar Sifrei Lubavitch, Inc., 312 F.3d 94 (2d Cir. 2002).

Metro-Goldwyn-Mayer Studios, Inc. v. Grokster, Ltd., 259 F.Supp.2d 1029 (C.D. Cal. 2003), aff'd 380 F.3d 1154, (9th Cir. Cal. 2004), vacated and remanded, 545 U.S. 913 (2005).

Metro-Goldwyn-Mayer Studios, Inc. v. Grokster, Ltd., 545 U.S. 913 (2005).

National Association of Government Employees / International Brotherhood of Police Officers v. BUCI, 118 F.Supp.2d 126 (D. Mass. 2000).

New Kids on the Block v. News America Pub., Inc., 971 F.2d 302 (9th 1992).

New Era Publications International, ApS v. Carol Publishing Group, 904 F.2d 152 (2d Cir. 1990), stay denied 497 U.S. 1054, cert. denied 498 U.S. 921 (1990).

New Era Publications International, ApS v. Henry Holt and Co., Inc., 695 F. Supp. 1493 (S.D.N.Y. 1988).

New York Times Co. v. Tasini, U.S. 533 U.S. 483 (2001).

Nunez v. Caribbean International News Corp., 235 F.3d 18 (1st Cir. 2000).

NXIVM Corp. v. Ross Institute, 364 F.3d 471 (2d Cir. 2004).

Perfect 10, Inc. v. Amazon.com, Inc., 508 F.3d 1146 (9th Cir. 2007).

Peter Letterese and Associates, Inc. v. World Institute of Scientology Enterprises, Inc., 533 F.3d 1287 (11th Cir. 2008).

Princeton University Press v. Michigan Document Services, 99 F.3d 1381(6th Cir. 1996), cert. denied, 520 U.S. 1156 (1997).

ProCD Inc. v. Zeidenberg, 86 F.3d 1447 (7th Cir. 1996).

Ringgold v. Black Entertainment Television, Inc., Home Box Office, Inc., 126 F.3d 70 (2d Cir. 1997).

Robinson v. Random House, Inc., 877 F.Supp. 830 (S.D.N.Y. 1995).

Rogers v. Koons, 960 F.2d 301 (2d Cir.), cert. denied 506 U.S. 934 (1992).

Rubin v. Brooks/Cole Pub. Co., 836 F.Supp. 909 (D. Mass. 1993).

S&L Vitamins, Inc., v. Australian Gold, Inc., 521 F.Supp.2d 188 (E.D.N.Y. 2007).

Salinger v. Colting, WL 1916354 (S.D.N.Y. 2009).

Salinger v. Random House, Inc., 811 F.2d 90 (2nd Cir.), cert. denied 493 U.S. 1094 (1987).

SCQuARE Intern., Ltd. v. BBDO Atlanta, Inc., 455 F.Supp.2d 1347 (N.D. Ga. 2006).

Sega Enterprises Ltd. v. Accolade, Inc., 977 F.2d 1510 (9th Cir. 1992).

Sony Computer Entertainment America, Inc. v. Bleem, LLC, 214 F.3d 1022 (9th Cir. 2000).

Sony Computer Entertainment, Inc. v. Connectix Corp., 203 F.3d 596 (9th Cir. 2000), cert. denied 531 U.S. 871 (2000).

Sony Corporation of America v. Universal City Studios, Inc., 464 U.S. 417 (1984).

Sundeman v. Seajay Society, Inc., 142 F.3d 194 (4th Cir. 1998).

Suntrust Bank v. Houghton Mifflin Co., 268 F.3d 1257 (11th Cir. 2001), rehearing and rehearing en banc denied 275 F.3d 58 (11th Cir. 2001).

Ticketmaster, Corp. v. Tickets.com, Copy. L. Rep. (CCH) ¶28,146 (C.D. Calif. 2000).

Twentieth Century Music Corp. v. Aiken, 422 U.S. 151 (1975).

Twin Peaks Productions, Inc. v. Publications International Ltd., 996 F.2d 1366 (2d Cir. 1993).

Ty, Inc. v. Publication International Ltd., 292 F.3d 512 (7th Cir. 2002), cert. denied 537 U.S. 1110 (2003).

UMG Recordings, Inc. v. MP3.com, Inc., 92 F.Supp.2d 349 (S.D.N.Y. 2000).

United Feature Syndicate, Inc. v. Koons, 817 F.Supp. 370 (S.D.N.Y. 1993).

Universal City Studios, Inc. v. Corley, 273 F.3d 429 (2d Cir. 2001).

Universal Gym Equipment, Inc. v. ERWA Exercise Equipment Ltd., 827 F.2d 1542 (Fed. Cir. 1987).

U.S. v. American Soc. of Composers, Authors and Publishers, 599 F.Supp.2d 415 (S.D.N.Y. 2009).

United States v. Elcom, Ltd., 203 F. Supp. 2d 1111 (N.D. Cal. 2002).

Video Pipeline, Inc. v. Buena Vista Home Entertainment, Inc., 342 F.3d 191 (3d Cir. 2003), cert. denied 540 U.S. 1178 (2004).

Warner Brothers Entertainment, Inc. v. RDR Books, 575 F.Supp.2d 513 (S.D.N.Y. 2008).

World Wrestling Federation Entertainment, Inc. v. Big Dog Holdings, Inc., 280 F.Supp.2d 413 (W.D. Pa. 2003).

Worldwide Church of God v. Philadelphia Church of God, Inc., 227 F.3d 1110 (9th Cir. 2000).

Wright v. Warner Books, 748 F.Supp. 105 (S.D.N.Y. 1990).

References: Secondary Sources

Austin, B., & Taylor, K. (2003). Four scenarios concerning fair use and copyright costs: Electronic reserves at the University of Colorado, Boulder. *Journal of Interlibrary Loan, Document Delivery & Information Supply, 13*(3), 1–13.

Baker, J. B. (2009). Contracting to supplement fair use doctrine. *University of Memphis Law Review, 39*(Spring), 757–792.

Band, J. (2007a). *Educational fair use today.* Retrieved December 14, 2009, from www.arl.org/bm~doc/educationalfairusetoday.pdf

Band, J. (2007b). Google and fair use. *Journal of Business & Technology Law, 3*(1), 1–27.

Band, J. (2008). How fair use prevailed in the *Harry Potter* case. Retrieved December 14, 2009, from www.arl.org/bm~doc/harrypotterrev2.pdf

Baksik, C. (2006). Fair use or exploitation? The Google book search controversy. *portal: Libraries and the Academy, 6*(4), 399–415.

Beard, J. J. (1974). The copyright issue. *Annual Review of Information Science and Technology, 9,* 381–411.

Becker, G. H. (2003). *Copyright: A guide to information and resources* (3rd ed.). Lake Mary, FL: Gary H. Becker.

Beebe, B. (2008). An empirical study of U.S. copyright fair use opinions, 1978–2005. *University of Pennsylvania Law Review, 156*(January), 549–624.

Buttler, D. K. (1999). CONFU-sed: Security, safe harbors, and fair-use guidelines. *Journal of the American Society for Information Science, 50*(14), 1308–1312.

Casamiquela, R. J. (2002). Contractual assent and enforceability in cyberspace. *Berkeley Technology Law Journal, 17,* 475–495.

Conference on Fair Use. (1998). *Final report to the Commissioner on the conclusion of the Conference on Fair Use.* Washington, DC: U.S. Patent and Trademark Office.

Conley, N. J. (2009). Circumventing rights controls: The token crack in the fair use window left open by Congress in Section 1201 may be open wider than expected—technically speaking. *Chicago-Kent Journal of Intellectual Property, 8*(Spring), 297–316.

Crews, K. D. (1993). *Copyright, fair use, and the challenge for universities: Promoting the progress of higher education.* Chicago: University of Chicago Press.

Crews, K. D. (1999). Electronic reserves and fair use: The outer limits of CONFU. *Journal of the American Society for Information Science, 50*(14), 1320–1323.

Dames, K. M. (2005). Copyright clearances: The high stakes of fair use. *Online, 29*(6), 38–42.

Electronic Frontier Foundation. (2009). *Fair use principles for user generated video content.* Retrieved December 14, 2009, from www.eff.org/issues/ip-and-free-speech/fair-use-principles-usergen

Frazier, K. (1999). What's wrong with fair-use guidelines for the academic community? *Journal of the American Society for Information Science, 50*(14), 1353–1357.

Gasaway, L. N. (1997). The White Paper, fair use, libraries and educational institutions. *Serials Librarian, 31*(1/2), 211–220.

Gasaway, L. N. (1999). Guidelines for distance learning and interlibrary loan: Doomed and more doomed. *Journal of the American Society for Information Science, 50*(14), 1337–1341.

Hanratty, E. (2005). Google library: Beyond fair use? *Duke Law & Technology Review, 10.* Retrieved December 14, 2009, from www.law.duke.edu/journals/dltr/articles/pdf/2005 dltr0010.pdf

Heller, J. S. (2002). Copyright, fair use and the for-profit sector. *Information Outlook, 6*(5), 6–8, 10, 12, 14.

Heller, J. S. (2004). *The librarian's copyright companion.* Buffalo, NY: William S. Hein & Co.

Henderson, K. A., Spinello, R. A., & Lipinski, T. A. (2007). Prudent policy? Reassessing the Digital Millennium Copyright Act. *Computers and Society*, *37*(2), 25–40.

Henslee, W. (2009). You can't always get what you want, but if you try sometimes you can steal it and call it fair use: A proposal to abolish the fair use defense for music. *Catholic University Law Review*, *58*(Spring), 663–700.

Hoffman, G. M. (2001). *Copyright in cyberspace: Questions and answers for librarians*. New York: Neal Schuman.

High, E. (2009). Holding history hostage: Fair use in the context of historical documentary. *Temple Political and Civil Rights Law Review*, *18*(Spring), 753–781.

Hines, M., & Beckles, T. (2005). *Will fair use survive? Free expression in the age of copyright control*. New York: Brennan Center for Justice, New York University School of Law.

Keplinger, M. S. (1980). Copyright and information technology. *Annual Review of Information Science and Technology*, *15*, 3–33.

Landes, W. M., & Posner, R. A. (2003). *The economic structure of intellectual property law*. Cambridge, MA: Harvard University Press.

Lawrence, J. S., & Timberg, B. (1989). *Fair use and free inquiry: Copyright law and the new media* (2nd ed.). Norwood, NJ: Ablex.

Levering, M. (1999). What's right about fair-use guidelines for the academic community? *Journal of the American Society for Information Science*, *50*(14), 1313–1319.

Lipinski, T. A. (2005). *Copyright law and the distance education classroom*. Lanham, MD: Scarecrow.

Lipinski, T. A. (2006). *The complete copyright liability handbook for librarians and educators*. New York: Neal Schuman.

McCrann, M. (2009). A modest proposal: Granting presumptive fair use protection for musical parodies. *Roger Williams University Law Review*, *14*(Winter), 96–125.

Melamut, S. J. (2000). Pursuing fair use, law libraries, and electronic reserve. *Law Library Journal*, *92*, 157–192.

Melamut, S. J., Thibodeau, P. L., & Albright, E. E. (2000). Fair use or not fair use: That is the electronic reserves question. *Journal of Interlibrary Loan, Document Delivery & Information Supply*, *11*(1), 3–28.

Metcalfe, A., Diaz, V., & Wagoner, R. (2003). Academe, technology, society, and the market: Four frames of reference for copyright and fair use. *portal: Libraries and the Academy*, *3*(2), 191–206.

Nimmer, D. (2008). *Copyright illuminated: Refocusing the diffuse U.S. statute*. New York: Wolters Kluwer.

Nimmer, R. T., & Dodd, J. D. (2008). *Modern licensing law, 2008–2009 Edition*. St. Paul, MN: West Publishing.

Ou, C. (2003). Technology and copyright issues in the academic library: First sale, fair use and the electronic document. *Portal: Libraries and the Academy*, *3*(1), 89–98.

Patry, W. F. (1995). *The fair use privilege in copyright law*. Washington, DC: BNA, Inc.

Patterson, L. R. (1997). Fair use for teaching and research: The folly of *Kinko's* and *Texaco*. In L. N. Gasaway (Ed.), *Growing pains: Adapting copyright for libraries, education and society* (pp. 351–376). Littleton, CO: Fred B. Rothman.

Pressman, R. R. (2008). Fair use: Law, ethics and librarians. *Journal of Library Administration*, *4*, 89–110.

Rivera-Morales, N. A. (1999). Fair-use guidelines: A selected bibliography. *Journal of the American Society for Information Science, 50*(14), 1353–1357.

Rupp-Serrano, K. (1997). Copyright and fair use: A policy analysis. *Government Information Quarterly, 14*(2) 155–172.

Russell, C. (2003). Fair use under fire. *Library Journal, 128*(13), 32–34.

Samuelson, P. (2009). Unbundling fair uses. *Fordham Law Review*, 77(April), 2537–2621.

Schlosser, M. (2006). Fair use in the digital environment: A research guide. *Reference & User Services Quarterly, 46*(1), 11–17.

Schragis, S. (2001). Do I need permission? Fair use rules under the federal copyright law. *Publishing Research Quarterly, 16*(4), 50–63.

Sharp, J. (2002). Coming soon to pay-per-view: How the Digital Millennium Copyright Act enables digital content owners to circumvent educational fair use. *American Business Law Journal, 40*, 1–81.

Sinofsky, E. R. (1984). *Off-air videotaping in education: Copyright issues, decisions, implications*. New York: R.R. Bowker.

Spoo, R. (2002). Current copyright law and fair use. *Journal of Scholarly Publishing, 33*(3), 125–147.

Thatcher, S. G. (2006). Fair use in theory and practice: Reflections on its history and the Google case. *Journal of Scholarly Publishing, 37*(3), 215–229.

Thatcher, S. G. (2009). From the university presses: Is "functional" use "transformative" and hence "fair"? A copyright conundrum. *Against the Grain, 21*(3), 66–69.

Trosow, S. E. (2001). When is a use a fair use? University liability for educational copying. *portal: Libraries and the Academy, 1*(1), 47–57.

U.S. Congress. House of Representatives. (1992). Report No. 102–836, 102nd Congress, 2nd Session. Washington, DC: U.S. Government Printing Office. Reprinted, United States Code Congressional and Administrative News (pp. 2553–2563). St. Paul, MN: West Publishing. (also available in Westlaw at 1992 WL 199748).

U.S. National Commission on New Technological Uses of Copyrighted Works. (1978). *Final report of the National Commission on New Technological Uses of Copyrighted Works*. Washington, DC: Library of Congress.

Weil, B. H. (1975). Copyright developments. *Annual Review of Information Science and Technology, 10*, 359–381.

Wiant, S. K. (1997). Users' rights to photocopy: The impact of *Texaco* and *Michigan Document Services*. In L. N. Gasaway (Ed.), *Growing pains: Adapting copyright for libraries, education and society* (pp. 315–349). Littleton, CO: Fred B. Rothman.

Index